Justice as Message

Justice as Message

Expressivist Foundations of International Criminal Justice

CARSTEN STAHN

OXFORD
UNIVERSITY PRESS

OXFORD
UNIVERSITY PRESS

Great Clarendon Street, Oxford, OX2 6DP,
United Kingdom

Oxford University Press is a department of the University of Oxford. It furthers the University's objective of excellence in research, scholarship, and education by publishing worldwide. Oxford is a registered trade mark of Oxford University Press in the UK and in certain other countries

First Edition published in 2020

Impression: 1

Published in the United States of America by Oxford University Press
198 Madison Avenue, New York, NY 10016, United States of America

British Library Cataloguing in Publication Data
Data available

Library of Congress Control Number: 2019957834

ISBN 978–0–19–886418–9

Printed and bound by
CPI Group (UK) Ltd, Croydon, CR0 4YY

Preface

'Just a castaway', an 'island lost at sea'.[1] International criminal justice is about messages. Messages are present anywhere: in regulation, adjudication, and institutional practice. Some of them are directed at specific audiences. Others are coded or sent to unknown recipients, similar to messages in a bottle. In existing scholarship, surprisingly little attention has been paid to the fundamental question of how international criminal justice creates social meaning. Lawyers have a natural inclination to stay inside their comfort zones. Mainstream legal discourse tends to sideline the philosophical, sociological, criminological, or psychological underpinnings of law. These foundations are treated at the margins. They are mostly reflected as *obiter dicta* in legal reasoning or sentencing decisions. They are often taken for granted in prosecutorial strategy, outreach or legacy work, or even regarded with suspicion. Pragmatism prevails.

This study seeks to diversify perspectives. It inquires how legal norms and practices produce meaning. Law is a way of making sense of the world. Many of the types of violations or crimes that trigger international criminal justice are performative. They are social acts that carry real or symbolic meanings. They assert power, entail certain statements or messages to audiences, or seek to transform social reality. Part of their power is related to their perception. If this premise is correct it is only natural to look at the functions of international criminal law and its processes through a broader lens.

International criminal justice is a hallmark of social performance. It is a form of communicative and performative power. Messaging and performative elements are inherent in interpretation, norm production, institutional practices, or prevention and punishment.

International criminal justice involves legal scripting, acting, dramatic timing, and spectacle. It draws audiences in and makes others 'witness' to past events. Law-making or regulation is partially a counter-message to violence, anxiety, fear, or disorder. Legal adjudication involves narratives and storytelling. Almost any international criminal trial sets the stage for new narrative and stories and creates novel audiences. It speaks through legal expression, re-enactment, images, and aesthetics. The creation of a new institution is a performative act which carries symbolic and transformative meaning. Arrest or the delivery judgment are dramatic moments which seek to shape public conscience. Criminal proceedings have theatric features. They involve a plot, role play, and audiences. Punishment is partly

[1] The Police, 'Message in a Bottle', Reggatta de Blanc (1979).

a ritual with a demonstrative effect through which the international community seeks to (re)confirm its own foundations.

In the existing legal literature, these elements are typically discussed under the label of 'expressivism'. The notion has become a common term in criminal law theory or transitional justice in order to reflect the communicative or didactic features of criminal law and punishment or its contribution to history and remembrance. An increasing number of articles and textbooks cover individual aspects or contain general references to the concept, but there is no comprehensive treatment of expressivism as a theory and its link to conceptions of justice. Individual contributions have stressed the communicative dimensions of punishment, the educative function of trials, or the symbolism of institutions. However, few attempts have been made to put the various pieces of the puzzle together.

This book engages with expressivism in a holistic way. It examines its role as a method of international law, its space in justice theory, and its articulation in practice. It does not seek to defend expressivism as an overarching justification of international criminal justice. Instead, it argues that many of the paradoxes, tensions, and limitations of the field can be understood better through the study of the social functions of international norms and institutions, including communicative relations and performative elements.

This broader perspective sheds a new light on many facets of international criminal justice. It shows that the whole is more than the sum of its parts. Justice cannot be reduced to legal rationality but occurs through signals, communication, affective bonds, or emotion. This is partially reflected in the old maxim that justice must not only 'be done', but 'seen to be done' and—one should add—'felt to be done'. The value of international criminal justice goes far beyond its tangible or visible output, or its immediate legal reception. Factors, such as performance, the ritual-like features of the legal process, the playful character of the law, the communicative relations created through agency, voice, and listening, and the aspirational dimensions of international criminal justice are essential to the experience of international criminal justice. The intersubjective process of communication, the deliberative culture reflected in justice discourse, and the engagement with different interlocutors (e.g. offenders, victims, affected communities, members of different professions) are important elements of the process of creating justice. Messages are not only a means to an end but partly an end in themselves.

At the same time, the use of expressivist techniques and justifications requires critical scrutiny. Speaking is a form of power. The process of messaging creates new power relations. Spoken words may suppress alternative ideas. Legal notions create distances. Messages need to be translated, both in the lingual and cultural sense, in order to create intended meanings. The emphasis on educational or didactic rationales may carry paternalistic features. Court-driven images or communications may be easily perceived as marketing tools or create inflated expectations. This may undermine expressivist effects. The organization of the trial as a form of adversarial combat between parties may create obstacles to mutual engagement and listening, or cultivate cognitive dissonance. Defendants have a right to remain silent and cannot be forced to show remorse or repentance. International criminal institutions themselves must remain open to social learning.

The cover image of the book, portraying the Dock at Nuremberg in 1946, reflects many of the hopes and aspirations associated with the international criminal justice (e.g., order over chaos, equality before the law), the role of public shaming, as well as some of the inherent limits of communicative relationship of historical trials. It draws on the personal impressions of the artist, Dame Laura Knight, who attended the trial as a War Correspondent. This book is, in the largest sense, an invitation to lawyers to think beyond the silos of the legal discipline and to engage with the multidisciplinary foundations and possibilities of the international criminal justice project. It draws on the footprints of many pioneering scholars from multiple fields (e.g. sociology, law, political science, criminology, history, psychology) who have laid important theoretical groundwork for this study.

This work is derived from a habilitation thesis (*Habilitationsschrift*) at the Faculty of Law of Humboldt University Berlin, my former *alma mater*. I owe particular gratitude to my academic mentor and teacher, Professor Christian Tomuschat, who has served as guide and inspiration over the past two decades, and Professor Luís Greco.

The manuscript has benefited from many actual and virtual conversations with scholars and practitioners in the field, as well as friends and colleagues at the Grotius Centre for International Legal Studies and Queen's University Belfast School of Law, my second academic home.

Special thanks to my colleagues Joseph Powderly, Darryl Robinson, Cale Davis, Ciara Laverty, Rafael Braga da Silva, and Paula Baldini Miranda da Cruz who have inspired ideas, commented on individual aspects of the book, or supported writing, editing and figures, as well as the participants of the ICC Scholar Forum, jointly convened by the Whitney R. Harris World Law Institute (Washington University School of Law) and the Grotius Centre, who have served as invaluable sounding board for ideas.

I am also grateful to my new colleagues at Queen's University Belfast (e.g. Robin Hickey, Kieran McEvoy, Louise Mallinder, Luke Moffett, Rachel Killean, Cheryl Lawther, Lauren Dempster, and Yassin Brunger) who shaped my thinking on many of the transitional justice aspects of the work and provided me with the necessary time and space to finish this writing project.

I am very grateful to Merel Alstein who has supported the idea of this manuscript from its outset, as well as the excellent team at Oxford University Press who made this book a reality.

I hope that this book will serve as basis for on continuing conversation on merits and critiques of international criminal justice as a field across disciplines.

The Hague and Belfast,
March 2020

Contents

List of Figures

Table of Cases

DOMESTIC CASES

EXTRAORDINARY CHAMBERS IN THE COURTS OF CAMBODIA

EUROPEAN COURT OF JUSTICE

INTER-AMERICAN COURT OF HUMAN RIGHTS

INTERNATIONAL CRIMINAL COURT

INTERNATIONAL COURT OF JUSTICE

INTERNATIONAL CRIMINAL TRIBUNAL FOR RWANDA

INTERNATIONAL CRIMINAL TRIBUNAL FOR THE FORMER YUGOSLAVIA

INTERNATIONAL MILITARY TRIBUNALS

INTERNATIONAL RESIDUAL MECHANISM FOR CRIMINAL TRIBUNALS

SPECIAL COURT FOR SIERRA LEONE

SPECIAL TRIBUNAL FOR LEBANON

Table of Legislation

TABLE OF DOCUMENTS

List of Abbreviations

ASP	Assembly of State Parties
AU	African Union
CAR	Central African Republic
CDF	Civil Defence Forces
CIA	Central Intelligence Agency
DRC	Democratic Republic of Congo
EAC	Extraordinary African Chambers
ECCC	Extraordinary Chambers in the Courts of Cambodia
ECJ	European Court of Justice
ECOWAS	Economic Community of the West African States
EU	European Union
EULEX	European Union Rule of Law Mission in Kosovo
FARC	Fuerrzas Armadas Revolucionarias de Colombia
GA	United Nations General Assembly
IACtHR	Inter-American Court of Human Rights
ICC	International Criminal Court
ICJ	International Court of Justice
ICRC	International Committee of the Red Cross
ICTR	International Criminal Tribunal for Rwanda
ICTY	International Criminal Tribunal for the Former Yugoslavia
IHL	International Humanitarian Law
ILA	International Law Association
IMT	International Military Tribunal
ISIS	Islamic State of Iraq and the Levant
JCE	Joint Criminal Enterprise
KLA	Kosovo Liberation Army
KSC	Kosovo Specialist Chambers and Specialist Prosecutor's Office
NATO	North Atlantic Treaty Organization
NGO	Non-Governmental Organizations
OAS	Organisation of American States
OHCHR	Office of the United Nations High Commissioner for Human Rights
OTP	Office of the Prosecutor
PPT	Permanent People's Tribunal
RAF	Rwandan Armed Forces
RPF	Rwandan Patriotic Front
RUF	Sierra Leonean Revolutionary United Front
SCSL	Special Court for Sierra Leone
SITF	EULEX Special Investigative Task Force
STL	Special Tribunal for Lebanon

TEU	Treaty on European Union
TRC	Sierra Leonean Truth and Reconciliation Mission
TWAIL	Third World Approaches to International Law
UN	United Nations
UNESCO	United Nations Educational, Scientific and Cultural Organization
UNMIK	United Nations Interim Administration Mission in Kosovo
UNWCC	United Nations War Commission
VSS	Victim Support Section

Introduction

Law speaks.[1] It is an act of communication, that is, a process of transferring meaning. This understanding goes back to ancient times. It can be traced back to the story of Moses, who received the Ten Commandments from God on two tablets on Mount Sinai.[2] These 'tables of the law' were reportedly written with the 'finger of God'. They embodied spoken word. This revelation of law through speech initiated a covenant between God and humanity.

International criminal justice bears synergies with this biblical story. It embodies aspirational norms and values, which are often grounded in faith, in order to organize international society. It involves transfer of meaning. We hear about international criminal justice, read it, feel it, and see it being performed. These communicative foundations are often sidelined in contemporary studies. There is a rich literature on the institutionalization and content of international criminal law. But the broader justification of its *raison d'être*, and how international criminal justice represents itself[3] and produces meaning, remain understudied.[4] These processes can only be understood through multidisciplinary perspectives.

International criminal justice is created through discursive relations.[5] It operates through networks, sites,[6] and geographies[7] of justice. It can be understood as

[1] Mary Ann Glendon, *Abortion and Divorce in Western Law* (Cambridge, MA: Harvard University Press, 1987), 8 ('tells stories about the culture that helped to shape it and which it in turn helps to shape').

[2] See Alan Watson, 'Two Early Codes, The Ten Commandments and the Twelve Tables: Causes and Consequences' (2004) 25 *Journal of Legal History* 129–49.

[3] See Peter Goodrich, 'Specters of Law: Why the History of the Legal Spectacle Has Not Been Written' (2011) 1 *UC Irvine Law Review* 773–812, 779.

[4] For an exception, see Tim Meijers and Marlies Glasius, 'Trials as Messages of Justice: What Should Be Expected of International Criminal Courts?' (2016) 30 *Ethics & International Affairs* 329–447; Marlies Glasius, 'It Sends a Message': Liberian Opinion Leaders' Responses to the Trial of Charles Taylor' (2015) 13 *JICJ* 419–47; Mark A. Drumbl, 'The Expressive Value of Prosecuting and Punishing Terrorists: Hamdan, the Geneva Conventions, and International Criminal Law' (2007) 75 *George Washington Law Review* 1165–99; Barrie Sander, 'The Method is the Message: Law, Narrative Authority and Historical Contestation in International Criminal Courts', (2018) 19 *Melbourne Journal of International Law* 299–334; Barrie Sander, 'The Expressive Turn of International Criminal Justice': A Field in Search of Meaning' (2019) 32 *LJIL* 851–72; Immi Tallgren, 'Come and See? The Power of Images and International Criminal Justice' (2017) 17 *International Criminal Law Review* 259–80.

[5] Nesam McMillan, 'Imagining the International: The Constitution of International as a Site of Crime, Justice and Community' (2016) 25 *Social & Legal Studies* 163–80.

[6] See iCourts, 'The Global Sites of International Criminal Justice (JustSites)', at https://jura.ku.dk/icourts/research/justsites/ defining 'justice sites' as 'localities in which the political, legal and professional activities that collectively create international criminal justice are developed'.

[7] See generally, Nicholas K. Blomley, *Space, and the Geographies of Power* (New York, NY: The Guilford Press, 1994); Leila Ullrich, 'Beyond the "Global–Local Divide"' (2016) 14 *JICJ* 543–78; Dustin N. Sharp, 'Addressing Dilemmas of the Global and the Local in Transitional Justice' (2014–2015) 29 *Emory International Law Review* 71–118.

Justice as Message. Carsten Stahn, Oxford University Press (2020). © Carsten Stahn.
DOI: 10.1093/oso/9780198864189.001.0001

a particular form of governance, which diffuses criminal authority across different institutions, both above and below the level of the State,[8] as a special type of authority[9] in relation to macro criminality,[10] or a as a field, a framework to understand relations between agents and constituencies and their experiences.[11] In its most radical form, it might be defended as a belief system[12] that is grounded in faith and perpetuated through symbols,[13] routines, and expression of values.

This field is still defining its identity. Its contours, goals, and justifications of international criminal justice[14] remain disputed. Some view it as a response 'system' to mass atrocity crime.[15] Others regard it as a 'transnational field' which draws on strands from diplomacy, human rights advocacy, and criminal justice.[16] Others adopt an agent-based definition, defining it as 'a complex subject made up of the totality of persons (lawyers, academics, administrators) and institutions (NGOs, journals, and of course tribunals) invested at any one point in the field and that seek to make sense of it'.[17] It is marked by contestation of ideas, divergent interests, and clashes of power.[18]

[8] On links to humanitarian governance, see Sara Kendall, 'Beyond the restorative turn' in Christian de Vos, Sara Kendall, and Carsten Stahn (eds), *Contested Justice: The Politics and Practices of International Criminal Court Interventions* (Cambridge: Cambridge University Press, 2015), 352–76; Kjersti Lohne, 'Penal Humanitarianism Beyond the Nation State: An Analysis of International Criminal Justice' (2018) *Theoretical Criminology* 1–18; Sara Kendall and Sarah Nouwen, 'International Criminal Justice and Humanitarianism', University of Cambridge Faculty of Law Research Paper No. 69/2018, December 2018.

[9] It bears public features. As Larry May and Shannon Fyfe have argued, 'criminal law, unlike contract law, for instance, is not grounded in the consent of the parties—one cannot merely decide whether or not to be subject to criminal laws'. See Larry May and Shannon Fyfe, *International Criminal Tribunals: A Normative Defense* (Cambridge: Cambridge University Press, 2017), 79.

[10] The term goes back to Herbert Jäger, *Makrokriminalität, Zur Kriminologie kollektiver Gewalt* (Frankfurt: Surhrkamp, 1989). For a critique, see Michael Walter, 'Zur Reichweite des Konzepts Kriminalität—Einige Überlegungen zur Makrokriminalität Herbert Jägers' (1993) 25 *Kriminologisches Journal* 117–33.

[11] See Fréderic Mégret, 'International Criminal Justice as a Juridicial Field' (2016) 13 *Champ pénal/Penal Field* 3. This understanding may be related to Pierre Bourdieu's work on the juridical field as a social space. Pierre Bourdieu, 'The Force of Law: Toward a Sociology of the Juridical Field' (translated by R. Terdiman), (1987) 38 *Hastings Law Journal* 805–53. Bourdieu has argued that the 'juridical field' is an area of structured, socially patterned activity or 'practice that is governed by 'habitus', symbolic power, specific forms of cultural 'capital', and struggle of agents over authority.

[12] See Jean D'Aspremont, *International Law as Belief System* (Cambridge: Cambridge University Press, 2017); David Koller, 'The Faith of the International Criminal Lawyer' (2007) 40 *NYU Journal of International Law & Policy* 1019–69.

[13] Symbols represent larger ideas and "evoke an attitude, a set of impressions, or a pattern of events associated ... with the symbol'. See Murray Edelman, *The Symbolic Uses of Politics* (Chicago, IL: University Illinois Press, 1985) 6.

[14] Mirjan Damaška, 'What Is the Point of International Criminal Justice?' (2008) 83 *Chicago-Kent Law Review* 329–65.

[15] Gideon Boas, 'What is international criminal justice?' in Gideon Boas, William A. Schabas, and Michael P. Scharf (eds), *International Criminal Justice: Legitimacy and Coherence* (Northampton, MA: Edward Elgar Publishing, 2012), 1–24.

[16] Peter Dixon and Chris Tenove, 'International Criminal Justice as a Transnational Field: Rules, Authority and Victims' (2013) 7 *International Journal of Transitional Justice* 393–412, 395.

[17] Frédéric Mégret, 'The Anxieties of International Criminal Justice' (2016) 29 *LJIL* 197–221, 199.

[18] Immi Tallgren, 'The Sensibility and Sense of International Criminal Law' (2002) 13 *EJIL* 561–95.

Some of the foundations are under critique.[19] Even more than other fields, international criminal justice faces an ever-growing volume of expectations from different actors and constituencies, such as UN organs, political agents, non-governmental organizations (NGOs), victim groups, and affected societies. It is associated with ideals of equality before the law, truth, justice for victims, and effective remedies for violations, and seeks to promote such ideals through normative expression, communicative processes, performative practices (e.g. trials and procedures), and messages about accountability and repair. In public discourse, it is presented as a potential solution to all kinds of societal conflict, ranging from the protection of civilians to electoral politics, gender biases, or specific patterns of victimization. However, the institutions, procedures, and resources of international criminal justice are often at odds with these ambitions.[20]

The field navigates between two major poles, namely the idea of crime control, which involves defence of the public order, peace, and security, and the role of due process and fairness, which protects the liberty of persons and safeguards against abuse of power.[21] It is a deeply relational project.[22] It draws justification from state consent but seeks to represent a broader range of interests, ranging from protection of victims and defendants to broader collective or even community interests. It defines itself in relation to different constituencies: its founding bodies, states, societies, communities, victims, defendants, and humanity as global constituency.[23]

International criminal justice has been surprisingly pragmatic and non-committal in relation to justice theories.[24] As Frédéric Mégret has noted, the

[19] There is a sense of realism, if not skepticism about the future of international criminal justice. See, for example, Cherif M. Bassiouni, 'The ICC—Qui vadis?' (2006) 4 *JICJ* (2006) 421–7; David Luban, 'After the Honeymoon: Reflections on the Current State of International Criminal Justice' (2003) 11 *JICJ* 505–15; Christian Tomuschat, 'The International Criminal Court at Age Ten' (2012) *32 Human Rights Law Journal* 15–24; Christian Tomuschat, 'Zehn Jahre Internationaler Strafgerichtshof' (2012) 39 *Europäische Grundrechte Zeitschrift* 673–81.

[20] For a critical account, see, Christine Schwöbel (ed.), *Critical Approaches to International Criminal Law: An Introduction* (Abingdon: Routledge, 2014); Barrie Sander, 'International criminal justice as progress: From faith to critique' in Morten Bergsmo, Cheah Wui Ling, Song Tianying, and Yi Ping (eds), *Historical Origins of International Criminal Law: Volume 4* (Brussels: Torkel Opsahl Academic EPublisher, 2015), 749–834; Frédéric Mégret, 'International Criminal Justice: A Critical Research Agenda' in Schwöbel, 'Critical Approaches', 17–53; Dov Jacobs, 'Sitting on the Wall, Looking in: Some Reflections on the Critique of International Criminal Law' (2015) 28 *LJIL* 1–11; Gerry Simpson, 'War crimes: A critical introduction' in Timothy L.H. MacCormack and Gerry J. Simpson (eds), *The Law of War Crimes: National and International Approaches* (The Hague: Kluwer International) 1–30; Gerry Simpson, 'History of histories' in Kevin J. Heller and Gerry Simpson (eds), *The Hidden Histories of War Crimes Trials* (Oxford: Oxford University Press, 2013), 1–9, 8–9.

[21] On this account in domestic law, see Herbert L. Packer, 'Two Models of the Criminal Process' (1964) 113 *University of Pennsylvania Law Review* 1–68.

[22] On a relational justification of international criminal justice, see Adil Ahmad Haque, 'Group Violence and Group Vengeance: Toward a Retributivist Theory of International Criminal Law' (2005) 9 *Buffalo Criminal Law Review* 273–328.

[23] On ICC relations, see Gerhard Werle and Moritz Vormbaum, 'African States, the African Union, and the International Criminal Court: A Continuing Story' (2017) 60 *German Yearbook of International Law* 17–42.

[24] See Frédéric Mégret, 'What Sort of Global Justice is "International Criminal Justice"' (2015) 13 *JICJ* 77–96; Sarah M.H. Nouwen and Wouter G. Werner, 'Monopolizing Global Justice: International

project 'has less of a theory of its global justice than a theory of its fairness to, notably, defendants'.[25] It has been mainly understood as 'the theory of its institutions (primarily the tribunals) and its legal practices, rather than something that needs to be specifically understood in terms of justice'.[26]

Broadly speaking, the field may be associated with four different concepts of justice: (i) retributive justice, which focuses on the idea that criminal law provides 'what is due' to the defendant and safeguards certain general interest in crime control;[27] (ii) restorative justice, which sees the virtue of criminal adjudication in its ability to restore the rights of victims and affected communities, the potential rehabilitation of offenders and the transformation of the *status quo*;[28] (iii) distributive justice, which relates criminal justice to the just allocation of benefits and burdens, including decisions on resource allocation and assignment of rights and responsibilities to different justice agents;[29] and (iv) expressivist justice, which emphasizes the communicative and performative dimensions of criminal justice.[30]

Some people see international criminal justice as an emancipatory project to enhance the well-being of humankind.[31] Others look at it as if it is some sort of evil design deployed to target the State, or a cause, rather than a solution, to the world's problems.[32] Claims of victor's justice[33] or imperial critiques never fully went away or they appear in novel forms.[34] Socio-legal scholars

Criminal Law as Challenge to Human Diversity' (2015) 13 *JICJ* 157–76. See also Steven Ratner, *The Thin Justice of International Law: A Moral Reckoning* (Oxford: Oxford University Press, 2015).

25 Mégret, 'What Sort of Global Justice' 77.

26 Ibid.

27 See Alexander K.A. Greenawalt, 'International Criminal Law for Retributivists' (2014) 35 *University of Pennsylvania Journal of International Law* 969–1044; Adil Ahmad Haque, 'Retributivism: The Right and the Good' (2013) 32 *Law & Philosophy* 59–82.

28 See generally Carrie Menkel-Meadow 'Restorative Justice: What Is It and Does It Work?' (2007) 3 *Annual Review of Law and Social Science* 161–87; Adam J. MacLeod, 'All for One: A Review of Victim-Centric Justifications for Criminal Punishment' (2008) 13 *Berkeley Journal of Criminal Law* 31–64.

29 Mégret, 'What Sort of Global Justice' 83.

30 Margaret deGuzman, 'Choosing to Prosecute: Expressive Selection at the International Criminal Court' (2012) 33 *Michigan Journal of International Law* 265–320; Robert D. Sloane, 'The Expressive Capacity of International Punishment: The Limits of the National Law Analogy and the Potential of International Criminal Law' (2007) 43 *Stanford Journal of International Law* 39–94.

31 On international criminal justice and peace, see Frédéric Mégret, 'International Criminal Justice as a Peace Project' (2018) 29 *EJIL* 835–58; see Kirsten Sellars, *Crimes against Peace in International Law* (Cambridge: Cambridge University Press, 2013).

32 On different conceptions of world order, see Christian Tomuschat, 'World Order Models. A Disputation with B.S. Chimni and Yasuaki Onuma' (2006) 8 *International Community Law Review* 71–9.

33 See, for example, Telford Taylor, *The Anatomy of the Nuremberg Trials: A Personal Memoir* (New York, NY: Alfred A. Knopf, 1992), 641. The International Criminal Tribunal for Rwanda has been criticized for failing to look crimes committed by the Rwandan Patriotic Front ('RPF').

34 Asad G. Kiyani, 'Group-Based Differentiation and Local Repression: The Custom and Curse of Selectivity' (2016) 14 *JICJ* 939–57; Carsten Stahn, 'Justice civilisatrice? The ICC, post-colonial theory, and faces of 'the local' in Christian De Vos, Sara Kendall, and Carsten Stahn (eds), *Contested Justice: The Politics and Practice of International Criminal Court Interventions* (Cambridge: Cambridge University Press, 2015) 46–84.

have pointed out the risks and exclusionary effects of international criminal justice.[35]

One of the most striking dilemmas of international criminal justice is the strong discrepancy between expectation and reality. Antonio Cassese has famously compared international criminal justice to a 'giant' without legs. This image contrasts with the wide, and sometimes excessive, expectations that are voiced in discourse.[36] State agents, victims, and NGOs expect it to produce quick and tangible outcomes and results than can be measured in quantitative and qualitative turns. International criminal justice is portrayed as an instrument to bring atrocity within the realm of the law and to promote social change. The very function of the project has been strongly linked to a logic of enforcement. This has not only benefits but also downsides.

As Christian Tomuschat has cautioned, global challenges, such as peace or justice, cannot necessarily be solved through the creation of new legal rights and obligations. It would be wrong to assume that better protection can be secured simply 'by establishing centralized mechanisms with comprehensive responsibilities'.[37] Strategic communications of NGOs which seek to expand or stretch the realm of international criminal justice artificially may create false expectations or contribute to anti-criminal justice rhetoric.[38] The focus on rights and enforcement may sideline more complex and subtle effects, such as its broader impact on knowledge production or the transformation of discourse, which are often sidelined. The disconnect between reality and ambition creates not only a factual but also a normative problem. The failure of institutions to deliver the justice they promise may lead to loss of faith, mission creep, or produce silences.[39] Payam Akhavan has warned that 'the rise of international criminal justice in the nascent phase of its existence' and 'the projection of exaggerated normative fantasies on to this seeming panacea' have 'invariably given way to its perceived decline'.[40]

Traditionally, international criminal justice has been explained through classical rationales of punishment, such as retributive or consequentialist

[35] One of the most intriguing critiques is that it empowers global actors or specific elites rather than providing meaningful justice to affected communities. See Asad G. Kiyani, 'International Crime and the Politics of Criminal Theory: Voices and Conduct of Exclusion' (2015) 48 *NYU Journal of International Law & Politics* 129–208, 187.

[36] See Antonio Cassese, 'On the Current Trends towards Criminal Prosecution and Punishment of Breaches of International Humanitarian Law' (1998) 9 *EJIL* 2–17, 13 ('the ICTY remains very much like a giant without arms and legs—it needs artificial limbs to walk and work').

[37] See Christian Tomuschat, *Human Rights: Between Idealism and Realism* (Oxford: Oxford University Press, 2014), 431; Christian Tomuschat, 'Internationaler Menschenrechtsschutz—Anspruch und Wirklichkeit' (2008) 56 *Vereinte Nationen* 195–200.

[38] See Megan A. Fairlie, 'The Hidden Costs of Strategic Communications for the International Criminal Court' (2016) 51 *Texas International Law Journal* 282–319, 319.

[39] On crimes of silence, see Gerard J. Libaridian (ed.), *A Crime of Silence: The Armenian Genocide* (London: Zed Books, 1985) 243.

[40] Payam Akhavan, 'The Rise, and Fall, and Rise, of International Criminal Justice (2013) 11 *JICJ* 527–36, 529.

arguments. However, these theories have remained vulnerable. Deterrence is difficult to establish empirically.[41] International criminal justice cannot be justified by the number of criminal trials or the severity of punishment. It remains highly selective in its enforcement. It is partly rooted in a culture of faith. As Immi Tallgren has noted, if arguments of 'utility and rationality' were stripped from the discourse on the justification of international criminal justice, one of its main defences would be its potential ability to serve as 'a symbol and as a model'.[42]

Expressivist theories have seen a renaissance in legal discourse over past decades in both Anglo-American doctrine[43] and continental law systems[44] that is sometimes referred to as the 'expressive turn'.[45] Expressivism is grounded in the idea that law has value because of its ability to convey social meaning.[46] It stresses the function of criminal law to articulate and reinforce social norms (e.g. by signalling 'societal reproach')[47] and send different types of messages. This idea may be traced back to the Nuremberg trials,[48] which were associated with the idea that criminal proceedings can 'affirm respect for law, reinforce a moral consensus, narrate history, and educate the public'[49] or transform society.[50] It has become part of the methods of international law. Expressivist theories provide a novel lens to understand processes of norm diffusion,[51] the symbolic value and limits of institutions,[52]

[41] Meijers and Glasius, 'Trials as Messages of Justice' 431.

[42] Tallgren, 'The Sensibility and Sense of International Criminal Law' 592–3.

[43] It has a rich tradition in domestic criminal law, in particular in relation to punishment. See Joel Feinberg, 'The Expressive Theory of Punishment' (1965) 49 *The Monist* 397–423; Alan Strudler, 'The Power of Expressive Theories of Law' (2001) 60 *Maryland Law Review* 492–505; Elizabeth S. Anderson and Richard H. Pildes, 'Expressive Theories of Law: A General Restatement' (2000) 148 *University of Pennsylvania Law Review* 1504–75.

[44] It is *inter alia* reflected in the works of Günther Jakobs, Tatjana Hörnle, Klaus Günther, and Claus Roxin. See Claus Roxin and Luís Greco, *Strafrecht Band I: Allgemeiner Teil* (München: C.H. Beck, 2020). See **section 1.1.4**. See also Tobias Zürcher, *Legitimation von Strafe: Die expressive-kommunikative Straftheorie zur Rechtfertigung von Strafe* (Tübingen: Mohr Siebeck, 2014); Daniela Demko, 'An Expressive Theory of International Punishment for International Crimes' in Florian Jessberger and Julia Geneuss (eds), *Why Punish Perpetrators of Mass Atrocities?* (New York: Cambridge University Press, 2020), 176–96.

[45] Sander, The Expressive Turn of International Criminal Justice 851.

[46] Expressivist theory has been applied in several legal field, including environmental law, public law and criminal law. See generally Cass R Sunstein, 'On the Expressive Function of Law' (1996) 133 *University of Pennsylvania Law Review* 2021–54, 2024; Dan M. Kahan, 'What Do Alternative Sanctions Mean?'(1996) 63 *The University of Chicago Law Review* 591–653, 597.

[47] Diane Marie Amann, 'Group Mentality, Expressivism, and Genocide' (2002) 2 *International Criminal Law Review* 93–143, 120.

[48] Christian Tomuschat, 'The Legacy of Nuremberg' (2006) *JICJ* 830–44.

[49] Mark A. Drumbl, *Atrocity, Punishment and International Law* (Cambridge: Cambridge University Press, 2007) 12.

[50] Lawrence Douglas, *The Memory of Judgment: Making Law and History in the Trials of the Holocaust* (New Haven, CT: Yale University Press, 2001), 41.

[51] See Amann, 'Group Mentality, Expressivism, and Genocide' 120.

[52] De Guzman, 'Choosing to Prosecute' 315. On expressivist theory and affirmation of faith in the rule of law, see Harmen van der Wilt, 'Why international criminal lawyers should read Mirjan Damaška' in Carsten Stahn and Larissa van den Herik (eds), *Future Perspectives on International Criminal Justice* (The Hague: TMC Asser Press, 2010), 44–57.

or the recognition of specific forms of harm. For instance, regional systems, such as the EU or the Inter-American system on human rights, rely on legal messaging[53] in order to foster macro goals or promote the internalization of norms via domestic acceptance and application.

Expressivism has developed into one the leading theories to understand the foundations of international criminal justice[54] and its symbolic and communicative functions.[55] It is inherent in the relational aspects of accountability. It may explain both some of the aspirations of international criminal justice[56] as well as some of its paradoxes (e.g. high social relevance, despite selectivity,[57] normative authority despite non-compliance).[58] It offers a framework to understand how a comparatively limited system of justice (e.g. in terms of arrest, prosecutions, or punishment) may be socially significant. It is linked to the continuous effort of the field to present an alternate reality and justify its own existence in a state of normative uncertainty.

Critical legal scholarship has insisted that international law operates not only through rules and norms, but through 'argumentative practices'.[59] Expressivism is part of such methods. It may be defined as a process of creating meaning through communicative actions and representational practices, including symbolic expression. It encompasses a wide range of communicative acts.[60] It includes not only

[53] On expressivism in the EU context, see Jenia Iontcheva Turner, 'The Expressive Dimension of EU Criminal Law' (2012) 60 *American Journal of Comparative Law* 555–83; Nikolas P. Sellheim, 'The Voice of Disapproval: The Expressive Function and Paradox of the EU Seal Regime' (2006) 8 *The Polar Journal* 224–42. On the Inter-American context, see Jessie Allen, 'Theater of International Justice' (2012) 3 *Creighton International & Comparative Law Journal* 121–47.

[54] See *inter alia* Drumbl, *Atrocity, Punishment and International Law* 17, 175–6; Salif Nimage, 'An International Conscience Collective? A Durkheimian Analysis of International Criminal Law' (2007) 7 *International Criminal Law Review* 561–619; Barrie Sander, 'Justifying international criminal punishment: A critical perspective' in Morten Bergsmo and Emiliano J. Buis (eds), *Philosophical Foundations of International Criminal Law: Foundational Concepts* (Brussels: Torkel Opsahl Academic EPublisher, 2019), 167–240, 192–225; Kirsten J. Fisher, *Moral Accountability and International Criminal Law, Holding Agents of Atrocity Accountable to the World* (London: Routledge, 2011), 49–65. On expressivism and international law, see Alex C. Geisinger and Michael Ashley Stein, 'A Theory of Expressive International Law' (2007) 60 *Vanderbilt Law Review* 77–131.

[55] See, Larry May and Shannon Fyfe, *International Criminal Tribunals: A Normative Defense* (Cambridge: Cambridge University Press, 2017), 61–4.

[56] For an aspirational account, see Saira Mohamed, 'Deviance, Aspiration, and the Stories We Tell: Reconciling Mass Atrocity and the Criminal Law' (2015) 124 *Yale Law Journal* 1628–89, 1674. See also Bill Wringe, 'Why Punish War Crimes?' (2006) 25 *Law and Philosophy* 159–91.

[57] The STL has argued that '[c]riminal investigation and prosecution ... is unavoidably selective in any system, even where prosecuting reported crimes is expressed to be legally "mandatory"'. See STL, *Prosecutor v. Ayyash et al.*, Decision on the Defence Challenges to the Jurisdiction and Legality of the Tribunal, STL1101/PT/TC, 27 July 2012, para. 87.

[58] On paradoxes, see Kerstin Bree Carlson, 'International Criminal Law and Its Paradoxes: Implications for Institutions and Practice' (2017) 5 *Journal of Law and Courts* 33–53.

[59] See Martti Koskenniemi, 'Methodology of International Law' in Rüdiger Wolfrum (ed.), *The Max Planck Encyclopedia of Public International Law, Volume VII* (Oxford: Oxford University Press, 2007) 124–30, 124

[60] On justice as dialogue, see Kenneth A. Rodman, 'Justice as a Dialogue Between Law and Politics: Embedding the International Criminal Court within Conflict Management and Peacebuilding' (2014) 12 *JICJ* 437–69.

classical forms of lingual expression, such as messages, speech acts, or narratives,[61] but also signs and performative actions which render authority visible[62] and make 'justice seen'.[63] It takes into account that international criminal law embodies and enacts social norms and alters social identities and relationships.[64]

Expressivism has close links to performative theory.[65] International criminal justice is a form of social performance.[66] It relies on public demonstration, symbolic action, role play and spectacle (e.g. captivation) in order to contribute to its own authority. It does not only draw attention to atrocity crime but 'draws' audiences 'in' through various types of communication (e.g. language, images, or symbolic representation).[67] It uses 'symbolic capital', 'discourse, narrative, logic', and 'performance' in order to produce social meaning, transforms 'bystanders into participants, spectators into audience', proposes alternative readings of reality, or triggers political action.[68] Its success depends partly on its way of representation, that is via 'expression, articulation, style, presence'.[69]

This work marks an attempt to understand the expressive function of international criminal justice as well as its risks,[70] and critiques,[71] among other issues its focus on the communicator[72] rather than the recipient of justice,[73] its tendency of

[61] Anette Bringedal Houge, 'Narrative Expressivism: A Criminological Approach to the Expressive Function of International Criminal Justice' (2019) 19 *Criminology & Criminal Justice* 277–93.

[62] Performance is not only crucial to politics but inherent in legal processes. See Julie Stone Peters, 'Legal Performance Good and Bad Law' (2008) 4 *Culture and the Humanities* 179–200, 180 ('performance makes authority visual, palpable, bodily (accessible to the senses). In this sense, it obviates the rational justifications for authority it offers . . . and transcends the demand for rational justification).

[63] Shoshana Felman, *The Juridical Unconscious: Trials and Traumas in the Twentieth Century* (Cambridge: Harvard University Press, 2002), 162.

[64] Ibid., 20.

[65] The idea that certain acts are performative goes back to speech act theory (e.g. Austin), but has gained broader reception in social sciences and social-legal studies. See generally Simon Shepherd, *The Cambridge Introduction to Performance Theory* (Cambridge: Cambridge University Press, 2016). On how performance and theatricality relate to law, see Julie Stone Peters, 'Law as performance: Historical interpretation, objects, lexicons, and other methodological problems' in Elizabeth S. Anker and Bernadette Meyler (eds), *New Directions in Law and Literature* (New York, NY: Oxford University Press, 2017), 193–209.

[66] See Jeffrey C. Alexander, Bernhard Giesen, and Jason L. Mast, *Social Performance: Symbolic Action, Cultural Pragmatics, and Ritual* (Cambridge: Cambridge University Press, 2009).

[67] On emotion in meaning production, see Kamari Clarke, *Affective Justice* (Durham and London: Duke University Press, 2019), 19–20.

[68] See David E. Apter, 'Politics as theatre: An alternative view of the rationalities of power' Alexander, Giesen, and Mast (eds), *Social Performance*, 218–56, 225.

[69] Ibid., 227.

[70] One risk of expressivism is that it may spread certain 'conceptions about atrocity and its causes, dictating in turn, a constrained conception of justice and the return to order through criminal law'. See Doris Buss, 'Performing Legal Order: Some Feminist Thoughts on International Criminal Law' (2011) 11 *International Criminal Law Review* 409–23, 423.

[71] For a critique of expressivist theory, see Matthew D. Adler, 'Expressive Theories of Law: A Skeptical Overview' (2000) 148 *University of Pennsylvania Law Review* 1363–500, 1369–70.

[72] See Meijers and Glasius, 'Trials as Messages of Justice' 439. In practice, there are often discrepancies between the intended meaning of legal acts and procedures, and their public and social reception in affected societies. On the 'unreceptive offender' problem, see Wringe, 'Why Punish War Crimes?' 81.

[73] A common objection is that expressivism treats offenders as a means to an end. A counterargument is that expressivism addresses the offender as citizen and member of a community. See **section 1.2.4**.

treating the offender as a means to an end or its potential detraction from the core function of the trial.[74] It argues that expressivism is not only related to the punitive functions of international criminal justice[75] but represented in a whole spectrum of practices: norm expression and diffusion (e.g. criminalization, internalization); institutional meanings, practices, and policies; legal procedures and punishment, and repair of harm. It shows that expressivism is a *modus operandi* rather than a comprehensive justice theory.[76] The values or morality expressed need to be grounded elsewhere.[77] Expressivism can only be understood through the interplay of law with other disciplines, such as social psychology,[78] organizational theory, or semiotics (the science of signs).[79] This framework provides a basis for an understanding of justice as message, that is as a communicative process.[80]

Chapter 1 traces the multidisciplinary foundations of expressivist theory. The origins of expressivism lie in sociology (e.g. Emile Durkheim) and communicative theories of criminal law (e.g. Joel Feinberg, Antony Duff). These ideas have been developed in contemporary criminal law doctrine (e.g. Günther Jakobs, Andrew von Hirsch, Tatjana Hörnle, Claus Roxin), transitional justice (e.g. Mark Osiel, Pablo de Greiff), and international criminal law.[81] The chapter develops a contemporary theorization of expressivism. It argues that expressivism is rooted in a 'communicative cycle' (Klaus Günther) between norms as messages, crimes as messages, and judicial responses. This triad provides an explanation for the functioning of expressivism. It can be divided into norm expression and diverse types of agent-related expression. Their application involves different tensions: empirics versus faith, power-related critiques, instrumentalism, and mediation of messages.

Chapter 2 analyses how international criminal justice engages in norm expression in relation to criminalization and crime.[82] Expressivist theory suggests that international criminal justice can serve as a means to instil norms and values in

[74] On symbolism, see Marina Aksenova, 'Symbolism as a Constraint on International Criminal Law' (2017) 30 *LJIL* 475–99.

[75] On denunciatory expressivism, see Bill Wringe, *An Expressive Theory of Punishment* (London: Palgrave Macmillan, 2016).

[76] For instance, the fact that international criminal courts and tribunals may use morality and emotive language in their reasoning as part of communication does not per se mean that this is the right thing to do.

[77] As critics have cautioned, expressivists may fall into the trap of writing 'as if "expressiveness" [would] eo ipso' justify the reasoning or interpretation adopted. See Anthony Skillen, 'How to Say Things with Walls' (1980) 55 *Philosophy* 509–23, 520–1.

[78] On international criminal law and psychology, see Gideon Boas and Pascale Chifflet, *International Criminal Justice* (Cheltenham: Elgar, 2017), 93–135.

[79] Charles Morris, *Foundation of the Theory of Signs* (Chicago, IL: University of Chicago Press, 1938).

[80] On the foundations of communicative action, see Jürgen Habermas, *The Theory of Communicative Action, Volume 1, Reason and the Rationalization of Society* (Boston, MA: Beacon Press, 1984); Jürgen Habermas, *The Theory of Communicative Action, Volume 2, System and Lifeworld: A Critique of Functionalist Reason* (Boston, MA: Beacon Press, 1987).

[81] See **sections 1.4 and 1.2**.

[82] According to constructivist approaches, norms evolve in cycles, for example through emergence, consolidation, and internalization. See Martha Finnemore and Kathryn Sikkink, 'International Norm Dynamics and Political Change' (1998) 52 *International Organization* 887–917.

international society through communicative justice and persuasion. The chapter demonstrates that contemporary practice shifts between norm expression and norm entrepreneurship.[83] It relates norm expression to the imperfect structure of international law[84] and the performative nature of crimes. It argues that norm expression is partially a counter-performance to crimes. It shows that international criminal justice has captured a new zone[85] and forms of social behaviour through thematic investigations and prosecutions (e.g. sexual and gender-based violence,[86] child soldiers, cultural property) and legal practice relating to core crimes (genocide, crimes against humanity, war crimes, aggression).[87] It illustrates how legal agents have used rhetorical techniques (e.g. narration, storytelling and imagery) to reformulate some of the premises of underlying bodies of law (e.g. human rights law, international humanitarian law, and the law of the use of force). This transformation exposes international criminal justice to certain risks of normative overreach.

Chapter 3 examines the space of expressivism in institutional practices. As Jelena Subotić has shown, what trials and institutions signify may sometimes be more important than whom they try or what conviction they achieve.[88] The chapter demonstrates that the very act of reacting to atrocities, and institutionalization itself, has expressive meaning. Sometimes the 'medium is the message'.[89] For instance,

[83] On the dilemma of entrepreneurship, see Tshepo Madlingozi, 'On Transitional Justice Entrepreneurs and the Production of Victims' (2010) 3 *Journal of Human Rights Practice* 208–28.

[84] International criminal justice struggles to counter ideologies or system criminality through individual trials. Unlike in the domestic context, criminal behaviour is often marked by conformity to domestic or local norms, rather than norm deviance. These factors may explain why norm expression has particular value in international criminal justice. See Alette A. Smeulers, 'Punishing the Enemies of All Mankind' (2008) 21 *LJIL* 971–93, 976–81.

[85] French sociologist Henri Lefebvre has argued that space is a form of social production which involves physical, mental, and lived dimensions. See Henri Lefebvre, *The Production of Space* (translated by Donald Nicholson-Smith) (Oxford: Blackwell, 1991), 349. On social space as a bounded combination of social institutions and structures, see also Christian Fuchs, 'Henri Lefebvre's Theory of the Production of Space and the Critical Theory of Communication' (2019) 29 *Communication Theory* 129–50.

[86] Feminist and gender justice approaches have offered critical re-readings of law and policies. See Judith Gardam, 'A Feminist Analysis of Certain Aspects of International Humanitarian Law' (1992) 12 *Australian Year Book of International Law* 265–78; Judith Gardam, 'Woman and the Law of Armed Conflict: Why the Silence?' (1997) 46 *ICLQ* 55–80; Valerie Oosterveld, 'Feminist Debates on Civilian Women and International Humanitarian Law' (2009) 27 *Windsor Year Book of Access to Justice* 385–402; Christine Chinkin, 'Feminist Interventions into International Law' (1997) 19 *Adelaide Law Review* 13–24.

[87] On foundations of international crimes, see Larry May, *Crimes Against Humanity: A Normative Account* (Cambridge University Press, 2005); Kai Ambos, 'The Overall Function of International Criminal Law—Striking the Right Balance Between the Rechtsgut and the Harm Principles: A Second Contribution Towards a Consistent Theory of ICL' (2015) 9 *Criminal Law and Philosophy* 301–29; David Luban, 'A Theory of Crimes Against Humanity' (2004) 29 *Yale Journal of International Law* 85–167; Christopher Macleod, 'Towards a Philosophical Account of Crimes Against Humanity' (2010) 21 *EJIL* 281–302.

[88] Jelena Subotić, *Hijacked Justice: Dealing with the Past in the Balkans* (Ithaca, NY: Cornell University Press, 2016).

[89] On this idea in the context of media law, see Daithí Mac Síthigh, *Medium Law* (London: Routledge, 2018) 145–50.

institutions such as the Nuremberg or Tokyo tribunals, the *ad hoc* tribunals, or the Special Tribunal for Lebanon (STL) marked not only a reaction to silences or neglects of the past. They reflected a sentiment that a specific case had to be made in light of the circumstances of the time (e.g. in relation to genocide, terrorism, etc.).[90]

Throughout history, the very establishment of institutions has sent different signals, such as memory and remembrance, shame and apology, renewal of community relations, hope and belief, or protest. One of the unique powers of international criminal courts and tribunals lies in their broad audience and their ability to 'send messages', shape debates and discourse, and influence the generation and perception of norms. Speech act theory is helpful to understand the various meanings of institutional action. Many institutional acts carry meaning that goes beyond their immediate juridical significance. Practices such as outreach and legacy strategies involve strong didactic rationales. They are often more geared towards one-sided expression, rather than two-way communication or mutual learning.

Chapter 4 explores the role of expressivism in criminal procedures,[91] including their role as 'show trials'.[92] Many theorists claim that the justification of international criminal justice does not emanate solely from the authority underlying its creation but from the central function of proceedings.[93] For instance, sociologist Niklas Luhmann has stressed that procedures gain value through inter-subjective communication and social interaction and the contribution of agents to the 'ceremonial' features of proceedings.[94] Criminal procedures share certain symbolic features that allow international justice agents to constitute themselves as 'moral community'. They are not only a means to decide on guilt or innocence of defendants but involve communicative relationships with parties, participants, and spectators.[95] Antony Duff has claimed that '[t]he aim of the trial is not just to make an

[90] On Nuremberg, see Kim C. Priemel, *The Betrayal: The Nuremberg Trials and German Divergence* (Oxford: Oxford University Press, 2016). See also Frédéric Mégret, 'Nuremberg and the Contemporary Commitment to International Criminal Justice', *Völkerrechtsblog*, 22 February, 2017, https://voelkerrechtsblog.org/nuremberg-and-the-contemporary-commitment-to-international-criminal-justice/. On the importance of occasion in history, see Peter Burke, 'Performing History: The Importance of Occasions' (2005) 9 *Rethinking History* 35–52.

[91] One of the contradictions of international criminal justice is that international crimes are extraordinary while the procedures to investigate and prosecute offender are ordinary. See Miriam J. Aukerman, 'Extraordinary Evil, Ordinary Crime: A Framework for Understanding Transitional Justice' (2002) 15 *Harvard Human Rights Journal* 39–97.

[92] A show trial is more focused on the audience rather than the defendant. On the fine line between 'show trials' and political trials, see Judith N. Shklar, *Legalism: Law, Morals, and Political Trials* (Cambridge, MA: Harvard University Press, 1986); Milner S. Ball, 'The Play's the Thing: An Unscientific Reflection on Courts Under the Rubric of Theater (1975) 28 *Stanford Law Review* 81–115, 85.

[93] For example, David Luban, 'Fairness to rightness: Jurisdiction, legality, and the legitimacy of international criminal Law' in Samantha Besson and John Tasioulas (eds), *The Philosophy of International Law* (Cambridge: Cambridge University Press, 2010), 569–88; Mirjan Damaška 'Reflections on Fairness in International Criminal Justice' (2012) 10 *JICJ* 611–20.

[94] Niklas Luhmann, *Legitimation durch Verfahren* (Frankfurt: Suhrkamp 1983). He speaks of ceremonial integration of parties. Ibid., 114.

[95] On trials as a catalyst for public debate, see Carlos Santiago Nino, *Radical Evil on Trial* (New Haven, CT: Yale University Press, 1996); Mark Osiel, *Mass Atrocity, Collective Memory and the Law* (New Brunswick: Transaction Publishers, 1997). See also Iavor Rangelov, *Nationalism and the Rule*

accurate determination of the facts' but 'to engage with the defendant in a rational process of argument and judgment'.[96]

The chapter examines to what extent international criminal proceedings enable discursive justice. It draws on performative theories (e.g. Julie Stone Peters) and semiotics (e.g. Susan Tiefenbrun) to show that proceedings have symbolic, narrative, didactic, and transformative functions. As Julie Stone Peters has argued, the concept of 'performance' is useful, because it 'reveals the triangularity of the law–interpreter–audience relationship' and 'the centrality of the audience to legal determinations'.[97] Performative theory helps to understand legal practice in a more holistic way, namely through the lens of 'actors, stages, scripts and audiences'.[98] It sheds light on social realities, the 'multiplicity of actors and audiences', the importance of voice, and their 'different understandings, motivations and goals'.[99]

The chapter demonstrates how different agents in the criminal process (e.g. Prosecution, witnesses, Defence, victims, judges) have used narratives to convey messages to different audiences. It argues that international criminal proceedings encompass more performative rather than truly discursive elements, due to their adversarial structures. Such performances go beyond 'theatre' in a derogatory sense.[100] They may play a positive role beyond setting legal precedents or enhancing the consistency of law. The very repetition of trials is a means of 'creating and naturalizing structures of experience', that is, an 'antithesis of the arbitrary'.[101]

Chapter 5 engages with the question of how wrong is expressed and remedied through punishment and reparation ('remedial expression'). One of the paradoxes of international criminal justice is that the ability of perpetrators to do harm is far greater than their ability to repair damage. Traditionally, punishment is seen as the main instrument to remedy wrong. In international criminal justice, punishment goes beyond the individual. It is related to a wide range of social and political factors, such as incapacitation, deterrence (specific and general), reform, retribution, restitution, and communication.[102]

of Law: Lessons from the Balkans and Beyond (Cambridge: Cambridge University Press 2014), 51 ('Deliberative justice starts with the stories and interpretations offered by the participants in the courtroom drama; it is sparked by the trial, but takes on a life of its own.').

[96] Antony Duff, *Trials and Punishments* (Cambridge: Cambridge University Press, 1991), 35.

[97] Stone Peters, 'Legal Performance Good and Bad Law' 196.

[98] Gabrielle Lynch, *Performances of Justice: The Politics of Truth, Justice and Reconciliation* (Cambridge: Cambridge University Press, 2018) 20.

[99] Ibid, 21.

[100] See Allen, 'Theater of International Justice' 121. On the difference between law and theatre, see Marett Leiboff, 'Theatricalizing Law' (2018) 30 *Law & Literature* 351–67; Nicole Rogers, 'The Play of Law: Comparing Performance in Law and Theatre' (2008) 8 *Queensland University of Technology Law Journal* 429–43

[101] See Kate Leader, 'The Trial's the Thing: Performance and Legitimacy in International Criminal Trials' (2018) *Theoretical Criminology* 1–17, 7–8.

[102] See generally Florian Jessberger and Julia Geneuss (eds), *Why Punish Perpetrators of Mass Atrocities?* (New York: Cambridge University Press, 2020).

These different goals pull in different directions and cannot all be realized at the same time.

The chapter argues that expressivism is a justice theory, rather than a punishment theory. It does not offer a full justification for criminal sanction (e.g. imprisonment) on its own, but relies on preventive rationales and deontic factors to justify punishment. It provides a mid-way between retributive and preventive accounts, by focusing on messages about the value of norms, the denunciation of crimes, the allocation of responsibility (based on culpability), and the acknowledgement of harm. This work shows that international criminal justice is more a project of accountability rather than a narrow punitive undertaking.[103] Some of the unique features of punishment do not lie not in the length of sentences but in the publicity of proceedings. Interests of victims are built into the foundations of punishment. Expressivism provides a mid-way between retributive and educational accounts of punishment by focusing on messages about the value of norms, the denunciation of crimes, and the acknowledgment of harm. As Mark Drumbl put it: 'The expressivist punishes to strengthen faith in rule of law among the general public, as opposed to punishing simply because the perpetrator deserves it or because potential perpetrators will be deterred by it.'[104]

Reparations add to punishment by expressing responsibility for wrongdoing to victims of crime and highlighting specific types of harm caused through crime.[105] Like punishment itself, they are an imperfect means to acknowledge responsibility, recognize victimhood, or remedy harm caused through crimes. They are rather a means to help to restore trust about civility and inspire commitment to a social contract among citizens, aimed at preventing future crimes.

Chapter 6 connects expressivism to justice discourse and different dimensions of justice. It claims that expressivism has a more complex role in international criminal justice than publicly admitted. It argues that the concept marks in the most general way an attempt to constitute a community, based on shared experiences and beliefs. It is a method to formulate community aspirations, create social meaning, and give content and form to law. The chapter then develops strengths and weaknesses of the idea of justice as communicative process.

[103] According to modern understandings, the function of international criminal law is not to brand perpetrators as enemies or threats that can be targeted outside the international legal system but rather as members of a normative community that are asked to account for their crimes. See Antony Duff, 'Responsibility, Citizenship and Criminal Law' in Antony Duff and Stuart P. Green (eds), *Philosophical Foundations of Criminal Law* (Oxford: Oxford University Press, 2011), 125–48, 143.

[104] Drumbl, *Atrocity, Punishment and International Law* 173. See also Meijers and Glasius, 'Trials as Messages of Justice' 437–8 ('The trial is a way to reaffirm legal order, establish truths, recognize the wrongs committed to the victims, and educate the public at large. It is not only a message about the crimes but also about the system of justice.').

[105] See generally Margaret Urban Walker, 'The expressive burden of reparations: putting meaning into money, words and things' in Alice MacLachlan and Allen Speight (eds), *In the Wake of Conflict: Justice, Responsibility and Reconciliation* (New York, NY: Springer, 2013), 205–25.

International criminal justice is constituted through social dynamics. It is a form of knowledge production.[106] It bears ritualistic features.[107] Like human rights law,[108] the field forms a sort of 'secular religion'.[109] It is characterized by social interaction and repetition, aimed at creating 'the basis for beliefs, thinking, morality, and culture'.[110] It institutes a forum for accountability that passes judgment and communicates values. It provides a way to deal with the unbearable nature and reality of international crimes. It draws on embellishments and alternate realities.[111] It relies on moral aspirations ('should be'), potentialities ('could be'), or fictions ('as if') to create shared moral and legal spaces.[112] Normative, institutional, procedural, or remedial expression are deemed to foster reproduction.[113] They seek to encourage public follow-up, initiate replication in international or domestic contexts, build networks of compliance, or foster civil courage or resilience to international crimes.[114]

Expressivism provides a novel lens to explain many of the complexities, weaknesses, and hidden contradictions of international justice. It challenges purely legalistic understandings. For example, legal norms and institutions speak not only through the (rudimentary) language of law, but through symbols, narratives, performances, and repetition.[115] Certain core notions, like evil, humankind,

[106] See Mikkel Jarle Christensen, 'The Emerging Sociology of International Criminal Courts: Between Global Restructurings and Scientific Innovations' (2015) 63 *Current Sociology Review* 825–49, 835–8.

[107] Rituals can be 'defined as culturally transmitted symbolic codes which are stylized, regularly repeated, dramatically structured, authoritatively designated, and intrinsically valued'. See Frederick Bird, 'The Nature and Function of Ritual Forms: A Sociological Discussion' (1980) 9 *Studies in Religion* 387–402, 388. See also Adam B. Seligman, Robert P. Weller, Michael J. Puett, and Bennett Simon, *Ritual and its Consequences: An Essay on the Limits of Sincerity* (New York, NY: Oxford University Press, 2008), Catherine Bell, *Ritual Theory, Ritual Practice* (New York, NY: Oxford University Press, 1992); Stanley J. Tambiah, 'A Performative Approach to Ritual' (1979) 65 *Proceedings of the British Academy* 113–69, 119.

[108] On human rights, see Marie-Bénédicte Dembour, *Who Believes in Human Rights? Reflections on the European Convention* (Cambridge: Cambridge University Press, 2006), 2; Hilary Charlesworth and Emma Larking (eds), *Human Rights and the Universal Periodic Review: Rituals and Ritualism* (Cambridge: Cambridge University Press, 2014).

[109] See generally Benjamin Authers, Hilary Charlesworth, Marie-Bénédicte Dembour, and Emma Larking, 'Introduction to Humanity Rituals Special Issue' (2018) 9 *Humanity: An International Journal of Human Rights, Humanitarianism, and Development* 63–74, 64; Anne Orford, 'Ritual, Mediation and the International Laws of the South' (2007) 16 *Griffith Law Review* 353–74.

[110] Erika Summers-Effler, 'Ritual theory' in Jan E. Stets and Jonathan H. Turner (eds), *Handbook of the Sociology of Emotions* (New York, NY: Springer, 2007), 135–53.

[111] Seligman et al., *Ritual and its Consequences* 27 ('ritual is a means of performing the way things ought to be in conscious tension to the way things are in such a way that this ritualised perfection is recollected in the ordinary, uncontrolled, course of things').

[112] Seligman et al., *Ritual and its Consequences* 7–8.

[113] See also Authers et al., 'Introduction to Humanity Rituals Special Issue' 65 ('By creating an "as if" world, ritual brings that world into being. Once the ritual has come to a close, participants may continue to act in a manner consistent with its construction.').

[114] See generally Yves Dezalay and Bryant Garth (eds), *Lawyers and the Construction of Transnational Justice* (New York, NY: Routledge, 2012).

[115] On trials as shaming rituals, see Harold Garfinkel, 'Conditions of Successful Degradation Ceremonies' (1961) 61 *American Journal of Sociology* 420–4; James Cockayne, 'Hybrids or Mongrels? Internationalized War Crimes Trials as Unsuccessful Degradation Ceremonies' (2005) 4 *Journal of Human Rights* 455–73.

deterrence, retribution, or individual criminal responsibility are repeated like mantras. Their apparent incontestability provides a means to gain empathy and shield critiques.[116]

Storytelling is an important element of normative and procedural expression. Stories play a crucial law in the performance of justice. They serve as 'aids to selecting from a superfluity of information and to filling in gaps in that information; they are a vehicle for introducing judgements of value; and, above all, they provide essential frames of reference for organizing, evaluating and interpreting evidence'.[117]

Judgments and legal decisions use narratives, imagery, and expressivist language to appeal to the affective dimensions of audiences. They present alternative 'ways of seeing', invoke narratives of progress,[118] or use collective narration in order to create authoritative narratives[119] and engage audiences in the performance of justice.

Institutions are collective platforms to reflect, digest, or acknowledge moral failures. They assert power, create potential path dependencies, and communicate a sense of guardianship of international criminal justice. Procedures relate not only to participants in proceedings but also a broader public audience. They are performed at symbolic spaces.[120]

Punishment serves not only to inflict a punitive sanction on the offender but to publicly express condemnation and repudiation. The reiteration of these practices is deemed to have an integrative effect.[121] It is meant to organize social relations, offer a common discursive space, strengthen social ties, and build international criminal justice as a field through re-enactments. Ultimately, this practice 'performs and makes manifest an unrealized and perhaps unrealizable ideal of justice', but 'one that we nevertheless wish to preserve as the normative ideal for real time'.[122]

[116] For a critique, see Ann Sagan, 'African Criminals/African Victims: The Institutionalised Production of Cultural Narratives in International Criminal Law' (2010) 39 *Millennium—Journal of International Studies* 3–21.

[117] See William Twining, 'Lawyers' stories' in William Twining (ed.), *Rethinking Evidence: Exploratory Essays* (Cambridge: Cambridge University Press, 2006), 286–331, 308.

[118] See Renana Keydar, '"Lessons in Humanity": Re-evaluating International Criminal Law's Narrative of Progress in the Post 9/11 Era' (2019) 17 *JICJ* 229–57.

[119] Timothy William Waters, 'Dead man's tale: Deriving narrative authority from the terminated Milošević trial' in Timothy William Waters (ed.), *The Milošević Trial—An Autopsy* (Oxford: Oxford University Press, 2013), 297–300.

[120] On connections between law and political space, see Chris Adrian Butler, 'Critical Legal Studies and the Politics of Space' (2009) 18 *Social & Legal Studies* 313–32.

[121] German doctrine has coined the term 'integrative prevention' in order to reflect this ambition. See Jens Christian Müller-Tuckfeld, *Integrationsprävention: Studien zu einer Theorie der gesellschaftlichen Funktion des Strafrechts* (Frankfurt: Peter Lang, 1998).

[122] Danielle Celermajer, 'Mere Ritual? Displacing the Myth of Sincerity in Transitional Justice Rituals' (2013) 7 *International Journal of Transitional Justice* 286–305, 299.

In the widest sense, expressivism helps to understand international criminal justice as a 'realistic utopia'.[123] This notion has been developed in philosophies of justice (e.g. John Rawls)[124] and human rights (e.g. Jürgen Habermas)[125] to deal with the tension between universal aspiration and practical limitations, including the connection between morality and politics. It has direct relevance to international criminal justice.[126] Expressivism embraces normative ideals of international criminal justice but cautions against an idealism that is detached from political and social conditions. It provides a more modest foundation for international criminal justice than consequentialists accounts.

However, the concept also carries risks. Expressivism is a form of power. It may over-promise. Some of the alleged goals of expressivism, such as moral education, societal transformation, empowerment of victims, or cathartic features of criminal trials rely on complex social and cognitive processes that are ambitious and difficult to verify.[127]

Existing practices remain strongly focused on norm projection, institutional messaging, or demonstration effects.[128] This may have unintended negative side effects. Critics argue that expressivist practices may erase alternative accounts of truth, produce new social hierarchies and power relations, and pay limited attention to real-life interests of immediate victims of crimes.[129] Normative projection and the creation of novel relational spaces triggers broader social responsibilities.

The communicative structures require rethinking. International criminal justice often lacks a bonded community in local settings. The relationship between the 'messenger' and its diverse audiences, the reception of messages, and channels of dialogue and persuasion have received far less attention. Messages are heavily

[123] It may be defined as an 'an account of the world which is utopian in so far as it does not reflect existing social arrangements, but realistic in so far as it does not contravene anything we know about human nature'. See Chris Brown, 'The Construction of a "Realistic Utopia"': John Rawls and International Political Theory' (2002) 28 *Review of International Studies* 5–21, 7.

[124] John Rawls, *The Law of Peoples* (Cambridge, MA: Harvard University Press, 1999).

[125] Jürgen Habermas, 'The Concept of Human Dignity and the Realistic Utopia of Human Rights' (2010) 41 *Metaphilosophy* 464–80.

[126] See Antonio Cassese (ed.), *Realizing Utopia: The Future of International Law* (Oxford: Oxford University Press, 2012), Terry Tomsky, 'Towards a Realistic Utopia: Literary Representations of the International Criminal Tribunal for the Former Yugoslavia' (2016) 22 *Australian Journal of Human Rights* 123–42; Fannie Lafontaine, 'Universal Jurisdiction—the Realistic Utopia (2012) 10 *JICJ* 1277–302.

[127] Some of the 'rituals' that international criminal justice provides seek to shape consciousness and generate affect and cognitive change, but are not followed by action. They create 'feelings, ideas, and images that follow their own law'. See Emile Durkheim, *The Elementary Forms of Religious Life* (translated by K. Fields) (New York, NY: Free Press, 1995) 426.

[128] For a defence, see Bill Wringe, 'Rethinking Expressive Theories of Punishment: Why Denunciation is a Better than Communication or Pure Expression' (2017) 174 *Philosophical Studies* 681–708.

[129] Bhupinder S. Chimni, 'The Rituals of Human Rights Bodies: A View from the Global South'. Paper delivered at 'The Rituals of Human Rights' Workshop, Centre for International Governance and Justice, RegNet, Australian National University, Canberra, Australia, 25–27 June 2014.

encrypted and require interpretation to be understood. Speakers themselves require cognitive ability and social learning, including the will 'to learn from the wider public they are supposed to serve'.[130] There is a need for more two-sided communication, the more international criminal institutions affect social reality and the concrete lives of people.[131]

[130] Marlies Glasius, 'Do International Criminal Courts Require Democratic Legitimacy?' (2012) 23 *EJIL Democratic Legitimacy* 43–66, 61.
[131] See Sloane, 'Expressive Capacity of International Punishment' 55, who argues that the focus lies on the 'penal interests and values of the international community as a collective, not local political and social orders'; Meijers and Glasius, 'Trials as Messages of Justice' 441–2.

1
International Criminal Justice and Expressivist Theory

Expressivism is a concept that transcends disciplines. It has gained ground in the legal literature in the second half of the twentieth century.[1] However, its roots are much older. Expressivism has played an important role in aesthetic theory and the philosophy of art.[2] For instance, in his famous essay on 'What is Art?', Leo Tolstoy defined art as the expression of emotion by the artist to the audience through a medium, that is through words, paint, or music.[3] His theories were later developed by British philosopher Robin George Collingwood who defended a more cognitive theory. He argued that art can be distinguished from representational art or entertainment by the fact that it does not simply convey a message or express an emotion but involves a process of cognitive discovery (e.g. learning) or stimulation (e.g. expressive imagination) by the artist and the viewer. Collingwood accepted that the role of the audience is not merely passive ('receptive'), but 'collaborative'.[4] He stated that the artist 'undertakes his artistic labour not as a personal effort on his own private behalf, but as a public labour on behalf of the community to which he belongs'.[5] Other theorists have claimed that art's meaning is produced predominantly in the viewer rather than the artwork itself.

In the legal field, expressive theories have started to be invoked in general theories of law[6] and domestic justifications of punishment since the 1960s.[7] They have

[1] Andrew Koppelman, 'On the Moral Foundations of Legal Expressivism' (2001) 60 *Maryland Law Review* 777–84; Matthew X. Etchemendy, 'New Directions in Legal Expressivism' (2016) 22 *Legal Theory* 1–22. On traces of expressivism in Hart's work, see Kevin Toh, 'Hart's Expressivism and His Benthamite Project' (2005) 11 *Legal Theory* 75–123.

[2] Gordon Graham, *Philosophy of the Arts: An Introduction to Aesthetics*, 2nd edn (London: Routledge, 2000), 33 et seq.

[3] See Leo Tolstoy, *What is Art* (Oxford: Oxford University Press, 1930). His theory was criticized for reducing art to the artists 'original emotions' ('naïve expressivism') and ignoring that art can express messages or emotions that the artist never felt or intended. See Gordon Graham, 'Expressivism' in Berys Gaut and Dominic Lopes (eds), *The Routledge Companion to Aesthetics*, 3rd edn (London: Routledge, 2013), 106–15.

[4] Robin George Collingwood, *Principles of Art* (New York, NY: Oxford University Press, 1938), 324.

[5] Ibid., 314–15.

[6] Elizabeth S. Anderson and Richard H. Pildes, 'Expressive Theories of Law: A General Restatement' (2000) 148 *University of Pennsylvania Law Review* 1504–75, 1503; Matthew D. Adler, 'Expressive Theories of Law: A Skeptical Overview' (2000) 148 *University of Pennsylvania Law Review* 1363–500, 1364.

[7] Ted Sampsell-Jones, 'Culture and Contempt: The Limitations of Expressive Criminal Law' (2003) 27 *Seattle University Law Review* 133–90.

Justice as Message. Carsten Stahn, Oxford University Press (2020). © Carsten Stahn.
DOI: 10.1093/oso/9780198864189.001.0001

received support by the rise of the law and literature movement which has stressed the performative features of law and legal cultures.[8] According to these understandings, law operates not merely 'within a paradigm of one-dimensional rationality' but it triggers a communicative process.[9] Expressivists insist that 'law works by what it says in addition to what it does'.[10]

Expressivist theory has gained prominence in domestic justice due to the rise of civil society movements[11] and a 'communicative turn of modern societies'.[12] It changed perceptions relating to the relationship between State authority, the offender, and victims. Expressivism was applied to different aspects of criminal justice: the justification of punishment, rational engagement with the offender,[13] or the sending of messages to the broader social community of the offender and the victim.[14] As Antony Duff has claimed, expressivism has a broader basis than communication of punishment and sentencing. It is able to justify trials by other reasons than punishment. For instance, expressivists would argue that where a 'defendant dies shortly after conviction, or for some other reason cannot be punished, justice has still to be done by his trial, since he has been held to account'.[15]

Criminal law theorists (e.g. Tatjana Hörnle) have distinguished at least two major forms of expressivism: (i) norm-oriented expression which is directed at a general public and geared at reaffirming moral values and normative appeals through punishment; and (ii) agent-based expression which derives the virtue of punishment from its ability to send messages to different types of actors (e.g. the perpetrator, victims).[16]

[8] James Boyd White, *The Legal Imagination: Abridged Edition* (Chicago, IL: University of Chicago Press, [1973] 1985), xiii ('The law makes a world. And the law in another sense, as the profession we teach and learn and practice, is a kind of cultural competence: an art of reading the special literature of the law and an art of speaking and writing—of making compositions of one's own—in this language. It is a branch of rhetoric.').

[9] Mark van Hoecke, *Law as Communication* (Oxford: Hart Publishing, 2002), 10.

[10] Richard H. McAdams, 'A Focal Point Theory of Expressive Law', 86 *Virginia Law Review* 1649–729, 1650–1.

[11] Jeffrey Alexander, *The Civil Sphere* (Oxford: Oxford University Press, 2006).

[12] See Klaus Günther, 'Criminal Law, Crime and Punishment as Communication', Normative Orders Working Paper 02/2014, 3–4, at https://d-nb.info/1054399557/34, also published in Andrew. P. Simester, Antje du Bois Pedain, and Ulfrid Neumann (eds), *Liberal Criminal Theory. Essays for Andreas von Hirsch* (Oxford: Hart Publishing, 2014), 123–40.

[13] Antony Duff, *Punishment, Communication, and Community* (Oxford: Oxford University Press, 2001).

[14] Bill Wringe, *An Expressive Theory of Punishment* (London: Palgrave Macmillan, 2016); Antony Duff, 'Penal Communities' (1999) 1 *Punishment & Society* 27–43; Antony Duff, 'Penance, Punishment and the Limits of Community' (2003) 5 *Punishment & Society* 295–312. For an exploration of the limits, see Marguerite Schinkel, 'Punishment as Moral Communication: The Experiences of Long-Term Prisoners' (2014) 16 *Punishment & Society* 578–97.

[15] Antony Duff, 'Authority and Responsibility in International Criminal Law' in Samantha Besson and John Tasioulas (eds), *The Philosophy of International Law* (Oxford: Oxford University Press, 2010) 589–604, 598.

[16] See Tatjana Hörnle, *Straftheorien* (Tübingen: Mohr Siebeck, 2017), 31–6.

In international criminal justice, expressivism has gained acceptance as a theory only recently.[17] Specific forms of expressivism (e.g. the expressive functions of judgments) may be traced back to the origins of international criminal adjudication. For example, Lawrence Douglas has shown in his *Memory of Judgment* that expressive language can be found in many historical judgments.[18] However, a fuller understanding of the different forms and functions of expressivism emerged only through contemporary studies of the multiple faces of justice agents, their effects, and constituencies across multiple disciplines (e.g. law, international relations, victimology, and sociology).

In international criminal justice, expressivism is related to a broader public, including the offender, victims, local groups, and international society.[19] Some authorities place the emphasis on the role of the criminal process to affirm law or values. For instance, Antonio Cassese has argued that the *raison d'être* of international criminal law lies in value expression or strengthening of protected interests towards a broader public.[20] Others pay greater attention to the didactic and communicative features of criminal law, including its role in persuasion and internalizing values. One of the virtues of expressivist theory is that it may explain some of the unique features and paradoxes of the field and the limitations of legalism in relation to international crimes.

1.1 Origin and Foundations of Expressivist Theory

Many of the conceptual foundations of expressivist theory are grounded in sociology. Expressivism tends to see criminal law as an instrument to transmit values and change attitudes.[21] It fits within theories of communication action. For instance, Jürgen Habermas has argued that communicative processes occur not only through language but also through signs and symbols.[22] Niklas Luhmann has claimed that law marks an autopoietic[23] social system that constitutes and

[17] The rediscovery expressivism is *inter alia* related to the emancipation of international criminal law as a juridical field and the growing consciousness of the role of international criminal courts and tribunals as social agents.

[18] Lawrence Douglas, *The Memory of Judgment: Making Law and History in the Trials of the Holocaust* (New Haven, CT: Yale University Press, 2001).

[19] Tim Meijers and Marlies Glasius, 'Trials as Messages of Justice: What Should Be Expected of International Criminal Courts?' (2016) 30 *Ethics & International Affairs* 329–447, 442–4.

[20] Cassese calls this 'universal values legitimacy'. See Antonio Cassese, 'The Legitimacy of International Courts and Tribunals and Their Current Prospects' (2012) 25 *LJIL* 491–501, 497.

[21] Kirsten J. Fisher, *Moral Accountability and International Criminal Law, Holding Agents of Atrocity Accountable to the World* (London: Routledge, 2011), 49–65, 59.

[22] See Jürgen Habermas, *The Theory of Communicative Action, Volume 1, Reason and the Rationalization of Society* (Boston, MA: Beacon Press, 1984); *Volume 2, System and Lifeworld: A Critique of Functionalist Reason* (Boston, MA: Beacon Press, 1987).

[23] Autopoiesis refers to 'self-creation' or 'self-making'.

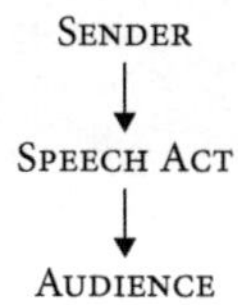

Figure 1 Tripartite relationship

reproduces itself through communication.[24] Expressivism acknowledges that justice occurs not merely as a sequence of events and procedures but functions within a discursive space. It builds on the idea that law derives its meaning not only from intent of legal agents but also from its reading, perception, and understanding by different agents in light of existing social norms.[25]

Expressivists argue that the law itself is not 'silent' but is constructed through communicative relationships. Logically, expressivism requires three elements: a sender, a speech act, and an audience.

1.1.1 The communicative cycle

In the criminal justice context, expressivism has been associated with at least three different functions: (i) its ability to denounce the wrong done by the offenders and harm caused to victims; (ii) the capacity to highlight the communicative and performative aspects of trials; and (iii) the possibility to identify messages sent through action.[26]

It involves three layers of communication: the criminal norm, which contains a normative statement;[27] the crime itself, which may be read as a message;[28] and trial and punishment, which seek to answer such messages.[29] It is thus based on a communicative cycle.

[24] Niklas Luhmann, *Das Recht der Gesellschaft* (Frankfurt: Suhrkamp, 1993), 61. Luhmann has argued that law is a system of communication which is self-establishing and reproducing. See Niklas Luhmann, *Einführung in die Systemtheorie* (Heidelberg: Carl Auer-Verlag, 2017). Punishment serves not only as a means to enforce norms but to demonstrate them. See also Niklas Luhmann, 'What is Communication?' (1992) 2 *Communication Theory* 251–9. On Luhmann's idea of autopoiesis, see Hugh Baxter, 'Niklas Luhmann's Theory of Autopoietic Legal Systems' (2013) 9 *Annual Review of Law and Social Science* 167–84.

[25] Klaus Günther, *Schuld und kommunikative Freiheit* (Frankfurt: Klostermann, 1995).

[26] Maria Elander, 'The Victim's Address: Expressivism and the Victim at the Extraordinary Chambers in the Courts of Cambodia' (2013) 7 *International Journal of Transitional Justice* 95–115, 100–1.

[27] Duff, *Punishment, Communication, and Community* 80 ('In claiming authority over the citizens, it claims that there are good reasons, grounded in the community's values for them to eschew such wrongs... It speaks to the citizens as members of the normative community.').

[28] See Günther, 'Criminal Law, Crime and Punishment as Communication' 6 ('the crime itself, insofar as it was committed by a rational and communicative agent, has a communicative meaning').

[29] On punishment as speech act, see Roman Hamel, *Strafen als Sprechakt. Die Bedeutung der Strafe für das Opfer* (Berlin: Duncker & Humblot, 2009).

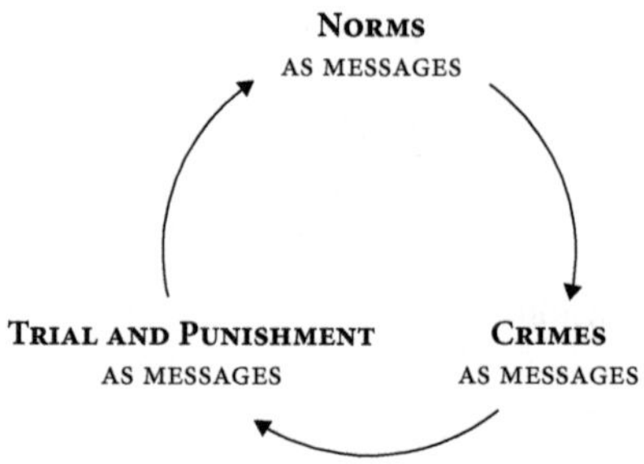

Figure 2 Communicative cycle

Communication consists of a message sent by an addresser to an addressee.[30] The message, sent in code, requires a contact between addresser and addressee that may be made orally, visually, or otherwise. If the message does not refer to a context that is mutually understood between the addressee and the addresser (who presumably share the convention upon which this code depends), the message will not make sense.

1.1.1.1 Expressive norms

The recognition of the expressive nature of norms is a first key element of the communicative cycle. Criminal norms do not only provide authorization for agents to exercise criminal powers or to inflict punishment. Philosophers like Jeremy Bentham have established that criminal norms express values, establish authority over citizens, and contain appeals for law-abiding behaviour.[31] They entail value judgments, that is messages about behaviours that should be avoided and correspondingly that a sanction will be applied in case of violation.[32] This understanding is reflected in modern constitutional systems. In democracies, criminal norms are

[30] A theory of communication has been developed by Russian-American linguist Roman Jakobson. He has argued that an act of communication requires six elements, or factors of communication, that are necessary for communication to occur: (i) context (e.g. an environment in which the message takes place); (ii) a sender; (iii) a receiver; (4) a contact; (5) a common code; and (6) a message. See Roman Jakobson 'Linguistics and poetics' in Thomas Sebeok (ed.), *Style in Language* (Cambridge, MA: M.I.T. Press, 1960), 350–77.

[31] Cass R. Sunstein, 'On the Expressive Function of Law' (1996) 133 *University of Pennsylvania Law Review* 2021–54, 2021; Anderson and Pildes, 'Expressive Theories of Law' 1504 ('Expressive theories tell actors—whether individuals, associations, or the State—to act in ways that express appropriate attitudes toward various substantive values.').

[32] See Jeremy Bentham, *An Introduction to the Principles of Morals and Legislation*, James H. Burns and Herbert L.A. Hart (eds) (London: Athlone Press, 1970), 307 ('The constitutional branch is chiefly employed in conferring, on particular classes of persons, powers, to be exercised for the good of the whole society, or of considerable parts of it, and prescribing duties to the persons invested with those powers.').

formed through collective deliberative procedures and aimed at influencing the behaviour of individuals. They reflect generalized interests and speak to citizens as members of a normative community.[33]

In international law, these communicative structures are more diffuse and decentralized. However, many international criminal norms are expressive in character and have a strong normative appeal. They are grounded in moral norms and certain commonly protected interests. Their formulation in treaty instruments, statutory frameworks, UN resolutions, judicial decisions, or soft law instruments is meant to form a normative community and to persuade states, non-actors, and individuals to behave in accordance with these behavioural standards.

As Christoph Möllers has argued,[34] norms are not merely prohibitive or restrictive in nature but also enabling. They are 'operating codes'. They articulate 'possibilities', provide incentives to act, and facilitate practices that would otherwise not exist. Many norms in international criminal justice are expressive in this sense.[35] They express wrongs and carry meaning and legal significance in themselves, irrespective of the consequences that they entail.[36] They communicate values or desirable forms of behaviour. They incentivize norm addresses to regard prohibitions as a 'cherished' good.[37] Crimes or non-deviant behaviour diminish that expressive value.

Norms, such as the prohibition of aggression, genocide, crimes against humanity, or war crimes, are marked by a certain degree of indeterminacy. This leaves space for pluralist understandings or evolution of meaning. For instance, the very concept of crimes against humanity involves many different individual crimes that raise cultural sensitivities. Notions such as aggression, war crimes, or genocide provide an umbrella for a whole range of protected norms and prohibited acts. However, the use of a common framework for such categories of crimes itself has expressive value. It signals that there is 'in fact a single label for very different norms' that involves a 'common presupposition', namely that these matter legally and morally.[38]

[33] See also Günther, 'Criminal Law, Crime and Punishment as Communication' 14 ('[the legal norm] is not a generalised will viewed from nowhere, detached from the real interests of individual citizens, but the result of a public deliberation about interests').

[34] See Christoph Möllers, *Die Möglichkeit der Normen: Über eine Praxis jenseits von Moralität und Kausalität* (Berlin: Suhrkamp, 2015).

[35] On human dignity as expressive norm, see Tarunabh Khaitan, 'Dignity as an Expressive Norm: Neither Vacuous Nor a Panacea' (2012) 32 *Oxford Journal of Legal Studies* 1–19.

[36] Ibid., 4, 'Expressions matter morally qua expressions, independently of the consequences or other (non-expressive) aspects of the action itself.'

[37] See also Emily Kidd White, 'Till Human Voices Wake Us: The Role of Emotions in the Adjudication of Dignity Claims' (2014) 3 *Journal of Law, Religion and State* 201–39, 213.

[38] Khaitan, 'Dignity as an Expressive Norm' 19.

1.1.1.2 The crime as expression

The 'crime' is a second element in the communicative chain. As been argued in domestic criminal law theory (e.g. Georg Friedrich Hegel,[39] Günther Jakobs[40]), a crime is not only a natural act, involving material and mental elements, but a social act which carries a certain normative meaning. For instance, Hegel viewed punishment as the 'other half' of crime. He noted that crimes demonstrate an assault on rights that posit a 'new law'.[41] He famously argued that 'the crime is to be annulled, not because it is the producing of an evil, but because it is the infringement of the right as right'.[42]

Contemporary accounts view crimes as a special type of speech act, namely as a communicative act that sends a message of objection, defiance, or negligence towards the criminal norm.[43] It does not operate in a vacuum, but takes on a specific meaning. It may be understood as 'a violation of a norm of criminal law, a violation of legally protected interests or goods, a harm to others which is legally prohibited'.[44]

The commission of a crime does not per se negate the existence of the criminal norm. But it may imply that the perpetrator placed his or her own interests above other competing interests that are protected by the criminal norm.[45] In certain cases (e.g. terrorism), the crime might involve an outright rejection of the norm or the order that represents. In other contexts, it might entail a more subtle challenge: a different weighing of protected interests or a claim of superiority which infringes on the rights of victims.[46] For instance, crimes may affect the status and power balance between offenders, victims, and society as a whole. They may violate

[39] Hegel has argued that a crime is an expressive act which posits the existence of a new norm. See Georg Friedrich Hegel, *Elements of the Philosophy of Right, §§ 100–101: Justice*, Allen W. Wood (ed.), translated by H.B. Nisbet (Cambridge: Cambridge University Press, 1991), 126.

[40] Günther Jakobs has compared a crime to a speech act, namely a declarative statement by the offender which calls into question the validity of a criminal norm. See Günther Jakobs, 'Strafrecht zwischen Funktionalismus und Prinzipiendenken' (1995) 107 *Zeitschrift für die gesamte Strafrechtswissenschaft* 843–76, 844 ('Erst im kommunikativen Verständnis der Tat als normwiedersprechende Behauptung und der Strafe als normbestätigende Antwort mag sich ein umumgehbarer und in dem Sinn vernünftiger Zusammenhang zeigen.').

[41] On Hegel, see Markus Dubber, 'Rediscovering Hegel's Theory of Crime and Punishment' (1994) 92 *Michigan Law Review* 1577–621, 1607 ('Punishment responds not to crime's subjective aspect—the infliction of a loss on a particular victim—but to its objective aspect—the affront to right as such manifested in the criminal act.').

[42] Hegel, *Elements of the Philosophy of Right*, § 99. For a critique of Hegel, see Larry May, *Crimes Against Humanity: A Normative Account* (Cambridge: Cambridge University Press, 2005), 222–4.

[43] On the view that criminal behaviour carries a meaning, see Jakobs, 'Strafrecht zwischen Funktionalismus und Prinzipiendenken' 844.

[44] Günther, 'Criminal Law, Crime and Punishment as Communication' 8.

[45] Not all crimes may be viewed as an attack on criminal norms or protected interests or as action that places individual interests over societal interests. For instance, in some cases, the underlying norm may be outdated. Other crimes may be driven by competing societal interests. The 'crime as expression' can also have a transformative effect, that is bring about a decriminalization of conduct.

[46] See Daniel Farnham, 'A Hegelian Theory of Retribution' (2008) 39 *Journal of Social Philosophy* 606–24, 620 ('In wrongdoing that involves both damage to acknowledgement and realization of a person's value, there is an elevation of one person above another that constitutes subjugation or mastery.').

values that victims expect to share with the offender or that are common to a group or society. This is particularly compelling in international criminal justice, where many offences coincide with human rights violations or are understood as crimes against humanity.

One problem of a communicative understanding of crime is that it involves a strong degree of attribution: the message sent may not necessarily correspond to what the perpetrator had in mind. It must often be inferred from the social context. The social meaning of the crime is thus virtually created through the criminal process (i.e. charges, trial, sentencing).

1.1.1.3 Trial and punishment as expression

Trial and punishment are a third element in the communicative sequence. They provide to some extent 'reactive attitudes'[47] or an 'answer' to the message of the crime. If norms entail behavioural commands, and crimes entail express or implicit challenges to such commands, then trial and punishment are essential means to counter such messages. They may be conceived as public objections to the violations of norms, and the messages sent through crimes. A failure to respond may destabilize faith in the common order or make public authorities complicit in the violation.

Trials entail a whole range of messages that extend beyond punishment. They 'speak' to the citizens as members of the normative community. They serve to reinforce belief in the validity of norms, articulate the public understanding of the acts of the perpetrator, and to engage the offender, the victim, and society in discourse over wrongdoing. The judgment is essentially a reasoned public speech act. It articulates the social meaning of the crime in the language of law and identifies the consequences of the action.[48]

Punishment is the last step in this communicative cycle. It is deemed to satisfy public expectations, express wrongdoing, and induce future compliance. It might reflect a certain legislative intent (e.g. in case of mandatory sentencing requirements) or an expression by the sentencing authority. Punishment is often less

[47] See Tobias Zürcher, *Legitimation von Strafe: Die expressive-kommunikative Straftheorie zur Rechtfertigung von Strafe* (Tübingen: Mohr Siebeck, 2014), 106. On 'reactive attitudes', see Peter F. Strawson, 'Freedom and Resentment' in Peter F. Strawson, *Freedom and Resentment and other Essays* (London: Methuen, 1974) 1–25.

[48] ICC President Chile Eboe-Osuji relied on this communicative understanding in the aftermath of the Gbagbo acquittal. He noted: '[Punishment] does not tell the whole story of the meaning of accountability ... accountability means first and foremost an assurance that no one is above the law. It means primarily that everyone, regardless of their station in life, must answer to the law.' He qualified judicial performance as the articulation of a counter-proposition. He stated: '[T]he dispensation of accountability then presents the counter-norm, which requires everyone—regardless of station or stature—to answer questions in the manner of reasonably founded allegations of wrongdoing made against them.' Remarks at Ceremony for Opening of Judicial Year by Judge Chile Eboe-Osuji, Friday, 18 January 2019, 2, at https://www.icc-cpi.int/itemsDocuments/190118-opening-judicial-year-president-stat_ENG.pdf. Ibid., 3.

communicative in nature than the criminal process itself since it often entails social exclusion of the perpetrator (i.e. imprisonment). It is increasingly connected to the idea of accountability towards victims (e.g. through victim participation, impact statements, or reparation).[49]

This general structure is helpful to understand the functioning of criminal justice in classical liberal structures (e.g. democratic societies). It takes into account the norm-affirmative function of criminal law in society and the role of individuals as equal, rational, and communicative subjects.

International criminal law differs partly from domestic contexts. It has a more rudimentary regulatory framework, limited enforcement powers, a more selective punishment culture, and a less developed sentencing practice.[50] But it shares many precepts of the classical liberal trial model. It relies heavily on normative appeal to State agents, non-State actors and individuals, in order to maintain its validity. Trial and punishment may thus even gain more symbolic value.[51]

1.1.2 Durkheim: Criminal law as expression of a collective conscience

Many of the sociological foundations of expressivist theory can be traced back to French sociologist Emile Durkheim.[52] Durkheim understood punishment not strictly in the sense of state control but as a form of social expression. He related criminality to conceptions of collective conscience and morality of society. He viewed law an instrument of expressing moral attitudes in society. He feared that phenomena such as economic crises might destabilize a society more than classical murder crimes. He claimed that repression of crime constitutes an expression of collective beliefs and sentiments of a specific society. He saw criminality as an attack on such beliefs and punishment as an instrument to reaffirm social solidarity. Thus, according to Durkheim, the evil nature of criminality lies not so much in the crime itself but in its destructive effect on common beliefs. Key ideas are reflected in his famous work, *Division of Labor in Society* (1893), which was written at the height of industrialization. He argued that the 'true function' of punishment is 'to maintain social cohesion intact, while maintaining all its vitality in the common conscience'.[53]

[49] Jo-Anne Wemmers, 'Where Do They Belong? Giving Victims a Place in the Criminal Justice Process' (2009) 20 *Criminal Law Forum* 395–416; Tatjana Hörnle, 'Die Rolle des "Opfers in der Straftheorie und im materiellen Strafrecht"' (2006) 19 *Juristenzeitung* 950–7.

[50] See **section 6.1**.

[51] See **section 4.1**.

[52] See generally Steven Lukes, *Emile Durkheim: His Life and Work: A Historical and Critical Study* (Stanford, CA: Stanford University Press, 1973).

[53] Emile Durkheim, *The Division of Labour in Society* (translated by George Simpson) (New York, NY: The Free Press, 1947), 108.

His work was partly a reaction to the threats of liberalism to commonly shared beliefs and the moral order in society. It has close links to the idea that certain crimes affect the common conscience of a global community,[54] which emerged in the twentieth century.

Durkheim regarded judicial institutions as legitimate guardians of collective beliefs who are entitled to express to outrage to attacks on morality and collective conscience. He accepted that punishment extends beyond rational determination of guilt. He associated punishment with expression of feeling, that is a 'passionate reaction',[55] through which society condemns criminal behaviour.

In later works (e.g. *Moral Education*), Durkheim stressed the demonstrative effects of punishment.[56] His conception of punishment was thus less concerned with the offender than with the message and social meaning of punishment. His ideas on the links between criminal law and religions mirror contemporary debates on the faith-based nature of international criminal justice as a project.[57] His work stressed the value of punishment to the community itself. The originality of Durkheim's approach in relational to modern accounts of international criminal justice lies in the fact that he accepted that punishment reflects in part 'society's pure expressivist urge to manifest itself to itself'.[58] It is guided by the hope that adjudication may contribute to the formation of a universal social solidarity.

Several aspects of Durkheim's theory have been criticized. Some scholars have challenged Durkheim's central assumption that punishment as such promotes 'social solidarity'.[59] For example, Michel Foucault has argued that punishment is more about the assertion of power and control than about social bonding.[60] Other scholars have questioned the basic premise of Durkheim's view that law and punishment reflect commonly shared beliefs. For instance, David Garland has noted that 'it is not "society as a whole" that enacts laws and punishes offenders but, rather, legislative elites and professional functionaries, whose particular priorities and concerns may prompt an enacted version of social morality that is not universally shared'.[61]

More recently, Durkheim's theory has also been challenged from the perspective of democratic legitimacy. It takes a rather uncritical approach to the role of courts

[54] Immi Tallgren, 'The Durkheimian Spell of International Criminal Law?' (2013) *71 Revue interdisciplinaire d'études juridiques* 137–69, 149.

[55] Durkheim, *The Division of Labour in Society* 90.

[56] Emile Durkheim, *Moral Education* (New York, NY: The Free Press, 1961), 176.

[57] Tallgren, 'Durkheimian Spell of International Criminal Law' 169.

[58] See Frédéric Mégret, 'Practices of Stigmatization' (2013) 76 *Law and Contemporary Problems* 287–318, 290.

[59] See David Garland, 'Sociological Perspectives on Punishment' (1991) 14 *Crime and Justice* 115–65, 125.

[60] Foucault argued that institutions of punishment are about power and control, rather than rehabilitation. See Michel Foucault, *Discipline and Punish: The Birth of the Prison* (New York, NY: Pantheon Books, 1978).

[61] Garland, 'Sociological Perspectives on Punishment' 125–6.

as such. It assumes they have a representative role and that they are able to express a collective conscience in relation to society as a whole, without investigating their limitations. The approach 'suggests a democratic outcome (judgments "naturally" expressing the will of the people) without requiring a democratic input to guarantee the outcome'.[62]

The merit of Durkheim lies in the fact that he paved the way for a broader understanding of punishment, which is rooted in 'cultural practices' and based on 'a complex pattern of regulatory, expressive and significatory effects'.[63]

1.1.3 Expressivist justifications of punishment in domestic law

In the course of the twentieth century, expressivist theory was mostly developed in contemporary domestic settings. It is reflected not only in Anglo-American scholarship but also in continental criminal law doctrine.[64]

1.1.3.1 Expressivist accounts of punishment

In the 1960s, Joel Feinberg clarified the expressive foundations of punishment.[65] He made the point that punishment has per definition an expressive function. He distinguished punishment from penalties. He argued that punishment has an expressive function that penalties lack.[66]

Feinberg stressed that punishment expresses not only the moral evil of the defendant but a broader social objection to criminal behaviour. He recognized that punishment has a symbolic function. It expresses a collective form of reprobation in relation to wrongdoing. He identified four key dimensions that are inherent in the expression of punishment: (i) the authoritative disavowal of the crime; (ii) symbolic non-acquiescence; (iii) the affirmation of the law to encourage law-abiding behaviour; and (iv) the absolution of others through punishment, which relieves others of suspicion and blame.[67] These four elements explain why punishment is a morally correct response to criminal behaviour. They are not only linked to the criminal sentence but the trial as a process. They provide to some extent an 'intrinsic' justification of expressivism, namely the value of expressing disapproval of

[62] Marlies Glasius, 'Do International Criminal Courts Require Democratic Legitimacy?' (2012) 23 *EJIL Democratic Legitimacy* 43–66, 54.

[63] See David Garland, 'Frameworks of inquiry in the sociology of punishment' (1990) 41 *British Journal of Sociology* 1–15, 10.

[64] See **section 1.1.4**.

[65] Joel Feinberg, 'The expressive function of punishment' in Joel Feinberg (ed.), *Doing and Deserving* (Princeton, NJ: Princeton University Press, 1970), 95–118.

[66] He stated that '[punishment] ... has a symbolic significance largely missing from other penalties'. See Feinberg, 'The expressive function of punishment' 400.

[67] Ibid., 401–8.

crime through punishment.[68] The inherently expressivist nature of criminal justice is illustrated by the negative, that is, the absence of punishment. As noted in scholarship: '[A] decision not to punish wrongdoers ... is also expressive: it communicates to the victim and to the wider society the idea that such treatment, and the status it attributes to the victim, are appropriate.'[69]

Feinberg's reasoning was developed in a number of works that defended the idea of 'punishment as censure'.[70] They have grounded expressivism in the obligation of a community to 'denounce' unlawful conduct of agents through punishment. Punishment may, for instance, signal the distance between the offender and the community whose rights have been violated. Others have built on Durkheim's work to argue that the purpose of punishment is to express 'appropriate emotional reactions to wrongdoing', for example moral outrage over the conduct.[71]

One of the weaknesses of Feinberg's argument was that it failed to offer a full explanation of the value of expressivism in relation to the punishment of the offender. Such a justification was provided by educational theories of punishment. For instance, Jean Hampton has argued that crimes entail an inherent claim of moral superiority by the offender over victims that is discarded by punishment.[72] She stressed that punishment has important demonstrative purposes. She claimed that punishment reinstates the equality of victims and defendants, since it 'negates the evidence of superiority implicit in the wrongdoer'.[73]

Others have argued that punishment is an act that translates the expression of condemnation into a language that offenders understand.[74] For instance, Igor Primoratz has claimed that 'merely verbal condemnation is not likely to reach its immediate addressee and to be fully understood by him'.[75] '[I]f society's condemnation of their misdeeds is really to reach [the criminals], if they really are to

[68] On 'intrinsic expressivism', see also Igor Primoratz, 'Punishment as Language' (1989) 64 *Philosophy* 187–205, 201–2; Barrie Sander, 'Justifying international criminal punishment: A critical perspective' in Morten Bergsmo and Emiliano J. Buis (eds), *Philosophical Foundations of International Criminal Law: Foundational Concepts* (Brussels: Torkel Opsahl Academic EPublisher, 2019), 167–240, 196 ('Intrinsic expressivist accounts seek to justify punishment by identifying some internal or inherent connection between crime and the symbolic character of punishment.').

[69] Jean Hampton, 'Correcting Harms versus Righting Wrongs: The Goal of Retribution' (1992) 39 *UCLA Law Review* 1659–1702, 1684–1685.

[70] On 'censure theory', see Jean Hampton, 'An expressive theory of retribution' in Wesley Cragg (ed.), *Retributivism and Its Critics* (Stuttgart: F. Steiner Verlag, 1992), 1–25; Andrew von Hirsch, 'Proportionality in the Philosophy of Punishment: From "Why Punish?" to "How Much?"' (1990) 1 *Criminal Law Forum* 259–90; Andrew von Hirsch, *Censure and Sanctions* (Oxford: Oxford University Press, 1993), Thaddeus Metz, 'Censure Theory and Intuitions about Punishment' (2000) 19 *Law and Philosophy* 491–512.

[71] Peter Königs, 'The Expressivist Account of Punishment, Retribution, and the Emotions' (2013) 16 *Ethic Theory Moral Practice* 1029–1049.

[72] Jean Hampton, 'The Moral Education Theory of Punishment' (1981) 10 *Philosophy & Public Affairs* 208–38, 223–30.

[73] Jean Hampton, 'The retributive idea' in Jeffrie. G. Murphy and Jean Hampton (eds), *Forgiveness and Mercy* (New York, NY: Cambridge University Press, 1988), 111–61, 129.

[74] Primoratz, 'Punishment as Language' 199–200; Michael Davis, 'Punishment as Language: Misleading Analogy for Desert Theorists' (1991) 10 *Law and Philosophy* 311–22.

[75] Primoratz, 'Punishment as Language' 200.

understand how wrong their actions are, it will have to be translated into the one and only language they understand (i.e., punishment).'[76]

These accounts largely failed to address the question to what extent there are viable alternative ways of denunciation or censure other than criminal punishment[77] (i.e. victim–offender mediation, alternative restorative forms of justice, non-criminal sanctions).

1.1.3.2 Communicative theories

Traditional expressive justifications of punishment were partly one-sided, that is, 'pure, non-communicative' types of expressivism.[78] They have focused on the act of expression of blame and reaffirmation of the law rather than its reception. This narrow focus has been challenged by communicative accounts which justify punishment as a method of communication. Antony Duff is among the most prominent defenders of a communicative theory of punishment.[79] He has argued that expressivism is not merely a 'one-way activity', but a 'two-way process that seeks to actively engage the other'.[80] He claimed that expressivist justifications require a process communication through which the condemnatory message is conveyed:

> Our reasons for maintaining such a system of law have to do with the prevention of crime and the good of the community but we do not simply use citizens or criminals as means to these ends: the law addresses all the citizens as rational moral agents, seeking their assent and their understanding; and punishment is part of that continuing dialogue.[81]

Duff has insisted that punishment must be expressed to a particular audience. He treated the criminal trial as a forum in which members of a common polity hold offenders accountable for public wrongs.[82]

Duff built on the tradition of Hegel who viewed punishment as a means to honour the defendant.[83] He developed classical theories which recognized that

[76] Ibid.

[77] See Joshua Glasgow, 'The Expressivist Theory of Punishment Defended' (2015) 34 *Law and Philosophy* 601–31, 614 et seq.

[78] Glasgow, 'The Expressivist Theory of Punishment Defended' 608.

[79] Duff, 'Punishment, communication and community' in Derek Matravers and Jonathan E. Pike (eds), *Punishment, Communication and Community* (London: Routledge, 2003), 387–407.

[80] Duff, 'Authority and Responsibility in International Criminal Law' 593.

[81] Duff, *Trials and Punishments* 238.

[82] See Duff, 'Authority and Responsibility in International Criminal Law' 595 ('Crimes are "public" wrongs, not in the sense that they harm the "public" as distinct from any individual victims, but in the sense that they are wrongs that concern the "public", i.e. all members of the polity, in virtue of their shared membership; the criminal trial is the forum in which we formally call each other to account, as citizens', for such wrongs.').

[83] In the early nineteenth century, Hegel viewed punishment as engagement with the perpetrator as rational being. He criticized Feuerbach's justification of punishment by psychological coercion. See Hegel, *Elements of the Philosophy of Right*, § 99 ('right and justice must have their seat in freedom and

punishment should build on a common bond of rationality between victim and offender. He stressed that offenders need to be treated as a rational agent. He justified the distinct expressive effects of the trial by the fact the defendant is called to answer charges 'as an active participant in the process who will receive and respond to the communication'.[84] Punishment becomes thus a way of rational communication which sends a message of disapproval to a particular offender. This communicative approach seeks to induce offenders to recognize the wrongfulness of acts: 'Punishment ... aims at the goals of repentance, reform and reconciliation. These goals are to be pursued by a communicative process of imposing penitential burdens on offenders, in order to promote remorse or regret of wrongdoing.'[85]

Duff's communicative account differs from classical retributive accounts in its motivation of sentencing. According to classical theories of retribution, the sanction must be proportionate to the guilt and defendant and the gravity crime. Communicative theories adopt a slightly different logic. Duff's theory suggests that in cases where wrongdoing is not admitted, the penalty inflicted must be serious enough to express appropriate condemnation for the conduct in question and to persuade the perpetrator that the actions are wrong.[86] According to Duff, punishment is thus an instrument to reconcile the offender with his wrong and with society. It must be strong enough to be felt by the offender. The defendant is, to a certain extent, an agent of its own punishment.

Duff's approach broke new ground since it deviated from mere denunciatory theories. But it has met a number of objections. It has been criticized for its predominant focus on punishment as communication with the offender, and its limited attention to other audiences, such as victims and societies affected by wrongdoing.

Other theorists have adopted a wider understanding. For instance, Bill Wringe has made the point that the 'intended audience may be considerably wider—not just, or even primarily the wrongdoer, but the society itself or even the world at large'.[87] He has argued that expressive acts of punishment should be directed towards the community in which both offender and victim are members and the public at large as additional audience.[88] He has insisted that punishment sends a message that 'certain norms are in force and that transgressions against them are viewed seriously'.[89]

will, and not in that lack of freedom at which the threat is directed. To justify punishment in this way is like raising one's stick at a dog; it means treating a human being like a dog instead of respecting his honour and freedom.'). See also Dubber, 'Rediscovering Hegel's Theory of Crime and Punishment' 1583.

[84] Duff, *Punishment, Communication, and Community* 79.
[85] Ibid., 107.
[86] John Tasioulas, 'Punishment and Repentance' (2006) 81 *Philosophy* 279–322.
[87] Wringe, 'Why Punish War Crimes?' 178.
[88] See also Meijers and Glasius, 'Trials as Messages of Justice' 433.
[89] Wringe, *Expressive Theory of Punishment* 24.

Communicative theories have struggled to deal with the dilemma of 'unreceptive audiences', that is the problem of reaching persons who are unable or unwilling to engage with the message that is communicated. Educative theories, which are aimed at moral improvement of individuals through punishment, may encounter dilemmas of paternalism.[90] Not all forms of expression may trigger full two-sided communication, engaging a sender and a concrete audience. Some audiences may stay indifferent to the communication or unwilling to learn. As Joshua Glasgow has noted, 'if the sole justification for punishment is to communicate with the offender, then there is no justification for punishing any of these uncommunicative offenders'.[91]

This had led to more relaxed versions of communicative theory which rely on awareness of an audience and intended interaction but do not require that the message reaches the audience or achieves the desired result (e.g. recognition of wrongdoing and remorse by the offender).[92] According to this understanding, the communication may lie in the moral and legal affirmation that the behaviour deserves punishment, and in the message that society sends to itself (e.g. expression of norms).

1.1.4 Expressivism and continental criminal law doctrine

In contemporary continental criminal law doctrine, expressivism has gained ground as a means to go beyond the traditional dichotomy between deontological accounts, which seek to justify punishment by its inherent value (e.g. retribution, response to wrongdoing), and consequentialist accounts, which look at the beneficial effects of punishment (e.g. crime reduction). It is reflected in a growing number of works in Romano-Germanic doctrine,[93] including German, Spanish, and Latin-American scholarship.[94]

[90] On a normatively oriented expressive theory, see Hörnle, *Straftheorien*, 30.

[91] Glasgow, 'The Expressivist Theory of Punishment Defended' 605.

[92] Ibid., 603–4.

[93] For a survey, see Claus Roxin and Luís Greco, *Strafrecht Band I: Allgemeiner Teil* (München: C.H. Beck, 2020), 37–44; Claus Roxin, 'Prevention, censure and responsibility: The recent debate on the purposes of punishment' in Simester, Bois-Pedain, and Neumann (eds), *Liberal Criminal Theory: Essays for Andreas von Hirsch*, 23–42; Hörnle, *Straftheorien* 21–43; Frank Saliger, 'Über das kommunikative Element in neueren, insbesondere expressiven Straftheorien' in Frank Saliger, Young-Whan Kim, Shing I Liu, Christos Mylonopoulos, Keiichi Yamanaka, Yongliu Zheng, Juarez Tavares and Osman Isfen . (eds), *Rechtsstaatliches Strafrecht: Festschrift für Ulfrid Neumann zum 70. Geburtstag* (Heidelberg: C.F. Müller, 2017), 689–700; Jens Christian Müller-Tuckfeld, 'Expressionistische Straftheorie' in Wolfgang Ludwig-Mayerhofer (ed.), *Soziale Ungleichheit, Kriminalität und Kriminalisierung* (Opladen: Leske & Budrich, 2000), 263–87; Klaus Günther, 'Die symbolisch-expressive Bedeutung der Strafe—Eine neue Straftheorie jenseits von Vergeltung und Prävention?' in Cornelius Prittwitz, Michael Baurmann, Klaus Günther, Lothar Kuhlen, Reinhard Merkel, Cornelius Nestler, and Lorenz Schulz (eds), *Festschrift für Klaus Lüderssen zum 70. Geburtstag* (Baden-Baden: Nomos, 2002), 205–20; Günther Jakobs, *System der strafrechtlichen Zurechnung* (Frankfurt: Klostermann Vittorio, 2012) 13 et seq. (arguing that crime and punishment are connected in a speech/answer relationship); Philipp Bruckmann, 'Sinn und Unsinn gegenwärtiger Vergeltungstheorien—überholt, hilfreich oder notwendig zur Legitimation staatlicher Strafe?' (2019) 2 *Kriminalpolitische Zeitschrift* 105–18.

[94] Gabriel Pérez Barbéra, 'Problemas y Perspectivas de las Teorías Expresivas de la Pena' (2014) 4 *InDret—Revista para el Análisis del Derecho* 1–44; Carlos Gómez-Jara Díez, 'La retribución

Expressivism seeks to mitigate some of the empirical dilemmas of consequentialist theories of punishment, but its remains sceptical of justifying punishment for its own sake.[95] It is thus in line with the growing trend towards 'mixed accounts'[96] which allow differentiation, such as the German unifying theory (*Vereinigungsth eorie*),[97] which accommodates different schools: absolute conceptions of punishment, which derive justification of punishment from wrongdoing (i.e. breaking the law, *punitur quia peccatum est*) and relative conceptions of punishment, which rely on punishment to minimize the commission of crimes (*punitir ne peccetur*).[98] Mixed accounts recognize that punishment as such is justified by certain beneficial effects (e.g. norm recognition, prevention), while cautioning that consequential accounts must be subject to constraints (e.g. in relation to the offender)[99] and face empirical difficulties (e.g. nothing 'works').[100] For instance, threat of punishment and enforcement of sentences are guided by preventive purposes, while the infliction of a penalty on the offender carries retributive elements (e.g. expression of censure). Expressive theories emphasize the communicative dimensions of retribution and prevention. They place more emphasis on the meaning of punishment rather than its effects.

1.1.4.1 Günther Jakobs' norm-oriented expressivism

Many of the doctrinal foundations of expressivism have been shaped by Günther Jakobs,[101] who defended a communicative model of criminal law,[102] drawing

comunicativa como teoría constructivista de la pena: ¿El dolor penal como constructo comunicativo?' (2008) 2 *InDret—Revista para el Análisis del Derecho* 1–31, Federico León Vargas, 'El rol de la retribución en una teoría de la pena como institución regulativa' (2015) 21 *Revista Ius et Praxis* 171–216.

[95] Markus Dubber, 'Theories of Crime and Punishment in German Criminal Law' (2006) 53 *American Journal of Comparative Law* 679–707, 704–6.

[96] For instance, contemporary retributive theories do not treat retribution as an absolute premise, but link its necessity by certain social rationales (e.g. societal peace). See Tonio Walter, 'Vergeltung als Strafzweck: Prävention und Resozialisierung als Pflichten der Kriminalpolitik' (2011) 7 *Zeitschrift für Internationale Strafrechtsdogmatik* 636–47. Andrissek has developed a retributive theory of general prevention. See Tobias Andrissek, *Vergeltung als Strafzweck* (Tübingen: Mohr Siebeck, 2017). Similarly, consequentialist accounts recognize their own limits.

[97] See BVerfGE 45, 187 (253). On the mixed theory in Anglo-American literature, see also Herbert L.A. Hart, 'Prolegomenon to the Principles of Punishment' (1960) 60 *Proceedings of the Aristotelian Society* 1–26.

[98] The dispute goes back to the controversy between Karl Binding, a proponent of a norm-based school (Karl Binding, *Strafrechtliche und strafprozessuale Abhandlungen. Erster Band*, 1915 (reprint: Berlin: Duncker & Humbolt, 2013)) and Franz von Liszt, who argued that punishment should protect legal goods (Franz von Liszt. *Lehrbuch des Deutschen Strafrechts* (Berlin/Leipzig: De Gruyter, 1921)).

[99] On side constraints, see Herbert L.A. Hart, *Punishment and Responsibility* (Oxford: Oxford University Press, 2008) 8–11.

[100] On the 'nothing works' doctrine, see Robert Martinson, 'What Works? Questions and Answers about Prison Reform' (1974) 35 *The Public Interest* 22–54.

[101] Günther Jakobs, *Staatliche Strafe: Bedeutung und Zweck* (Paderborn: Ferdinand Schöningh Verlag, 2004) 24 et seq.

[102] For a discussion, see Daniel Ohana, 'Günther Jakobs's Feindstrafrecht: A dispassionate account' in Markus Dubber (ed.), *Foundational Texts in Modern Criminal Law* (Oxford: Oxford University

on Luhmann's understanding that communication about norms is an essential element of modern societies.[103] Jakobs understood criminal law not only as an instrument of moral reprobation but as a discursive code which ensures coordination between actors in society and stabilizes normative expectations.[104] He argued that criminal law can only perform its function in society if the members of that society recognize the validity of legal norms and are loyal to the law.[105] He advocated an expressive-preventive conception of punishment.

1.1.4.1.1 Contributions

Jakobs made several important contributions to expressivist theory. The first one is his theorization of crime as an act of communication that signals meaning. Jakobs understood crimes less as an attack on legal goods rather than as an attack on the normative fabric of society, communal values, and respect of law.[106] He recognized that not only words but human behaviour conveys meaning. He clarified the social semantics of criminal acts.[107] He distinguished acts of nature, which lack the ability to undermine validity of norms, and communicative acts, through which the offender participates in creation of social meaning.[108] According to Jakobs, criminal wrongdoing is thus comparable to a spoken sentence, namely an assertion or statement which calls into question the criminal norm.[109] For instance, Jakobs qualified homicide as an assertion by the offender not to honour the right to life of the victim.[110] He acknowledged that the meaning expressed does not necessarily depend on the intent of the offender.[111] This understanding was later extended by Gudrun Ingeborg Puppe who argued that crimes may not only entail a statement but also act as a sign.[112]

Press, 2014) 353–71; Daniel Ohana, 'Trust, Distrust and Reassurance: Diversion and Preventive Orders Through the Prism of Feindstrafrecht' (2010) 73 *Modern Law Review* 721–51.

[103] Niklas Luhmann, *A Sociological Theory of Law* (London: Routledge, 1985); Niklas Luhmann, *Law as a Social System* (Oxford: Oxford University Press, 2004).

[104] Jakobs, *Staatliche Strafe* 30.

[105] Günther Jakobs, *Strafrecht: Allgemeiner Teil*, 2nd edn (Berlin: Walter de Gruyter, 1991) 9–10.

[106] See Günther Jakobs, *Der strafrechtliche Handlungsbegriff* (München: C.H. Beck, 1992) 44 ('Sich-schuldhaft-zuständig-Machen für einen Normgeltungsschaden'). See also Urs Kindhäuser, 'Handlungs—und normtheoretische Grundfragen der Mittäterschaft' in Joachim Bohnert, Christof Gramm, Urs Kindhäuser, Alfred Rinken, and Gerhard Robbers (eds), *Verfassung—Philosophie—Kirche, Festschrift für Alexander Hollerbach zum 70. Geburtstag* (Berlin: Duncker & Humblot, 2001) 627–55, 638 ('Kommunikationsakt mangelnder Normanerkennung').

[107] Jakobs, *Der strafrechtliche Handlungsbegriff* 30, 32 et seq, 44.

[108] Jakobs, *System der strafrechtlichen Zurechnung* 17 et seq.

[109] See Jakobs, *Strafrecht: Allgemeiner Teil* 9; Jakobs, *System der strafrechtlichen Zurechnung* 13 et seq.

[110] Jakobs, *System der strafrechtlichen Zurechnung* 13, note 4.

[111] For example, a drunk driver may signal through behaviour that he or she considers other things to be more important than lives of others. See Jakobs, *Strafrecht: Allgemeiner Teil* 9.

[112] Gudrun Ingeborg Puppe, 'Strafrecht als Kommunikation' in Erich Samson, Friedrich Dencker, Peter Frisch, Helmut Frister, and Wölfram Reiß (eds), *Festschrift für Gerald Grünwald zum 70. Geburtstag* (Baden-Baden: Nomos, 1999), 469–93, 473.

Second, Jakobs provided a social justification of punishment.[113] He justified punishment as an act of social confirmation, namely as a demonstration of norm affirmation which reminds the offender and fellow citizens that the wrongdoing is unacceptable and will not be tolerated. Punishment has thus both a symbolic-expressive[114] and a preventive function: it demonstrates that society lives up to its expectation to maintain and enforce norms[115] and it seeks to remind the perpetrator of the duty to remain loyal to the law as a citizen of society.

One of the main innovations of Jakobs' approach is that it alleviated punishment theory partly from the dilemma of empirical grounding.[116] He argued that norm affirmation inherent in punishment, that is the expression of contradiction to the attack on the validity of the norm, is beyond empirical falsifiability.[117] It is not an aim of punishment but a consequence of it, a way of creating meaning.[118] There is no case in which it does not occur.

1.1.4.1.2 Critiques

Jakobs' communicative approach has established important foundations of expressivist theory, but it has also raised critiques. A first objection is that it is too norm-oriented. It assumes too easily that criminal wrongdoing conveys a message relating to the negation of the norm. Wrongdoing may express a social condition. Jakobs' theory uses a simplified model of communication. It assumes that wrongdoing carries a fixed and objective meaning that can be identified.

A second critique is the limited integration of inter-subjective forms of communication. Under Jakobs' model, the offender is seen predominantly as the sender of a normative message rather than as a moral agent. The pain inflicted on the offender is a means to remove threats of norm erosion.[119] The interests of victims are largely blended out: they are passive subjects.

An additional weakness is the strong focus on a rational justification of punishment. Critics note that punishment does not only affirm legal norms but also expresses a societal reaction. For instance, Winfried Hassemer has argued that punishment does not necessarily affirm the violated norm but a culture of humane

[113] Günther Jakobs, 'Strafbegründung und positive Generalprävention' in Peter Siller and Bertram Keller (eds) *Rechtsphilosophische Kontroversen der Gegenwart* (Baden: Nomos, 1999) 135–8.

[114] On punishment as symbolic act, see Günther Jakobs, *Norm, Person, Gesellschaft* (Berlin: Duncker & Humblot, 2008) 111–16.

[115] Jakobs, *Staatliche Strafe* 26–30.

[116] Bernhardo Feijoo Sánchez, 'Positive Generalprävention. Gedanken zur Straftheorie Günther Jakobs' in Michael Pawlik and Rainer Zaczyk (eds), *Festschrift für Günther Jakobs* (Köln: Heymann, 2007), 75–95, 88 et seq.

[117] Günther Jakobs, 'Das Strafrecht zwischen Funktionalismus und "alteuropäischem" Prinzipiendenken' 844–5.

[118] Ibid., 844 ('nicht empirisch fassbar ist insbesondere die Bestätigung der Identität; denn sie ist nicht Folge des Verfahrens, sondern seine Bedeutung').

[119] Jakobs, *Norm, Person, Gesellschaft* 114 ('Der Strafschmerz hebt die Gefahr der Erosion auf; seine Legitimation gründet demgemäß auf im Synallagma von Verhaltensfreiheit und Folgenverantwortung.').

engagement with deviance.[120] Psychological approaches suggest that punishment is also an experience which may express 'we' feelings or emotive solidarity.[121] In some circumstances (e.g. illiberal or autocratic regimes), the reaffirmation of norms may not be a virtue but may have counterproductive effects.[122]

Finally, Jakobs' argument on the lack of need for empirical grounding is open to critique. The symbolic expressive function of punishment, that is its expression of the validity of the norm, may be inherent. But the second dimension of punishment, its role to strengthen society's trust in legal norms and ensure that the citizens act according to the law (i.e. the 'exercise in norm recognition'), is a question of degree and thus subject to empirical inquiry.[123]

1.1.4.2 Communication of censure (Von Hirsch, Hörnle, Günther)

A second group of scholars have relied on the idea that expression of censure is a main purpose of punishment.[124] This approach emerged as a response to broadly construed preventive justifications of punishment (e.g. crime control models). It usually combines retributive and preventive elements.[125] It insists that punishment should be justified by censure-related arguments in relation to offenders[126] and/or broader preventive rationales in relation to society. It is regarded as an advance over classical retributive approaches because of its communicative orientation. The sanction is treated as an act of communication, rather than as a form of control. Punishment is not only related to arguments of 'just desert', removal of unfair advantages,[127] or pay back of debt to society, but a means to communicate censure or condemnation to offenders that they deserve. Censure implies culpability but gives meaning to punishment. It places greater weight on the role of citizens as communicative actors[128] in the justification of punishment than the affirmation of the validity of norms. It treats punishment not only as a form of moral reprobation for wrong but recognizes the offender as an agent capable of moral deliberation.

[120] Winfried Hassemer, *Einführung in die Grundlagen des Strafrechts*, 2nd edn (München: Beck, 1990) 334.

[121] Jens Christian Müller-Tuckfeld, *Integrationsprävention: Studien zu einer Theorie der gesellschaftlichen Funktion des Strafrechts* (Frankfurt: Peter Lang, 1998), 348.

[122] Ibid., 68.

[123] Hassemer, *Einführung in die Grundlagen des Strafrechts* 326.

[124] Jean-Claude Wolf and Ignace Haaz, 'Strafe als Tadel? Argumente pro und kontra' in Andreas Von Hirsch, Ulfrid Neumann, and Kurt Seelmann (eds), *Strafe—Warum? Gegenwärtige Strafbegründungen im Lichte von Hegels Straftheorie* (Baden-Baden: Nomos, 2011) 69–77.

[125] Tatjana Hörnle and Andreas von Hirsch, 'Positive Generalprävention und Tadel' (1995) 142 *Goltdammer's Archiv für Strafecht* 261–82.

[126] For a pure retributive expressive theory, see Frauke Rostalski, *Der Tatbegriff im Strafrecht* (Tübingen: Mohr Siebeck, 2019), 27.

[127] Robert Nozick, *Philosophical Explanations* (Cambridge, MA. Harvard University Press, 1981) 363–4.

[128] See Günther, *Schuld und kommunikative Freiheit* 245–58.

This understanding may be traced back to the works of Andreas von Hirsch.[129] He argued that punishment is grounded in both prevention and censure. He regarded censure as a primary purpose of punishment which must be deserved (i.e. a proportionate reaction)[130] and offer a way for reform. Censure involves different dimensions: communication of wrongdoing, acknowledgment of harm, or even calls for remorse and healing (e.g. repentance). It is directed at the offender, victims, and the general public as a third party. It expresses disapprobation of crime, acknowledges that the perpetrator caused harm, and gives others a reason to avoid such conduct because it is presented as being morally wrong.

This account was developed by Tatjana Hörnle. She expressly qualified expressivism as a separate doctrine of punishment which defies classical notions (e.g. absolute or relative theories).[131] She expressed reservations towards purely norm-oriented expressive theories and emphasized the vital role of victims in expressive theory: acknowledgment and condemnation of wrong serve not only the interests of the general public but also reflect the legitimate interests of victims in punishment.[132] Expressivism is thus grounded in the interests of victims to see justice being done, which are exercised through the state as trustee and medium.[133] Her approach strengthened the claim that restorative features, including reparation, should be seen as an inherent part of the expressive function of criminal law.[134] Hörnle also addressed the problem that expressive disapproval of an act (e.g. through words and symbols) is not necessarily punishment. She argued that penal sanction ('hard treatment') is a necessary element of communication, in order to convey different degrees of censure and signal disapprobation that is taken seriously and exceeds words (e.g. shaming).

Klaus Günther viewed expressivism as a means to overcome a justification of punishment based on retribution and repression and emphasized the symbolic-expressive nature of punishment.[135] He defended censure-based approaches of punishment based on their deliberative features, that is their structure and

[129] Andrew von Hirsch, *Censure and Sanctions* (Oxford: Oxford University Press, 1993); Antje du Bois-Pedain and Anthony E Bottoms, *Penal Censure: Engagements Within and Beyond Desert Theory* (Oxford: Hart, 2019).

[130] Von Hirsch, *Censure and Sanctions* 15.

[131] Tatjana Hörnle, 'Expressive Straftheorien' in Thomas Hilgers, Gertrud Koch, Christoph Möllers, and Sabine Müller-Mall (eds), *Affekt und Urteil* (Paderborn: Wilhelm Fink, 2015) 143–58; Hörnle, *Straftheorien* 31–43.

[132] Tatjana Hörnle, 'The role of victims' rights in punishment theory' in Bois-Pedain and Bottoms (eds), *Penal Censure*: 207–26, 207.

[133] Hörnle, *Straftheorien* 41.

[134] Lyane Sautner, *Opferinteressen und Strafrechtstheorien: Zugleich ein Beitrag zum restorativen Umgang mit Straftaten* (Innsbruck: Studien Verlag, 2010); Johannes Kaspar, Wiedergutmachung und Mediation im Strafrecht (Münster: LIT Verlag, 2004) 63.

[135] Günther, 'Die expressiv-symbolische Bedeutung der Strafe' 205–20.

public performance.[136] He argued that communicative theories detach punishment from 'political justification'. Punishment should be understood as a process of communication with offenders and victims about criminal norms and reasons for their rejection. Hard treatment and, in particular, imprisonment, are non-communicative.[137] Punishment and expression of censure are justified by the inter-subjective nature of criminal judgments, their public nature, and reasons. It is partly a communication of society with itself.[138]

One of the weaknesses of censure-based approaches is that they are rather backward- than forward-looking. They focus on public disapproval of the crime and the communicative process related thereto rather than preventive purposes. Another risk is the moralization of punishment. The conception of punishment as censure has something paternalistic. It stands in contrast to the neutral role of the judge and the liberal foundations of trials.[139] Opponents stress that the State should not be entitled to limit the rights and freedoms of citizens simply based on moral or philosophical views.[140] It is questioned whether expression of emotions such as 'outrage, anger, feelings of revenge, feelings of retaliation or retribution' should be part of the censure function.[141]

1.1.4.3 Positive general prevention and expressive theory of punishment

A third group of authorities ground expressive justifications of punishment in theories of 'positive general prevention'.[142] Such theories have a gained a prominent place in German doctrine in order to avoid the normative and empirical dilemmas of consequentialist approaches. They imply that punishment is more about 'meaning something', rather than 'accomplishing something'.

Positive general prevention was developed in German doctrine to extend prevention beyond mere discouragement of crime to integrative purposes.[143] According to general prevention theories, punishment has a socially integrative function which goes beyond protection of legal goods. It serves to demonstrate the inviolability of the legal order and to strengthen the population's loyalty to the law.

[136] Klaus Günther, 'Crime and Punishment as Communication' 123–39.
[137] Ibid. 133–25.
[138] Ibid., 131.
[139] Roxin and Greco, *Strafrecht Band I: Allgemeiner Teil* 39.
[140] Ibid. 50.
[141] See Danila Demko, 'An Expressive Theory of International Punishment for International Crimes' in Florian Jessberger and Julia Geneuss (eds), *Why Punish Perpetrators of Mass Atrocities?* (New York: Cambridge University Press, 2020) 176–96, 189.
[142] See **section 5.1.2.2**. See generally Karl Schumann, Positive Generalprävention (Heidelberg: C.F. Müller, 1989), Winfried Hassemer, 'Variationen der positiven Generalprävention' in Bernd Schünemann, Andrew von Hirsch, and Nils Jareborg (eds), *Positive Generalprävention: Kritische Analyses im deutsch-englischen Dialog* (Heidelberg: C.F. Müller, 1998) 29–50, 43; Michael Baurmann, 'Vorüberlegungen zu einer empirischen Theorie der positiven Generalprävention' (1994) 141 *Goltdammer's Archiv für Strafrecht* 368–84.
[143] Müller-Tuckfeld, *Integrationsprävention*.

Its justification may be grounded in different arguments, the protective duties of states, or duties of loyalty of citizens towards the State and community.[144]

General prevention is rarely defended as justification of punishment in its own right. Critics note that it is more a rationalization of practice than a justification of penal authority. It does not justify punishment as an institution. It is morally impermissible to punish an offender simply in order to reinforce the moral inhibitions of citizens. As Markus Dubber has cautioned, positive general prevention can justify any mode of expression that signifies 'communal solidarity under common norms through communal condemnation', including public shaming.[145] Punishment could be replaced by educative measures in order to achieve the social effects of societal integration.[146] Sociologically, the ignorance of crimes of others might be more conducive to purposes of norm recognition than their revelation through punishment.[147]

Scholars have thus adopted dialectical or complementary accounts which combine preventive justifications with culpability-based considerations. For instance, in their influential treatise on the General Part of German Criminal Law, Claus Roxin and Luís Greco have advocated a prevention oriented punishment theory which integrates culpability. Punishment serves purposes of special or general prevention. But penal authority is limited by culpability which serves as a side constraint against excessive punishment.[148]

Conceptually, it is artificial to draw categorical distinctions between expressive and preventive justifications of punishment, as is sometimes suggested in doctrine.[149] Positive general prevention is an essence an expressive theory of punishment.[150] It places the emphasis on communication with the general public (e.g. through criminalization in laws, public pronouncement of judgments in the name of society, and messages about enforcement through sentencing), in addition to communication with the offender. This type of communication involves symbolic expression, rituals,[151] and speech acts. As Roxin has argued, the 'expressive

[144] On loyalty duties, see Michael Pawlik, *Person, Subjekt, Bürger. Zur Legitimation von Strafe* (Berlin: Duncker & Humblot, 2004) 83 et seq.

[145] See Dubber, 'Theories of Crime and Punishment in German Criminal Law' 705.

[146] See Luís Greco, *Lebendiges und Totes in Feuerbachs Straftheorie* (Berlin: Duncker & Humblot Verlag, 2009) 398 et seq.

[147] Heinrich Popitz, *Über die Präventivwirkung des Nichtwissens* (Tübingen: Mohr, 1968).

[148] See Roxin and Greco, *Strafrecht Band I: Allgemeiner Teil* 44–56.

[149] See Hörnle, *Straftheorien*, 2011, 58; Zürcher, *Legitimation von Strafe* 127; Bruckmann, 'Sinn und Unsinn gegenwärtiger Vergeltungstheorien' 117–18.

[150] See also Axel Montenbruck, *Deutsche Straftheorie: Ein Lehrbuch*, 1st edn (Berlin: ISBN 978-3-96110-050-7, 2017), 210, arguing that the expressive and communicative character of punishment has a general preventive orientation since a community constitutes itself through communication and cooperation. . See also Andreas Werkmeister, 'The Individual and the International Community: An Outline for a Combined Meso Preventive Theory of International Punishment' in Florian Jessberger and Julia Geneuss (eds), *Why Punish Perpetrators of Mass Atrocities?* (New York: Cambridge University Press, 2020) 228–57, 249–50.

[151] Christoph Bennett, *The Apology Ritual: A Philosophical Theory of Punishment* (Cambridge: Cambridge University Press, 2008).

function of punishment' is thus 'a legitimate penal aim alongside the preventive goals of punishment'.[152] It communicates the re-socializing aims of punishment. It may be justified by the idea of accountability, namely 'responsibility for wrongdoing'.[153] As part of the responsibility for the crime, the offender must accept that the example set through punishment is 'also intended to discourage others from committing crimes', to 'reassure the general population', and to restore the 'disturbed civil peace'.[154]

1.1.5 Expressivism and transitional justice

In the 1990s, expressivist theories have gained particular attention in the field of transitional justice. In the context of political transitions from conflict to peace, accountability and punishment gain partially different meanings than in classical peacetime settings. They are not only oriented towards the past but linked to transformative goals, such as democratic reform, societal reconciliation, or socio-economic progress. These very rationales are under constant scrutiny and public attention. The idea of a 'just peace' may involve concessions and compromises. It requires not only a 'win–win' for each side but certain sacrifices. Steven James Barela and Alexis Keller have called this the 'principle of renouncement'.[155] This has an impact on the role of punishment. As Lily Rueda Guzman and Barbora Holá have noted, punishment is 'no longer an end in and of itself, or the reaction of a society to a criminal offence or an ethical response to the crimes. Instead, it is an instrument to achieve broader social goals.'[156]

Expressivism has particular attraction in this context, since it provides a legitimization for criminal justice that goes beyond offenders. It addresses some of the conflicting interests that criminal punishment faces in conflict and post-conflict transitions. It captures some of the performative aspects of accountability processes, including their ability to convey certain important social meanings of processes of transition (e.g. the move from crime to restoration of legality and order and the construction of a new identity).[157] As Doris Buss has noted, 'transitional

[152] Roxin, 'Prevention, censure and responsibility' 41 .

[153] Ibid., 41.

[154] Ibid., 23, 37.

[155] Steven James Barela and Alexis Keller, 'Justice, Peace and Jus Post Bellum' (2015) 7 *Amsterdam Law Forum* 98–107, 107. They argue that 'just peace' is a 'human experience that requires a visible and obvious rapprochement on the human level and that requires visible sacrifices from both parties.

[156] See Lily Rueda Guzman and Barbora Holá, 'Punishment in Negotiated Transitions: The Case of the Colombian Peace Agreement with the FARC-EP' (2019) 19 *International Criminal Law Review* 127–59, 135

[157] See, for example, Diana Taylor, *Disappearing Acts: Spectacles of Gender and Nationalism in Argentina's 'Dirty War'* (Durham, NC: Duke University Press, 1997); Catherine M. Cole, *Performing South Africa's Truth Commission: Stages of Transition* (Bloomington, IN: Indiana University Press, 2010).

justice mechanisms can be seen as performing or enacting certain kinds of understandings not just of the issues at hand, but also the larger processes of "transition"; the rebirth of the nation after a period of political violence/conflict'.[158]

Expressive accounts of criminal justice coincide with some of the rationales that transitional justice doctrine embrace (e.g. accountability for past wrongs, search for the truth, restoration of the rights of victims, transformation of public institutions). They do not only emphasize the value of punishment as a measure of retribution but also see criminal justice as part of a broader process of public acknowledgment of wrong, trust-building vis-á-vis victims and affected communities, and prevention of future atrocities.

The debate shifted from the mere justification of punishment to a consideration of the expressive role of accountability proceedings and criminal trials more broadly. Scholars began to draw attention to the symbolic functions of legal institutions and communicative value of trials. The transformative dimensions of expressivist and communicative approaches gained further importance. Transitional justice mechanisms, including criminal trials, were regarded as potential means to educate and alter people's behaviour and attitudes.[159] Trials were seen as an instrument to bring out a judicial truth, publicly engage with the past, promote rights of victims, and allow discursive engagement. Expressivism was more closely related to theories on reconciliation.

A central contribution to the contemporary understanding of the role of expressivist theories was made by Mark Osiel.[160] Osiel examined the effects of the Eichmann and Argentinean junta trials in the 1980s on 'collective memory'.[161] He challenged Durkheim's view that the expressivist dimensions of criminal punishment are per se solidarity-enhancing. He argued that Durkheim's conception only works in the rare context where members of society share a common view of justice. He stressed that the positive expressive effects of criminal justice do not necessarily flow from the educational effects of punishment of offenders but rather from the discursive features of trials. He argued that criminal trials might promote public discussion in 'ways that foster the liberal virtues of toleration, moderation, and civil respect'.[162]

[158] Doris Buss, 'Performing Legal Order: Some Feminist Thoughts on International Criminal Law' (2011) 11 *International Criminal Law Review* 409–23, 413.

[159] See also Gerhard Werle and Moritz Vormbaum, *Transitional Justice: Vergangenheitsbewäl tigung durch Recht* (Berlin: Springer, 2018), 35–6 ('Solche Maßnahmen senden ein Signal an die Bevölkerung und sollen dazu beitragen, Vertrauen in die neue staatliche Führung, Verwaltung und Justiz zurückzugewinnen.').

[160] Mark Osiel, *Mass Atrocity, Collective Memory, and Law* (New Brunswick: Transaction Publishers, 1997) 36–55.

[161] On the notion see Joachim J. Savelsberg and Ryan D. King, 'Law and Collective Memory' (2007) 3 *Annual Review Law Social Science* 189–211, 191 ('Collective memory, a term coined in the classic work of French sociologist Maurice Halbwachs, refers to knowledge about that past that is shared, mutually acknowledged, and reinforced by a collectivity—from small informal groups to formal organizations to nation states and global communities.')

[162] Osiel, *Mass Atrocity, Collective Memory and the Law* 2.

Osiel used the concept of 'civil dissension' to explain the paradoxes of criminal prosecutions.[163] He demonstrated that atrocity trials have 'decidedly not' been 'simple and unmediated reflections of moral sentiments universally felt within society toward the accused'.[164] He admitted that such trials may trigger conflicting interpretations of history and opposing visions of justice. He argued that the judicial task 'is to employ the law of evidence, procedure and professional responsibility to recast the courtroom drama in terms of the "theatre of ideas" where large questions of collective memory and even national identity are engaged'.[165]

The central claim of his theory is that the expression of divergent views may trigger public discussion beyond the courtroom and stimulate reflection on wrongs of the past and future norms. He that argued that such civil dissension might allow some form of 'discursive solidarity' in divided societies.[166] This solidarity does not rely on consensus but rather on engagement with difference,[167] namely 'civil engagement in disagreements'[168] and 'a recognition that society's members often disagree radically regarding their conceptions of justice and the good and that they nevertheless recognize a need to settle upon a common scheme of association and cooperation'.[169]

Osiel's theory defended the expressive value of trials by its deliberative features. He stressed the need to hold 'liberal show trials' in order to overcome trauma after conflict.[170] The weakness of Osiel's approach is that it relied strongly on a classical 'liberal trial model' and democratic structures as a prerequisite for deliberative recovery. It presupposes the existence of a society that is willing to respect the 'other' and tolerate difference, despite opposite or conflicting views of events and facts.[171] It does not necessarily function in contexts where such conditions do not exist. Examples, such as the former Yugoslavia, have shown that expressive trials may fail to overcome prejudices emanating from ethnic division. Factors, such as lack of security or ethnic, religious, or other biases may impede 'discursive solidarity'.[172] Expressivism becomes ambivalent if defendants manage to detract from their individual responsibility and turn the trial into a forum for the judgment of collective identities.[173]

163 Ibid., 36.
164 Ibid., 36.
165 Ibid., 3
166 Ibid., 50.
167 See also Mirjan Damaška, 'What Is the Point of International Criminal Justice?' (2008) 83 *Chicago-Kent Law Review* 329–65, 346 ('Reconciliation and genuine social solidarity do not require locating an elusive consensus but, rather, finding a way to live with the absence of consensus.').
168 Osiel, *Mass Atrocity, Collective Memory and the Law* 48.
169 Ibid., 51.
170 Ibid., 3.
171 See David A Crocker, 'Democracy and Punishment: Punishment, Reconciliation, and Democratic Deliberation' (2002) 5 *Buffalo Criminal Law Review* 509–49.
172 See generally Nevin T. Aiken, *Identity, Reconciliation and Transitional Justice: Overcoming Intractability in Divided Societies* (London: Routledge 2014).
173 Izabela Steflja, 'The Production of the War Criminal Cult: Radovan Karadžić and Vojislav Šešelj at The Hague' (2018) 46 *Nationalities Papers* 52–68.

Later works have been more critical.[174] For instance, Pablo de Greiff acknowledged that trials may '*persuade* offenders and others about the wrongfulness of certain kinds'.[175] But he argued that expressivist justifications require an account of 'what is *just,* in the sense of being equally in the interest of all'[176] and are dependent on a 'broader political theory' of deliberative democracy.[177]

Colleen Murphy has defended a relational account of transitional justice which takes into account interpersonal relations, such as 'political relationships among citizens and between citizens and officials'.[178] She argued that the 'just pursuit of transformation' requires the establishment of relationships that are 'predicated on mutual respect for agency'[179] and 'reciprocity',[180] including measures promoting the rule of law, political trust and 'relational capabilities' of agents.[181] Her theory has tied expressivism to acts of recognition, acknowledgment, and respect.[182]

Jaya Ramji-Nogales has turned the attention to some of the weaknesses of expressivist theories in transitional justice contexts, including discrepancies between 'sender' and 'recipient' audience. Criminal trials are often 'top-down' mechanisms, entrenched in binary structure, or detached from 'local' context. There is thus a risk that the 'message received' may differ from the 'message intended'.[183] From an expressivist perspective, it is thus important to engage not only with the offender but to incorporate the perspective of the victims.[184] Victim involvement is crucial in several respects, namely to help perpetrators recognize the wrongfulness of their acts, and to relate the messages of trials

[174] Some scholars have openly questioned whether the expressivist aspects of trials may foster reconciliation. On empathy as condition of reconciliation, see Jodi Halpern and Harvey M. Weinstein, 'Rehumanizing the Other: Empathy and Reconciliation' (2004) 26 *Human Rights Quarterly* 561–83. See also Laurel Fletcher and Harvey Weinstein, 'Violence and Social Repair: Rethinking the Contribution of Justice to Reconciliation' (2002) 24 *Human Rights Quarterly* 573–639, 588.

[175] Pablo De Greiff, 'Deliberative Democracy and Punishment' (2002) 5 *Buffalo Criminal Law Review* 373–403, 375.

[176] Ibid., 402.

[177] Deliberative democracy is a space in which 'free and equal citizens (and their representatives) justify decisions in a process in which they give one another reasons that are mutually acceptable and generally with the aim of reaching decisions that are binding in the present on all citizens but open to challenge in the future'. It relied on the premise that citizens owe each other justification for the laws that govern society. See Amy Gutman and Dennis Thompson, *Why Deliberative Democracy?* (Princeton, NJ: Princeton University Press, 2004), 7.

[178] Colleen Murphy, *Conceptual Foundations of Transitional Justice* (Cambridge: Cambridge University Press, 2017), 121, 160.

[179] Ibid., 121.

[180] Ibid., 121.

[181] Ibid., 160.

[182] See also Ruti Teitel, *Globalizing Transitional Justice: Contemporary Essays* (New York, NY: Oxford University Press, 2014).

[183] Jaya Ramji-Nogales, 'Designing Bespoke Transitional Justice: Pluralist Process Approach' (2010) 32 *Michigan Journal of International Law* 1–72, 8.

[184] Ibid., 17.

closer to their constituencies. Truth commissions and locally based restorative justice mechanisms may provide more direct forums of communicative justice than trials.[185]

Social scientists have highlighted the complex interrelation between institutional 'legitimacy' and processes of internalization.[186] The communicative function of a trial is highly dependent on the acceptance of the trial as a legitimate forum. Such consensus may be lacking. Public confidence in institutions may be lost after conflict. It needs to be earned.[187] For a successful performance of expressivist functions, it is essential that 'the community whose norms are at issue must trust those who aim to alter these norms, and individuals with authority in the message-receiving communities must participate in the process of clarifying and establishing new social norms'.[188]

Transitional justice theory has further shed a different light on the dilemma of punishment. In domestic justifications of punishment, expressivist rationales have been used to justify imprisonment as the most visible form of censure for wrongdoing.[189] In transitional contexts, alternative approaches to imprisonment have gained broader prominence in order to promote broader strategies of conflict resolution. As Paul Seils has noted, often 'the best that can be hoped for is an approximation whereby a significant degree of condemnation and social persuasion for reform is achieved'.[190]

More efforts have been made to express condemnation of wrongdoing in alternative ways such as public acknowledgment of wrong, direct encounter with victims, exclusions from political office, reparations, and alternative or suspended sentences. Expressivist theories have thus taken a new turn, including more victim-centred conceptions of expressivism.[191]

[185] See generally Jonathan Doak, 'The Therapeutic Dimension of Transitional Justice: Emotional Repair and Victim Satisfaction in International Trials and Truth Commissions' (2011) 11 *International Criminal Law Review* 263–98.

[186] Tom R. Tyler, 'Multiculturalism and the Willingness of Citizens to Defer to Law and to Legal Authorities' (2000) 25 *Law & Social Inquiry* 983–1019, 985.

[187] See also Paul Seils, 'Squaring Colombia's Circle: The Objectives of Punishment and the Pursuit of Peace', *ICTJ Briefing*, June 2015, 14 at https://www.ictj.org/sites/default/files/ICTJ-COL-Briefing-Punishments-2015.pdf).

[188] Ramji-Nogales, 'Designing Bespoke Transitional Justice' 8.

[189] On the logic, see Dan M. Kahan, 'The Anatomy of Disgust in Criminal Law' (1998) 96 *Michigan Law Review* 1621–1657, 1641 ('On expressive grounds serious crimes strike us as such that is, as crimes and as serious—not just because they impair another's interests, but because they convey that the wrongdoer doesn't respect the true value of things. To express condemnation, then, society must respond with a form of punishment that unequivocally evinces the community's repudiation of the wrongdoer's valuations.').

[190] Seils, 'Squaring Colombia's Circle' 13.

[191] See Maria Elander, 'The Victim's Address: Expressivism and the Victim at the Extraordinary Chambers in the Courts of Cambodia' (2013) 7 *International Journal of Transitional Justice* 95–115, 95.

1.1.6 The turn to expressivism in international criminal justice

The formal recognition of expressivist theories in international criminal justice is a relatively recent paradigm.[192] This reluctance may be explained by several factors: the high degree of pragmatism inherent in the formation of international criminal law as a field, the general lack of theorization, fears about its perception a symbolic, rather than as a 'real' project, and hesitations by members of the field to engage with the broader socio-legal factors justifying international criminal justice as a project.

The turn to expressivism is partly a result of the failure of traditional justice theories to deal with the unique features and paradoxes of international criminal justice.[193] International criminal justice has traditionally lacked enforcement agents akin to State authorities in the domestic context. Expressivism is an instrument to gain 'buy-in' for authority. It has not only been used to support the justification for punishment but also to compensate for the selectivity of international criminal justice or the absence of punishment.[194]

Condemnation has been associated early on with rationales such as expressing morality or contributing to historical record. For instance, the Nuremberg Tribunal relied on moral outrage to justify its own basis. It did not hide its symbolic value. Judicial language was shaped by expressivist vocabulary. This is vividly illustrated by Jackson's opening remarks: 'What makes this inquest significant is that these prisoners represent influences that will lurk in the world long after their bodies have turned to dust. We will show them to be living symbols of racial hatreds, of terrorism and violence, and of the arrogance and cruelty of power.'[195]

The International Military Tribunal (IMT) made certain findings that did not carry immediate consequences for defendants. It dealt with incidents that it did not punish. The approach was strongly guided by the ambition to nourish the emergence of new norms.[196]

Expressivism became a means to compensate for certain limitations, such as the lack of existing 'hard' law or principles or selective enforcement. As Diane Amann

[192] See also Sander, 'The Expressive Turn of International Criminal Justice'.

[193] Domestic justifications of expressivism cannot be directly transposed to the international context. See Sander, 'Justifying International Criminal Punishment' 240.

[194] See Diane Marie Amann, 'Group Mentality, Expressivism, and Genocide' (2002) 2 *International Criminal Law Review* 93–143, 121–2.

[195] Nuremberg Trials, Opening Address for the United States, Nazi Conspiracy & Aggression, Volume I (United States Government Printing Office, Washington, 1946), 115.

[196] Former Dutch Judge at Tokyo, Bert Röling, recognized this in his subsequent analysis of the post-war experience: 'The purpose was not to punish all cases of criminal guilt, but to give expression to the abhorrence of what had happened. The exemplary punishments served the purpose of restoring the legal order, that is of reassuring the whole community that what they had witnessed for so many years was criminal behavior.' Bert Röling, 'Aspects of criminal responsibility for violations of the laws of war' in Antonio Cassese (ed.), *The New Humanitarian Law of Armed Conflict* (Naples: Editoriale Scientifica, 1979), 199–231, 206.

put it, throughout much of the second half of the twentieth century 'expression without enforcement was all that occurred in international criminal law'.[197] It was guided by the belief that condemnation and norm affirmation are important rationales per se, even if they are not constantly enforced in society.

Contemporary theories have revealed the complexity of expressivist justifications, their means of expression, and their limitations.

A classical conceptual problem of the use of expressivist rationales in international criminal justice is the distance between 'sender' and 'audiences'. Norms and actors of international criminal justice have traditionally been more detached from their envisaged audiences than their domestic counterparts.[198] For instance, offenders are not necessarily part of the same community as those who seek to inflict judicial punishments.[199] The delivery of criminal justice itself has thus a broader communicative function. As Martti Koskenniemi has argued, it 'enables the community ritually to affirm its guiding principles and thus to become a workable 'moral community'.[200]

International criminal justice involves more demonstration than restoration. Expressivism is designed to limit the geographical and 'moral distance' to victims and crimes. It affirms the 'difference from the moral universe in which the crimes could occur precisely through its meticulous procedures and standards of evidence, and a humane punishment at the end'.[201] 'The message is one of respect for basic human rights and of nonviolent conflict resolution, and an exercise in the rule of law—all key ingredients for the (re)establishment of a well-functioning society.'[202]

1.1.6.1 Law affirmation and expressive value of punishment

The most classical claim is that expressivism has a strong functional role in international criminal justice since it serves to affirm the value of law or punishment.

As Frédéric Mégret has claimed, in international criminal justice, crimes are not only adjudicated for the crimes sake (e.g. to comply with a duty to investigate or prosecute) but to affirm something bigger: 'What shocks us about the commission of crimes is not that they are crimes, but that their commission contradicts our deeply held beliefs.'[203]

[197] See Amann, 'Group Mentality, Expressivism and Genocide' 121.

[198] See Mark Drumbl, 'Collective Violence and Individual Punishment: The Criminality of Mass Atrocity' (2005) 99 *Northwestern University Law Review* 539–610, 593.

[199] Bill Wringe, 'War crimes and expressive theories of punishment: Communication or Denunciation?' (2010) 16 *Res Publica*, 119–33, 125.

[200] See Martti Koskenniemi, 'Between Impunity and Show Trials' (2002) 6 *Max Planck Yearbook for United Nations Law* 1–36, 10.

[201] Meijers and Glasius, 'Trials as Messages of Justice' 438.

[202] Ibid.

[203] Mégret, 'Practices of Stigmatization' 289.

Drawing on Durkheim, Edward Wise has argued shortly after the adoption of the International Criminal Court (ICC) Statute that the 'function of criminal law in affirming and strengthening feelings of social solidarity and community' seems 'peculiarly apt—indeed stunningly apt—when we consider the likely effects of the Rome Statute'.[204]

There is a close interrelation between rationality and empathy in the expression of core crimes. Adjudication of atrocity violence touches the very limits of the law. The social meaning of crimes often extends their legal significance. Some crimes defy comprehension and or lie beyond reason. This discrepancy has encouraged the use of expressivist language, language that conveys a moral opinion on an issue that is not strictly necessary to decide a case.[205] For instance, notions such as genocide cannot be reduced to law. There is a certain 'genocide mystique'.[206] Tribunals have tended to treat it as a 'symbol, not just a legal category'.[207] Courts have attempted to reflect the exceptional nature of atrocity crime in certain narrative hierarchies, with 'genocide' or 'aggression' at the peak of condemnation, and others (crimes against humanity, war crimes) at the lower echelon.[208]

Judges have used expressive language to reach audiences beyond parties and participants in legal proceedings. They have understood their role and mandate in adjudication not only in a technical legal sense but rather as part of a broader epistemic community ('international judicial community').[209] This broader understanding has served as a vehicle to address broader audiences, such as a global legal community, 'would-be perpetrators,' actual and potential victims of crime, and affected societies.[210]

As Rosa Aloisi and James Meernik have shown in their comparative study of judgments, judges have 'spoken to history'[211] and 'intentionally' relied on expressivism to 'speak to the whole of humanity',[212] 'place the suffering of victims into a historical context',[213] and 'help achieve the tribunal's aims of advancing justice, peace and reconciliation'.[214]

The expressive function of law and the close nexus between moral and legal argument[215] is reflected in progressive readings of the law.[216] The history of

[204] Edward M. Wise, 'The International Criminal Court: A Budget of Paradoxes' (2000) 8 *Tulane Journal of International and Criminal Law* 261–81, 267.
[205] See Rosa Aloisi and James Meernik, *Judgment Day* (New York: Cambridge University Press, 2017) 129.
[206] William Schabas, *Unimaginable Atrocities: Justice, Politics, and Rights at the War Crimes Tribunals* (Oxford: Oxford University Press, 2012), 117.
[207] Payam Akhavan, *Reducing Genocide to Law* (Cambridge: Cambridge University Press, 2012) 176.
[208] Amann, 'Group Mentality, Expressivism and Genocide', 128–31.
[209] Aloisi and Meernik, *Judgment Day* 149.
[210] Ibid., 198.
[211] Ibid., 198.
[212] Ibid., 149
[213] Ibid., 149.
[214] Ibid., 198.
[215] On moral foundations, see Victor Tadros, *The Ends of Harm: The Moral Foundations of Criminal Law* (Oxford: Oxford University Press, 2012).
[216] For a full account, see **section 3.2**.

international criminal justice is replete with examples where judges have partly acted as 'judicial entrepreneurs' to avoid or reduce legal gaps, promote humanity-based readings of law, reach broader audiences, or attempt to leave a legal legacy through judgments, which extends beyond the number of cases or trials.[217] Expressivist language has in particular been used in relation to the branding of crimes and sentencing, the most emotive part of judicial reasoning. The ability to express norms and commitment to them has become recognized as a central feature of international criminal justice.[218] Some have even gone so far as to argue that international criminal tribunals can 'contribute most effectively to world public order as self-consciously expressive penal institutions', namely by 'publicly condemning acts deplored by international law, acting as an engine of jurisprudential development at the local level, and encouraging the legal and normative internalization of international human rights and humanitarian law'.[219]

For instance, David Luban has claimed that 'norm projection' is the most 'promising justification' of international criminal institutions. He sees the virtue of trials in the fact that they are 'expressive acts broadcasting the news that mass atrocities are, in fact, heinous crimes and not merely politics by other means'.[220] This view is in line with claims that international criminal justice is mainly a way to speak 'truth to power'[221] rather than a project of social justice.

The expressive function of punishment extends beyond the infliction of a penalty. The traditional assumption that punishment involves a proportionate condemnatory message to the defendant is problematic in international criminal justice.[222] International sentences may be lighter than their domestic counterparts or less painful to the defendant in light of their modalities of enforcement. The sentencing objectives invoked in judgments to justify penalties serve often more as an affirmation of the functions of international criminal justice as such[223] rather than as a basis for the calculation of proportionate punishment of individuals.[224]

[217] Aloisi and Meernik, *Judgment Day* 151.

[218] See Fisher, *Moral Accountability and International Criminal Law* 62.

[219] Robert D. Sloane, 'The Expressive Capacity of International Punishment: The Limits of the National Law Analogy and the Potential of International Criminal Law' (2007) 43 *Stanford Journal of International Law* 39–94, 44.

[220] David Luban, 'Fairness to rightness: Jurisdiction, legality, and the legitimacy of international criminal law' in Samantha Besson and John Tasioulas (eds), *The Philosophy of International Law* (Cambridge: Cambridge University Press, 2010), 569–88, 576.

[221] Martti Koskenniemi, *The Gentle Civilizer of Nations, The Rise and Fall of International Law 1870–1960* (Cambridge: Cambridge University Press, 2001).

[222] Aloisi and Meernik, *Judgment Day* 117.

[223] Traces of an expressivist function of punishment were articulated by the ICTY in *Nikolić*. The Chamber went beyond classical sentencing rationales. It argued that '[o]ne of the main purposes of a sentence imposed by an international tribunal is to influence the legal awareness of the accused, the surviving victims, their relatives, the witnesses and the general public in order to reassure them that the legal system is implemented and enforced. Additionally, the process of sentencing is intended to convey the message that globally accepted laws and rules have to be obeyed by everybody… This fundamental rule fosters the internalisation of these laws and rules in the minds of legislators and the general public.' *Prosecutor v. Nikolić*, Sentencing Judgment, IT-94-2-S, 18 December 2003, para. 139.

[224] Aloisi and Meernik, *Judgment Day*, 188.

The expressive function of punishment is related to other factors, such as affirmation of the authority 'to punish through the law', the special stigma associated with international punishment, or its publicity.[225]

1.1.6.2 Expressivist features of trials

Expressive theories have gained scholarly attention in the context of the study of the functions and rationales of criminal trials. Expressive justifications have been developed to complement purely retributive accounts of international criminal justice. They provide an instrument to take into the collective nature of violence and the limitations of international criminal justice. Retribution 'fails' as a punishment theory in international criminal justice since 'too few people or entities receive just deserts while many powerful states and organizations automatically are absolved of any responsibility'.[226]

Trials have important demonstration effects.[227] They exceed classical moral education theory which has focused on the defendant as the primary audience of moral education.[228] As Mark Drumbl has stated, international criminal justice involves 'popular trials' that 'define a debate, remind us of the content and value of law, or serve as intergenerational "signposts" in history'.[229]

Lawrence Douglas has shown in his study of the *Eichmann* and *Demjanjuk* trials that law and history are closely interrelated.[230] Judicial proceedings often mark a tribute to history and memory, in light of their specific set-up and orchestration. They are used 'not simply to punish extreme crimes but to demonstrate visibly the power of the law to submit the most horrific outrages to its sober ministrations'.[231] In this way, they visualize the 'neutral authority of the rule of law'.[232]

[225] Ibid., 188. For a full account of expressive punishment', see **section 5.1**.

[226] Mark Drumbl, 'Collective Violence and Individual Punishment: The Criminality of Mass Atrocity' 588.

[227] There is a tension between the expressivist features of international criminal justice, including its norm affirmative, and the narrow legal focus on individuals. Narrative functions are curtailed by a number of factors, such as 'selective truths' or 'management strategies'. See Amann, 'Group Mentality, Expressivism and Genocide' 133.

[228] See Fisher, *Moral Accountability and International Criminal Law* 60.

[229] Drumbl, *Atrocity, Punishment, and International Law* 175. Drumbl has defended a realistic account of expressivism which recognizes the inherent limits of atrocity trials. He has argued that international criminal justice should reach beyond 'high-profile criminal trials' in order to reduce its expressive vulnerabilities'. Ibid., 177.

[230] The framework and methodology of the judicial process differs from historical methods of inquiry. But what happens in the courtroom may become part of history. Evidence, testimony and narrative accounts reflected in the judgment may contribute to historical clarification. The question is thus not whether proceedings contribute to the production of history but rather how they do it. See **section 4.2.1.3**.

[231] See Douglas, *The Memory of Judgment* 41. Douglas makes a powerful argument that the *Eichmann* and *Demjanjuk* trials, as well as the trials of Klaus Barbie and Holocaust denier Ernst Zundel, were aimed to do justice both to the defendants and to the history and memory of the Holocaust.

[232] Ibid.

Trials are a medium through which the legal system stages itself,[233] and a stage for the production of competing narratives—and sometimes different layers of 'truth'. They involve both performance, that is the 'showing of justice', and 'performativity',[234] that is 'the doing of justice'.[235] Performative aspects relate *inter alia* to speech, truth-finding, or testimony.[236] Factors, like the publicity of arrest, the drama of the courtroom, or the suspense surrounding the delivery of judgment, are part of the performance of justice, the process of enacting law and making justice visible.

The connection between the performative aspects of trials and the production of international criminal justice has gained more explicit attention.[237] Trials have been branded as 'spectacles of legality'.[238] Some of the historical value of the *Eichmann* trial was seen in its social reorganization of the 'public sphere', namely its reframing of victim identity in public consciousness and its inclusion of stories of survivors.[239]

Feminist scholarship has highlighted some of the benefits of the performative aspects of trials, such as their ability to serve as a 'theatre of renewal'.[240] Expressive rationales provide a normative foundation to highlight stereotypes and neglects regarding sexual and gender-based violence. They may render sexual and gender-based violence visible, highlight specific types of harms, or signal the need for greater global investigation or prosecution.[241] For instance, the 'drama of charging and convicting individuals of sexual violence crimes' has been instrumental in

[233] See Marina Aksenova, 'The role of international criminal tribunals in shaping the historical accounts of genocide' in Uladzislau Belavusau and Aleksandra Gliszczyńska-Grabias (eds), *Law and Memory: Towards Legal Governance of History* (Cambridge: Cambridge University Press, 2017), 48–69, 58.

[234] The notion of performativity may be traced back to Judith Butlers work famous work *Gender Trouble: Feminism and the Subversion of Identity* (New York, NY: Routledge, 1990).

[235] Başak Ertür, *Spectacles and Spectres: Political Trials, Performativity and Scenes of Sovereignty* (Birkbeck, University of London, PhD thesis, 2015), 19 at http://bbktheses.da.ulcc.ac.uk/110/1/cp_Ertur_PhD.pdf.

[236] See **sections 4.1. and 4.2.**

[237] See Saira Mohamed, 'Deviance, Aspiration, and the Stories We Tell: Reconciling Mass Atrocity and the Criminal Law' (2015) 124 *Yale Law Journal* 1628–89, 1633 ('these courts can serve as sites of storytelling, providing both an opportunity to derive insights into how individuals choose to perpetrate crimes and an occasion for articulating how we hope people will behave in the most hopeless of circumstances').

[238] Douglas, *The Memory of Judgment* 41.

[239] Shoshana Felman, *The Juridical Unconscious: Trials and Traumas in the Twentieth Century* (Cambridge: Harvard University Press, 2002), 126–7 ('Victims were thus for the first time gaining what as victims they precisely could not have: authority, that is to say, semantic authority over themselves and over others.').

[240] Buss, 'Performing Legal Order' 414.

[241] See Margaret deGuzman, 'Giving Priority to Sex Crime Prosecutions: The Philosophical Foundations of a Feminist Agenda' (2011) 11 *International Criminal Law Review* 515–28, 526 ('While all national systems treat murder as a serious crime—probably the most serious—sex crimes are often viewed as unworthy of official or judicial attention. Expressive theories thus support giving priority to sex crimes for international prosecution because the norms prohibiting those crimes are significantly less well-established than the norms prohibiting killing.').

promoting 'gendered understandings of international legal order and disorder'.[242] As Doris Buss has argued, in international criminal prosecutions, 'rape and other forms of sexual harm are identified *as harms*, they are prosecuted *as crimes*, and they result in punishment through years of incarceration for those found guilty'.[243] International criminal cases 'have generated substantial "official" and scholarly knowledge about the gendered effects of conflict'.[244]

Critics of expressivism note that functions such as expression of moral outrage, norm projection, or broader didactic aims (e.g. contributions to history or memory) may detract from the core function of trials or weaken their legitimacy.[245]

1.1.6.3 Expressivism and selective choice

International criminal justice has a strong signalling effect in relation to the use of adjudicative authority, distributions of burden and blame, and use of resources. Fréderic Mégret has called this the 'representational function of international criminal justice'.[246] Trials do not only express the nature of crimes that are adjudicated. They highlight the very constituencies that are affected by them, the value accorded to investigation and prosecution, forum choices, burden sharing, and allocation of resources. Trials fulfil these functions not merely 'by what they do' but 'also merely by what they are'.[247] Based on their forms and features, they may send very different messages:

> By virtue of a trial being held internationally, one sends a strong signal that the international community is ultimately the community of reference for international crimes, the yardstick of universalized understanding of the abominable. By virtue of a trial being organized domestically, one solidifies the vision of certain crimes being above all anchored in a domestic trajectory—which they may well be in certain circumstances and deserve to be treated as such.[248]

Expressivism has been used as an argument to counter some of the dilemmas arising from the selectivity of practice.[249] For example, scholars like Margaret deGuzman have argued that problems of choice and limitations of investigation, prosecution, and punishment in international criminal justice may be set into

242 Buss, 'Performing Legal Order' 423.
243 Ibid., 414.
244 Ibid., 414.
245 See **section 1.2.4**.
246 Fréderic Mégret, 'In Defense of Hybridity: Towards a Representational Theory of International Criminal Justice' (2005) 38 *Cornell International Law Journal* 725–51, 743.
247 Ibid.
248 Ibid.
249 See Mohammad Hadi Zakerhossein, *Situation Selection Regime at the International Criminal Court: Law, Policy, Practice* (Cambridge: Intersentia, 2017), 408 ('Expressivism allows the Court to function in an exemplary and selective manner.').

perspective by expressivism.[250] The main virtue of expressivism is that it may explain how a relatively rudimentary system, with limited resources and enforcement powers, may carry a high degree of social relevance and contribute to goals that exceed its capacity.

Theoretically, all international crimes are worthy of condemnation. But only a fraction receive attention, in light of the scope of jurisdiction, applicable legal filters, prosecutorial discretion, available evidence, and resource constraints. Both the selection of situations and the framing of charges are processes with a deeply expressive function. They contain messages about what types of conflicts, criminality, incidents, and perpetrators ought to be chosen for international investigation and prosecutions, and what prioritizations should be drawn.[251]

Expressivism is an inherent element of charging policy. It serves to justify thematic preferences. For example, the ICC Office of the Prosecutor (OTP) has argued that charges should, 'whenever possible', constitute a 'representative sample of the main types of victimisation and of the communities which have been affected by the crimes' in a relevant situation.[252] But it has left a very wide space to select charges based on alternative criteria, such as their lack of attention at the global scale.[253] The choice of charges is also determined by considerations as to what type of criminality ought to be more systematically investigated and prosecuted globally. For instance, environmental crime is a key area in which charges may have a strong global signalling effect.

However, this methodology also faces critiques. There is considerable dispute towards whom messages should be directed. One of the risks of expressivist charging is that it may privilege global audiences. For example, DeGuzman has claimed that 'for the ICC, as a normative matter, global expression is the most appropriate role for the institution.'[254]

[250] Margaret DeGuzman, 'Choosing to Prosecute: Expressive Selection at the International Criminal Court' (2012) 33 *Michigan Journal of International Law* 265–320, 265.

[251] For instance, existing ICC Policy Papers on Preliminary Examinations and Case Selection and Prioritisation are replete with expressivist justifications to counter selectivity critiques. See OTP, Policy Paper on Preliminary Examinations, November 2013, paras 105–106, at http://www.legal-tools.org/doc/acb906/pdf/. The choice of situations is defended by 'gravity'. The ICC has taken into account factors, such as the messages sent through crimes, and their impact, in applying the notion. In the Comoros situation, the Pre-Trial Chamber relied *inter alia* on the 'international concern caused by the events at issue' to justify its sufficient gravity. See Pre-Trial Chamber I, Decision on the request of the Union of the Comoros to review the Prosecutor's decision not to initiate an investigation, ICC-01/13-34, 16 July 2015, para. 48. See also **section 4.2.2**.

[252] OTP, Policy Paper on Case Selection and Prioritisation, 15 September 2016, para. 45, at https://www.icc-cpi.int/itemsDocuments/20160915_OTP-Policy_Case-Selection_Eng.pdf.

[253] The Policy Paper on Case Selection and Prioritization states: 'The Office will pay particular attention to crimes that have been traditionally under-prosecuted, such as crimes against or affecting children as well as rape and other sexual and gender-based crimes. It will also pay particular attention to attacks against cultural, religious, historical and other protected objects as well as against humanitarian and peacekeeping personnel. In so doing, the Office will aim to highlight the gravity of these crimes, thereby helping to end impunity for, and contributing to the prevention of, such crimes.' Ibid., para. 46.

[254] DeGuzmann, 'Choosing to Prosecute' 316. Ibid., 312 ('ICC should focus on its expressive impact at the global level in the hopes that its various justifying aims will be indirectly achieved as the norms it promotes are strengthened and entrenched throughout the world.').

This premise is contested by critics who fear that such a global orientation may re-entrench equality divides or marginalize competing visions of justice (e.g. Third World Approaches to International Law (TWAIL)).[255] Opponents caution that international criminal justice should primarily address the offender, affected communities, or local victims.[256]

1.1.6.4 Expressivism and social production of reality

International criminal justice involves social production.[257] It seeks to attract sympathy to its own cause through images and appeals to relieve human suffering. [258] International criminal agents do not only apply, interpret, or enforce the law but they also produce new facts and realities, forms of power, and symbolic orders. The field constitutes itself through judicial and non-judicial forms of expression (e.g. imagery),[259] inside and outside the courtroom.

The setting of the courtroom has high symbolic importance. It represents respect of authority and obedience to law.[260] The use of crime labels and the choice of sites of intervention produces certain stigmas and narratives. It presents 'the other' predominantly as a site of conflict, evil, and violence. It relies on many ideal types, such as the image of the villain perpetrator or the 'victim' that needs to be saved.[261] For instance, international prosecutors have been described as the 'embodiment of the crusading knight in shining linen on hand to save disempowered victims from the savagery of their own'.[262]

[255] See Makau Mutua, 'What is TWAIL?' 94 *American Society of International Law Proceedings* (2000) 31–9; Antony Anghie and Bhupinder S. Chimni, 'Third World Approaches to International Law and Individual Responsibility in Internal Conflict' (2003) 2 *Chinese Journal of International Law* 77–103.

[256] See Damaška, 'What's the Point', 349 arguing that the priority of international criminal courts should be to establish effective lines of communication with local audiences.

[257] On law as performance, see Jack M. Balkin and Sanford Levinson, 'Law as performance' in Michael Freeman and Andrew D.E. Lewis (eds), *Law and Literature* (New York: Oxford University Press, 1999), 729–51 ('Legal interpretation—which includes adjudication, enforcement, and offering legal advice—is a social activity that shapes, directs, and normalizes the thought and behavior of others. Legal interpretation affects its "audience": it does things with them and to them. Hence performance always brings with it special responsibilities to the audience.').

[258] On emotion and atrocity, see Thomas Brudholm and Johannes Lang, 'Introduction: Emotions and mass atrocity' in Thomas Brudholm and Johannes Lang (eds), *Emotion and Mass Atrocity* (Cambridge: Cambridge University Press), 1–20, Neta C. Crawford, 'Institutionalizing Passion in World Politics: Fear and Empathy' (2014) 6 *International Theory* 535–57.

[259] Tallgren, 'Come and See?' 259.

[260] On symbolism of courts and their architecture, see Judith Resnik, Dennis E. Curtis, and Allison Anna Tait, 'Constructing courts: Architecture, the ideology of judging, and the public sphere' in Anne Wagner and Richard K. Sherwin (eds), *Law, Culture & Visual Studies* (Dordrecht: Springer, 2013), 515–45. See also Nigel Eltringham, 'Spectators to the Spectacle of Law: The Formation of a "Validating Public" at the International Criminal Tribunal for Rwanda' (2012) 77 *Ethnos: Journal of Anthropology* 425–45.

[261] See **section 4.2.2.**

[262] John Reynolds and Sujith Xavier, '"The Dark Corners of the World": TWAIL and International Criminal Justice' (2016) 14 *JICJ* 959–83, 965.

International criminal justice creates novel subjectivities and frames with which other actors need to engage. The articulation of crimes, criminal agents, and groups attaches different forms of stigmatization to conduct.[263] These labels are particularly powerful because they are illustrated through testimony, evidence, and public proceedings.

Notions of victimhood are often associated with certain characteristics, such as vulnerability, powerlessness, disadvantages, abuse, and fear. Such images are part of the expressive function. They are deemed to gather broader social consensus around acknowledgment and condemnation of atrocity and reaffirmation of humanist values. They convey messages about the identity and 'mission' of international criminal justice and the type of victims and crimes that should be its subjects. They are amplified through channels of public information, outreach, and media.[264]

Socio-legal scholars have used the notion of 'spectacles' to characterize this type of social production, that is, the construction of events and characters through real and imagined images. For instance, Christine Schwöbel-Patel has argued that international criminal justice involves imagery and performance that evokes 'a particular (stereo-)type in our collective imagination' and appeals to specific audiences (e.g. fundraisers, donors).[265] Immi Tallgren has stressed the interplay between imagery and a 'commodification of suffering'. She has compared image production to a purifying ritual:

> [The] power [of international criminal justice] lies in bringing to view suffering of individuals or groups identified, suffering presumably caused by suspects identified, too, all of them becoming characters in a narrative with chronological sequences that can be 'evidenced', to create a beginning and an end. The power culminates in shaping the focus: this is the suffering that gets selected, it passes through the elaborate international criminal justice procedural rites, is purified, and becomes confirmed as worthy of concern ... Images of 'justice being done' may appear to wipe away both crimes and suffering and complicities not directly visible.[266]

According to this logic, the performance of trials serves to absolve humanity itself from guilt and evil.[267]

263 Mégret, 'Practices of Stigmatization' 295–316.

264 Daniel Joyce, 'Human Rights and Mediatization of International Justice' (2010) 23 *LJIL* 507–27.

265 Christine Schwöbel-Patel, 'Spectacle in International Criminal Law: The Fundraising Image of Victimhood', (2016) 2 *London Review of International Law* 247–74, 249–50.

266 Tallgren, 'Come and See?' 277.

267 On shame and apology in the institutional history, see **section 3.1.1.2**.

1.1.6.5 Expressivism and the problem of communication

The creation of social meanings is a highly complex process. It is dependent on context and influenced by many intermediate factors. Communicative action operates in a complex inter-subjective context.[268]

Some theoretical guidance on the function of expressivism may be derived from modern speech act theory. Speech acts are communicative activities that seek to leave an impression by the speaker on others and their environment.[269] Speech act theory posits that language and communication entail performative speech acts.[270] It goes back to the works of British philosopher John Austin and US scholar John Searle.[271]

Austin and Searle have distinguished different types of speech acts: locutionary, illocutionary, and perlocutionary acts. The locutory act is the act of uttering the sentence. Illocutionary acts refer to what is expressed through speech action. They are linked to the speaker, that is the intended significance of an act. Perlocutionary acts concern the consequences of speech acts, that is what follows from speech. They relate to the effect on the listener (e.g. persuasion, fear, inspiration), including thoughts, emotions, or physical acts.[272]

Speech act theory has relevance to the understanding of adjudication and enforcement. Judicial proceedings involve a whole range of different speech acts. Some of them declaratory, others are communicative in nature. Certain legal acts, such as the pronouncement of the judgment or legal processes may be considered as illocutionary speech acts.

The connection between expressivism and speech act theory starts to be reflected in legal scholarship. For instance, Roman Hamel has argued that the judgment in a criminal law trial constitutes a declarative speech act.[273] A similar argument applies to the act of punishment. It may be viewed as non-verbal speech act. Tobias Zürcher has made the point that criminal enforcement may be viewed as a perlocutionary speech act, aimed at the offender and the respective domestic society.[274]

However, in practice, expressivism continues to face serious methodological challenges. Expressivist justifications tend to imply that legal actions can be

[268] Habermas, *Theorie des kommunikativen Handelns*, vol I, 391, 395.

[269] German linguist Philip Wegener spoke of linguistic action (*sprachliches Handeln*). See Philip Wegener, 'Der Wortsatz' (1921) 39 *Indogermanische Forschungen* 1–26. John Austin referred to 'doing things with words'.

[270] As John Searle put it: 'speaking a language is engaging in a rule-governed form of behaviour Searle'. See John Searle, *Speech Acts: An Essay in the Philosophy of Language* (Cambridge: Cambridge University Press, 1969) 22.

[271] John Langshaw Austin, *How to do Things with Words* (Oxford: Clarendon Press, 1962); John Searle, *Speech Acts: An Essay in the Philosophy of Language*.

[272] For a typology, see also **section 4.2.1**.

[273] Hamel, *Strafen als Sprechakt* 128, 152–3.

[274] See Zürcher, *Legitimation von Strafe* 133 et seq.

translated into a coherent set of messages. But there is often no mutual understanding of speaker and hearer. What is expressed may differ from the content that is intended to be communicated. For example, the meaning that is conveyed is deeply linked to specific social conventions, rituals, and habits. 'Outsiders' who are not acquainted with these customs, or are hostile to them, may fail to understand the message or read it differently.

Criminal proceedings involve message pluralism. They may produce more or different messages than anticipated. For instance, the Prosecution, the Defence, victims, and judges all speak with a different voice and may convey conflicting messages. The messages that are sent are often 'one-sided' acts of expression rather than mutual processes of engagement.[275]

In international criminal justice, it is less clear than in a domestic context which target audience is supposed to be reached. International justice agents often assume that there is a receptive audience. But it is unclear whether the intended audience is actually 'listening' and how the messages conveyed are actually received.[276] There is limited empirical research as to whether trials have indeed managed to convey intended messages.[277]

There are mediation problems. Messages must cross different types of borders (e.g. physical, lingual or culturally borders) to be received locally. As Marina Aksenova has observed, even 'new forms of communication powered by modern technologies' do not 'ensure a straightforward dialogue whereby a message is publicly broadcast and delivered to the recipients with its content unchanged'.[278] Any information 'goes through a variety of filters that shape its meaning before it reaches the addressee'.[279] Judgments and proceedings may thus be perceived very differently by different audiences. Punishment can entail a form of disapproval but it can divide society.

1.2 A Contemporary Theorization

Expressivism remains undertheorized as a concept. It plays an important role in the practice of international criminal justice.[280] However, there are still conceptual divides and normative confusion. The concept is understood differently by different authors and across fields. For instance, transitional justice scholarship

[275] On the divide between 'expressivist' and 'communicative' accounts, see Wibren Van der Burg, 'The Expressive and Communicative Functions of Law, Especially with Regard to Moral Issues' (2001) 20 *Law and Philosophy* 31–59.

[276] Glasius, 'It Sends a Message' 423 ('[Expressivism] does not examine whether, in fact, society is listening whether there is an attentive audience for the messages enunciated.').

[277] Glasius, 'It Sends a Message' 446–7.

[278] Marina Aksenova, 'Symbolism as a Constraint on International Criminal Law' (2017) 30 *LJIL* 475–99, 484.

[279] Ibid.

[280] Sloane, 'The Expressive Capacity of International Punishment' 70.

offers different perspectives on key normative elements (e.g. the role of symbolism, historical clarification, educative rationales, and orientation of punishment) than classical criminal law doctrine.

Many foundations of expressivist theory have been developed in domestic law. They require certain adjustments in the international context. For instance, speaker and audience problems are more acute. In domestic contexts, it is common to distinguish two different forms of expressivism: (i) norm expression and (ii) person- and audience-related expression.[281] This distinction is more blurred in international criminal justice since it relies on wider and more loosely defined community structures than does domestic jurisdiction. Expressivism governs partly different speech relations and faces different critiques.[282] It is thus necessary to revisit some of the existing theories and critiques.

1.2.1 Dual foundation

The general distinction between norm expression and person-related expressivism (Hörnle) applies not only to domestic criminal law but is also useful to understand international criminal justice. [283] Norm expression is, in essence, one-directional. It is focused on sending messages rather than dialectical communication. It expresses the intention of the sender and seeks to foster application and compliance through the message.[284] Direct communication is related to the recipient. It may involve two-way communication. Such types of interactions have gained broader significance in international criminal justice with the development of fair trial rights and the recognition of victims as agents in the criminal process.[285]

1.2.1.1 Norm expression

Norm expression is grounded in the idea that international criminal justice serves to restore confidence in norms that have been violated. This rationale has a long

[281] See **section 1.1.4**.

[282] It relies on the communication of meaning about 'power, authority, legitimacy, normality, morality, personhood, social relations, and a host of other matters'. See David Garland, *Punishment and Modern Society: A study in Social Theory* (Chicago, IL: University of Chicago Press, 1990), 252.

[283] See also Demko, 'An Expressive Theory of International Punishment for International Crimes' 180.

[284] Zürcher, *Legitimation von Strafe*, 168. The assumption that international criminal justice contributes to norm affirmation through declaratory speech acts is open to critique. It may easily take on paternalistic features. For instance, the idea that international criminal justice marks a project of 'civilizing' or emancipating society has remained suspicious in the eyes of those affected. See **section 2.2.4**.

[285] Paul Roberts and Nesam McMillan, 'For Criminology in International Criminal Justice' (2003) 1 *JICJ* 315–38; Jennifer L. Balint, 'The Place of Law in Addressing International Regime Conflicts' (1996) 59 *Law & Contemporary Problems* 103–26, 113; Mark A. Drumbl, 'Toward a Criminology of International Crime' (2003) 19 *Ohio State Journal on Dispute Resolution* 263–82; Susanne Karstedt, 'Comparing Cultures, Comparing Crime: Challenges, Prospects and Problems for a Global Criminology' (2001) 36 *Crime, Law & Social Change* 285–308.

tradition in legal philosophy. For instance, Immanuel Kant has argued that a crime deserves to be punished since it is an attack on the security and protection of victims and members of society.[286] Hegel famously justified punishment as an act of negation, namely as a measure which protects the law against its own negation ('*Negation der Negation*').[287] He argued that a crime is an act that proposes a new norm and punishment a 'cancellation of crime'.[288] Punishment needs to deny the crime because it would otherwise 'become valid'.[289]

Hegel's negation theory offers a useful theoretical starting point for understanding norm expression, but it has certain limitations from a legal perspective. For instance, not all crimes involve an intentional attack on norms. Nor do crimes abolish norms in the technical sense. Critics rightly insist that a norm does not lose its validity because it is violated by offenders.

Contemporary legal scholars have developed the idea of punishment as a response to crimes. Most prominently, Günther Jakobs has argued that the function of criminal law is to 'contradict the contradiction' of norms which define the identity of society. He has developed a norm-oriented expressive theory which regards punishment as an act of norm affirmation ('*Einübung in Normanerkennung*').[290]

This argument has been echoed at the international level. [291] As David Luban has noted, international criminal justice involves both (i) norm affirmation (i.e. affirmation of existing norms) and (ii) norm projection (i.e. the articulation of new codes of behaviour) in response to crime.[292]

International crimes are often characterized by State policies or systematically orchestrated violence. They involve structured or organized attacks on social order (i.e. armed conflict, 'systematic or widespread attack' against the civilian population) or international society (e.g. act of aggression). These contextual factors distinguish them from ordinary crimes. If a crime breaches a general norm, 'everyone is affected by it'.[293] Based on this argument, international criminal justice may be

[286] On Kant as modern retributivist whose penal theory is focused on 'civic respect for persons as citizen', see Sarah Holtman, 'Kant, Retributivism, and Civic Respect' in Mark White (ed.), *Retributivism: Essays on Theory and Policy* (Oxford: Oxford University Press), 107–27.

[287] On Hegel's penal theory, see Thom Brooks, 'Hegel on crime and punishment' in Thom Brooks and Sebastian Stein (eds), *Hegel's Political Philosophy: On the Normative Significance of Method and System* (Oxford: Oxford University Press, 2017), 202–21.

[288] Hegel, *Philosophy of right* § 101 ('The cancellation [Aufheben] of crime is retribution in so far as the latter, by its concept, is an infringement of an infringement.').

[289] Hegel, *Philosophy of right*, § 99 ('cancellation [Aufheben] of the crime, which would otherwise be regarded as valid').

[290] See **section 1.1.4.1**; Günther Jakobs, *Schuld und Prävention* (Tubingen: Mohr, 1976), 10. For a critique, see Hendrik Schneider, *Kann die Einübung in Normanerkennung die Strafrechtsdogmatik leiten? Eine Kritik des strafrechtlichen Funktionalismus* (Berlin: Duncker & Humblot, 2004).

[291] Demko, 'An Expressive Theory of International Punishment'.

[292] See also **section 2.1**.

[293] See Pablo De Greiff, 'Articulating the links between transitional justice and development justice and social integration' in Pablo de Greiff and Roger Duthie (eds), *Transitional Justice and Development: Making Connections* (New York, NY: International Centre for Transitional Justice, 2009), 28, 43.

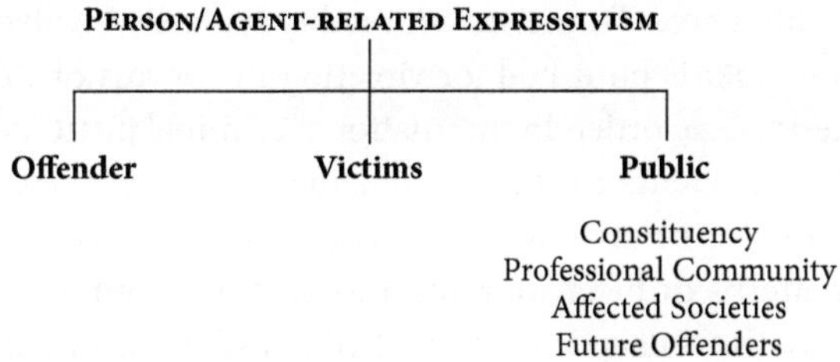

Figure 3 Person/agent-related expression

viewed as an attempt to reinforce the trust of society in international legal norms and to inspire human beings to obey the law.

1.2.1.2 Person- and audience-related expression

Person- and audience-related types of expression involve more directed speech acts towards specific audiences. Domestic theories have typically focused on the role of trials as means of communication with agents in proceedings, namely the offender and victims. However, in international criminal justice, this framing is too narrow. The broader 'human-interpersonal' dimensions lie at the core of expressivist foundations at the international level.[294] The scope of addressees extends to communication with a 'broader public', which includes constituencies, professional communities, affected societies, and future offenders. This type of interaction has more synergies with norm expression.

1.2.1.2.1 International criminal justice as communication with the offender

International criminal justice contains speech acts towards offenders. Trials involve not only an expression of moral blameworthiness but also communication with offenders.[295] They seek to influence behaviour of offenders, including acknowledgment of wrong. Communication is essential to achieve purposes of punishment. It reflects a recognition of the autonomy and dignity of the offender. Lawful behaviour cannot be enforced through pressure and coercion alone, but requires persuasion. Communicative structures are reflected in several features of international criminal proceedings, including the recognition of the central role of the Defence throughout different stages of the criminal process, who is called to 'answer' the case,[296] the encouragement of guilty pleas, and agreement in relation to facts and evidence at trial or sentencing considerations.

Many of the justifications for defending communicative accounts of trial in domestic settings also apply to international criminal justice. However, there are

[294] Demko, 'An Expressive Theory of International Punishment' 180.
[295] Duff, 'Authority and Responsibility in International Criminal Law' 594–7.
[296] Ibid., 594 ('responsible agent, who should be called to answer').

some structural differences. Domestic criminality typically involves norm-defiant behaviour. The offender is punished for violating the norms of a common polity, namely the domestic legal order. In international criminal justice, the argument of norm defiance by the offender is more problematic. It often involves punishment for partially law-abiding behaviour, namely conduct that is in conformity with domestic laws or patterns of behaviour, but in violation of international norms or rules of behaviour. The didactic function of trial and punishment transcends the individual. The communication expressed through punishment may address a broader collectivity than the offender. In many instances, international criminal justice has a strongly representational function. The offender is not so much punished in its capacity as an individual but rather as representative of a particular collective structure, that is a government, military structure, armed group, or a criminal organization.[297]

The need for re-socialization may be less acute. Criminological research (*Täterforschung*) has shown that many atrocity crimes are heavily conditioned by social context, such as hierarchical relationships, structures of obedience, group dynamics, or organizational routines which rationalize behaviour.[298] For instance, historian Christopher Browning has shown that many German perpetrators were not Nazi fanatics but 'ordinary men' who grew into their roles through peer pressure and group dynamics.[299] He has divided offenders into four categories: ideologues ('true believers'), political leaders who orchestrate crime and believe in their cause; 'apolitical' professionals and experts who become involved in their commission; middle or lower-level bureaucrats or functionaries; and ordinary members of society who became complicit. Social psychologists have argued that perpetrator behaviour in relation to atrocity crime is often determined by structures of 'obedience'.[300] Many offenders lose these incentives or conformity pressures when they are detached from the relevant context or structure.[301] Some benefits may follow from the sheer distance to crimes and criminal structures.

Moral re-education is not necessarily a primary goal but, at best, an effect of trials and punishment.[302] The premise that trials serve to restore morality is often

[297] See Mégret, 'Practices of Stigmatization' 305.

[298] Herbert Jäger, *Verbrechen unter totalitärer Herrschaft* (Frankfurt: Suhrkamp Verlag, 1982).

[299] Christopher R. Browning, *Ordinary Men: Reserve Police Battalion 101 and the Final Solution in Poland* (New York, NY: Harper Collins, 1992).

[300] Herbert C. Hamilton and V. Lee Hamilton, *Crimes of Obedience: Toward a Social Psychology of Authority and Responsibility* (New Haven, CT: Yale University Press, 1989).

[301] Barbora Holà, Joris van Wijk, and Jessica Kelder, 'Effectiveness of international criminal tribunals: Empirical assessment of rehabilitation as sentencing goal' in Nobuo Hayashi and Cecilia Bailliet (eds), *The Legitimacy of International Criminal Tribunals* (Cambridge: Cambridge University Press), 351–75, 375.

[302] See generally Margaret Walker, *Moral Repair: Reconstructing Moral Relations after Wrongdoing* (New York, NY: Cambridge University Press, 2006).

not as clear-cut as assumed. Offenders are not always 'evil-intending persons'.[303] As social scientists Alan Page Fiske and Tage Shakti Rai have argued, violence is often 'morally motivated' (virtuous violence), namely aimed at improving social relationships, at the least in the moral universe of the offender.[304] This makes the idea of moral education highly complex in relation to politically motivated crime. The legal process, the judgment, and the act of punishment may be aimed at persuading the offender to acknowledge wrongdoing. But this is not strictly required by the legal process. Defendants cannot be compelled to show repentance or engage in reconciliation.[305]

1.2.1.2.2 International criminal justice as communication with victims

Victims form a second audience of intended messages. Over past decades, it has become more common to view international criminal justice a means of communication with victims.[306] This is a consequence of the rise of victim-related justifications of criminal trials and punishment.[307]

In many contemporary contexts, victims cannot only appear as witnesses for either of the parties but act as autonomous agents in proceedings. The Special Tribunal for Lebanon (STL), the Extraordinary Chambers in the Courts of Cambodia (ECCC), and ICC have elaborate provisions on victim participation. They can either intervene as civil parties (*partie civile* model) or as participants in criminal proceedings (criminal model).[308]

There are compelling arguments in favour of victim-related expressivism. International criminal justice needs to express itself to victims. Delivering justice to victims is one of its principal causes. Without taking into account the interests of

[303] See Arne Johan Vetlesen, 'Social science and the study of perpetrators' in Thomas Brudholm and Johannes Lang (eds), *Emotions and Mass Atrocity* (Cambridge: Cambridge University Press, 2018), 104–20, 105.

[304] Alan P. Fiske and Tage S. Rai, *Virtuous Violence* (Cambridge: Cambridge University Press, 2015), xxii.

[305] International criminal justice differs in this respect from truth and reconciliation proceedings, which seek to promote acceptance of wrong or victim–offender mediation. Defendants have a right to remain silent. A judge cannot order an apology by the perpetrator, nor forgiveness by victims. This is part of the liberal trial model. It requires respect of the autonomy of the defendant and victims. It rests on the assumption that only people can build or repair social relations. It may require respect of the will of those who choose not to acknowledge responsibility or not to forgive. See **sections 4.3 and 4.4.**

[306] Tatjana Hörnle, 'The role of victims' rights in punishment theory' in Antje du Bois-Pedain and Anthony E Bottoms (eds), *Penal Censure: Engagements Within and Beyond Desert Theory* (Oxford: Hart, 2019), 207–26; Hörnle, 'Die Rolle des Opfers in der Straftheorie und im materiellen Strafrecht' 950–8.

[307] This movement started at the domestic level in the 1960s. It has gained ground in international criminal justice over the past two decades, with more extensive provision for victim participation and reparation in international treaties and procedural regimes of international criminal courts and tribunals (e.g. ICC, STL, ECCCC, Extraordinary African Chambers in Senegal). See **section 4.3.5.**

[308] See generally Brianne McGonigle Leyh, *Procedural Justice? Victim Participation in International Criminal Proceedings* (Antwerp: Intersentia, 2011), 33–91.

victims, international criminal justice is likely to lose public confidence. Criminal trials and punishment may *inter alia* express the wrong and harm inflicted to victims and mark an act of solidarity with their suffering.[309]

Typically, this type of interaction is more mediated than communication with offenders.[310] Victim participation is more discretionary.[311] Victims have a legitimate interest in criminal sanction, but no individual right to punishment.[312] The type of engagement with victims depends on the nature and protected interests of crimes. Communicative relationships are limited. Not all crimes have individual victims.[313] In many contexts, the messages sent through international criminal justice address victims as abstract or collective entities.[314]

Messages can take different forms. In some cases, the message is an expression of care and solidarity, which seeks to restore a certain sense of trust. It shows that the international community cares about what happened to victims[315] or that law prevails over anarchy. Other acts may be addressed more directly towards individualized victims. For instance, the judgment, punishment, and award of reparation may contain more direct speech acts towards victims. A criminal conviction signals that 'there is no justification or excuse' for imposing harm or suffering on victims.[316] The attribution of responsibility to the offender for a particular crime is not only directed towards the latter, but also a communication towards victims affected by crimes.[317]

[309] Nimaga, 'An International Conscience Collective' 609 ('From the Durkheimian standpoint the victims need to be present in the court proceedings, not as mere "objects of discussion" but as active pursuers of their interests, as witnesses and/or onlookers. Only in this way can there be efforts to restore their humanity that was so blatantly denied them by their victimizers.').

[310] See also **section 4.3.5**.

[311] Participation is grounded in their right of access to justice, to hear the truth, and to receive reparation for wrongdoing.

[312] Punishment remains a prerogative and duty of public authority. For a discussion, see David Alm, 'Crime Victims and the Right to Punishment' (2019) 13 *Criminal Law, Philosophy* 63–81, 76 ('such a "right" would be very thin indeed. In the first place it is derived from a more fundamental right (to equal treatment), which tends to elicit the thought that the real cause of the frustrated victim's reaction is the unequal treatment rather than the non-punishment as such.').

[313] Elander, 'Expressivism and the Victim at the ECCC' 114.

[314] On the role of fictions, see Kamari Clarke, 'The Rule of Law Through Its Economies of Appearances: The Making of the African Warlord' (2011) 18 *Indiana Journal of Global Legal Studies*, 7–40; Kamari Clarke, *Fictions of Justice: The International Criminal Court and the Challenge of Legal Pluralism in Sub-Saharan Africa* (Cambridge: Cambridge University Press, 2010), 105–9.

[315] A classic example is the defence of a 'victim-oriented perspective' in the preamble of the UN Basic Principles and Guidelines on the Right to a Remedy and Reparation for Victims of Gross Violations of International Human Rights Law and Serious Violations of International Humanitarian Law. It is a Durkheimian act of solidarity *par excellence*. It justifies the right to a remedy for victims as an act of 'human solidarity' by the 'international community' with 'victims of violations of international law, including violations of international human rights law and international humanitarian law, as well as with humanity at large'. See Preamble, General Assembly resolution 60/147 of 16 December 2005.

[316] Klaus Günther, 'Positive General Prevention and the Idea of Civic Courage in International Criminal Law' in Florian Jessberger and Julia Geneuss (eds), *Why Punish Perpetrators of Mass Atrocities?* (New York: Cambridge University Press, 2010) 213–28, 225.

[317] See Demko, 'An Expressive Theory of International Punishment' 194.

1.2.1.2.3 International criminal justice as communication with a 'broader public': A typology

One important difference between international and domestic criminal justice is the broad spectrum of secondary audiences.[318] Many communicative acts of international criminal justice are geared at a broader public and more indeterminate audiences.[319] As Diane Amann has put it:

> The intended audience of such exhortations is not just the wrongdoer of most concern to deterrence and retributive theorists. It is also the Everyone of most interest to expressive theorists: the law-abider and the lawmaker, the activist and the private citizen, and even the potential victim, today and tomorrow.[320]

This 'public' comprises international institutions, states, civil society actors, or individuals, even if they are not direct victims of crimes. For instance, the Special Court for Sierra Leone (SCSL) Trial Chamber stated in the *Taylor* case that the aim of judgment was not only to 'influence the legal awareness of the accused, the surviving victims, their relatives, [and] the witnesses' but also 'the general public in order to reassure them that the legal system is implemented and enforced'. It stated that 'sentencing is intended to convey the message that globally accepted laws and rules have to be accepted by everyone'.[321]

Messages sent to the broader 'public' generally tend to be more one-dimensional and may be oriented towards the future. This 'public' may be divided into different sub-categories of audiences.

The most direct communicative audience are stakeholders, agents who are part of the constituency of international criminal justice. Many communicative acts are directed towards entities to whom justice actors are answerable. This includes the funding bodies or governance organs of international justice institutions. For instance, most ICC acts 'speak' not only to a specific actor in proceedings but also to states and other actors who form the ICC system. Many messages of these messages are inherent, or follow certain codes of action or informal answer/response schemes that are set by principal–agent dynamics. They may reply to previous communications, critiques, or challenges, answer formal or 'unspoken' expectations, or form part of a systemic or structured dialogue that is repeated over time, or part of routine functioning or institutional governance.[322]

[318] See also Volker Nerlich, 'Audiences of the International Criminal Court' (2019) 19 *International Criminal Law Review* 1046–56, 1050. He includes the 'general public' in and outside situation countries, the 'broader "legal community" of lawyers, academics etc. interested in international criminal law' and the 'stakeholder audience of diplomats, states, NGOs, etc'.

[319] See Luigi D.A. Corrias and Geoffrey M. Gordon, 'Judging in the Name of Humanity: International Criminal Tribunals and the Representation of a Global Public' (2015) 13 *JICJ* 97–112.

[320] Amann, 'Group Mentality, Expressivism, and Genocide' 124.

[321] See *Prosecutor v. Taylor*, Sentencing Judgment, SCSL-03-01-T, 30 May 2005, para. 16. See also *Nikolić*, Sentencing Judgment, para. 139.

[322] See **section 3.2**.

For example, a trial judgment is not only a retributive measure (e.g. a determination on guilt and innocence) but also a multifaceted speech act. It contains implicit statements about the efficiency/inefficiency of the Court as a whole, expressions regarding fair or unfair treatment of defendants, justifications regarding the use of resources, acknowledgment of the limitations of ICC processes, or normative appeals for action, etc. It is addressed to a multiplicity of actors such as the Assembly of States Parties, authors of referrals (e.g. States, Security Council) or communications to the Court (e.g. non-governmental organizations (NGOs)), actors who have made submissions to the Court in proceedings, or even third states who are affected by decisions.

A second, broader audience are the professional communities that form international criminal justice as a field. They include not only international organizations, other courts and tribunals, and NGOs, but also professional bodies and individuals (e.g. former staff members, academics, etc.).[323] They form the 'invisible college'[324] of international criminal justice.[325] These relations are often less structured or hierarchical. There may be no formal legal bonds. Interaction is interest-based rather than driven by formal channels of accountability. The audiences are addressed because they have an interest in the matter at stake, or might serve as force multiplier for the cause at stake. They typically use the 'same language' as the 'speaker'. The act of communication is often more one-directional. The message is an invitation to engage.

A third audience is affected societies. This notion includes not only states or public institutions who have a nexus to atrocities but groups and individuals who are affected, irrespective of whether they are participating in proceedings. This relationship is delicate.[326] These audiences may be particularly attentive or averse to messages. Messages may have to cross physical, linguistic, or cultural boundaries. There are often no preconfigured channels of communication. Important aspects may get 'lost in translation' or be altered due to the high degree of mediation on the process of communication. Legal or factual statements may be dominated by politics, or struggle to address deeply unequal and undemocratic contexts. Special efforts are required to relay content and set messages into context. Mere one-sided

[323] For instance, in the Al Bashir Jordan immunity decision, the ICC issued a Questions and Answer Document which replied to certain critiques made on legal blogs. It directly addressed lawyers engaging in public commentary. See 'Q & A regarding Appeals Chamber's 6 May 2019 Judgment in the Jordan Referral Re Al Bashir Appeal', ICC-PIOS-Q&A-SUD-02/01/19_Eng, May 2019, at https://www.icc-cpi.int/itemsDocuments/190515-al-bashir-qa-eng.pdf.

[324] Oscar Schachter, 'The Invisible College of International Lawyers', (1977) 72 *Northwestern University Law Review* 217–26.

[325] See generally Claus Kress, 'Towards a Truly Universal Invisible College of International Criminal Lawyers' FICHL Occasional Paper Series No. 4 (Brussels: Torkel Opsahl Academic EPublisher, 2014).

[326] See generally Jane E. Stromseth, 'The International Criminal Court and Justice on the Ground' (2011) 43 *Arizona State Law Journal* 427–45; Rosalind Shaw and Lars Waldorf, with Pierre Hazan (eds.), *Localizing Transitional Justice: Interventions and Priorities after Mass Violence* (Stanford, CA: Stanford University Press, 2010).

outreach or presentation of law and facts through global, national, or local media is often not enough. Speech acts may require additional acts of 'translation' and broader communication channels.[327]

A fourth audience is potential perpetrators and victims who may be at risk of similar types of actions. This audience is more indeterminate. It encompasses addresses that are not yet know. This type of communication relies on the assumption that the message is able to influence the future social behaviour of individuals. For instance, the very process of norm affirmation or expression contains not only a positive statement about what the norms are or ought to be but also an implicit command to behave accordingly. This behavioural command is the unspoken consequence of the legal act.

It contains 'negative' and 'positive' dimensions. The 'negative' one is an appeal to potential future offenders not to violate the norm. It aims at encouraging individuals not to commit or assist in crimes. The 'positive' message seeks to encourage active prevention of violations. It implies that every individual should show disobedience to violations and fail to comply with domestic norms, orders, or systems of law that are incompatible with international criminal law.[328] It fortifies the idea that international criminal law protects all human beings from criminal violations by others and empowers them to show civil courage[329] and resistance against behaviour that violates international norms.

Finally, some messages are directed at the broader community of states or a fictive international community. They are aimed at building solidarity among states. The messages themselves mark an attempt to create a sort of global 'collective conscience'.

1.2.2 Roles

Expressivism is useful to understand the foundations of international criminal justice. It has at least two important general roles. It provides (i) an explanatory model for international criminal justice, which recognizes some of its limitations

[327] For instance, studies of the Charles Taylor trial suggest that the messages of the judgment have predominantly reached social, political, and legal elites rather than ordinary citizens or victims. See Marlies Glasius and Tim Meijers, 'Constructions of Legitimacy: The Charles Taylor Trial' (2012) 6 *International Journal of Transitional Justice* 247–52; Glasius, 'It Sends a Message' 443.

[328] This 'positive' dimension may be grounded in the Kantian's idea of cosmopolitan law, namely the theory that international criminal justice serves as a 'world citizen law'. See Klaus Günther and Vasco Reuss, 'Legitimation des Völkerstrafrechts in Deutschland—Völkerstrafrecht als Bürgerstrafrecht' in Christoph Safferling and Stefan Kirsch (ed.), *Völkerstrafrechtspolitik—Praxis des Völkerstrafrechts* (Berlin: Springer, 2014), 127–63.

[329] Vasco Reuss, 'Zivilcourage als Strafzweck des Völkerstrafrechts? Betroffenenbelange aus teleologischer Perspektive (2012) 45 *Kritische Justiz* 241–60; Vasco Reuss, *Zivilcourage als Strafzweck des Völkerstrafrechts: Was bedeutet Positive Generalprävention in der globalen Zivilgesellschaft?* (Berlin: LIT, 2012). See also Günther, 'Positive General Prevention and the Idea of Civic Courage in International Criminal Law' 213–28.

and paradoxes, and (ii) it allows a differentiated vision of the justification of criminal procedures and punishment.

1.2.2.1 Explaining paradoxes and tensions

One of the strengths of expressivist theory is that it is able to explain the paradoxes and tensions of international criminal justice.[330] The focus on communication and sender–audience relations is able to offer a theory of international criminal justice, which places some of the perceived weaknesses and contradictions of the field into perspective.

Expressivism is useful to understand the limitations of criminal proceedings. It helps to deconstruct overinflated ambitions about 'truth' and 'reconciliation'. It is able to explain that a criminal process may have valuable didactic functions (e.g. cognitive discovery) even though it is received differently by different agents or produces 'multiple' stories or versions of 'truth' in society.[331] It mitigates some (but not all) of the empirical dilemmas of international punishment.[332] As rightly observed by Danila Demko, it 'focuses more on the significance of the symbolic and communicative factor as such', the 'communicative content and relationship aspects of international punishment' and 'on those aspects that can be influenced'.[333]

It can also explain how international criminal justice may be meaningful, although it is selective in application[334] and limited in enforcement. International criminal justice aims at the equal application of the law to all perpetrators.[335] But this does not mean that all of them need to investigated or prosecuted internationally. Expressivism recognizes that the power of international criminal courts and tribunals lies in their transparency and persuasion, that is, their unique ability to denounce the wrong, reinforce international norms, or signal accountability problems that deserve broader attention internationally or domestically.[336] This may enhance a sense of 'shared responsibility'.[337]

330 See Darryl Robinson, 'Inescapable Dyads: Why the International Criminal Court Cannot Win' 28 *LJIL* 323–47, 333–43; Kerstin Carlson, 'International Criminal Law and its Paradoxes: Implications for Institutions and Practice, (2017) 5 *Journal of Law and Courts* 33-53, 37-41.

331 See **section 4.2.1.3.**

332 Demko, 'An Expressive Theory of International Punishment' 183.

333 Ibid.

334 Selectivity has been described as the 'original sin' of international criminal justice, See Pierre Hazan, *Justice in the Time of War* (College Station, TX: Texas A&M University Press, 2004), 36.

335 Jonathan Hafetz, *Punishing Atrocities through a Fair Trial: International Criminal Law from Nuremberg to the Age of Global Terrorism* (Cambridge: Cambridge University Press, 2018) 156.

336 This type of expression may make it more difficult for states, including 'big and powerful actors' to ignore atrocities. See Damaška, 'What's the Point?' 363.

337 On shared responsibility in relation to atrocity crime, see Gentian Zyberi, 'Responsibility of states and individuals for mass atrocity crimes' in André Nollkaemper and Ilias Plakokefalos (eds), *The Practice of Shared Responsibility in International Law* (Cambridge: Cambridge University Press, 2017), 235–62.

1.2.2.2 Complementing punishment theories

Expressivism provides a more realistic account for existing punishment theories. Classical rationales do not operate in the same way for international crimes as they do for ordinary domestic crime.[338] For example, the nature of international crimes makes it difficult to rely on the idea of the retribution in the classical sense (the Latin '*retribuo*', 'I pay you back'), that is, punishment as pay-back for crimes. Expressivism is not a justification for punishment per se. It relies on preventive and retributive considerations to justify non-communicative aspects of punishment (e.g. detention, imprisonment).[339] But it provides nuances and additions to the justification trials and punishment. By viewing punishment as a message, it provides a different grounding for retribution,[340] prevention, and restorative justice.[341] It allows greater differentiation in relation to stakeholders and addresses of international criminal justice.

According to an expressivist logic, punishment does not require certainty in relation to sentencing rationales (e.g. deterrence, certainty) but rather expresses an aspiration to reach them, a 'desire to minimize crime' or make the offender 'pay' for crimes.[342] This approach is able to explain some of the realities of sentencing. Sentencing is not an arithmetic exercise but is shaped by beliefs and inner convictions. Expressivism recognizes that judges partly rely on sentencing rationales in order to state or affirm their belief in them.

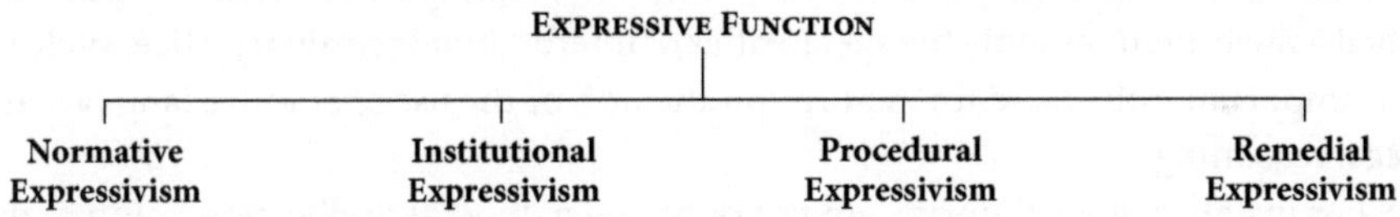

Figure 4 The expressive function

338 See Kai Ambos, *Treatise on International Criminal Law: Volume III: International Criminal Procedure* (Oxford: Oxford University Press, 2016), 47 ('one may even argue that macrocriminals are perfectly socialized since they commit the criminal acts demanded from them by the criminal system they are part of').

339 See Werkmeister, 'The Individual and the International Community', 243–4; Puppe, 'Strafrecht als Kommunikation' 475.

340 The relationship between expressivism and retribution is widely debated. Some scholars view them as alternative concepts. Others stress their links. See Michael S. Moore, 'Justifying Retributivism' (1993) 27 *Israel Law Review* 15–49; Nathan Hanna, 'Say What? A Critique of Expressive Retributivism' (2008) 27 *Law and Philosophy* 123–50.

341 Jean Hampton, 'An expressive theory of retribution' 1–25. See **section 5.1.2**.

342 See Anthony Skillen, 'How to Say Things with Walls' (1980) 55 *Philosophy* 509–23, 513. On expressivism and aspiration, see Mohamed, 'Deviance, Aspiration, and the Stories We Tell' 1628, 1677–80.

1.2.3 The expressive function: A novel typology

Expressivism is not only a theory but a structural feature of international criminal justice. Matthew Edward has called this 'applied legal expressivism'.[343] It manifests itself in very different types of activity such as the establishment of norms and institutions or concrete aspects of practice, including criminal procedure, sentencing, legacy, or outreach. This feature, that is, the way in which international criminal justice defines itself through different expressive acts and communicative relationships, may be referred to as the expressive function of international criminal justice. It is part of a perpetual process of self-legitimization.[344] It encompasses intended and unintended actions. It encompasses different phenomena that will be treated in more detail in subsequent chapters: normative expressivism, institutional expressivism, procedural expressivism, and remedial expressivism.

These four lenses provide an umbrella to illustrate the diversity of communicative acts and their interrelations. They are also useful to understand the critiques and limits of international criminal justice.

1.2.3.1 Normative expressivism

A first element of the expressive function is what may be called normative expressivism.[345] Normative expressivism refers to the way in which international criminal justice contributes to processes of norm affirmation and norm life cycles.

It builds on the communicative sequence between norms as messages, crimes as messages, and trials and punishment as messages, highlighted earlier.[346] It helps to shed a novel light on some the specificities of international criminal justice, such as the important role of judges in norm production or the use of emotive language in legal reasoning.

For instance, if legal norms are not only understood as application commands but also as messages, it is easy to explain why judges serve not only as a '*bouche de la Loi*' but as norm interpreters and promoters.[347] Norm expression becomes an inherent function of judicial activity. Adjudication is, to some extent, an answer

[343] See Matthew Edwards, 'Legal Expressivism: A Primer', SSRN Paper, 16 March 2009, 2, at http://dx.doi.org/10.2139/ssrn.1361101.

[344] International criminal justifies itself as a project to its stakeholders through discourse and messages, partly in order to respond to critique or 'backlash'. On the ICC experience, see Laurence R. Helfer and Anne E. Showalter, 'Opposing International Justice: Kenya's Integrated Backlash Strategy against the ICC' (2017) 17 *International Criminal Law Review* 1–46.

[345] See also Meijers and Glasius, 'Trials as Messages' 433.

[346] See **section 1.1.1**.

[347] The active role of judges is one of the trademarks of international criminal justice. At the international level, there is no global legislator. Judicial activity involves a high degree of norm projection. Máximo Langer has referred to this as 'managerial judging'. See Máximo Langer, 'The Rise of Managerial Judging in International Criminal Law' (2005) 53 *American Journal of Comparative Law* 835–909. See also Shane Darcy and Joseph Powderly (eds), *Judicial Creativity at the International Criminal Tribunals* (Oxford: Oxford University Press, 2010).

to the messages contained in the underlying norms. It is partly a means to instil norms and values in communities for the prevention of future atrocities and to build solidarity.[348]

The communicative sequence helps to understand the turn to morality and emotive language in international criminal justice.[349] If crimes are deemed to contain messages, judicial activity is an act of inferring such messages from the acts of the perpetrator and countering such messages through public condemnation. The very messages inherent in crimes defy the boundaries of legalism. They cannot be reduced to pure legal form. The use of emotive language, and appeal to morality, is part of the process of translating the message of the crime into legal notions, and the judicial response to the message.[350] It is to some extent a relief valve. It uses morality and emotion as an attempt to grapple with the limits of the law[351] and to answer the message of the crimes in a way that other audiences (e.g. victims, the defendant, future perpetrators) can understand. This widens the authority of judges and adjudicators. It makes them agents of social production.

1.2.3.2 Institutional expressivism

Institutional expressivism is a second element of the expressive function. It reflects the meaning created through the creation and operation of institutions. David Luban has compared international criminal justice institutions to 'news broadcasting' agencies.[352] However, institutions convey messages beyond what they say and do. Often, the choice of an institutional response to crime carries in itself a certain meaning.[353] It expresses a message. For instance, the establishment of an international criminal institution, as opposed to domestic jurisdiction or a transitional justice forum, has symbolic significance.[354] The individual, institutional design entails a statement about distributive choices. It sends *inter alia* messages about who should be investigated or prosecuted. The 'medium' (i.e. the institution or justice forum) is to some extent 'the message' itself.[355]

[348] Jose E. Alvarez, 'Rush to Closure: Lessons of the Tadić Judgment' (1997–1998) 96 *Michigan Law Review* 2031–2112, 2085.

[349] In empathy in law and punishment, see Markus Dubber, *The Sense of Justice* (New York, NY: New York University Press, 2006).

[350] See Amanda Potts and Anne Lise Kjær, 'Constructing Achievement in the International Criminal Tribunal for the Former Yugoslavia (ICTY): A Corpus-Based Critical Discourse Analysis' (2016) 29 *International Journal for the Semiotics of Law* 525–55, 552.

[351] Aloisi and Meernik, *Judgment Day* 151 ('[judges] are judicial entrepreneurs with a moral as well as a legal mission to use the vehicle of their judgments to speak to human values that transcend legal necessities').

[352] Luban, 'Fairness to Rightness' 576.

[353] See **section 3.1**.

[354] This symbolic significance is often downplayed in institutional discourse. Institutions seek to portray themselves as active agents, or drivers of normative change, rather than as symbols.

[355] For instance, the ICTY recognized in *Erdemović* that 'the International Tribunal is a vehicle through which the international community expresses its outrage at the atrocities committed' See *Prosecutor v. Erdemović*, Sentencing Judgement, IT-96-22-Tbis, 5 March 1998, para. 21.

1.2.3.3 Procedural expressivism

Procedural expressivism is a third type of expressivism. It relates to the ways in which international criminal justice manifests itself through procedures and to the messages that are connected to such procedures.[356]

The idea that a trial is a performative ritual with symbolical value goes back to Durkheim. It has gained modern reception in transitional justice discourse and international criminal justice. Many scholars claim that criminal proceedings have an important didactic function since they expose wrongdoing and harm caused to social values. They have been described as 'public spectacles'[357] or theatres of renewal. They signal 'the end of one thing (crime) and the restoration of another (legality)'.[358]

Trials also send messages about fair treatment.[359] They have important symbolic functions for victims. They do not only recognize their harm but bestow a broader sense of equality between victim and offender.[360] This is important for societal purposes. As Paul Seils has noted, 'bringing those responsible for planning systematic crimes face-to-face with their victims humanizes the crimes'.[361] It destroys 'the "respectability vacuum" that senior officials may attempt to place between themselves and the deeds of their foot soldiers'.[362]

1.2.3.4 Remedial expressivism

Remedial expressivism is a fourth dimension of the expressive function. It is broader than punishment. It includes expressive elements of criminal sanction and modalities of repairing harm.[363]

Expressivism leaves space for a broader punitive theory. It recognizes that punishment is not only an instrument to inflict suffering on offenders but a means to express moral condemnation. It relates punishment to the publicity of condemnation, and its potential impact on the offender, rather than an absolute measure of severity, or a specific form of penalty. This flexibility is an asset in the context of mass violence. It provides some room for alternative forms of punishment, including accountability mechanisms involving truth-telling, justice towards

[356] See below chapter 4.
[357] Osiel, *Mass Atrocity, Collective Memory and the Law* 2.
[358] Buss, 'Performing Legal Order' 414.
[359] For instance, the Nuremberg trials marked an expression of fairness towards defendants, which stood in stark contrast to earlier proposals for summary executions. Today, fairness has a broader meaning. It relates not only to fair trial protections for the defendant, but fairness as a structural principle of proceedings. See Yvonne McDermott, *Fairness in International Criminal Trials* (Oxford: Oxford University Press, 2016).
[360] Expressivist theory provides an important conceptual justification for victim participation. It justifies the active role of victims as a response to a claim of superiority made by the defendant through the commission of the crime. See **section 4.3.5**.
[361] Seils, 'Squaring Colombia's Circle' 12.
[362] Ibid.
[363] See below chapter 5.

victims, or sanctions relating to the civic status of the offender. It is able to take into account structural critiques of imprisonment as penalty.[364]

Victim redress may have similar expressive effects. It places the focus to a greater extent on repair of harm, rather than punitive sanction. For instance, reparations are speech acts to victims. They clarify that perpetrators 'owe' something to victims and that society cares about them.[365] As Fréderic Mégret has noted, reparations involve a distinct set of messages: 'In the same way sentencing someone to a more or less harsh punishment sends a discreet signal about the gravity of the facts at stake, awarding more or less reparations sends a signal about the gravity of the harm sustained.'[366]

1.2.4 Objections and critiques

Expressivism remains a contested concept, not only in the arts and sciences but also in law. It meets, at least, four principal objections, in the area of international criminal justice: (i) empirical challenges; (ii) power-related critiques; (iii) instrumentalism; and (iv) mediation of messages. They need to be addressed if expressivism is developed as a concept.

1.2.4.1 Empirics versus faith

One of the weaknesses of expressivism is its limited empirical grounding. Expressivism is not only concerned with the conveyance of meaning but also with the production of consequences. This requires understanding of the social and cognitive processes underlying expression and reception. Expressivism is innovative from the perspective of behavioural economics since it proposes that law can sometimes induce changes in behaviour simply by expression alone. For instance, legal economist Richard McAdams has argued that theorists should stop implicitly assuming that law 'matters only because legal sanctions affect the costs of behavior': 'The law influences behavior expressively, as by influencing beliefs about approval patterns. interest groups will seek to capture the expressive power of law as a means of expanding their influence over the behavior of others.'[367]

[364] For instance, critics have questioned whether imprisonment is the most adequate sanction to remedy sexual crimes, given that prisons are often environments that are 'dehumanizing, racist, homophobic, and inherently violent themselves. See Constance Backhouse, 'A feminist remedy for sexual assault: A quest for answers' in Elizabeth Sheehy (ed.), *Sexual Assault Law in a Post-Jane Doe Period*, Vol II (Ottawa: University of Ottawa Press, 2012) 725–39.

[365] Matiangai V.S. Sirleaf, 'Beyond Truth and Punishment in Transitional Justice' (2014) 54 *Virginia Journal of International Law* 223–96, 234, arguing that reparations 'send signals to victims, and to society more generally, that the successor regime is committed to respecting victims' and fellow citizens' rights'.

[366] Frédéric Mégret, 'Reparations Before the ICC: The Need for Pragmatism and Creativity' ICC Forum 6 February 2012, at https://iccforum.com/reparations#Megret.

[367] Richard McAdams, 'An Attitudinal Theory of Expressive Law' (2000) 79 *Oregon Law Review* 339–90, 389–90.

1.2.4.1.1 Expressivism and compliance studies

Expressivist theory is grounded in assumptions about social benefits. Most efforts have been made to demonstrate the beneficial effects of the expressive function of law in the area of law enforcement. Law and economics scholarship suggests that there is some evidence that the mere presence of law may enhance compliance in specific fields. Legislation may express popular preferences and beliefs.[368] In some areas, law has changed behaviour through provision of information rather than penalty. For instance, Maggie Wittlin has argued that the passage of seatbelt law in the United States has changed societal behaviour through its publicity effect, even beyond the prospect of sanction.[369] Smoking is another area, where regulation has changed behaviour, based on risks and belief in the credibility of public information rather than sanction. Patrick Funk has relied on Swiss data to show that in some 'public good areas', such as cantonal voting, 'even a sanctionless law targeting at the civic duty might have a bigger impact on behaviour than actions which affect the coast of provision for the public good'.[370]

Similar experiences have been made in international adjudication. For instance, Tom Ginsberg and Richard McAdams have argued that there is overall a high compliance rate with International Court of Justice (ICJ) decisions, even in the absence of enforcement power, 'because the decisions make one outcome focal or provide an important signal of the state of the world, either of which facilitates the parties in ordering their own affairs'.[371]

McAdams has made the most comprehensive effort to analyse expressive effects in practice in his study on the 'Expressive Powers of Law'.[372] He has developed a rational choice model of expressive power based on the study of criminal, civil, and arbitral mechanisms. He has argued that law may alter behaviour through expressive effects in two ways, namely through its coordinating function, that is its ability to express a 'focal point', around which affected stakeholders (e.g. individuals or states) can coordinate their behaviour in accordance with expectations,[373] and its information function (e.g. the mere passage of law), which enables them to change beliefs and behaviour.[374]

[368] Ibid., 358.

[369] Maggie Wittlin, 'Bucking Under Pressure: An Empirical Test of the Expressive Effects of Law' (2011) 28 *Yale Journal on Regulation* 419–69, 456.

[370] Patricia Funk, 'Is There an Expressive Function of Law? An Empirical Analysis of Voting Laws with Symbolic Fines' (2007) *American Law and Economics Review* 135–59.

[371] Tom Ginsburg and Richard McAdams, 'Adjudicating in Anarchy: An Expressive Theory of International Dispute Resolution' (2004) 45 *William & Mary Law Review* 1229–1339.

[372] Richard H. McAdams, *The Expressive Powers of Law: Theories and Limits* (Cambridge, MA. Harvard University Press, 2015).

[373] Ibid., 5.

[374] Ibid., 6, 136.

1.2.4.1.2 Empirical challenges

In international criminal justice, there are only limited empirical studies on expressivism; that is, the behavioural effects of the expression of new norms (norm expression), or reception of messages sent through adjudication and punishment on perpetrators, victims, and the broader public.

The effects of norm expression are only starting to be understood. Experiences, such as the ICC Statute, show that the adoption of a new multilateral treaty has an important signalling effect, even before its entry into force or ratification. It may influence domestic norms or stimulate the adoption of a new law in the domestic sphere. The act of ratification by states has expressive effects and may alter beliefs through inferential mechanisms. Treaty ratification and compliance may send signals to other states and different constituencies inside state systems. Alex Geisinger and Michael Stein have called this the 'ratification effect'.[375] It may arguably 'provide information on what the majority of a State believes and thus serve to change or reinforce what citizens will sanction socially and, in the case of some democratic regimes, affect politicians' willingness to act'.[376]

However, treaty regimes are limited in international criminal law. Many foundations have been clarified through expressive adjudication. In this context, expressivist effects are more difficult to establish.

Social science research has shown that individuals may often be more influenced by social pressures or extra-legal factors than prospects of punishment. There are some indications that judicial action has an impact as to how individuals frame social and political issues.[377] Some studies suggest that norm expression in international criminal justice has indirect benefits, namely through its interaction with human rights regimes, transnational judicial discourse, and the mobilization of civil society networks.[378] For instance, international criminal justice may not directly deter individual behaviour,[379] but can strengthen civil networks and raise

[375] Geisinger and Stein, 'A Theory of Expressive International Law' 102.

[376] Ibid., 101.

[377] Harold Koh has argued that the most effective form of compliance is 'not the imposition of external sanction, but the inculcation of internal obedience'. See Harold Hongju Koh, 'How Is International Human Rights Law Enforced?' (1999) 74 *Indiana Law Review* 1397–1418, 1401.

[378] In recent years, the concept of 'social deterrence' has gained prominence in explaining compliance with human rights norms. See Geoff Dancy and Kathryn Sikkink, 'Ratification and Human Rights Prosecutions: Toward a Transnational Theory of Treaty Compliance' (2012) 44 *New York University Journal of International Law and Politics* 751–990; Thomas Risse, Steve C. Ropp, and Kathryn Sikkink (eds), *The Power of Human Rights: International Norms and Domestic Change* (Cambridge: Cambridge University Press, 1999).

[379] As Hyeran Jo and Beth A. Simmons have argued, the concept of social deterrence has relevance for international criminal justice. Hyeran Jo and Beth A. Simmons, 'Can the International Criminal Court Deter Atrocity?' (2016) 70 *International Organization* 443–75. Payam Akhavan speaks of 'socio-pedagogical influence of judicial stigmatization'. See Payam Akhavan, 'The Lord's Resistance Army Case: Uganda's Submission of the First State Referral to the International Criminal Court' (2005) 99 *AJIL* 403–21, 419.

the profile of accountability actors who promote the cause of international criminal justice.[380] It can also potentially serve to construct normative beliefs.

However, the effects of agent- or person-related expressivism are less well documented. The impact of messages sent through trial and punishment on individuals are influenced by numerous motivational and cognitive factors, including social identity[381] and cognitive biases. They depend on social psychology, including empathy and the perception and interpretation of judicially constructed narratives by individuals. Even a clear message may not necessarily result in persuasion since persuasion requires a willingness to engage.[382]

International criminal justice poses specific challenges in relation to behavioural change since it is highly emotive[383] and deals with collective violence. Criminality cuts across ethnic, religious, and national lines, affects social identity, and poses delicate tensions between individual and collective responsibility. It is strongly marked by 'conflicting thoughts or beliefs'. The very context of armed conflict and political may alter perceptions of identity and victimization.[384] Social scientists have demonstrated that external threat or armed conflict may intensify patterns of national or social self-identification inside groups, displace former perceptions, and provide a ground for feelings of collective victimization.[385] Under certain circumstances, structured intergroup contact may recreate trust and the ability to show empathy.[386] But attitudes are often marked by cognitive resistance. Longitudinal studies on post-conflict dynamics suggest that mutual engagement across communities requires 'some awareness and sense of past ingroup culpability by members of a 'perpetrator' group'.[387]

[380] For instance, the ICC system 'encourages member states to improve their capacity to reduce, detect, and prosecute such crimes domestically'. See Jo and Simmons, 'Can the International Criminal Court Deter Atrocity?', 469.

[381] Emily Shaw, 'The Role of Social Identity in Resistance to International Criminal Law: The Case of Serbia and the ICTY', Berkeley Program in Soviet and Post-Soviet Studies, Working Paper (2003), 21, at https://escholarship.org/uc/item/27g2v7bz ('If individuals have been made to feel more homogenous as a result of a threat perceived to be inescapable, there is a good chance they will carry this feeling over to the post-threat environment and continue to identity with the nationalist position.').

[382] Fletcher and Weinstein, 'Violence and Social Repair' 573.

[383] For instance, genocide is grounded in 'emotions of fear, humiliation, hatred, and hope for an imagined Community'. See Neta C. Crawford, 'Fear, hope, and the formation of specific intention in genocide' in Thomas Brudholm and Johannes Lang (eds), *Emotions and Mass Atrocity* (Cambridge: Cambridge University Press, 2018), 42–63, 46.

[384] Diane Orentlicher, *Some Kind of Justice: The ICTY's Impact in Bosnia and Serbia* (Oxford: Oxford University Press, 2018), 227–31.

[385] Shaw, 'The Role of Social Identity in Resistance to International Criminal Law', 12–13; Daniel Bar-Tal, Lily Chernyak-Hai, Noa Schori, and Ayelet Gundar, 'A Sense of Self—Perceived Collective Victimhood in Intractable Conflicts' (2009) 91 *International Review of the Red Cross* 229–58, 247.

[386] Sabina Cehajić and Rupert Brown, 'Silencing the Past: Effects of Intergroup Contact on Acknowledgment of In-Group Responsibility' (2010) 1 *Social Psychological and Personality Science* 190–6.

[387] Rupert Brown and Sabina Cehajić, 'Dealing with the Past and Facing the Future: Mediators of the Effects of Collective Guilt and Shame in Bosnia and Herzegovina' (2008) 38 *European Journal of Social Psychology* 669–84, 682.

Scholarship in social psychology has used the notion of 'cognitive dissonance'[388] to explain resistance to behavioural change. As Stuart Ford[389] and others[390] have argued, this notion has particular relevance to understanding the social impact of international criminal justice on individuals or groups. Exposure to law and facts concerning international crimes may cause psychological discomfort between altering propositions. Individuals develop strategies to reduce this dissonance in different ways, by rejecting one proposition as false, or by trying to develop new rationalizations that reconcile the different propositions. Change of attitudes is often compromised by 'confirmation bias', that is, disposition of affected agents 'to search for, recall, and interpret information in a way that has a tendency to confirm their existing beliefs'.[391]

For instance, surveys relating to the impact of the SCSL suggest that the choice of the indictments and perpetrators 'can have a large negative effect on how the court is perceived by affected groups that identify with one of the "sides" in the conflict'.[392]

Studies relating to the *Taylor* trial indicate that attitudes of victims may easily be influenced by different visions of the underlying conflict, including a discrepancy between what they see as the most serious crimes and the actual crimes charged.[393]

Similar experiences characterize the impact of the International Criminal Tribunal for the Former Yugoslavia (ICTY) in Serbia, Bosnia, or Croatia. Groups have continued to regard themselves as 'victims' of atrocities by the other side while showing reluctance to assume responsibility for their own wrongs.[394]

This makes is difficult to trace behavioural changes in short-term intervals. The generation that was involved in crime may not be fully ready to 'face' responsibility, or persevere in its beliefs.[395] The expressivist elements of trials and punishment must often reach a certain 'tipping point' before they reach victims and perpetrators.[396] The fact that expressivism works in practice might

388 Leon Festinger, *A Theory of Cognitive Dissonance* (Evanston, IL: Row, Peterson, & Co., 1957); David Matz and Wendy Wood, 'Cognitive Dissonance in Groups: The Consequences of Disagreement' (2005) 88 *Journal of Personality and Social Psychology* 22–37.

389 Stuart Ford, 'A Social Psychology Model of the Perceived Legitimacy of International Criminal Courts: Implications for the Success of Transitional Justice Mechanisms' (2012) 45 *Vanderbilt Journal of Transnational Law* 405–76, 427.

390 See Orentlicher, *Some Kind of Justice* 226–37.

391 Ford, 'Social Psychology Model' 434.

392 Ibid., 447.

393 See Glasius, 'It Sends a Message' 446.

394 Orentlicher, *Some Kind of Justice* 232–157.

395 On the Nuremberg, Frankfurt Auschwitz, and Majdanek trials in Germany, see Mark A. Wolfgram, 'Didactic War Crimes Trials and External Legal Culture: The Cases of the Nuremberg, Frankfurt Auschwitz, and Majdanek Trials in West Germany' (2014) 26 *Global Change, Peace & Security* 281–97, 281 ('While these trials certainly affected the external legal culture, through radio, television, theater plays, films, and other forms of popular culture, the lessons Germans learned were not always the ones that prosecutors had hoped for.').

396 Orentlicher, *Some Kind of Justice* 235.

even more difficult to show in international criminal justice than in domestic law.[397]

At present, expressivism navigates between faith and fact.[398] It is still largely a normative proposition. As in the context of general prevention, it is erroneous to refute expressivism simply because it has not been fully proven empirically.[399] It is a useful construct, even if it cannot be fully shown empirically. It fosters belief and hope in international criminal justice.[400] As Aloisi and Meernik have written, international criminal justice institutions have used 'messaging' 'because it satisfies the need to send a message to those whose lives have been violated by international crimes, signal the importance of the human rights and humanity of the victims, and can increase the resonance and perhaps even the legitimacy of international justice'.[401]

Criminological scholarship on general prevention suggests that the impact of norm expression on behavioural attitudes may differ according to a number of factors, such as distinctions between different types of protected norms (*malum in se, malum prohibitum*) and the motivational factors underlying their commission, differences among persons, rendering them 'more or less unsusceptible to the moral influences of the law', societal context, including social pressures, legal control, or attitudes towards law (*Rechtsbewußtsein*), and the influence of conflicting 'group norms' on individual behaviour.[402]

In scholarly discourse, there is a certain 'move from faith to science'.[403] Some scholars have suggested that expressivism has 'utility as an empirical theory'.[404] For instance, Meijers and Glasius found that expressivism 'can take the form of an empirically testable hypothesis about the potential of institutions to send messages to a public, with a measurable effect on its behavior or beliefs'.[405] This finding has been based on studies of individual international criminal trials (e.g. *Charles Taylor, Karadžić*). But the devil is in the detail.

[397] See also Tim Meijers and Marlies Glasius, 'Expression of Justice or Political Trial? Discursive Battles in the Karadžić Case (2013) 35 *Human Rights Quarterly* 720–52, 751 with reference to 'the stage, which unlike in domestic trials cannot be assumed to be uncontested'. See also Deirdre Golash, 'The justification of punishment in the international context' in Larry May and Zachary Hoskins (eds), *International Criminal Law and Philosophy* (Cambridge: Cambridge University Press, 2010) 201–23, 223.

[398] See generally Carsten Stahn, 'Between "Faith" and "Facts": By What Standards Should We Assess International Criminal Justice?' (2012) 25 *LJIL* 251–82.

[399] See Johannes Andenaes, 'General Preventive Effects of Punishment' (1966) 114 *University of Pennsylvania Law Review* 949–83, 955–57.

[400] On the role of 'hope', see Margaret Urban Walker, 'Hope(s) after genocide' in Brudholm and Lang (eds), *Emotion and Mass Atrocity*, 211–33, 216–20.

[401] Aloisi and Meernik, *Judgment Day* 119–20.

[402] See Andenaes, 'General Preventive Effects of Punishment' 957–60.

[403] See Mark Drumbl, 'The future of international criminal law and transitional justice' in William Schabas, Yvonne McDermott, and Niamh Hayes (eds), *Ashgate Research Companion to International Criminal Law* (Farnham: Ashgate, 2013), 531–45, 541.

[404] Glasius, 'It Sends a Message' 447.

[405] Meijers and Glasius, 'Trials as Messages' 432.

There are differences between types of expressivism, target audiences, and the nature of messages. For instance, empirical research on social deterrence seems to indicate that messages sent through trials and punishment may reach certain global audiences and alter behavioural patterns.[406] Experiences in transitional justice suggest that trials may have certain positive effects on affected societies. In some cases, messages of accountability have reached relevant audiences, although the legitimacy of the institution was contested. Psychological studies from the Rwandan genocide indicate that facts and information about atrocities offer survivors 'hope' for preventing future violence since they clarify that 'the horror of their experience might be a comprehensible, even predictable, outcome of human processes rather than of incomprehensible evil'.[407]

But there are also many counterfactuals. Messages may be interpreted differently by the recipient than the sender. The impact on defendants and victims may be divisive. Often behavioural change is influenced by other contextual factors and emerges only gradually over time. The conditions under which norm- and agent-related expression may reach target audiences require therefore more verification and testing.

1.2.4.2 Power-related critiques

Expressivism continues to face objections because of its close relationship to power. The relationship between punishment and power is complex. Expressivism tries to reinforce the claim that punishment is not solely about the infliction of physical power over defendants. It tries to counter messages about display of power through a legal process,[408] or to 'speak truth to power'. The message 'is one of respect for basic human rights and of non-violent conflict resolution, and an exercise in the rule of law'.[409]

[406] See Beth A. Simmons and Hyeran Jo, 'Measuring Norms and Normative Contestation: The Case of International Criminal Law' (2019) 4 *Journal of Global Security Studies* 18–36, 18 ('Assessing evidence of norms beyond states leads us to conclude that the core ICL norms are robust, but their practical and institutional applicability are still contested)', 21 ('ICL norms are reiterated and enacted, partly because almost nobody wants to be seen as in favor of genocide. Norm robustness is almost certainly related to the inherent nature of and abhorrence surrounding atrocity that ICL norms are designed to counter. These underlying values contribute to broad and diverse support, and consequently to norm robustness, even when norms are violated in specific circumstance.'); Beth A. Simmons and Allison Marston Danner, 'Credible Commitments and the International Criminal Court' (2010) 64 *International Organization* 225–56.

[407] See Ervin Staub, Laurie A. Pearlman, Alexandra Gubin, and Athanase Hagengimana, 'Healing, Reconciliation, Forgiving and the Prevention of Violence after Genocide or Mass Killing: An Intervention and Its Experimental Evaluation in Rwanda' (2005) 24 *Journal of Social and Clinical Psychology* 297–334, 327–8.

[408] See Meijers and Glasius, 'Trials as Messages' 437 ('Punishment should not be a mere display of power of one over the other. This is exactly the kind of message criminal courts should counter. Showing brute force rather than reasons and respect for legal norms would, instead of reaffirming the legal (and moral) order, be a continuation of the conflict by other means.').

[409] Meijers and Glasius, 'Trials as Messages' 438.

However, expressivism comes itself with various manifestations of power. As Pierre Bourdieu has argued, language is not solely a means of communication but also a form of power through which individuals pursue their own interests.[410] Expressivist practices involve a strongly 'propositional' dimension and a high degree of social engineering. This makes them vulnerable to different power-related critiques.

The work of sociologists, such as Norbert Elias or Michel Foucault on the dynamics and complexities of power in criminal systems, is helpful to understand some of the dilemmas of expressivism.[411] Elias has identified links between punishment and changes in societal behaviour in his theory of the 'civilizing process'.[412] He has argued that changes in the penal system of societies are intrinsically linked to changes in manners in cultures, including sentiments about civilization and 'decivilization'.[413] Foucault has shed a new light on power relations in his famous work, *Discipline and Punish*, which examined the evolution of Western penal systems and forms of social control in disciplinary institutions. Foucault argued that the penal systems involve subtle forms of control and domination that go beyond repressive power and functional subordination.[414] He developed his broader theory of power in his concept of 'governmentality'. He suggested that institutions exercise power and influence behaviour through the production of knowledge and initiation of discourses that are internalized by individuals. Foucault's understanding is important for the understanding of justice processes since it implies that juridical practices create new forms of subjectivities and subjects.[415]

1.2.4.2.1 Empowering the speaker

A fundamental critique of the expressive function of punishment is that it serves the predominantly the communicator rather than the recipient of messages.[416]

[410] Pierre Bourdieu, *Language and Symbolic Power* (Cambridge, MA. Harvard University Press, 1991).

[411] See Felix Driver, 'Power, Space, and the Body: A Critical Assessment of Foucault's Discipline and Punish' (1985) 3 *Environment and Planning* 425–46.

[412] See Norbert Elias, *The Civilizing Process: The History of Manners* (London: Blackwell, 1969); Norbert Elias, *The Civilizing Process: State Formation and Civilization* (London: Blackwell, 1982).

[413] On Elias, see John Pratt, 'Norbert Elias, the Civilizing Process and Penal Development in Modern Society' (2011) 59 *Sociological Review* 220–40; Jonathan Fletcher, *Violence and Civilization: An Introduction to the Work of Norbert Elias* (Cambridge: Polity Press, 1997); Pieter Spierenberg, *The Spectacle of Suffering* (Cambridge: Cambridge University Press, 1984);

[414] Foucault, *Discipline and Punish: The Birth of the Prison.*

[415] See generally Michel Foucault, 'The Subject and Power' (1982) 8 *Critical Inquiry* 777–95. On Foucault's concept of governmentality and the ICC, see Gozde Turan, '"Responsibility to Prosecute" in an Age of Global Governmentality: The International Criminal Court' (2016) 5 *Cooperation and Conflict* 20–37.

[416] See Sloane, 'Expressive Capacity of International Punishment', 85. See also Amann, 'Group Mentality, Expressivism, and Genocide' 124 ('The intended audience of such exhortations is not just the wrongdoer of most concern to deterrence and retributive theorists. It is also the Everyone of most interest to expressive theorists: the law-abider and the lawmaker, the activist and the private citizen, and even the potential victim, today and tomorrow.').

Viewing adjudication as a communicative exercise aimed at norm projection poses legitimacy challenges. Expressivism may be used as a strategic tool or form of exercise of control.[417] As Anthony Skillen has noted, 'if a person or institution represents itself, through punishment, as holding to certain values, then the question arises as to whether this is true'.[418] What 'can represent can misrepresent'.[419]

The application of norm expression in the Durkheimian sense in international criminal justice causes unease from the perspective of those who are submitted to the proposition. The idea that criminal justice serves an expressive instrument to constitute a moral community or to legitimize the existence a global justice system has something disturbing. It involves a risk that legal determinations produce questionable readings of norm acceptance.

As critics of expressivism have argued, 'legislatures, courts, agencies, and other legal institutions do not possess mental states, independent of the mental states of the persons that make up these institutions'.[420] Norm expression is strongly shaped by institutional interests. It involves multiple forms of power: signalling of decisional power, implicit claims over discursive space, meaning, and semantics, ownership over knowledge, or control over the broader framing of a problem (e.g. as a human right, criminal law or security issue). It marks a form of 'social control'.[421] For instance, norm affirmation in and through criminal adjudication is often more than simply an articulation of the existing status quo, designed to restore the trust of audiences in the existence of norms. It provides a language for articulating violations, contains implicit action commands for individuals or even creates a new status quo, a speech act which 'constitutes the change in the world to which it refers'.[422] It is thus a form of productive power.

Such a power raises fears and anxieties. Expressive power may clash with the limits of adjudication. For instance, third states might be concerned if an institution like the ICC, or a domestic court exercising universal jurisdiction, engages in universal norm expression. Such expressions (e.g. findings on customary law or general principles) may postulate a vision of universality that is grounded in the perspective of the 'speaker', rather than the lens of the multiple addressees affected. Normative aspirations may disregard differences between and within societies or

[417] See also Sander; 'The expressive turn of international criminal justice' 17, referring to the 'instrumental expressive potential of international criminal law in the context of concrete struggles for social and political change'.

[418] Skillen, 'How to Say Things with Walls' 521.

[419] Ibid.

[420] Adler, 'Expressive Theories of Law' 1389.

[421] On 'social control' and 'social disciplining' see Sheilagh Ogilvie, '"So That Every Subject Knows How to Behave": Social Disciplining in Early Modern Bohemia' (206) 48 *Comparative Studies in Society and History* 38–78.

[422] Adler, 'Expressive Theories of Law' 1395. Adler distinguishes 'descriptive speech-acts-actions' where the 'speaker intends to get the hearer to believe some proposition', 'directive speech-acts-actions' where the 'speaker intends to get the hearer to do something' and 'declarations' where the 'speech-act itself constitutes the change in the world to which it refers'.

create new economies of knowledge. It is important to subject processes of norm affirmation to public scrutiny, provide adequate structures to challenge assumptions, and create space for cognitive learning, based on feedback and reception.

These dilemmas are even more acute in the context of agent-related expressivism. Adjudication action expresses legal rights and obligations and frames the scope of civil liberties or responsibilities (e.g. the duty to make reparation). It contains determinations what acts constitute a crime, who is a 'criminal', who qualifies as a victim, and it provides a concrete meaning to notions of responsibility and victimization. Such determinations involve not only repressive power towards the defendant but more nuanced and diversified forms of power. The very use of symbols, images, and legal notions alters social reality, attributes meaning and status to individuals, or introduces certain hierarchies. This makes it necessary to institute checks and balances to 'guard the guardian'. Persons subjected to power should be given a voice in such determinations.

1.2.4.2.2 Global orientation of messages

The orientation of messages is a further point of concern. In international criminal justice, messages are strongly oriented towards a global public, that is, international institutions, states, etc. International criminal courts and tribunals are generally more inclined to 'speak' to global audiences since they depend on state authority or other multilateral organizations and are likely to receive positive reception by like-minded agents (e.g. institutions sharing a commitment to international human rights norms and the rule of law). Some authors (e.g. deGuzman) have expressly advocated that sentencing should contribute to global norm expression.[423] Communication with affected societies is more burdensome since it is impeded by spatial or cultural distances. Inside affected societies, social and political elites are easier to reach than local actors.

This limited focus is a weakness from a justice perspective. Expressivism reinforces the risk that justice agents address a global constituency rather than the offender or local constituencies. A focus on global knowledge production, assertion of universal standards, and the creation of new subjectivities may make international criminal justice complicit in the creation of a new order that reduces social complexity or marginalizes alternative understandings. It may privilege global over local conceptions of justice, create frictions in relation to 'what is perceived as just' by those involved, or produce new inequalities or dependencies. There is a need to relate expressive practices more closely to local institutions and agents of the social communities where crimes have been committed.

[423] Margaret M. deGuzman, 'Proportionate Sentencing at the ICC' in Carsten Stahn (ed.), *The Law and Practice of the International Criminal Court* (Oxford: Oxford University Press, 2015), 932–62, 957–8 Margaret M. deGuzman, 'Choosing to Prosecute' 316 ('for the ICC, as a normative matter, global expression is the most appropriate role for the institution').

1.2.4.3 Instrumentalism

Expressivism creates fears because of its risks of instrumentalization.[424] Classical liberal conceptions of criminal justice derive its every foundation from non-instrumentalism, including the need to treat the defendant as an end in itself rather than a means to an end. Pure retributivists who place the emphasis entirely on the culpability of the offender, have remained sceptical towards expressivism, because it may cause tensions in relation to fairness and due process.

Some scholars have argued that educational functions should not be treated as sentencing rationales since this may conflict with the protection of human dignity. For instance, German scholar Peter Badura has taken the view that general prevention should not be recognized as a sentencing factor.[425] He has relied on Kant's reservations towards the 'instrumentalization' of individuals to support this claim: The perpetrator should not be punished based on the hypothetic imagined effects of the crime, that is as a means of deterring crimes by others.[426] This position has some merit. Human dignity may be read to imply that trial and punishment should not be used for expressivist purposes only. The non-instrumentalization thesis provides an important argument against the recognition of expressivism as sole justification of punishment. The ICTY expressly recognized this premise in *Kunarac*.[427] However, in reality, the conflict may be less pronounced than asserted.

Badura's view relies on a due process-dominated vision of criminal justice. Most systems try to reconcile the human dignity of the offender with considerations of crime control, warranted by the protection of rights of others. In legal practice, expressivism has been mostly used in combination with other punishment rationales, such as retribution. Expressivism and non-instrumentalism are thus not irreconcilable per se. Many forms of expressivism are not strictly related to the defendant.

According to modern accounts, expressivism is not only concerned with ideas of crime control but inherently related to the protection of due process. The offender is treated as 'someone who is able to respond within the communicative process of punishment'.[428] Communication of fairness is one of the inherent parts

[424] Darryl Robinson, 'The Identity Crisis of International Criminal Law' (2008) 21 *LJIL* 925–63, 931 ('using the accused as an object in a didactic exercise rather than respecting autonomy and fairness').

[425] Peter Badura, 'Generalprävention und Würde des Menschen' (1964) 19 *Juristenzeitung* 337–44.

[426] Ibid., 343–4. Justifying punishment by the ambition to send a message clashes with the Kantian moral premise that wrongdoers should not be treated as mere 'means' of punishment (i.e. as a means to obtain some societal benefit), but rather as ends in themselves. See Immanuel Kant, *The Metaphysics of Morals* (Mary Gregor ed. and trans., 1991) (1797), 140–1 ('Punishment by a court ... can never be inflicted merely as a means to promote some other good for the criminal himself or for civil society ... For a man can never be treated merely as a means for the purposes of another or be put among the objects of rights to things.').

[427] *Prosecutor v. Kunarac, Kovac and Vukovic*, Judgment, IT-96-23-T& IT-96-23/1-T, 22 February 2001, para. 840 (*Kunarac* Trial Judgment) ('[A] sentence should in principle be imposed on an offender for his culpable conduct—it may be unfair to impose a sentence on an offender greater than is appropriate to that conduct solely in the belief that it will deter others.)

[428] Werkmeister, 'The Individual and the International Community' 253.

of expressivism. The emphasis lies on the justice process rather than punishment as outcome. For instance, an acquittal may serve an important function from an expressivist perspective.

Some expressivist theories even strengthen the case against instrumentalism. For instance, Duff's call for a view of trials as communicative engagement with the offender is a direct challenge to enemy-based conceptions of criminal law. Excluding perpetrators from the realm of criminal law conflicts with the message that trials need to respect the dignity of offenders and treat them as equal subjects.[429] As Andreas Werkmeister has observed, the 'international community would contradict itself in a (hypothetical) discourse about the justification of punishment if it is communicating to the offender that dignity does not exist in the normative universe of International Criminal Law'.[430] It cannot 'refer to an inherent human dignity to establish punitive power but not stick to this concept when it comes to the criminal offender'.[431]

1.2.4.4 Mediation of messages

A final objection relates to the strong degree of mediation of messages, the fact that information goes through a variety of filters that shape its meaning before it reaches the addressee. Mediation is a key element in expressivism. It remains critically underdeveloped in contemporary understandings.

Expressivist theory seems to imply that criminal trials and procedures are able to send clear and coherent messages that may have a didactic effect on audiences. But the reality is often more blurry and confusing. Criminal adjudication involves a wide range of messages, including normative, institutional procedural and remedial messages. These messages are expressed through different mediums: legal acts, such as judgments or decisions, institutional policies or practices, the role of the courtroom as a stage, pleadings, testimonies, and images, or even silences. Some of the messages are conveyed directly through a physical or legal 'speech act' or an image. Others lack active speech action (e.g. silence) or are expressed in indirect ways (e.g. courtroom symbolism).

The process of mediation creates problems in relation to inter-subjectivity and the role of the recipient in the communicative process. Expressivism relies on an active audience. Most messages are not directly accessible to the recipient but require a process of rationalization, interpretation, or inference by the recipient.[432]

[429] Raimond Gaita, *Good and Evil: An Absolute Conception* (London: Routledge, 2004), 2 ('even the most terrible evil doers are owed this respect as human beings and that we owe it to them because we are human beings').

[430] Andreas Werkmeister, 'International criminal law as a means to fight the '*hostes humani generis*'? On the dangers of the concept of enemy criminal law' in Mark Fenwick and Stefan Wrbka (eds), *Legal Certainty in a Contemporary Context* (Singapore: Springer, 2016), 179–91, 187.

[431] Ibid., 187.

[432] On audience and interpretation, see audience to interpretation, see generally Andrea Bianchi, 'The game of interpretation in international law: the players, the cards, and why the game is worth the

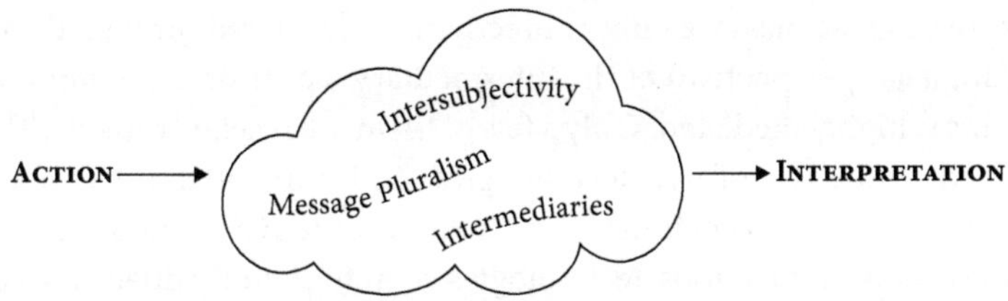

Figure 5 Mediation and transformation of messages

For instance, a legal decision may not in itself convey a clear message. The content must be inferred through interpretation or reading between the lines.[433] Understanding the message may require consideration of multiple acts by different speakers at the same time, or contextualization of speech acts. For example, a message relating to punishment may not be inferred from the sentence alone but is connected to the images and public ritual of punishment in a public forum before a global audience. In the context of silence (e.g. a decision not to act), the message is virtually created in the mind of the audience. The audience attributes social meaning to inaction.

These difficulties are reinforced by the plurality of messages. Often, one and the same forum may send a plurality of messages. In some cases, the meaning of messages may be obstructed by conflicting opinions. For instance, split judicial decision, with contradictory opinions or adverse witness statements at trial, may lack a coherent message. In other cases, one message can only be understood through different acts. Due to the plurality of perspectives in criminal proceedings, many of the more complex messages can only be understood in the context of a chain of events, that is as reaction to moves or strategies from a different actor. For instance, a message about fairness of a trial requires consideration of messages by different speakers: the Defence, judges, and the Prosecution. This requires good knowledge of the trial and its context. In the absence of such knowledge and expertise, the message may be inaccessible.

Messages are transformed throughout the communicative process. Many messages are abstract or need to be translated, not only in a linguistic but also a broader normative sense, in order to become eligible to communication. This translation is typically not done by the 'speaker' but either by the recipient or through intermediaries. The role of intermediaries widens the scope of recipients. One key challenge is the discrepancy between 'sender' and 'intermediary'. Senders lose control over the content of the message in the transmission process. In many contexts,

candle' in Andrea Bianchi, Daniel Peat, and Matthew Windsor (eds), *Interpretation in International Law* (Oxford: Oxford University Press, 2015) 34–59, 36–9.

[433] See section 4.1.

recipients receive the message only indirectly, namely filtered through the medium (i.e. the language/perspective) of the intermediary. For instance, communication with victims is highly mediated. Only a few of them are reached directly. This trend is reinforced by the rise of new technologies. As Immi Tallgren has noted: 'In a high-tech version of Durkheimian functionalism, the ICC would rely on media and modern communications technologies to reflect individual and collective representations reaffirming beliefs and values threatened by serious international crimes.'[434]

Many recipients receive messages in shortened, mediated or altered form. Messages are conveyed through media, such as television, radio, or newspapers, NGO statements, blogs or social media (Twitter, Facebook). This diversity increases the number of potential addresses but it may compromise norm dissemination and truth-telling:

> Some of these media, in particular donor-supported non-profit initiatives, have a mandate to fulfill some of the expressivist purposes of conveying truths, recognizing victims, educating the public, and reaffirming the rule of law ... Others, such as professional journalists, will be primarily interested in finding angles they believe will attract their target audiences. Yet another group may be affiliated with particular political factions in society.[435]

In such contexts, it becomes unclear whether the message can be attributed to the 'sender' or the 'intermediary'. 'Senders' may be required to develop their own channels to 'broadcast' messages, clarify their content, or correct misrepresentations. These dynamics must be better understood in order to explain expressivist effects in a reliable way.

434 Tallgren, 'Durkheimian Spell of International Criminal Law' 160
435 Meijers and Glasius, 'Trials as Messages' 442.

2

Norm Expression

Norm Affirmation, Norm Projection, and Storytelling

International criminal justice is closely related to norm expression.[1] Norms may be defined as 'intersubjective standards and practices that create moral (and sometimes legal) claims'.[2] International criminal justice represents a normative system which affirms, strengthens, or produces belief in legal norms.[3] It involves moral norm projection (e.g. the establishment of a 'common civility') since it is 'concerned with radically immoral and unethical conduct, where moral and ethical norms can be seen to coincide'.[4] As Markus Dubber has noted, what 'is at stake is not only criminal guilt', but 'moral guilt, or ethical deviance, through violation of norms of the human moral/ethical community'.[5]

Crimes may be deemed to 'shatter normative expectations fundamental to our sense of agency in the world'.[6] International criminal justice is designed to create an ideal for aspiration, namely an argument for norm-compliant behaviour,[7] through regulation, adjudication, and punishment. It establishes responsibilities and declares wrongs.

The history of international criminal justice has shown that norm expression may be an important asset even in the absence of universal enforcement or

[1] Marlies Glasius, 'Do International Criminal Courts Require Democratic Legitimacy?' (2012) 23 *EJIL Democratic Legitimacy* 43–66, 56.

[2] See Beth A. Simmons and Hyeran Jo, 'Measuring Norms and Normative Contestation: The Case of International Criminal Law' (2019) 4 *Journal of Global Security Studies* 18–36, Beth A. Simmons and Hyeran Jo, 'Measuring Norms and Normative Contestation: The Case of International Criminal Law' (2019) 4 *Journal of Global Security Studies* 18–36, 19.

[3] See Jean D'Aspremont, *International Law as Belief System* (Cambridge: Cambridge University Press, 2017).

[4] Markus Dubber, 'Common Civility: The Culture of Alegality in International Criminal Law' (2011) 24 *LJIL* 923–36, 933.

[5] Ibid.

[6] As Pablo de Greiff explains: 'The expectations that get broken whenever human rights are violated are not just whimsical ones; they are based on general norms—that is, they are expectations whose satisfaction we reasonably feel entitled to. These norm-based expectations are the manifestation of the basic structure, the ground or framework, of our agency. They are expectations about, for example, what constitutes legitimate treatment of others and at the hands of others, about situations in which it is "normal" to expect the assistance of others, about the state being the guarantor, rather than the violator, of fundamental rights, and so on'. See Pablo De Greiff, 'Articulating the links between transitional justice and development justice and social integration' in Pablo de Greiff and Roger Duthie (eds), *Transitional Justice and Development: Making Connections* (New York, NY: International Centre for Transitional Justice, 2009), 42.

[7] Saira Mohamed, 'Deviance, Aspiration, and the Stories We Tell: Reconciling Mass Atrocity and the Criminal Law' (2015) 124 *Yale Law Journal* 1628–9, 1628.

Justice as Message. Carsten Stahn, Oxford University Press (2020). © Carsten Stahn.
DOI: 10.1093/oso/9780198864189.001.0001

punishment. Important legal instruments have remained 'dormant' over the decades. In some cases, agents have started to act in accordance with the message of norms, although 'there is no risk of punishment'.[8]

Norm expression as a phenomenon cannot be understood without a broader understanding of its context. In domestic settings, norm expression is enshrined in a structured compliance system which includes community-defined regulatory norms and accepted law enforcement institutions. Laws reflect the values of a determined society. Adjudication and punishment mark a response to messages contained in legal and social norms and crimes challenging protected interests. Expressivism is thus grounded in societal expectations and rational choices by agents and institutions.

In international criminal justice, the context is less structured. Norms are often contested, more diffuse, or imperfect in the first place. Adjudication and punishment reflect the values and norms of a more abstract, pluralist, or even fictive society (*civitas maxima*).

Norm expression has retrospective and prospective features. It is often a reaction to past wrongdoing and seeks to reaffirm belief in norms or to contribute to a process of normative transformation. It is part of a continuing effort to bring some order into international relations (i.e. to move from anarchy to society),[9] stigmatize violations, and contribute to prevention.

The way in which norms are expressed has received limited attention in contemporary literature.[10] Guidance may be drawn from scholarship in international relations. Finnemore and Sikkink have developed a life cycle model to explain norm dynamics of social transformation. They have distinguished three different stages: 'norm emergence', that is the framing of issues by stakeholders to reach a broader audiences; a process of 'norm cascade', in which ideas begin to be generally accepted as norms; and 'norm internalization' where agents mobilize support for universal adherence and domestic implementation.[11] The first stage involves 'persuasion by norm entrepreneurs', the second attempts to 'socialize' others 'to become norm followers' (e.g. socialization, demonstration), and the third stage the maturation of a status in which the inherent propositions are followed and taken for granted (e.g. institutionalization).[12] This typology is useful for understanding the complexities of norm expression in international criminal justice.

[8] Diane Marie Amann, 'Group Mentality, Expressivism, and Genocide' (2002) 2 *International Criminal Law Review* 93–143, 122.

[9] Jason Ralph, 'Anarchy is what criminal lawyers and other actors make of it: International criminal justice as an institution of international and world society' in Steven C. Roach (ed.), *Governance, Order, and the International Criminal Court* (Oxford: Oxford University Press, 2009), 133–53.

[10] For an alternative 'narrative' account, see Anette Bringedal Houge, 'Narrative Expressivism: A Criminological Approach to the Expressive Function of International Criminal Justice' (2019) 19 *Criminology & Criminal Justice* 277–93.

[11] Martha Finnemore and Kathryn Sikkink, 'International Norm Dynamics and Political Change' 887–917.

[12] Ibid, at 895.

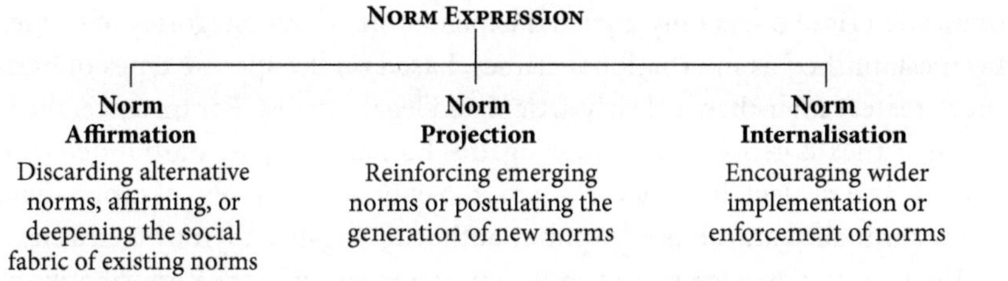

Figure 6 Dimensions of norm expression

2.1 Structural Context

Norm expression is part of a cycle involving an interplay between norms, crimes, and punishment as messages. It involves at least three key dimensions: classical norm affirmation, that is, appeals to comply with existing criminal norms, deepen their social fabric, and discard alternative norms; measures to reinforce emerging norms or to generate new norms (processes of norm projection); and/or calls for internalization.

The starting point of a communicative cycle between norm, crime, and punishment is not always the invalidation of a clear pre-existing norm through the crime, but the horror and shock caused by criminality as a phenomenon. Response through trial and punishment is guided by selectivity, an urge to control crime, and an attempt 'to embody and, thereby, to constitute a new, global political community'.[13] Propositions related to norm internalization are didactive.

2.1.1 Crimes as performances

Norm expression is strongly driven by the nature of criminality. International crimes often carry an element of concreteness and immediacy that triggers an expressive urge. This urge is influenced by several factors, including context and sociological rationales.

In legal discourse, international crimes are typically seen to be worthy of condemnation because of their systematicity, scale, or impact on victims,[14] or their contradiction to common interests.[15] However, the alleged gravity in relation to

[13] Luigi D.A. Corrias and Geoffrey M. Gordon, 'Judging in the Name of Humanity: International Criminal Tribunals and the Representation of a Global Public' (2015) 13 *JICJ* 106.

[14] The contextual elements of crimes are used to distinguish them from ordinary crimes.

[15] For example, Judge Cançado Trindade has qualified '[g]rave breaches of human rights and of international humanitarian law, amounting to international crimes' as 'anti-juridical acts'. See ICJ, *Jurisdictional Immunities of the State (Germany v. Italy)*, Judgment, 3 February 2012, Dissenting Opinion of Judge Cançado Trindade, para 129.

domestic crime offers only a partial explanation. Many categories of crimes have been established as international crimes, based on the specific types of harm that they create, rather than a clearly articulated legal interest. For instance, the idea to brand crimes as genocide or crimes against humanity is partly grounded in a sense of historical neglect. It marks an attempt to express the cruelty of group dynamics, state criminality, and abuses by public authorities against their own citizens.

The turn to norm expressivism is in part a reaction to the performative aspects of crimes. The core crimes (genocide, crimes against humanity, war crimes, aggression) have a strong performative character.[16] Typically, crimes are theorized in a bipolar way, namely through the relationship of perpetrator and victim. As David Luban has argued, almost any crime can be theorized as entailing an 'expressive content' in the relationship between victim and perpetrator:

> Crimes committed by one person against another ... express the moral falsehood that I, the perpetrator, am 'high' and you, the victim, are 'low'—that I am the sort of person who gets to do things like that to others, or you are the sort of person to whom others get to do it or both.[17]

The expressive dimensions of core crimes go further. They involve an agent, a target, and an audience. The social meaning conveyed through the crime is often as important as the material act, the *mens rea*, or any physical harm caused to victims. The identity of the crime results even more than in a domestic context from the interplay between agent, target, and audience. As Saira Mohamed has noted, for 'individuals in conflict settings, participation in group crime may fortify a sense of community and belonging when society is otherwise disintegrating'.[18]

International crimes produce their meaning not only in the relationship between the perpetrator and immediate target but through context and the relationship to the prospective audience. They are both local and global crimes. They are often not only a direct attack on victims or 'the local society' but also an assault on 'the international community at large or the international order' whose law is violated.[19]

The performative dimensions have gained some dimension in domestic criminology. American sociologist Edwin Sutherland has suggested that criminal behaviour is grounded in interactions and communication with other people.[20]

[16] See generally Judith Butler, *Excitable Speech: A Politics of the Performative* (New York, NY: Routledge, 1997).

[17] See David Luban, 'State criminality and the ambition of international criminal law' in Tracy Isaacs and Richard Vernon (eds), *Accountability for Collective Wrongdoing* (New York, NY: Cambridge University Press, 2012), 61–91, 71.

[18] Mohamed, 'Deviance, Aspiration, and the Stories We Tell' 1628.

[19] Miriam J. Aukerman, 'Extraordinary Evil, Ordinary Crime: A Framework for Understanding Transitional Justice' (2002) 15 *Harvard Human Rights Journal* 39–97, 46.

[20] On differential association theory, see Edwin Sutherland, *Principles of Criminology* 4th edn. (Philadelphia, PA: J.B. Lippincott, 1947) 6–7.

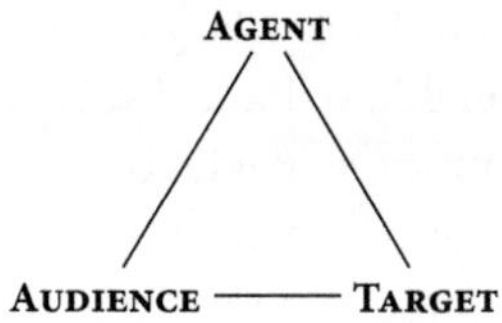

Figure 7 International crimes as performative speech acts

Symbolic interactionism has generated an emerging strand of research on 'narrative criminology',[21] that is, 'the study of the role the telling and sharing of stories play in committing, upholding and effecting desistance from crime and other harmful acts'.[22] Jack Katz, one of the early defenders of cultural criminology,[23] has argued that crimes involve storytelling and can be viewed as narrative plots. He noted that crimes 'generally cannot occur without the people involved using narratives about crime—an understanding of the phases and transitions among phases—to make the crimes happen'.[24]

This also applies to international crimes. Social science research has stressed the 'performative qualities of violence'.[25] Violence does not simply occur but is often communicative in nature, directed towards something or someone, either directly or indirectly. It is 'a set of actions, whether verbal or physical, personal or institutional, that is performed or imagined by social beings under specific historical conditions for concrete reasons'.[26]

Similar considerations apply to atrocity-related international crimes. They have a performative character.[27] They may generate particular effects through their utterance and commission.

The performative dimensions of crimes have been shown in relation to group and gang violence in domestic settings. Perpetrators often engage in violent acts in such contexts, in order to gain a sense of security or identity, conform to social

[21] Lois Presser and Sveinung Sandberg, *Narrative Criminology: Understanding Stories of Crime* (New York, NY: NYU Press, 2015).

[22] Sveinung Sandberg and Thomas Ugelvik, 'The Past, Present, and Future of Narrative Criminology: A Review and an Invitation' (2016) 12 *Crime Media Culture* 129–36.

[23] Jack Katz, *Seductions of Crime: The Moral and Sensual Attractions of Doing Evil* (New York, NY: Basic Books, 1988).

[24] Jack Katz, 'Culture within and Culture about Crime: The Case of the "Rodney King Riots"' (2016) 12 *Crime Media Culture* 233–51, 235. Ibid., 234.

[25] Teresa Koloma Beck, 'The Eye of the Beholder: Violence as a Social Process' (2011) 5 *International Journal of Conflict and Violence* 345–56; David Riches, 'The phenomenon of violence' in David Riches (ed.), *The Anthropology of Violence* (Oxford: Basil Blackwell, 1986) 1–27, 8.

[26] Jefffrey Stevenson Murer, 'Understanding collective violence: the communicative and performative qualities of violence in acts of belonging' in Ilias Bantekas and Emmanouela Mylonaki Bantekas (eds), *Criminological Approaches to International Criminal Law* (Cambridge: Cambridge University Press, 2014) 287–315, 288.

[27] Klejda Mulaj, 'Violence of War, Ontopology, and the Instrumental and Performative Constitution of the Political Community' (2017) 44 *Review of International Studies* 64–82.

expectations or demonstrate loyalty to a larger collectivity.[28] Many of the existing core crimes under international law share similar dynamics. They are collective crimes, shaped by group dynamics, struggles over identity, purported social gains, or strivings for power. Criminality is driven by the interplay between contextual, group-level, and individual-level factors. Crimes express authority and will. Offenders may gain social capital by violating human rights norms or criminal prohibitions, as long as they abide by the expectations of the larger collective to which they belong or purport to belong. The public 'reading' of crimes has particular relevance. International crimes require a 'spectacle' and a 'spectator'. As Klejda Mulaj has observed, atrocity crime can be viewed as 'a boundary-creation mechanism' which 'unmakes an old order to remake a new one'.[29] Many crimes claim narrative territory or space in societal discourse. Their performative nature increases with the multiplication of discursive forums and the range of new media and technology to communicate.

Performative features are inherent in genocide, crimes against humanity, war crimes, and the crime of aggression

2.1.1.1 Performative dimensions of genocide

Genocide is a highly expressive crime. It involves an attack on the collective character of victims. Criminological studies have shown that genocide is not only a material attack, carried out with intent to destroy another national, ethnical, racial, or religious group, but a statement about civic value. It is driven by complex macro dynamics (e.g. conflict, political or ideological struggles, declining state structures, failures of colonial policies, lack of accountability).[30] It involves psychological factors, such as processes of 'authorization, routinization, and dehumanization of the victim' which contribute not only to 'to the weakening of moral restraints' but also to 'the dehumanization of the victimizer', who may feel lesser personal responsibility or human empathy.[31] The utterance of genocidal intent produces 'us versus them' divisions that cause 'expressive harm'.[32]

The underlying criminal acts are deemed to express or reinforce certain messages.[33] The most classical example is incitement to genocide. It involves physical speech acts (e.g. inflammatory discourse) or rituals, symbols, or racial epithets to

[28] Murer, 'Understanding collective violence' 313–315.

[29] Mulaj, 'Violence of War' 70.

[30] Nicole Rafter, *The Crime of All Crimes: Toward a Criminology of Genocide* (New York, NY: New York University Press 2016).

[31] Herbert C. Kelman, 'Violence without Moral Restraint: Reflections on the Dehumanization of Victims and Victimizers' (1973) *Journal of Social Issues* 25–61, 29, 52.

[32] See Adil Ahmad Haque, 'Group Violence and Group Vengeance: Toward a Retributivist Theory of International Criminal Law' (2005) 9 *Buffalo Criminal Law Review* 273–328, 315.

[33] For a collective action theory of genocide see John Hagan and Wenona Rymond-Richmond, 'The Collective Dynamics of Racial Dehumanization and Genocidal Victimization in Darfur' (2008) 73 *American Sociological Review* 875–902.

'stage' confrontation. It is criminalized as an inchoate crime, because 'denigrating speech and inciting speech' may 'enhance a climate of intolerance that facilitates the persecution of protected groups'.[34] The message of incitement is the crime. It is based on 'a communication that is made with a view to persuading the addressee(s) to commit an offence'.[35] The International Criminal Tribunal for Rwanda (ICTR) convicted Simon Bikindi, a famous Rwandan singer, for inciting genocide through anti-Tutsi songs urging Hutus to 'exterminate [the Tutsis] quickly'.[36]

Genocidal destruction carries important symbolical meaning. It expresses and produces divides between collectivities, that is, 'in-groups' and out-groups'.[37] It marks an act of distinction, namely a process of 'othering' and a reinforcement of the offender's own collective identity.[38] It often involves attempts to destroy culture, identity, and composition of protected groups or to 'purify' a human group or territory through collective genocidal plans or policies.[39] It is accompanied by verbal or non-verbal acts of degradation or discrimination towards victims[40] which are directed to local, national, or international audiences.

The meaning of genocidal acts stems partly from meanings that others attach to them. Genocide involves not only speech acts about atrocity by the perpetrator but also messages about gravity. Genocide expresses not only the 'fact of wrongdoing' but rather a certain level of wrongdoing. Victims may be 'deeply disappointed when their own suffering is acknowledged as "mere" crimes against humanity'.[41]

Genocidal practices draw greater attention to audiences. They send particular signals to global audiences, that is, 'those who care about others being subjected to mass murder, as well as those individuals and organizations that are in a position to do something concrete to help disseminate a call for action and/or to actually put a plan into action to attempt to halt it'.[42]

[34] Richard A. Wilson, *Incitement on Trial: Prosecuting International Speech Crimes* (Cambridge: Cambridge University Press, 2017), 285 ('Such speech may convince an elite of the rightness of its strategy and raise the likelihood that a population will feel less empathy towards members of the out-group and be more willing to morally justify violence.').

[35] Joseph Jaconelli, 'Incitement: A Study in Language Crime' (2018) 12 *Criminal Law and Philosophy* 245–65.

[36] *Prosecutor v. Bikindi*, Judgment, ICTR-01-72-T, 2 December 2008, paras 266, 422, 426.

[37] Edward Day and Margaret Vandiver, 'Criminology and Genocide Studies: Notes on What Might Have Been and What Still Could Be' (2000) 34 *Crime, Law & Social Change* 43–59, 50.

[38] Murer, 'Understanding collective violence' 314.

[39] Jacques Semelin, *Purify and Destroy: The Political Uses of Massacre and Genocide* (New York, NY: Columbia University Press, 2007).

[40] This link to context is directly expressed in the ICC Elements of Crime which require that the conduct must 'take place in the context of a manifest pattern of similar conduct directed against that group or was conduct that could itself effect such destruction'. See ICC Elements of Crime, Art. 6 Genocide.

[41] William Schabas, 'The law and genocide' in Donald Bloxham and A. Dirk Moses (eds), *The Oxford Handbook of Genocide Studies* (Oxford: Oxford University Press, 2010), 123–42, 126, 135.

[42] Samuel Totten, 'A matter of conscience: Part II' in Samuel Totten (ed.), *Advancing Genocide Studies: Personal Accounts and Insights from Scholars in the Field* (New Brunswick, NJ: Transaction Publishers 2015) 229–66, 252.

2.1.1.2 Performative dimensions of crimes against humanity

Crimes against humanity share similar features. They are deemed to 'victimize' humanity as a whole, even though the physical acts of crimes may be territorially confined. They involve murder-type and persecution-related elements. Criminologists suggest that they have their 'origins in the experience of extreme strain caused by insecurity, deprivation, political and economic oppression and/or military occupation' which 'undermine societal level and inter-group solidarity and ... drive individuals to rely more heavily on narrowly defined "us versus them" primary-group affiliations'.[43]

Crimes against humanity are strongly goal-oriented. Criminality is intrinsically linked to specific political or organizational structures. The notion was originally linked to state policies, including crimes by governments against its own population.[44] But it has been extended to a broader range of organizations. Crimes against humanity represent not merely attacks on certain legally protected goods or interests. Their significance lies in their organization and systematicity, that is the link to a more regular pattern and policy involving public or private resources. The close link to organizational structures gives them performative dimensions. Individual acts must be seen in the context of system criminality and interaction. Group think, organizational dynamics, lack of social control (e.g. abuse of public authority), and the interplay between macro and micro factors shape the criminogenic conditions that facilitate crimes against humanity.[45]

Crimes against humanity defy traditional criminological theories. They are not only the result of anomie, lawlessness, or the weakness of social norms[46] or social pressures inducing crime.[47] They are the very expression of norms through policies and patterns of conduct. They require a whole machinery in order to be committed. They may be expressed in state legislation, regulatory acts, or practices. The message of crimes against humanity may be inscribed in the acts, that is the 'attack'

[43] Daniel Maier-Katkin, Daniel P. Mears, and Thomas J. Bernard, 'Towards a Criminology of Crimes against Humanity' (2009) 13 *Theoretical Criminology* 227–55, 241–2.

[44] Rudolph Rummel has coined the term 'democide' to express this. See Rudolph J. Rummel, *Democide: Nazi Genocide and Mass Murder* (New Brunswick, NJ: Transaction, 1992).

[45] Dawn L. Rothe and Christopher W. Mullins, 'Toward a Criminology of International Criminal Law: An Integrated Theory of International Criminal Violations' (2009) 33 *International Journal of Comparative and Applied Criminal Justice* 97–118

[46] Criminality is sometimes explained by the lack of regulation or integration into society. On Durkheim's anomie theory, see Stephen R. Marks, 'Durkheim's Theory of Anomie' (1974) 80 *American Journal of Sociology* 329–63.

[47] Strain theorists argue that society creates pressures on individuals to realize socially accepted goals. See Robert Merton, 'Social Structure and Anomie' (1938) 3 *American Sociological Review* 672–82. For instance, Robert Merton's argued that individuals receive messages about 'what is normal' from societal institutions. See Robert Merton, *Social Theory and Social Structure* (Glencoe, IL: The Free Press, 1957), 132. On strain theory of crime and deviance, see Daniel S. Murphy and Matthew B. Robinson, 'The Maximizer: Clarifying Merton's Theories of Anomie and Strain' (2008) 12 *Theoretical Criminology* 501–21.

on the civilian population, the policies (e.g. explicit instructions or strategic plans), or result from meanings that victims associated with these acts.

Crimes against humanity may be aimed at 'producing greater individual submission to authority and acceptance of social roles'[48] or reinforcing 'belief systems that dehumanize others, justify or recommend violence, and associate 'higher' values with immediate self-interest'.[49] As David Luban has argued, crimes against humanity may be characterized in the broadest sense as an attack on 'humanness', including the role of individuals as social and political beings.[50]

The human body becomes a site through which violence and power are transmitted. For instance, public display of torture, execution, and violence by non-state armed groups, such as the Islamic State of Iraq and the Levant (ISIS), marks an attempt to weaken and challenge state authority. Killings or abductions (i.e. enforced disappearances) carry significant meaning. They are often an instrument used to instil fear or demonstrate control.[51] Civilians are used as tools to disseminate certain messages to the public. Other crimes (e.g. apartheid, persecution) involve processes of distinction and exclusion. The importance of the crime lies in the transmission of these messages, the reshaping of minds or the reorganization of society.

Crimes, like ethnic cleansing or forced displacements of people, are driven by messages about territory and identity. They mark an attack on human diversity. They postulate identity of territory and the population that controls it.

2.1.1.3 Performative dimensions of war crimes

War crimes involve both collective and individual human action.[52] They are not only violent acts but acts with symbolic and performative meaning that affect the dynamics of conflict. This is *inter alia* reflected in the idea of 'theatre of war'.[53] As Vincenzo Ruggiero has noted: 'Wars are foundational events, as they establish international hierarchies and domestic order. They are crucial for the constitution of identities and for the provision of collective memory in national contexts, as war efforts mobilize unselfish feelings, encourage the formation of common sensibilities and shared goals.'[54]

48 Daniel Maier-Katkin, Daniel P. Mears, and Thomas J. Bernard, 'Towards a criminology of crimes against humanity' (2009) 13 *Theoretical Criminology* 227–55, 244.

49 Ibid., 246.

50 David Luban, 'A Theory of Crimes Against Humanity' (2004) 29 *Yale Journal of International Law* 85–167.

51 On the performative nature violence by drug cartels, see Andrew Lantz, 'The Performativity of Violence: Abducting Agency in Mexico's Drug War' (2016) 25 *Journal of Latin American Cultural Studies* 253–69, 264.

52 War crimes have enjoyed relatively limited attention in criminology. See Ruth Jamieson, *The Criminology of War* (Farnham: Ashgate, 2014).

53 On war crimes as theatre, see Simon Chesterman, 'Never Again ... and Again: Law, Order, and the Gender of War Crimes in Bosnia and Beyond' (1997) 22 *Yale Journal of International Law* 299–343, 311.

54 Vincenzo Ruggiero, 'War and the death of Achilles' in Sandra Walklate and Ross McGarry (eds), *Criminology and War: Transgressing the Borders* (New York, NY: Routledge, 2015), 21–37, 27.

From the point of view of the morality of war, war crimes may be deemed to constitute a violation of a 'soldier's code of honour' or crimes against humans.[55] From a behavioural perspective, they produce a new reality and transforms identities. They affect power balances or social orders, influence reciprocal behaviour in warfare, or communicate the meaning and cruelty of conflict to civilians.

Game theorists and conflict researchers have argued that armed conflict is closely related to audiences and strongly driven by practices of 'signalling'.[56] This implies the sending of signals of strength and commitment to opponents or the attempt to broaden the scope of potential supporters. Some acts provide meaning or justification for military operations or armed conflict. They seek to intimidate the adversary in conflict or imitate or conceal earlier crimes. Others constitute manifestations of control and power over people or persons. They may signal control over territory or provide a means to keep the conflict alive. Again others may send messages to bystanders or silence victims.

In traditional legal discourse, victims and objects are seen as consequences or casualties of warfare. But the reality is more complex. The very meaning of the crime is created through attacks on soldiers, civilians, protected persons, or protected spaces. As studies on experiential dimensions of warfare have shown, the 'human body is a unit that has agency in war and is also the target of war's violence'.[57]

Messages of crimes are conveyed through different sites: through 'the bodies of individuals', 'territory', or other affected actors (e.g. bystanders, international organizations).[58] Persons or places are not only harmed in the physical sense but take on different roles or identities through the crime. Third actors are affected. They may no longer be able to remain neutral but are forced to become involved.

It is impossible to provide an exhaustive survey of the expressivist dimensions of war crimes. However, many individual crimes involve performative elements. The conflict is virtually a global stage to express messages, which affects group dynamics or comes with certain benefits or forms of recognition.

Expressivism may be part of the tactics of warfare. Many crimes related to means and methods of warfare are expressive in nature: they convey a message through the crime. A prime example is the crime of spreading terror.[59] Historically, aerial

[55] See Larry May, *After War Ends: A Philosophical Perspective* (New York, NY: Cambridge University Press, 2012), 69; Larry May, *War Crimes and Just War* (New York, NY: Cambridge University Press, 2012).

[56] Thomas C. Schelling, "The Strategy of Conflict: Prospectus for a Reorientation of Game Theory (1958) 2 *Journal of Conflict Resolution* 203–64; James D. Fearon, 'Rationalist Explanations for War' (1995) 49 *International Organization* 379–414; Harrison Wagner, 'Bargaining and War' (2000) 44 *American Journal of Political Science* 469–84, 470.

[57] Christine Sylvester, *War as Experience: Contributions from International Relations and Feminist Analysis* (New York, NY: Routledge Press, 2013) 65.

[58] Mulaj, 'Violence of War' 69.

[59] See Marlies Glasius, 'Terror, terrorizing, terrorism: Instilling fear as a crime in the cases of Radovan Karadzic and Charles Taylor' in Dubravaka Zarkov and Marlies Glasius (eds), *Narratives of Justice In and Out of the Courtroom: Former Yugoslavia and Beyond* (The Hague: Springer, 2014), 45–61.

bombardment was used for the purpose of terrorizing the civilian population. In the conflict in Sierra Leone, rebels of the Revolutionary United Front (RUF) fired loud shots in order to create fear among civilians and conquer towns and villages more easily. In the former Yugoslavia, Bosnian Serb troops used sniping and shelling of civilians in Sarajevo as a means of spreading terror. In many contemporary atrocity contexts, 'ritual executions' have become a performative tool of extremists groups. They reach global audiences through cell phones or video documentation. The gravity of such practices does not necessarily result from the individual attack or the immediate harm caused but rather from the intended consequences, that is, an ulterior message sent through the act.

Other war crimes involve comparable performative features. Hostage-taking marks not only an attack on the physical liberty of the victim but also a speech act to the opponent or a demonstration of power.[60] For instance, hostage-taking by the Revolutionary Armed Forces of Colombia (FARC) in the Colombian conflict was an instrument to send a message to the Colombian security forces.[61] ISIS took hostages not only as an instrument to gain ransom or to prevent an attack but to convey a message to journalists or aid workers: to stay out of the conflict.[62]

Attacks on peacekeepers or humanitarian personnel convey similar meanings.[63] They have significantly expanded over the past decades. They are often 'staged' for a broader audience. The respective entities are not targeted because of their combat force but rather due to their symbolic meaning or the anticipated political consequences. The crime is deemed to create a sense of insecurity and to provoke a withdrawal of foreign engagement. For instance, the attacks on UN troops by Somali militias in Mogadishu were deemed to make the United Nations more reluctant to intervene in the conflict. They prompted the United States and European countries to withdraw their forces from Somalia in March 1994.[64] The International Criminal Court (ICC) recognized expressly in the Darfur situation that the attack killing twelve members of the African Union Mission in Sudan carried gravity because it 'severely disrupted' the mission and affected 'its mandated protective roles

[60] The International Convention against the Taking of Hostages labels the taking of hostages as 'an offence of grave concern to the international community'. Hostage-taking must be geared at compelling 'a third party, namely, a State, an international intergovernmental organization, a natural or juridical person, or a group of persons, to do or abstain from doing any act as an explicit or implicit condition for the release of the hostage'. See Article 1 of International Convention against the Taking of Hostages, GA Res. 146 (XXXIV), UN GAOR, 34th Sess., Supp. No. 46, at 245, UN Doc A/34/46 (1979), entered into force 3 June 1983.

[61] On Mexican cartel violence, see Lantz, 'The Performativity of Violence' 253.

[62] On counterterrorism strategies, see Beatrice de Graaf, *Evaluating Counterterrorism Performance. A Comparative Study* (London: Routledge 2011).

[63] On the jurisprudence of the SCSL, see James Sloan, 'Peacekeepers under Fire: Prosecuting the RUF for Attacks against the UN Assistance Mission in Sierra Leone' (2010) 9 *The Law and Practice of International Courts and Tribunals* 243–93.

[64] In the background, see Report of the Commission of Inquiry Established pursuant to Security Council Resolution 885 (1993) to Investigate Armed Attacks on UNOSOM II Personnel, UN Doc S/1994/653, 1 June 1994.

with respect to millions of Darfurian civilians in need of humanitarian aid and security'.[65]

Sexual violence and offences against children involve a distinct set of messages. They entail a partial reversal of the social order through war. Crimes against children include the 'war crimes of child recruitment and use', including abductions, 'sexual and gender-based crimes' committed against children or their families, and 'attacks against buildings dedicated to education and health care'.[66] They are particularly grave because of their long-term and intergenerational impact. They mark an attack on the social fabric of a given society in war, and human development and behaviour over the life course.

The importance of sexual and gender-based violence often reaches beyond acts of a sexual nature.[67] It targets socially constructed gender roles or seeks to reorder societal roles, status, and relationships of power. It uses the human body as a site to express power, cause trauma, attack 'family' bonds or the self-dignity of survivors. Some scholars have described rape as a 'crime of biological warfare'.[68] However, the impact of sexual and gender-based violence is much broader. It may be an instrument to challenge the roles of males and females in a particular society, to affect reproductive capacity, or to alter the ethnic composition of a population.

Attacks against certain protected objects and targets include performative, symbolic, or communicative dimensions. They are often used for purposes of 'signalling'.[69] They may constitute a means to justify violence or armed conflict, based on different identities or ideologies. As Mark Drumbl has noted: 'Intentionally attacking cultural property, like other forms of persecution, is often an initial step in what can mutate into something far more endemic. These attacks may be a trigger to dehumanize, demoralize, and depict the victim group as lacking culture and thereby as unworthy.'[70]

For instance, in the Yugoslav conflict, attacks on religious buildings or cultural property were partly a means to express superiority and destroy identity. Religious sites, such as churches, mosques, and minarets were targeted as symbols of another culture or ethnicity, rather than to gain a military advantage or prevent individuals

[65] *Prosecutor v. Abu Garda*, Decision on the Confirmation of Charges, ICC-02/05-02/09, 8 February 2010, para. 33.

[66] See OTP, Policy on Children, November 2016, para. 19, at https://www.icc-cpi.int/iccdocs/otp/20161115_OTP_ICC_Policy-on-Children_Eng.PDF.

[67] See OTP, Policy Paper on Sexual and Gender-Based Crimes, June 2014, para 16 ('Gender-based crimes are not always manifested as a form of sexual violence. These crimes may include non-sexual attacks on women and girls, and men and boys, because of their gender, such as persecution on the grounds of gender.').

[68] Beverly Allen, *Rape, Warfare: The Hidden Genocide in Bosnia-Herzegovina and Croatia* (1996), 121–32

[69] See generally Patty Gerstenblith, 'The Destruction of Cultural Heritage: A Crime Against Property or a Crime Against People?' (2016) 15 *John Marshall Review of Intellectual Property Law* 336–93.

[70] See Mark Drumbl, 'From Timbuktu to The Hague and Beyond: The War Crime of Intentionally Attacking Cultural Property' (2017) 17 *JICJ* 77–99, 92.

from returning to their homes. The most famous example is the destruction of the bridge of Mostar. As social scientists have noted:

> The prime reason for the attack was that Mostar—and the bridge especially—symbolized a multi-ethnic and multi-religious society living in peace ... This symbolism constituted an obstacle for the creation of a nationalist Croatian state in Bosnia and Herzegovina, with Mostar as the intended capital. The destruction of the bridge was thus an attack on the idea of a future multi-ethnic nation.[71]

The destruction of the Timbuktu sites in 2012 was driven by similar motives. As the Office of the Prosecutor (OTP) noted in pre-trial proceedings, what was 'at stake' here was 'not just walls and stones'.[72] The destruction marked an act of protest and resistance, guided by religious ideology. Al Mahdi openly acknowledged this in his admission of guilt. He noted that he 'was influenced by a group of deviant people from Al-Qaeda and Ansar Dine', who 'were able to influence' him and carry him 'in their evil wave through actions that affected the whole population' of Timbuktu.[73] The Trial Chamber openly acknowledged the performative nature of the attack in the Reparation Order. It noted that the 'destruction of international cultural heritage' carries 'a message of terror and helplessness; it destroys part of humanity's shared memory and collective consciousness; and it renders humanity unable to transmit its values and knowledge to future generations'.[74]

A further example is the pillaging of archaeologic sites. Such sites are highly in symbolic nature. Their exploitation or destruction is often not a random act of looting but a 'message crime'. The physical object itself becomes the medium to transmit a message. A key example is the destruction of cultural symbols in Palmyra marked an attack on Syrian cultural diversity. According to the UN Educational, Scientific and Cultural Organization (UNESCO), the conduct was guided by the objective 'to deprive the Syrian people of its knowledge, its identity and history'.[75]

The environment is subject to similar concerns. It is often targeted in international conflicts or civil warfare in order to send 'signals' to the adversary or a broader public. In the first Gulf War in 1991, Saddam Hussein set Kuwait's oil fields on fire to cover the retreat of forces and destroy economic capacity.[76] In

[71] Johan Brosché, Mattias Legnér, Joakim Kreutz, and Akram Ijla, 'Heritage under Attack: Motives for Targeting Cultural Property during Armed Conflict' (2017) 23 *International Journal of Heritage Studies* 248–60, 252.

[72] *Prosecutor v. Al Mahdi*, Transcript, Confirmation of Charges Hearing, 1 March 2016, 13.

[73] *Prosecutor v. Al Mahdi*, Transcript, Trial, 22 August 2016, 9.

[74] *Prosecutor v. Al Mahdi*, Reparations Order, ICC-01/12-01/15, 17 August 2017, para. 22 (*Al Mahdi* Reparations Order).

[75] See UNESCO, 'Director-General Irina Bokova firmly condemns the destruction of Palmyra's ancient temple of Baalshamin, Syria', 2015, at https://en.unesco.org/news/director-general-irina-bokova-firmly-condemns-destruction-palmyra-s-ancient-temple-baalshamin.

[76] On environmental protection, see Carsten Stahn, Jens Iverson, and Jennifer Easterday (eds), *Environmental Protection and Transitions from Conflict to Peace* (Oxford: Oxford University Press, 2017).

Rwanda and Yugoslavia, parties to the conflict used the environment as a weapon of war. ISIS forces burnt oil fields and factories in Iraq, which released toxins and contaminated drinking water. Similar damage occurs in civil war: 'Insurgents often use tropical forests as home bases and hiding grounds; counter-insurgency forces often respond by slashing and burning forests and by polluting rivers, viewing both as legitimate theaters of operations.'[77] Harm to humans or objects is thus not merely a consequence of conflict, as typically presented in war crimes law, but rather part of processes of signalling and communication between actors involved in conflict.

2.1.1.4 Performative dimensions of aggression

The crime of aggression is closely related to the demonstration of power. Aggression has a signalling effect on the world stage. At Nuremberg, the crime of aggression was branded as the 'supreme international crime,' because it affected the entire world.[78] It carries meanings about the scope and limits of use of force in international relations and the very role of war as institution.

From a criminological perspective, aggression is even more a 'state crime' than other crimes because it requires state involvement, that is, an unlawful state act aggression.[79] Acts of aggression use state structures and coercive means to demonstrate power.[80] They mark an attack on different interests: peace, security sovereignty, or human rights.

Acts of aggression differ in scope. Some acts during the Second World War have 'resulted in the loss of millions of lives' while others (e.g. 'the invasions of Austria and Czechoslovakia') have 'resulted immediately in little loss of life because the victims submitted without resistance.'[81]

Aggression may send multiple messages in addition to violations of territorial integrity or taking of control over territory or lives of people. Classical wars of aggression signal imperial ambitions, militarist ideologies, or global political-economic power. Judge Pal highlighted these broader dimensions in his dissent of the crime of aggression at Tokyo. He situated aggression in the perpetuation of patterns of colonial rule, violence, and inequality among nations. He argued that efforts to criminalize aggression would create a new global order that reproduces

[77] See Mark Drumbl, 'Waging war against the world: The need to move from war crimes to environmental crimes' in Jay E. Austin and Carl E. Bruch (eds), *The Environmental Consequences of War* (Cambridge: Cambridge University Press, 2000), 620–46, 631.

[78] Danilo Zolo, 'Who is Afraid of Punishing Aggressors? On the Double-Track Approach to International Criminal Justice' (2007) 5 *JICJ* 799–807.

[79] Ronald C. Kramer and Raymond J. Michalowski , 'War, Aggression and State Crime: A Criminological Analysis of the Invasion and Occupation of Iraq' (2005) 45 *British Journal of Criminology* 446–69.

[80] Mark Drumbl, 'The Push to Criminalize Aggression: Something Lost Amid the Gains?' (2009) 41 *Case Western Law Research Journal of International Law* 291–319

[81] Quincy Wright, 'The Law of the Nuremberg Trial' (1947) 41 *AJIL* 38–72, 44.

existing power structures and validates the maintenance of colonialism in the name of a universal community.[82]

Modern of acts of aggression that fall short of a full-fledged war of aggression (e.g. interventions, indirect forms of aggression) have similar effects. They entail implicit statements about the legality or acceptance of use of force as an instrument to solve global problems, or relevance of the global institutional architecture. Unilateral acts of aggression, or military operations carried out without authorization or valid legal mandate, mark an attack on the global security system and the international legal order, even if they are carried out for humanitarian purposes. This reflected in the semantics surrounding the use of force. They constitute a form of 'organizational deviance' in criminological terms. They do not necessarily defy classical state authority, but the global system of international peace and security with its law and institutions. They often rely on images of crisis, sacrifice, and solution to justify deviance. This is framed in terms of exceptionalism, heroic narratives, aimed at attracting empathy, use of binaries (e.g. demonization of inaction), or narratives of progress (e.g. 'old' versus 'new').[83]

Ultimately, the messages associated with acts of aggression may lead to a loss of social control. One of the specific dangers of aggression is that they may trigger uncontrollable consequences. The very initiation of acts of aggression may cause a chain of events that is difficult to control or predict.[84] It may set in motion a spiral of violence, unpredictable countermeasures, or a sequence of war crimes, even in cases where there may have a legitimate reason to use coercive force in the first place.

2.1.1.5 Mode of commission and/or contribution as expression

The expressive nature of criminality may not only derive from the nature of crimes and their political context but also from their modes of commission.[85] The process of committing international crimes, that is, from planning to execution, is highly decentralized. Certain messages result from the way in which crimes are perpetrated through collective structures, the 'how'. Crimes are often committed as part of a system or network of criminality.[86] They are part of collective action in

[82] Elizabeth S. Kopelman, 'Ideology and International Law: The Dissent of the Indian Justice at the Tokyo War Crimes Trial' (1991) 23 *New York University Journal of International Law and Politics* 373–444; Latha Varadarajan, 'The Trials of Imperialism: Radhabinod Pal's Dissent at the Tokyo Tribunal' (2015) 21 *European Journal of International Relations* 793–815.

[83] See Anne Orford, 'Muscular Humanitarianism: Reading the Narratives of the New Interventionism' (1999) 10 *EJIL* 679–711.

[84] Frédéric Mégret, 'What is the specific evil of aggression?' in Claus Kress and Stefan Barriga (eds), *The Crime of Aggression: A Commentary* (Cambridge: Cambridge University Press, 2017) 1398–453, 1418.

[85] On modes of liability in the ICC context, see Gerhard Werle, 'Individual Criminal Responsibility in Article 25 ICC Statute' (2007) 5 *JICJ* 953–73.

[86] Herbert Jäger, *Makrokriminalität, Zur Kriminologie kollektiver Gewalt* (Frankfurt: Surhrkamp, 1989).

which structures or the state itself may turn into a 'repressive and destructive machine'.[87] They involve leaders, mid-level perpetrators, followers, and executioners. Sometimes, the way of commission entails a 'statement' of its own.[88] The criminality lies partly in the abuse of power and the use of such structures.[89] Crimes are facilitated through techniques, such as the creation of spatial distance, use of authority, peer pressure, or degradation of victims.

Some crimes, such as incitement to genocide, are directly committed through speech.[90] However, in many contexts, the expressive nature of crimes results from a combination of factors, such as speech acts, political communications, or abuses of authority. Criminality is grounded in the structural relationship to the crime rather than physical proximity to it. For example, leadership criminality, that is, the responsibility of political or military leaders,[91] is tied to political ideology, use of hierarchies, or networks of power. This structural connection is reflected in expanded concepts of co-perpetration, such as joint criminal enterprise (JCE)[92] or joint control over the crime, which ground responsibility in objective elements, such as structural control over the crime ('*Tatherrschaft*') (ICC)[93] and/or subjective elements, that is, a common plan or agreement with an 'an element of criminality' (JCE).

[87] David Martínez Osorio, 'Manual Contextual Analysis of Criminal Investigations by the National Analysis and Context Division of the Attorney General's Office' June 2014, 10 at https://www.ictj.org/sites/default/files/ICTJ-Report-DINAC-2014.pdf.

[88] Social science research suggests that there connection between such speech acts and political violence: 'Violence is most likely to result when charismatic speakers in positions of authority explicitly call for immediate violence against targeted groups, in a context where inter-group violence has occurred previously and where the current situation is tense and the speakers' audience is fearful of being attacked itself.' Richard A. Wilson, 'The Hartford Guidelines on Speech Crimes in International Criminal Law' *EJIL Talk*, 31 August 2018, at https://www.ejiltalk.org/the-hartford-guidelines-on-speech-crimes-in-international-criminal-law/.

[89] It relies on communicative structures, authority, and networks of power. For instance, a telephone phone call or the signing of a document can constitute murder.

[90] See generally Gregory Gordon, *Atrocity Speech Law* (Oxford: Oxford University Press, 2017). Other speech acts may fall short of incitement to genocide but contribute to the crime of persecution, or amount unlawful forms of complicity. Shannon Fyfe, 'Tracking Hate Speech Acts as Incitement to Genocide in International Criminal Law' (2017) 30 *LJIL* 523–48; Richard A. Wilson, 'Inciting Genocide with Words' (2015) 36 *Michigan Journal of International Law* 278–320. Complicity as a category of criminal responsibility may capture 'rogue politicians, media personalities and other individuals who incite others to commit crimes but who may not hold elected office or occupy a position of military command'. See Richard Ashby Wilson and Matthew Gillett, *The Hartford Guidelines on Speech Crimes in International Criminal Law* (The Hague: Peace and Justice Initiative, 2018) 72.

[91] Héctor Olásolo, *The Criminal Responsibility of Senior Political and Military Leaders as Principals to International Crimes* (Oxford: Hart, 2009).

[92] On the development of JCE, see Antonio Cassese, 'The Proper Limits of Individual Responsibility under the Doctrine of Joint Criminal Enterprise' (2007) 5 *JICJ* 109–33.

[93] According to the ICC, it captures 'those to whom essential tasks have been assigned—and who, consequently, have the power to frustrate the commission of the crime by not performing their tasks—can be said to have joint control over the crime'. See *Prosecutor v. Lubanga*, Decision on the confirmation of charges, ICC-01/04-01/06-803-tEN, 29 January 2007, para. 347.

These doctrines were initially developed based on state criminality, such as Nazi structures.[94] However, they have been gradually extended to informal structures of power, which rely more on trust, group cohesion, or social pressures (*de facto* authority), rather than *de jure* control. They include organizational forms of control, that is use of organized structures of power (Claus Roxin),[95] in order to prevent subordinates are used 'as a mere gear in a giant machine'.[96]

In other cases, crime is facilitated through crime-conducive role models, disciplinary pressures,[97] or flawed organizational cultures. For example, crimes of mid-level or lower-level perpetrators may be partly 'crimes of obedience'.[98] Such structures are common in military and paramilitary groups, governmental bureaucracies, or business structures. The abuse of positions of authority may prevent soldiers, civil servants, or other persons to question orders and disobey authority.[99]

2.1.2 The constitutive function of norm expression

Norm expression is partly a reaction to the performative features of crimes and the signals associated with them. As Durkheim noted, from a moral point of view, the crime may be 'an anticipation of the morality to come, a progression towards what will be'.[100] Norm expression is a social response. It seeks to respond to the rationalization and commodification of violence and the risk that crimes become accepted because they are not prohibited or sanctioned. It is in certain respects a 'counter-performance'. If crimes are deemed to destroy a political community, norm expressivism has the opposite function, namely to maintain, build, or reconstitute

[94] Jäger, *Verbrechen unter totalitärer Herrschaft*; Claus Roxin, 'Crimes as Part of Organized Power Structures' (2011) 9 *JICJ* 193–205.

[95] Hans Vest, *Genozid durch organisatorische Machtapparate* (Baden Baden: Nomos Verlagsgesellschaft, 2002)

[96] *Prosecutor v. Katanga and Ngudjolo Chui*, Decision on the Confirmation of Charges, 30 September 2008, ICC-01/04-01/07-717, para. 515.

[97] The giving of orders expresses a relationship of authority between the speaker and audience. Ordering is criminalized as mode of liability in cases where it has a 'direct and substantial effect' on the commission of the crime.

[98] Herbert C. Kelman and V. Lee Hamilton, *Crimes of Obedience: Toward a Social Psychology of Authority and Responsibility* (New Haven, CT: Yale University Press, 1989).

[99] International criminal justice seeks to counter such practices inter alia through principle of superior responsibility, which seeks to encourage responsible leadership in military and civilian structures. See Guénaël Mettraux, *The Law of Command Responsibility* (Oxford: Oxford University Press, 2009); Volker Nerlich, 'Superior Responsibility under Article 28 ICC Statute' (2007) 5 *JICJ* 665–82.

[100] See Emile Durkheim, 'The rules of sociological method' in Steven Lukes (ed.), *The Rules of Sociological Method and Selected Texts on Sociology and its Method* (New York, NY: The Free Press, 1982), 31–163, 102.

it. It seeks to build shared expectations about appropriate behaviour for actors with a given identity. The point is to express that behaviour that may 'conform with the politics of a criminal regime' can 'still be deviant from the standpoint of an international community'.[101]

Norm expression introduces a different discursive space for the messages sent through crimes. Symbolism and performance are part of this process. Legal regulations or judicial actions perform or enact certain kinds of understandings. They facilitate self-recognition, community recognition, or even a manifestation of order,[102] that is, the creation of a global society with belief in the protection of human rights and common values.

This trend to communicate legal and social meaning, enact order, or constitute greater normative consensus is reflected in many fields. For instance, the laws of war 'do not merely seek to regulate the battlefield'.[103] They are also 'part of its symbolic maintenance and even construction as a particular space defined by the norms that apply to it'.[104]

The regulation of international crimes is strongly linked to the establishment of order. It defines the subjects that are subject to this order and frames the response, including civic and state duties (e.g. prevention, obligation to investigate or prosecute), as well as public sanction. As Simon Chesterman has claimed, new categories of international crimes have emerged because they 'serve *a performative* function (as "theater") as retribution, as deterrence, and more generally as the cathartic experience of absolution that is needed to validate the order so grievously shattered by the violations prosecuted'.[105]

The form in which international criminal law reacts to violations and messages differs from case to case. It does not necessarily always correspond to the gravity or harmfulness of the crime. It is shaped by many extra-legal considerations, such as power, historical context or regional differences. For example, some of the judgments of the International Criminal Tribunal for the former Yugoslavia (ICTY) and the ICTY have been deemed to 'constitute' a new 'form of political recognition for women' because they recognized the harms experienced by women in wartime and treated them 'seriously by an international community that previously ignored them'.[106]

[101] Salif Nimage, 'An International Conscience Collective? A Durkheimian Analysis of International Criminal Law' (2007) 7 *International Criminal Law Review* 561–69, 593.

[102] Corrias and Gordon, 'Judging in the Name of Humanity' 102.

[103] Frédéric Mégret, 'War and the Vanishing Battlefield' (2011) 9 *Loyola University Chicago International Law Review* 131–55, 135.

[104] Ibid.

[105] Chesterman, 'Never Again' 323.

[106] Doris Buss, 'Performing Legal Order: Some Feminist Thoughts on International Criminal Law' (2011) 11 *International Criminal Law Review* 409–23, 414.

2.2 Expressivism and Norm Transformation

Legal responses (e.g. laws, regulations, judicial acts, or other communicative acts) are not always fully connected to the crime as a sociological phenomenon. The messages and signals expressed through crimes are often difficult to discern, may have different meanings, or require interpretation or translation. International norms and institutions read and interpret meanings of crimes and identify potential communicative responses.[107] For instance, law-makers or judges interpret social reality and give social and legal meaning to crimes. They have a dual role. They are some extent the 'narrators' of the messages of crimes that they critique and they build counter-narratives.

2.2.1 The diverse roles of legal agents

Norm expression attaches a new frame to the physiology of human conduct and crime, filters events, makes causal connection, creates new rubrics, or sets action and messages in a broader context. The nature and message of the crime are revealed through the eyes of the spectator and through the prism of different agents contributing to the process of normative expression. This process involves identity creation, norm consolidation, and transformation.[108]

French philosopher Jacques Derrida, who is most well-known for his work on deconstruction, recognized the performative function of law in his theory of law and justice.[109] He wrote in his essay on the 'Force of Law':

> The very emergence of justice and law, the instituting, founding and justifying moment that institutes law implies a performative force, that is to say always an interpretative force and a call to faith: not in the sense that law would be in the service of force, ... but rather in the sense of law that would maintain a more internal, more complex relation to what one calls force, power or violence.[110]

[107] Hanneke van Schooten, 'Towards a New Analytical Framework for Legal Communication' (2014) 27 *International Journal for the Semiotics of Law* 425–61, 433 ('A legal rule, in its most basic and essential form, is a sequence of linguistic signs expressing a meaning content—a mental construction, communicative in function, transferred from sender to receiver and aimed at an observable effect, that is, materialization in the factual world.').

[108] Mikkel J. Christensen, 'From Symbolic Surge to Closing Courts: The Transformation of International Criminal Justice and its Professional Practices' (2015) 34 *International Journal of Law, Crime and Justice*, 609–25.

[109] See Simon Glendinning, 'Derrida and the Philosophy of Law and Justice' (2016) 27 *Law Critique* 187–203.

[110] Jacques Derrida, 'Force of law: The mystical foundation of authority' in Jacques Derrida, *Acts of Religion* (ed., Gil Anidjar) (New York, NY: Routledge, 2002), 230–98, 241.

Derrida's logic applies to normative expression. It is inherently performative in nature. This interactive function of text and language has been recognized by the law and literature movement. It has acknowledged that '[l]aws oppress and protect; grant and deny rights; acknowledge or repudiate one's humanity, moral worth or entitlement; create spheres of violence or intimacy; and create feelings of misery, deprivation, safety or respect'.[111]

Norm expression can occur in different forms. It may be formal and evaluative, aimed at judging or condemning messages sent through crimes.[112] Expression can also be less formal. As proponents of New Haven School have acknowledged, 'speaking the law' may contribute to norm expression.[113] International criminal courts and tribunals are platforms of knowledge production. They not only interpret and apply legal rules in the narrow legal sense but 'communicate publically and ceremonially to society what it wants its norms and principles to be'.[114]

Many aspects of norm expression are shaped by a multiplicity of voices and agents, including Judges, the Prosecution, the Registry, other participants in legal processes, or NGOs. Their statements not only gain weight due to their substantive content but also 'because they are 'uttered in a specific legal context' by actors that enjoy 'a special status assigned by law'.[115] Anette Bringedal Houge has coined the term 'narrative expressivism' to reflect the close connection between legal expression and performance. It captures a type of norm expression in international criminal justice 'that emphasizes its *stories*, not its truths, its *understandings*, not its punishments, its descriptions and explanations, not its normative evaluation and judgment'.[116]

These dimensions are often sidelined in mainstream legal analysis since are they considered to be 'alien' to the objectivity and formality of the legal process. But they are part and parcel of legal discourse and the workings methods of international criminal justice. They are *inter alia* reflected in the contextual information of situations and cases in legal proceedings, *obiter dicta* in decisions, the use of individual

[111] Robin West, 'Communities, Texts, and Law: Reflections on the Law and Literature Movement' (1998) 1 *Yale Journal of Law & the Humanities* 129–56, 154.

[112] For example, former ICJ judge Manfred Lachs acknowledged the inherently expressive nature of judgments in relation to dispute settlement: '[Y]ou do not only decide the dispute between state A and state B, you perform an educational function. You indicate to states A and B how their dispute should be solved, but you also give a wider background to all nations so that similar issues, or related issues, should be solved in a similar way.' See Garry Sturgess and Philip Chubb, *Judging the World: Law and Politics in the World's Leading Courts* (Sydney: Butterworths, 1988), 89

[113] Michael Reisman, 'International Lawmaking: A Process of Communication (1981) 75 *American Society of International Law Proceedings* 101–20.

[114] See Beatrice de Graaf, 'Terrorists on Trial: A Performative Perspective', Expert Paper, 30 March 2011, 1, 5, at https://www.icct.nl/download/file/ICCT-de-Graaf-EM-Paper-Terrorism-Trials-as-Theatre.pdf.

[115] See Wouter Werner, 'What's Going On? Reflections on Kratochwil's Concept of Law' (2016) 44 *Millennium: Journal of International Studies* 258–68, 266.

[116] Houge, 'Narrative Expressivism' 284.

opinions as frames of reference,[117] moral expressions of outrage, non-judicial forms of communication (e.g. press releases, statements), or governance processes that contribute to the formation of international criminal justice as a field (e.g. treaty negotiations, decision-making processes in international organizations, etc.). Such practices 'visualize' and 'produce' new spaces and intersubjectivities that are conducive to normative transformation.[118] They convey meanings of violation, respect, or compassion.

Law and literature scholarship has opened new pathways for the understanding of expressivism through its analysis of law as a form of rhetoric and narration.[119] It emerged in the 1970s,[120] partly in response to rational choices approaches in law and economics. James Boyd White, one of the founding figures of the law and literature movement, developed a performative theory of legal rhetoric in his classic work, 'The Legal Imagination'.[121] He argued that law is an art of 'speaking and writing', geared at 'establishing meaning and constituting community in language'.[122] According to this theory, a 'law is . . . always more than just a text. It is also, potentially, a communicative and interactive tool of violence, violation, compassion, nurturance or respect.'[123]

Narrative techniques involve the ordering of the underlying material in a specific way or sequence, and the presentation of content in the form of a 'coherent story'.[124] They also deploy rhetorical features.

International criminal justice relies heavily on rhetorical strategies to appeal not only to immediate perpetrators and victims but also a broader target audience. Legal acts and decisions have used three classical pillars of Aristotle's rhetoric (*logos, ethos*, and *pathos*),[125] in order to persuade actual or imagined audiences.[126] *Logos* is connected to logic and reason. It is inherent in legal reasoning

[117] On the ICJ, see Geoff Gordon, 'Innate Cosmopolitan Dialectics at the ICJ: Changing Perceptions of International Community, the Role of the Court, and the Legacy of Judge Álvarez' (2014) 27 *LJIL* 309–30.

[118] See Nesam McMillan, 'Imagining the International: The Constitution of International as a Site of Crime, Justice and Community' (2016) 25 *Social & Legal Studies* 163–80, 167.

[119] For a survey, see Andrea Bianchi, *International Law Theories* (Oxford: Oxford University Press, 2016) 287–310.

[120] See Peter Brooks and Paul Gewirtz, *Law's Stories: Narrative and Rhetoric in the Law* (New Haven, CT: Yale University Press, 1996); Monika Fludernik, 'A Narratology of the Law? Narratives in Legal Discourse' (2014) 1 *Critical Analysis of Law: Critical Analysis of Law and the New Interdisciplinarity* 87–109.

[121] See James Boyd White, *The Legal Imagination: Abridged Edition* (Chicago, IL: University of Chicago Press, [1973] 1985), xiii.

[122] James Boyd White, *When Words Lose Their Meaning* (Chicago, IL: University of Chicago Press, 1984), xi.

[123] Robin West, 'Community, Texts, and the Law' 129, 154.

[124] See Lawrence Stone, 'The Revival of Narrative: Reflections on a New Old History' (179) 85 *Past & Present* 3–24.

[125] On Aristotle and speech, see also Wilson, *Incitement on Trial* 225–7.

[126] See Fabiana Pinho, 'On logos, pathos and ethos in judicial argumentation' in Liesbeth Huppes-Cluysenaer and Nuno M.M.S. Coelho (eds), *Aristotle on Emotions in Law and Politics* (Berlin: Springer, 2018), 133–43.

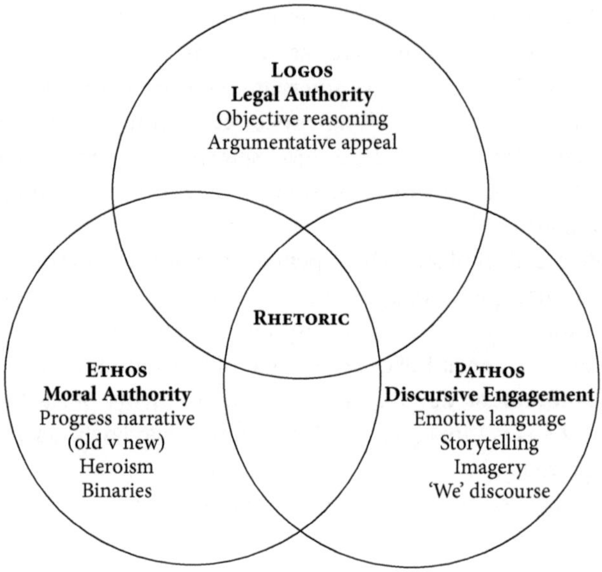

Figure 8 Expressivist rhetoric

and argumentation. *Ethos* relies on ethical appeal, including means to enhance the credibility of the speaker in the eyes of the audience. *Pathos* involves emotional appeal. It seeks to create an affective bond with the audience.[127]

These three modes of the rhetoric persuasion are part and parcel of normative expressivism, the broadcasting of 'messages and norms' in order to 'construct a consensus across a given society'.[128]

Legal argument is grounded in objective reasoning, that is, its embedding in a normative framework (*logos*). However, the discourse involves many rhetorical features aimed at enhancing the legitimacy of the 'speaker' (*ethos*). This includes arguments bolstering moral authority (e.g. reputational gains, alignment with socially constructed values), the portrayal of international criminal justice as a history of progress, notions of heroism, or strategies countering victimization. It is full of *pathos* and seeks to mobilize emotional support. This is *inter alia* reflected in use of emotive language, reliance on emotionally charged images and techniques of storytelling which frame legal reasoning in an appealing storyline in order to make it more attractive to audiences.

[127] On audience and persuasion, see Peter Goodrich, 'Rhetoric as Jurisprudence: An Introduction to the Politics of Legal Language' (1984) 4 *Oxford Journal of Legal Studies* 88–122, 95–96.

[128] See Birju Kotecha, 'The Art of Rhetoric: Perceptions of the International Criminal Court and Legalism' (2018) *LJIL* 939–62, 944

Norm expression is related to all stages of the 'norm cycle'. It has been used to describe or affirm a state of affairs ('norm affirmation'), institute a new *status quo* through juridical expression ('norm projection'), or to commit others do so something (internalization).

The first two types ('norm affirmation' and 'projection') are most expressive in nature, that is, they are aimed at expressing certain normative standards that individuals and states should abide by in response to criminality. They produce certain ideals, convey empathy or blame, promote adherence to practices, or seek to build a new normative community. The last shares broader communicative features. It goes beyond normative production by the 'speaker', involves discourse with subjects,[129] and relies on the participation of affected subjects. It remains critically underdeveloped.

2.2.2 Techniques of norm affirmation

Expressive norm affirmation is a response to the idea that crimes affect individuals as fellow citizens or as part of a global community. Global prohibition regimes emerged partly because they 'give force and symbolic representation to the moral values, beliefs and prejudices of those who make the laws'.[130] International criminal courts and tribunals have used expressive norm affirmation 'because it satisfies the need to send a message to those whose lives have been violated by international crimes, signal the importance of the human rights and humanity of the victims, and can increase the resonance and perhaps even the legitimacy of international justice'.[131]

2.2.2.1 Structural parameters

The process of normative expression is closely related to expressions of morality and the ethics of justice (*ethos*). International criminal justice is not only composed of positive rules. Its alleged vocation goes much further. It seeks 'to represent and enact humanity's, or the international community's, rejection of and opposition to inhumanity, suffering and injustice'.[132]

[129] On communication in the domestic context, see Wibren Van der Burg, 'The Expressive and Communicative Functions of Law, Especially with Regard to Moral Issues' (2001) 20 *Law and Philosophy* 31–59, 48–50.

[130] Ethan Nadelman 'Global Prohibition Regimes: The Evolution of Norms in International Society' (2009) 44 *International Organization* 479–526, 481

[131] Aloisi and Meernik, *Judgment Day* 119–20. On the judicial function and expressivism, see also Joseph Powderly, *Judges and the Making of International Criminal Law* (Leiden: Martinus Nijhoff, 2020) 405–9.

[132] See McMillan, 'Imagining the International' 171.

Expressive practices focus strongly on the affirmation of a global humanity.[133] They produce, imagine, and shape the contours of a global humanity 'through the performative declaration of certain acts' as crimes against humanity or other international crimes and 'the framing of the pursuit of accountability for such acts'.[134]

The strong turn to *ethos* as a rhetorical technique is partly linked to the structure of international criminal law. Unlike in domestic law, where many crimes are codified or part of centuries of judicial practice, the notion of a crime is less settled in international criminal law. Some legal space for normative expression is provided by the relaxed framing of the *nullum crimen sine lege* principle in relation to international crimes.[135] It allows trial of crimes that are criminalized under the 'general principles of law recognized by the community of nations'.[136] Judges made clear that it does not prevent courts 'from interpreting and clarifying the elements of a particular crime'.[137]

Communicative space for norm affirmation is offered by open legal constructs. A good example is the famous Martens Clause, contained in the Preamble of the 1899 Hague Convention with respect to the laws and customs of war on land, which derives protection from the 'laws of humanity and the dictates of public conscience'.[138] The clause provides a vehicle for humanitarian expressivism and norm affirmation. It suggests that the laws of armed conflict 'do not simply provide a positive legal code' but also 'a moral code'.[139] It provides a 'bridge' between *lex lata* and 'dictates of public conscience'.[140] As Judge Shahabuddeen put in its dissenting opinion in the *Advisory Opinion on Nuclear Weapons:*

> The Martens Clause provided authority for treating the principles of humanity and the dictates of public conscience as principles of international law, leaving the precise content of the standard implied by these principles of international law to be ascertained in the light of changing conditions, inclusive of changes in the means and methods of warfare and the outlook and tolerance levels of the international community.[141]

[133] Mikkel Jarle Christensen, 'The Emerging Sociology of International Criminal Courts: Between Global Restructurings and Scientific Innovations' (2015) 63 *Current Sociology Review*, 837–41.
[134] McMillan, 'Imagining the International' 167.
[135] Mohamed Shahabuddeen, 'Does the Principle of Legality Stand in the Way of Progressive Development of Law?' (2004) 2 *JICJ* 1007–17.
[136] Article 15 (2) ICCPR.
[137] *Prosecutor v. Milutinovic*, Decision on Motion Challenging Jurisdiction, No. IT-99-37-AR72, 21 May 2003, para. 38.
[138] See generally Theodor Meron, 'The Martens Clause, Principles of Humanity, and Dictates of Public Conscience' (2000) 94 *AJIL* 78–89.
[139] See Rupert Ticehurst, 'The Martens Clause and the Laws of Armed Conflict' (1997) 317 *International Review of the Red Cross* 125–34, 130.
[140] Jared Wessel, 'Judicial Policy-Making at the International Criminal Court: An Institutional Guide to Analyzing International Adjudication' (2006) 44 *Columbia Journal of Transnational Law* 377–452, 390.
[141] ICJ, *Legality of the Threat or Use of Nuclear Weapons*, Advisory Opinion, 8 July 1996, Dissenting Opinion of Judge Shahabuddeen, 1996 ICJ Reports, 226, 406.

Although there are different interpretations[142] as to what extent the clause provides an interpretive device or a source of law (e.g. a general principle),[143] it specifies at a minimum that where a rule 'is not sufficiently rigorous or precise', it must be 'defined with reference to those principles and dictates'.[144] The natural law foundations of the clause ('principles of humanity', 'dictates of public conscience') facilitated the emergence of the notion of 'crimes against humanity'[145] and served as an incentive for the development of international law.[146]

The reference to 'public conscience'[147] has strong synergies with Durkheim's concept of 'collective conscience'. It embraces the idea that public conscience comes before positive law and that legal expression may convey a collective sense of what is right or wrong. It suggests that states cannot behave 'wholly regardless of public and world opinion'.[148] It is reflected in other instruments, such as the Universal Declaration of Human Rights ('conscience of mankind'), weapons conventions,[149] and the preamble of the ICC Statute which refers to the 'conscience of humanity'. The concept provides a tool for expressivist vocabulary. International institutions have used it to present themselves as 'authorized interpreters of collective sentiments'.[150] They have invoked the concept to speak on behalf of humanity, promote the humanitarian foundations of international humanitarian law, and develop international criminal justice. A good example is the *Furundžija* judgment, a landmark decision in which the ICTY developed the definition of rape as a weapon of war on 'Human Rights Day', based on general principles of international law. It noted:

> The general principle of respect for human dignity is the basic underpinning and indeed the very raison d'être of international humanitarian law and human rights

[142] Michael Salter, 'Reinterpreting Competing Interpretations of the Scope and Potential of the Martens Clause' (2012) 17 *Journal of Conflict & Security Law* 403–37.

[143] See ICTY, *Prosecutor v. Martić*, Review of the Indictment Pursuant to Rule 61, ICTY-95-11-PT, 13 March 1996, para. 13 ('elementary considerations of humanity . . . constitute the foundations of the entire body of international humanitarian law applicable to all armed conflict').

[144] *Prosecutor v. Kupreskić et al.*, Judgment, IT-95-16-T, 14 January 2000, para. 525 (Kupreskić Trial Judgment).

[145] Kerstin von Lingen, 'Fulfilling the Martens clause: debating crimes against humanity, 1899–1945' in Fabian Klose and Mirjam Thulin (eds), *Humanity: A History of European Concepts in Practice from the 16th Century to the Present* (Göttingen: Vandenhoeck & Ruprecht, 2016), 187–208.

[146] Antonio Cassese, 'The Martens Clause: Half a Loaf or Simply Pie in the Sky?' (2000) 11 *EJIL* 187–216.

[147] Michel Veuthey, 'Public Conscience in International Humanitarian Action' (2003) 22 *Refugee Survey Quarterly* 198–201.

[148] Meron, 'The Martens Clause' 85.

[149] For example, Convention on Prohibitions or Restrictions on the Use of Certain Conventional Weapons Which May be Deemed to be Excessively Injurious or to Have Indiscriminate Effects, Geneva, 10 October 1980, UNTS Vol. 1342, p. 137; Convention on the Prohibition of the Use, Stockpiling, Production and Transfer of Anti-Personnel Mines and on their Destruction, 18 September 1997, UNTS Vol. 2056, p. 211.

[150] See Immi Tallgren, 'The Durkheimian Spell of International Criminal Law?' (2013) 71 *Revue interdisciplinaire d'études juridiques* 137–69, 33.

> law; indeed in modern times it has become of such paramount importance as to permeate the whole body of international law. This principle is intended to shield human beings from outrages upon their personal dignity, whether such outrages are carried out by unlawfully attacking the body or by humiliating and debasing the honour, the self-respect or the mental well-being of a person.[151]

The affirmation of the existence of international crimes has changed the perception of the role of the state in international affairs. Sovereignty has, to some extent, become a *bête-noire* in and through international criminal law.[152] In the context of international criminal law, the image of the state is often loaded with negative connotations. Representations are shaped by shadows of the Holocaust. The 'state' is often presented as a hierarchical unitary entity or as a bureaucracy that hides behind the notion of sovereignty to evade obligations. It is portrayed as a non-accountable human rights offender that needs to be tamed by law. For instance, in *Kanyabashi*, the ICTR went back to statements in the trial of Hans Frank in 1946 to disregard sovereignty claims. It compared 'the principle of State sovereignty' to a 'mask' that protects defendants. Once 'this mask removed, the man's responsibility reappears'.[153]

Many normative changes in international law are related to imagery or symbolic language.[154] Storytelling plays a central role in norm affirmation. Generally, law tends to present itself as 'neutral and dispassionately analytical'.[155] But norm affirmation is conveyed through narration, involving a speaker and an audience, a plot ordering and facts and law, turn-taking, and persuasion.[156] Legal concepts are often connected to narratives. Narratives involve a narrator, an audience, and a specific purpose. In legal discourse, they 'minimally include agents with human-like subjectivity, involve changes or a description of human-like experience, and

[151] *Prosecutor v. Furundžija*, Judgment, IT-95-17/1-T, 10 December 1998, para. 183 (*Furundžija* Trial Judgment).

[152] See Robert Cryer, 'International Criminal Law vs State Sovereignty: Another Round?' (2005) 16 *EJIL* 979–1000, 981.

[153] *Prosecutor v. Kanyabashi*, Decision on Defence Motion on Jurisdiction, ICTR-96-15-T, 18 June 1997, para. 34.

[154] Maks Del Mar, 'Metaphor in International Law: Language, Imagination and Normative Inquiry' (2017) 86 *Nordic Journal of International Law* 170–95.

[155] A good illustration is the 1995 *Tadić* Interlocutory Appeal decision. The Appeals Chamber noted: 'one cannot but rejoice at the thought that, universal jurisdiction being nowadays acknowledged in the case of international crimes, a person suspected of such offences may finally be brought before an international judicial body for a dispassionate consideration of his indictment by impartial, independent and disinterested judges coming, as it happens here, from all continents of the world'. See ICTY, *Prosecutor v. Tadić*, Decision on the Defence Motion for Interlocutory Appeal on Jurisdiction, IT-94-AR72, 2 October 1995, para. 62 (*Tadić* Interlocutory Appeal 1995). See also Richard Delgado, 'Storytelling for Oppositionists and Others: A Plea for Narrative' (1989) 87 *Michigan Law Review* 2411–41, 2440.

[156] Meir Sternberg, 'If-plots: Narrativity and the law-code' in John Pier and José Angel García Landa (eds), *Theorizing Narrativity* (Berlin: De Gruyter, 2008), 29–108, 38 ('law … incorporates the narrativities of repetition and quotation among its makings, workings, aids to processing and understanding').

take place in some identifiable space and time'.[157] They contain stories (e.g. about facts or sequence of events) and discourse about the context through which a legal rule is to be seen.[158]

As Andrea Bianchi has noted, storytelling is at the heart of the legal profession. It is 'the medium by which we perform our profession's multifarious tasks, and the key to our success, or lack thereof, in the discipline'.[159]

International criminal justice is a prime illustration of this interconnectivity. It constantly uses narratives that seek to represent and form international law. These narratives affect subjectivities. They express moral principles or frame stories about the impact of legal norms and institutions that affect others as subjects. The choice of semantics and text itself has a 'community-building' function in the Durkheimian sense.[160] It is meant to draw in the reader and to persuade the target audience, in order to create a shared space between author, reader and intended audience. It creates a certain culture in relation to the use of legal argument. It defines specific roles and relations and establishes means and methods of discourse. In this way, it creates a 'rhetorical community over time'.[161]

The image of 'piercing the veil' is one of the best illustrations of norm expression. It is reflected in the *Nuremberg* dictum, according to which 'crimes against international law are committed by men, not by abstract entities'.[162] It shaped the individualist orientation of criminal law. It branded a new strand of thought according to which international law is said to pierce 'the veil of national sovereignty'.[163] International criminal law was viewed as a 'shield' of protection against state arbitrariness. The image framed a 'cult of the individual'.[164] The individual

[157] See Greta Olsen, 'On narrating and troping the law: the conjoined use of narrative and metaphor in legal discourse' in Michael Hanne and Robert Weisberg (eds), *Narrative and Metaphor in the Law* (Cambridge: Cambridge University Press, 2018), 19–36, 23.

[158] Bernard S. Jackson, *Law, Fact and Narrative Coherence* (Merseyside: Deborah Charles Publications, 1988).

[159] Andrea Bianchi, 'International Adjudication, Rhetoric and Storytelling' (2018) 9 *Journal of International Dispute Settlement* 28–44, 33.

[160] West, 'Community, Texts, and the Law' 131.

[161] James Boyd White, 'Law as Language: Reading Law and Reading Literature' (1981–82) 60 *Texas Law Review* 415–45, 441.

[162] Trial of the Major War Criminals before the International Military Tribunal, vol. I, Nürnberg 1947, 223 in 41 *AJIL* 221. For a critique, see Gerry Simpson, 'Men and abstract entities: Individual responsibility and collective guilt in international criminal law' in André Nollkaemper and Harmen van der Wilt (eds), *System Criminality in International Law* (Cambridge: Cambridge University Press, 2009), 69–100.

[163] See, for example, Henry T. King Jr, 'The Meaning of Nuremberg' (1998) 30 *Case Western Reserve Journal of International Law* 143–8, 147; Leora Bilsky, 'Hannah Arendt's judgement of bureaucracy' in Marco Goldoni and Christopher McCorkindale (eds), *Hannah Arendt and the Law* (Oxford: Hart Publishing, 2012), 271–90, 280; Luban, 'Theory of Crimes Against Humanity' 117 ('pierce the veil of sovereignty through international criminal law').

[164] Emile Durkheim, *Professional Ethics and Civic Morals*, trans. C Brookfield (London: Routledge & Kegan Paul, 1957) 54, 69–70, 172. See Nimaga, 'An International Conscience Collective' 618 ('The emergence of international criminal law pointed towards a new stage in the development of criminal law, one based on the drive towards internationalisation inherent in the cult of the individual.').

came to be seen as an 'end' in itself, and the state as a means to foster human interests.[165]

This development is reflected in the seminal *Tadić* Interlocutory Appeal decision. It is a paradigm example of normative expressivism and 'post-national narratives'. The ICTY contrasted the idea of sovereignty with human rights protection, as if the two were opposite poles, with one being a reminiscent of the past and the other a guideline for the future.[166] It relied on changing conceptions of sovereignty to defend the idea of primacy over domestic jurisdiction. It stated in dramatic terms:

> It would be a travesty of law and a betrayal of the universal need for justice, should the concept of State sovereignty be allowed to be raised successfully against human rights. Borders should not be considered as a shield against the reach of the law and as a protection for those who trample underfoot the most elementary rights of humanity.[167]

Thus language plays with the image of the morally conscientious reader who cannot but consent with the morality of argument.

2.2.2.2 Norm affirmation and storytelling

Norm expression has underpinned the genesis of most core crimes as international crimes. Statutes, legal decisions, and doctrines have been used in a narrative fashion, namely to actively support norm affirmation. Many foundational instruments or judgments are shaped by legal argumentation and rhetoric features that seek to gain 'buy in' from audiences and alter behaviour.[168]

2.2.2.2.1 Peace narratives underlying the crime of aggression

The very origins of the crime of aggression were strongly grounded in expressive norm affirmation.[169] The Nuremberg and Tokyo judgments were counter-performances to the 'evils' of the Second World War. The formal story behind the turn to criminal law was not only one of justice but also one of appeasement. The events of the Holocaust were viewed through the lens of aggressive war. For instance, Robert Jackson argued in his opening address that 'getting rid of the

[165] See Anne Peters, *Beyond Human Rights: The Legal Status of the Individual in Public International Law* (Cambridge: Cambridge University Press, 2016), 115–65.
[166] 1995 *Tadić* Interlocutory Appeal, para. 97.
[167] Ibid., para. 58.
[168] Darryl Robinson and Gillian MacNeil, 'The Tribunals and the Renaissance of International Criminal Law: Three Themes' (2016) 110 *AJIL* 191–211.
[169] See also Tom Dannenbaum, *The Crime of Aggression, Humanity, and the Soldier* (Cambridge: Cambridge University Press, 2018) 55–7.

influence of free labor, the churches, and the Jews was to clear their obstruction to the precipitation of aggressive war'.[170]

International criminal justice was presented as a 'peace' project.[171] Aggression was expressly qualified a crime against peace. Charges were constructed around major episodes of war. The relaxed approach towards the *nullum crimen sine lege* principle (i.e. its characterization as a mere 'principle of justice') allowed it to combine moral condemnation with expressive norm affirmation in order to qualify the Nuremberg Charter as an 'expression of International Law existing at the time of its creation'.[172] The reasoning was built on the assumption that 'substantive provisions of international criminal law existed at the level of an international conscience collective, albeit in unconscious form'.[173] The Nuremberg judgment made express reference to the 'the conscience of the world' in order to justify that 'resort to a war of aggression is not merely illegal, but is criminal'.[174] Nuremberg used a specific narrative to justify this claim. It presented war as an act of institutional deviance and an attack on the sanctity of treaties. The judgment argued that the 'solemn renunciation of war as an instrument of national Policy' in the Briand–Kellogg Pact 'necessarily involve[d] the proposition that such a war is illegal in International Law and that those who plan and wage such a war, with its inevitable and terrible consequences, are committing a crime in so doing'.[175]

It qualified aggressive war as an attack on a 'series of pacts and treaties', including the commitment to peaceful settlement of disputes under the Covenant of the League of Nations, which had reaffirmed in a resolution in 1927 that a 'war of aggression can never serve as a means of settling international disputes, and is, in consequence, an international crime'.[176]

The International Military Tribunal (IMT) took a shortcut to arrive at a morally convenient solution. It used an *a fortiori* argument to make a finding on illegality by arguing that 'those who wage aggressive war are doing that which is equally illegal, and of much greater moment than a breach of one of the rules of the Hague Convention'.[177]

It relied on the image of aggression as 'supreme international crime' that contains 'within itself the accumulated evil of the whole' in order to mark a transition from the just war tradition to a legal prohibition of warfare—a *jus contra bellum*.

[170] See Nazi Conspiracy & Aggression, Volume I, Chapter VII, Office of the United States Chief Counsel for Prosecution of Axis Criminality (Washington, DC: United States Government Printing Office, 1946), 144.
[171] Mégret, 'International Criminal Justice as a Peace Project' 835–58.
[172] Trial of the Major War Criminals before the International Military Tribunal, vol. I, 218.
[173] Nimaga, 'An International Conscience Collective' 604.
[174] Trial of the Major War Criminals before the International Military Tribunal, vol. I, 222.
[175] Ibid., 220.
[176] Ibid., 222.
[177] Ibid., 221.

The Tokyo Tribunal was more divided on the peace narrative.[178] Judge Röling argued in his dissent that aggression is comparable to a political crime and that the 'dominant principle in the crime against peace is the dangerous character of the individual'.[179] He submitted that it did not constitute a 'true crime before and in the beginning of this war', but might 'compel the nations to take the legal steps to achieve the maintenance of peace' in the future.[180] Judge Pal developed a fundamentally different narrative. He claimed that international law must first change its *status quo*, that is, establish 'rules effecting peaceful changes' and target 'the actual plague of imperialism' before the 'introduction of criminal responsibility' for warfare.[181] Otherwise, it 'would be nothing but 'an ideological cloak, intended to disguise the vested interests or the interstate sphere and to serve as first-line for their defense'.[182]

Pal's argument made it clear that the Nuremberg peace narrative and its claim of global conscience is vulnerable to critique since it silences the diversity of opinion and entrenches existing structural inequalities in the international legal system.

2.2.2.2.2 Changing narratives of genocide

The affirmation of crimes like genocide and crimes against humanity in the aftermath of the Second World War gave a new meaning to the idea of abuse of state power. The crimes were theorized as a betrayal of trust and obligations by a state towards its own population. David Luban has captured this image most vividly when arguing that 'crimes against humanity are not just horrible crimes' but 'crimes of politics gone cancerous'.[183]

Norm expression has been used as an instrument to make these crimes 'speakable'[184] and to affirm their existence in law. Genocide is a compelling example. Genocide carries a greater stigmatizing effect than a crime such as extermination, which is part of crimes against humanity. The genesis of crime is fuelled by expressivist language.[185] General Assembly (GA) Resolution 96(1), adopted immediately after confirmation of the principles of international law embraced by the Nuremberg Charter and judgment, affirmed that 'genocide is a crime under

[178] See Barrie Sander, 'The Method is the Message: Law, Narrative Authority and Historical Contestation in International Criminal Courts', (2018) 19 *Melbourne Journal of International Law* 299–334, 23.

[179] International Military Tribunal for the Far East (IMTFE), Judgment, Opinion Justice Röling, 12 November 1948, 49, at https://www.legal-tools.org/doc/fb16ff/pdf/.

[180] Ibid., 45.

[181] IMTFE Judgment, Dissentient Judgment of Justice Pal, 239, at https://www.legal-tools.org/doc/b0d708/pdf/.

[182] Ibid., 240–1.

[183] Luban, 'Theory of Crimes against Humanity' 117.

[184] *Prosecutor v. Krajisnik*, Judgment, IT-00–39-T, 27 September 2006, para. 1146 ('No sentence, however harsh, will never be able to rectify the wrongs, and will be able to soothe only to a limited extent the suffering of the victims, their feelings of deprivation, anguish, and hopelessness.').

[185] Amann, 'Group Mentality, Expressivism and Genocide' 99.

international law which the *civilized world* condemns'.[186] It justified its criminalization by the fact that it denies the 'right of existence of entire human groups' and 'shocks the conscience of mankind'.[187]

The preamble of the 1948 Genocide Convention reads like an implicit recognition of historical failure. It recognizes that 'genocide has inflicted great losses on humanity' at 'all periods of history' and expresses a determination to 'liberate mankind from such an odious scourge'.[188] This language provided moral comfort for legal condemnation. The concept of genocide reflected in the Convention was considerably narrower than initially imagined by Lemkin. It was more closely related to the idea of physical-biological destruction, rather than destruction of group identity. For a long time, scholars claimed that it marked more a 'symbolic' act than a 'legislative' instrument.[189]

In *Krstić*, the first genocide conviction of the ICTY in relation to Srebrenica, the tribunal openly struggled with 'the indulgence of expressing how it feels about what happened in Srebrenica'.[190] The Appeals Chamber stated that 'the law must not shy away from referring to the crime committed by its proper name ... genocide'.[191]It singled out the 'special condemnation' of genocide. It held:

> The crime is horrific in its scope; its perpetrators identify entire human groups for extinction. Those who devise and implement genocide seek to deprive humanity of the manifold richness its nationalities, races, ethnicities and religions provide. This is a crime against all of humankind, its harm being felt not only by the group targeted for destruction, but by all of humanity.[192]

The judgment gave a partly new meaning to genocide in legal terms. It confirmed that genocide is not a 'game of numbers' but can be committed against a part of the protected group, even in small territorial enclaves—something that William Schabas has called 'localized genocide'.[193]

Narrative expressivism became a means to preserve facts for posterity. The Trial Chamber expressly used the words of Nuremberg Prosecutor Telford Taylor in order to stress the importance of the judgments to document the violations 'in detail'. It insisted that it is 'important that these incredible events be established by

186 See GA Resolution 96 (I) of 11 December 1946, para. 1.

187 Ibid., preamble.

188 Genocide Convention Preamble.

189 Jack Nusan Porter, 'What is genocide? Notes towards a definition' in Jack Nusan Porter (ed.), *Genocide and Human Rights: A Global Anthology* (Lanham, MD: University Press of America 1982) 2–33, 7.

190 *Prosecutor v. Krstić*, Judgment, IT-98-33-T, 2 August 2001, para. 2 (*Krstić* Trial Judgment).

191 *Prosecutor v. Krstić*, IT-98-33-A, Judgment, 19 April 2004, para. 37 (*Krstić* Appeal Judgment)

192 Ibid., para. 36.

193 William Schabas, 'Was Genocide Committed in Bosnia and Herzegovina? First Judgments of the International Criminal Tribunal for the Former Yugoslavia Schabas' (2001) *25 Fordham International Law Journal* 23–53, 42.

clear and public proof so that no one can ever doubt that they were fact and not fable'.[194] It stated that 'no words of comment can lay bare the saga of Srebrenica more graphically than a plain narrative of the events themselves'.[195]

2.2.2.2.3 *The malleable foundations of crimes against humanity and sexual and gender-based violence*

The concept of crimes against humanity emerged largely through expressive norm affirmation.[196] As Salif Nimaga has noted, the very concept in itself is one of the clearest illustrations of the Durkheimian heritage in international criminal law. It 'constitutes the paradigmatic case of the protection of values that result from the cult of the individual as it is precisely the aspect of the individual shared with all of humankind that is protected here'.[197]

The notion developed without treaty foundation and without a clear articulation of the underlying interests protected. It had a gap-filling function. The notion was used to bridge gaps left by the traditional laws of war.[198] The naissance of the term may be traced back to 1915,[199] but it gained relevance as legal concept as a reaction to new dimensions of 'state criminality' in the aftermath of the Second World War.[200] The term was coined by a hub of different lawyers (e.g. Czech jurist Bohuslav Ecer, Egon Schwelb) in the United Nations War Crimes Commission (UNWCC) in 1944. As Karin van Lingen has noted, it was essentially '[e]xiled lawyers and Jewish emigrés' who 'changed the perception of international law into a protector, as they put more weight on the experience of violence and victim's voices than on the earlier approach of protecting states from violence'.[201]

194 *Krstić* Trial Judgment, para. 95.

195 *Krstić* Trial Judgment, para. 2.

196 See generally Kerstin von Lingen, 'Defining crimes against humanity: The contribution of the United Nations War Crimes Commission to international criminal law, 1944–1947' in Morten Bergsmo, Wui Ling Cheah, Ping Yi (eds), *Historical Origins of International Criminal Law* (Brussels: Torkel Opsahl Academic EPublisher, 2014), 475–506; Beth van Schaack, 'The Definition of Crimes against Humanity: Resolving the Incoherence' (1998–1989) 37 *Columbia Journal of Transnational Law* 787–850; Lindsay Moir, 'Crimes Against Humanity in Historical Perspective' (2006) 3 *New Zealand Yearbook of International Law* 101–30.

197 Nimaga, 'An International Conscience Collective' 594–5.

198 See Schwelb, 'Crimes against Humanity' 206.

199 A famous declaration made by France, the United Kingdom, and Russia in 1915 condemned Armenian atrocities as 'crimes against humanity and civilization'. See Michelle Tusan, '"Crimes against Humanity": Human Rights, the British Empire and the Origins of the Response to the Armenian Genocide' (2014) 119 *American Historical Review* 47–77.

200 See ICC, PTC I, Decision Pursuant to Article 15 of the Rome Statute on the Authorization of an Investigation into the Situation in the Republic of Kenya, ICC-01/09-19, 31 March 2010 (Kenya Authorization Decision), Dissenting Opinion Judge Kaul, para. 61 (the '[D]rafters of the London Conference ... recognized in 1945 that the commission of crimes against civilian populations according to a State policy necessitated the adoption of crimes against humanity as a new category of crimes under international law. The intolerable risks and threats for humankind emanating from such State policy required international criminalization and international enforcement.').

201 Kerstin von Lingen, 'Legal Flows: Exiled Lawyers' Contribution towards the Concept of "Crimes against Humanity"' (2018) *Modern Intellectual History* 1–19, 18.

The term was allegedly suggested by Hersch Lauterpacht to Robert Jackson.[202] In the UNWCC, Ecer even took the position that crimes against humanity should be considered as the most important category crime, since they are 'the most real cause of all the other crimes ... the malum in se'.[203] The Nuremberg Charter used the term for the first time in the technical use. Jackson tried to ground it in existing international principles. He noted:

> The application of this law may be novel because the scope of the Nazi activity has been broad and ruthless without precedent. The basic principles to be applied, however, are not novel and all that is needed is a wise application of those principles on a sufficiently comprehensive scale to meet the situation. International law must develop to meet the needs of the times just as the common law has grown, not by enunciating new principles but by adapting old ones.[204]

Nuremberg linked crimes against humanity to warfare in order to bring them within accepted categories of law. The Nuremberg Tribunal justified crimes against humanity essentially by the idea that they were an instrument of warfare. It stated:

> [F]rom the beginning of the war in 1939 war crimes were committed on a vast scale, which were also crimes against humanity; and insofar as the inhumane acts charged in the Indictment, and committed after the beginning of the war, did not constitute war crimes, they were all committed in execution of, or in connection with, the aggressive war, and therefore constituted crimes against humanity.[205]

The Nuremberg definition reduced the scope of crimes against humanity in order to constrain its articulation as a new category of crime. It related the concept of crimes against humanity to peace and security considerations.[206] However, the historical significance of the concept went far beyond this. The very notion embodied an entirely new strand of accountability. It criminalized a 'horrific novelty of the twentieth century', namely crimes by a state against its own people.[207] At the ICC, the 'abuse' argument was expressly invoked to justify ICC authority to adjudicate crimes against humanity.[208]

[202] William Schabas, *Unimaginable Atrocities: Justice, Politics, and Rights at the War Crimes Tribunals* (Oxford: Oxford University Press, 2012), 51.

[203] Von Lingen, 'Defining Crimes against Humanity' 492.

[204] Report of Robert H. Jackson, United States Representative to the International Conference on Military Trials, London 1945, 28, 37.

[205] Trial of the Major War Criminals before the International Military Tribunal, vol. I, 254–5.

[206] Robert Dubler, 'What's in a Name: A Theory of Crimes against Humanity' (2008) 15 *Australian International Law Journal* 85–107, 91–2.

[207] Luban, 'Theory Crimes against Humanity' 94.

[208] Judge Kaul stated: 'If leaders of a State who normally have the duty to uphold the rule of law and to respect human rights engage in a policy of violent attacks against a civilian population, it is the community of States which must intervene and prevent, control and repress this threat to the peace,

The notion of crimes against humanity captures a great variety of individual crimes. Many of them are a reaction to changing patterns of violence. The recognition of the crime of apartheid as crime against humanity is a paradigm example of affirmative norm expression. Its history bears some resemblance to genocide.[209] It is a reaction to institutionalized forms of oppression. In 1970, GA Res. 2627 compared apartheid to 'Nazism' and declared it as a crime 'against the conscience and dignity of mankind'.[210] It defined it as a stand-alone crime in the Apartheid Convention. As noted in scholarship,[211] the main impact of the Convention is not that it outlawed conduct that was previously considered to be lawful but rather its stigmatization of apartheid practices: 'In classifying apartheid as an international crime, the international community declared that systematic racial discrimination is abhorred and unacceptable ... it stigmatizes the specific practice and educates individuals and states by reminding them of apartheid and the international response to it.'[212] Its inclusion on the ICC Statute is mainly a tribute to South African initiatives which sought to 'demonstrate the international community's disapprobation, and to provide a specific label for the prosecution of such acts'.[213]

Other crimes have contributed to a norm-nurturing process. They did not per se mark new criminalizations but promote a thicker counter-norm. Classical examples are slavery, torture, or sexual and gender-based violence. Slavery and torture have a long historical tradition in international law. Many forms of sexual violence are outlawed by domestic law. The branding as crime against humanity has broadened criminalization or contributed to a broader social movement, aimed at reducing tolerance of violations.

For instance, the ban of slavery has a long history in international criminal justice. The 1926 Slavery Convention outlawed 'chattel' slavery, that is the assertion of title over individuals and their treatment as a form of movable property. In modern history, the criminalization of forms of slavery has been significantly extended beyond classical 'slave trade' and legal ownership to modern forms of exploitation.[214] Post-Second World War cases dealt with forced labour programmes.

security and well—being of the world.' See Kenya Authorization Decision, Dissenting Opinion Judge Kaul, para. 63.

[209] In practice, apartheid has for a long time remained dead letter. Its criminalization is grounded in 'affirmation, exclamation, or denunciation'. See Roger Clark, 'Crimes against humanity and the Rome Statute of the International Criminal Court' in Mauro Politi and Giuseppe Nesi (eds), *The Rome Statute of the International Criminal Court—A Challenge to Impunity* (Aldershot: Ashgate 2001) 75–93, 88.

[210] GA Res. 2627 of 20 October 1970, para. 7.

[211] Adriaan Barnard, 'Slegs Suid Afrikaners—South Africans only?: A Review and Evaluation of the International Crime of Apartheid' (2009) 7 *New Zealand Journal of Public and International Law* 317–66, 344.

[212] Ibid., 343, 345.

[213] Darryl Robinson, 'Defining Crimes Against Humanity at the Rome Conference' (1999) 93 *AJIL* 43–57 fn 74..

[214] Harmen van der Wilt, 'Slavery Prosecutions in International Criminal Jurisdictions' (2016) 14 *JICJ* 269–83.

Martin Borman was convicted at Nuremberg for his role in the German slave labour programme. The US Military Tribunal held in the *IG Farben* case that the 'use of concentration camp labour and forced foreign workers at Auschwitz, with the initiative displayed by the officials of Farben in the procurement and utilization of such labour, is a crime against humanity'.[215]

The Tokyo Tribunal convicted several Japanese defendants for slave labour imposed on prisoners of war and on conscripted civilians. However, it failed to qualify the subjugation of 'comfort women' as slavery.[216] The implicit story was that 'males' and detainees subjected to forced labour fit the bill of classical slavery, while 'female sexual slavery during wartime simply did not resemble the accepted rubric of chattel enslavement'.[217] Modern practice has extended the scope of slavery as a crime against humanity to various contemporary forms of slavery 'which are also based on the exercise of any or all of the powers attaching to the right of ownership'.[218] They include enslavement and related practices, such as sexual slavery. The ICTY Appeal Chamber identified a list of indicators, such as 'control of someone's movement, control of physical environment, psychological control, measures taken to prevent or deter escape, force, threat of force or coercion, duration, assertion of exclusivity, subjection to cruel treatment and abuse, control of sexuality and forced labour'.[219] Sexual slavery has been recognized as a distinct form of enslavement. It has been distinguished from 'forced marriage'.[220] The distinction applied to human trafficking has become more fluid.[221]

Such clarifications make only a modest contribution to the anti-slavery movement but they are important from the perspective of 'norm expression'.[222] As Valerie Osterveld has noted: 'Naming is an important expressive tool of the law, and the recognition of forced marriage or conjugal slavery as prohibited acts within crimes against humanity authoritatively transformed a previously legally unacknowledged experience into acknowledged wrongs.'[223]

Norm expression helped counter classical gender prejudices, such as the perception of narratives of female slavery as a form of prostitution or gratification in

[215] US Military Tribunal, Trial of Carl Krauch and Twenty-Two Others (I.G. Farben Trial), Judgment of 29 July 1948, 53.

[216] Patricia V. Sellers, 'Wartime Female Slavery: Enslavement?' (2011) 44 *Cornell International Law Journal* 115–42, 119–20.

[217] Ibid., 120.

[218] *Prosecutor v. Kunarac*, Judgment, IT-96-23& IT-96-23/1-A, 12 June 2002, para. 117 (*Kunarac* Appeal Judgment).

[219] Ibid., para. 119.

[220] Neha Jain, 'Forced Marriage as a Crime Against Humanity' 6 *Journal of International Criminal Justice* (2008) 1013–32.

[221] Nina Tavakoli, 'A Crime that Offends the Conscience of Humanity: A Proposal to Reclassify Trafficking in Women as an International Crime' (2009) 9 *International Criminal Law Review* 77–98.

[222] Van der Wilt, 'Slavery Prosecutions' 282.

[223] Valerie Oosterveld, 'Evaluating the Special Court for Sierra Leone's gender jurisprudence' in Charles C. Jalloh (ed.), *The Sierra Leone Special Court and Its Legacy: The Impact For Africa and International Criminal Law* (Cambridge University Press, 2014), 234–59, 250.

exchange for protection.[224] It also provided guidance and criteria to national audiences by clarifying 'society's reproach of the perpetrator' and 'different forms of suffering of victims'.[225]

The crime of torture carries a particular stigma. Torture is associated with abuse of power, demonstration of cruelty, and infliction of unnecessary suffering on helpless victims. Torture does not only cause harm to individuals. Its detrimental effect lies in the fact that it damages trust in authority and institutions.[226] It is inherently connected to 'state identity' and 'ethical standing' and is a moral taboo.[227] In criminological terms, the commission of torture is often facilitated by the 'construction of a separate reality'.[228] Such an environment is created through practices such as 'authorization, routinization and dehumanization'[229] and processes of 'cognitive neutralization' which reduce resilience by bystanders.[230] The branding of torture as a crime against humanity has served as an instrument to deconstruct such parallel realities. Torture was already recognized as a crime against humanity after the Second World War in Allied Control Council Law No. 10. But its prohibition has solidified. Perhaps the clearest illustration is the *Furundžija* case, in which the ICTY affirmed the nature of torture as a '*jus cogens*' norm. The Tribunal stated that the crime '*signals* to all members of the international community and the individuals over whom they wield authority that the prohibition of torture is an absolute value from which nobody must deviate'.[231]

The crime was thus construed as a counter-norm to a 'torture sustaining reality'.[232] The judgment added that 'the value of freedom from torture is so great that it becomes imperative to preclude any national legislative act authorising or condoning torture or at any rate capable of bringing about this effect'.[233]

The ICTY further recognized that the scope of application of torture is not restricted to public officials, thereby extending the scope of potential perpetrators beyond the Convention against Torture.[234] Later, norm affirmation was used as a counter-narrative to lower standards in the 'war on terror'. For instance, in its request for authorization of an investigation in relation to Afghanistan, the OTP qualified certain officially authorized US Central Intelligence Agency (CIA)

224 Sellers, 'Wartime Female Slavery' 142.
225 Van der Wilt, 'Slavery Prosecutions' 282.
226 On the link to civilization, see Andrew Linklater, 'Torture and Civilisation' (2007) 21 *International Relations* 111–18, 112.
227 See Jamal Barnes, 'The 'War on Terror' and the Battle for the Definition of Torture' (2016) 30 *International Relations* 102, 104; David Sussman, 'What's Wrong with Torture?' (2005) 33 *Philosophy & Public Affairs* 1–33.
228 Ronald D. Crelinsten, 'The World of Torture: A Constructed Reality' (2003) 7 *Theoretical Criminology* 293–318.
229 Ibid., 300–2.
230 Ibid., 303.
231 *Furundžija* Trial Judgment, para. 154.
232 Crelinsten, 'The World of Torture' 299.
233 *Furundžija* Trial Judgment, para. 150.
234 See *Kunarac* Appeal Judgment, para. 148.

'interrogation techniques' as torture (e.g. 'waterboarding', 'rectal rehydration', 'rectal feeding').[235] The move, and the publicity of information related to it, served as instruments to strengthen the robustness of the anti-torture norm, even in the absence of actual prosecutions.

The prohibition of sexual and gender-based violence has evolved with the growth of the feminist movement[236] and growing attention to the gendered dimensions of conflict in the Yugoslav and Rwandan conflicts. Norm expression became a tool to respond to the lack of investigation and prosecution in previous decades and gendered stereotypes in the laws of war, which branded rape and sexual violence as an attack on a woman's honour and modesty. Sexual and gendered-based violence was not framed as an ordinary sex crime (i.e. unrestrained sexual behaviour of individuals) but as an instrument of conflict and an attack against the international community.[237]

International criminal law has shaped a predominant contemporary narrative according to which sexual violence is a strategy or tactic of war.[238] The ICTY qualified the 'rape of any person' in the *Čelebići* case as a 'despicable act which strikes at the very core of human dignity and physical integrity'.[239] The *Akayesu* judgment recognized 'genocidal rape'. It stressed the fact that women were targeted during the genocide because of both their ethnicity and their gender.[240] The Special Court for Sierra Leone (SCSL) clarified that RUF fighters used sexual violence to terrorize civilians into submission to the RUF[241] and rendered the first international conviction for sexual slavery as crime against humanity.[242] The contribution of the SCSL is 'expressive in nature': 'By labeling the gender-based violence suffered by women and girls as forced marriage/conjugal slavery and sexual slavery, and by naming the rape that was carried out against women, girls, men, and boys as criminal, these violations were publicly and internationally acknowledged as wrongs.'[243]

The branding of sexual and gender-based violence as a crime is marked by specific narratives. There is a tendency to consider international criminal law as the

[235] ICC, Public redacted version of 'Request for authorisation of an investigation pursuant to article 15', 20 November 2017, ICC-02/17-7-Conf-Exp, ICC-02/17, 20 November 2017, para. 245.
[236] Janet Halley, 'Rape at Rome: Feminist Interventions in the Criminalization of Sex-Related Violence in Positive International Criminal Law' (2008) 30 *Michigan Journal of International Law* 1–124.
[237] Paul Kirby, 'Ending Sexual Violence in Conflict: the Preventing Sexual Violence Initiative and its Critics' (2015) 91 *International Affairs* 457–72.
[238] Paul Kirby 'How is Rape a Weapon of War?' (2012) 19 *European Journal of International Relations* 797–821
[239] *Prosecutor v. Mucić et al.*, Judgment, IT-96-21-T, 16 November 1998, para. 495.
[240] Sherrie L. Russell-Brown, 'Rape as an Act of Genocide' (2003) 21 *Berkeley Journal of International Law* 350–74.
[241] See *Prosecutor v. Sesay, Kallon and Gbao*, Judgment, SCSL-04-15-T, 2 March 2009, para. 1348 (RUF Trial Judgment).
[242] The RUF trial judgment entered the first ever convictions for forced marriage as a crime against humanity. RUF Trial Judgment, paras 1472–1473. The AFRC appeal judgement developed the Special Court's jurisprudence on forced marriage.
[243] Oosterveld, 'Evaluating the Special Court for Sierra Leone's Gender Jurisprudence' 259.

main frame or 'a panacea for conflict-related sexual violence'.[244] Sara Meger speaks of a 'fetishization of sexual violence'.[245] The basic premise is that attacks against gendered structures and norms in society can be addressed through the instrument and language of law, most notably through 'stricter enforcement of policies, norms, and codes of conduct to curtail this behavior'.[246]

Such imageries are reflected in practice. For instance, ICC Prosecutor Fatou Bensouda has qualified the *Bemba* judgment as an expressive act which 'has highlighted the critical need to eradicate sexual and gender-based crimes as weapons in conflict'.[247] These formulations may be read to imply that conflict-related forms of sexual violence require more attention than other forms of gender-based violence.

Norm expression has focused strongly on banning specific forms of sexual and gender-based violence.[248] Less attention has been paid to subjects and victims. Some decisions appear to imply that sexual violence is graver than other forms of conflict-related violence or that it constitutes the most reprehensible form of gender-based violence. The idea that sexual violence is worse than other forms of violence in conflict is represented in the reasoning of the *Ntaganda* decision. The ICC Trial and Appeals Chambers held that 'there is never a justification to engage in sexual violence against any person; irrespective of whether or not this person may be liable to be targeted and killed under international humanitarian law'.[249]

The majority of the Pre-Trial Chamber defended the view that 'the prohibition on rape itself' has 'attained jus cogens status under international law'.[250] It specified that '[a]s a consequence of the prohibition against rape and sexual slavery being peremptory norms, such conduct is prohibited at all times, both in times of peace and during armed conflicts, and against all persons, irrespective of any legal status'.[251]

Existing discourses have used images that attract empathy for criminalization. The story of sexual violence is often told as a story of victimization rather than

[244] Anette Bringedal Houge and Kjersti Lohne, 'End Impunity! Reducing Conflict-Related Sexual Violence to a Problem of Law' (2017) 51 *Law and Society Review* 755–89.

[245] Sara Meger, 'The Fetishization of Sexual Violence in International Security' (2016) 60 *International Studies Quarterly* 149–59.

[246] Ibid., 150.

[247] OTP, Statement of the Prosecutor of the International Criminal Court, Fatou Bensouda, regarding the conviction of Mr Jean-Pierre Bemba, 21 March 2016, at https://www.icc-cpi.int/Pages/item.aspx?name=otp-stat-bemba-21-03-2016.

[248] Meger, 'The Fetishization of Sexual Violence' 152.

[249] *Prosecutor v. Ntaganda,* Second decision on the Defence's challenge to the jurisdiction of the Court in respect of Counts 6 and 9, ICC-01/04-02/06, 4 January 2017, para. 49; *Prosecutor v. Ntaganda*, Judgment on the appeal of Mr Ntaganda against the 'Second decision on the Defence's challenge to the jurisdiction of the Court in respect of Counts 6 and 9', ICC-01/04-02/06 OA5, 15 June 2007, para. 65. The Appeals Chamber rejected the Defence claim that this interpretation would involve 'judicial activism' or a "substantial and unjustified extension of the scope of war crimes law'. Ibid., para. 67.

[250] Ibid., para. 51. See also David S. Mitchell, 'The Prohibition of Rape in International Humanitarian Law as a Norm of Jus Cogens: Clarifying the Doctrine' (2005) 15 *Duke Journal of Comparative Law & International Law* 219–57.

[251] Ibid., para. 52.

survival. It focuses on expression of harm and suffering. The image of sexual violence as a weapon of war puts the emphasis on the magnitude of violations rather than their causes.[252] It produces clear binaries: evil perpetrators and innocent victims. Such stories are easy to 'market'. They attract broad public attention but may simply belie the complexity of the underlying problems.[253]

2.2.2.2.4 War crimes law as a story of humanization

Norm expression has broadened the scope of war crimes and changed narratives about international humanitarian law.[254] International criminal law has told the story of the laws of war as a story of 'humanization'[255] rather than as a story of mutual obligations in 'war'. Classical understandings have grounded the laws of war in ideas reciprocity, necessity, and codes of honour. As noted in scholarship, '[t]he rationale underlying the prohibition of war crimes, especially in the beginning, was governments' desire to protect their own nationals. It was based on a logic of self-restraint in one's own interest, as every exaggeration in war times holds the danger of reprisals.'[256]

Law and economics scholars have emphasized the contract-like features of obligations and grounded compliance in mutual expectations.[257] International criminal courts and tribunals have adopted a predominantly 'humanitarian' perspective. They analysed and applied international humanitarian law through the specific lens of criminal justice and its goals (i.e. 'substantive justice and equity', interest of victims), rather than state interests and practice.[258] For instance, in *Kunarac*, the ICTY held:

> In the field of international humanitarian law, and in particular in the context of international prosecutions, the role of the state is, when it comes to accountability,

[252] Meger, 'The Fetishization of Sexual Violence' 153.

[253] Severine Autesserre, 'Dangerous Tales: Dominant Narratives on the Congo and Their Unintended Consequences' (2012) 111 *African Affairs* 202–22.

[254] Amanda Alexander, 'A Short History of International Humanitarian Law' (2015) 26 *European Journal of International Law* 109–38; Shane Darcy, *Judges, Law and War: The Judicial Development of International Humanitarian Law* (Cambridge: Cambridge University Press, 2014); Nobuo Hayashi, 'Performance of international criminal courts and tribunals' in Theresa Squatrito, Oran R. Young, Andreas Follesdal, and Geir Ulfstein (eds), *The Performance of International Courts and Tribunals* (Cambridge: Cambridge University Press, 2018), 154–90.

[255] Theodor Meron, 'The Humanization of Humanitarian Law' (2000) 94 *AJIL* 239–78; Theodor Meron, 'The Humanization of the Law of War' in Theodor Meron (ed.), *The Making of International Criminal Justice: A View from the Bench* (Oxford: Oxford University Press, 2012), 42–61; Ruti Teitel, *Humanity's Law* (New York, NY: Oxford University Press, 2011). See also Nobuo Hayashi, 'Is the Yugoslav Tribunal guilty of hyper-humanising international humanitarian law?' in Nobuo Hayashi and Cecilia Bailliet (eds), *The Legitimacy of International Criminal Tribunals* (Cambridge: Cambridge University Press, 2017) 179–205.

[256] Nimage, 'An International Conscience Collective' 598.

[257] Eric Posner, 'A Theory of the Laws of War' (2003) 70 *University of Chicago Law Review* 297–317.

[258] For a critique, see Kenneth Anderson, 'The Rise of International Criminal Law: Intended and Unintended Consequences' (2009) 20 *EJIL* 331–58, 343 ('international criminal tribunals undermine reciprocity. And reciprocity still matters.').

> peripheral. Individual criminal responsibility for violation of international humanitarian law does not depend on the participation of the state and, conversely, its participation in the commission of the offence is no defence to the perpetrator.[259]

This has created alliances with human rights concepts and the natural law foundations of international humanitarian law.[260] International criminal law was presented as a counter-project to warfare and its means and methods. War crimes law has served as a 'gentle civilizer' of international humanitarian law as a discipline.[261] International adjudication adjusted conventional rules established in 1949 and 1977 cover contemporary conflicts. It moved from relative to more absolute protections.

Judge Gabrielle McDonald delivered a passionate justification for this approach. She noted:

> As war itself has changed, the laws of war should follow. Yet, because the international community has clung passionately, politically, to the immovable rock of State sovereignty that keeps alive and keeps dominant archaic perceptions of warfare, the pace of the law has been far slower than the pace of the war.[262]

Evolutive interpretation provided a means to establish new narratives and recast certain foundations.[263] The *ad hoc* tribunals branded international humanitarian law as a 'rudimentary branch of law' that needed to be built through a coherent legal system through judicial decisions.[264] This starting point served as a basis to justify normative change as progression. The tribunals portrayed normative transformation as norm affirmation. They presented innovations in law as reflecting pre-existing customary international law.[265]

A key example of this methodology is *Kupreskić* judgment.[266] The Chamber relied on the Martens Clause to argue that this is 'an area where opinio iuris sive

[259] *Kunarac* Trial Judgment, para. 470.

[260] See generally Christian Tomuschat, 'Human Rights and International Humanitarian Law' (2010) 21 *EJIL* 15–23.

[261] Tamàs Hoffmann, 'The gentle humanizer of humanitarian law—Antonio Cassese and the creation of the customary law of non-international armed conflict' in Carsten Stahn and Larissa van den Herik (eds), *Future Perspectives on International Criminal Justice* (The Hague: T.M.C. Asser Press 2010), 58–80.

[262] Gabrielle Kirk McDonald, 'The Eleventh Annual Waldemar A. Solf Lecture: The Changing Nature of the Laws of War' (1998) 156 *Military Law Review* 30–51, 50–1.

[263] See Alliston Danner, 'When Courts Make Law: How the International Criminal Tribunals Recast the Laws of War' (2006) 59 *Vanderbilt Law Review* 1–65.

[264] 1995 *Tadić* Interlocutory Appeal, para. 119.

[265] Alexander Zahar, 'Civilizing civil war: Writing morality as law at the ICTY' in Bert Swart, Alexander Zahar, and Göran Sluiter (eds), *The Legacy of the International Criminal Tribunal for the Former Yugoslavia* (Oxford: Oxford University Press, 2011), 469–505.

[266] *Kupreskić* Trial Judgment, para. 527.

necessitatis may play a much greater role than usus'.[267] It presented customary law as a fluid and malleable concept. It specified that 'principles of international humanitarian law may emerge through a customary process under the pressure of the demands of humanity or the dictates of public conscience, even where State practice is scant or inconsistent'.[268]

The Chamber argued that this 'new' approach towards the establishment of custom was justified by the transformation of humanitarian law and the 'humanisation of armed conflict'.[269] It used this argument to stress the 'absolute character of obligations' imposed by fundamental rules of international humanitarian law[270] and the ban of reprisals against civilians as a 'barbarous means of seeking compliance with international law'.[271] It held:

> [W]hile reprisals could have had a modicum of justification in the past, when they constituted practically the only effective means of compelling the enemy to abandon unlawful acts of warfare and to comply in future with international law, at present they can no longer be justified in this manner.[272]

The argument of humanization provided a frame to fill gaps. It is an example of 'affective' dimensions of justice, that is, the use of emotion and empathy to reinforce attachment to normative statements.[273] The *Tadić* decision used only a limited amount of facts and authority to establish individual criminal responsibility in non-international armed conflict. It developed a narrative that made it morally objectionable to disagree with its findings. It stated:

> [E]lementary considerations of humanity and common sense make it preposterous that the use by States of weapons prohibited in armed conflicts between themselves be allowed when States try to put down rebellion by their own nationals on their own territory. What is inhumane, and consequently proscribed, in international wars, cannot but be inhumane and inadmissible in civil strife.[274]

This reasoning played with sentiments of empathy and guilt. It found that the 'general essence of' the rules of the law of international armed conflict 'has become

[267] Ibid., para. 527.
[268] Ibid.
[269] Ibid., para. 529.
[270] Ibid., para. 519.
[271] Ibid., para. 529.
[272] Ibid., para. 530.
[273] See Arie Freiberg, 'Affective Versus Effective Justice: Instrumentalism and Emotionalism in Criminal Justice' (2001) 3 *Punishment & Society* 265–78.
[274] 1995 *Tadić* Interlocutory Appeal, para. 119.

applicable to internal conflicts'.[275] Judges thereby changed 'the perception of what the law was'.[276]

This type of 'narrative expressivism' is a recurring feature in international criminal justice. It is a technique to conceal potential conflicts with the principle of legality. The ICTY opened a door for such a methodology in *Aleksovski*. It noted that the principle of legality

> does not prevent a court, either at the national or international level, from determining an issue through a process of interpretation and clarification as to the elements of a particular crime; nor does it prevent a court from relying on previous decisions which reflect an interpretation as to the meaning to be ascribed to particular ingredients of a crime.[277]

International criminal courts and tribunals have used this technique to limit means and methods of warfare. They have often resorted to narrative process tracing, a combination of storytelling and drawing of links between possible causes and outcomes ('process tracing')[278] as method, in order to support norm adaptation. This technique involves the identification and selection of relevant historical events, their organization in a logically narrative structure, and subsequent explanation of the relevant legal outcome.

For instance, in *Galić*, the ICTY rejected the idea that 'terror comes with war'. It 'expressed' the customary nature of the crime of spreading terror amongst the civilian population. It relied on a progressive reading of practice. Treaty law failed to define the infliction of terror as a war crime. The Trial Chamber used a particular narrative technique, namely the identification of 'trends' to justify a conviction. It narrated developments from the Commission on Responsibilities in 1919 to the Geneva Law and domestic legislation to trace a thickening plot of criminalization.[279] It relied on a 'continuing trend of nations criminalising terror as a method of warfare'.[280] The Chamber thereby mixed legal analysis with causal inferences about the unfolding of events or situations over time. This type of narrative expressivism was challenged in dissenting opinions by Judge Neto-Navia[281] and Judge Schomburg,[282] but was ultimately upheld on appeal.[283]

[275] Ibid., para. 126.

[276] Françoise Hampson, 'Relevance for the prosecution of violations of international humanitarian law' in Larry Maybee and Benarji Chakka (eds), *Custom as a Source of International Humanitarian Law* (New Dehli: ICRC, 2006), 103–14, 109.

[277] *Prosecutor v. Aleksovski*, Judgment, IT-95-14/1-A, 24 March 2000, para. 127.

[278] David Collier, 'Understanding Process Tracing' (2011) 44 *Political Science & Politics* 823–30.

[279] See *Prosecutor v. Galić*, IT-98-29-T, Judgment, 5 December 2003, paras 86–134.

[280] For a critique, see *Prosecutor v. Galić*, Dissenting Opinion Schomburg, para. 21 ('The use of the term "trend" clearly indicates that at the time of the commission of the crimes in question, this development had not yet amounted to undisputed state practice.').

[281] See *Prosecutor v. Galić*, Separate and Partially Dissenting Opinion of Judge Nieto-Navia, para. 113.

[282] *Prosecutor v. Galić*, Dissenting Opinion Schomburg, para. 21.

[283] *Prosecutor v. Galić*, Judgment, IT-98-29-A, 30 November 2006, para. 94. See also fn. 297.

The SCSL deployed a similar methodology to determine that child enlistment constitutes a separate war crime under customary law that differs from forcible recruitment of children or using them in combat. The Appeals Chamber constructed a particular narrative in the *Norman* case to justify that the prohibition crossed the threshold from illicit conduct under international humanitarian law to a war crime. It is 'narrative expressivism' at its best. The Chamber defined three critical historical junctures, the 1980s, the period from 1990 to 1994, and finally the time from 1994 to 1996, in order to demonstrate a change of 'conscience' and affirm the customary nature of the norm in line with the temporal jurisdiction of the SCSL.[284] It first developed a particular historical narrative, in order to define a two-year 'turning point' when the norm under international law arguably turned into a crime. It then validated its own reasoning by adding that 'the fact that child recruitment still occurs and is thus illegally practiced does not detract from the validity of the customary norm'.[285] The weakness of this line of argument was exposed by Justice Robertson. He argued that NGOs were starting to campaign for a crime of enlistment at 'about this time'[286] and that even Secretary-General still had doubts in 1996 whether the crime of enlisting was captured by customary law.[287] He noted that '[t]he enlistment of children of fourteen years and below to kill and risk being killed in conflicts not of their making was abhorrent to all reasonable persons in 1996 and is abhorrent to them today. But abhorrence alone does not make that conduct a crime in international law'.[288]

The ICC consolidated the elements of the crime in *Lubanga*. As has been aptly observed, the trial marked 'an attempt to contribute to the establishment and confirmation of the international community's normative foundations'.[289]

Another vivid illustration of the practice to frame the laws of war as instruments of humanization is the acceptance of intra-party protection by the ICC in *Ntaganda*. Traditionally, international humanitarian law deals with protection

[284] *Prosecutor v. Norman*, SCSL-2004-14-AR72(E), Decision on Preliminary Motion Based on Lack of Jurisdiction (Child Recruitment), 31 May 2004, paras 50–51. The Chamber stated: 'Custom takes time to develop. It is thus impossible and even contrary to the concept of customary law to determine a given event, day or date upon which it can be stated with certainty that a norm has crystallised. One can nevertheless say that during a certain period the conscience of leaders and populations started to note a given problem. In the case of recruiting child soldiers this happened during the mid-1980s. One can further determine a period where customary law begins to develop, which in the current case began with the acceptance of key international instruments between 1990 and 1994. Finally, one can determine the period during which the majority of states criminalized the prohibited behaviour, which in this case, as demonstrated, was the period between 1994 and 1996. It took a further six years for the recruitment of children between the ages of 15 and 18 to be included in treaty law as individually punishable behaviour. The development process concerning the recruitment of child soldiers, taking into account the definition of children as persons under the age of 18, culminated in the codification of the matter in the CRC Optional Protocol 1. The overwhelming majority of states ... did not practise recruitment of children under 15 according to their national laws and many had, whether through criminal or administrative law, criminalized such behaviour prior to 1996.'

[285] Ibid., para. 51.

[286] *Prosecutor v. Norman*, Dissenting Opinion of Justice Robertson, para. 35.

[287] Ibid., para. 34.

[288] Ibid., para. 9.

[289] Nimaga, 'An International Conscience Collective' 617

against harm by the opposing side. In *Ntaganda*, the ICC extended protection under war crimes law to intra-party violence, that is, crimes committed against members of the own side. The SCSL had discarded this type of protection, arguing that the 'law of international armed conflict was never intended to criminalise acts of violence committed by one member of an armed group against another'.[290]

This argument implied that intra-party crimes fall essentially within the disciplinary or criminal jurisdiction under domestic law. The ICC challenged this understanding with respect to sexual violence committed against child soldiers. Trial Chamber VI argued that such a limited understanding of protection 'is contrary to the rationale of international humanitarian law, which aims to mitigate the suffering resulting from armed conflict'.[291]

It stated:

> It ... cannot be the case that by committing a serious violation of international humanitarian law by incorporating ... children under the age of 15 into an armed group, the protection of those children under that same body of law against sexual violence by members of that same armed group would cease as a result of the prior unlawful conduct reach of international humanitarian law.[292]

The Appeals Chamber followed this approach. It rejected the assumption that the concept of war crimes 'is generally limited to cases where victims are nationals of the opposing party'.[293] It noted: '[I]nternational humanitarian law does not contain a general rule that categorically excludes members of an armed group from protection against crimes committed by members of the same armed group'.[294]

The process of norm affirmation is often grounded in 'constitutionalist' textures and semantics. It contains determinations and demarcations in relation to other legal regimes. For instance, international criminal courts and tribunals have been eager to stress that arguments relating to the just cause for the resort to armed violence (e.g. *jus ad bellum*) have no place in the determination of individual criminal responsibility. Several judgments have made it clear that the principle of humanity requires protection for victims in all circumstances, irrespective of the side to which they belong. The ICTY reaffirmed the 'fundamental distinction in international law between the rules governing a State's right to resort to armed force (*jus ad bellum*) and the rules applicable in armed conflict (*jus in bello*)'.[295]

[290] RUF Trial Judgment, para. 1453.

[291] *Prosecutor v. Ntaganda*, Second decision on the Defence's challenge to the jurisdiction of the Court in respect of Counts 6 and 9, para. 48.

[292] Ibid., para. 53.

[293] *Prosecutor v. Ntaganda*, Judgment on the appeal of Mr Ntaganda against the 'Second decision on the Defence's challenge to the jurisdiction of the Court in respect of Counts 6 and 9', ICC-01/04-02/06 OA5, 15 June 2017, para. 62.

[294] Ibid., para. 63.

[295] *Prosecutor v. Boškoski and Tarčulovski*, Judgment, IT-04-82-A, 19 May 2010, para. 44.

It clarified that 'military operations in self-defence do not provide a justification for serious violations of international humanitarian law'.[296] The SCSL rejected the defence of necessity in relation to war crimes and crimes against humanity in *Fofana and Kondewa*. It argued that such a defence would 'negate the norms and fundamental principles protecting persons not taking part in hostilities and the victims of armed conflicts'[297]:

> [V]alidating the defence of Necessity in International Criminal Law would create a justification for what offenders may term and plead as a 'just cause' or a 'just war' even though serious violations of International Humanitarian Law would have been committed. This . . . would negate the resolve and determination of the International Community to combat these crimes which have the common characteristics of being heinous, gruesome or degrading of innocent victims or of the civilian population that it intends to protect. [298]

The Trial Chamber added expressivist language to reinforce the didactic rationales of sentencing. It expressed the hope that the judgment would 'send a message to future pro-democracy armed forces or militia groups that notwithstanding the justness of propriety of their cause, they must observe the laws of war in pursuing or defending legitimate causes, and that they must not recruit or use children as agents of instruments of war'.[299]

References to notions, such as *jus cogens*, non-derogable rights, or principles of humanity, are part of expressive strategies. They introduce express or implicit hierarchies. They associate norms of international criminal justice with a higher degree of 'normativity'.[300] They suggest that the underlying norms are 'intransgressible' or universally shared. A good example is the qualification of torture as a *jus cogens* norm in *Furundžija*. The ICTY used it to clarify a 'hierarchy of rules in the international normative order'.[301] It noted that the prohibition 'enjoys a higher rank in the international hierarchy than treaty law and even "ordinary" customary rules'.[302]

Such a branding has not only juridical but also expressive meaning. It is a narrative technique with a signalling function.[303] It creates a new framework of reference in an attempt to bring order to chaos and produce a counter-narrative to the messages of crimes.

296 *Prosecutor v. Kordić and Čerkez*, IT-95-14/2-T, Judgment, 26 February 2001, para. 452.

297 *Prosecutor v. Fofana and Kondewa*, Sentencing Judgment, SCSL-04-14-T, 9 October 2007, para. 78.

298 Ibid., para. 79.

299 Ibid., para 96.

300 Martti Koskenniemi, '"The Lady Doth Protest Too Much": Kosovo, and the Turn to Ethics in International Law' (2002) 65 *Modern Law Review* 159–75.

301 *Furundžija* Trial Judgment, para. 153.

302 Ibid., para. 153.

303 Andrea Bianchi, 'Human Rights and the Magic of Ius Cogens' (2008) 19 *EJIL* 491–508.

Such narrative techniques provide an additional affective dimension to processes of norm affirmation. They extend their reach beyond a specific geographical or historical context. They are a means of nourishing social values, stabilizing norms, or imagining and producing 'a community of humanity'.[304]

2.2.3 Techniques of norm projection

The boundaries between norm affirmation and norm projection are porous. There is only a fine between the two. At the domestic level, norms are often pre-existing. At the international level, the normative structure is more diffuse.

International criminal justice has traditionally shared strong synergies with what Ethan Nadelmann has called 'transnational moral entrepreneurship', that is, the transmission of moral views that 'transcend the state', depoliticize the individual, and emphasize 'the existence of an international society of human beings sharing common moral bond'.[305] It has not only defended the preservation of specific norms but attached novel meanings to them or projected change in order to transform the consciousness of individuals and communities.

International criminal courts and tribunals have, to some extent, served as 'epistemic engines'[306] and architects of the social meaning of crimes.[307] The very process of affirming the global existence of a norm may entail its very 'scripting' as a crime or capture new forms of social behaviour.[308] Norm projection labels conduct as an offence and involves behavioural commands. As David Luban has noted, it may project 'new norms' to the 'wider world' or convey messages that 'politics' must 'never again cross moral lines that heretofore it has always crossed'.[309] It suggests that the respective norm should be recognized, applied, and protected by states, and obeyed by institutions and individuals.

Norm projection has a strongly transformative dimension. It positions the law as a response to violation and harm which warrants redress and prevention. It postulates 'what the world is, what it might be and what it ought to be as part of an on-going process to progress from an imperfect reality to an imagined alternative'.[310]

304 McMillan, 'Imagining the International' 173

305 Nadelmann, 'Global Prohibition Regimes' 482, 484.

306 Jakob v. H. Holtermann, 'International Criminal Tribunals as Epistemic Engines Or Why Legal Truth Is Not Sui Generis', *Humanity*, 6 July 2017, at http://humanityjournal.org/wp-content/uploads/2017/07/04.-Holtermann-International-Criminal-Tribunals.pdf.

307 Lawrence Lessig, 'The Regulation of Social Meaning' (1995) 62 *University of Chicago Law Review* 943–1045, 951.

308 See Hugo van der Merwe, *The Transformative Value of International Criminal Law* (PhD Dissertation, Stellenbosch 2012) 338.

309 David Luban, 'State criminality and the ambition of international criminal law' 75.

310 Hugo Van der Merwe, *The Transformative Value of International Criminal Law* (PhD Dissertation, Stellenbosch 2012), 369.

It institutes a new set of communicative relations. The legal concept of the crime is to some extent a code. It offers a new way of looking at social reality. It introduces a common language and a broader 'responsibility for the suffering of others'.[311] It is deemed to encourage resilience against offences.

Like norm affirmation, norm projection is closely related to narration and narrative techniques.[312] It presents corrective counter-readings to existing narratives or generates new narratives. It is facilitated by the 'open texture' of legal rules[313] and the absence of a unified theory of international crimes or modes of liability.[314] Many fundamental legal notions (e.g. 'policy', 'armed conflict') lack an 'ordinary meaning'. Crimes are presented as being evil in themselves (*malum in se*). This structure has allowed norm expansion. The meaning of norms has been adjusted to new contexts or extended through 'tying', that is, association with other normative regimes, or use of precedent, that is, invocation and distinction of comparable cases. Judicial reasoning is thus 'a type of storytelling and story-matching whereby the law evolves through the analogical extrapolation from one story to the next'.[315]

Norm projection has been driven by a range of different argumentative techniques, including removal of ambiguity and inconsistency, process tracing, gap filling, and collective narration.

2.2.3.1 Solving ambiguity and inconsistency

A classical way to steer normative transformation is to trace shortcomings in the law and to remedy them through legal construction and shifting meanings. This narrative technique has been used on multiple occasions. A key example is the extension of the scope of application of crimes against humanity to non-state actors.

The scope of application of crimes against humanity has been interpreted in light of different readings of the policy element. This legal notion is indeterminate. It can be associated with a range of meanings, ranging from state-centred readings of crimes against humanity to interpretations contesting its relevance for modern readings of the crime.[316] According to a historical understanding, crimes against humanity were primarily associated with state violations. They were read as criminalized human rights abuses by states.[317] This meaning was gradually altered. International criminal courts and tribunals have reinterpreted and extended this

[311] McMillan, 'Imagining the International' 170.

[312] See Richard Posner, 'Legal Narratology' (1997) 64 *University of Chicago Law Review* 737–47.

[313] Herbert L.A. Hart, *The Concept of Law* (Oxford: Clarendon Press, 1994), 128.

[314] Robert Cryer, 'The ad hoc Tribunals and the law of command responsibility: A quiet earthquake' in Shane Darcy and Joseph Powderly (eds), Judicial Creativity at the International Criminal Tribunals (Oxford: Oxford University Press, 2010), 159–83.

[315] Marjolein Cupido, 'The Casuistry of International Criminal Law: Exploring A New Field of Research' (2015) 44 *Netherlands Journal of Legal Philosophy* 116–32, 127.

[316] The ICTY questioned the relevance of the policy element in the *Kunarac* Appeal Judgment, para. 98.

[317] William A. Schabas, 'State Policy as an Element of International Crimes' (2008) 98 *Journal of Criminal Law & Criminology* 953–82, 981.

understanding. They have used different narrative arguments to explain a wider meaning of the policy element.

The *Tadić* Trial judgment Chamber told the story of transformation of policy element as a tale of changing patterns of organization.[318] It first articulated the 'traditional conception', according to which 'a policy must be present but that the policy must be that of a State, as was the case in Nazi Germany'.[319] It justified this by the original focus on 'state's institutions, personnel and resources' in the commissions of crimes. It then stressed its unique role as 'the first international tribunal to consider charges of crimes against humanity alleged to have occurred after the Second World War'.[320] It framed a counter-narrative, based on historic development. It stated: 'While this may have been the case during the Second World War, and thus the jurisprudence followed by courts adjudicating charges of crimes against humanity based on events alleged to have occurred during this period, this is no longer the case'.[321]

The Chamber then acted as engineer of a novel normative meaning. It equated organizations with territorial control to states. It ruled that 'the law in relation to crimes against humanity has developed to take into account forces which, although not those of the legitimate government, have de facto control over, or are able to move freely within, defined territory'.[322]

It also mentioned in an *obiter dictum* that the policy element might cover a 'terrorist group or organization'.[323] This reasoning is in line with the broad interpretation of the concept of armed conflict which covers protracted armed violence between a state and an armed group, or even between two armed groups.

The ICC developed this line of argument in the famous *Kenya Authorization* decision.[324] The majority found that 'organizations not linked to a State may, for the purposes of the Statute, elaborate and carry out a policy to commit an attack against a civilian population'.[325] It used a partly different narrative to justify this outcome. It did not rely so much on the argument of institutional transformation but rather on the capacity of non-stators to commit human rights abuses. It claimed that 'the formal nature of a group and the level of its organization' should not serve as 'defining criterion'. Instead, 'a distinction should be drawn on whether a group has the capability to perform acts which infringe on basic human values'.[326] It implied that

318 *Prosecutor v. Tadić*, Opinion and Judgment, IT-91-1-T, 7 May 1997, para. 654 (*Tadić* Trial Judgment).

319 Ibid.

320 Ibid.

321 Ibid.

322 Ibid.

323 Ibid. This position was confirmed in *Prosecutor v. Blaskić*, Judgment, IT-95-14-T, 3 March 2000, para. 205 ('with de facto power or organized in criminal gangs').

324 See Gerhard Werle and Boris Burghardt, 'Do Crimes Against Humanity Require the Participation of a State or a 'State-Like' Organization?' (2012) 10 *JICJ* 1151–70.

325 Kenya Authorization Decision, para. 92.

326 Ibid., para. 90.

crimes against humanity might be committed by 'private individuals with de facto power or organized in criminal gangs or groups'.[327] This marked a seismic shift, namely the recognition that 'national and transnational conflicts between states and destructive private organizations crimes'[328] may, in a case-by-case basis, give rise to crimes against humanity.

Judge Kaul adopted yet another narrative in his dissent. He interpreted 'historic experience' in a different way.[329] He questioned as to whether the concept of crimes against humanity should not be assimilated 'to any infringement of human rights'. He traced the transformation of the policy argument as a history of evolving jurisdiction and the distinction between international and domestic crimes. He argued that the policy element encompasses only certain 'non-state organizations', namely 'state-like entities'.[330] According to his view, crimes against humanity are deemed to 'protect the international community against the extremely grave threat emanating from such policies'.[331]

He defended the limitation of the policy element to 'state-like actors' by the need to maintain differences between legal rubrics of crimes, namely 'between international crimes and ordinary crimes; between those crimes subject to international jurisdiction and those punishable under domestic penal legislation'.[332]

All of these three readings offered a different way of looking at social reality, but gave a partly novel meaning to crimes against humanity.

2.2.3.2 Narrative process tracing

Narrative process tracing is a second way to promote norm projection. It involves the weaving of a certain legal narrative, through accelerated narration, selection and emphasizing of certain events (while leaving out others), their placement in a logical and ordered sequence (plot), and the tracing of influences, based on inferences, in order to frame legal argument. It bears synergies with pedagogic narrations of history which rely on techniques, such as periodization and causal sequencing, in order to frame historic narratives.[333]

327 Ibid., para. 91.

328 See Claus Kress, 'On the Outer Limits of Crimes against Humanity: The Concept of Organization within the Policy Requirement: Some Reflections on the March 2010 ICC Kenya Decision' (2010) 23 *LJIL* 855–73, 873 referring to a 'third generational step' of international criminal law.

329 Kenya Authorization Decision, Dissenting Opinion Judge Kaul, para. 61. He traces history as follows: 'Since 1945, the experience of other mass crimes committed in various parts of the world has confirmed, time and again: each time when it is a State which adopts or practices a policy to attack a civilian population, quite regularly the same apocalyptic threat of mass crimes reappears or materializes. This was the case in particular with the Khmer Rouge "crimes against humanity" committed in Cambodia, with the mass poisoning of Kurds in Halabja in 1988, with the Rwanda crisis in 1994 and other mass crimes such as the ones in former Yugoslavia in the 90ies of the last century.' Ibid., para. 62.

330 Ibid., para. 67.

331 Ibid., para. 63.

332 Ibid., para. 65.

333 See Jean d'Aspremont, 'Critical Histories of International Law and the Repression of Disciplinary Imagination' (2019) 7 *London Review of International Law* 89–115.

2.2.3.2.1 Terrorism as international crime

A prominent example is the STL decision on the international crime of terrorism. It is a hallmark of expressive norm projection and legal storytelling. It illustrates how courts may create a novel crime through legal narration.

The STL Appeals Chamber started its analysis with an acknowledgment of the expressive features of legal texts. It admitted that statutes may be presumed to be 'speaking'.[334] It noted that interpretation may involve an 'exercise of construction',[335] since judges are 'not permitted to resort to a non-liquet', that is to declare that it is 'impossible for them to reach a decision' because the point at issue is unclear.[336] It then applied this methodology in its reasoning.

The Chamber justified the use of evolutive interpretation to frame terrorism as a crime through progress-related narratives. It delineated a clear distinction between past and present. The judgment contrasted an 'old international community' with the reality of 'modern international courts'.[337] It presented the past as a world of 'deference to state sovereignty' in which 'individuals did not play any role and there did not yet exist intergovernmental organisations such as the United Nations tasked to safeguard such universal values as peace, human rights, self-determination of peoples and justice'.[338]

It construed contemporary reality as a counter-vision to the past, namely as a world in which 'the interests of the world community tend to prevail over those of individual sovereign states; universal values take pride of place restraining reciprocity and bilateralism in international dealings; and the doctrine of human rights has acquired paramountcy throughout the world community'.[339]

In the following step, the STL developed the concept of terrorism as an international crime through process tracing. It traced legal instruments in a periodic way and constructed the elements of the crime through legal patchworking and didactic narration. It derived a 'commonly shared agreement' from policy considerations (e.g. the 'fight' against international terrorism) and a mix of different sources: treaties, UN practice, state practice, and general principles of law. It ordered treaty law in a progressive sequence. It referred to 'a long line of terrorism-related conventions'[340] and used the 1999 International Convention for the

[334] STL, Interlocutory Decision on the Applicable Law: Terrorism, Conspiracy, Homicide, Perpetration, Cumulative Charging (STL-11-01/I/AC/R176bis), Appeals Chamber, 16 February 2011, para. 21 (STL Interlocutory Appeal Applicable Law), para. 21. The STL drew on UK Supreme Court, *Yemschaw v. London Borough of Hounslow* [2011] UKSC 3, 26 ('statutes will generally be found to be ... always speaking'). For a critical discussion, see Ben Saul, 'Legislating from a Radical Hague: The United Nations Special Tribunal for Lebanon Invents an International Crime of Transnational Terrorism' (2011) 24 *LJIL* 677–700.

[335] Ibid., para. 19.

[336] Ibid., para. 23.

[337] Ibid. para. 29.

[338] Ibid., para. 29.

[339] Ibid. para. 29.

[340] Ibid., para. 89.

Suppression of the Financing of Terrorism, which 'provides the UN's clearest definition of terrorism', as anchor point.[341] It then developed the elements of an international crime of terrorism through attitude tracing, including analysis of national legislation and international attitude of states.

The core element of the reasoning of the judgment relies on an understanding of customary law that bears strongly expressivist features. The Chamber noted:

> To turn into an international crime, a domestic offence needs to be regarded by the world community as an attack on universal values (such as peace or human rights) or on values held to be of paramount importance in that community; in addition, it is necessary that States and intergovernmental organisations, through their acts and pronouncements, sanction this attitude by clearly expressing the view that the world community considers the offence at issue as amounting to an international crime.[342]

In its methodology, the STL borrowed from the approaches of the *ad hoc* tribunals, including the *Furundžija, Kunarac,* and *Tadić* judgments.[343] It defined terrorism a criminal action 'that aims at spreading terror or coercing governmental authorities and is a threat to the stability of society or the State'.[344] It claimed that this notion 'is so deeply embedded in the legislation of so many diverse countries, that one is warranted to conclude that those countries share the same basic view of terrorism and are not in the least likely to depart from it'.[345]

The judgment then delivered the corresponding historical narrative. It drew parallels with the development and transformation of war crimes law. The Chamber relied on the *Tadić* criteria to determine that there is individual criminal responsibility for an international crime of terrorism in peacetime. The relevant passage is a paradigm example of historical legal storytelling for purposes of norm projection. The Chamber constructed individual criminal responsibility through process tracing. It stated:

> [C]riminalisation of terrorism has begun at the domestic level, with many countries of the world legislating against terrorist acts and bringing to court those allegedly responsible for such acts. This trend was internationally strengthened by the passing of robust resolutions by the UN General Assembly and Security Council condemning terrorism, and the conclusion of a host of international treaties banning various manifestations of terrorism and enjoining the contracting parties to cooperate for the repression of those manifestations. As a

341 Ibid., para. 88.
342 Ibid., para. 91.
343 Ibid., paras 91 and 103.
344 Ibid., para. 97.
345 Ibid., para. 97.

> result, those States which had not already criminalised terrorism at the domestic level have increasingly incorporated the emerging criminal norm into domestic penal legislation and case-law, often acting out of a sense of international obligation. The characterisation of terrorism as a threat to international peace and security through UN Security Council 'legislation' strengthens this conclusion. It is notable that the Security Council has generally refrained from characterising other national and transnational criminal offences (such as money laundering, drug trafficking, international exploitation of prostitution) as 'threats to peace and security'. The difference in treatment of these various classes of criminal offences, and the perceived seriousness of terrorism, bears out that terrorism is an international crime classified as such by international law, including customary international law, and also involves the criminal liability of individuals.[346]

This narrative was used to justify the anticipated result, namely to brand international terrorism as a crime that results from an international law-making process rather than judge-made law. The entire construction has strong synergies to legal fiction. The recognition of terrorism as international crime in peacetime has remained contested.[347]

As Thomas Weigend has cautioned, the broad framing of terrorism for expressivist purposes has negative effects. It coins an image of a 'universal terrorist' and may lead to 'overuse of the label of terrorism'.[348] *Mens rea* can easily be inferred from harm. It is better to 'err on the side of moderation' in order 'to avoid disproportional intrusions into protected areas of individual privacy as well as a devaluation of terrorism through an inflationary use of this term'.[349]

2.2.3.2.2 Immunity exception in relation to international court

The ICC Appeals Chamber used a similar method in its immunity decision in the *Jordan Referral re Al Bashir Appeal*. The issue as to whether there are exception to immunities for international crimes is an 'emotive' one. As Dire Tladi has noted: '[I]t is a microcosm for the long-standing battle for the soul of international law: will international law—at its core—protect sovereignty and the immunity implied by it or will it pursue a brave new world by promoting accountability and justice for the victims of atrocity crimes.'[350]

[346] Ibid., para. 104.

[347] See Gerhard Werle and Florian Jessberger, *Principles of International Criminal Law* (Oxford: Oxford University Press, 2014), 48–49.

[348] See Thomas Weigend, 'The Universal Terrorist: The International Community Grappling with a Definition' (2004) 4 *JICJ* 912–32.

[349] Ibid., 932.

[350] See Dire Tladi, 'The International Law Commission's Recent Work on Exceptions to Immunity: Charting the Course for a Brave New World in International Law? (2019) 32 *LJIL* 169–87, 187.

The Appeals Chamber presented immunity as a 'relic" of a bygone era'.[351] It established a broad international court exception that goes beyond the ruling of the International Court of Justice (ICJ) *Arrest Warrant* case. The ICJ started from the premise that immunity can serve as a bar to the exercise of criminal jurisdiction in inter-state relations, since immunity does not mean impunity.[352] The ICC flipped the starting point. It did not operate from the premise that immunity is the rule in relation to the prosecution of international crimes before an international court but implied that the very existence of an immunity rule would need to be positively shown.[353] The ICJ had marked an opening in this direction by noting that immunity does not hinder 'criminal proceedings before certain international criminal courts, where they have jurisdiction'.[354] This reference covered tribunals established under Chapter VII and treaty systems in which states accepted the inapplicability of immunities. The ICC extended this logic. It argued that 'there is neither State practice nor opinio juris that would support the existence of Head of State immunity under customary international law vis-à-vis an international court'.[355]

This approach is novel since it indicates the absence of a rule of customary law in relation to international criminal courts and tribunals. It means that immunities of Heads of State, including those of non-Party States, are irrelevant in the triangular relationship between the ICC, state parties, and non-Party states (e.g. Sudan), whenever the Security Council refers a situation to the Court.

The decision itself is a paradigm example of norm projection.[356] The Appeals Chamber relied on historical process tracing and emplotment (i.e. the assembly of a series of events into a narrative with a plot) in order to arrive at this result, the absence of a rule of customary international law providing Heads of States immunity from the jurisdiction of international courts.

Like the *ad hoc* tribunals, the Appeals Chamber balanced stability in international relations against the need to avoid 'impunity for violations of fundamental human rights'.[357] It framed international law as a post-Westphalian order. The Joint Concurring Opinion of Judges Eboe-Osuji, Morrison, Hofmański, and Bossa stated:

> [S]ince the end of World War II, international law has, to all intents and purposes, evolved away from its Westphalian roots in relation to individuals.

[351] *Prosecutor v. Al Bashir*, Judgment in the Jordan Referral re Al-Bashir Appeal, ICC-02/05-01/09 OA2, 6 May 2019, Joint Concurring Opinion of Judges Eboe-Osuji, Morrison, Hofmański and Bossa, ICC-02/05-01/09-397-Anx1-Corr, para. 135.

[352] ICJ, *Arrest Warrant of 11 April 2000 (Democratic Republic of the Congo v. Belgium)*, Judgment, 14 February 2002, para 60.

[353] *Prosecutor v. Al Bashir*, Judgment in the Jordan Referral re Al-Bashir Appeal, para. 116.

[354] Ibid., para. 61.

[355] *Prosecutor v. Al Bashir*, Judgment in the Jordan Referral re Al-Bashir Appeal, para. 113.

[356] For a defence of the reasoning under customary law with reference to the 'aspiration of an equal enforcement of the law' and the ICC's 'expressive function to the world', see Claus Kress, *Preliminary Observations on the ICC Appeals Chamber's Judgment of 6 May 2019 in the Jordan Referral re Al-Bashir Appeal* (Brussels: Torkel Opsahl Academic EPublisher, 2019) 24–5.

[357] Ibid., para. 147.

> Regardless of the imperfections of that evolution, human beings now have recognised rights and duties that the human agents of States may no longer violate, without provoking questions of accountability on the international stage.[358]

The judgment ordered 'judicial pronouncements' in a specific sequence in order to answer the question as 'whether or not a rule of customary international law has as such "crystallized"'.[359] The Joint Concurring Opinion of Judges Eboe-Osuji, Morrison, Hofmański, and Bossa argued that 'customary international law has never evolved to recognise immunity—even for Heads of State—before an international court exercising jurisdiction over crimes under international law'.[360]

The judgment built a progressive historical line from the First World War, the Nuremberg Charter and Principles,[361] to the Genocide Convention,[362] the *ad hoc* tribunals as 'milestones',[363] and the *Taylor* judgment, in order to arrive at the conclusion that 'the sovereign equality of states does not prevent a Head of State from being prosecuted before an international criminal tribunal or state'.[364]

The method of narrative process tracing is clearly illustrated by the Joint Concurring Opinion of Judges Eboe-Osuji, Morrison, Hofmański, and Bossa. The Opinion used a three-step approach. It first traced the 'nascence of a "New International Law' Norm Rejecting Immunity before International Tribunals' in the 'twilight days of World War I',[365] based on 'trend that had emerged in the consciousness of international law'.[366] It then used Nuremberg as a hallmark in order to establish the 'consolidation of the International Norm Rejecting Immunity before International Tribunals'.[367] It concluded with the affirmation of a general 'Anti-Immunity Norm',[368] for which the distinction between functional and personal immunity is immaterial.[369]

358 *Prosecutor v. Al Bashir*, Joint Concurring Opinion of Judges Eboe-Osuji, Morrison, Hofmański, and Bossa, para. 192.

359 *Prosecutor v. Al Bashir*, Judgment in the Jordan Referral re Al-Bashir Appeal, para. 113.

360 *Prosecutor v. Al Bashir*, Joint Concurring Opinion of Judges Eboe-Osuji, Morrison, Hofmański, and Bossa, para. 66.

361 *Prosecutor v. Al Bashir*, Judgment in the Jordan Referral re Al-Bashir Appeal, paras 103 and 104.

362 Ibid., para. 105.

363 Ibid, para. 107.

364 Ibid., para. 109.

365 *Prosecutor v. Al Bashir*, Joint Concurring Opinion of Judges Eboe-Osuji, Morrison, Hofmański, and Bossa, para. 76.

366 Ibid., para. 150.

367 Ibid., para. 151.

368 Ibid., para. 175.

369 Ibid., para. 176 ('commission of international crimes is not part of the job description of the Head of State. The primary justification for leadership of State is protection of the population, which by necessity precludes the commission of international crimes against them.').

The Appeals Chamber invoked community notions and preventive rationales in order to justify the outcome. It stressed the benefits international courts, which 'act on behalf of the international community as a whole' over domestic jurisdictions: 'While the latter are essentially an expression of a State's sovereign power, which is necessarily limited by the sovereign power of the other States, the former, when adjudicating international crimes, do not act on behalf of a particular State or States.'[370]

It then grounded duties of cooperation in the nature of crimes. It found there is an 'obligation erga omnes to prevent, investigate and punish crimes that shock the conscience of humanity'.[371]

The decision is thus a classic in expressivist norm projection. It is customary law by narration. A critical aspect of this type of narration lies in what it leaves out. The Chamber relied heavily on the early history of international criminal law. It disregarded the lack of actual state practice regarding the prosecution of Heads of State (e.g. Versailles), focused on statements a few selected 'enlightened' states and judgments, and ignored contrary practice (e.g. Malabo Protocol, statements challenging the duty to arrest).

The methodology adopted by the Chamber failed to explain how the absence of immunity can be justified in relation to states that do not consent to the jurisdiction of an international criminal court.[372] The fact that a Head of State enjoys no immunity before a treaty-based international criminal court, such as the ICC, does not per se mean that this exclusion also applies automatically in the horizontal relationship between state parties and non-state parties.[373]

2.2.3.3 Gap filling as narrative

A third narrative technique to foster norm projection is gap filling. It involves at least two logical steps: the framing of an issue as a gap, and the presentation of norm projection as a remedy to mitigate the problem or transform the *status quo*.

This technique has inspired the development of international criminal law. The 'gap' argument has played an important role in legal discourse. The turn to international criminal law was initially justified as a response to an 'enforcement gap' at the domestic level, that is, the lack of domestic jurisdiction over offences, or the unavailability of domestic justice. Later, the 'gap' argument returned in modified form. International criminal law was justified as an anti-impunity project, a means

[370] *Prosecutor v. Al Bashir*, Judgment in the Jordan Referral re Al Bashir Appeal, para. 115. See also Joint Concurring Opinion of Judges Eboe-Osuji, Morrison, Hofmański, and Bossa, para. 59: An 'international court exercises the jurisdiction of no one sovereign. It exercises the jurisdiction of all the concerned sovereigns inter se, for their overall benefit.'

[371] Ibid., para. 123.

[372] The Joint Concurring Opinion of Judges Eboe-Osuji, Morrison, Hofmański, and Bossa deals with this argument in relation to Security Council referrals at ibid., paras 339–340.

[373] The decision is ambiguous in this regard. Ibid., paras 10–12.

to close 'impunity gaps'.[374] It was seen as a remedy to broader structural problems, such as lack of 'peace' or 'rule of law' deficits. An illustration is the *Nikolić* judgment, in which the Trial Chamber expressed the hope that the 'Tribunal and other international courts are bringing about the development of a culture of respect for the rule of law and not simply the fear of the consequences of breaking the law'.[375]

The idea of breaking a 'culture of impunity' serves as a strong incentive for expressive norm transformation. The development of the concept of individual criminal responsibility is grounded in this logic. The turn to individual responsibility was presented as an alternative to collective guilt. It was meant to address the gaps and shortcoming of state responsibility. Robert Jackson stressed this point in his Nuremberg opening address. He stated

> This principle of personal liability is a necessary as well as logical one if international law is to render real help to the maintenance of peace. An international law which operates only on states can be enforced only by war because the most practicable method of coercing a state is warfare ... Only sanctions which reach individuals can peacefully and effectively be enforced.[376]

Individual responsibility was thus framed as a counter-instrument to collective responsibility. This line was later taken up by the ICTY. It branded individual criminal responsibility forcefully as an alternative to vengeance.[377]

A similar method was used to establish new modes of liability. For example, in *Tadić* the ICTY developed the concept of joint criminal enterprise (JCE) in part to fill structural gaps in relation to responsibility for collective crimes. JCE as a concept combines features from different legal traditions. The ICTY grounded the concept formally in Second World War case law. But the branding of the doctrine entailed strong narrative elements. The Appeals Chamber introduced a novel categorization of joint commission of crimes, based on historical patterns encountered in the Second World War. It distinguished three distinct 'categories of collective criminality':[378] (i) JCE I, grounded in collective action according to a common plan with a criminal purpose, such as the famous *Einsatzgruppen*; (ii) JCE II, which is modelled after the so-called concentration camp cases[379] (i.e. a system of ill-treatment and intent to further the common design of ill-treatment[380]);

[374] See Theodor Meron, 'Closing the Accountability Gap: Concrete Steps Toward Ending Impunity for Atrocity Crimes' (2018) 112 *AJIL* 433–51.

[375] *Nikolić* Sentencing Judgement, para. 89.

[376] Opening Address for the United States, Nazi Conspiracy & Aggression, Vol. I (Washington, DC: United States Government Printing Office, 1946) 168.

[377] *Prosecutor v. Aleksovski*, IT-95-14/1-A, Judgment, 24 March 2000, para. 185 ('[Retribution] is not to be understood as fulfilling a desire for revenge but as duly expressing the outrage of the international community at these crimes.').

[378] *Prosecutor v. Tadić*, Judgment, IT-94-1-A, 15 July 1999, para. 195 (*Tadić* Appeal 1999).

[379] Ibid., para. 202.

[380] Ibid., para. 220.

and (iii) the more elusive form of JCE III, which relates to responsibility for crimes which are outside the scope of the common plan (i.e. a natural and foreseeable consequence of it).[381]

Tadić presented these three forms on an equal level and affirmed their basis in customary law. But the recognition of JCE III marked an extension of the parameters of co-perpetration. The *Tadić* narrative, with its equal historical treatment of the three forms of JCE, gained ground in the jurisprudence of the *ad hoc* tribunals and the SCSL. However, it was later challenged by the Extraordinary Chambers in the Courts of Cambodia (ECCC). The ECCC questioned whether the authority cited in *Tadić* supported the legal narrative. It contested the customary nature of JCE III.[382]

In the *Čelebići* case, the ICTY relied on the 'gap' logic to develop the doctrine of superior responsibility. It noted that the doctrine of command responsibility has a basis in military law, but it found that it 'ha[d] not been applied by any international judicial organ' since the Second World War.[383] It extended the scope of liability to civilian commanders, despite limited historical precedent.[384] The extension of the doctrine transformed the scope of civic duties. It implied that the duties of civilian superiors are not restricted to their own direct participation in crime but cover responsibilities to ensure his or her subordinates are not committing crimes. This line of argument transposed due diligence and professional duties from classical public authority-based structures to more decentralized private relationships.

2.2.3.4 Collective narration

Norm projection is deeply shaped by collective forms of narration. It involves collective processes of scripting of norms. Each judgment and decision is a narrative act, a speech act, that defines history and frames a sequence of events that shapes norm production. The success of legal storytelling is influenced by collective dynamics and reproduction. It bears synergies with collective novel writing. Ronald Dworkin has introduced the metaphor of the chain novel to explain this phenomenon. He argued that legal agents are narrators and interpreters of the law, whose actions contribute to a storyline and collective novel composed by a sequence of authors.

381 Ibid., para. 220.

382 ECCC, *Prosecutor v. Thirith, Sary and Samphan*, Decision on the Appeals Against the Co-Investigating Judges Order on Joint Criminal Enterprise, 20 002/19-09-2007-ECCC/OCIJ (PTC38), 20 May 2010, para. 51 ('the Tadic Appeals Chamber wrongly determined that JCE liability existed under customary international law as it relied on too few cases, 131 and the treaties it relied upon do not actually provide support for JCE liability as claimed because they were not in existence in 1975–79').

383 *Prosecutor v. Delalić et al.*, Judgment, IT-96-21-T, 16 November 1998, para. 340 (*Delalić et al.*, Trial Judgment).

384 Judge Röling had cautioned at Tokyo that 'a Tribunal should be very careful in holding civil government officials responsible for the behaviour of the army in the field'. See ICTR, *Prosecutor v. Musema*, Judgment and Sentence, ICTR-96-13-T, 27 January 2000, para. 134.

Dworkin made this argument in relation to legal interpretation. Dworkin described interpretation as a performative exercise in which legal agents build on previous narratives and clarify understandings within a logic and chronology that has emerged as 'point or value' in practice.[385] He argued that '[e]ach judge must regard himself, in deciding the new case before him, as a partner in a complex chain enterprise of which these innumerable decisions, structures, conventions, and practices are the history'.[386] In *Law's Empire*, he compared norm production to process in which 'a group of novelists writes a novel seriatim'. He wrote: '[E]ach novelist in the chain interprets the chapter he has been given in order to write a new chapter, which is then added to what the next novelist receives, and so on.'[387]

Dworkin's image of 'chain production' has been criticized.[388] Opponents have stressed the autonomy of individual agents in the 'chain'. For instance, Stanley Fish has argued that each contributor to the discourse shapes history and sets in motion a new chain.[389] However, Dworkin's basic idea, namely that legal agents contribute to an overall story and use their discursive power to enhance certain common ideas, has significant appeal in the context of norm projection. Judicial reasoning often relies on 'plots' or 'quasi-plots' in order to frame an argument in a logical way.[390]

International criminal justice has partly developed as a normative system through processes of collective legal storytelling, in which each agent made its contribution to a common plot in the line of previous 'chapters'. A good example is the gradual ban of rape. It emerged through a line of judgments that were in conversation with each other and contributed to a common storyline, like a 'chain novel'. The involvement of different agents (e.g. ICTR, ICTY, and SCSL) in a common plot framed an elastic definition of the form and harms of rape that exceeds many domestic legal prohibitions, a gradual eradication of consent as a defence, and a gender-neutral conception of sexual violence. This narrative paved the way for a differentiated understanding of sexual and gender-based violence and more harm-specific criminalization.

The *ad hoc* tribunals, the SCSL, and later the ICC constructed a modern narrative thread which recognized rape as 'one of the worst sufferings a human being can inflict upon another'.[391] They refined contemporary narratives through a line

[385] Ronald Dworkin, 'Law as interpretation' in W.J. Thomas Mitchell (ed.), *The Politics of Interpretation* (Chicago, IL: University of Chicago Press 1963) 249–70, 264.

[386] Ibid., 263.

[387] Ronald Dworkin, *Law's Empire* (Cambridge, MA: Harvard University Press, 1986), 229.

[388] Judith M. Schelly, 'Interpretation in Law: The Dworkin-Fish Debate (or, Soccer amongst the Gahuku-Gama)' (1985) 73 *California Law Review* 158–80.

[389] Stanley Fish, 'Working on the Chain Gang: Interpretation in the Law and in Literary Criticism, (1982) 9 *Critical Inquiry* 201–16.

[390] Simon Sterns draws an analogy to Paul Ricoeur's concept of quasi plots. See Simon Stern, 'Narrative in the legal text: Judicial opinions and their narratives' in Michael Hanne and Robert Weisberg (eds), *Narrative and Metaphor in the Law* (Cambridge: Cambridge University Press, 2018), 121–39, 134 ('Judicial opinions, even more than the writings of historiams, traffic in quasi plot.').

[391] *Kunarac* Trial Judgment, para. 655

of cases that questioned historical understandings and rewrote legal approaches through mutual engagement with each other. The 'opening chapter' was *Akayesu*. The judgment broke new ground because it defined rape in broad terms, namely as 'a physical invasion of a sexual nature, committed on a person under circumstances which are coercive'.[392] The Chamber viewed rape essentially as 'aggression that is expressed in a sexual manner'.[393] It refused to give a detailed description, since 'the central elements of the crime of rape cannot be captured in a mechanical description of objects and body parts'.[394] This narrative sought to accommodate evolving norms of criminal justice. *Akayesu* also offered new perspectives in relation to relevance of victim consent. In domestic laws, rape is sometimes defined as 'non-consensual intercourse'. Domestic approaches rely on the assumption that individuals are free and autonomous agents who are able to make rational and informed choices. *Akayesu* challenged the feasibility of this logic in relation to atrocity crime situations. It implied that true consent is impossible in coercive circumstances.

ICTY case law developed this plot. It offered a more 'mechanical' definition of rape, in light of the principle of legality and the distinction between rape and serious sexual assault. The *Furundžija* judgment built on *Akayesu* but offered a more specific definition ('sexual penetration')[395] based on general principles of law.[396] It argued that rape requires coercion or force or threat of force against the victim or a third person. It included forced sex into the definition. It held that rape could constitute torture.[397] In *Kunarac*, the first case involving rape as crime against humanity, the ICTY refined the definition offered in *Furundžija*. It branded rape as a violation of sexual autonomy. It stated that the 'basic principle which is truly common to these legal systems is that serious violations of sexual autonomy are to be penalised'.[398] It recognized that consent does not serve as a defence if the 'victim has been subjected to or threatened with or has reason to fear violence, duress, detention or psychological oppression'.[399] The SCSL specified that the *Kunarac* definition 'is broad enough to be gender-neutral as both men and women can be victims of rape'.[400] Together, this line of decisions re-scripted the narratives towards rape. It marked a dramatic move 'away from norms that conceived of sexual violence as a violation of a man's property rights over a woman,

[392] *Prosecutor v. Akyesu*, Case No ICTR-96-4-T, 2 September 1998, para. 598 (*Akayesu* Trial Judgment).
[393] *Prosecutor v. Musema*, Judgement and Sentence, ICTR-96-13-A, 27 January 2000, para. 228.
[394] *Akayesu* Trial Judgment, para. 597.
[395] *Furundžija* Trial Judgment, para 185.
[396] Ibid., paras 176–177.
[397] Ibid., para. 163.
[398] *Kunarac* Trial Judgment, para. 457.
[399] Ibid., para. 464.
[400] RUF Trial Judgment, para. 146.

to norms that come closer to respecting the human dignity and bodily integrity of the victims themselves'.[401]

This collective narrative may gradually foster a new awareness that sexual crimes are not merely sexual acts without or against the will of a person, but attacks on sexual identity or functions.[402]

A similar process is emerging in relation to sexual violence against men and men boys.[403] It is a story of collective engagement with 'silences'. Traditionally, international humanitarian law has failed to address sexual violence against male victims. Such abuses have been treated as a form of bodily harm, torture, other inhumane acts or outrages on personal dignity, rather than sexual violence. Men were mostly seen as perpetrators rather than victims. Prosecutors have been reluctant to bring charges for rape of male victims.[404] Only the Statute of the SCSL and the Rome Statute have expressly branded other forms of sexual violence than rape as sexual crimes. Gendered stereotypes surrounding sexual violence have made it difficult to regard men and boys as victims and to recognize their gendered harm, such as loss of identity, 'feminization', or 'homosexualization'.[405] As Chris Dolen has noted, 'where rape is construed as a violation of women who are regarded as the property of men it is difficult to see men as victims'.[406]

Sexual violence against men and boys has mostly been treated as mere form of violence, rather than a sexual crime per se, due to cultural myths, shame, or reluctance of male victims to come forward, or the general characterization of sexual acts as 'abuse' or 'torture' in testimony.[407] This representation of male sexual violence conveys stereotypes about the presumed invulnerability of men and 'harms women by reinforcing a viewpoint that equates "female" with "victim" '.[408]

[401] K. Alexa Koenig, Ryan Lincoln, and Lauren Groth, 'The Jurisprudence of Sexual Violence' Berkeley Human Rights Centre, May 2011, 14.

[402] See generally Fionnuala Ní Aoláin, 'Gendered Harms and their Interface with International Criminal Law' (2014) 16 *International Feminist Journal of Politics* 622–46.

[403] Sandesh Sivakumaran, 'Lost in Translation: UN Responses to Sexual Violence Against Men and Boys in Situations of Armed Conflict' (2010) 92 *International Review of the Red Cross* 259–77; Sandesh Sivakumaran, 'Sexual Violence Against Men in Armed Conflicts' (2007) 18 *EJIL* 253–76; Solange Mouthaan, 'Sexual Violence Against Men and International Law :Criminalising the Unmentionable' (2013) 13 *International Criminal Law Review* 665–95; Dustin Lewis, 'Unrecognized Victims: Sexual Violence Against Men in Conflict Settings Under International Law' (2009) 27 *Wisconsin International Law Journal* 1–49.

[404] For instance, the SCSL focused on charges of sexual violence against women and girls in the cases against the Armed Forces Revolutionary Council and Charles Taylor.

[405] Dubravka Zarkov, 'The body of the other man—sexual violence and construction of masculinity, sexuality and ethnicity in the croatian media' in Caroline O.N. Moser and Fiona C. Clark (eds), *Victims, Perpetrators or Actors? Gender, Armed Conflict and Political Violence* (London: Zed Books, 2001), 69–82, 77.

[406] Chris Dolan, 'Into the Mainstream: Addressing Sexual Violence Against Men and Boys in Conflict', 14 May 2014, 2, at https://reliefweb.int/sites/reliefweb.int/files/resources/Into_The_Mainstream-Addressing_Sexual_Violence_against_Men_and_Boys_in_Conflict.pdf.

[407] Kirsten Campbell, 'The Gender of Transitional Justice: Law, Sexual Violence and the International Criminal Tribunal for the Former Yugoslavia' (2007) 1 *International Journal of Transitional Justice* 411–32, 425 ('men appear to testify to conflict and women testify to rape').

[408] Anne-Marie De Brouwer, 'The Importance of Understanding Sexual Violence in Conflict' (2015) 48 *Cornell Journal of International Law* 639–49.

It stands in contrast with 'the potential for positive expressivism in international criminal law'.[409]

Some of the stereotypes and shortcomings have been addressed through a range of international decisions and practices.[410] The *ad hoc* tribunals and the SCSL have defined the act in a gender-neutral fashion, covering rape committed against women, girls, men, and boys.[411] The drafters of the Rome Statute added an explicit footnote to that effect to the Elements of rape, specifying that the term 'invasion' is 'intended to be broad enough to be gender-neutral'. The ICTY struggled to articulate the sexual nature of male rape,[412] but demonstrated various forms of male sexual violence in its judgments. It noted *inter alia* that 'the act of [forced fellatio] could constitute rape for which liability could have been found if pleaded in the appropriate manner'.[413]

In Sierra Leone, charges for sexual violence-related mostly to women and girls.[414] The SCSL criticized this in the RUF trial judgment. The Trial Chamber openly acknowledged that the Prosecution 'restricted its pleadings on sexual violence in the Indictment to crimes committed against "women and girls," thereby excluding male victims of sexual violence'.[415] But it addressed sexual violence against men in its judgment. It stated that fighters used 'perverse methods of sexual violence against women and men of all ages' in order to 'break the will of the population and ensure their submission to AFRC/RUF control'.[416]

The *Bemba* case was the first case which dealt intensively with stigmas of male rape. The OTP noted in its closing statements that men were raped in order to challenge their power and leadership and humiliate them within their communities. The Pre-Trial Chamber acknowledged in the Confirmation Decision that that 'civilian women and men were raped'.[417] The Trial Judgment marked the first conviction for male rape as a specific charge.[418]

409 Valerie Oosterveld, 'Sexual Violence Directed Against Men and Boys in Armed Conflict or Mass Atrocity: Addressing a Gendered Harm in International Criminal Tribunals' (2014) 10 *Journal of International Law and International Relations* 107–28, 115.

410 Helen Touquet and Ellen Gorris, 'Out of the Shadows? The Inclusion of Men and Boys in Conceptualisations of Wartime Sexual Violence' (2016) 24 *Reproductive Health Matters* 36–46.

411 *Akayesu* Trial Judgment, para 598; *Kunarac* Trial Judgment, para 460.

412 On male rape, see Ruth Graham, 'Male Rape and the Careful Construction of the Male Victim' (2006) 15 *Social & Legal Studies*, 187–208

413 *Prosecutor v. Mucić et al.* IT-96-21, Trial Judgment, 16 November 1998, para. 1066.

414 In the *Taylor* and *AFRC* cases, the Trial Chamber found that it was unable to address sexual violence against men in light of the limited charges of the Prosecution.

415 RUF Trial Judgment, para. 1303.

416 Ibid., paras 1347–1348.

417 *Prosecutor v. Bemba*, Decision pursuant to Article 61(7)(a) and (b) of the Rome Statute on the Charges of the Prosecutor Against Jean-Pierre Bemba Gombo, ICC-01/05-01/08, 15 June 2009, para. 286.

418 See *Prosecutor v. Bemba*, Judgment pursuant to Article 74 of the Statute, ICC-01/05-01/08, 21 March 2016, para. 633.

In the *Ongwen* case, the charges confirmed related to crimes against women and girls, but the Legal Representatives of Victims stressed the need to hear evidence relating to sexual violence against men. They noted that 'sexual violence committed by the LRA was not limited to violence against women and girls. A significant number of male participating victims were either victims of rape, forced to carry out rapes, or forced to abuse the corpses of killed abductees in sexualised ways.'[419]

They relied on case law of the ICTY and ICTR to argue that male rape was part of the crimes charged, since it constitutes a form of torture.[420] They also identified some of the gendered dimensions of harm.

> The true nature of the crime is the humiliation, emasculation, homo-sexualisation and 'feminisation' of the victim. Sexual violence against men (as with women) in conflict settings is usually motivated significantly less by sexual gratification than by an attempt to exert power and dominance over the victim and the victim's community.[421]

The *Ntaganda* Trial judgment entered a conviction for rape committed by UPC/FPLC soldiers against men.[422] It clarified expressly that the term 'invasion' in the Court's legal framework 'includes same-sex penetration, and encompasses both male and/or female perpetrators and victims.'[423]

There is thus an emerging line of decisions and practices which seek to counter existing biases and gaps and to demonstrate that sexual violence against men and boys should no longer be downplayed as an ordinary form of physical abuse. This collective rewriting of narratives is a tool to reveal otherwise hidden forms of harm.

2.2.4 Techniques of internalization

A third type of norm expression relates to norm internalization. As David Luban has observed, substantive norm affirmation or projection are not the only forms of advancing 'moral learning.'[424] Norms that are not enforced may easily become

[419] *Prosecutor v. Ongwen*, Victims' requests for leave to present evidence and to present victims' views and concerns in person, ICC-02/04-01/15, 2 February 2018, para. 16.

[420] *Prosecutor v. Ongwen*, Request for reconsideration of the 'Decision on the Legal Representatives for Victims Requests to Present Evidence and Views and Concerns and related requests', ICC-02/04-01/15, 12 March 2018, para. 13.

[421] *Prosecutor v. Ongwen*, Victims' requests for leave to present evidence and to present victims' views and concerns in person, para. 17.

[422] *Prosecutor v. Ntaganda*, Judgment, ICC-01/04-02/06-2359, 8 July 2019, paras 945–948.

[423] Ibid., para. 933.

[424] David Luban, 'After the Honeymoon: Reflections on the Current State of International Criminal Justice' (2003) 11 *JICJ* 505–15, 512.

moot. This is why 'the devolution of the norm from international to local institutions is equally important'.[425]

Norm internalization involves more than just narration or a 'broadcasting' of norms. It is deemed to bridge the distance between 'speaker' and the 'audience'. It creates incentives for norm acceptance and non-repetition of violations. It involves integration of norms into an internal value system. Norms become intersubjective.[426] They are related to intended audiences and deemed to inform habitus or ordinary routine.[427] This dimension remains one of the weak spots of international criminal justice.

2.2.4.1 Understandings of norm internalization

Norm internalization can be understood in different ways. In legal scholarship, it is associated with a 'process by which nations incorporate international law concepts into domestic practice'.[428] Internalization takes place when norms are reflected in executive action, legislative action or judicial interpretation. As Harold Koh has argued, it is often a transnational process which is shaped by cycles of interaction, interpretation, internalization, and obedience.[429] It creates a growing sense of legal obligation and recognition of international legal principles. It differs from coercion-based forms of compliance which are grounded in motives of punishments or reward.[430] It increases reputational costs related to violations, both internationally and domestically.[431]

In the social sciences, norm internalization is viewed as a didactic process that involves social learning and cognitive change. It is a multi-step process which translates external norms into shared norms and corresponding goals, intentions, and actions. For instance, political internalization occurs through norm acceptance by political elites and their application in policies. Social internalization is emerging when society and individuals relate to norms and values and conform to them as a set of shared norms. It results in a higher degree of intolerance with

[425] Ibid., 511.

[426] Finnemore and Sikkink, 'International Norm Dynamics and Political Change' 914.

[427] Habitus relates to preferences or dispositions through which persons connect to the social world. On Bourdieu's conception, see Jason D. Edgerton and Lance W. Roberts, 'Cultural Capital or Habitus? Bourdieu and Beyond in the Explanation of Enduring Educational Inequality' (2014) 12 *Theory and Research in Education* 193–220.

[428] Dana Zartner, 'Internalization of international law' in *Oxford Research Encyclopedia, International Studies* (Oxford: Oxford University Press), 1. See also Sarah H. Cleveland, 'Norm Internalization and U.S. Economic Sanctions' (2001) 26 *Yale Journal of International Law* 1–91, 26.

[429] Harold Hongju Koh, 'Internalization Through Socialization' (2005) 54 *Duke Law Journal* 975–82; Harold Hongju Koh, 'How Is International Human Rights Law Enforced?' (1999) 74 *Indiana Law Review* 1397–418, .

[430] Harold Hongju Koh, 'The 1998 Frankel Lecture: Bringing International Law Home' (1998–1999) 35 *Houston Law Review* 623–81, 642–3

[431] See George W. Downs and Michael A. Jones. 'Rational Choice and International Law: Reputation, Compliance and International Law' (2002) 31 *Journal of Legal Studies* 95–114; Robert O. Keohane, 'Rational Choice Theory and International Law: Insights and Limitations' (2002) 31 *Journal of Legal Studies* 307–19.

regard to norm violation.[432] Norm-abiding behaviour is gradually felt as an appropriate course of action, while deviant behaviour is perceived as wrong or lacking public legitimacy.

A crucial step in internalization is 'translation'. For instance, new norms may 'have to fight their way into institutional thinking'.[433] Norm translation is a means to facilitate the transfer of a norm from one context to another and to counter norm resistance.[434] It provides an instrument to address concerns and objections against the norm and to adjust it. This step is often blended out in expressivist practices, which are oriented towards emulation, that is, repetition and imitation, rather than integration into context.

2.2.4.2 Legal parameters

Norm internalization is a long-term process. It relies on communicative power and the persuasiveness of information or communication. It is closely related to the rationale of prevention. As Payam Akhavan has stated, criminal sanctions serve to 'instill voluntary or "good faith" respect for just conduct by discrediting inhumane or unjust conduct', while norm internalization may be deemed to encourage 'habitual or subliminal conformity with the law'.[435]

In international criminal law, the existing formal infrastructure to foster norm internalization is limited. International law has traditionally paid limited attention to norm internalization since it was deemed to fall within the domestic sphere of states. Several international conventions contain formal legal duties to incorporate treaty provisions into domestic law.[436] However, most conventions in the field of international criminal law are 'suppression' treaties. They proscribe a duty to criminalize certain forms of conduct in order to 'suppress' crimes, while leaving it within the discretion of states how to implement this duty.[437] For instance, the Geneva Conventions are 'suppression' treaties. The mandate states to 'enact any legislation necessary to provide effective penal sanctions for persons

[432] Giulia Andrighetto, Daniel Villatoro, and Rosaria Conte, 'Norm Internalisation in Artificial Societies' (2010) 23 *AI Communications* 325–39, 337.

[433] Ole Elgström, 'Norm Negotiations: The Construction of New Norms Regarding Gender and Development in EU Foreign Aid Policy' (2000) 7 *Journal of European Public Policy* 457–76, 458.

[434] Andrea Schneiker, 'NGOs as Norm Takers: Insider–Outsider Networks as Translators of Norms' (2017) 19 *International Studies Review* 381–406, 383; Aaron Boesenecker and Leslie Vinjamuri, 'Lost in Translation? Civil Society, Faith-Based Organizations and the Negotiation of International Norms' (2011) 5 *International Journal of Transitional Justice* 345–65.

[435] Payam Akhavan, 'Justice in the Hague, Peace in the Former Yugoslavia? A Commentary on the United Nations War Crimes Tribunal' (1998) 20 *Human Rights Quarterly* 737–816, 741.

[436] Christian Tomuschat, 'The duty to prosecute international crimes committed by individuals' in Hans-Joachim Cremer, Thomas Giegerich, Dagmar Richter, and Andreas Zimmermann (eds), *Tradition und Weltoffenheit des Rechts: Festschrift für Helmut Steinberger* (Berlin: Springer, 2002), 315–29; Kevin Jon Heller, 'What Is an International Crime? (A Revisionist History)' (2017) 58 *Harvard International Law Journal* 353–420, 391.

[437] Neil Boister, 'Human Rights Protections in the Suppression Conventions' (2002) 2 *Human Rights Law Review* 199–227.

committing' grave breaches'. However, they do not 'explicitly require such prosecutions to reflect the international nature of the crimes committed'.[438] Crimes against humanity are only partially captured by existing treaty regimes. The Genocide Convention brands genocide as an international crime, but relies on the traditional suppression logic, by requiring states to 'enact, in accordance with their respective Constitutions, the necessary legislation to give effect to the provisions of the present Convention'.[439] No treaty requires criminalization of aggression.

In terms of legal obligation, states retain flexibility as to norm internalization. As the ICTY noted in *Hadzihasanović*:

> [S]ince the end of World War II, majority practice seems to provide more than enough freedom in prosecuting international crimes solely under domestic criminal law as ordinary criminal offences. As such, many defendants have been prosecuted in national jurisdictions for ordinary crimes, although they were committed in the context of armed conflicts and therefore liable to be characterised as war crimes.[440]

The ICC Statute did not break this logic. It does not contain an express duty to implement crimes into domestic law. The principle of complementarity reaffirms that national authorities have the primary responsibility for investigating and prosecuting atrocity crimes. But it serves mostly as an incentive for states to approximate substantive criminal law in the area of core crimes. It encourages processes of approximation indirectly, namely through norm expression, articulation of practices, and policy incentives for states to avoid the exercise of ICC jurisdiction. There is, at best, an 'obligation of result' in relation to criminalization. Domestic crime definitions may be wider or more restrictive than ICC crimes.[441] The lack of domestic internalization is not sanctioned per se but offers the ICC the possibility to act.

In practice, many states domesticate crimes for expressivist purposes. For instance, Belgium gave such a justification in relation to the criminalisation of genocide. It stated:

> [T]he inclusion of a criminalisation of genocide in national criminal law is important because of its symbolic value, in the sense that the perpetrators of a

[438] See Ward Ferdinandusse, 'The Prosecution of Grave Breaches in National Courts' (2009) 7 *JICJ* 723–41, 729. See also *Prosecutor v. Hadzihasanović and Kubura*, Judgment, IT-01-47-T, 15 March 2006, para. 260 (*Hadzihasanović* Trial Judgment).

[439] Article 5 of the Convention on the Prevention and Punishment of the Crime of Genocide, UNTS Vol. 78, p. 277.

[440] *Hadzihasanović* Trial Judgment, para. 256.

[441] See Julio Bacio Terracino, 'National Implementation of ICC Crimes' (2007) 5 *JICJ* 421–40.

> genocide will be punished for committing that specific offence, obviating the need for the criminal Judge to convict on the basis of other characterisations such as criminal homicide or murder. The effect of a conviction for genocide and its preventative nature will be reinforced. [442]

Similarly, the obligation to prevent crimes is only partially regulated in existing treaties. It is related to due diligence duties of states. The contours of duties of prevention, in particular the scope of positive duties and their extraterritorial dimensions remain contested.[443] The ICJ established that the duty to prevent is separate from the duty to punish.[444] It argued in the *Genocide* case that the duty to prevent the crime of genocide is not only tied to territorial or personal jurisdiction but applies even in relation to extraterritorial events. It found that a state violates this obligation in cases where it 'manifestly failed to take all measures to prevent genocide which were within its power, and which might have contributed to preventing the genocide'.[445]

It added that the scope of the duty depends on geographic, political, and other links to the persons or groups at issue.[446]

The ILC framed the obligation to prevent more cautiously in the Draft Articles on Crimes Against Humanity. It did not assert a general obligation of states to prevent crimes against humanity outside their borders in line with the ICJ test. It merely stated that

> [e]ach State also undertakes to prevent crimes against humanity, in conformity with international law, including through: (a) effective legislative, administrative, judicial or other preventive measures, such as education and training programmes, in any territory under its jurisdiction; and (b) cooperation with other States, relevant intergovernmental organizations and, as appropriate, other organizations.[447]

[442] Belgian Senate, Report of the Justice Commission on the Law for the Punishment of Genocide, enforcing the Convention on the Prevention and Punishment of the Crime of Genocide of 9 December 1948, 1 December 1998, No. 1-749/3, para. II, (A) and (B). See also Ward Ferdinandusse, *Direct Application of International Criminal Law in National Courts* (The Hague: TMC Asser Press, 2005) 209.

[443] Article 2 of the UN Convention against Torture (UNTS Vol. 1465, p. 85) obliges contracting parties to prevent torture 'in any territory under its jurisdiction'. Article 1 of the Inter-American Convention against Forced Disappearances involves a broader obligation 'to cooperate' to 'prevent the forced disappearance of persons'. The Convention on the Suppression and Punishment of the Crime of Apartheid (UNTS Vol. 1015, p. 243) contains a duty 'prevent any encouragement of the crime of apartheid'.

[444] ICJ, *Application of the Convention on the Prevention and Punishment of the Crime of Genocide* (*Bosnia and Herzegovina v. Serbia and Montenegro*), Judgment of 26 February 2007, para. 425 ('two distinct yet connected obligations').

[445] Ibid., para. 230.

[446] Ibid.

[447] See Article 4 of the Draft Articles. See ILC, Fourth report on crimes against humanity, A/CN.4/725, 18 February 2019, 129. For a discussion, see William A. Schabas, 'Prevention of Crimes Against Humanity' (2018) 16 *JICJ* 705–28.

A breach of the obligation to prevent is not a 'criminal violation' but a factor relevant in the assessment of state responsibility.

2.2.4.3 Communicative techniques

International criminal courts and tribunals have sought to overcome the limitations of existing legal frameworks and to foster legal norm internalization through communicative techniques, including persuasion, and social interaction.[448] They have *inter alia* relied on arguments of common identity, convergence of interests, symbolic meaning, or structures of interaction, in order to encourage norm internalization, including norm observation irrespective of external sanction.

2.2.4.3.1 Common identity

A first strategy of norm internalization is the grounding of norms in a common system.[449] The embedding encourages the emergence of common identity and reinforces consistent application. States are more likely to internalize norms if they correlate to their identity. As Bruce Broomhall has argued, the 'entrenchment of international criminal law as a regular feature of the international system' is closely related to 'the development of a deeply rooted culture of accountability that leads to a convergence of perceived interests and of behaviour on the part of the States responsible for enforcing this law'.[450]

International criminal courts and tribunals have presented some of their weaknesses as strengths and relied on the idea of a system to enhance norm internalization. For instance, the ICC has defined itself not only as a treaty-based court but as a system of justice. The OTP has used this image expressly in its prosecutorial strategy. It has stressed the converging interests between the Court and states, arguing that a 'Court based on the principle of complementarity ensures . . . an interdependent, mutually reinforcing international system of justice'.[451]

The system argument has been developed in ICC jurisprudence. In the Myanmar context, the Pre-Trial Chamber described the ICC as 'legal-judicial-institutional entity which has engaged and cooperated not only with States Parties, but with a large number of States not Party to the Statute as well'.[452]

It then compared the ICC to the United Nations in terms of objective international personality. It relied on the famous passage of the ICJ in the *Reparations* case[453] and applied it to the Court. It noted: '[M]ore than 120 States, representing

[448] See generally on OTP Policies, Kotecha, 'The Art of Rhetoric' 947–60.

[449] Paul F. Diehl, Charlotte Ku, and Daniel Zamora,'The Dynamics of International Law: The Interaction of Normative and Operating Systems' (2003) 57 *International Organization* 43–75.

[450] Bruce Broomhall, *International Justice and the International Criminal Court: Between Sovereignty and the Rule of Law* (Oxford: Oxford University Press, 2003), 3.

[451] ICC, OTP, Report on Prosecutorial Strategy, 14 September 2006, 5.

[452] ICC, Decision on the "Prosecution's Request for a Ruling on Jurisdiction under Article 19(3) of the Statute, ICC-RoC46(3)-01/18, 6 September 2018, para. 48.

[453] ICJ, *Reparation for Injuries Suffered in the Service of the United Nations*, Advisory Opinion, [1949] ICJ Rep. 174, p. 185'.

the vast majority of the members of the international community, had the power, in conformity with international law, to bring into being an entity called the "International Criminal Court", possessing objective international personality, and not merely personality recognized by them alone.'[454] This *dictum* sent a message that the ICC is a quasi-universal treaty system in which mutual interests converge.

The system argument has gained practical application in relation to cooperation. International courts have used George Scelle's image of 'role splitting' (*dedoublement fonctionnel*)[455] in order to address their own limitations and stress the role of states in norm implementation. Scelle postulated that states are community agents and act on behalf of the international community, when they enforce international law.[456] This theory implies that states act on behalf of the tribunal when they enforce their decisions. The ICC used this idea to underscore cooperation duties in the context of the controversy over immunity in interstate-relations. It held that 'when cooperating' with the ICC and 'therefore acting on its behalf', States Parties 'are instruments for the enforcement of the *jus puniendi* of the international community whose exercise has been entrusted to this Court when States have failed to prosecute those responsible for the crimes within its jurisdiction.'[457]

This reasoning strengthens the idea of a shared sense of identity between the ICC and its members in order to foster commitment to cooperation and enforcement of norms.[458] It seeks to gain additional 'buy in' from states, in order to encourage norm internalization, even in areas where is legal contestation.

The idea of a system has further been used to extend strategies of prevention beyond existing legal frameworks. Crime prevention relies on a tripartite relationship involving perpetrators, victims, and third parties. This is sometimes referred to as the 'prevention triangle'.[459] International criminal justice has placed particular emphasis on systemic prevention and the role of third-party actors in this triangular

[454] ICC, Decision on the "Prosecution's Request for a Ruling on Jurisdiction under Article 19(3) of the Statute, para. 48.

[455] See Antonio Cassese, 'Remarks on Scelle's Theory of "Role Splitting" (dedoublement fonctionnel) in International Law' (1990) 1 *EJIL* 210–31.

[456] Antonio Cassese applied this to international criminal justice, when arguing that the ICTY 'needs artificial limbs to walk and work' and that 'these artificial limbs are state authorities'. See Antonio Cassese, 'On the Current Trends towards Criminal Prosecution and Punishment of Breaches of International Humanitarian Law' (1998) 9 *EJIL* 2–17, 13.

[457] *Prosecutor v. Al Bashir*, Corrigendum to the Decision Pursuant to Article 87(7) of the Rome Statute on the Failure by the Republic of Malawi to Comply with the Cooperation Requests Issued by the Court with Respect to the Arrest and Surrender of Omar Hassan Ahmad Al Bashir, ICC-02/05-01/09, 13 December 2011, para. 46.

[458] On the argument of states as trustees of community interests, see Kress, 'Preliminary Observations on the ICC Appeals Chamber's Judgment', 15–16.

[459] Fred Grünfeld, 'The role of bystanders in Rwanda and Srebrenica: Lessons learned' in Alette Smeulers and Roelof Haveman (eds), *Supranational Criminology: Towards a Criminology of International Crimes* (Antwerp: Intersentia, 2008), 457–86, 458

relationship. It has used expressivist language to push prevention strategies beyond their narrow confines.[460]

Post-war justice after the Second World War was deeply concerned about preventing future wars. It associated the establishment of crimes against peace with emergence of preventive strategies. At Nuremberg, Jackson drew particular attention to this point. He stated:

> Personal punishment, to be suffered only in the event the war is lost, will probably not be a sufficient deterrent to prevent a war . . . the ultimate step in avoiding periodic wars . . . is to make statesmen responsible to law . . . [I]f it is to serve a useful purpose it must condemn aggression by any other nations, including those which sit here now in judgment.[461]

At Tokyo, Joseph B. Keenan, Chief Prosecutor of the International Prosecution Section, relied on a collective 'we' in order to stress third-party duties. He noted that 'our specific purpose is to contribute all we soundly [can] towards the end—the prevention of the scourge of aggressive war'.[462]

The use of 'we' is a common rhetoric figure in international criminal law.[463] It is both an instrument to remove distance to crimes through expression of a 'shared emotion' (*pathos*) and tool to build solidarity and create a responsive community. It fits within Durkheim's conception of the creation of a moral community through law. As Immi Tallgren has noted, in international criminal law, the 'we' 'continuously reconstitutes itself in expressing its punitive feelings'.[464] If, however, the 'we' remains 'silent on crime, the collective beliefs and sentiments fade, endangering the existence of an audible 'we'.[465]

In the *Lubanga* case, the first trial of the ICC, Prosecutor Luis Moreno-Ocampo used prevention as a central argument to justify the focus on child soldiers. The expressivist logic of the case is clearly reflected in an OTP press release, justifying the trial:

> Regardless of the outcome of the proceedings, this case represents a huge step in the struggle against these serious crimes against children. Child conscription destroys

[460] On rhetoric in prosecutorial opening statements, see Damien Rogers, *Law, Politics and the Limits of Prosecuting Mass Atrocity* (New York, NY: Palgrave Macmillan, 2018), 85–102; id. 'Prosecutors opening statements: The rhetoric of law, politics, and silent war' in Nobuo Hayashi and Cecilia Bailliet, *The Legitimacy of International Criminal Tribunals* (Cambridge: Cambridge University Press, 2017), 325-350.

[461] Robert Jackson, Nuremberg Trials, Opening Address for the United States, Nazi Conspiracy & Aggression, Volume I (Washington DC: United States Government Printing Office, 1946), 172.

[462] For a full analysis of rhetoric of law, politics and war in Jackson's and Kennan's openings, see Rogers, *Chief amongst the Angels? International Prosecutors and the Moralist Project* 131–52.

[463] Immi Tallgren, 'The Voice of the International: Who is Speaking?' (2015) 13 *JICJ* 135–55.

[464] Ibid., 148.

[465] Ibid.

> the lives and futures of thousands of children around the world. This case will contribute to exposing the problem and in stopping these criminal practices.[466]

At the opening of the trial, Ocampo reiterated this argument. He noted that 'the aim [of the trial] is to end impunity and contribute to the prevention of future crimes': 'If convicted, Thomas Lubanga's sentence will send a clear message: The era of impunity is ending.'[467]

Preventive objectives are frequently echoed in sentencing decisions. For instance, both the ICTY and the SCSL have stated that one of the 'main purposes of a sentence is to influence the legal awareness of the accused, the surviving victims, their relatives, the witnesses and the general public in order to reassure them that the legal system is implemented and enforced'.[468] Additionally, 'sentencing is intended to convey the message that globally accepted laws and rules have to be obeyed by everybody'.[469]

This language gives third-party actors a role in the 'prevention triangle' that is far less well articulated in legal norms. It reiterates the message that bystanders cannot remain neutral in relation to violations. The implicit or explicit use of 'we' notions is deemed to influence the psychology of recipients and to animate resistance to crimes.

2.2.4.3.2 Conformity with existing domestic norms

A second strategy to foster norm internalization is their alignment with existing domestic systems. International norms are more likely to gain acceptance in domestic systems if they are grounded in existing domestic norms. For instance, legal internalization becomes easier 'when the format, substance, and ideas behind the international rules closely mimic the state's own domestic law'.[470] It is thus common to ground norm affirmation and projection in domestic consent or to grant leeway for some degree of deference. In this way, the underlying norms are gradually brought in alignment with domestic goals, intentions, and actions.

A classical example is the approach towards crimes against humanity. The concept was presented as an extension of existing domestic norms. The synergies to domestic law were used to downplay its novel nature on the international plane and to reinforce its implementation. The ICTY used this technique in *Tadić*, when

[466] ICC, Press Release, 'Child soldier charges in the first International Criminal Court case', The Hague, 28 August 2006, ICC-OTP-20060828-157-En, at http://www.rscsl.org/Clippings/2006/2006-08/pc2006-8-29.pdf, 13–14.

[467] See Opening statement Lubanga, 26 January 2009, at https://www.icc-cpi.int/NR/rdonlyres/89E8515B-DD8F-4251-AB08-6B60CB76017F/279630/ICCOTPSTLMO20090126ENG2.pdf.

[468] *Nikolić* Sentencing Judgment, para. 139; *Taylor* Sentencing Judgment, para. 16.

[469] Ibid.

[470] Zartner, 'Internalization of international law' 14–15 ('states whose legal traditions are founded on religious legal traditions often have very different societal understandings of law and do not accept external law created by nonreligious authorities that may contradict their religious beliefs').

it justified the customary nature of crimes against humanity. It stated that the use of crimes against humanity in the Nuremberg Charter marked 'the first technical use of the term', but did not introduce 'a novel concept'.[471]

The ICC Statute has been branded as an affirmation of existing law rather than as a projection of new norms. This is reflected in the preamble of the Statute. It recalls that 'it is the duty of every State to exercise its criminal jurisdiction over those responsible for international crimes'.[472] This framing lends support to the view that the statutory duties are grounded in pre-existing obligations. It makes internalization easier.

International criminal courts and tribunals have been reluctant to challenge domestic implementation of crimes. The *ad hoc* tribunals have exercised restraint in judging domestic implementing legislation. The ICTY held that 'there is no rule, either in customary or in positive international law, which obligates states to prosecute acts which can be characterised as war crimes solely on the basis of international humanitarian law, completely setting aside any characterisations of their national criminal law'.[473]

Both tribunals formulated domestic prosecution under an international crime label as an incentive. They have defined conditions for the transfer of cases to domestic jurisdictions under Rule 11*bis* and cooperation schemes designed to facilitate sharing of evidence with domestic actors. In this context, judges argued that they would be unable to transfer cases back to domestic jurisdictions in case of ordinary criminal prosecution. The ICTR Appeals Chamber clarified that Norway's proposed prosecution of genocide as mass murder under the general provisions of its criminal code would fail to reflect the gravity of genocide.[474] It thereby stressed the symbolic value of international criminal prosecution.[475]

The ICC has refused to assume the role of a supervisory organ of domestic implementing legislation. It has specified its approach in the Libyan cases. It noted that a state must not necessarily investigate or prosecute a crime under an international crime label in order to bring a successful admissibility challenge. The Appeals Chamber stated that 'there is no requirement in the Statute for a crime to be prosecuted as an international crime domestically' since it is 'the alleged conduct, as opposed to its legal characterisation, that matters'.[476] It introduced

[471] *Tadić* Trial Judgment, para. 618.

[472] Para. 6 of the preamble.

[473] *Hadzihasanović* Trial Judgment, para. 260.

[474] *Prosecutor v. Bagaragaza*, Decision on Prosecutor's extremely urgent motion for revocation of the referral to the Kingdom of the Netherlands pursuant to Rule 11bis (F) and (G), ICTR 2005-86-11bis, 17 August 2007, para.14.

[475] See also *Prosecutor v. Bagaragaza*, Decision on Rule 11bis Appeal, ICTR-05-86-AR11bis, 30 August 2006, para. 18 and para. 19 arguing that it could not 'sanction the referral of a case to a jurisdiction for trial where the conduct cannot be charged as a serious violation of international humanitarian law'.

[476] *Prosecutor v. Gaddafi and Al-Senussi*, Judgment on the appeal of Mr Abdullah Al-Senussi against the decision of Pre-Trial Chamber I of 11 October 2013 entitled 'Decision on the admissibility of the case against Abdullah Al-Senussi', ICC-01/11-01/11-565, 24 July 2014, para. 119

a 'mirror' image in order to determine the admissibility assessment. It held that '[w]hat is required is a judicial assessment of whether the case that the State is investigating sufficiently mirrors the one that the Prosecutor is investigating'.[477]

The 'mirror' image is nowhere expressly in the Statute. It serves as an incentive for national institutions to model their case strategy after the ICC in order to challenge admissibility. The ICC implies that domestic investigations and prosecutions must cover the 'same underlying incidents'.[478]

This line of jurisprudence projects domestic implementation of crimes as an asset for states without forcing them to act. The 'mirror' image is essentially a rhetoric invention to encourage norm internalization through procedural carrots and sticks. One of its downsides it that may foster 'imitation', rather than internalization. As Sarah Nouwen has shown, it might lead to superficial implementation or artificial legal constructs that remain detached from social reality in conflict or post-conflict settings.[479]

2.2.4.3.3 Establishment of communicative structures

A third technique to stimulate norm internalization is the establishment of communicative structures to encourage norm support and trigger self-enforcement.[480] It has been developed rather late in international criminal justice and remains rudimentary.[481]

International criminal justice relies on the premise that norm projection and interaction with states will internalize a commitment to criminal accountability and provide incentives to prosecute international crimes. ICC Prosecutor Ocampo formulated this vision for the ICC when taking office. He argued that the absence of cases would be a major indicator of the functioning of the ICC as a system.[482] However, there are relatively few treaty regimes with governance mechanisms that foster long-term norm support. International criminal courts and tribunals go in

[477] *Prosecutor v. Gaddafi and Al-Senussi*, Judgment on the appeal of Libya against the decision of Pre-Trial Chamber I of 31 May 2013 entitled 'Decision on the admissibility of the case against Saif Al-Islam Gaddafi', ICC-01/11-01/11-547-Red, 21 May 2014, para. 73 (*Gaddafi* Appeal Judgment).

[478] Ibid., para. 72.

[479] Sarah Nouwen, *Complementarity in the Line of Fire:The Catalysing Effect of the International Criminal Court in Uganda and Sudan* (Cambridge: Cambridge University Press, 2013), 413. For instance, in situations, such as Libya, Kenya or Uganda, ICC action has triggered the adoption of new domestic legislation in relation to core crimes. However, internal implementation processes were guided by the aim to avoid external ICC intervention, rather than longer term rationales of norm internalization. The interaction between the Court and domestic jurisdictions was thus essentially an action/response game driven by the intent to avoid ICC interference, rather than a process of social learning

[480] Amrita. Kapur, 'The Value of International–National Interactions and Norm Interpretations in Catalysing National Prosecutions of Sexual Violence' (2016) 6 *Oñati Socio-legal Series* 62–90.

[481] Yvonne Dutton, 'Bridging the Legitimacy Divide: The International Criminal Court's Domestic Perception Challenge' (2017) *56 Columbia Journal of Transnational Law* 70–122.

[482] ICC, Ceremony for the solemn undertaking of the Chief Prosecutor of the International Criminal Court, Statement made by Mr Luis Moreno-Ocampo 16 June 2003, 3 ('complementarity implies that the absence of trials before this Court, as a consequence of the regular functioning of national institutions, would be a major success').

and out or move from situation to situation. Communicative structures are typically limited to complementarity strategies,[483] cooperation, monitoring schemes, and outreach.[484] In practice, NGOs have served as compliance and internalization 'entrepreneurs', promoting the advancement of norms of international criminal justice in society.[485] This mediation poses risks for internalization. It may distort the meaning of the message or impede critical engagement with norm projection.[486] As Fréderic Mégret has shown, NGOs may be tempted to advocate for over-compliance,[487] that is, articulate maximalist positions in relation to internalization that do not always offer the best systemic fit for domestic systems.

2.2.4.3.4 Engagement with civic duties in legal discourse

In some instances, legal acts or decisions contain speech acts that are directly oriented towards norm internalization by individuals. Some judgments have addressed civic duties of individuals in order to encourage norm-abiding behaviour.[488] The decisions appeal to ideals of integrity, honour, morality, and professionalism in order to challenge individual predispositions and encourage resistance to crime.

The Nuremberg judgment made this argument in general terms. It stated that 'individuals have international duties which transcend the national obligations of obedience imposed by the individual State'.[489]

The trials under Control Council Law No. 10 applied this logic to different professions and fields of society. The so-called Doctors' trial (*United States of America vs. Karl Brandt et al.*) relied on the 'ethics of the medical profession' in order to condemn Nazi experiments. The judgment countered utilitarian justifications of Nazi experiments (e.g. their alleged benefit for the 'good of society') by reference to the

[483] The ad hoc tribunals or the SCSL have developed strategies to foster domestic internalization as part of their completion strategy. These mechanisms are 'quasi'-complementarity schemes, aimed to encourage greater self-enforcement of norms after the closure of the tribunals. At the ICC, complementarity offers room for the Prosecutor and the Court to engage with ongoing domestic justice discourses and to encourage processes of normative adaptation. See **section 3.2.2.**

[484] Victor Peskin, 'Courting Rwanda: The Promises and Pitfalls of the ICTR Outreach Programme' (2005) 3 *JICJ* 950–61, 953. Outreach has been associated with broader educational rationales, namely to 'produce greater judicial accountability, demonstrate that judicial arbitrariness is no longer acceptable, educate on the rule of law, enable deterrence of future crimes and promote peace and reconciliation'. Philipp Schulz, 'Discussing Community-Based Outreach Activities by the International Criminal Tribunal for Rwanda' (2017) *11 Journal of Eastern African Studies* 347–66, 354.

[485] Schneiker, 'NGOs as Norm Takers' 381.

[486] Internalization often requires an additional act of 'translation' to the context. This step may get lost through NGO advocacy.

[487] See Fréderic Mégret, 'Too much of a good thing?: Implementation and the uses of complementarity' in Carsten Stahn and Mohamed El Zeidy (eds), *The International Criminal Court and Complementarity: From Theory to Practice* (Cambridge: Cambridge University Press, 2010), 361–90, 367–76, referring to implementation as a 'Trojan horse'.

[488] On civil courage, see generally Günther, 'Positive General Prevention and the Idea of Civic Courage in International Criminal Law' 220.

[489] Trial of the Major War Criminals before the International Military Tribunal, vol. I, Nürnberg 1947, 223.

cardinal value of consent. It stated: 'The duty and responsibility for ascertaining the quality of the consent rests upon each individual who initiates, directs or engages in the experiment. It is a personal duty and responsibility which may not be delegated to another with impunity.'[490]

The *Justice* trial (*United States of America v. Josef Altstötter et al.*) addressed the professional duties of the legal profession, that is crimes committed in the name of law.[491] Prosecutor Telford Taylor clarified this objective in his opening remarks of the case. He noted that the conduct of judges and officials of the Nazi judicial system was 'a dishonor to their profession.'[492] He stated that defendants could 'no more escape that responsibility by virtue of their judicial robes than the general by his uniform.'[493]

The judgment recognized that the Nazi system divided judges into 'one of two categories', namely those 'who still retained ideals of judicial independence and who administered justice with a measure of impartiality and moderation' and those 'who with fanatical zeal enforced the will of the Party with such severity that they experienced no difficulties and little interference from party officials.'[494] For the second category, it created an exception to the general doctrine of judicial immunity, according to which judges should not be held personally liable for their judicial actions. It justified this exception on the ground that the respective entities 'resembled administrative tribunals acting under directives from above in a quasi-judicial manner.'[495]

Judith Shklar concluded that the Nuremberg trials re-instilled a sense of legality into the legal profession. She noted that the trials 'induced the German legal profession to rediscover and publicly proclaim anew the value of the principle of legality in criminal law which for so many years had been forgotten and openly disdained.'[496]

International criminal law has made it clear that soldiers have a duty to engage with norms that postulate contradictory behaviour. Post-Second World War case law has clarified that soldiers cannot blindly follow authority. It assumes that

[490] *United States of America v. Karl Brandt et al.* (Case I) November 21, 1946—August 20, 1947, 2 Trials of War Criminals Before the Nuremberg Military Tribunals under Control Council Law No. 10, 181–2 (1949).

[491] See generally Hans Petter Graver, *Judges Against Justice: On Judges When the Rule of Law is Under Attack* (Heidelberg: Springer, 2015).

[492] *United States of America vs. Josef Altstötter et al.*, Opening Statement for the Prosecution (Telford Taylor), Transcript, 35 at http://nuremberg.law.harvard.edu/transcripts/3-transcript-for-nmt-3-justice-case?seq=37.

[493] Ibid.

[494] *United States of America v. Josef Altstötter et al.*, Trials of War Criminals Before the Nuernberg Military Tribunals Under Control Council Law No. 10, Nürnberg, October 1946-April 1949: Case 3: Justice Case (Washington: United States Government Printing Office, 1949), 1024–5.

[495] Ibid.

[496] Judith N. Shklar, *Legalism: Law, Morals, and Political Trials* (Cambridge, MA: Harvard University Press, 1986), 165–6.

'the soldier is a reasoning agent, and therefore capable of appraising the orders he receives'.[497]

The concept of command responsibility has been recognized as a 'key form of liability' for military to civilian commanders (e.g. *Čelebići*), since it provides a 'critical tool to ensure the principle of responsible command' and contributes to prevention.[498]

The *Erdemović* case dealt with the limits of the professional duties of soldiers in its discussion of the defence of duress in relation to atrocity crime. Judges McDonald and Vohrah rejected the availability of duress as a defence to the killing of civilians, based on the special responsibility of soldiers. Judge Cassese challenged this reasoning in his dissent, which later prevailed in the framing of duress under Art. 31 of the ICC Statute.[499]

The ICTR engaged with the duties of religious leaders in the case against Athanase Seromba, a Roman-Catholic priest, who became complicit in the decision to bulldoze the Nyange church that resulted in the deaths of the at least 1,500 displaced ethnic Tutsi. He was convicted of genocide and extermination as a crime against humanity. The Trial Chamber argued that his 'training as a priest and his experience within the church' should have 'enabled him to understand the reprehensible nature of his conduct during the events'.[500] It qualified the abuse of a 'position of trust' as an aggravating factor in sentencing.[501]

All of these decisions mark attempts to influence norm internalization by individuals through judicial reasoning and rhetoric. They seek to increase an internalized social commitment to norms which contributes to prevention.

2.3 Conclusions

Norm expression is a double-edged sword. It is beyond doubt one of the strongest functions of international criminal justice. It is part of the methods of the field. It is inherently connected to the performative dimensions of international crimes. It serves to construct the social and legal meaning of crimes and to provide a counter-performance to the messages inherent in the commission of crimes. It has an important function in a liberal conception of criminal justice which derives the legitimacy of criminal law and its coercive powers from the idea of the protection of a *civitas maxima* and citizen consent. As Luhmann has argued, law as system

[497] Paola Gaeta, 'The Defence of Superior Orders: The Statute of International Criminal Court versus Customary International Law' (1999) 10 *EJIL* 172–91, 178.

[498] See OTP, Policy Paper on Case Selection and Prioritisation, para. 44.

[499] See *Prosecutor v. Erdemović*, Judgment, IT-96-22-A, 7 October 1997, Separate and Dissenting Opinion of Judge Cassese, para. 47.

[500] *Prosecutor v. Seromba*, Judgment, ICTR-2001-66-I, 13 December 2006, para. 385.

[501] Ibid., para. 390.

requires cognitive openness. It derives stability and validity from the possibility of variation or transformation.[502] Expressive power is necessary to adjust law to changing social circumstances and to facilitate public discourse over the meaning and effects of norms. As in a domestic context, international criminal norms 'are, by definition, laws over which citizens disagree'.[503]

Norm expression serves two important roles. It seeks to 'advance constructive public dialogue around criminal justice norms, particularly (but not exclusively) those that have generated expressive conflict', and to compel justice agents to 'regularly revisit and reconsider' the 'real-world consequences' of international norms.[504] It has been used as an instrument to justify and promote normative change in relation to all three stages of the life cycle of norms: norm affirmation, norm projection, and internalization.

The way in which it has been used sheds a fresh light on the very conception of the field. It challenges the traditional view that law is neutral and dispassionate.[505] The argument that practices are simply grounded in law is a rhetorical technique to discard criticism. A more structural analysis of the field shows that Aristotle's three foundational elements of rhetoric (*logos*, *ethos*, and *pathos*) have enjoyed an important space in legal discourse on international criminal justice since its inception.

Rationality and positivist legal reasoning have been combined with discursive strategies to enhance the image and legitimacy of the speaker in the eyes of prospective audiences and to encourage norm internalization. Due to the lack of axiomatic legitimacy and the virtual nature of a *civitas maxima*, legal agents have relied on rhetorical techniques to enhance their authority and create a new normative reality. Progress narratives, heroism, and binaries (e.g. evil perpetrator versus innocent 'victim') are part of the rhetorical arsenal of self-justification. 'We' narratives, emotive language, and reliance on images[506] are communicative techniques to engage audiences. In particular, 'legal storytelling' is important to promote norm affirmation, norm projection, and norm internalization. For instance, judgments like *Tadić* or *Akayesu* were so successful in norm promotion because they told normative change in the form of a story. Storytelling is not only a way of structuring argument[507] but a means to engage the reader and encourage continued writing of a narrative plot. Storytelling fills an abstract argument with feeling. As Richard Delgado has argued, this has an inclusive effect: 'Stories

[502] See Niklas Luhmann, *Soziologische Aufklärung Vol. 1: Aufsätze zur Theorie sozialer Systeme* (Heidelberg: Springer, 2009), 224, 227.

[503] See Nirej Sekhon, 'The Pedagocgcal Prosecutor' (2014) 44 *Seton Hall Law Review* 1–46, 34.

[504] Ibid., 32.

[505] See Aloisi and Meernik, *Judgment Day* 59.

[506] Douzinas Costas and Lynda Nead, 'Introduction,' in Douzinas Costas and Lynda Nead (eds), *Law and the Image: The Authority of Art and the Aesthetics of Law* (Chicago, IL: University of Chicago Press, 1999), 1–15.

[507] Bianchi, 'International Adjudication, Rhetoric and Storytelling' 43.

humanize us.... They allow us to see how the world looks from behind someone else's spectacles.'[508]

Techniques such as process tracing and framing legal developments in the form of a story have a double function. They create a bond with hearers and audiences (the 'out group') and invite them to see the world through others' eyes. This bond may trigger reconnaissance effects and encourage the group to participate in the discourse or challenge assumptions. Storytelling also has certain benefits for members of the 'in group', the initiated hearers or future 'storytellers'. It helps them to digest reasoning and may encourage the writing of further stories. For example, Dworkin's image of collective 'novel writing' is useful to understand some of the jurisprudential developments in relation to norm progression in international criminal justice.

In the widest sense, normative expressivism is about claiming space. As noted by socio-legal researchers, the concept of 'space' plays an important role in the legal discipline. It is 'clearly no longer the context or the background, but an active factor in constructing subjectivity and societal presence'.[509] For instance, rendering a judgment has few immediate effects in itself. The judgment gains importance because it involves claims about the role of the speaker and its space in legal discourse and signals which norms, concepts, or institutions ought to serve as a framework of reference in discourse.[510]

The creation of legal doctrine through a pattern of cases has an educational orientation. It communicates rules of behaviour to society. It can be considered 'as a form of "training" that initiates those who undergo training in the practice of criminal judicial interpretation or construction'.[511]

Affective dimensions of justice tend to be downplayed in legal discourse,[512] but they play an important role in norm expression. The sociology of affect[513] suggests that norm expression and, in particular, norm internalization are only effective if they are also affective. Affection reinforces notions of solidarity and social

[508] Delgado, 'Storytelling for Oppositionists and Others' 2440.

[509] Andreas Philippopoulos-Mihalopoulos, 'Spatial Justice: Law and the Geography of Withdrawal' (2010) 6 *International Journal of Law in Context* 201–16, 206.

[510] See Alex Jeffrey, 'Justice Incomplete: Radovan Karadžić, the ICTY, and the Spaces of International Law' (2009) 27 *Environment and Planning D: Society and Space* 387–402, 399 ('The documentation and broadcast of the trials at the ICTY ... produce a range of new sites of justice. In simple terms, the quotidian accounts ... help to locate the process of justice within the corridors, trial chambers, and cells of Tribunal's headquarters at The Hague ... But in addition to these formal spaces of judicial process, the ICTY's proceedings are projected through television, radio, and Internet broadcasts to wider publics across the world.'

[511] Ferry de Jong, 'The End of Doctrine? On the Symbolic Function of Doctrine in Substantive Criminal Law' (2011) 7 *Utrecht Law Review* 8–45, 41.

[512] See generally Susan A. Bandes and Jeremy A. Blumenthal, 'Emotion and the Law' (2012) 8 *Annual Review of Law and Social Science* 161–81; Markus Dubber, 'Making Sense of the Sense of Justice' (2005) 53 *Buffalo Law Review* 815–58.

[513] Freiberg, 'Affective Versus Effective Justice' 265–78, 267–9; Sean Watson, 'Policing the Affective Society: Beyond Governmentality in the Theory of Social Control' (1999) 8 *Social & Legal Studies* 227–51.

commitment to norms. Expressivism is likely to have greater resonance among norm resistant audiences if it combines rational argument with use of emotions, narratives, and symbols. Such elements provide an affective–emotional frame in which to determine legal expression.

One of the problems of normative expressivism in international criminal justice is the lack of proper communicative frame. Normative expressivism is closely related to processes of socialization and affirmation of identity. Attachment to norms requires mutual engagement, rather than mere expression. David Luban has stressed that the expressivist accounts remain weak because it carries 'a dangerous vagueness about who exactly belongs to the intended audience of its message'.[514] However, the structural problem goes much deeper. Norm expression suffers a certain degree of self-circularity and lacks an 'ideal speech situation', as Jürgen Habermas put it, that is, a space where 'undistorted communication' is possible.

Norm expression is deemed to achieve certain rationales and results through interaction. The means of seeking a mutual understanding between speaker and audience or countering critiques, or encouraging critical self-reflection are limited. In substance, normative expressivism has remained subject to 'power' critiques. It has been perceived as a non-inclusive (e.g. Western) or even hegemonic exercise by some of those who are affected by the projected norms. It involves unresolved questions about the authority of the 'speaker'. For instance, there are concerns to what judges or NGOs should serve as norm entrepreneurs at all, charged with the task to 'make human rights, justice and peace universal'.[515] They are not necessarily 'neutral transmitters of general social values'[516] but are guided by interests of their own. Internalization can only occur 'through local legitimation and support'.[517]

Some of the ways in which *ethos* and *pathos* are invoked in discursive structures are deeply problematic. 'We' discourse is subject to manipulation. As critics have argued, the fundamental question 'remains whether, how and in whose name international law responds when the outrage upon humanity begins'.[518] Concepts, such as the 'civilized world' or 'conscience of mankind' may cause estrangement. For instance, US Prosecutor Keenan noted at Tokyo that Japan had 'declared war on civilization'.[519] Such 'high-flown references to natural law and legalism' were 'completely lost' on Japanese society.[520] The reference to a unified 'humanity' in

[514] Luban, 'State criminality and the ambition of international criminal law' 76.

[515] See Tallgren, 'The Voice of the International' 145.

[516] See Emile Durkheim, *The Division of Labour in Society* (George Simpson trans., New York, NY: The Free Press, 1947), 37.

[517] Zartner, 'Internalization of international law' 14.

[518] Tallgren, 'The Voice of the International' 145.

[519] On the influence of the Commonwealth on the trial, see Yuki Takatori, 'America's' War Crimes Trial? Commonwealth Leadership at the International Military Tribunal for the Far East, 1946–48, (2007) 35 *Journal of Imperial and Commonwealth History* 549–68.

[520] See Harmen van der Wilt, 'Crimes against humanity: A category hors concours in international criminal law?' in Britta van Beers, Luigi Corrias, and Wouter G. Werner (eds), *Humanity across International Law and Biolaw* (Cambridge: Cambridge University Press, 2014), 25–41, 32.

order to justify norm projection may mask legitimate differences or create oversimplification. It seems to imply that 'humanity' sits in judgment over 'inhumanity'.

The use of narrative techniques and storytelling may have negative implications. It relies on fiction, may sell certain elements as law through speech, or sideline alternative readings. For instance, placing a central focus on humanization and progressive criminalization in the context of the history of international humanitarian law may produce certain counterproductive results. It may reduce 'attention to the rest of the laws of war—the corpus of the laws of war not devoted to liability at all, let alone criminal liability for individuals'.[521]

A good example is investigations. The emphasis on criminalization of violations may prioritize criminal investigations from the start and sideline other fact-finding methods to secure compliance with international humanitarian law and address the concerns of victims.[522] The collective dimensions of warfare may get lost through a criminalization narrative. As Kenneth Anderson has cautioned, '[w]ar is an activity between groups, not individuals, and a law predicated upon individual rights misapprehends something when it moves to disregard the question of sides, groups, and parties to a conflict in favour of seeing it as a matter of individual rights and individual liability'.[523] Collective legal story-telling *à la Dworkin*, that is, chain scripting, may re-entrench such effects over time.

The role of legal agents as 'meaning engineers' is inherent in the legal process, but requires careful scrutiny. Certain images have been used in problematic ways or reinforced stereotypes. For instance, the branding of perpetrators as enemies of humankind creates stigmas that contradict norm projections in relation to fairness and impede norm internalization.

Pathos-driven discourse on victims causes dilemmas in relation to 'commodification' of harm.[524] It involves ethical conflicts since it involves the taking of ownership over 'harm and suffering'. As critics have noted, violence is not only committed 'by 'the immediate victims or perpetrators' but also by 'dissociated possessors' who 'have the power and resources to articulate the threat within their own frames of reference and context'.[525]

Such images may generate artificial distinctions or produce novel inequalities. One illustration is the contemporary focus on sexual and gender-based violence. It has been significantly influenced by norm expression in international criminal justice. It has been criticized for 'orienting international aid programs toward

[521] See Anderson, 'The Rise of International Criminal Law' 346.

[522] See Mark Lattimer, 'The Duty to Investigate Civilian Deaths in Armed Conflict: Looking Beyond Criminal Investigations', *EJIL Talk*, 22 October 2018, at https://www.ejiltalk.org/the-duty-to-investigate-civilian-deaths-in-armed-conflict-looking-beyond-criminal-investigations/#more-16568.

[523] Anderson, 'The Rise of International Criminal Law' 349.

[524] McMillan, 'Imaging the International' 173 ('this community is one dependent on suffering and inhumanity to visualise its contours and affirm its existence').

[525] Meger, 'Fetishization of Sexual Violence' 152.

emergency care for female victims of sexual violence and strengthening criminal justice response to this specific form of violence, rather than to all violent crime'.[526]

The process of norm internalization is dependent on many intermediate factors, such as accessibility, translation of norms into context, and openness to discourse. These factors differ greatly among global audiences.

This leaves a divided picture. Normative expression involves both benefits and concerns. As Immi Tallgren has noted:

> There are signs of an eventual strengthening and stretching out of a reciprocal and solidary we- union animated by public concern for human suffering and desires for peace and justice. Yet the prognosis is overshadowed by the potentially fatal damage by a tumour of inequality in the shape of the continuous concentration of exclusive legal competence and political, military and economic power in a few states, driven by their relations of conflict and mutual control.[527]

[526] Meger, 'Fetishization of Sexual Violence' 155.
[527] Tallgren, 'The Voice of the International' 155.

3

Institutional Expression

The Medium as Message

Expressivism goes beyond the portrayal of norms and their internalization. The establishment of institutions and their functioning carry important meanings, irrespective of their output or concrete contribution to the genesis or perception of norms. As Robert Cover has argued:

> No set of legal institutions or prescriptions exists apart from the narratives that locate it and give it meaning. For every constitution there is an epic, for each decalogue a scripture. Once understood in the context of the narratives, that give it meaning, law becomes not merely a system of rules to be observed, but a world in which we live.[1]

Institutions are symbolic and behavioural systems that define social and legal meanings. They shape behaviour, choices, and perceptions. This insight may be traced back to Durkheim. He recognized the symbolic dimensions of justice institutions. He argued that that formal organizational structures possess and create symbolic meaning through acts of representation and rituals. From a Durkheimian perspective, law and legal enforcement mechanisms 'become tools to confront the past, reestablish moral boundaries, and provide an institution through which the public can express sentiments concerning right and wrong, similar to monuments and memorials'.[2]

Durkheim's thinking has influenced modern institutional theories.[3] Institutions are grounded in systems of knowledge, beliefs, and moral authority.[4] As of the 1970s, institutionalist theorists have sought to explain organizational structures not only through rationalist or functionalist arguments but also through symbolic factors or rational myths.[5]

1 Robert M. Cover, 'The Supreme Court, 1982 Term—Foreword: Nomos and Narrative' (1983) 97 *Harvard Law Review* 4–68, 5.

2 Joachim J. Savelsberg and Ryan D. King, 'Law and Collective Memory' (2007) 3 *Annual Review Law Social Science* 189–211 202.

3 See Frank Dobbin, 'How Durkheim's theory of meaning-making influenced organizational sociology' in Paul Adler (ed.), *Oxford Handbook of Sociology and Organization Studies: Classical Foundations* (New York, NY: Oxford University Press, 2009), 200–22.

4 See Philip Selznick, 'Foundations of the Theory of Organization' (1948) 13 *American Sociological Review* 25–35.

5 See generally Thomas B. Lawrence, 'Institutional Strategy' (1999) 25 *Journal of Management* 161–88.

Justice as Message. Carsten Stahn, Oxford University Press (2020). © Carsten Stahn.
DOI: 10.1093/oso/9780198864189.001.0001

John Meyer and Brian Rowan situated institutions in a social context. They argued that symbolic factors are crucial elements in the process of adopting organizational structures and in maintaining their legitimacy and 'survival' over time. They noted that organizations rely on structures that symbolize commitment to rationality and fairness and use practices that are grounded in 'myth and ceremony'.[6] Their argument framed a fundamental premise of organizational theory, namely the idea that organizations enhance their chances of survival by acting in line with external expectations.[7]

In the 1980s, Paul DiMaggio and Walter Powell developed this line of thought in their study of the social factors driving institutionalization.[8] They claimed that myths, rituals, and conventions are essential elements in the spread and interaction of organizational structures. They clarified that institutional context tends to render institutions similar to each other in terms of form, structure, and practice. They used the notion of 'isomorphism' to describe this phenomenon. The concept recognizes that conformity pressures arise from political factors (e.g. the need to appear legitimate in the eyes of powerful actors, 'coercive isomorphism'), social influences of the profession, 'normative isomorphism'), and mimetic factors, such as the urge to 'copy' practices of other organizations that are considered to be successful or legitimate (mimetic isomorphism').

Other organizational theorists have stressed the linkages between organizational structures and symbolic systems. For instance, Calvin Morrill has noted that 'social structure cannot exist without symbolic systems, which individuals use to make sense of, maintain, and change social structure, while symbolic systems cannot exist for long without 'plausibility structures, which root symbols in behavioral patterns'.[9]

Modern institutionalist theories have placed greater emphasis on agency of institutions.[10] They have insisted that institutional influences reach beyond conformity pressures and ceremonial elements. They have clarified that organizations may resist collective social beliefs and actively shape their social environment (e.g. institutional entrepreneurship).[11]

[6] See John Meyer and Brian Rowan, 'Institutionalized Organizations: Formal Structure as Myth and Ceremont' (1977) 83 *American Journal of Sociology* 340–63.

[7] See Thomas B. Lawrence and Masoud Shadnam 'Institutional theory' in Wolfgang Donsbach (ed.), *The International Encyclopedia of Communication* (Oxford: Blackwell Publishers, 2008) 2288–93

[8] See Paul Di Maggio and Walter Powell, 'The Iron Cage Revisited—Institutional Isomorphism and Collective Rationality in Organizational Fields' (1983) 48 *American Sociological Review* 147–60.

[9] Calvin Morrill, 'Conflict Management, Honor, and Organizational Change' (1991) 97 *American Journal of Sociology* 585–621, 586.

[10] See John W. Meyer, 'World Society, Institutional Theories, and the Actor' (2010) 36 *Annual Review of Sociology* 1–20.

[11] Steve Maguire, Cynthia Hardy, and Thomas B. Lawrence, 'Institutional Entrepreneurship in Emerging Fields: HIV/AIDS Treatment Advocacy in Canada' (2004) 47 *Academy of Management Journal* 657–79.

In international criminal justice, these insights from institutional theory have received limited attention. The institutional history of international criminal justice tends to be told in functional terms, i.e., in terms of functions (e.g., peace-maintenance[12], retribution, restoration of victims' rights), different justice models or through the lens of a series of successive generations. This functionalist account is incomplete. Expressivist dimensions are an important part of institutional foundations and dynamics of international criminal justice.[13] They are significant in at least three respects: (i) they are partly behind the turn to institutions; (ii) they explain identities of the form and nature of specific institutions; and (iii) they form a cornerstone of institutional practices.[14]

3.1 Expressivism and the Making of Institutions

International criminal justice has traditionally been embedded in broader geopolitical considerations. The making of international criminal justice institutions is an inherently political process. Such institutions are not only legal entities but also historical and cultural objects.[15] Contemporary intellectual histories are dominated by instrumentalist narratives. The value of institutions is justified by comparative advantages, strategic rationales, or effectiveness arguments. A defining criterion of utility and performance is to go beyond symbolism. Symbolic meaning is recognized in relation to aesthetics, court architecture, or design. But the notion is almost a blasphemy in the genealogy of international criminal justice. It is associated with weaknesses, such as lack of institutional power, the absence of meaning, or limited impact in the real world.

The focus on measurable social functions, such as defence of public goods or global commons, tends to overshadow the complex socio-pedagogical function of institutions. Symbolic function is an important element in itself.[16] Sociological theories suggest that almost any action has symbolic elements.[17] For example, mere presence carries meaning. The act of creating an institution is a powerful spectacle.

[12] Danilo Zolo, 'Peace through Criminal Law' (2004) 2 *JICJ* 727–34.

[13] Mikkel Jarle Christensen, 'The symbolic economy of international criminal justice: Shaping the discourse of a new field of law' in Joanna Nicholson (ed.), *Strengthening the Validity of International Criminal Tribunals* (Leiden: Brill, 2018) 74–98; Mikkel Jarle Christensen, 'From symbolic surge to closing courts' in Joanna Nicholson (ed.), *Strengthening the Validity of International Criminal Tribunals*, 609–25.

[14] For instance, the 'survival' instinct is clearly reflected in outreach and legacy strategies.

[15] Frédéric Mégret, 'The Legacy of the ICTY as Seen Through Some of its Actors and Observers' (2011) 3 *Göttingen Journal of International Law* 1011–52.

[16] Emanuela Fronza and Juliette Tricot, 'Fonction symbolique et droit pénal international :une analyse du discours des Tribunaux pénaux internationaux' in Emanuela Fronza and Stefano Manacorda (eds), *La justice pénale internationale dans les décisions des Tribunaux ad hoc* (Paris/Milan: Dalloz/Giuffré, 2003), 292–309. See also Diane Bernard, *Trois propositions pour une théorie du droit international pénal* (Brussels: Presses de l'Université Saint-Louis, 2014)

[17] Joel M. Charon, *Symbolic Interactionism* 10th edn (Upper Saddle River, NJ: Pearson, 2011), 48–53.

It constitutes new relationships and involves communication or expressions of solidarity. The creation of a new legal institution or the transfer of jurisdiction to an international entity is a communicative act.[18] It entails certain messages about the legalization of the public space or the protection of certain norms and principles.

The symbolic function is closely linked to non-rational factors and faith,[19] that is, belief in an international community or humanity, and their enactment through 'rituals, symbols and mythologies'.[20] Its mobilizing effect extends beyond punishment or establishment of discipline and order. The making of institutions is often meant to shape habits among states and civil societies, encourage mimetic practice, or enact new ideals. International criminal justice bears ritualistic features, since institutions are associated with hope to 'create a practiced repertoire of appropriate responses or dispositions, from which individuals can thence, when the world presents novel situations, generate normatively appropriate responses'.[21]

3.1.1 The turn to institutions

The very turn to novel institutions is strongly influenced by emotive factors, such as outrage, passion, or guilt, and inspired by utopian ideals. Durkheim's conception of criminal law as societal reaction to crime offers a compelling addition to instrumentalist explanations of international criminal justice institutions. Durkheim placed the idea of a common conscience logically before the notion of crime. He argued that 'we must not say that an action shocks the common conscience because it is criminal, but rather that it is criminal because it shocks the common conscience. We do not reprove it because it is a crime, but it is a crime because we reprove it.'[22]

This construction changes perspectives on the functions of laws and institutions. It turns some of the existing thinking around. It sees institutions as an act reaffirming networks of community existing beyond nations, rather than mere legal creations. Technically, it is thus not the legal notion of the crime, which triggers a response, but the attack on solidarity and a common social environment. In Durkheim's view, laws 'have done nothing but codify, organize, and systematize' spontaneous 'reactions to deviant behaviour'.[23]

[18] Salif Nimage, 'An International Conscience Collective? A Durkheimian Analysis of International Criminal Law' (2007) 7 *International Criminal Law Review* 605–7.

[19] See Diane Bernard, 'Faut-il croire en le droit (international pénal)? Religion et symbolique dans le projet de justice internationale pénale' (2016) 13 *Penal Field* 1–39

[20] Immi Tallgren, 'The faith in humanity and international criminal law' in Monica Garcia-Salmones Rovira, Martti Koskenniemi, and Paolo Amorosa (eds), *International Law and Religion* (Oxford: Oxford University Press, 2017), 334–62, 335.

[21] See Danielle Celermajer, 'Mere Ritual? Displacing the Myth of Sincerity in Transitional Justice Rituals' (2013) 7 *International Journal of Transitional Justice* 286–305, 297.

[22] Emile Durkheim, *The Division of Labor in Society* (New York, NY: Macmillan, 1933), 81.

[23] See Emile Durkheim, *Moral Education* (New York, NY: Free Press, 1961), 181.

This vision challenges some of the classical rational models of institutionalism and managerial approaches. It views international criminal justice institutions not only as technocratic and administrative structures, that is, exercises of regulatory authority by states to manage certain global problems, but as 'passionate' reactions to threats to social life and communal networks.[24]

This approach provides a fuller explanation of the institutional development of international criminal justice. It recognizes that the process of establishment of institutions has important communicative and community-building functions. It entails messages about norms and their enforcement and the interaction and co-ordination of different community networks.

Based on such a vision of behaviour, the turn to international criminal institutions may not only be explained by rational and legal formalist criteria but also through the expression of signals. Sometimes the 'medium is the message'. The act of establishment may convey different messages, such as (i) signals of memory and remembrance ('Never again'); (ii) expressions of shame and apology; (iii) acts of re-creation and renewal of community relations; (iv) manifestations of hope and belief; and (v) articulations of protest (Figure 9).

This typology of messages offers a frame to understand major institutional creations and critiques in the history of international criminal justice over the past century. The turn to institutions and their evolution over time is driven by one or several of these factors simultaneously. The type of message that is expressed may evolve or take on different priorities and nuances throughout the lifecycle of

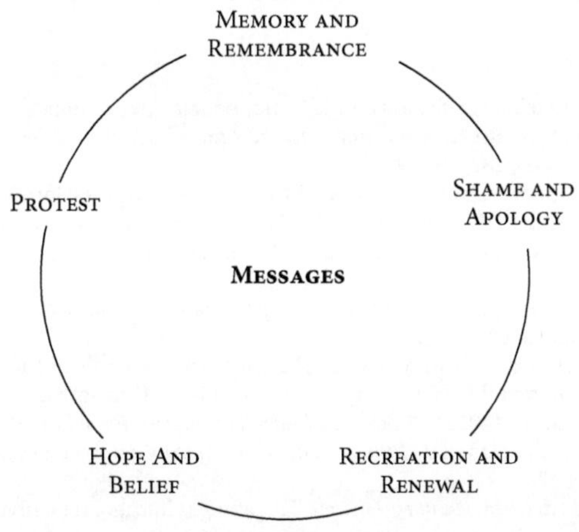

Figure 9 The medium as message

[24] See also Nimage, 'An International Conscience Collective' 605 (The claim is that ... crimes not merely temporally preceded the establishment of these Tribunals, but that they were a causal factor for that establishment).

institutions. One institution may reflect different messages at the same time. The main argument can be illustrated through a few examples from institutional history, ranging from the second half of the twentieth century to today.

3.1.1.1 Signals of memory and remembrance

From a sociological point of view, international criminal justice institutions may be perceived as symbols against forgetting. This is reflected in the slogan 'Never again', which has played a crucial role in lobbying for responses to atrocity crime.[25] It is inherently connected to the horrors of the Holocaust or the Latin American dictatorships. The 'Never again' message was part and parcel discourse of the Nuremberg trial.[26] It is reflected in the preamble of the Genocide Convention ('liberate mankind from such an odious scourge') and the adoption of the Nuremberg Principles. In Latin America, 'Nunca más' became the official title of the Report of the Argentine National Commission on the Disappeared,[27] and a more general slogan to deal with the consequences of atrocity crime. It is reflected in the promotion of the 'right to truth' as a means to allow societies understand past violations and avoid repetition of crimes.[28] According to this logic, institutions represent, as Mark Drumbl put it 'intergenerational signposts in history'.[29] They connect history to memory and serve as symbols of remembrance.[30] For instance, many of the judgments of the Inter-American Courts of Human Rights on enforced disappearances contributed to the formation of 'regional memory'.[31]

Messages of memory and remembrance have played an important role in relation to the justification of international criminal justice institutions and atrocity trials.[32] Justice is 'in part a form of remembrance'.[33] There is a close

[25] Antonio Cassese, 'Quelques réflexions sur la justice pénale internationale' in Emanuela Fronza and Stefano Manacorda (eds), *La justice pénale internationale dans les décisions des tribunaux ad hoc* (Paris/Milan: Dalloz/Giuffrè, 2003), 283–94, 290–1

[26] Opening Address for the United States, Nazi Conspiracy & Aggression, Volume I, (Washington, DC: United States Government Printing Office, 1946) 115 ('the wrongs we seek to condemn and punish have been so calculated, so malignant and so devastating that civilization cannot tolerate their being ignored—because it cannot survive their being repeated').

[27] See Nunca más (never again): A Report by Argentina's National Commission on Disappeared People (London: Faber & Faber, 1986).

[28] On the 'right to truth' see Yasmin Naqvi, 'The Right to the Truth in International Law: Fact or Fiction? (2006) 88 *International Review of the Red Cross* 245–73; Dermot Groome, 'The Right to Truth in the Fight against Impunity' (2011) 29 *Berkeley Journal of International Law* 175–99.

[29] See Mark A. Drumbl, *Atrocity, Punishment and International Law* (Cambridge: Cambridge University Press, 2007), 175.

[30] See generally Paul Ricoeur, *Memory, History, Forgetting* (Chicago, IL: University of Chicago Press, 2004); Savelsberg and King, 'Law and Collective Memory' 189.

[31] See Moshe Hirsch, 'The Role of International Tribunals in the Development of Historical Narratives' (2018) 20 *Journal of the History of International Law* 391–428, 418.

[32] Mark J. Osiel, 'Ever Again: Legal Remembrance of Administrative Massacre' (1995) 144 *University of Pennsylvania Law Review* 463–704; Donald Bloxham, *Genocide on Trial: War Crimes Trials and the Formation of Holocaust History and Memory* (New York, NY: Oxford University Press, 2001).

[33] James Booth, 'The Unforgotten: Memories of Justice' (2001) 95 *American Political Science Review* 777–91.

interrelation between justice agents and 'collective memory', memories that may not be grounded in individual experiences but are shaped by collective processes of memory construction.[34] As Moshe Hirsch has noted, courts contribute to practices of 'collective memory':

> Decisions of international tribunals occasionally function as carriers of collective memory, particularly among professional groups. Such judgements occasionally include a description of the relevant historical events.... And vice versa, adjudicators are commonly influenced by the relevant historical narratives prevailing in their social group.[35]

Legal action may relate to past events, as well as the future, that is they may influence how history and events should be remembered in the future.

3.1.1.1.1 The long shadow of the Holocaust

Many institutions and trials serve as spaces of memory. A striking example is the institutional treatment of the 'ethos of Nuremberg' and its silences. Nuremberg is often associated with the Holocaust.[36] The Nuremberg trials were meant to affect collective memory.[37] However, they dealt only marginally with the Holocaust as such.[38] The history of the mass extermination of European Jews was largely blended out.[39] Much of the evidence was left untouched. Victim communities felt that the trials lacked 'human aspect' since they failed to hear testimony from survivors. The trials did not create a new era of international criminal jurisdiction.[40] Their effects were not immediate but long term.[41] Nuremberg was followed

[34] See Moshe Hirsch, *Invitation to Sociology of International Law* (Oxford: Oxford University Press, 2015) 58–88

[35] See Moshe Hirsch, 'The Role of International Tribunals in the Construction of Collective Memories', Hebrew University of Jerusalem, Research Paper No. 08-16, November 2016, 3.

[36] Gary Bass, *Stay the Hand of Vengeance: The Politics of War Crimes Trials* (Princeton, NJ: Princeton University Press, 2000), 148. On the Holocaust as 'global construct', see Jeffrey C. Alexander, 'On the Social Construction of Moral Universals: The 'Holocaust' from War Crime to Trauma Drama' (2002) 5 *European Journal of Social Theory* 5–85, 6.

[37] Stephan Landsman, *Crimes of the Holocaust* (Philadelphia, PA: University of Pennsylvania Press 2005), 6–7.

[38] Donald Bloxham 'The Eichmann Trial Fifty Years On' (2011) 29 *German History* 265–82, 279 ('the idea, which features in some of the transitional justice literature, of the trial of the major war criminals as a crucible of extensive international and (thus) German confrontation with the Holocaust, is nothing but a 'Nuremberg imaginaire', though it is no less powerful an inspiration for being illusory'). On Holocaust memory, see Daniel Levy and Natan Sznaider, *The Holocaust and Memory in the Global Age*, translated by Assenka Oksiloff (Philadelphia, PA: Temple University Press, 2006).

[39] See Michael Marrus, *Nuremberg War Crimes Trial of 1945–1946* (Boston, MA: Bedford, 1997); Bloxham, *Genocide on Trial.*

[40] David Fraser, *Law after Auschwitz: Towards a Jurisprudence of the Holocaust* (Durham, NC: Carolina Academic Press, 2005).

[41] Susanne Karstedt, 'The Nuremberg Tribunal and German society: International justice and local judgment in post-conflict reconstruction' in David A. Blumenthal and Timothy L.H. McCormack (eds), *The Legacy of Nuremberg: Civilising Influence or Institutional Vengeance?* (Leiden: Martinus Nijhoff Publishers, 2008), 13–36.

by a period of 'relative' silence.[42] The educative effect on German society remained limited.[43] Societal studies suggest that public discussion in West Germany about the Holocaust 'remained extremely muted until after 1978'.[44] The ethos of 'Nuremberg' was institutionalized later, namely through national proceedings of the 1960s. These trials were driven by an urge to rebuild collective memory and community. They had important symbolic meaning, due to the absence of an international legal infrastructure.

The *Eichmann* trial brought the Holocaust back into public consciousness. It marked an attempt to recreate memory and remembrance. The Attorney General, Gideon Hausner, expressed the historic significance at the beginning of the trial. He said: 'I am not standing alone. With me are six million accusers ... Their blood cries out, but their voice is not heard.'[45]

Hannah Arendt acknowledged that history 'stood in the center of the trial'.[46] The trial relied on universal jurisdiction and signalled 'the importance of situating international trials in venues with a meaningful organic connection to the crimes'.[47] It was as much a tale of jurisdiction as a collective tale of mourning'.[48] It added testimonies of survivors to the Nuremberg record and gave a voice to victims, which

[42] In his famous work on *German Guilt* (*Die Schuldfrage*), published in 1946, Karl Jaspers distinguished criminal, political, moral, and metaphysical guilt. See Karl Jaspers, *The Question of German Guilt*, trans. E. B. Ashton (New York: Capricorn Books, 1961 [1947]). He saw Nuremberg as an opportunity to promote cosmopolitan principles on individual criminal responsibility and a return to ideals of the Enlightenment. But legal engagement with Nazi criminality was marginal until the 1960s. See Peter Reichel, *Vergangenheitsbewältigung in Deutschland: Die Auseinandersetzung mit der NS-Diktatur von 1945 bis heute* (München: C.H. Beck, 2001). Accountability was at best approached in an abstract way. Many former Nazis were integrated into society. See Helmut König, *Die Zukunft der Vergangenheit. Der Nationalsozialismus im politischen Bewusstsein der Bundesrepublik* (Frankfurt: Fischer, 2003). See also Samuel Moyn, *The Last Utopia* (Cambridge, MA: Harvard University Press, 2010), 7 ('contrary to conventional assumptions, there was no widespread Holocaust consciousness in the postwar era, so human rights could not have been a response to it); Bloxham in 'The Eichmann Trial Fifty Years On' 266 ('any survey of general historiography from the 1950s and 1960s will reveal the marginal status of Nazi genocide in mainstream historical thought, while in all affected European countries, genocide was subsumed within larger political narratives of suffering and sacrifice').

[43] See Mark A. Wolfgram, 'Didactic War Crimes Trials and External Legal Culture: The Cases of the Nuremberg, Frankfurt Auschwitz, and Majdanek Trials in West Germany' (2014) 26 *Global Change, Peace & Security* 281–97, 284 ('it is difficult to detect any significant increase in the social discussion of the Nazi persecution of the Jews until the very end of the 1970s, long after the conclusion of the Nuremberg trials and more than a full decade after the conclusion of the Frankfurt Auschwitz trials, and during the Majdanek trial, which was widely ignored until January 1979'). See also Donald Bloxham, 'Milestones and mythologies: The impact of Nuremberg' in Patricia Heberer and Jürgen Matthäus (eds), *Atrocities on Trial: Historical Perspectives on the Politics of Persecuting War Crimes* (Lincoln, NE: University of Nebraska Press, 2008), 263–82 ('Nuremberg as a re-education, democratizing success story is a misleading representation, and its deployment in the Iraq connection doubly unfortunate').

[44] Wolfgram, 'Didactic war crimes trials and external legal culture' 296.

[45] Lawrence Douglas, *The Memory of Judgment: Making Law and History in the Trials of the Holocaust* (New Haven, CT: Yale University Press, 2001), 151.

[46] See Arendt, Hannah, *Eichmann in Jerusalem: A Report on the Banality of Evil* (New York, NY: Penguin, 1977), 19.

[47] Lawrence Douglas in 'The Eichmann Trial Fifty Years On' (2011) 29 *German History* 265–82, 269.

[48] Shoshana Felman, *The Juridical Unconscious: Trials and Traumas in the Twentieth Century* (Cambridge: Harvard University Press, 2002) 129.

complemented documentary and filmic evidence. As Lawrence Douglas noted, 'many survivors came forward to record their story for posterity. In this regard, the trial assumed the quality of an oral history project.'[49]

The proceedings were highly emotive in many respects, namely 'the affirmation of the state of Israel as the owner of the tragedy of holocaust, the controversial abduction of Eichmann, the critical views on the legality of prosecuting Eichmann, the emotional force of parts of the testimony in the presence of many victims'.[50]

The trial became a site of memory. It had several effects: it disrupted a prevailing 'sense that people had in the 1950s that World War II was over'; it produced a fuller picture of the Holocaust; and it marked 'the first in a renewed wave of Nazi trials that lasted at least into the 1980s'.[51]

The Eichmann case led to a re-engagement with the past by German courts in the mid-1960s in the Frankfurt Auschwitz trials (1963–1965)[52] and Majdanek trials in Düsseldorf in the mid-1970s.[53] These trials marked a departure from a *de facto* policy of non-prosecution (i.e. amnesty, clemency) in the 1950s. According to historians, they broke a 'wall of silence'[54] and entailed to some extent to a 're-discovering' of the Holocaust.[55] They faced some resentment by the public[56] but initiated greater acknowledgment of the past ('*Vergangenheitsbewältigung*')[57] and distance from what Ralph Giordano has called the 'second guilt' of the war,[58] namely the lack of engagement with crimes. Susanne Karstedt qualified them as a moment of collective memory:

> [T]he Auschwitz Trial in Frankfurt . . . was the key event . . . and watershed experience for the German society. It illuminated the horror of the death camps and the Holocaust in all graphic detail, the victims had a real presence in Germany for the first time, and the media coverage was extensive. It became a defining moment for

[49] Douglas in 'The Eichmann Trial Fifty Years On' 273. Douglas argues that 'the Eichmann trial must be seen as a crucial moment of transition that helped usher the lived experience of victims and survivors to the centre of the international criminal trial'. Ibid.

[50] Immi Tallgren, 'The Durkheimian Spell of International Criminal Law?' (2013) *71 Revue interdisciplinaire d'études juridiques* 137–69, 161–2.

[51] Devin Pendas in 'The Eichmann Trial Fifty Years On' (2011) 29 *German History* 265–82, 270.

[52] Rebecca Wittmann, *Beyond Justice: The Auschwitz Trial* (Cambridge, MA: Harvard University Press, 2005).

[53] See Wolfgram, 'Didactic war crimes trials and external legal culture' 286–96; Marina Aksenova, 'The Role of International Criminal Tribunals in Shaping the Historical Accounts of Genocide' in Uladzislau Belavusau and Aleksandra Gliszczyńska-Grabias (eds), *Law and Memory: Towards Legal Governance of History* (Cambridge: Cambridge University Press, 2017), 48–69, 53–4.

[54] Devin Pendas, 'Seeking Justice, Finding Law: Nazi Trials in Postwar Europe' (2009) 81 *The Journal of Modern History* 347–68, 367.

[55] Bloxham in 'The Eichmann Trial Fifty Years On' 266.

[56] Devin Pendas, *The Frankfurt Auschwitz Trial, 1963–1965: Genocide, History, and the Limits of the Law* (Cambridge: Cambridge University Press, 2006), 286–7.

[57] See generally Gerhard Werle and Moritz Vormbaum, *Transitional Justice: Vergangenheitsbewältig ung durch Recht* (Berlin: Springer, 2018).

[58] Ralph Giordano, *Die zweite Schuld oder Von der Last Deutscher zu sein* (Hamburg: Rasch und Röhring, 1987).

> the identity of the younger generation—who were not directly involved, and it allegedly shaped the students' movement in Germany.[59]

The very term 'Holocaust' gradually became 'a universal symbol of evil in the Western world'.[60]

3.1.1.1.2 The ECCC as forum of collective memory

Another striking example of collective memory through trial is the ECCC. It provides an effort to create a shared perception of the past.[61] The legacy of the Khmer Rouge regime divided Cambodian society. The tribunal was set up more than three decades after the facts. Pardons and amnesties were key instruments in the strategy to defeat the regime. The Extraordinary Chambers in the Courts of Cambodia (ECCC) symbolized the attempt to come to terms with the past through judicial means. The defendants were in their eighties during the proceedings. The point of the ECCC was not so much to inflict retributive punishment on the individual defendants but to clarify the structures and atrocities underlying the Khmer Rouge regime and acknowledge historical victims.[62]

The jurisdiction was limited to the period between 1975 and 1979 and excluded violence by other others before and after the regime. The focus was placed on senior leaders. This made it possible to present the ECCC as a project to gain critical distance to the past, foster reconciliation or even consider lower offenders as victims.[63] The framing of jurisdiction marginalized broader contextual factors, such as 'French colonialism, the Vietnam War, Vietnamese, Thai, and Asian regional interest, Soviet, US, and Chinese geopolitical interests, class antagonisms, poverty, landlessness, Cold War politics, and the US interference in and carpet-bombing of Cambodia during the civil war'.[64] Nuon Chea, second-in-command to Pol Pot, criticized the tribunal for focusing on the 'body of the crocodile', rather than its 'head and tail'.[65] This imagery sought to tell an alternative history.

[59] Susanne Karstedt, 'The Life Course of Collective Memories: Persistency and Change in West Germany between 1950 and 1970' (2009) 165 *Polish Sociological Review* 27–38, 35.

[60] See Savelsberg and King, 'Law and Collective Memory' 200. See generally Alexander, 'On the Social Construction of Moral Universals' 5–85.

[61] See Peter Manning, *Transitional Justice and Memory in Cambodia: Beyond the Extraordinary Chambers* (New York, NY: Routledge, 2017); Peter Manning, 'Reconciliation and Perpetrator Memories in Cambodia' (2015) 9 *International Journal of Transitional Justice* 386–406; Michelle Caswell, 'Khmer Rouge Archives: Accountability, Truth, and Memory in Cambodia' (2010) 10 *Archival Science* 25–44.

[62] See David Chandler, 'Cambodia Deals with its Past: Collective Memory, Demonisation and Induced Amnesia' (2008) 9 *Totalitarian Movements and Political Religions* 355–69.

[63] See ECCC Outreach poster, at https://www.eccc.gov.kh/sites/default/files/publications/poster-senior-big%20EN.jpg. See also Peter Manning, 'Governing Memory: Justice, Reconciliation and Outreach at the Extraordinary Chambers in the Courts of Cambodia' (2011) 5 *Memory Studies* 165–81, 166–7.

[64] See Alexander Hinton, *The Justice Facade: Trials of Transition in Cambodia* (Oxford: Oxford University Press 2018), 43.

[65] Hinton, *The Justice Façade* 41.

Themes such as breaking silence and 'amnesia' in relation to Cambodia's killing fields figured prominently in tribunal representations. One of the slogans to defend the tribunal put it expressly: 'It's time to set the record straight'.[66] Proceedings served to bring out collective memory through truth-finding, victim participation, and symbolic punishment. They were deemed to have a therapeutic effect.[67] The ECCC constituted 'an institutional attempt to respond to victims' grief and communities' losses'.[68]

Legal proceedings were closely connected to the reproduction and framing of memories. Case 001 (the *Duch* case) focused on events relating to detention camp S-21, which was called the 'Asian Auschwitz'.[69] The trial used documentary evidence and witness testimony to reconstruct and renew memory of S-21.[70] The case brought out new details about the operation of S-21. Duch admitted his responsibility for tortures and execution. He said:

> I would like to make it clear that I am legally responsible for the crimes committed at S-21, especially the acts of torture and the executions in the camp ... As a perpetrator, I know that I am personally guilty before the entire Cambodian people and nation, before the families of all the victims who lost their lives at S-21.[71]

Like Eichmann, he presented himself as 'a mere puppet in the criminal regime'. He said that as director of S-21, he did not 'dare to seek any alternatives to obeying the orders from the upper echelon'.[72] This half-hearted apology left victims divided. Critics have noted that 'by focusing on the years of Khmer Rouge rule in Cambodia', the 'case ultimately produced a "truth" bleached of historical process and an understanding of the factors that enabled the Khmer Rouge to rise to power'.[73]

Case 002 brought out regime atrocity. Peter Manning has noted that the 'interplays between Prosecution and Defence in Case 002' marked 'attempts to prove or refute—specific genres of memory claim—the roles of "senior leaders" on the basis of their position and authority within the Communist Party of Kampuchea

[66] See ECCC Outreach poster, at http://www.eccc.gov.kh/sites/default/files/publications/poster-record-big%20EN.jpg.

[67] See generally Claire Moon, 'Healing Past Violence: Traumatic Assumptions and Therapeutic Interventions in War and Reconciliation' (2009) 8 *Journal of Human Rights* 71–91. On victim visibility in proceedings, see Rachel Killean, 'Constructing victimhood at the Khmer Rouge Tribunal: Visibility, selectivity and participation' (2018) 24 *International Review of Victimology* 273–96.

[68] Maria Elander, 'The Victim's Address: Expressivism and the Victim at the Extraordinary Chambers in the Courts of Cambodia' (2013) 7 *International Journal of Transitional Justice* 95–115, 102.

[69] Chandler, 'Cambodia Deals with its Past' 361.

[70] Manning, *Transitional Justice and Memory in Cambodia*, 80.

[71] Compilation of statements of apology made by Kaing Guek Eav alias Duch during the proceedings, Transcript of 31 March 2009, p. 52, line 14 to p. 56 line 21, at https://www.eccc.gov.kh/sites/default/files/publications/Case001Apology_En_low_res.pdf.

[72] Ibid.

[73] Alexander Hinton, 'Justice and Time at the Khmer Rouge Tribunal: In Memory of Vann Nath, Painter and S-21 Survivor' (2014) 8 *Genocide Studies and Prevention: An International Journal* 7–17, 11.

command structure'. [74] In this way, they 'characterize a central genre of memory claim at work at tribunals: that knowledge of the past, as a set of memories and artifacts, can be objectively reproduced as a set of unequivocal facts'.[75]

The public attention to proceedings was significant. The number of visitors exceeded that of other tribunals. In Case 002/01, judges ruled that the presence of the defendants at trial was necessary due to the enormous public interest in proceedings.[76]

The rendering of the judgment in Case 002/02 against Nuon Chea and Khieu Samphan, former head of state, marked a landmark moment. David Scheffer, the former UN Secretary General's special expert on assistance to the Khmer Rouge trials, described it expressly as a 'Nuremberg moment' for Cambodia. He stated that the 'verdict is essentially the Nuremberg judgement for the ECCC and thus carries very significant weight for Cambodia, international criminal justice, and the annals of history'.[77]

The defendants were convicted for genocide and crimes against humanity committed between 1977 and 1979. The qualification of the crimes of the Khmer Rouge as genocide was controversial. The Genocide Convention limits genocide to four protected groups: racial, national, ethnic, and religious groups. Many killings focused on the part of a national group, the 'new people'. They targeted regime opponents inside the Khmer majority group. Experts remained divided to what extent the targeting of the quasi-entirety of a population satisfies the group definition. Some authorities claimed that inclusion of killings of 'Khmers by Khmers' would overstretch the definition.[78] Others argued that the group definition is not by itself limited to minority groups and coined the term 'auto-genocide' to capture the phenomenon.[79] The judgment in case 002/02 was of historical significance. It found that

> during the Democratic Kampuchea period there existed a policy to target the following groups in order to establish an atheistic and homogenous society without class divisions by abolishing all ethnic, national, religious, racial, class and cultural differences: Cham, Vietnamese, Buddhist and former Khmer Republic officials (including civil servants and military personnel) and their families.[80]

[74] Manning, *Transitional Justice and Memory in Cambodia* 80.

[75] Ibid.

[76] Rachel Hughes, 'Ordinary Theatre and Extraordinary Law at the Khmer Rouge Tribunal' (2015) 33 *Environment and Planning D: Society and Space* 714–31, 725.

[77] See AFP, 'Khmer rouge leaders found guilty of genocide in landmark ruling, 16 November 2018, at https://www.dailymaverick.co.za/article/2018-11-16-khmer-rouge-leaders-found-guilty-of-genocide-in-landmark-ruling/.

[78] William Schabas, 'Problems of International Codification: Were the Atrocities in Cambodia and Kosovo Genocide?' (2001) 35 *New England Law Review* 287–302, 291.

[79] Hurst Hannum, 'International Law and Cambodian Genocide: The Sounds of Silence' (1989) 11 *Human Rights Quarterly* 82–138, 111–12.

[80] ECCC, Summary of Judgement, Case 002/02, Case File No. 002/19-09-2007/ECCC/TC, 16 November 2018, para. 26.

It recognized crimes against two minority groups as genocide, namely attacks against the Cham Muslim people[81] and people of Vietnamese origin.[82] It thereby associated events on Cambodia with the formal label of genocide.

The judgment also qualified the notorious state-arranged marriages during the regime as 'forced marriages'. It argued that they constituted a crime against humanity against both, 'men and women'.[83] It noted:

> There existed a nationwide policy to regulate family building and marriage, which was implemented by Party cadres at all administrative and military levels. The CPK designed this policy, replacing the role of parents in the selection of a suitable spouse, forcing couples to marry and forcing the production of children, for the purpose of increasing the country's population within 10 to 15 years.[84]

It thereby branded the Communist Party of Kampuchea's policy of forced marriage as a crime on a national scale.

The ECCC served as a public forum for collective memory. It recollected facts, events, and persons from memory through proceedings, witness testimony, and participation of victims and survivors in the trials. It contributed to the creation of memory in society, through its rituals and performative practices. Its expressive role extended not only to the international community but mostly to local groups. The close nexus to collective memory is illustrated by the testimony of former S-21 survivor, Vann Nath, in the *Duch* trial.[85] His artistic work played a key role in understanding the story of the years. When asked by the presiding judge why he wanted to testify, he argued that his testimony was motivated by the prospect of contributing to memory and to educate future generations. He said:

> I determined if one day I survived and had freedom, I would compile the events to reflect on what happened so that the younger generation knew and would know of our suffering. … So I had to reveal, I had to write, I had to compile, and it can be served as a mirror to reflect to the younger generation of the lives of those who were accused with no reason, who committed no wrong, and that they were punished that way. That was the very suffering that we received and the suffering that we had because we told them the truth and they did not believe it.[86]

[81] Ibid., para. 30.
[82] Ibid., para. 34.
[83] Ibid., para. 40.
[84] Ibid., para. 40.
[85] His wrote a memoir entitled 'A Cambodian Prison Portrait: One Year in the Khmer Rouge's S-21 Prison'. See generally Y-Dang Troeung, 'Human Rights and the Literary Self-Portrait: Vann Nath's A Cambodian Prison Portrait: One Year in the Khmer Rouge's S-21' (2015) 19 *Rethinking History* 235–51.
[86] Trial Chamber, Extraordinary Chambers in the Courts of Cambodia, 'Transcript of Trial Proceedings—Kaing Guek Eav 'Duch' Public' Trial Day 35, 29 June 2009, 54–5..

Using institutions as sites of collective memory may frame national consciousness, but it also carries risks.[87] For instance, one of the downsides is the impact on Defence rights. The pressure to break silences or mark a rupture ('never again') may increase the symbolic importance of securing convictions. Moreover, there is a deeper societal critique relating to memory construction through international justice institutions. Such institutions may not serve so much as sites of local memory or remembrance, but rather as memory producers for 'an imagined internationalized constituency'.[88] Critics note that such memory-writing involves 'the appropriation of specific historical events to produce global narratives about the significance of these occurrences for those who did not directly endure them'.[89]

3.1.1.2 Expressions of shame and apology

The establishment of other institutions carries meanings of shame and apology. Traditionally, international criminal institutions are presented as 'powerful symbols that convey moral, social, as well as legal approbation of the guilty and the political objectives that drove them to commit their misdeeds'.[90] However, the very act of creation may also symbolize a different type of collective conscience, that is, feelings of shame[91] and guilt by the creators.[92]

Criminologists have stressed that shame and guilt have communicative powers or even certain reintegrative functions.[93] This logic also applies to institutional processes. The turn to new justice mechanisms in the 1990s can be regarded as a response to failures of the international community.[94] It marked an attempt to institute 'relations of global responsibility for the suffering of others'.[95]

As structural critiques of international criminal law have brought out, many of the conflicts that gave rise to the establishment of international criminal

[87] Michelle Staggs Kelsall, 'Symbolic, Shambolic or Simply Sui Generis? Reflections from the Field on Cambodia's Extraordinary Chambers' (2009) 27 *Law Context: A Socio-Legal Journal* 154–77, 159–62.

[88] Nesam McMillan, 'Remembering "Rwanda"' (2016) 12 *Law, Culture and the Humanities* 301–28, 325.

[89] Ibid., 327 and 328.

[90] Laurel Fletcher, 'From Indifference to Engagement: Bystanders and International Criminal Justice' (2005) 26 *Michigan Journal of International Law* 1013–95, 1028–9.

[91] On 'shame' see Robert F. Drinan, *The Mobilization of Shame: A World View of Human Rights* (New Haven, CT: Yale University Press, 2001); Saira Mohamed, 'Shame in the Security Council' (2013) 90 *Washington University Law Review* 1191–254

[92] See Robert D. Sloane, 'The Expressive Capacity of International Punishment: The Limits of the National Law Analogy and the Potential of International Criminal Law' (2007) 43 *Stanford Journal of International Law* 39–94, 46.

[93] John Braithwaite, *Crime, Shame and Reintegration* (Cambridge: Cambridge University Press, 1989), 55 ('Reintegrative shaming means that expressions of community disapproval ... are followed by gestures of reacceptance into the community of law-abiding citizen'); Mark Drumbl, 'Punishment Postgenocide: From Guilt to Shame to "Civis" in Rwanda' (2000) 75 *New York University Law Review* 1221–326, 1258–63.

[94] Tina Rosenberg, 'Conference Convocation' (1998) 13 *American University International Law Review* 1383–411, 1407.

[95] Nesam McMillan, 'Imagining the International: The Constitution of International as a Site of Crime, Justice and Community' (2016) 25 *Social & Legal Studies* 163–80, 170.

institutions have been shaped by post-colonial continuities, direct or indirect political influences of major powers, or external economic interests. The push towards problem-solving through criminal institutions is often interconnected with moral dilemmas of complicity, bystander responsibility, or failures of prevention. Scholars of Third World Approaches to International Law (TWAIL) have insisted that 'any attempt to identify responsibility' for tragedies and 'to create systems of accountability' should also look at the roles that 'other international actors played in promoting and exacerbating the situation'.[96]

3.1.1.2.1 The ad hoc *tribunals as 'purification ritual'*

The establishment of the *ad hoc* tribunals was marked by this ambiguity. The International Criminal Tribunal for the former Yugoslavia (ICTY) and the International Criminal Tribunal for Rwanda (ICTR) were not created based on selfless idealism but borne out of mixed motives, including self-interest and feelings of guilt.[97] As Laura Bingham has noted, 'one aim of the Tribunals at the time of creation involved not the reality but the image of a tribunal—the semaphoric weight of the institution in the abstract'.[98] Their development can be traced 'in part to the shameful failure of states to muster the collective political will to prevent or forestall systematic human rights atrocities' in the Balkans and Rwanda.[99]

The ICTY struggled with the perception that its creation was 'just another cynical ploy to assuage the guilty conscience of the West—a sop for the international community's loss of faith in failing either because of unwillingness or inability, to stop the Balkan's carnage'.[100]

The Security Council sat on reports on atrocities for more than a year before the establishment of the ICTY. Voices in the Council differed from calls for more decisive intervention, fears of interference with peace initiatives, and scepticism towards a judicial response.[101] When Resolution 808 was adopted, Madeleine Albright famously referred back to the spirit of the Nuremberg Principles. She said:

> There is an echo in this Chamber today ... By its action today, with Resolution 808 (1993), the Security Council has shown that the will of this Organization can be exercised, even if it has taken nearly half of a century for the wisdom of our earliest principles to take hold.[102]

[96] Antony Anghie and Bhupinder S. Chimni, 'Third World Approaches to International Law and Individual Responsibility in Internal Conflict' (2003) 2 *Chinese Journal of International Law* 77–103, 90.

[97] David P. Forsythe, 'International Criminal Courts: A Political View' (1997) 15 *Netherlands Quarterly of Human Rights* 5–19, 8 ('The Court did not reflect a sea change in international moral solidarity, but rather a confluence of varying political calculations.').

[98] Laura Bingham, 'Strategy or Process—Closing the International Criminal Tribunals for the Former Yugoslavia and Rwanda' (2006) 24 *Berkeley Journal of International Law* 687–717, 690.

[99] See Sloane, 'Expressive Capacity of International Punishment' 47.

[100] See Mirko Klarin, 'The Tribunal's Four Battles' (2004) 2 *JICJ* 546–57, 547.

[101] Forsythe, 'International Criminal Courts: A Political View' 8.

[102] Verbatim Record, UN Doc. S/PV. 3175, 22 February 1993, 11.

The statements made during the adoption of SC Resolution 827 (1993) reflect a sense of blame and apology. For instance, Venezuela stated:

> Too many grave violations of human rights have taken place in many parts of the world while those responsible for them have escaped the hand of justice, such as the Khmer Rouge in Cambodia and the warlords in Somalia; Sudan, Iraq and Haiti are other instances. But there comes a time when one must ask oneself: If we do not act now, when will we? If we do not act in a case such as this, when will we act?[103]

The establishment of a tribunal was partly an instrument to mitigate the failure to prevent or constrain atrocities at the doorsteps of Europe. Gary Bass put it drastically when arguing that Security Council action marked 'an act of tokenism by the world community, which was largely unwilling to intervene in the ex-Yugoslavia but did not mind creating an institution that would give the *appearance* of moral concern.'[104]

The Bosnian Ambassador to the United Nations noted that the ICTY was an 'alternative to real immediate measures to confront the crime or the criminals.'[105] The perceived institutional message was: 'Don't worry about it. What we are going to do is make sure that all the criminals are brought to justice. And this will teach everyone a lesson, that this should not happen again.'[106]

Cynics have noted that the choice of a legal response was a 'euphemism for inaction.'[107] The establishment of the Tribunal was seen as an excuse not to deploy a robust military peace operation.[108]

Feelings of guilt and shame were magnified by the drastic failure to prevent the atrocities in Srebrenica, which occurred while the Tribunal was already in place. The UN Secretary-General recognized the collective failure of the international community in the self-critical report, 'Fall of Srebrenica' in 1999.[109] The report started with a statement by ICTY Judge Riad which had qualified events at Srebrenica as 'scenes from hell, written on the darkest pages of human history.'[110]

[103] Verbatim Record, UN. Doc. S/PV.3217, 25 May 1993, 7.

[104] Bass, *Stay the Hand of Vengeance* 207.

[105] Payam Akhavan, 'Justice in the Hague, Peace in the Former Yugoslavia? A Commentary on the United Nations War Crimes Tribunal' (1998) 20 *Human Rights Quarterly* 737–816, 745.

[106] Ibid.

[107] Gary Bass, *Stay the Hand of Vengeance: The Politics of War Crimes Trials* (Princeton, NJ: Princeton University Press, 2000)
215.

[108] See Fréderic Mégret, 'Politics of International Criminal Justice' 1272.

[109] Report of the Secretary-General pursuant to General Assembly resolution 53/35: The fall of Srebrenica, UN Doc. A/54/549, 15 November 1999.

[110] Ibid., para. 2, with reference to a press release issued by the ICTY (CC/PIO/026-E), The Hague, 16 November 1995.

The Secretary-General acknowledged collective responsibility for the events: 'The international community as a whole must accept its share of responsibility for allowing this tragic course of events by its prolonged refusal to use force in the early stages of the war.'[111]

The report pointed specifically to failures of the Security Council, the Contact Group, and 'Governments which contributed to the delay in the Use of Force', as well as by the UN Secretariat and the 'mission in the field'.[112] But it stated that the 'primary and most direct responsibility' lies with the 'architects and implementers of the attempted genocide in Bosnia', including Karadžić and Mladic who were indicted by the ICTY.[113] The report deplored 'the inadequacy of symbolic deterrence in the face of a systematic campaign of violence'[114] and stressed the importance of criminal prosecutions: 'The men who have been charged with this crime against humanity reminded the world and, in particular, the United Nations, that evil exists in the world.'[115]

The exercise of individual criminal responsibility by the ICTY became thereby almost inevitably a remedy to make up for collective failure and to supplement the limited channels for state responsibility. It symbolized the need to address the 'scope of the evil'[116] inflicted on victims through criminal prosecution of individuals. The ICTR expressly justified the very 'attribution of individual criminal responsibility' as 'a fundamental expression of the need for enforcement action by the Security Council'.[117]

This heavy symbolic baggage was challenged by defendants who came to be seen not only as offenders of their own crimes but as symbols of state criminality.[118] In *Tadić*, the ICTY's first case, Defence counsel Michail Wladimiroff pointed to the dangers of treating defendants as 'guinea-pigs'.[119] He stated:

> [T]he lack of defined and public criteria has blown the case against Dusko Tadic out of all proportion. Already the danger seems evident that the case is viewed as a symbol of everything that happened in the area, and that Dusko Tadic has been portrayed as the prototype of a war criminal.[120]

[111] Ibid., para. 501.
[112] Ibid., para. 501.
[113] Ibid., para. 501.
[114] Ibid., para. 505.
[115] Ibid., para. 506.
[116] Ibid., para. 503.
[117] *Prosecutor v. Kanyabashi*, Decision on Defence Motion on Jurisdiction, para. 34.
[118] Gerry Simpson, 'Men and abstract entities: Individual responsibility and collective guilt in international criminal law' in André Nollkaemper and Harmen van der Wilt (eds), *System Criminality in International Law* (Cambridge: Cambridge University Press, 2009), 69–100, 95.
[119] *Prosecutor v. Tadić*, IT-94-1, Trial Transcript, 7 May 1996, pp. 53–4 ('there is no room for experiments with a defendant as a guinea-pig').
[120] Ibid., 56.

A similar argument was later made by the *Orić* Defence team:

> [N]o good policy is served to be set by saying, well, if wrongs were done, we have to convict the accused of something. Our client is not a scapegoat for any wrongs done, and it's not as if a criminal trial is a failure if it results in a complete acquittal, although some seem to think so.[121]

Other critics have noted that the branding of Srebrenica as a 'symbol of evil' provided a political legitimization 'for the U.S.-NATO attack on and dismantling of Yugoslavia, colonial occupations in Bosnia and Kosovo, and justification for "humanitarian intervention" more broadly'.[122]

The ICTR was established under similar circumstances.[123] Its 'story' is inherently connected to 'renewed importance of Western emotional engagement and practical intervention in African contexts in the postcolonial era'.[124] Its establishment was requested by Rwanda after the international community had turned its back on atrocities. The creation was partly prompted by guilt over non-intervention by the West.[125] The Report of the independent inquiry into the actions of the United Nations during the 1994 genocide in Rwanda made this point bluntly in 1999. It stated: 'The United Nations failed the people of Rwanda during the genocide in 1994. It is a failure for which the United Nations as an organization, but also its Member States, should have apologized more clearly, more frankly, and much earlier.'[126]

The United States was reluctant to act following the attacks on peacekeepers in Somalia in 1993. France played an ambiguous role. It had supported the Hutu-dominated Habyarimana government and Hutu Interahamwe before 1994. During the genocide, it called for the creation of Operation Turquoise. This French-led mission was meant to save lives and protect civilians but it indirectly protected genocide perpetrators.[127] The lack of invocation of the term 'genocide' demonstrated the reluctance of the international community to take responsibility. Some of the deeper ethnic divisions fuelling the genocide were rooted in colonial heritage.

Rwanda called for the establishment of the tribunal, but ultimately felt compelled to vote against the final text of Resolution 955 (1994). In its explanation

121 *Prosecutor v. Orić*, Trial Transcript, 10 April 2006, p. 16583.

122 Edward S. Herman, 'The Approved Narrative of the Srebrenica Massacre' (2006) *19 International Journal for the Semiotics of Law* 409–34, 434.

123 See also Christian Tomuschat, *Human Rights: Between Idealism and Realism* (Oxford: Oxford University Press, 2014), 381; Nesam McMillan, '"Our Shame": International Responsibility for the Rwandan Genocide' (2008) 28 *Australian Feminist Law Journal* 3–28, 12.

124 McMillan, 'Remembering "Rwanda"' 322.

125 Romeo Dallaire, *Shake Hands with the Devil: The Failure of Humanity in Rwanda* (New York, NY: Carrol & Graf Publishers, 2003).

126 Report of the Independent Inquiry into the actions of the United Nations during the 1994 genocide in Rwanda, UN Doc. S/1999/1257, 16 December 1999, p. 51.

127 Hazel Cameron, 'The French Connection: Complicity in the 1994 Genocide in Rwanda' (2015) 8 *African Security* 96–119.

of the vote in the Security Council, it directly pointed to some of the failures. It stated that 'the international community, through its diplomatic representatives and international organizations in Kigali, as well as many reports by human rights organizations, was well aware of these massacres and cannot claim that it became cognizant of the situation only in the wake of the tragedy of April 1994'.[128]

Rwanda blamed major powers for their inaction. It noted on the record that 'when the genocide began', the international community (which had troops in Rwanda) 'could have saved hundreds of thousands of human lives by, for example, establishing humanitarian safe zones'.[129] But international actors 'decided instead to withdraw [their] troops from Rwanda and to abandon the victims to their butchers'.[130]

The statements by delegations supporting the establishment of the ICTR in the Security Council reflect a desire to turn the page and use international criminal justice as a means to remedy shortcomings.

The United States admitted that the role of the Security Council in the crisis 'has not been immune from criticism'.[131] France openly referred to as 'genocide'.[132] Other states linked the establishment of the tribunal to arguments of failure. For instance, New Zealand stated: 'After witnessing the genocide in Rwanda, on a scale reminiscent of that which occurred during the Second World War, we believe that the response could be no less than it was in Nuremburg or Tokyo decades ago or in respect of war crimes in the former Yugoslavia last year.'[133] Argentina expressly invoked 'never again' language. It noted that 'the establishment of the Tribunal is a 'clear message that the international community is not prepared to leave unpunished the grave crimes committed in Rwanda' and that 'the international community could not remain silent and inactive'.[134] The Russian delegate stated that, following the footsteps of the ICTY, the ICTR would 'give yet another clear and unequivocal signal to the effect that the international community will not tolerate serious violations of norms of international humanitarian law and disregard for the rights of the individual'.[135]

The ICTR as an institution is thus a symbol of its own.[136] It reflects the interconnection between justice and shame and apology. The creation of the Tribunal entails not only a message about Rwanda and expression of solidarity with victims of atrocities but also an act of redemption of the international community to

[128] Verbatim Record, 3453rd meeting, S/PV.3453, 8 November 1994, 15.
[129] Ibid., 14.
[130] Ibid.
[131] Ibid., 17.
[132] Ibid., 3.
[133] Ibid., 4.
[134] Ibid., 8.
[135] Ibid., 2.
[136] See also Bingham, 'Strategy or Process' 695 ('the "international community" (filtered through the prism of the Security Council) envisioned a tribunal for Rwanda as a powerful expressive mechanism to invoke in response to the inhumanity of the situation').

itself (i.e. a 'purification ritual').[137] It marked a step to accommodate pressures and address frictions that were shaped by colonial practices. It was later followed by other gestures signalling a share in responsibility. For instance, in 1998, former US President Bill Clinton expressed an apology to genocide survivors at the airport in Kigali. He stated:

> It may seem strange to you here, especially the many of you who lost members of your family, but all over the world there were people like me sitting in offices, day after day after day, who did not fully appreciate the depth and speed with which you were being engulfed by this unimaginable terror.[138]

After the ICTR assumed its operations, several states (e.g. Belgium, Switzerland, Germany, Canada, Finland, Norway, Sweden, the Netherlands, and France) gradually started to exercise jurisdiction over Rwandan genocide cases in their own domestic courts.

ICTR adjudication left many gaps. It failed to address crimes of the mainly Tutsi Rwandan Patriotic Front (RPF). It did not elaborate broader historical lines of inquiry or complicity, such as 'how the legacy of Belgian colonialism and French neocolonialism, the policy and practice of external development aid programmes and the continued supply of arms to Rwanda throughout the genocide also contributed to the conditions in which the massacres occurred'.[139]

3.1.1.2.2 The symbolism of the Kosovo Specialist Chambers

A third example of the close link between failure, shame, and apology and institutional creativity is the establishment of the Kosovo Specialist Chambers and Specialist Prosecutor's Office. The institution emerged in the shadow of shortcomings of the ICTY and international institutions in Kosovo (United Nations Interim Administration in Kosovo (UNMIK) and the European Union Rule of Law Mission in Kosovo (EULEX)). The Kosovo war took place while the ICTY was in existence. However, the tribunal pursued only a limited number of Kosovo-related cases. It held three cases relating to Serb defendants and two cases against Kosovo Albanians. Ramush Haradinaj, former commander of the Kosovo Liberation Army (KLA) and later Prime Minister of Kosovo, was acquitted twice. The acquittals resonated with dominant narratives in Kosovo, according to which the KLA was 'a liberation force that fought for justice and independence from decades of

[137] McMillan, 'Imagining the International' 170 ('The experience of the Rwandan genocide is understood to have caused 'sorrow' to more than its direct victims and be a source of "bitter regret" and "shame" for those who failed to prevent it.').

[138] Text of President Clinton's address to genocide survivors at the airport in Kigali, Rwanda, as provided by the White House, 25 March 1998, at https://www.cbsnews.com/news/text-of-clintons-rwanda-speech/.

[139] See McMillan, 'Imaging the International' 172.

brutal Serbian repression'.[140] Allegations of crimes committed by NATO during the air campaign were not investigated. International institutions in Kosovo relied on cooperation with political powers in Kosovo, including former KLA leaders. For a long time, few efforts were made to investigate crimes by KLA members against the Serbian population or certain Albanian Kosovars. As Dominik Zaum has noted, the prospect of international justice has 'polarised rather than reconciled': 'Neither in Serbia, nor in Kosovo has there been public support to try one of their own for war crimes. Serb authorities were for a long time very reluctant to cooperate with the ICTY, and Albanian indictees have generally been portrayed locally as war heroes rather than suspected criminals.'[141]
UNMIK and EULEX only handled 32 cases and left more than 900 cases to local prosecutors.[142] This created a gap and a legitimacy problem.

In 2000, these failures were openly addressed in a report by former Swiss prosecutor, Dick Marty on 'Inhuman treatment of people and illicit trafficking in human organs in Kosovo' to the Council of Europe ('Marty Report').[143] The report acknowledged a glaring victor's justice dilemma.[144] It stated:

> The appalling crimes committed by Serbian forces, which stirred up very strong feelings worldwide, gave rise to a mood reflected as well in the attitude of certain international agencies, according to which it was invariably one side that were regarded as the perpetrators of crimes and the other side as the victims, thus necessarily innocent.[145]

The report stressed the need to address this failure. It noted: 'There cannot and must not be one justice for the winners and another for the losers. Whenever a conflict has occurred, all criminals must be prosecuted and held responsible for their illegal acts, whichever side they belonged to and irrespective of the political role they took on.'[146]

[140] Anton Vukpalaj, 'Acquittals at the International Criminal Tribunal for the Former Yugoslavia (ICTY) in 2012–2013: The Domestic Implications' (2018) 10 *Studies of Transition States and Societies* 37–49, 38.

[141] Dominik Zaum, 'International Justice and the Prevention of Atrocities, Case Study: Kosovo', European Council on Foreign Relations Background Paper, November 2013, 3, at https://www.ecfr.eu/page/-/IJP_Kosovo.pdf.

[142] Humanitarian Law Center Kosovo, *An Overview of War Crime Trials in Kosovo 1999–2018* (Pristina: HLC Kosovo, 2018), at http://www.hlc-kosovo.org/wp-content/uploads/2018/10/HLC-Kosovo-An-overview-of-war-crime-trials-in-Kosovo-1999-2018.pdf.

[143] Council of Europe, Committee on Legal Affairs and Human Rights, 'Inhuman treatment of people and illicit trafficking in human organs in Kosovo', AS/Jur (2010) 46, 12 December 2010 ('Marty Report').

[144] See generally James Meernik, 'Victor's Justice or the Law?: Judging and Punishing at the International Criminal Tribunal for the Former Yugoslavia' (2003) 47 *Journal of Conflict Resolution* 140–62; Victor Peskin, 'Beyond Victor's Justice? The Challenge of Prosecuting the Winners at the International Criminal Tribunals for the Former Yugoslavia and Rwanda' (2005) 4 *Journal of Human Rights* 213–31.

[145] Marty Report, para. 13.

[146] Ibid., para. 15.

The Marty Report criticized international institutions for promoting 'short-term stability at any price' and thereby 'sacrificing some important principles of justice'.[147]

Based on these findings, the EULEX established a Special Investigative Task Force (SITF) to carry out further investigation of crimes. It recommended the establishment of a new judicial mechanism. It was set up by a national law, Law No. 05/L-053, following an exchange of letters between the President of Kosovo and the High Representative of the European Union.[148] The Chief Prosecutor of the Task Force, Clint Williamson, said: 'What our investigations has done, and what this court will do, is to fill the void left by the ICTY's jurisdictional limitations'.[149]

The establishment of the Kosovo Specialist Chambers and Specialist Prosecutor's Office thus symbolizes to some extent shame and regret about the failures of previous international institutions to shed light on serious criminal offences committed during the Kosovo war.[150] The very act of creation entails a message, namely a reminder about the importance of prosecuting the 'victors of a war'. In domestic laws, such as the law on reparations, KLA fighters are predominantly viewed as martyrs.[151] Kosovo Specialist Chambers may ultimately create a different narrative about the role of the KLA and the image of the war as 'war of liberation'.[152]

3.1.1.3 Re-creation and renewal of community relations

In some cases, the significance of the establishment of institutions lies in their ability to recreate and renew community relations. The act of creation symbolizes a transformation. Durkheim used the concept of 'collective effervescence' to describe such moments of social organization. It refers to moments in which a community comes together to recharge its relations and bonds and to express its commitment to values that become institutionalized through collective practices. Durkheim argued that collective effervescence is inherently creative in nature and may produce new ideas of morality, in particular in 'revolutionary or creative epochs'. The main idea is reflected in his work, *Elementary Forms of Religious Life*:

147 Ibid., para.10.

148 Assembly of the Republic of Kosovo, Law on Specialist Chambers and Specialist Prosecutor's Office, Law No. 05/L-053, 3 August 2015.

149 Statement of the Chief Prosecutor of the Special Investigative Task Force, 29 July 2014, at http://www.balkaninsight.com/en/file/show/Statement_of_the_Chief_Prosecutor_of_the_SITF_EN.pdf.

150 See Ismet Hajdari, 'A New Era for Justice in Kosovo' 12 January 2017, at https://www.boell.de/en/2017/01/12/new-era-justice-kosovo ('What is important regarding the Special Court is that it must not repeat the mistakes made by UNMIK and EULEX, nor be brought into any connection with them. This particularly goes for EULEX—if one wants the Special Court to succeed, there must be no continuity between it and EULEX, since the largest (and most expensive) civilian mission in the history of the European Union has been such a failure.').

151 Law No. 04/L-054 on the Status and the Rights of the Martyrs, Invalids, Veterans, Members of Kosovo Liberation Army, Civilian Victims of War and Their Families, available at: https://gzk.rks-gov.net/ActDocumentDetail.aspx?ActID=2793.

152 See Prishtina Insight, 'The "specter" of the Special Court hangs over Kosovo', 17 October 2018, at https://prishtinainsight.com/the-specter-of-the-special-court-hangs-over-kosovo/.

> Under the influence of some great collective shock in certain historical periods, social interactions become much more frequent and active ... People live differently and more intensely than in normal times. The changes are not simply of nuance and degree; man himself becomes something other than what he was.[153]

Creative effervescence is 'a phenomenon during which new ideas in morality can emerge, as well as ideal conceptions of society'.[154]

3.1.1.3.1 Nuremberg and Tokyo as peace projects

Such moments have occurred in the history of international criminal justice. Nuremberg and Tokyo are key examples.[155] They marked moments of symbolic re-enactment which changed social and normative structures in times of high emotional intensity. These trials 'made a case that needed to be made after this war and those crimes'.[156] They may be understood as 'colossal event[s] in international politics that aimed at carrying out a dramatic change from war to peace'.[157] This is reflected in the rhetoric of the trials and the strong focus on crimes against peace. Through the trials, the Allied powers sought to promote an ethical and political vision that departed from the conduct and ideology of defeated powers.[158] Ultimately, the trials were meant to prevent a recurrence of Nazi structures and Japanese imperialism. The invocation of the crime marked an attempt to 'juridify the logic of war'.[159]

As Yuki Takatori has noted:

> the Allies hoped that by trying and punishing the former rulers of Germany and Japan (including even those who might claim to have no blood on their hands), and by revealing their folly and cruelty, they would 'educate' the people, causing them to reject all that the men who had led them represented and leaving an indelible impression on the consciousness of the defeated nations.[160]

153 Emile Durkheim, *The Elementary Forms of Religious Life* (New York, NY: Free Press, 1995), 212–13.

154 Tim Olaveson, 'Collective Effervescence and Communitas: Processual Models of Ritual and Society in Emile Durkheim and Victor Turner' (2001) 26 *Dialectical Anthropology* 89–124, 101.

155 See Mégret, 'International Criminal Justice as a Peace Project' 840 ('Nuremberg and, to a lesser extent, Tokyo were in a sense the culmination of this movement of belief in the centrality of crimes against peace to the international legal order.').

156 See Frédéric Mégret, 'Nuremberg and the Contemporary Commitment to International Criminal Justice', https://voelkerrechtsblog.org/nuremberg-and-the-contemporary-commitment-to-international-criminal-justice/.

157 See Yuki Takatori, 'Remembering the War Crimes Trial: The Tokyo Trial view of history' in Sven Saaler and Wolfgang Schwentker (eds), *The Power of Memory* in Modern Japan (Folkestone: Global Oriental 2008), 78–95, 92.

158 Kim C. Priemel, *The Betrayal: The Nuremberg Trials and German Divergence* (Oxford: Oxford University Press, 2016).

159 Lawrence Douglas, 'From IMT to NMT: The emergence of a jurisprudence of atrocity' in Kim C. Priemel and Alexa Stiller (eds), *Reassessing the Nuremberg Military Tribunals: Transitional Justice, Trial Narratives, and Historiography* (New York, NY: Berghahn Books, 2012) 276–95, 280.

160 Takatori, 'Remembering the War Crimes Trial' 92.

Nuremberg was later used as the catalyst moment for the creation of the *ad hoc* tribunals. Symbolism played an important role in this context. For instance, the United Nations-established Commission of Experts to inquire into the events of the Rwandan genocide noted that the Nuremberg trials 'symbolized the possibility that trials could actually be carried out and punishment enforced in modern times'.[161]

3.1.1.3.2 The STL as symbol of curbing terrorism through law

The establishment of the Special Tribunal for Lebanon (STL) was guided by similar motives. It is inherently connected to the ambition to 'tame' terrorism through law. The idea of an international terrorism court has a long historical trajectory. It was first discussed in the 1930s, but lay dormant for decades.[162] It re-emerged in the shadow of 9/11 when terrorist acts and extreme forms of violence by non-state actors were perceived as a challenge to existing rubrics of international law and as a threat to the social equilibrium in international society. The Security Council started to take quasi-legislative action in order to strengthen global protection against terrorism.[163] Counter-terrorism conquered a broader space in UN action. The creation of the STL was more than a reaction to the terrorist attacks in Lebanon. It symbolized an intent to shape a more comprehensive framework for the criminalization of terrorism and complemented ongoing efforts inside the UN system.

The strategic importance of the STL was acknowledged by former Legal Counsel Nicholas Michel, one of the key architects of the tribunal. He noted: '[T]he creation of a special tribunal was requested not only to respond to the killing of one individual, former Prime Minister Hariri, on 14 February 2005. The context indicates far broader peace and security dimensions and implications.'[164] The symbolic nature is reflected in statements made at the adoption of Security Council Resolution 1757.[165] In this resolution, the Council used its powers under Chapter VII to set in motion the entry into force the Agreement between the United Nations and Lebanon on the Tribunal, which had been

[161] UN Security Council, 'Preliminary report of the Independent Commission of Experts established in accordance with Security Council resolution 935 (1994)', Annex to Letter, dated 1 October 1994, from the Secretary-General addressed to the President of the Security Council, Doc No S/1994/1125, para 127.

[162] Ignacio de la Rasilla, 'An International Terrorism Court *in nuce* in the Age of International Adjudication' (2017) 1 *The Asian Yearbook of Human Rights and Humanitarian Law* 76–108.

[163] SC Res. 1373 (2001), UN Doc. 28 September 2001, UN Doc. S/RES/1373 (2001). See Paul C. Szasz, 'The Security Council Starts Legislating' (2002) 96 *AJIL* 901–5; Stefan Talmon, 'The Security Council as World Legislature' (2005) 99 *AJIL* 175–93.

[164] See Nicolas Michel, 'The creation of the Tribunal in its context' in Amal Alamuddin, Nidal Nabil Jurdi, and David Tolbert (eds), *The Special Tribunal for Lebanon: Law and Practice* (Oxford: Oxford University Press, 2014) 10–31, 15.

[165] SC 1757 (2007), S/RES/1757, adopted by the Security Council at its 5685th meeting, on 30 May 2007.

blocked in the Lebanese parliament. Several states emphasized the global significance of the tribunal.

Slovakia justified its support for the Tribunal based on the belief 'that impunity should not be allowed and tolerated'.[166] It stated that [t]he rule of law must be respected everywhere and by everybody. The establishment of the Tribunal is necessary for a thorough investigation of the cases of politically motivated violence—in fact, terrorism.'[167]

Other delegations addressed the link to global deterrence. The United States argued that the Resolution marks a 'commitment to the principle that there shall be no impunity for political assassinations in Lebanon or elsewhere'.[168] It stated that '[t]he Tribunal will also serve to deter future political assassinations'.[169]

Lebanon adopted a similar line. It praised the resolution as a general victory for justice, rather than 'a victory of one party over another'.[170] It added that the Tribunal 'will certainly act as a deterrent to terrorist activities'.[171]

The STL was formally mandated to apply Lebanese substantive criminal law, but the statute left leeway to 'depart from the application and interpretation of national law by national courts under certain conditions'.[172] The Appeals Chamber used this in the Interlocutory Appeal Decision on the Applicable Law in which it defined terrorism as an international crime for the first time. In the decision, it expressly qualified 'the crime of terrorism' as the 'Tribunal's principal raison d'être'.[173] The branding of terrorism as international crime remains contested as judicial precedent, but it stands as one of the most important institutional legacies of the STL, namely the ideal to curb acts of political terrorism in peacetime and in wartime through the instrument of criminal law.[174] According to an expressivist logic, such an affirmation is an important message in itself, irrespective of whether it results in convictions by the STL.

3.1.1.3.3 The SCSL and the dichotomy between peace and justice

The Special Court for Sierra Leone (SCSL) marked an institutional experiment to overcome the traditional dichotomy between peace and justice.[175] It deviated from the model of the *ad hoc* tribunals for the former Yugoslavia and Rwanda through its close interrelation with a parallel truth and reconciliation process. It stood, like no other previous institution, as a symbol that peace and justice should be seen as

166 Verbatim Record, 5685th meeting, 30 May 2007, S/PV.5685, 7.

167 Ibid., 7.

168 Ibid., 7.

169 Ibid., 7.

170 Ibid., 9.

171 Ibid., 9.

172 STL Interlocutory Appeal Applicable Law, para. 39.

173 Ibid., para. 42.

174 See generally Harmen van der Wilt, 'The legacy of the Special Tribunal for Lebanon' in Alamuddin, Jurdi, and Tolbert (eds), *The Special Tribunal for Lebanon: Law and Practice*, 268–87.

175 Charles C. Jalloh and Vincent O. Nmehielle, 'The Legacy of the Special Court for Sierra Leone' (2006) 30 *Fletcher Forum of World Affairs* 107–24.

being complementary to each other.[176] It was the first internationalized court that operated alongside a Truth and Reconciliation Commission (TRC). It symbolized the development of a 'two-pronged transitional justice approach', and 'an ad hoc division of labour in which the SCSL focused on criminal guilt, and the TRC focused on peacebuilding and democratization, with a particular emphasis on sexual violence and youth'.[177]

The Lomé Peace Agreement, which put an end to the conflict in Sierra Leone, provided for a TRC[178] and a sweeping amnesty and pardon clause, which was deemed to apply to 'to all combatants and collaborators in respect of anything done by them in pursuit of their objectives'.[179] At the time of the signing of the agreement, there was a widespread sentiment that this was the 'price to pay' for peace.[180] The Special Representative of the Secretary-General entered a reservation regarding the amnesty provision. But the agreement was welcomed by the Security Council in Resolution 1260 of 20 August 1999. The pragmatic stance is reflected in the statement of the UK. It noted:

> The Lomé Agreement is not perfect. The inclusion of a blanket amnesty for those who have committed appalling atrocities has rightly caused concern. But this was one of many hard choices that the Government and the people of Sierra Leone had to make in the interests of securing a workable agreement.[181]

Violations of the peace agreement and obstructions of the peace process by RUF led to a complete turnaround one year later. On 14 August 2000, the Security Council requested the Secretary-General in Resolution 1315 to create an independent special court with 'jurisdiction over persons who bear the greatest responsibility for the commission of the crimes'.[182]

The establishment of the Special Court broke the image of a binary choice between a 'peace' track and a 'justice' track.[183] The Court and the TRC coexisted as independent entities with 'distinct', yet 'related functions'.[184] The interplay caused

[176] See Alpha Sesay, 'To compete or to complement? Assessing the relationship between the Sierra Leone Special Court and the truth and reconciliation' in Charles Jalloh (ed.), *The Sierra Leone Special Court and its Legacy* (Cambridge: Cambridge University Press, 2014) 481–501, 497.

[177] See Rebekka Friedman, *Competing Memories* (Cambridge: Cambridge University Press, 2017) 93.

[178] Lomé Agreement, Art. 26.

[179] Lomé Peace Agreement, Art. 9 (2).

[180] See Avril McDonald, 'Sierra Leone's Shoestring Special Court, (2002) 84 *International Review of the Red Cross* 121–43, 123 ('the price of peace was complete impunity for all those who had committed serious violations of international humanitarian law').

[181] SC Resolution 1260, Verbatim Record, S/PV.4035, 20 August 1999, 4.

[182] See para. 3 of SC Resolution 1315, 14 August 2000, UN Doc S/RES/1315 (2000).

[183] See generally Juan E. Méndez and Jeremy Kelley, 'Peace-making, justice and the ICC' in Christian de Vos, Sara Kendall, and Carsten Stahn (eds), *Contested Justice: The Politics and Practice of International Criminal Court Interventions* (Cambridge: Cambridge University Press, 2015) 479–95, 479–95.

[184] Letter dated 12 January 2001 from the Secretary-General addressed to the President of the Security Council, UN Doc. S/2001/40, para. 9 ('care must be taken to ensure that the Special Court for

some frictions in practice,[185] but ultimately, the model gained importance as an 'example of how a TRC could operate alongside a Court' while respecting the role of traditional institutions in reconciliation and peacebuilding.[186] The core message was that there is room for a two-track approach in institutional terms, and a conceptual need for it, since it represents 'two distinct understandings of the causes of conflict', namely 'one which stresses long-term historical antecedents and structural root causes, and the other which stresses the responsibility of individuals'.[187]

William Schabas, who served on the TRC, compared the relationship to house repair. He noted:

> The Truth and Reconciliation Commission is the plumber, and the Special Court is the electrician. The two trades work in different parts of the house, on different days, at different stages of the construction, and using different tools and materials. Nobody would want to live in a finished house that lacked either electricity or plumbing.[188]

The Special Court carried multiple symbolic meanings.[189] The courtroom and the trials virtually symbolized the 'emergence from the moral and physical degradation of the war'.[190] The Court relied heavily on outreach, which was considered as the '[c]rown jewel of the SCSL',[191] in order to 'make legal proceedings a part of Sierra Leone's national discourse and heritage'.[192] However, its very existence highlighted at the same time the limits of the justice process and the need to apply different approaches to prevention and conflict transformation.

3.1.1.4 Manifestation of hope and belief

A fourth message associated with the creation of institutions is the expression of hope and belief.[193] Often the very act of creation has symbolic meaning as a form

Sierra Leone and the Truth and Reconciliation Commission will operate in a complementary and mutually supportive manner, fully respectful of their distinct but related functions').

185 See Sesay, 'To compete or to complement?' 497 ('issues relate mainly to collaboration between the two institutions, discussions around primacy or exercise of powers, information sharing, witness protection, the Commission's access to detainees in the custody of the Court, and the establishment of an institutional relationship').

186 Kirsten Ainley, Simone Datzberger, Rebekka Friedman, and Chris Mahony, *Ten Years On: Transitional Justice in Post-Conflict Sierra Leone* (London: LSE, 2013) 17.

187 Ibid., 37–8.

188 William Schabas, 'The Relationship between Truth Commissions and International Courts: The Case of Sierra Leone' (2003) 25 *Human Rights Quarterly* 1035–66, 1065.

189 Former SCSL President, Justice Renate Winter, qualified the Special Court as 'an exemplary model of international justice'. See Security Council, Verbatim Record, 6163rd meeting, 16 July 2009, S/PV.6163, 3.

190 See Rachel Kerr and Jessica Lincoln, *The Special Court for Sierra Leone Outreach, Legacy and Impact*, Final Report February 2008 (London: King's College, 2008) 5.

191 Antonio Cassese, 'Report on the Special Court for Sierra Leone' 12 December 2006, para. 270.

192 See Security Council, 6163rd meeting, 16 July 2009, S/PV.6163, 3.

193 On utopia and hope, see Ernst Bloch, *The Principle of Hope* (Cambridge, MA: MIT Press, 1986).

of projection and imagination of ideas.[194] Many scholars have drawn attention to the parallels between criminal justice and religion and the 'faith'-based underpinnings of international criminal justice.[195] They are connected to theories of 'social idealism'.[196] A compelling example is the creation of the ICC. It represents the incarnation of the cosmopolitan dream of reimagining international society, based on ideals of humanity and universality.[197] It reflects the desire of a collective conscience ('conscience of humanity')[198] and stands as a symbol against the constraints of realism and *realpolitik*. It has been considered as a utopian project, that is, a 'realist utopia', since its inception.[199] It embraces many macro objectives, such as universality, 'end to impunity', or global 'enforcement of international justice' that are ideal states rather than measurable institutional objectives. They are open-ended and subject to constant improvement. By definition, they cannot be fully reached, since they are subject to change.

3.1.1.4.1 Utopian foundations of idea of an international criminal court

The historical foundations of the idea go back to the inter-war period when networks of individuals and non-state actors (e.g. the International Law Association (ILA) and the International Committee of the Red Cross (ICRC)) sought to rethink international relations and state power.[200] The efforts to create an international criminal court are grounded in at least three distinct traditions, which share different interests and ideologies, namely the pacifist movement which saw international justice as an instrument to foster peace settlement of disputes and pacification of international relations, the humanitarian movement which was concerned with the humanization of warfare, and the emerging human rights movement, which saw international criminal justice as a means to strengthen rights of groups (e.g. minorities) or individuals.[201] All three traditions associated

[194] See Kenneth Anderson, 'The Rise of International Criminal Law: Intended and Unintended Consequences' (2009) 20 *EJIL* 331–58, 335 (qualifying the ICC as 'symbol of both the promise of international law and its stunning shortcomings').

[195] See Tallgren, 'The faith in humanity and international criminal law' 334; Bernard, 'Faut-il croire en le droit (international pénal)?' 1.

[196] Iain Scobbie, 'The holiness of the heart's affection: Philip Allott's theory of social idealism' in Alexander Orakhelashvili (ed.), *Research Handbook on the Theory and History of International Law* (Cheltenham: Elgar 2011), 168–97.

[197] Cosmopolitanism is grounded in the belief that 'that every human being has a global stature as an ultimate unit of moral concern'. See Thomas W. Pogge, 'Cosmopolitanism and Sovereignty' (1992) 103 *Ethics* 48–75, 49.

[198] See para. 2 of the preamble of the ICC Statute.

[199] See generally Antonio Cassese (ed.), *Realizing Utopia: The Future of International Law* (Oxford: Oxford University Press, 2012); Isabel Feichtner, 'Realizing Utopia through the Practice of International Law' (2012) 23 *EJIL* 1143–57.

[200] On networks, see Roger Cotterrell, 'The concept of crime and transnational networks of community' in Valsamis Mitsilegas, Peter Alldridge, and Leonidas Cheliotis (eds), *Globalisation, Criminal Law and Criminal Justice: Theoretical, Comparative and Transnational Perspectives* (Oxford: Hart, 2015), 7-23

[201] See Mark Lewis, *The Birth of the New Justice, The Internationalization of Crime and Punishment, 1919–1950* (Oxford: Oxford University Press, 2014), 5–7.

international criminal justice with goals and aspirations that exceed its actual capacities.

Pacifists supported the idea of an international criminal court based on beliefs that it would strengthen protection against war. In the 1920s, Romanian jurist, Vespasian Pella, developed a criminological justification for this claim. He argued that a global criminal court would serve as an instrument to prevent aggressive war and sanction crimes of states.[202] However, in practice, international criminal justice has struggled with the criminalization of aggression, that is a ban of the use of force in inter-state relations ('negative peace'). Throughout much the second half of the twentieth century, criminalization has been focused on *jus in bello* violations rather than *jus ad bellum* considerations. The ICC Statute and the Kampala Conference did not involve a radical reimagining of the concept of the crime of aggression, but rather confirmed of the *status quo*, based on GA Resolution 3314 (1970).[203] Individual criminal responsibility serves only to a limited extent as an instrument to contribute to broader aspirations of 'positive peace', that is the ambition to contribute to conflict transformation or democratic peace. Peace versus justice dilemmas are inherent in the operation of international criminal justice and cannot be meted out as such. Peace is mostly an imagined ideal, which inspires hope and orientation, rather than a tangible, functional objective.

Similar discrepancies between aspiration and reality have emerged to exist in relation to the humanitarian tradition. The first proposal for a permanent international criminal court was made by Gustave Moynier, one of the founders of the ICRC, in 1872. He suggested the creation of an international judicial body in order to deal with prevention and punishment of violations of the Geneva Convention of 22 August 1864.[204] Already at the time, legal scholars (e.g. Francis Lieber) questioned whether individual criminal responsibility is the best method to prevent violations and secure protection for victims of war.[205] They argued that other methods, such as inter-state arbitration, fact-finding on violations, protection of humanitarian relief, or education should gain priority.[206] Later, Jean Pictet argued in his commentary on the Fundamental Principles of the Red Cross that '[o]ne cannot be at one and the same time a champion of justice and charity'.[207]

The tensions persist until today. In international criminal justice, humanization of warfare or protection of victims of war are not primary goals per se. They are tied to investigations and prosecutions. Methodologies differ. International criminal justice promotes transparency of procedures and publicizing of violations.

[202] Ibid., 105.
[203] Frédéric Mégret, 'International Criminal Justice as a Peace Project' (2018) 29 *EJIL* 835–58, 856.
[204] See Christopher Hall, 'The First Proposal for a Permanent International Criminal Court' (1998) 322 *International Review of the Red Cross* 57–74.
[205] Ibid., 63–4.
[206] Ibid.
[207] See Jean Pictet, *Commentary: Fundamental Principles of the Red Cross* (Geneva: International Federation of Red Cross and Red Crescent Societies, 1979), 22–3.

Humanitarian protection may rely on confidential dialogue and persuasion. There is thus no full congruence between international criminal justice and the humanitarian tradition.

The human rights movement supported the creation of the ICC because it offers prospects for a reimagination of various types of rights and human rights violations. Human rights non-governmental organizations (NGOs) were instrumental in the framing of crime definitions, jurisdiction, the rights of victims, and gender approaches, and most importantly the independent role of the Prosecutor.[208] But attempts to view the ICC primarily through the prism of individual or collective human rights or 'rights-based' approaches to accountability fail to recognize the complexity of international criminal justice, and the need to balance conflicting rights and obligations. For instance, rights of victims in relation to state violations cannot be simply transposed to criminal proceedings which are centred on individual criminal responsibility. A traditional human rights lens creates inflated expectations and fails to address the competing liberalisms inside the international criminal justice project.[209]

3.1.1.4.2 The ICC as modern Sisyphus

The actual establishment of the International Criminal Court (ICC) in the 1990s was marked by utopian features. When the Court was created, it was seen as part of a story of institutional progression. It symbolized moves from ad hocism to permanence, from selectivity to universality, and/or from politics to law:

> Nuremberg and Tokyo, or so the story goes, were imperfect but necessary experiments in establishing the idea of international criminal justice; the ICTY and ICTR were 'laboratories' for a more permanent engagement with international criminal trials; the ICC then heralds a new age leading to a horizon of universality of international criminal justice.[210]

The preamble of the Statute euphorically proclaims that 'peoples are united by common bonds, their cultures pieced together in a shared heritage'.[211] Many of the aspirations and projections of the Statute (e.g. universality, 'end of impunity', 'peace, security and well-being of the world') exceed institutional means or capacities or

[208] On the role of NGOs, see Helen Durham, 'The Role of Civil Society in Creating the International Criminal Court Statute: Ten Years On and Looking Back' (2012) 3 *International Humanitarian Legal Studies* 3–42; Zoe Pearson, 'Non-Governmental Organizations and the International Criminal Court: Changing Landscapes of International Law (2006) 39 *Cornell International Law Journal* 243–81.

[209] See Darryl Robinson, 'The Identity Crisis of International Criminal Law' (2008) 21 *LJIL* 925–63, 931.

[210] Mégret, 'International Criminal Justice as a Juridical Field' 43.

[211] See ICC Statute, preamble.

are based on myth or fiction.[212] The role of the ICC bears synergies with Homer's myth of Sisyphus, who is condemned to roll heavy rocks up a mountain for eternity.[213] The Court is expected to shoulder the global evil of atrocity crime.[214] Its task is never complete. It perpetually encounters perils and struggles to address them. Its action is shaped by repetition, ritual, and hope in the prospect of success.

Some scholars have recognized this symbolic institutional function of the ICC and its role in building and sustaining community relations. For instance, Edward Wise has argued that the 'primary significance' of the ICC lies in its 'symbolic' role, namely its ability to 'make a show of closing ranks against criminals' and 'to engage in the rituals of reprobation that the criminal trial and punishment represent'.[215] He has recognized that this 'symbolic' role does not make the ICC 'any less important', since 'symbols can have real effects'.[216]

A prime example is the argument of deterrence. It has not been proven to work. But the institutional existence of the ICC may be helpful to strengthen belief in the discouragement of crime. As Wise has noted:

> Deterrence is not simply a matter of intimidating potential offenders who consciously calculate the prospective costs and benefits of criminal activity. There is reason to believe it operates more subtly and indirectly, in part by helping to form and reinforce popular perceptions and social norms about what constitutes right and wrong, and in part, as Durkheim suggests, by serving as a symbolic affirmation of the ties that hold a community together and by fostering a sense that one is a law-abiding citizen.[217]

Others postulate that the 'symbolic function' should be regarded as an 'assumed purpose' of international criminal justice more generally, like 'retribution, reparation and prevention'.[218]

[212] Cotterrell, 'The concept of crime and transnational networks of community' 20 ('global consciousness as a basis of universal cultural authority for criminalisation is a myth, just as the idea of a global "international community" is a mythical foundation of a universal politico-legal authority').

[213] Jose A. Baez, 'An International Crimes Court: Further Tales of the King of Corinth' (1993) *23 Georgia Journal of International and Comparative Law* 289–325, Niamh Hayes, 'Sisyphus wept: Prosecuting sexual violence at the International Criminal Court' in William A. Schabas, Yvonne McDermott, and Niamh Hayes (eds), *Ashgate Research Companion to International Criminal Law: Critical Perspectives* (Farnham: Ashgate 2013), 7–44.

[214] For an analogy to the myth of the Titan Atlas, who was deemed to carry celestial heavens for eternity, and a critique of overabundance of goals , see Mirjan Damaška, 'What Is the Point of International Criminal Justice?' (2008) 83 *Chicago-Kent Law Review* 329–65, 331 ('Unlike Atlas, international criminal courts are not bodies of titanic strength, capable of carrying on their shoulders the burden of so many tasks.').

[215] Edward M. Wise, 'The International Criminal Court: A Budget of Paradoxes' (2000) 8 *Tulane Journal of International and Criminal Law* 261–81, 268.

[216] Ibid., 268.

[217] Ibid., 267.

[218] Julien Pieret and Marie-Laurence Hébert-Dolbec, 'International Criminal Justice as a Critical Project: Introduction' (2016) 13 *Penal Field* 1, 6.

3.1.1.5 Messages of protest and resistance

Certain other institutions reflect a message of discontent and protest. The idea that institutions and procedures stand as symbols of protest and resistance against atrocities has an established history in civil society. Popular early examples are 'people's tribunals' which articulate a different perspective on accountability, including messages about political accountability and recognition of voices that are otherwise not heard.[219]

3.1.1.5.1 Peoples' tribunals

People's tribunals have become a popular mechanism to express discontent about the failure of states to investigate violations in a formal legal forum. An early example is the 'Russell tribunal', which was convened by British philosopher Bertrand Russell and French philosopher Jean-Paul Sartre as a sign of protest against the failure to collect evidence and testimony regarding crimes associated with the military intervention in Vietnam. It was guided by the idea to 'speak truth to power'. It called itself 'the International War Crimes Tribunal'. It was composed of a jury of eminent persons, who acted as 'public conscience'. It was meant to formulate a 'counter-narrative' to the 'sovereignty-based paradigm of the Cold War, one based on empathy and identification with the victims of state and neo-imperial violence'.[220]

The tribunal lacked a formal legal basis. The authors saw the 'tribunal' as an expression of global outrage against historical injustice and as a starting point for an alternative history. Sartre insisted that the tribunal was not an instrument of moral condemnation but an attempt to judge policies in accordance with international laws.[221] It sought to make a case that criminality was not only grounded in individual actions but the result of a systematic policy. It is a symbolic tribunal *par excellence*. It sought to represent truths about accountability through the performance of justice. It has a ritualistic character:

> Given that the Tribunal gathered no specific 'accused' nor sought any punishment or retribution, it did not strive to produce any individual convictions ... it encourages us to evaluate the success of peoples' tribunals by considering their ritual function and potential influence on their participants and onlookers.[222]

[219] See generally Andrew Byrnes and Gabrielle Simm, *Peoples' Tribunals and International Law* (Cambridge: Cambridge University Press, 2017).

[220] Annette Weinke, 'The Eichmann Trial Fifty Years On' (2011) 29 *German History* 265–82, 280.

[221] Jean-Paul Sartre, 'Imperialist Morality' (1967) I/41 *New Left Review* 3–10, 5.

[222] Zachary Manfredi, 'Sharpening the Vigilance of the World: Reconsidering the Russell Tribunal as Ritual' (2018) 8 *Humanity* 75–91, 85

The Russell Tribunal was followed by a series of other civil society-led 'people's tribunals, including the establishment of a Permanent People's Tribunal (PPT), founded in 1979 by former Italian senator Lelio Basso. The PPT reflects the wish to express global consciousness about violations through civil society procedures. As Basso put it:

> The needs of public conscience can become a recognized source of law ... and a tribunal that emanates directly from the popular consciousness reflects an idea that will make headway: institutionalized powers and the people, from whom the former claim legitimacy in actual fact tend to diverge and only a truly popular initiative can try to bridge the gap between people and power.[223]

It looked into cases relating to Tibet, Western Sahara, Argentina, Eritrea, El Salvador, Afghanistan, and Guatemala.

The format of a people's tribunal often goes beyond traditional narratives. It provides an opportunity to narrate everyday experiences and illustrates the effects of power. Its value goes beyond legal justice. It has conquered its own space because it 'enables protest movements to symbolically harness this power to create an archive that gives credibility to dissenting perspectives and recognise subjects whose experience has been ignored or dismissed by law as irrelevant'.[224]

3.1.1.5.2 The Malabo Protocol as instrument of protest

The Malabo Protocol is a contemporary example of expression of discontent and protest.[225] Its history is loaded with institutional storytelling. The Protocol responds to critiques about the selectivity and Westernization of international justice.[226] It combines institutional creativity and utopian features with elements of resistance and protest. It was established with the aim to provide an alternative to existing international approaches including global criminal jurisdiction. It symbolizes an act of protest against some of the conventional approaches in international criminal justice and the practice of the ICC. It may be read as an attempt to correct 'perceived biases in international criminal justice'.[227] It is the result of a whole range of critiques voiced against the effects and inequalities of international and domestic jurisdiction.

[223] See the institutional slogan of the PPT, at http://permanentpeoplestribunal.org/?lang=en.

[224] Dianne Otto, 'Beyond Legal Justice: Some Personal Reflections on People's Tribunals, Listening and Responsibility' (2017) 5 *London Review of International Law* 225–49, 236.

[225] On the Protocol as 'counterjudicial narrative', see Kamari Clarke, *Affective Justice* (Durham and London: Duke University Press, 2019) 216–16.

[226] See generally Gerhard Werle and Moritz Vormbaum, *The African Criminal Court—A Commentary on the Malabo Protocol* (The Hague: TMC Asser Press, Springer, 2016); Vincent Nmehielle, '"Saddling" the New African Regional Human Rights Court with International Criminal Jurisdiction: Innovative, Obstructive, Expedient?', (2014) 7 *African Journal of Legal Studies* 7–42.

[227] Matiangai Sirleaf, 'The African Justice Cascade and the Malabo Protocol' (2017) 11 *International Journal of Transitional Justice* 71–91.

A first factor is the discontent about the exercise of universal jurisdiction, including the indictment of Rwandese officials in France and Spain.[228] The very establishment of the Protocol may be traced back to universal jurisdiction critiques, namely the perception by African states that they were 'singularly targeted in the indictment and arrest of their officials' and subject to 'double standards'.[229] In 2008, African Union (AU) Ministers of Justice and Attorney Generals expressed concerns against the way in which European States exercise universal jurisdiction. The AU adopted a formal 'decision on the abuse of universal jurisdiction' which criticized 'political nature and abuse of the principle of universal jurisdiction by judges from some non-African States against African leaders, particularly Rwanda'.[230] It stated that '[t]he abuse and misuse of indictments against African leaders have a destabilizing effect that will negatively impact on the political, social and economic development of States and their ability to conduct international relations'.[231]

The decision led to the creation of AU–EU Expert Report on the Principle of Universal Jurisdiction. It promoted the idea that 'African crimes' should be tried in Africa. It noted that

> states should, as a matter of policy, accord priority to territoriality as a basis of jurisdiction, since such crimes, while offending against the international community as a whole by infringing universal values, primarily injure the community where they have been perpetrated and violate not only the rights of the victims but also the general demand for order and security in that community.[232]

It recommended the extension of the jurisdiction of the African Court on Human and Peoples' Rights to 'international crimes such as genocide, crimes against humanity and war crimes'.[233] The creation of a regional body was reinforced by efficiency arguments, namely the intent to avoid delays in the prosecution by domestic courts, such as the initial stalemate over the trial of Habré in Senegal. The preamble of the Malabo Protocol recalled the 'Assembly Decision on Abuse of the Principle of Universal Jurisdiction'.[234]

A second important element is the controversy with the ICC over the Court's focus on African execution of warrants of arrest against heads of states, such as

[228] Matiangai Sirleaf, 'Regionalism, Regime Complexes and the Crisis in International Criminal Justice' (2016) 54 *Columbia Journal of Transnational Law* 699–778.

[229] Council of the European Union, AU–EU Expert Report on the Principle of Universal Jurisdiction, Doc. 8672/1/09 Rev.1, 16 April 2009, para. 34. Charles C. Jalloh, 'Universal Jurisdiction, Universal Prescription? A Preliminary Assessment of the African Union Perspective on Universal Jurisdiction' (2010) 21 *Criminal Law Forum* 1–65.

[230] Decision on the Report of the Commission on the abuse of the Principle of Universal Jurisdiction, Doc. Assembly/AU/14 (XI), Assembly/AU/ Dec.199(XIII), 1 July 2008, para. 5.

[231] Ibid., para. 5.

[232] See AU-EU Expert Report on the Principle of Universal Jurisdiction, Recommendation 9.

[233] Ibid., Recommendation 3.

[234] See Malabo Protocol, preamble.

Gaddafi and Al-Bashir, and the development of the Kenyan cases. The Malabo Protocol, with its call for 'African solutions to African problems', is partly a message of protest against the ICC. As Chacha Bhoke Murungu has noted, the 'call for establishment of a Criminal Chamber within the African Court to prosecute African individuals who commit international crimes in Africa' is closely linked to the 'AU decision not to cooperate with the ICC'.[235] At its meeting on 3 July 2009 in Sirte, Libya, the AU Assembly expressed concern over the 'unfortunate consequences' of the Al-Bashir warrant 'on the delicate peace processes underway in The Sudan'.[236] Insider voices note that these concerns 'directly influenced its decision to call on relevant AU organs to speed up the work on its request made earlier in the year, to investigate the prospects of vesting the ACJHR with a criminal prosecution mandate'.[237]

The AU regarded ICC warrants against acting heads of states and other high-ranking government officials as a threat to stability and peace in the region. It appealed to the Security Council to make a request under Article 16 to block investigations and prosecutions. When efforts in this multilateral context failed, it turned to the idea of a regional forum. It encouraged AU member states not to execute warrants of arrests. It promoted the Malabo Protocol as a regional forum to 'substitute and operate parallel to the ICC'.[238]

The Protocol ignores the role of the ICC. It uses silence as a means of protest. The Preamble notes that the Protocol will 'complement national, regional and continental bodies and institutions in preventing serious and massive violations of human and peoples' rights',[239] but fails to mention the ICC in this context. The states that the 'jurisdiction of the Court shall be complementary to that of the National Courts, and to the Courts of the Regional Economic Communities', without any single reference to the ICC.[240]

The Protocol might even be interpreted 'as a mechanism to prevent the ICC from exercising jurisdiction over senior government officials accused of committing crimes in Africa'.[241] It contains a sweeping immunity provision which states: 'No charges shall be commenced or continued before the Court against any

[235] Chacha Bhoke Murungu, 'Towards a Criminal Chamber in the African Court of Justice and Human Rights' (2001) 9 *JICJ* 1067–88, 1079.

[236] AU, Assembly of the African Union, Thirteenth Ordinary Session, held in Sirte Libya on 1–3 July 2009, para. 3.

[237] Kamari M. Clarke, Charles C. Jalloh, and Vincent O. Nmehielle, 'Origins and issues of the African Court of Justice and human and peoples rights' in Charles C. Jalloh, Kamari M. Clarke, and Vincent O. Nmehielle (eds), *The African Court of Justice and Human and Peoples' Rights in Context* (Cambridge: Cambridge University Press 2019) 1–54, 9.

[238] Amnesty International, 'Malabo Protocol: Legal and Institutional Implications of the Merged and Expanded African Court', AFR 01/3063/2016 (London: Amnesty International 2016), 9.

[239] Malabo Protocol, preamble.

[240] Malabo Protocol, Art. 46 H.

[241] Stuart Ford, 'Between hope and doubt: The Malabo Protocol and the resource requirements of an African criminal court' in Jalloh, Clarke, and Nmehielle (eds), *The African Court of Justice and Human and Peoples' Rights in Context*, 1076–100, 1083.

serving AU Head of State or Government, or anybody acting or entitled to act in such capacity, or other senior state officials based on their functions, during their tenure of office'.[242]

This clause is an institutional counter-message to Article 27 of the ICC Statute. It legitimates immunity for acting heads of states and other senior officials during terms of office. It may shield leaders from accountability.[243]

A third element of critique relates to deeper structural shortcomings of international criminal justice, such as its limited concern for the causes of conflict and everyday violations. The Protocol deviates from other international criminal justice instruments through its wider spectrum of criminality and its broadening of lines of responsibility. It 'seeks to disrupt some' of the classical 'baggage associated with ICL trials' through 'its ability to prosecute crimes that other ICL courts do not cover'.[244] It takes a slightly different ideological stance on accountability than other international instruments. It recognizes the role of corporate complicity and bystander responsibility in relation to atrocity crime in provisions on corporate criminal responsibility and illicit resource exploitation. These provisions signal the ambition to tell a broader story about accountability that is marginalized in other contexts. The Protocol also highlights the nexus between atrocity crimes and transnational crimes.[245] It includes crimes, such as mercenarism, corruption, money laundering, trafficking of humans, drugs and hazardous waste, and terrorism, alongside atrocity crimes. This broader focus is a response to corresponding silences in the ICC Statute and its ignorance of socio-economic causes of violence which are at the heart of human atrocity. The Protocol postulates a different vision of international criminal justice which is more closely in line with TWAIL critiques.

Such expression of protest and critique, and the formulation of alternatives frames, are helpful. It is a necessary response to the dream of a universal global court. As Judith Shklar has noted:

> The idea that all international problems will dissolve with the establishment of an international court with compulsory jurisdiction is an invitation to political indolence. It allows one to make no alterations in domestic political action and thought, to change no attitudes, to try no new approaches and yet appear to be working for peace.[246]

[242] Malabo Protocol, Art. 46H.

[243] Ademola Abass, 'The Proposed International Criminal Jurisdiction for the African Court: Some Problematical Aspects' (2013) 60 *Netherlands International Law Review* 27–50.

[244] Sirleaf, 'The African Justice Cascade and the Malabo Protocol' 86.

[245] See Neil Boister, 'Transnational crimes jurisdiction of the Criminal Chamber of the African Court of Justice and human and peoples' rights' in Jalloh, Clarke, and Nmehielle (eds), *The African Court of Justice and Human and Peoples' Rights in Context*, 336–61.

[246] Judith N. Shklar, *Legalism: Law, Morals, and Political Trials* (Cambridge, MA: Harvard University Press, 1986), 134.

3.1.2 Expressivism and the form of institutions

The legal form in which institutions are established is another important element of institutional expressivism. Its relevance goes far beyond formal legal authority. For instance, Jelena Subotić has claimed that 'international justice models may be adopted not for what they *do* but for what they *signify*, for their symbolic and normative properties'.[247]

According to an expressivist understanding, the function of international justice institutions is not only to try individuals but to brand 'crimes themselves as forms of reprehensible deviancy'.[248] Legal form is connected to affective dimensions of justice. If crimes are viewed as an attack on a common conscience, the form of institutional reaction matters. For example, the occurrence of a crime may be perceived as a tragic event which triggers a relational bond of responsibility. The institutional reaction entails messages about the *raison d'être* of the institution and the nature of the reaction to crimes. It carries meaning in itself. As Durkheim put it, 'since it is the common conscience which is attacked, it must be that which resists, and accordingly the resistance must be collective'.[249]

According to this logic, the institution becomes the 'medium' through which international society organizes itself.[250] Legal form is an element of the expressive reaction to crimes. Based on this vision, 'it makes all the difference whether the court acting in a specific case is a national or an international court':[251] 'The court's message is about 'power, authority, legitimacy, normality, morality, personhood, social relations', and all these elements depend as a reference point on the entity in whose name a court is acting.'[252]

Prosecution by an international institution carries particular signs of stigma. It implies that perpetrators are important enough and crimes are grave enough in order to warrant international attention. For instance, 'being prosecuted by the ICC is not just about being prosecuted at all, it is about being prosecuted by the ICC and in the process symbolically being designated as one of the gravest international criminals'.[253]

According to a simple application of Durkheim, expressivism might be read as a principled justification for a turn to international institutions. The relevant test is whether the gravity of the offence is adequately expressed in the institutional

[247] Jelena Subotić, *Hijacked Justice: Dealing with the Past in the Balkans* (Ithaca, NY: Cornell University Press, 2016), 24.

[248] See Frédéric Mégret, 'Practices of Stigmatization' (2013) 76 *Law and Contemporary Problems* 287–318, 305.

[249] Durkheim, *The Division of Labor in Society* 103.

[250] See also Nimage, 'An International Conscience Collective' 607 (the 'establishment of these courts marks a transition between the conception of a society of states and a community of mankind').

[251] See Nimage, 'An International Conscience Collective' 611.

[252] Ibid.

[253] Frédéric Mégret, 'What Sort of Global Justice is "International Criminal Justice"' (2015) 13 *JICJ* 77–96, 82.

reaction. Based on this test, international institutions would constitute the best response to international crimes since they reflect the international nature of the violation and the expression of outrage.[254] Such reasoning has *inter alia* been invoked by the former President of the SCSL, Justice Renate Winter, to justify international criminal jurisdiction. She has qualified international crimes as emotional events, namely as acts which create 'a tear in the common fabric of humanity'.[255] She then defended international prosecution as an ideal type of 'response of the international community'.[256] Ultimately, this form may serve to invite 'people and publics outside these geographical contexts to understand these events as occurrences that implicate and affect them'.[257]

The weakness of this approach is that it fails to recognize the diversity of messages and effects associated with institutional form, and some of the ambivalent effects of international structures. International crimes have a dual nature: they often share international and domestic features.[258] The choice of the legal form of institutions to investigate and prosecute does not only contain messages about the nature and impact of the underlying criminality but also statements about the different societies and constituencies affected by them. As Fréderic Mégret has argued, international criminal institutions 'represent the nature of the crimes they are judging, by designating and acknowledging the communities that are being affected by them'.[259]

This act of designation has enormous significance. It involves processes of inclusion and exclusion, choices in relation to legal geographies and implicit messages in relation to 'gravity' of crimes. Such messages arise not only from judicial action but from the sheer presence of institutions.

The label of an institution as being 'international' sends certain messages. Historically, 'international' has been understood as an antidote to 'domestic' institutions. International attributes were associated with ideas of moral superiority and a greater degree of impartiality and independence. For instance, in the context of Versailles, pleas for an international trial emerged because it was deemed to be unfeasible to try the former German Emperor before domestic courts.[260]

[254] Nirej Sekhon, 'Complementarity and Post-Coloniality' (2013) 27 *Emory International Law Review* 799–828, 814 ('when a conviction under ICL is secured, it symbolizes the broadest condemnation that can be leveled against an individual within a legal order').

[255] See Renate Winter, 'The Special Court for Sierra Leone' in Cherif. M. Bassiouni (ed.), *The Pursuit of International Criminal Justice: A World Study on Conflicts, Victimization, and Postconflict Justice*, Vol. 1. (Antwerp: Intersentia, 2010), 155–60, 155.

[256] Ibid., 155.

[257] McMillen, 'Imagining the International' 170.

[258] Frédéric Mégret, 'In Defense of Hybridity: Towards a Representational Theory of International Criminal Justice' (2005) 38 *Cornell International Law Journal* 725–51, 737 ('international crimes are never entirely international, nor are they ever purely domestic').

[259] Ibid., 743.

[260] Ferdinand Larnaude and Albert Geouffre de Lapradelle, 'Examen de la responsabilité pénale de l'empereur Guillaume II d'Allemagne' (1919) 46 *Journal du Droit International* 131–59, 152.

Justice Robert Jackson made a similar point about the virtue of internationalism at Nuremberg when noting that '[t]he common sense of mankind demands that law shall not stop with the punishment of petty crimes by little people'.[261]

The Nuremberg and Tokyo tribunals struggled with critiques that they were not 'international enough'. Both tribunals operated in the shadow of the law of occupation. International instruments were mixed with the *debellatio* doctrine or direct application of occupation authority (MacArthur). The Allied Powers tried to present them as being international as possible, in order to enhance their authority and expressivist impact.

The *ad hocs* were celebrated as archetypes of internationalism in light of their legal form. They constitute 'legalised expressions of a global sense of outrage' *par excellence*.[262] The ICTY was praised for its distinction from Nuremberg and Tokyo and its independence from domestic justice. It was described first 'truly international tribunal'. Antonio Cassese argued that it marked progress since it 'is an expression of the entire world community, not the long arm of four powerful victors'.[263]

The ICTR was hailed as an institution which translated crimes from the domestic sphere into the language of international law. It was said to have 'done more than any other institution to show that the genocide in Rwanda was not simply an irreducible African tribal specificity, but a crime amenable to international law's universalizing categorizations of abhorrent violence'.[264]

Those tribunals who were not purely international have relied on international features in order to stress their independent legal identity. For example, the SCSL qualified itself as an 'expression of the will of the international community'[265] which 'was established to fulfil an international mandate and is part of the machinery of international justice'.[266] It found in the *Taylor* Immunity decision that 'it is not a national Court of Sierra Leone and is not part of the judicial system of Sierra Leone, exercising judicial powers of Sierra Leone'.[267] The STL argued that it 'exists solely as a result of the passing of Security Council Resolution 1757'.[268]

The qualification as being 'international' entails certain messages. It conveys the idea of judicial independence, special juridical status, and power over domestic jurisdictions. It bears traces of 'institutional isomorphism'. It associated the SCSL and STL more closely with the form and tradition of the *ad hoc* tribunals, including

[261] Nuremberg Trials, Opening Address for the United States, Nazi Conspiracy & Aggression, Volume I (Washington, DC: United States Government Printing Office, 1946) 115.
[262] McMillen, 'Imagining the International' 168.
[263] Bass, 'Stay the Hand of Vengeance' 282.
[264] Mégret, 'In Defense of Hybridity' 737.
[265] *Prosecutor v. Taylor*, Decision on Immunity from Jurisdiction, para. 38.
[266] Ibid., para. 39.
[267] Ibid., para. 40.
[268] STL, Decision on the Defence Challenges to the Jurisdiction and Legality of the Tribunal, para. 50.

their jurisprudence. It ultimately symbolized power and a turn to the privileges, images, and rituals connected to international jurisdiction.

Over the past two decades, this clear juxtaposition between 'international' and 'domestic' has come under critique. It stands in contrast to competing prerogatives, such as the urge to demonstrate the multiplicity of affected constituencies, to reflect the 'domestic' grounding of crimes, and, most importantly, to bridge spaces[269] between different communities.

Studies on the relationship between geography and justice[270] have highlighted the important spatial dimensions of institutional expression, namely its ability to 'map relational space'.[271] Institutions are 'a site at which people and communities may be brought closer to the suffering of others'.[272] The turn to international institutions is deemed to 'lift justice out of its politicized national context',[273] but it sends ambivalent messages about proximity and distance to communities. It may create 'remote spaces of justice'.[274] The more an entity claims to be international in nature, the more difficult it becomes to argue that it is locally grounded at the same time.

It has become evident that creating an international jurisdiction may entail messages of disempowerment. For instance, for states like Rwanda, Bosnia, Croatia, and Serbia, it became crucial to adjudicate trials in a domestic legal setting in order to reclaim space, namely to show that they are politically stable, enjoy a fair and independent judicial system, or are on the path to democracy.

Critiques of the spatial and relational limits of international criminal jurisdictions have contributed to a renaissance of forms of hybridity. Hybrid legal forms have gained a new momentum because they are able to accommodate the political dimensions of international trials[275] or to reduce cultural or physical distances to sites of crimes and victims. The Court of Justice of the Economic Community of the West African States (ECOWAS Court) used the argument of hybridity in the *Habré* case to promote a wider space for accountability in terms of temporal jurisdiction. It argued that *Habré* could only be tried retroactively for crimes committed in Chad between 1982 and 1990 by an 'ad hoc special procedure of an international character'.[276]

[269] Space relates not only to territorial limitation or physical distance but is the product of interrelation and social production. See Doreen Massey, *For Space* (London: Sage Publications, 2005) 9.

[270] Jane Holder and Carolyn Harrison (eds), *Law and Geography* (Oxford: Oxford University Press, 2003).

[271] McMillen, 'Imagining the International' 170.

[272] Ibid.

[273] Ruti Teitel, *Transitional Justice* (Oxford: Oxford University Press, 2000), 33.

[274] See Alex Jeffrey, 'Justice Incomplete: Radovan Karadžić, the ICTY, and the Spaces of International Law' (2009) 27 *Environment and Planning D: Society and Space* 387–402, 399.

[275] See Harry Hobbs, 'Hybrid Tribunals and the Composition of the Court: In Search of Sociological Legitimacy' (2016) 16 *Chicago Journal of International Law* 482–522, 491.

[276] Court of Justice of ECOWAS, *Hissein Habré v. Republique du Senegal*, Judgment, 18 November 2010, para. 61.

Hybridity carries some of its own important symbolic meanings. It sends a counter-message to processes of the 'externalisation of justice'.[277] It is associated with greater respect of domestic ownership, closer proximity to local constituencies ('justice from below'), and the ability to respond more specifically to needs arising in the respective context. The very notion challenges conformity pressures and allows greater pluralism in institutional structures. It is at the same time associated with educational rationales, such as the 'development of the domestic justice system'[278] and hopes for 'long-term stability', including the creation of 'public confidence in the institutions'.[279] As the Office of the UN High Commissioner for Human Rights (OHCHR) put it, hybridity symbolizes the aspiration that 'the targeted international intervention that hybrid courts represent can leave behind more than just convictions, acquittals and "bricks and mortar"'.[280]

Ultimately, the 'hybrid' form is grounded in the belief that justice may emerge through complex processes of interactions between international and domestic constituencies. It is guided by the ambition that hybrid structures may 'convey to citizens a disapproval of violations and support for certain democratic values' inside domestic societies.[281] However, it also carries its own risks. It may bring institutions more closely back into the realm of domestic politics and signal lack of power. Hybridity may also convey 'negative perceptions of the local legal system', cause brain-drain from existing judicial structures, or postpone 'investment in the necessary domestic legal reforms'.[282]

The turn to regional forums carries yet another meaning. Like hybridity, regionalization attempts to bring institutions closer to the reality they seek to represent. But it captures an additional dimension, namely a special sense of affection. It implies that crimes attack a special sense of regional identity that goes beyond individual states and might differ from universalist traditions. This is closely reflected in the design of the Malabo Protocol. Its jurisdiction and definition of crimes are visibly adjusted to particular patterns of criminality that affect the continent (e.g. illicit exploitation of natural resources, corruption).[283] It clearly marks an attempt to create 'African solutions to African problems'.

The creation of the Kosovo Specialist Chambers through the exchange of letters with the European Union carries a similar symbolic meaning. This is expressed in the institutional framework. It relies on the European Convention on Human

[277] Chandra Lekha Sriram, 'Universal Jurisdiction: Problems and Prospects of Externalizing Justice' (2001) 12 *Finnish Yearbook of International Law* 47–70.

[278] See OHCHR, *Rule-of-Law Tools for Post-Conflict States: Maximizing the Legacy of Hybrid Courts* (Geneva: UN, 2008), 1.

[279] See OHCHR, *Rule-of-Law Tools for Post-Conflict States: Prosecution Initiatives* (Geneva: UN, 2006), 5.

[280] OHCHR, 'Maximizing the legacy of hybrid courts' 1.

[281] OHCHR, 'Maximizing the legacy of hybrid courts' 6.

[282] OHCHR, 'Maximizing the legacy of hybrid courts' 15.

[283] See **section 3.1.1.5.2.**

Rights as a meta-framework of constitutionality. Judicial activity is therefore subject to an additional lawyer of human rights scrutiny that lacked in other jurisdictions. It may be read as an implicit response to certain human rights critiques of other international criminal institutions.

3.2 An Expressivist Theory of Action

International criminal institutions are not unitary objects but rather 'a set of practices enacted through relationships between people, places, and institutions'.[284] Their role extends beyond providing justice in individual cases and adjudicating disputes. According to expressive theory, 'the expression of social values is an important function of the courts or, possibly, the most important function of the courts'.[285] It underpins nearly all aspects of their practice, consciously or unconsciously.

As institutional theorists have explained, the very existence of these institutions triggers patterns of self-perpetuation. They rely on speech acts to gain or convey authority, to convince others to follow their actions, or to consolidate their own legitimacy. They are even more dependent than domestic actors on persuasive authority, including symbols, myths, and rituals.[286]

3.2.1 Institutional action and speech act theory

Speech act theory is an important instrument to understand institutional practices. It provides a medium to understand and decipher the multiplicity of meanings.[287] It distinguishes different speech relations: relations between different speakers, relations between speakers and audiences, and changing roles in different speech contexts.[288]

[284] Caroline Desbiens, Alison Mountz, and Margaret Walton-Robert, 'Introduction: Reconceptualizi ng the State from the Margins of Political Geography' (2004) 23 *Political Geography* 241–366, 242.

[285] Robert Cooter, 'Expressive Law and Economics' (1998) 27 *Journal of Legal Studies* 585–608, 586.

[286] On the role of symbolism and rituals in the consolidation of rules, see Thomas Franck, *The Power of Legitimacy among Nations* (Oxford: Oxford University Press, 1990) 91–105. See also Tallgren, 'Durkheimian Spell of International Criminal Law' 161.

[287] See also Roman Hamel, *Strafen als Sprechakt. Die Bedeutung der Strafe für das Opfer* (Berlin: Duncker & Humblot, 2009), 128, 152–3.

[288] Speech act theory has been used to develop a communicative understanding of law. For instance, legal theorists have qualified regulation and adjudication in domestic systems as communicative action between different agents. They have distinguished (i) communication from state authorities (e.g. legislature) to subjects (e.g. citizens) through acts, such as laws, regulations, or adjudicative acts with an open texture; (ii) communications from citizens to authorities (e.g. through law-abiding or deviant behaviour); and (iii) speech acts between citizens (e.g. in court proceedings or parliamentary debates). See Wibren Van der Burg, 'The Expressive and Communicative Functions of Law, Especially with Regard to Moral Issues' (2001) 20 *Law and Philosophy* 31–59, 48. The degree of communication differs in each of these speech relations. It may be 'stronger and weaker', explicit, or implicit, but 'it is never completely

John Searle, the founder of modern speech act theory, has distinguished five general types of speech acts: (i) 'assertives' or representations, which describe a certain state of affairs (e.g. statements, descriptions, classifications, explanations, and clarifications); (ii) 'directives', which commit the addressee to do something (e.g. orders, commands, requests); (iii) 'commissives' which commit the speaker to a certain future action (e.g. promises, pledges, guarantees, contracts); (iv) 'expressives' which convey attitudes or emotions of the speaker; and (v) 'declarations' which change a *status quo* through performance (e.g. judicial pronouncements).[289]

All five types of speech acts recur on a routine basis in judicial action and legal discourse. For instance, criminal judgments and decisions make representations ('assertives'). They contain statements of facts, legal classifications, and explanations of judicial reasoning. As shown earlier,[290] the motivation of reasoning is often supplemented by emotive language ('expressives') which seeks to attract empathy. The tenor of decisions may change the *status quo* through its declaration. For example, a decision on jurisdiction may open or bar access to domestic or international legal remedies. A judgment on conviction or acquittal changes the *status quo* of the defendant.

Many judicial decisions are 'commissive' in the sense that they commit the acting legal agents or institutions to carry out future acts. For example, a criminal judgment may entail follow-up duties to release the defendant, to make provision for adequate enforcement of the sentence, to monitor imprisonment or review the sentence, or to consider reparation for victims.

Other types of decisions, such as warrants of arrest or requests for cooperation, are 'directive' since they commit the addressee to perform certain acts such as to arrest or detain persons, share evidence, provide access to crime sites or information, or to protect witnesses and victims.

Judgments and decisions convey messages not only through the words that they use but also through their silences and omissions. As speech act theorists have noted, silence may be 'an act of non-verbal communication that transmits any kind of meaning, depending on cultural norms of interpretation'.[291] It often gains bespoke meaning in its situational context. For instance, many institutional frameworks provide for discretion in order to protect decisional autonomy, facilitate

absent'. Ibid., 49. Proponents of the New Haven School have extended communicative theory to international law. They have argued that the international legal field operates through communication flows, symbols, and rituals. See Michael Reisman, 'International Lawmaking: A Process of Communication' (1981) 75 *American Society of International Law Proceedings* 101–20, 101.

[289] See John R. Searle, *Expression and Meaning: Studies in the Theory of Speech Acts* (Cambridge: Cambridge University Press, 1979) 1–29.

[290] See **section 3.3**.

[291] See Nuray Alagözlü and Sevgi Sahin, 'Silence as a Multi-Purpose Speech Act in Turkish Political Discourse' (2011) 15 *Procedia Social and Behavourial Sciences* 3008–13. See also Michal Ephratt, 'The Functions of Silence' (2008) 40 *Journal of Pragmatics* 1909–38.

case-specific solutions, or prevent an overload of cases. Silence may express a refusal to take a decision at this point in time or an intent not to proceed. The lack of reference to a particular category of crime, incident, or previous judicial decision may send a range of different messages, ranging from indecision to hidden disagreement.

3.2.1.1 Power and communication

Institutional action involves different types of communication and interaction.[292] The exercise of core criminal functions is governed by formal structures. It involves coercive power, creates new legal categories and notions, and produces knowledge or social meaning. It shapes the conduct and choices of other legal actors, social groups, or individuals.[293] Courtroom actions are primarily directed at participants to proceedings. However, they also serve to establish authority, build or portray identity, or persuade through demonstration. In this way, they become a form of governance.

Other types of actions, such as requests for cooperation, press releases and conferences, policy papers, summaries of judgments, outreach strategies, or legacy practices offer less formalized spaces for interaction. They are meant to establish relations with broader audiences, including affected populations, or are aimed at persuading through encouragement of public discourse. For instance, the ICC has developed a broad range of policy papers and governance reports that are geared towards illustrating institutional policies and speaking to audiences in a more flexible way than judicial acts. They may be used to increase 'soft power'.[294]

3.2.1.2 'Reading' institutional discourse

International criminal law creates a frame and common language in which speech acts are recognized and understood.[295] It establishes a behavioural system in which verbal and non-verbal actions acquire specific meanings.[296] For instance, a

[292] They are driven by conflicting prerogatives, namely the need to assert or extend power, in order to exercise criminal functions, and the need for dialogue and communicative space, in order to convey meanings, facilitate compliance, promote engagement with messages, or justify themselves towards constituencies.

[293] For instance, declaring a person as a 'criminal' brands the actions as crimes and stigmatizes the perpetrator 'in the name of the community that constitutes the relevant jurisdiction'. See Sekhon, 'Complementarity and Post-Coloniality', 814.

[294] For instance, the ICC has its own Twitter account (@IntlCrimCourt).

[295] John Austin uses the term 'felicity' conditions to describe the circumstances under which speech acts are commonly recognized by speaker and addressee. See John Langshaw Austin, *How to do Things with Words* (Oxford: Clarendon Press, 1962), 14–15 ('There must exist an accepted conventional procedure having a certain conventional effect, that procedure to include the uttering of certain words by certain persons in circumstance. The particular persons and circumstances in a given case must be appropriate for the invocation of the particular procedure invoked. The procedure must be executed by all participants both correctly and completely.').

[296] See also Winston P. Nagan and Craig Hammer, 'Communications Theory and World Public Order: The Anthropomorphic, Jurisprudential Foundations of International Human Rights' (2007) 47 *Virginia Journal of International Law* 725–805, 794 ('language in international law is accompanied by

sentence pronounced by an international criminal institution or a foreign state is recognized as a penalty and carries stigma, because speaker and addressee share a common understanding of the meaning of criminal procedures.

Many legal norms provide space for autonomous action, independent decision-making processes, or rational choice by legal actors (e.g. the duty to extradite or prosecute). The interpretation and application of these norms is a part of the process of communication about these norms and behavioural attitudes. States, non-state actors, and individuals communicate with each other through legal actions.[297] For example, the exercise of universal jurisdiction by one state expresses not only its own competence to act but also sends messages to various types of audiences (e.g. third states, NGOs, individuals) about the international nature or gravity of the crime, political commitment to act under the circumstances, or general willingness to comply with international norms, etc.

International and multilateral institutional frameworks are a means to organize communication and speech relations. Legal actions gain particular meanings in such contexts. States, individuals, or other entities may initiate specific types of interaction which require response through legal motions, statements, or conduct. Institutions address direct or indirect speech acts to their constituencies or other addresses (e.g. other institutions, individuals). Behaviour becomes a speech act through its institutional context, namely through its express or inferred meaning according to the rules, conventions, or codes of this institutional system.[298] For example, the application of norms by states or non-state actors and compliance with orders, requests, or decisions may signal loyalty, obedience, or commitment. Deviant behaviour may express disagreement. In some instances (e.g. the controversy over the ICC and Africa), institutions themselves become the site of public controversy over the role of norms and their application and meaning in a specific conflict.

The action and 'social infrastructure' of international criminal institutions create new speech relations. They may contribute to the formation of interpretive and professional communities.[299]

discrete intrinsic understandings, and employs signs and symbols of communication within an institutional framework in a global effort to express stable and well-understood messages').

[297] Reisman has defended a wider conception of law-making through communicative action. He argued that 'from the standpoint of communications theory, some law may indeed be made by specialized lawmaking institutions, but any communication between elites and politically relevant groups which shapes wide expectations about future behavior must be considered as functional lawmaking'. See Reisman, 'International Law-making: A Process of Communication' 107.

[298] Some meanings only emerge through action–response schemes or their embedding in legal rituals or conventions.

[299] Christensen, 'From symbolic surge to closing courts' 622 ('It is the social infrastructure of the wider field of practice, created precisely around the new tribunals, that now forms the basis for the social groups involved in the battle to recreate and rethink international criminal justice.').

3.2.2 Communicative practices

International criminal institutions use both unilateral expression and dialectic communication in order to maintain power and justify their existence towards affected subjects. Their action is driven by survival instinct and/or transformative rationales. The ability to realize goals and reach audiences depends heavily on interaction with different interlocutors, such as states, other international institutions, professional communities, victims, and affected society. Institutions are not only mandated to act but need to be seen to be acting in order to meet expectations.[300]

Communicative practices are shaped by a wide range of factors, including conformity pressures, rituals, and conventions (e.g. professional practices, institutional mimetics), the need to appear legitimate in the eyes of others, as well as forms of agency that are driven by self-preservation (e.g. demonstration of independence and impartiality, institutional entrepreneurship).

In some areas, such as jurisdiction or admissibility, international criminal institutions have tended to confirm their authority or maximize their powers in order to justify their existence or maintain the ability to act.[301] In other areas, such as the development of substantive law, the incentive to expand institutional power is constrained by the principle of legality.[302]

Self-presentation and 'marketing' are part of institutional strategies.[303] As Frédéric Mégret has observed, international criminal institutions are 'engaged in a constant effort to sell' their 'goals and achievements'.[304] Practice navigates between 'grandiose statements' about some of their alleged achievements, and 'sober reassessments' of their goals 'that seek to distance the project from some of the more outlandish claims made' in their name, in order to 'manage expectations'.[305] Lines of arguments shift. In situations where broader social objectives are difficult to achieve, institutions fall back to more classical rhetoric: 'less guarantor of social peace than independent and impartial, cosmopolitically constituted and humanitarian, professional and transparent, compassionate and fair manager of atrocity's aftermath'.[306]

[300] For a critical analysis, see Megan A. Fairlie, The Hidden Costs of Strategic Communications for the International Criminal Court' (2016) 51 *Texas International Law Journal* 282–319, 319 ('As the [ICC] struggles to meet its responsibilities and manage public expectations, civil society ought to adopt practices that enhance the way the ICC is viewed in the court of public opinion').

[301] See **section 3.2.2.1**.

[302] See, for example, Art. 22 ICC Statute.

[303] See Christine Schwöbel, 'The market and marketing culture of international criminal law' in Christine Schwöbel (ed.), *Critical Approaches to International Criminal Law* 264–80; Sophie Rigney, 'Postcard from the ICTY' in Jessie Hohmann and Daniel Joyce (eds), *International Law's Objects* (Oxford: Oxford University Press, 2018), 367–76.

[304] Mégret, 'International Criminal Justice as Juridical Field' 50.

[305] Ibid., 50.

[306] Ibid., 50.

Proponents of expressivist theories argue that international criminal justice contributes to crime control not only through threats and sanctions, but also through discourse. Some scholars regard the pedagogical role as an inherent obligation of prosecutors, grounded in a 'relation of public trust'.[307] For instance, Nirej Sekhon has argued that the expressive power of prosecutors 'does not depend upon obtaining convictions in particular cases' but rather on their ability to 'produce social and political meaning'[308] and to 'inform and educate citizens' for the 'purpose of impelling political dialogue'.[309]

Other scholars claim that the 'real potential' of international criminal justice lies in its didactic rationales, namely its 'interaction with policymakers, advocates and those working within national criminal justice system'.[310] They justify expressivist functions by the alleged ability of international criminal institutions to 'empower norm entrepreneurs such as advocates, prosecutors and judges to incorporate international conceptions into national practice', persuade 'governments to re-direct resources', or help 're-calibrate relations more broadly within society'.[311]

However, the didactic role is often ambivalent.[312] In light of the focus of criminal law on order and crime control, many speech acts are 'authority signals', i.e., 'communications[s] which attend the communication of policy content and control intention' and 'which indicate to the relevant audience that the communicators have the authority to proscribe'.[313]

The focus is on unilateral expression or symbolic meaning rather than dialectic communication. Discourse is often restricted to elites. Speech acts are often unilateral performances rather than cognitive processes.

A recurring problem is the discrepancy between the illocutionary force of speech acts, that is, the intended meaning of the speaker, and their perlocutionary effects, that is, the impact on the audience and real-life effects.[314]

[307] Nirej Sekhon, 'The Pedagogical Prosecutor' (2014) 44 *Seton Hall Law Review* 1–46, 33–4.

[308] Ibid., 17.

[309] Ibid., 33.

[310] Amrita Kapur, 'The Value of International-National Interactions and Norm Interpretations in Catalysing National Prosecutions of Sexual Violence' (2016) 6 *Oñati Socio-legal Series* 62–90, 62, 84.

[311] Ibid., 84.

[312] It is important to inquire more critically what type of 'pedagogy' is implied through speech acts. On 'critical pedagogies', see Jasmina Husanović, 'Resisting the culture of trauma in Bosnia and Herzegovina: Emancipatory lessons for/in cultural and knowledge production' in Dubravaka Zarkov and Marlies Glasius (eds), *Narratives of Justice in and out of the Courtroom: Former Yugoslavia and Beyond* (The Hague: Springer, 2014), 147–62, 154.

[313] See Reisman, 'International Lawmaking' 110.

[314] Each audience interprets the speech act in light of its own situational context. A single act may convey different meanings to different audiences. International criminal institutions are often unware of the complexity of messages or their differential meanings. Many legal acts convey more complex speech acts and social meanings that are disregarded in legal discourse. See Sekhon, 'Complementarity and Post-Coloniality' 815.

3.2.2.1 Expressivist dimensions of jurisdictional determinations

Jurisdictional decisions count among the most frequent and important decisions in international criminal justice. Jurisdictional challenges are typically the first objections that investigators, prosecutors, or judges face when exercising their powers. In a domestic setting, jurisdiction is tied to sovereignty and associated with 'the rightful authority to speak the law within a state's territory'.[315] In an international setting, it is tied to competence and delegated power.

All major international criminal courts and tribunals had to deal with jurisdictional disputes at the start. From a technical, legal perspective, jurisdictional determinations constitute an application of rules and principles on authority and competence by legal agents. They determine whether an entity is entitled to act, that is to take legal action, adjudicate conduct, or criminalize, or how far jurisdiction reaches in territorial, substantive, or temporal terms. However, their significance as speech acts goes far beyond the determination of legal competence.

Jurisdictional determinations are not only findings on institutional competence. They carry multiple meanings. They involve symbolic recognition that crimes have been committed. They decide over claims of individuals to access to justice.[316] They are speech acts about institutional identity, the scope of power, and relations to others. For instance, the famous jurisdictional decisions of the ICTY (*Tadić*),[317] ICTR (*Kanyabashi*),[318] or STL (*Ayyash et al.*)[319] were not only about determination of institutional authority but also about the identity of tribunals, their relationship to the Security Council, and the alleged emancipation of law from politics more broadly. They maximized the space of judicial authority and sought the shrink perception of external influence vis-á-vis tribunal critics.[320]

In inter-state relations, jurisdictional decisions represent claims or assertions of power which may exclude competing claims by other states or determine rights of access to justice of victims. They may have a broader systemic coordinating function by sending messages about the allocation of resources or potential 'divisions of labour'. For instance, universal jurisdiction is associated with the expression of a common conscience. Its exercise of jurisdiction is increasingly tied to a 'subsidiarity' test, according to which bystander states defer to the jurisdiction of the territorial state or the state of the nationality of the offender if they are able and

[315] See Devika Hovell, 'The Authority of Universal Jurisdiction' (2018) 29 *EJIL* 427–56, 438.

[316] Alex Mills, 'Rethinking Jurisdiction in International Law' (2014) 84 *BYIL* 187–239, 229.

[317] *Tadić* 1995 Interlocutory Appeal.

[318] *Prosecutor v. Kanyabashi*, Decision on the Defence Motion on Jurisdiction, 18 June 1997.

[319] *Prosecutor v. Ayyash et al.*, Decision on the Defence Challenges to the Jurisdiction and Legality of the Tribunal, 27 July 2012.

[320] See, for example, *Prosecutor v. Kanyabashi*, Decision on Defence Motion on Jurisdiction, para. 41 ('the judges of the Tribunal exercise their judicial duties independently and freely and are under oath to act honorably, faithfully, impartially and conscientiously as stipulated in rule 14 of the Rules. Judges do not account to the Security Council for their judicial functions.').

willing to prosecute.[321] This doctrine is modelled after complementarity in the ICC context. The articulation of an 'unable or unwilling' doctrine in universal jurisdiction introduces a messaging system in inter-state relations. It entails a speech act, namely a promise by states not to act unless the territorial or national state does not genuinely investigate or prosecute itself.[322]

The messaging function is even more developed in the ICC context. In the ICC, the exercise of jurisdiction is embedded in a broader system of speech acts. The OTP can act on its own motion, but it needs to notify states of its intention when it seeks to start investigations.[323] ICC jurisdiction can also be triggered by Security Council or state referrals. Such referrals are not only procedural prerequisites for the exercise of jurisdiction, but complex speech acts by the referring entities. They are 'directive' speech acts in the sense of Searle. They commit the ICC as institution to take follow-up action. They are often loaded with underlying political signals or hidden agendas.

For example, a decision by a state to refer a situation relating to its own territory or nationals is a statement about its own commitment to accountability. It entails an implicit message that the respective state is either unable or unwilling to act. The situational scope of jurisdiction described in a referral brands the scope of criminality. It contains messages about the 'geography of justice'. It produces a new framework of reference about the type of criminality that the state considers worthy of investigation of prosecution or the actors that it deems responsible. It may signal political will by the referring entity to cooperate with the ICC in relation to the situation and conduct described in the referral, but also create dependencies or open the ICC to manipulation (e.g. prosecution of non-state actors, ignorance of government criminality).[324]

Other referrals are messages that intend to create pressure on the OTP to act more expeditiously, or to blame it for inaction. For instance, in the context of Venezuela, a coalition of state Parties, including members of the 'Lima Group', have made a collective referral to the ICC after a situation was under consideration by the OTP in its own motion. The referral was a follow-up to a report by an expert panel of the Organisation of American States (OAS) which found that there were reasonable grounds to start investigations in relation to crimes against humanity.[325]

321 See Laura Burens, 'Universal Jurisdiction Meets Complementarity: An Approach towards a Desirable Future Codification of Horizontal Complementarity between the Member States of the International Criminal Court' (2016) 27 *Criminal Law Forum* 75–97.

322 The operation of this doctrine requires ongoing inter-state communication, verification, or monitoring.

323 See ICC Statute, Art. 18.

324 See Phil Clark, 'Chasing cases: The ICC and the politics of state referral in the Democratic Republic of Congo and Uganda' in Carsten Stahn and Mohamed El Zeidy (eds), *The International Criminal Court and Complementarity* (Cambridge: Cambridge university Press), 1180–203, 1202–3.

325 See Report of the General Secretariat of the Organization of American States and the Panel of Independent International Experts on the Possible Commission of against Humanity in Venezuela (Washington, DC: OAS General Secretariat, 2018).

The collective referral did not alter the potential scope of ICC jurisdiction, but was in essence aimed at inducing 'the Prosecutor to initiate an investigation more expeditiously' and asserting control in case of ICC inaction.[326]

In terms of their content, jurisdictional determinations are often not mere 'assertives' or representations in the sense of Searle's theory but rather 'declarative' speech acts. They change the *status quo*. They attach new vocabulary to social phenomena and construct a new 'crimino-legal sphere'. They may be deemed to 'produce international space and subjectivity'.[327] As Nesam McMillan has noted: 'It is through the performative declaration of certain acts as crimes against humanity and in the framing of the pursuit of accountability for such acts as a "plea of humanity to law" that a global humanity is productively named and imagined, its contours traced and its content defined.'[328]

Such determinations are 'not simply expressions of already existing global spaces and subjectivities'. Rather, 'they actively constitute the entities, geographies and social connections that they name'.[329] They carry strong expressive power since they involve authority claims and institute relations between normative communities.[330]

3.2.2.2 Complementarity as messaging

The complementarity principle, which determines the interplay between the ICC and domestic jurisdiction, has a strong communicative foundation.[331] It relies on a complex communicative structure which builds on messages, signals, and hypotheses in relation to behaviour. It developed into a 'managerial' system of interaction.[332] It may be viewed as a form of 'structured dialogue amongst technocratic elites at the international and national levels'.[333]

The 'mirror' image, introduced as part of the admissibility determination,[334] placed the ICC at the centre and states at the periphery in the discourse on the

[326] See Nicholas E. Ortiz, 'Understanding the State Party Referral of the Situation in Venezuela', *EJIL Talk*, 1 November 2018, at https://www.ejiltalk.org/understanding-the-state-party-referral-of-the-situation-in-venezuela/.

[327] McMillan, 'Imagining the International' 167.

[328] Ibid.

[329] Ibid.

[330] See also Hovell, 'Authority of Universal Jurisdiction' 455.

[331] The ICC Statute regulates complementarity mainly as admissibility device. However, its main function lies in its role as organizing framework of a broader system of justice. See Carsten Stahn, 'Complementarity: A Tale of Two Notions' (2008) 19 *Criminal Law Forum* 87–113.

[332] Traditionally, the exercise of ICC jurisdiction has been branded as a threat to sovereignty, akin to a 'sword' that hangs over the domestic. See Federica Gioia, 'State Sovereignty, Jurisdiction, and "Modern" International Law: The Principle of Complementarity in the International Criminal Court' (2006) 19 *LJIL* 1095–123.

[333] Sekhon, 'Complementarity and Post-Coloniality' 825.

[334] The ICC has clarified in its jurisprudence that state action must target the same 'case' and be accompanied by concrete investigative steps, in order to render a case inadmissible before the Court. This implies that states need to orient their own responses after ICC activity. It found that the ICC is automatically competent in cases of state inaction. See *Prosecutor v. Katanga*, Judgment on the Appeal of Mr

exercise of jurisdiction. Situation countries, such as Kenya, argued that this methodology 'send[s] out the wrong message to countries that are seeking to strengthen their national jurisdictions to fulfill their obligations under the Rome Statute'.[335]

The OTP has relied on complementarity to increase its expressive force. It has used it as a tool to strengthen its own leverage over domestic justice and to shape domestic approaches. It has developed a complex messaging system in which it actively used policy statements, progress reports, or benchmarks as 'carrots and sticks' to foster normative change in domestic jurisdictions under examination. It has developed the concept of 'positive complementarity' to encourage states to develop domestic accountability.[336]

This approach has a strong didactic underpinning. It implies that the OTP may use complementarity as a 'catalyst for compliance',[337] namely 'to educate, persuade, and prod states parties to undertake international criminal law investigations'.[338] Complementarity is thereby used to construct 'a new global system and order'[339] and persuade states and other actors to 'encourage to genuine national proceedings where possible'.[340]

These practices have exposed the ICC to critiques of institutional entrepreneurship.[341] 'Positive complementarity' gave non-state actors and NGOs greater space to become part of the discourse. The active use of conditionality conditions, promotion of 'capacity building', or rule-of-law toolkits increased the power of international NGOs and professional elites to insist on professionalization, standardization, and application of 'best practices' in domestic systems. They have used complementarity as an umbrella term to promote the 'universalization' of the ICC

Germain Katanga against the Oral Decision of Trial Chamber II of 12 June 2009 on the Admissibility of the Case, ICC-01/04-01/07 OA 8, 25 September 2009, para. 78.

[335] *Prosecutor v. Ruto, Kosgey and Sang* and *Prosecutor v. Muthuara, Kenyatta and Ali*, Application on the Behalf of the Government of the Republic of Kenya Pursuant to Article 19 of the ICC Statute, ICC-01/09-01/11 and ICC-01/09-02/11, 31 March 2011, para. 10. These critiques of the 'mirror' image were echoed by Judge Ušacka, who noted that 'such an approach could potentially preclude a State from focusing its investigations on a wider scope of activities and could even have the perverse effect of encouraging that State to investigate only the narrower case selected by the Prosecutor'. See *Gaddafi* Appeal Judgment, Dissenting Opinion of Judge Anita Ušacka, ICC-01/11-01/1 l-547-Anx2 (OA 4), paras 52 and 55.

[336] The Report of the Bureau on Complementarity defines 'positive complementarity' as 'all activities/actions whereby national jurisdictions are strengthened and enabled to conduct genuine national investigations and trials of crimes included in the Rome Statute'. See Assembly of States Parties, Report of the Bureau on Stocktaking: Complementarity, ICC-ASP/8/51, 18 March 2010, para. 16.

[337] See Jann Keffner, *Complementarity in the Rome Statute and National Criminal Jurisdictions* (Oxford: Oxford University Press, 2008), 309–40.

[338] Sekhon, 'Complementarity and Post-Coloniality' 825

[339] Mohammad Hadi Zakerhossein, *Situation Selection Regime at the International Criminal Court: Law, Policy, Practice* (Cambridge: Intersentia, 2017) 383.

[340] ICC, Paper on Some Policy Issues before the Office of the Prosecutor, September 2003, 5.

[341] See Padraig McAucliffe, 'From Watchdog to Workhorse: Explaining the Emergence of the ICC's Burden-sharing Policy as an Example of Creeping Cosmopolitanism' (2013) 14 *Chinese Journal of International Law* 259–96.

and a certain homogenization of justice approaches, and in particular in relation to the implementation of the Rome Statute.[342]

The effects are mixed. ICC investigations and prosecutions had limited 'demonstration' effects. In some contexts (e.g. Uganda, Democratic Republic of the Congo (DRC), Kenya), complementarity produced adverse or paradoxical consequences.[343] Domestic actors simply imitated the normative and procedural universe of the ICC. Implementation performed complementarity for 'predominantly international audiences'.[344] This has limited 'educational' value. Adjustment of national systems based on case-related strategic considerations may ultimately run counter to the objective of the Rome Statute, that is, to create a sustainable 'system of justice' and replicate failures of development policy (e.g. norm export, legal transplantation). ICC action in the DRC has created mixed reactions among domestic judicial actors. They felt that they were 'receiving mixed messages from the international community, which has invested heavily in legal reform but maintains that such reforms are insufficient to warrant domestic trials of high-profile suspects'.[345]

In practice, complementarity has tended to increase norm internalization in states that already have a strong domestic system. States with a weaker normative fabric have preferred to shift the accountability burden on the ICC rather than to advance domestic norm internalization.

Expressivist justifications of complementarity, that is the alleged benefits of international over domestic criminal law, faced socio-legal or post-colonial critiques. The use of complementarity language (e.g. 'unable' or 'unwilling') or emancipatory notions, such as capacity-building, has patronizing features. It is a form of knowledge production that may reduce the complexity of problems and steer distinctions between the 'able' and the 'unable', the 'knowing' and the 'unknowing', the 'progressive' and the 'regressive', and so on. It may create frictions between 'ordinary' justice and elitist international justice regimes. Presumed educational aspirations of international justice may deprive a domestic society of its own process of trial and error or foreclose alternative choices. Complementarity requires more investment in persuasion, rather than simple messaging. As critics have noted,

[342] On over-compliance, see Frédéric Mégret, 'Too much of a good thing?: implementation and the uses of complementarity' in Stahn and El Zeidy (eds), *The International Criminal Court and Complementarity*, 361–90, 367–76.

[343] For instance, Phil Clark has concluded that the ICC 'has failed to show itself to be technically superior to, and beholden to the same logistical and political challenges as, domestic courts [and] has weakened the capacity of national institutions to investigate and prosecute international crimes'. Phil Clark, *Distant Justice: The Impact of the International Criminal Court on African Politics* (Cambridge: Cambridge University Press, 2018) 185–6.

[344] See with respect to Uganda and Kenya, Christian de Vos, 'All roads lead to Rome: Implementation and domestic politics in Kenya and Uganda' in Christian De Vos, Sara Kendall, and Carsten Stahn (eds), *Contested Justice* (Cambridge: Cambridge University Press, 2015), 379–407, 406.

[345] Clark, *Distant Justice* 182.

the criminal trial may not be responsive to the psychic needs of those communities for which it is not an organic justice ritual. Worse, insisting that a criminal trial is the only acceptable form of a justice ritual may be reminiscent of colonial impositions of the not so distant past.[346]

3.2.2.3 Preliminary examinations as expressive speech acts

The ICC has developed rich imagery and a whole expressive machinery in order to defend its practices of preliminary examinations.[347] They constitute a hallmark of expressive practice. At other international criminal courts and tribunals, preliminary examinations had traditionally lesser importance, since the jurisdictional scope was predefined. At the ICC, policies and practices were largely developed through practices of the OTP.

The drafters of the Statute have devoted relatively limited attention to the issue.[348] The OTP virtually turned preliminary examinations into a novel procedural stage of its own.[349] It developed an elaborate system of assessment (i.e. a four-phase process) in its Regulations and Policy Papers which closely mirrors human rights monitoring. This process is designed to translate the complex reality of atrocity contexts into legal determinations, such as the determination of jurisdiction, the determination of the crime base, admissibility, or situational gravity.

ICC Prosecutor Bensouda branded preliminary examinations expressly as a 'messaging' technique. She noted that the 'level of [ICC] activity' in relation to preliminary examination is 'a sign of the state of the world where war, conflict and violence result in reported gross human rights violations'.[350]

Preliminary examinations are speech acts which signal concern about atrocities. They convey messages about the atrocities and the Court itself. They respond to societal expectations about ICC action: 'Each time a crisis erupts, the question asked is: "what is the International Criminal Court . . . doing about this?'[351]

In the widest sense, preliminary examinations deliver 'messages that the international community is not indifferent to the perpetration of unimaginable atrocities'.[352]

[346] Sekhon, 'Complementarity and Post-Coloniality' 815.
[347] See Morten Bergsmo and Carsten Stahn (eds), *Quality Control in Preliminary Examination* (Brussels: Torkel Opsahl Academic EPublisher, 2018); David L. Bosco, 'Discretion and State Influence at the International Criminal Court: The Prosecutor's Preliminary Examination' (2017) 111 *AJIL* 395–414; David L. Bosco, 'The International Criminal Court and Crime Prevention: Byproduct or Conscious' (2011) 19 *Michigan State Journal of International Law* 163–200.
[348] See ICC Statute, Article 15, para. 2.
[349] Carsten Stahn, 'Damned If You Do, Damned If You Don't: Challenges and Critiques of Preliminary Examinations at the ICC' (2017) 15 *JICJ* 413–34, 416–17.
[350] Presentation of the 2018 Annual Report on Preliminary Examination Activities, Seventeenth Session of the Assembly of States Parties, Opening remarks, 10 December 2018, 4, at https://www.icc-cpi.int/itemsDocuments/20181217-opening-remarks-otp_ENG.pdf.
[351] Ibid.
[352] Zakerhossein, *Situation Selection Regime at the International Criminal Court* 390.

The OTP has used preliminary examination as a technique to expand its own enforcement limitations and maximize its own impact in international relations. It noted its alleged preventive effect already in its early prosecutorial strategy: 'The mere monitoring of a situation can deter future crimes. It increases the risk of punishment even before trials begin. This effect is not limited to the situation under investigation but extends to all State Parties and reverberates worldwide.'[353]

Later, the OTP developed a more systematic early warning function, based on open-source information and proactive messaging. It includes a whole range of communicative practices, including letters, press releases and statements.[354] A famous example of direct communication comprises two letters sent by the OTP on 26 July and 7 August 2013 to Colombian authorities, cautioning against suspended sentences for those most responsible perpetrators of core crimes in the Legal Framework for Peace. They were compared to a 'letter bomb' by local news media.[355] They influenced the reasoning of the Colombian Constitutional Court which excluded full suspension of the execution of sentences for most responsible perpetrators of core crimes.[356] In other cases, the OTP addressed direct speech acts to individuals or groups or highlighted through crimes that are under-publicized, in order to enhance awareness.

Statements comprise a spectrum of different speech acts. In some cases, the OTP used statements to express condemnation. For instance, in the situation in Palestine, the OTP expressed concerns about potential crimes in Ghaza or 'the planned eviction of the Bedouin community of Khan al-Ahmar, in the West Bank' and felt 'compelled to remind all parties that the situation remains under preliminary examination'.[357] In other contexts, the Office issued direct warnings. For example, in 2016, Prosecutor Bensouda warned 'high officials of the Republic of the Philippines' that 'any person in the Philippines who incites or engages in acts of mass violence including by ordering, requesting, encouraging or contributing, in

353 Office of the Prosecutor, Report on Prosecutorial Strategy, 14 September 2006, 6.

354 See Ana Cristina Rodriguez Pineda, 'Deterrence or withdrawals? Consequences of publicizing preliminary examination activities' in Bergsmo and Stahn (eds), *Quality Control in Preliminary Examination, Vol.* 2, 321–93, 350–2.

355 'A "letter bomb"' ('"Una 'carta bomba'"), Semana, 17 August 2013, http://www.semana.com/nacion/articulo/una-carta-bomba/354430-3.

356 See Constitutional Court of Colombia, Decision C-579/13, 28 August 2013, at http://www.legal-tools.org/doc/d6139e/pdf/. On the impact of the ICC on the peace process in Colombia, see Courtney Hillebrecht, Alexandra Huneeus, and Sandra Borda, 'The Judicialization of Peace' (2018) 59 *Harvard International Law Journal* 279–330, 316 ('The impact of the courts' jurisdiction was to make the ongoing peace debate more infused with references to the guidance and constraints provided by international law, to make more actors at the domestic level aware of the international courts and laws, and, ultimately, to allow the manner in which these international norms were debated and understood to shift').

357 Statement of the Prosecutor of the International Criminal Court, Fatou Bensouda, regarding the Situation in Palestine, 17 October 2018, at https://www.icc-cpi.int/Pages/item.aspx?name=181017-otp-stat-palestine.

any other manner, to the commission of crimes within the jurisdiction of the ICC is potentially liable to prosecution before the Court'.[358]

In 2017, the Prosecutor noted in a statement that crimes in the Central African Republic 'must stop' and 'urge[d] all individuals and groups in the CAR engaged in violence, including those who appear to be linked to the anti-Balaka and ex-Seleka groups, to desist'.[359]

In other situations, the OTP appealed to parties not to engage in post-election violence. For instance, in 2018 Prosecutor Bensouda made an appeal 'to the Congolese people, and more particularly to the authorities, political actors, their supporters and sympathizers, to do their utmost to prevent and avoid any conduct of criminal violence contrary to the Rome Statute, anywhere and at any time'.[360]

Other statements comment on political events or explain OTP action. In 2016, the OTP 'welcomed' the announcement of the final peace agreement with FARC. The statement expressed 'the hope that this peace agreement will provide a basis for building lasting peace in Colombia'.[361]

Again, other speech acts are apologetic. For instance, in the context of the debate over accountability of ISIS, the OTP issued a clarificatory statement to reduce pressure of public opinion about ICC action. The statement sounded like an excuse. It acknowledged with *pathos* that 'crimes of unspeakable cruelty have been reported', but concluded that 'the jurisdictional basis for opening a preliminary examination into this situation is too narrow at this stage'.[362]

Ultimately, preliminary examinations are as much about sending messages as they are about making legal determinations about conflict or crime labels. They alert to crimes, make victims socially visible, or signal ICC monitoring. Their empirical effect on prevention is hard to measure. As Davis Bosco has argued, the 'court's prevention discourse may be as much about justification as strategy'.[363]

The approach is largely based on the belief that it is right and appropriate for the ICC to make such arguments. The OTP engages in these kinds of speech acts because it is expected to make them. Some of them have been informed by other

[358] Statement of the Prosecutor of the International Criminal Court, Fatou Bensouda concerning the situation in the Republic of the Philippines, 13 October 2016, at https://www.icc-cpi.int/pages/item.aspx?name=161013-otp-stat-php.

[359] Statement of the Prosecutor of the International Criminal Court, Mrs Fatou Bensouda, regarding increased violence in CAR: 'crimes must stop!', 23 May 2017, at https://www.icc-cpi.int/pages/item.aspx?name=160901-otp-stat-colombia.

[360] Statement by the Prosecutor of the International Criminal Court, Fatou Bensouda, on the recent pre-election violence in the Democratic Republic of Congo, 20 December 2018, at https://www.icc-cpi.int/Pages/item.aspx?name=20181220-ostat-prosecutor.

[361] Statement of ICC Prosecutor, Fatou Bensouda, on the conclusion of the peace negotiations between the Government of Colombia and the Revolutionary Armed Forces of Colombia—People's Army, 1 September 2016, at https://www.icc-cpi.int/pages/item.aspx?name=160901-otp-stat-colombia.

[362] Statement of the Prosecutor of the International Criminal Court, Fatou Bensouda, on the alleged crimes committed by ISIS, 8 April 2015, at https://www.icc-cpi.int/Pages/item.aspx?name=otp-stat-08-04-2015-1.

[363] Bosco, 'The International Criminal Court and Crime Prevention' 198.

motives, such as the will to detract from critique about the Court's own shortcomings, including its predominant focus on Africa or its lack of cases.[364] The speech acts are thus partly about the ICC itself, rather than aimed at 'education' or prevention per se.

Overall, the ICC has assumed too uncritically in its policies that prevention and 'positive complementarity' should be objectives of preliminary examinations. As Human Rights Watch has noted, the desire to steer national justice approaches through a policy on preliminary examinations may backfire over time: 'While the fact that a situation may come before the ICC initially provides an incentive for authorities to stop crimes or to start their own investigations, that leverage is likely to wane with the passage of time.'[365]

A survey from case studies (e.g. Colombia, United Kingdom, Georgia, Guinea) shows that is questionable whether the OTP 'can fundamentally alter political dynamics' on its own.[366] The impact of preliminary examinations is heavily dependent on factors that are not under ICC control, such as 'political support for accountability', the scope of the underlying crime base, 'public demand and interest in accountability', and the presence of international partners.[367] Deference to domestic justice may open the ICC to manipulation, delay justice, and complicate access to evidence at the investigation.

NGOs should exercise a certain degree of self-constraint in bringing communications under Article 15. The preliminary examination process is vulnerable to abuse for publicity purposes.[368] For instance, it is unhelpful to overload the ICC with communications in order to draw attention to a specific cause. Such communications may create misperception about the Court's mandate, divert resources, or even cause reputational damage.[369]

3.2.2.4 Investigation, case selection, and arrest as speech acts

Messages about the seriousness of crimes and blameworthiness of offenders can be expressed in many other ways than through judgment and punishment. Investigative acts, processes of case selection, or requests for arrest and surrender carry strong expressive meaning. They identify targets and sites of criminality, may attach stigma to acts, and contribute to the emergence of a 'broader global economy of shame'.[370]

364 Rodriguez Pineda, 'Deterrence or withdrawals' 363–70.

365 Human Rights Watch, ICC: Course Correction: Recommendations to the Prosecutor for a More Effective Approach to 'Situations under Analysis', 16 June 2011, https://www.hrw.org/news/2011/06/16/icc-course-correction.

366 Human Rights Watch, Pressure Point: The ICC's Impact on National Justice, May 2018, 9 at https://www.hrw.org/sites/default/files/report_pdf/ij0418_web_0.pdf.

367 Human Rights Watch, 'Pressure Point' 8–9.

368 Fairlie, 'Hidden Cost of Strategic Communications' 294–5.

369 See also Megan Fairlie, 'A Newly-Revealed Cost of Article 15 Communications' IntLawGrrls, 29 June 2018, at https://ilg2.org/2018/06/29/a-newly-revealed-cost-of-article-15-communications/.

370 Mégret, 'Practices of Stigmatization' 296.

3.2.2.4.1 Investigations as messages

Investigations are not only internal institutional practices but complex structural inquiries that involve key strategic choices, institutional interaction, a high degree of decision-making, interaction, and publicity. They produce new public frames of references, frame discourses on timing and form of justice, and involve decisions on resources and prioritization.

The start of investigations is often surrounded by publicity.[371] It does not only attract media interest but involves relations to providers of information, affected states, and potential witnesses. It gives a new quality and prominence to open-source material.[372] It involves visible investigative steps relating to crimes and individuals and the application of formal legal labels to criminal actions and procedures.

This publicity is broadly visible. For instance, Former ICC Prosecutor Luis Moreno Ocampo was widely criticized for his joint appearance with Ugandan President Museveni at a press conference in London after receiving the referral.[373] The decision as to (whether or not to) authorize an investigation in relation to *proprio motu* action is like a public ritual. It involves representations of victims and judicial determinations framing the scope of investigations that lay the foundations of future cases and trials. The decision is not only a signal to the Prosecutor, defendants, or states but a broader reaffirmation of the Court's authority in relation to a specific atrocity crime situation.[374] It produces effects in and by itself, irrespective of the outcome of investigations.

Generally, the start and closure of investigations involve a large degree of prosecutorial discretion. The decision when to proceed and not to proceed is closely linked to politics and strategy.[375] It is one of the most important speech acts about

[371] For a critique, see David L. Bosco, 'The International Criminal Court and Crime Prevention: Byproduct or Conscious' (2011) 19 *Michigan State Journal of International Law* 163–200, 181.

[372] On open source material and its impact on the ICC, see Lindsay Freeman, 'Law in Conflict: The Technological Transformation of War and its Consequences for the International Criminal Court', (2019) 51 *NYU Journal of International Law & Politics* 807–69.

[373] Victor Peskin, 'Caution and Confrontation in the International Criminal Court's Pursuit of Accountability in Uganda and Sudan' (2009) 31 *Human Rights Quarterly* 655–91, 656.

[374] In the situation in Afghanistan, the preliminary examination process involved determinations about the potential scope of responsibility of individuals of major powers in the conflict, the reach of a 'global battlefield' in the alleged 'war on terror', and linkages between conflict situations. The Pre-Trial Chamber held that the acts concerning persons captured elsewhere than Afghanistan lacked the nexus with an internal armed. See ICC, Decision Pursuant to Article 15 of the Rome Statute on the Authorisation of an Investigation into the Situation in the Islamic Republic of Afghanistan, ICC-02/17-33, 12 April 2019, paras 53–55. This understanding was reversed by the Appeals Chamber which defended a broader conception of the nexus requirement of war crimes. See ICC, Judgment on the appeal against the decision on the authorisation of an investigation into the situation in the Islamic Republic of Afghanistan, ICC-02/17 OA4, 5 March 2020, See paras 71–78.

[375] In Uganda, narratives remained divided over the progress of ICC investigations. The OTP claimed that its own action contributed to a dismantling of the LRA and reduced crime rates. Many stakeholders in the Juba peace process took the opposite view. They argued that the suspension or discontinuation of investigations might mark an 'important contribution to preventing future atrocities'. See Bosco, 'International Criminal Court and Crime Prevention' 183.

atrocity contexts and the exercise of prosecutorial discretion. It requires political savviness and familiarity with context. It sends messages about prioritization of situations and incidents. In some contexts, the ICC was criticized for pursuing sequenced rather than parallel investigations against the main actors involved in conflict.

Timing conveys messages about institutional commitment.[376] From a victim's perspective and 'the golden hour of evidence collection',[377] 'justice delayed' is often 'justice denied'. There are numerous instances in which the delay of investigations compromised the prospects of trials. For example, the lack of ICTY action against former Croatian President Franjo Tudjman allowed nationalist forces to maintain myths about the Homeland War in Croatia. At the ICC, the eleven-years-long preliminary examination relating to Afghanistan, followed by the Pre-Trial Chamber decision not to authorize an investigation, is a most cynical illustration of the dangers of justice delayed. The delay has been attributed to 'political factors', such as strategic interest and military presence of Western powers in the territory.[378] The Pre-Trial Chamber's failure to authorize an investigation was a wrong concession of law to *realpolitik*. The Chamber made authorization dependent on prospects of cooperation. It argued that the passage of time rendered the prospects of investigation illusory. It stated:

> [S]ubsequent changes within the relevant political landscape both in Afghanistan and in key States (both parties and non-parties to the Statute), coupled with the complexity and volatility of the political climate still surrounding the Afghan scenario, make it extremely difficult to gauge the prospects of securing meaningful cooperation from relevant authorities for the future, whether in respect of investigations or of surrender of suspects.[379]

This argument conflated two levels: investigation and enforcement. It deprived the Prosecutor of the possibility to gather a case and seek cooperation from non-compliant states. It provided an incentive for states to obstruct preliminary examinations and refuse to cooperate in order to avoid *proprio motu* investigations successfully. Almost a year later, this message was righly corrected by the ICC Appeals Chamber, which held that arguments relating to the interests of justice are not subject to judicial review in the authorization of proprio motu investigations.[380]

[376] Jean Galbraith, 'The Pace of International Criminal Justice' (2009) 31 *Michigan Journal of International Law* 79–143.

[377] See Anni Pues, 'Towards the 'Golden Hour'?: A Critical Exploration of the Length of Preliminary Examinations' (2017) 15 *JICJ* 435–53.

[378] See Bosco, 'Discretion and State Influence at the International Criminal Court' 412–13.

[379] Decision Pursuant to Article 15 of the Rome Statute on the Authorisation of an Investigation into the Situation in the Islamic Republic of Afghanistan, para. 94.

[380] ICC, Judgment on the appeal against the decision on the authorisation of an investigation into the situation in the Islamic Republic of Afghanistan, para. 46.

In other contexts, 'justice delayed' can be 'justice delivered'.[381] For instance, the experience of the Saddam Hussein trial suggests that a 'rush to conviction', in an attempt to turn the page, may be counterproductive. As Salem Chalabi, the former head of the Iraqi Special Tribunal said: 'Show trials followed by speedy executions may help the interim government politically in the short term but will be counterproductive for the development of democracy and the rule of law in Iraq in the long term.'[382]

Investigations imply messages about the allocation of resources and the economies of crime.[383] They are geared at mapping crime situations and patterns of criminality. They involve different cognitive exercises: 'casting the net' of internationally relevant criminality, 'discovering' potential cases, testing and exploring case hypotheses, and actual 'building' of cases.[384] The focus on specific themes, such as sexual or gender-based violence, protection of children, or environmental effects, signals what international agents care about and what they leave aside.

The conduct of investigations involves patterns of stigmatization.[385] Formally, defendants are protected by the presumption of innocence and other due process guarantees. However, the mere association with an investigation may carry a high degree of social condemnation or convey messages of 'guilt by association'.[386] Investigations involve the establishment of context and search for linkage evidence, including insider witnesses. Witnesses are often reluctant to cooperate because they fear intimidation or retaliation by perpetrators who often hold positions of power and authority.

3.2.2.4.2 Case selection as institutional expression

Case selection is one of the most controversial areas of institutional expression. As the STL noted: 'Criminal investigation and prosecution [....] is unavoidably selective in any system.... Selectivity is part of the history of international criminal jurisdictions, and an inevitable consequence of establishing an international criminal court or tribunal.'[387]

381 Alex Whiting, 'In International Criminal Prosecutions, Justice Delayed Can Be Justice Delivered' (2009) 50 *Harvard International Law Journal* 323–64.

382 See BBC, 'Iraq PM "seeks Saddam show trial"', 23 September 2004, at http://news.bbc.co.uk/2/hi/middle_east/3684052.stm.

383 See Stuart Ford, 'What Investigative Resources Does the International Criminal Court Need to Succeed?: A Gravity-Based Approach' (2017) 16 *Washington University Global Studies Law Review* 1–70, 22 ('each crime site that is part of the investigation represents a commitment to the expenditure of investigative resources').

384 See Dermot Groome, 'Evidence in cases of mass criminality' in Ilias Bantekas and Emmanouela Mylonaki (eds), *Criminological Approaches to International Criminal Law* (Cambridge: Cambridge University Press, 2014), 117–58, 121–2.

385 Mégret, 'Practices of Stigmatization' 299.

386 Quincy Wright, 'International Law and Guilt by Association' (1949) 43 *AJIL* 746–55; Marston Danner and Jenny S. Martinez, 'Guilty Associations: Joint Criminal Enterprise, Command Responsibility, and the Development of International Criminal Law' (2005) 93 *California Law Review* 75–169.

387 STL, Decision on Defence Challenges the Jurisdiction and Legality of the Tribunal, para. 87.

Because of this selectivity, case selection becomes a speech act about the 'gravity of crimes', the degree of responsibility of individuals or groups in a broader context, or the blameworthiness of individual conduct. For instance, the ICC has claimed that it should 'focus its investigations and prosecutions, in principle, on the most serious crimes within a given situation that are of concern to the international community as a whole'.[388]

Selection practices are often formally guided by the principle of objectivity; that is, they are meant to provide 'a representative sample of the main types of victimisation and of the communities which have been affected by the crimes in that situation'.[389] In practice, the desire to reflect 'the true extent of the criminality which has occurred within a given situation' must be balanced against available resources, access to evidence and the right of defendants to a speedy trial. This process inherently produces frictions. As Frederic Mégret has observed:

> When a group's crime of choice is never prosecuted, it sends a not-so-discreet signal that the crime is not quite as grave as others. Conversely, when a group's crime is the only one selected for prosecution, particularly in a context where many other crimes could have been prosecuted, the ICC is giving the crime considerable symbolic recognition.[390]

Audiences in affected societies may be more concerned about the balance of investigations and prosecutions among groups and actors than about individual responsibility. The SCSL has sought to mitigate this problem by developing distinct cases against each of the major factions in the conflict. Each case was thus aimed at expressing the relevant criminality of the respective group. The problem of this approach is that it may signal an equivalence of moral blame. At the ICTY, individual cases were largely seen through the prism of national or group identity.[391] The framing of the mandate of the Kosovo Specialist Chambers has been criticized for its focus on ethnic Albanians and KLA violence and leaving aside atrocities committed by Serbs.[392]

The focus on particular categories of charges may cause problems. Selection practices take into account the nature and 'manner of commission'. This includes

> the means employed to execute the crime, the extent to which the crimes were systematic or resulted from a plan or organised policy or otherwise resulted from

[388] Policy Paper on selection and prioritization, para. 35.

[389] Policy Paper on selection and prioritization, para. 45.

[390] Mégret, 'Practices of Stigmatization' 298.

[391] Frédéric Mégret, 'The Legacy of the ICTY as Seen Through Some of its Actors and Observers' 1041.

[392] See Oral Testimony of Dr Paul R. Williams given in front of US Congress, Ending Impunity in Kosovo: Closing the Accountability Gap for Crimes Committed during the Kosovo Conflict, 30 April 2019, 22 at https://docs.house.gov/meetings/FA/FA00/20190430/109398/HHRG-116-FA00-Wstate-WilliamsP-20190430.pdf.

> the abuse of power or official capacity, the existence of elements of particular cruelty, including the vulnerability of the victims, any motives involving discrimination held by the direct perpetrators of the crimes, the use of rape and other sexual or gender-based violence or crimes committed by means of, or resulting in, the destruction of the environment or of protected objects.[393]

It is controversial to what extent investigations should pursue a thematic approach in order to highlight under-represented categories of crimes. According to an expressivist logic, prosecutors might legitimately use their discretion to attach particular stigma to practices that are accepted as normal in some environments. This approach would allow an institution, for instance, to 'prioritize those crimes within its jurisdiction that are lesser known and where the educational impact can be maximized'.[394]

Some NGOs have advocated such an approach. For instance, the Women's Initiatives for Gender Justice has taken the position that selection of particular charges (e.g. sexual and gender-based violence) may be more important than the number of defendants.[395] The problem with this expressivist justification of selection is that it detracts from the principled commitment to representative charges and may justify extremely narrow cases for educational purposes. It prioritizes the didactic effect of global prevention over crime repression in the respective situational context. Rightly understood, institutional expression should not pitch these goals against each other but relate to both of them. It should combine didactic functions derived from repression, which require an in-depth examination of context and structure as well as representative charging, with more preventive rationales, allowing prioritization of particular charges for educational purposes (e.g. to inspire norm internalization).

One of the problems is that international institutions often lack the infrastructure and means to counter selectivity critiques due to their distance to communities. At the investigative stage, there is less open discursive structures with victims. Speech conditions are constrained. Prosecutors are the 'engine' of the case. They seek to persuade victims to testify as witnesses for the Prosecution or to provide information supporting their case. Prosecutorial choices create 'us versus them' divides or binary friend/enemy clusters.

These problems became evident in the debate on ICC and Africa. The OTP sought to counter the perception of bias in selection by stating that the choice of investigations is governed by 'gravity' rather than geographical distribution. But these policy explanations failed to reach audiences. As rightly observed,

393 Policy Paper on selection and prioritization, para. 40.
394 Bosco, 'The International Criminal Court and Crime Prevention' 192.
395 Letter from Brigid Inder, Executive Director of Women's Initiatives for Gender Justice, to Luis Moreno Ocampo, Chief Prosecutor of the Int'l Criminal Court, 2 http://www.iccwomen.org/news/docs/Prosecutor_Letter_August_2006_Redacted.pdf.

reliance on 'legal technicalities' did not produce the intended effect: 'The message must align the Court with and for victims, not the Court against senior leaders'.[396]

3.2.2.4.3 Arrest as messaging

The issuance of warrants of arrest and requests for arrest and surrender is a highly symbolic act. It sends a message about the need for enforcement to states. It involves naming and shaming of individual defendants on behalf of the 'international community', as a result of the outcome of the investigation.[397]

Arrest may trigger public protest and complex peace and justice dilemmas. For instance, many ICTY indictees were regarded as local heroes. When Ramush Haradinaj, the former Prime Minister of Kosovo, surrendered to the ICTY, even UN officials showed support for him.[398] UN Special Representative in Kosovo, Søren Jessen-Petersen, openly acknowledged that cooperation with the ICTY complicated political and security conditions in Kosovo.[399]

The stigma of arrest arises not only from the public branding of offences but also from the association with a history of institutional precedents. The very issuance of such acts is accompanied by societal expectations that are shaped by the identity of the acting institution. The defendant becomes an element and a product of this institutional history and a whole line of precedents. His or her actions come to be in light of deeds of others who have committed similar or even worse crimes. This creates risks of prejudice:

> Appearing in the seat of the accused, the seat previously occupied by others who have been convicted, and having one's picture taken and circulated the world over, framed by two square-jawed ICC security guards, already begins to shape the accused's body as that of a convict en puissance, rather than as an innocent in the wrong place.[400]

3.2.2.5 Cooperation as a speech act system

Cooperation is driven by action response schemes that convey messages about institutional interaction, compliance and solidarity in enforcement.[401] It contains

[396] Kip Hale, 'Sending the Right Message on the ICC', Huffington Post, 22 November 2016, at https://www.huffingtonpost.com/entry/sending-the-right-message-on-the-icc_us_58341e1ae4b0eaa5f14d4a56?ec_carp=8409142968280633509&guccounter=1.

[397] Mégret, 'Practices of Stigmatization' 309 ('An indictment by the ICC carries with it a certain stigma, a lot of stigma, and gives the impression that a country is in the category of a failed state.').

[398] In 2019, Haradinaj resigned again as prime minister after he was summoned for questioning by the Kosovo Specialist Prosecutor.

[399] Majbritt Lyck, 'International Peace Enforcers and Indicted War Criminals: The Case of Ramush Haradinaj' (2007) 14 *International Peacekeeping* 418–32, 423.

[400] Mégret, 'Practices of Stigmatization' 299.

[401] Christopher K. Lamont, *International Criminal Justice and the Politics of Compliance* (Farnham: Ashgate, 2010).

directive speech acts by requesting entities (e.g. orders, requests) to states or other actors, expressive responses by requested actors, and two-way communications. Cooperation by the requested entity manifests not only a sense of legal obligation but also trust in the institution.[402] It is a demonstration of faith in the law and underlying system (*Rechtstreue*), even in case of divergent opinion.

3.2.2.5.1 Cooperation as 'virtual' trial over compliance

In some regional contexts, such as the European Union, the idea of mutual trust has been institutionalized in the area of judicial assistance and cooperation as part of the development wider common judicial space between states.[403] However, in the relationship between international criminal institutions and states, this trust cannot be taken for granted but needs to be earned. International criminal justice relies even more than domestic judicial institutions on demonstration, incentives, and persuasion, in order to obtain cooperation.

Non-cooperation with international criminal institutions does not necessarily abrogate the law or moral authority,[404] but it sends out a damaging foreign policy message. It undermines expressive effects. As David Bosco has noted, 'unenforced indictments can serve to highlight the court's lack of enforcement power and, potentially, to diminish its ultimate preventive and deterrent effect'.[405]

In international criminal justice, enforcement requires different tools and strategies than at the domestic level. It depends heavily on networks, smart power, and diplomacy in relations between international criminal institutions, the requested state, and the international community. It is most likely to be effective 'not when states act out of a sense of legal obligation, but rather when there are shared expectations about the kinds of obligations created by an instrument and what the instrument requires of states'.[406]

The *ad hoc* tribunal could rely on top-down powers. However, in practice, cooperation worked based on a combination of strategies: naming and shaming, incentives for compliance, and negotiation. Due to the lack of enforcement power, the sensitivity of investigations and prosecutions, and pressures in domestic

402 Trust underlies and precedes cooperation.

403 As the European Court of Justice (ECJ) put it in the Opinion on the adherence of the EU to the European Convention on the Protection of Human Rights and Fundamental Freedom: 'This [EU] legal structure is based on the fundamental premise that each member state shares with all the other member states, and recognises that they share with it, a set of common values on which the EU is founded, as stated in Art. 2 TEU. That premise implies and justifies the existence of mutual trust between the Member States that those values will be recognised and, therefore, that the law of the EU that implements them will be respected.' See ECJ, Opinion 2/13 of the Court, 18 December 2014, para. 168.

404 Catherine Lu, 'The ICC as an institution of moral regeneration' in Joanna Harrington, Michael Milde, and Richard Vernon (eds), *Bringing Power to Justice? The Prospects of the International Criminal Court* (Montreal: McGill/Queen's University Press, 2006) 191–209.

405 Bosco, 'The International Criminal Court and Crime Prevention' 193.

406 Timothy L. Meyer, 'Towards a Communicative Theory of International Law', 2012) *13 Melbourne Journal of International Law* 921–39, 936–7.

politics, the *ad hoc* tribunals needed international support in order to insulate themselves from critique and obtain cooperation. The experience of ICTY cooperation has shown that 'the prospect of the government's arresting fugitives and sending them for a tribunal to trial can dominate a country's political life and sow instability by sparking anti-government protests and causing deep frictions in governing coalitions'.[407]

Victor Peskin has compared battles over cooperation to 'virtual' trials over compliance or obstruction of legal process.[408] Cooperation is a brokering process, marked by conflict and compromise. It is rarely successful 'without decisive international community intervention on behalf of war crimes tribunals—whether in the form of persuasion, incentives or coercion'.[409]

The ICC depends even more than other international courts and tribunals on communicative features to secure cooperation. It relies in many areas on voluntary state cooperation. It needs to 'persuade both the states that have and have not ratified the statute to become surrogate enforcers on behalf of the Court'.[410] This imposes severe constraints. As Kenneth Rodman has stressed, one of the weaknesses of international criminal justice is that the 'stigma associated with investigation and indictment by international tribunals' alone does not suffice to 'marginalize' leaders. It mostly succeeds in cases in which 'it reinforces a political commitment by powerful states to deploy coercive instruments for the same ends'.[411]

3.2.2.5.2 Techniques

International criminal institutions have particular means of exercising leverage to induce cooperation. Processes of naming and shaming (e.g. public exposure and condemnation) carry particular weight since they are amplified through international media and legal networks. However, they are not goals in themselves but rather a means to an end, namely to 'negotiate agreements for the handover of evidence, suspects and witnesses'.[412] Blaming a state for non-cooperation may mobilize political pressure and increase reputational costs of non-compliance, but it does not per se create conditions for cooperation. It is dependent on broader measures of persuasion.

Securing cooperation requires a full spectrum of communicative measures, including confrontation, negotiation, and conciliation. Confrontation 'signals the

[407] Victor Peskin, *International Justice in Rwanda and the Balkans: Virtual Trials and the Struggle for State Cooperation* (Cambridge: Cambridge University Press, 2012), 236.

[408] Ibid. 11. See also Peskin, 'Caution and Confrontation in the International Criminal Court's Pursuit of Accountability' 660.

[409] Peskin, *International Justice in Rwanda and the Balkans* 236.

[410] Ibid., 256.

[411] Kenneth A. Rodman, 'When Justice Leads, Does Politics Follow? The Realist Limits of Prosecutorial Agency in Marginalizing War Criminals' (2019) 17 *JICJ* 13–44, 40.

[412] Peskin, *International Justice in Rwanda and the Balkans* 239.

prosecutor's determination to counter state defiance', while 'conciliation can be an important way to leverage some co-operation.'[413]

Existing experiences suggest that excessive shaming can be counterproductive. It may harden opposition or denial in recalcitrant societies or strengthen nationalist forces through humiliation. In many instances, it has triggered an urge to reply in kind, that is, to engage in counter-shaming. For instance, Serbia and Croatia engaged in anti-ICTY campaigns in order to protect domestic narratives of the war.[414] Kenya was highly successful in mobilizing neo-colonial sentiments to counter ICC trials, using historical imagery and Western bias to try to deviate from commitments under the Rome Statute.

The option of recourse to the Security Council, the most powerful executive body in the international sphere, proved to be of limited value across institutions. It has been rarely used by the *ad hoc* tribunals.

The success of cooperation requires 'a long arm', diplomatic efforts, and compromises, such as confidential warrants of arrest, proper timing or postponement of requests of cooperation, a policy of gradually building up cases, and measures to minimize domestic political backlash.[415] For instance, the transfer and arrest of General Ante Gotovina to the ICTY was essentially prompted by the prospects of EU accession.

The ICC has developed a complex rhetoric strategy to gain 'buy in'. The OTP has gone beyond adversarial approaches to attract cooperation. It has actively garnered state consent to foster cooperation. It developed a policy of encouraging states to invite the ICC to start open investigations based on a referral.[416] This policy was driven by the hope that a non-confrontational approach would induce states to provide voluntary cooperation.

The OTP initially displayed caution in confronting non-state parties in order to refute allegations against an arbitrary exercise of power and avoid confrontation with major powers. It created a discursive forum, the Law Enforcement Network, in order to reduce the discrepancy between its own limited capacity and the statutory goal to 'end impunity' and facilitate domestic investigation and prosecution of cases not taken up by the ICC.[417] It practiced 'reverse cooperation', that is, sharing of evidence with states, in order to facilitate its own disengagement and pass the

[413] Peskin, 'Caution and Confrontation in the International Criminal Court's Pursuit of Accountability' 665.

[414] Peskin, *International Justice in the Rwanda and the Balkans* 113–16.

[415] Ibid., 239–43.

[416] See OTP, Report on the Activities Performed During the First Three Years (June 2003–June 2006), 12 September 2006, 7 '[W]hile proprio motu power is a critical aspect of the [OTP's] independence, the Prosecutor adopted the policy of inviting and welcoming voluntary referrals by territorial states as a first step in triggering the jurisdiction of the Court.'). For a critique, see Andreas Müller and Ignaz Stegmiller, 'Self-Referrals on Trial: From Panacea to Patient (2010) 8 *JICJ* 1267–94.

[417] See Patrícia Pinto Soares, 'Positive Complementarity and the Law Enforcement Network: Drawing Lessons from the Ad Hoc Tribunals' Completion Strategy' (2013) 46 *Israel Law Review* 319–38, 336.

burden to states.[418] For instance, in the context of Libya, the OTP collaborated with states and organizations to 'gather, exchange and analyse information in relation to alleged crimes committed against migrants', and provided assistance to 'national authorities to effectively conduct their own investigations and prosecutions'.[419]

In cases where the consensual approach faced its limits, such as Sudan, the OTP sought to leverage international support by states and NGOs in order to raise the ICC's profile and encourage cooperation. It used its appeal on other institutions as a force multiplier. In this way, non-cooperation turned from an issue between ICC and a non-cooperating state into an issue affecting the international community.

The most famous example is the dispute over non-cooperation in relation to the warrants of arrest for Omar Al Bashir. The OTP sought to refer the matter to the Assembly of States Parties and the United Nations[420] in order to put pressure on ICC state parties to arrest. These failures led to referrals in six instances.[421] All of them have remained unanswered by the Security Council, 'despite proposals from different States to develop a follow-up mechanism concerning the referral of States to the Security Council by the Court'.[422] This weakened trust in the viability of the ICC enforcement system. Council inaction sent the damaging message 'that a state can withhold cooperation without serious consequences'.[423] In the case of South Africa, the Pre-Trial Chamber ultimately decided not to refer the matter to the

[418] In the ICC, cooperation is a two-way street. It involves cooperation of states with the Court, and cooperation from the Court with states and other international actors. See Federica Gioia, 'Complementarity and "reverse cooperation"' in Stahn and El Zeidy (eds), *The International Criminal Court and Complementarity* 807–29.

[419] ICC, Sixteenth Report of the Prosecutor of the International Criminal Court to the UN Security Council Pursuant to UNSCR 1970 (2011), 2 November 2018, para. 34.

[420] See ICC, *Prosecutor v. Kenyatta*, Judgment on the Prosecutor's appeal against Trial Chamber V(B)'s 'Decision on Prosecution's application for a finding of non-compliance under Article 87(7) of the Statute', ICC-01/09-02/11 OA 5, 19 August 2015, para. 53.

[421] Pre-Trial Chamber I, Corrigendum to the Decision Pursuant to Article 87(7) of the Rome Statute on the Failure by the Republic of Malawi to Comply with the Cooperation Requests Issued by the Court with Respect to the Arrest and Surrender of Omar Hassan Ahmad Al Bashir, ICC-02/05-01/09-139-Corr, 13 December 2011; Pre-Trial Chamber I, Decision pursuant to Article 87(7) of the Rome Statute on the refusal of the Republic of Chad to comply with the cooperation requests issued by the Court with respect to the arrest and surrender of Omar Hassan Ahmad Al Bashir, ICC-02/05-01/09-140-tENG, 13 December 2011; Pre-Trial Chamber II, Decision on the Non-compliance of the Republic of Chad with the Cooperation Requests Issued by the Court Regarding the Arrest and Surrender of Omar Hassan Ahmad Al-Bashir, ICC-02/05-01/09-151, 26 March 2013; Pre-Trial Chamber II, Decision on the Cooperation of the Democratic Republic of the Congo Regarding Omar Al Bashir's Arrest and Surrender to the Court, ICC-02/05-01/09-195, 9 April 2014; Pre-Trial Chamber II, Decision on the non-compliance by the Republic of Djibouti with the request to arrest and surrender Omar Al-Bashir to the Court and referring the matter to the United Nations Security Council and the Assembly of the State Parties to the Rome Statute, ICC-02/05-01/09-266, 11 July 2016; Pre-Trial Chamber II, Decision on the non-compliance by the Republic of Uganda with the request to arrest and surrender Omar Al-Bashir to the Court and referring the matter to the United Nations Security Council and the Assembly of State Parties to the Rome Statute, ICC-02/05-01/09-267, 11 July 2016.

[422] See *Prosecutor v. Al Bashir*, Decision under Article 87(7) of the Rome Statute on the non-compliance by South Africa with the request by the Court for the arrest and surrender of Omar Al-Bashir, ICC-02/05-01/09, 6 July 2017, para. 138.

[423] Ibid., para. 239.

Council any more, *inter alia* because 'the past 24 meetings of the Security Council of the United Nations following the adoption of Resolution 1593 (2005)' have 'not resulted in measures against States Parties that have failed to comply with their obligations to cooperate with the Court'.[424]

The Assembly of States Parties relied on 'smart powers' in order to counter deviance and international indifference. It refined cooperative structures by developing general framework agreements for cooperation, strengthening coordination among national authorities, and clarifying the consultation procedure to resolve problems impeding compliance.[425] It also suggested the application of naming and shaming techniques to improve cooperation, such as the use of conditionality policies, targeted rewards and sanctions against individuals, financial asset recovery, and measures to isolate fugitives ('avoidance of non-essential contacts').

3.2.2.6 'Outreach' and 'inreach' practices

Institutional expressivism is most visible in the context of outreach.[426] As Kingsley Chiedu Moghalu, the former spokesperson of the ICTR, has noted, the 'impact of the tribunals beyond the forensic combat of the courtroom', including their perception, is 'just as important as what happens in their courtrooms'.[427]

International criminal institutions have deployed outreach as a technique to reduce the physical or temporal distance of judicial institutions to the context of crimes. It is a means to show that justice 'is seen to be done'[428] and to 'build positive, direct relationships with those affected by the crimes'.[429] It encompasses a range of different measures which are common across institutions:

> The production of leaflets and booklets in various languages; the transmission of (parts of) trial proceedings; the organization of seminars and town hall meetings

[424] Ibid.

[425] Article 97. The Pre-Trial Chamber ruled that 'consultations (whether requested or ongoing) between a State and the Court do not, as such, suspend or otherwise affect the validity of the Court's request for cooperation'. See *Prosecutor v. Al Bashir*, Decision under Article 87(7) of the Rome Statute on the non-compliance by South Africa with the request by the Court for the arrest and surrender of Omar Al-Bashir, para. 119.

[426] Janine N. Clark, 'International War Crimes Tribunals and the Challenge of Outreach' (2009) 9 *International Criminal Law Review* 99–106; Schulz, 'Discussing community-based outreach activities by the International Criminal Tribunal for Rwanda' 347–66; Varda Hussain, 'Sustaining Judicial Rescues: The Role of Outreach and Capacity-Building Efforts In War Crimes Tribunals' (2005) *45 Virginia Journal of International Law* 547–85.

[427] Kingsley Chiedu Moghalu, 'Image and Reality of War Crimes Justice: External Perceptions of the International Criminal Tribunal for Rwanda' (2002) 26 *Fletcher Forum of World Affairs* 21–48, 22.

[428] Norman Pentelovitch, 'Seeing Justice Done: The Importance of Prioritizing Outreach Efforts At International Criminal Tribunals' (2013) 39 *Georgetown Journal of International Law* 445–94; Philipp Schulz, 'Justice Seen is Justice Done'? Assessing the Impact of Outreach Activities by the International Criminal Tribunal for Rwanda (2016) 21 *Croatian International Relations Review* 63–93.

[429] Lal C. Vohrah and Jon Cina, 'The outreach program' in Richard May, David Tolbert, John Hocking, Ken Roberts, Bing Bing Jia, Daryl Mundis, and Gabriël Oosthuizen (eds), *Essays on ICTY Procedure and Evidence: In Honour of Gabrielle Kirk McDonald* (The Hague: Kluwer Law International, 2001) 547–57, 550.

to which court staff travel to give presentations; the appearance of court staff in local media (especially radio programs); and the arrangements to allow victims, civil society actors, journalists, local officials, and legal professionals to visit the courts and tribunals.[430]

3.2.2.6.1 Conceptual distinctions

Outreach occurs in different forms. Victor Peskin has distinguished two main categories: the 'transparency' model, which is aimed at building 'confidence and support for the institution's work' through dissemination of information;[431] and the 'engagement model', which seeks to facilitate interaction and dialogue with domestic society.[432]

The first one is outreach in the narrow sense, that is, measures to relay the work of institutions more closely to affected communities. It shares resemblance with expressivist action, such as marketing and self-promotion. It encompasses essentially one-sided communication aimed at transmitting knowledge. It is driven by social need, that is, to increase the demonstration effect of justice processes and procedures.

The second one is less self-focused and involves two-way communication with others.[433] It allows mutual dialogue and leaves more room for social dissension.[434] Wendy Lambourne has coined the term 'inreach' to describe this phenomenon. It is grounded in the insight that persuasion requires not only communication and translation of messages, but engagement with local audiences and affected communities. It involves 'obtaining ideas, opinions and feedback from local populations about their expectations and responses to the transitional justice process'.[435]

'Inreach' practices take into account how addressees understand and experience messages. They may contribute to a sustained dialogue based on trust and

[430] See also Marlies Glasius, 'Do International Criminal Courts Require Democratic Legitimacy?' (2012) 23 *EJIL Democratic Legitimacy* 43–66, 50, 64.

[431] Victor Peskin, 'Courting Rwanda: The Promises and Pitfalls of the ICTR Outreach Programme' (2005) 3 *JICJ* 950–61954.

[432] Ibid.

[433] For instance, the SCSL, the ICTR, and ICC field offices have developed strategies to engage in direct conversation with local actors on accountability approaches. See Yvonne Dutton, 'Bridging the Legitimacy Divide: The International Criminal Court's Domestic Perception Challenge' (2017) 56 *Columbia Journal of Transnational Law* 70–122, 92.

[434] On 'participation and public dialogue', see Payam Akhavan, '"Review: The International Criminal Court in Context: Mediating the Global and Local in the Age of Accountability"' (2003) 97 *AJIL* 712–21, 716.

[435] Wendy Lambourne, 'Justice After Genocide: Impunity and the Extraordinary Chambers in the Courts of Cambodia, (2013) 8 *Genocide Studies and Prevention: An International Journal* 29, 36. See also Wendy Lambourne, 'Outreach, inreach and civil society participation in transitional justice' in Phil Clark (ed.), *Critical Perspectives in Transitional Justice* (London: Intersentia, 2013), 235–61.

accommodate dissent, but they remain vulnerable to manipulation and subject to strict budgetary constraints.[436]

3.2.2.6.2 Historical development

Outreach was initially developed in response to a need to increase the visibility, accessibility, and understanding of investigative and prosecutorial practices. It was outreach in the classical sense, meant to inform public audiences about institutions and their work. It was designed to increase the public visibility of institutions, counter misperceptions, and connect the work more closely to local audiences. It evolved gradually through lessons learned.

Outreach was originally ignored in institutional designs and not treated as part of the core mandate. For example, Nuremberg and Tokyo lacked outreach programmes in the modern sense.[437] The *ad hoc* tribunals gradually introduced outreach work into their activity in order to respond to critiques and negative attitudes.

The ICTR developed an outreach programme four years after its establishment in order to counter perceptions in government and civil society that it was disconnected from the needs of victims and survivors.[438] Outreach was necessary to improve the image of the tribunal. In the early years of the ICTR, the relationship with the government of Rwanda was tense.[439] The ICTR was seen as competitor to the domestic system and alternative justice approaches. It received less attention in global media. Its image was shaped by negative perceptions, such as the 'prevailing stereotype of the African continent as one in perpetual crisis'.[440] Critics note that 'if the Tribunal's outreach programme' would 'have actually engaged its constituencies in a more participatory manner, rather than merely distributing partially outdated information', the 'results could theoretically be expected to be more positive'.[441]

At the ICTY, outreach activities started in 1999, five years after the establishment of the tribunal, under the initiative of former ICTY President Gabrielle Kirk

[436] On Rwanda, see Peskin, 'Courting Rwanda' 954 ('One danger is that dialogue will turn into a political chance for the government and closely aligned survivor groups to attack the Tribunal.'); on Kenya, see Dutton, 'Bridging the Legitimacy Divide' 92 ('State leaders can use their power to impede the ICC's ability to access their domestic audience.').

[437] Robert Jackson had prepared a 'Plan for the Public Relations Organization for the Trial of the Major War Criminals' in August 1945. See Gregory Townsend, 'Structure and management' in Luc Reydams, Jan Wouters, and Cedric Ryngaert (eds), *International Prosecutors* (Oxford: Oxford University Press 2012) 171–318, 184–6. It noted that 'one of the primary purposes of the trial is to document and dramatize for contemporary consumption and for history the means and methods employed by the leading Nazis in their plan to dominate the world and wage an aggressive war'. See John J. Michalczyk, *Filming the End of the Holocaust: Allied Documentaries, Nuremberg and the Liberation of the Concentration Camps* (London: Bloomsbury Academic, 2014) 11. Together with recordings of hearings, radio transmissions, and press releases, these efforts marked the beginning 'of what might fall within today's conception of outreach'. Townsend, 'Structure and Management' 185.

[438] Peskin, 'Courting Rwanda' 951.

[439] Moghalu, 'Image and Reality of War Crimes Justice' 29.

[440] Ibid., 35.

[441] Schulz, 'Justice Seen is Justice Done'? 362.

McDonald. They had an educative ambition, namely to 'combat these distortions' and to 'educate the public and the legal profession in the region'.[442] Before the creation of the outreach programme, the ICTY received a lot of global media attention but suffered from the negative image conveyed in local media. As David Tolbert noted, 'the tribunal's work was subject to gross distortions and disinformation in many areas in the former Yugoslavia. As a result, many misunderstood the tribunal and its work, and the tribunal became a political football for certain unscrupulous politicians in the region who cynically manipulated these misunderstandings.'[443] Gabrielle Kirk McDonald admitted that outreach was a means of self-protection, namely to 'provide a comprehensive pro-active information campaign stressing the [Tribunal's] impartiality and independence, as well as countering the endemic misconceptions that had prompted the widespread disillusionment with the Tribunal'.[444] It was initially financed through voluntary contributions by governments and NGOs. Later, it became associated with more ambitious goals, such as 'capacity-building', 'bridging the gap with local communities', or youth outreach.[445]

The outreach work of the SCSL has generally been considered as a 'gold standard'. The Court placed emphasis on outreach since the start in order to 'link the people of Sierra Leone with the Special Court'.[446] It started with 'Town Hall Meetings' and used a broad range of communicative means, including radio broadcasts, public screening of proceedings, booklets with illustrations ('The Special Court Made Simple'), and theatre performances. Despite certain critiques, such as the predominant visibility of the Prosecution,[447] the approach inspired outreach methods of other institutions, such as the ECCC or the ICC.

Today, it is more widely accepted that outreach is part of a broader responsibility of institutions towards the public that should not be outsourced to civil society solely.[448] It is part of an attempt to 'deliver justice' in a way that is visible 'in the country where the crimes took place'.[449]

3.2.2.6.3 Institutional practices

In practice, even some of the most ambitious outreach programmes have been marked by contradiction.

[442] Ibid., 13.

[443] David Tolbert, 'The International Criminal Tribunal for the Former Yugoslavia: Unforeseen Successes and Foreseeable Shortcomings', (2002) 26 *The Fletcher Forum of World Affairs* 7–19, 13.

[444] Gabrielle Kirk McDonald, 'Problems, Obstacles and Achievements of the ICTY' (2004) 2 *JICJ* 558–71, 569.

[445] See Matias Hellman, 'Challenges and limitations of outreach: From the ICTY to the ICC' in de Vos, Kendall, and Stahn (eds), *Contested Justice* 251–71, 253.

[446] Pentelovitch, 'Seeing Justice Done' 481.

[447] Ibid., 462–3.

[448] Ibid., 490. David Cohen, 'Hybrid Justice in East Timor, Sierra Leone, and Cambodia: Lessons Learned and Prospects for the Future' (2007) 43 *Stanford Journal of International Law* 1–38, 32.

[449] Kerr and Lincoln, *The Special Court for Sierra Leone, Outreach, Impact and Impact* 19.

Outreach practices operate on the premise that there is a direct connection between knowledge production and positive perception. They assume that transparency will increase public awareness and knowledge or trigger societal transformation. However, this assumption is often shaky. As critics have noted:

> [T]he way people receive and process information in reality is often far more complex and complicated as put forward in the theoretical argument, and may greatly vary among individuals ... such generalising assumptions do not reflect the whole complexity and diversification of how information is processed and opinions are formed, potentially further complicated through the psychological effects associated with experiences and inter-generational impact of armed conflict and genocide.[450]

Any potential 'educational effect' depends on diverse factors, such as the nature of information provided, the knowledge and credibility of the speaker (e.g. familiarity with context), and willingness by the audience to engage with facts and contrary opinion. Many international institutions have been criticized for using stereotypes or biases in discourse. The story of events told through judgments and legal motions is not 'neutral' but is shaped through the narratives of the parties, simplification of context, and expectations in relation to target audiences. Law's unique relationship to facts influences the way in which they expressed. As Refik Hodzić has noted provocatively, the 'Tribunal's judges have been and will always be more interested in what international law journals have to say about their judgments than the people to whose lasting peace they are supposed to be contributing'.[451]

The very way in which facts are produced may be problematic. For instance, ICTY staff and officials have been criticized for their failure 'to educate themselves adequately about the Balkans'.[452] Historical narratives have remained contested. Outreach may thus suffer not only from different interpretative frameworks or unreceptive audiences but from 'problems with the facts themselves'.[453]

Outreach is a mission with a cause. Information is combined with self-promotion. It is an attempt to persuade the constituencies (e.g. victims, survivors, and states) of particular interpretations of facts or values. It involves language and vocabulary that may create inflated expectations. For example, the SCSL claimed in its outreach that the work of the Court constitutes an 'unprecedented opportunity to contribute to the restoration of the rule of law'.[454] This had negative side

[450] Schulz, 'Justice Seen is Justice Done?' 361

[451] Refik Hodzić', 'Accepting a Difficult Truth: ICTY is Not Our Court' *Balkan Insight* 6 March 2013, www.balkaninsight.com/en/article/accepting-a-difficult-truth-icty-is-not-our-court.

[452] Diane Orentlicher, *Shrinking the Space for Denial: The Impact of the ICTY in Serbia* (New York, NY: Open Society Justice Institute, 2008), 22

[453] Cerstin Bree Carlson, *Model(ing) Justice: Perfecting the Promise of International Criminal Law* (Cambridge: Cambridge University Press, 2018), 154.

[454] Kerr and Lincoln, *The Special Court for Sierra Leone, Outreach, Impact and Impact* 9.

effects. Some audiences understood this message to 'mean that the SCSL would correct all of Sierra Leone's problems, especially in the criminal justice sector'.[455]

Promises to deliver 'reconciliation', domestic 'ownership', or capacity are all too often empty rhetorical slogans. They present judicial outputs as marketable goods and treat audiences as consumers. This approach does not necessarily create greater 'buy in' but may be counterproductive, since it creates expectations that institutions cannot meet.

An interview-based survey on the outreach, legacy, and impact of the SCSL has concluded that in Sierra Leone 'outreach appears to have been largely successful in disseminating basic information about the Court' but 'less successful, in terms of reaching beyond Freetown into the regions, engaging civil society, and addressing key concerns surrounding the Court's limited mandate, its procedure, including guarantees of international standards for fair trial, and its legacy'.[456]

The ICC developed a Strategic Plan for Outreach. It is the most direct reflection of the ICC's expressive function in Court policy documents. It states expressly that outreach communication 'should serve first of all to increase the confidence of these communities in the international criminal justice system'.[457]

The Strategic Plan defines different audiences as intended addressees of outreach: the 'general public', 'international, regional and local media', 'NGOs and civil society groups', 'victims', 'government/opposition' groups, 'traditional and religious leaders', and 'women, children and youth'.[458] It recognizes the importance of institutional messaging through outreach.[459] It formulates specific 'message themes' that should guide outreach. They are strongly 'self-focused', rather than 'other-focused'.

The first guideline states that 'messages' should 'maximize understanding and support for the Court, manage expectations, and situate the Court as part of a broader international justice system'.[460] The second guideline acknowledges that 'message themes' should 'pertain to the Court's attributes and the context in which it operates, highlighting, for example, its judicial role, the fairness, efficiency and impartiality of its proceedings, and the fact that the Court is mindful of the context in which it is active, and is responsive to victims'.[461] The third guideline specifies that messages 'should be tailored to specific audiences'.[462] Specific 'key messages' are supposed to be 'continuously repeated throughout the different judicial phases', in order to 'help reinforce basic ideas and to increase understanding of the Court'.[463]

455 Ibid., 9.
456 Ibid., 27.
457 ICC, Strategic Plan for Outreach of the International Criminal Court, ICC-ASP/5/12, 29 September 2006, para. 3.
458 ICC, Strategic Plan for Outreach, paras 48–58.
459 ICC, Strategic Plan for Outreach, para. 13.
460 Ibid., para. 46.
461 Ibid.
462 Ibid.
463 Ibid.

This approach illustrates some of the marketing-oriented features of outreach. The Court acts as a communicative enterprise that repeats certain institutional messages about accountability in order to showcase its performance and expand its authority. Outreach is geared at image promotion and presenting the ICC as a coherent 'brand' which appeals to international and local audiences. The message is 'to make the law as impartial and judicious as possible to ensure its separation from politics'.[464] The use and repetition of categoric message themes hide the fact that the interests of the Court do not necessarily coincide with 'those of the victims of violence that the court claims to represent'.[465] The Plan contemplates 'ongoing two-way communication process with audiences and partners on the ground', but mainly as a reactive tool, namely to review and reformulate messages sent. [466]

Cognitive dissonance between speaker and audiences has been a major problem in many contexts. For instance, in Sierra Leone, the record of the court remained contested, despite a comprehensive and ambitious outreach to local communities, because of ongoing misalignment between 'expectations of quick and efficient justice' and 'expectations regarding the Court's contribution to restoration of peace and justice in Sierra Leone'. [467]

'Inreach' is a means to enable institutions and audiences to understand mutual concerns and expectations better and to foster a sense of engagement of those affected by international criminal justice. It started initially with targeted road trips and conversations. It has gradually gained broader importance in institutional design (e.g. through participatory schemes) and field activities.

For example, the ICC Strategic Plan recognizes that outreach should also 'foster greater participation of local communities in the activities of the Court' and 'respond to the concerns and expectations expressed in general by affected communities and by particular groups within these communities'.[468] The Court has *inter alia* established field offices in situations in order to facilitate such discourse and interaction. This is complemented by novel participatory regimes, such as victim participation on proceedings, which may influence decision-making

This type of activity is guided by the hope that 'by fostering dialogue', outreach may 'produce greater judicial accountability, demonstrate that judicial arbitrariness is no longer acceptable, educate on the rule of law, enable deterrence of future crimes and promote peace and reconciliation'.[469]

However, in practice, there are many obstacles and challenges. Engagement often remains instrumental. The very process of starting dialogue may send

[464] See Joseph Hoover, 'Moral Practices: Assigning Responsibility in the International Criminal Court' (2013) 76 *Law and Contemporary Problems* 263–86, 264.

[465] Ibid., 285.

[466] ICC, Strategic Plan for Outreach, para. 46.

[467] Kerr and Lincoln, *The Special Court for Sierra Leone, Outreach, Impact and Impact* 9.

[468] ICC, Strategic Plan for Outreach, para. 13.

[469] Patrick Vinck and Phuong N. Pham, 'Outreach Evaluation: The International Criminal Court in the Central African Republic' (2010) 4 *International Journal of Transitional Justice* 421–42, 442.

discomforting messages. Images such as 'staff flying into remote regions on helicopters' and travel in 'white UN jeeps' create perceptions of 'superiority and difference'.[470] Reaching out to victims and survivors may be understood as an attempt to persuade them to act as witnesses. Those who appear may have their own political or material interests in engaging with international justice institutions. Many immediate victims care for their basic needs while they see 'the people indicted as being well looked after—given food, medical treatment and education'.[471]

The context may not be conducive to mutual learning. For example, outreach in Rwanda has shown that in 'a society where almost everyone has been affected in one way or another by large-scale genocidal violence', it proves 'tremendously difficult to educate about the genocide in a culturally and ethnically sensitive manner'.[472]

Moreover, outreach has often primarily reached certain social elite or the international community. Access to information may be impeded by structural inequalities. For instance, in Sierra Leone, there was 'a pervading sense of dislocation between Freetown compared to the rest of the country'.[473] In the Central African Republic, 'knowledge and awareness' about the ICC were 'on average, higher among members of an urban, male, educated and wealthy elite who have frequent access to the media and are targeted for informational meetings'.[474] If expressivist action is deemed to have an empowering effect on women, they 'must be informed about and understand the proceedings'.[475] 'Inreach' practices require more input from 'non-elite' groups.

3.2.2.7 Legacy discourse

Legacy discourse is an integral part of the institutional survival strategy of international criminal institutions.[476] It is driven by economic, identity-related, and psychological factors. The closure or disengagement of a judicial entity in a conflict situation is a threat from the perspective of organizational theory. It challenges the 'symbolic' value expressed through the act of creation.[477]

[470] Kerr and Lincoln, *The Special Court for Sierra Leone, Outreach, Impact and Impact* 21.

[471] Ibid., 23.

[472] Schulz, 'Justice Seen is Justice Done'? 362.

[473] Kerr and Lincoln, *The Special Court for Sierra Leone, Outreach, Impact and Impact* 18.

[474] Vinck and Pham, 'Outreach Evaluation' 439.

[475] Kerr and Lincoln, *The Special Court for Sierra Leone, Outreach, Impact and Impact* 18.

[476] On legacy, see Carsten Stahn, 'Legacy in international criminal justice' in Margaret M. deGuzman and Diane Marie Amann (eds), *Arcs of Global Justice: Essays in Honour of William A. Schabas* (Oxford: Oxford University Press, 2018) 271–86; Viviane Dittrich, 'Legacies in the making: Assessing the institutionalized legacy endeavour of the Special Court for Sierra Leone' in Jalloh (ed.), *The Sierra Leone Special Court and its Legacy* 663–91; Elizabeth Evenson and Alison Smith, 'Completion, Legacy and Complementarity at the ICC, in Stahn', *The Law and Practice of the International Criminal Court* 1259–96; Sara Kendall and Sarah Nouwen, 'Speaking of Legacy: Toward an Ethos of Modesty at the International Criminal Tribunal for Rwanda' (2016) 110 *AJIL* 212–32; Milena Sterio and Michael Scharf, *The Legacy of Ad Hoc Tribunals in International Criminal Law* (Cambridge: Cambridge University Press, 2019); van der Wilt, 'The legacy of the Special Tribunal for Lebanon' 268–87.

[477] See Bingham, 'Strategy or Process?' 691.

Legacy discourse seeks to address this concern. It involves not only documentation and representation but attempts to provide meaning to past events, frame future discourse, or gain 'influence over remembrance'.[478] It has become part of official strategy,[479] although it is not mentioned in the constitutive legal instruments of institutions.

More or less all international criminal courts and tribunals have followed the proposition that legacy 'requires a strategy and will not necessarily happen automatically or by osmosis'.[480] Legacy strategies are designed to provide a lasting impact beyond institutional closure or withdrawal from situations.[481] The symbolic momentum inherent in the creation of an entity changes or fades over time.[482] With closure and disengagement, institutions are under pressure to justify themselves in the eyes of their constituencies and to demonstrate their record. Legacy discourse looks back to performance and seeks to shape future relevance (e.g. archives).[483]

3.2.2.7.1 Historical development

The desire to leave a legacy may be traced back to post-war strategies. Jackson had prepared a 'Plan for the Public Relations Organization for the Trial of the Major War Criminals' in August 1945.[484] It noted that 'one of the primary purposes of the trial is to document and dramatize for contemporary consumption and for history the means and methods employed by the leading Nazis in their plan to dominate the world and wage an aggressive war'.[485] The trials involved different dimensions of legacy building. Legal legacy was a core instrument of Allied strategy. Both Nuremberg and Tokyo were 'revolutions in law'. Telford Taylor expressed this transformative ambition openly when noting that 'Nuremberg' is both what actually happened there and what people think happened, and the second is more important than the first ... [I]t is not the bare record but the ethos of Nuremberg with which we must reckon today.'[486]

[478] Viviane Dittrich, *Present at the Completion: Creating Legacies at the International Criminal Tribunals* (PhD thesis, London: London School of Economics and Political Science 2015), 26, at https://pdfs.semanticscholar.org/bc8a/cc18c1479823befbd80629334330785876 3e.pdf?_ga=2.33763940.493328000.1562574900-1872614660.1562574900.

[479] According to OHCHR, '[t]he need to leave a legacy is now firmly accepted as part of United Nations policy'. See OHCHR, *Rule of the Law Tools for Post-Conflict States* 5.

[480] OHCHR, *Rule of the Law Tools for Post-Conflict States* 41.

[481] Irene C. Lu, 'Curtain call at Closing: The Multi-Dimensional Legacy of the International Criminal Tribunal for Rwanda' (2013) 34 *University of Pennsylvania Journal of International Law* 859–99, 867.

[482] Bingham, 'Strategy or Process' 716 ('Imagery is a delicate and fickle thing, and symbols can rapidly take on new meaning in the eyes of the perceiver.').

[483] Ibid., 691.

[484] Gregory Townsend, 'Structure and management' in Reydams, Wouters, and Ryngaert (eds), *International Prosecutors* 184–86.

[485] See Michalczyk, *Filming the End of the Holocaust* 11.

[486] Telford Taylor, *Nuremberg and Vietnam: An American Tragedy* (Chicago, IL: Quadrangle Books, 1970) 13–14.

One of the breaking points in the Nuremberg trial was the screening of a documentary film, entitled 'Nazi Concentration Camps', which displayed the cruelty of Nazi violence, based on eyewitness testimony. It left an enduring imprint on defendants. This use of film material was part of a broader public relations strategy, identified before the trial, which included recordings of hearings, radio transmissions, and press releases. The Nuremberg Military Tribunal started early on to make plans for the publication of the judgement and archiving critical documents.[487] Immediately after the Nuremberg Judgement, on 11 December 1946, the UN General Assembly adopted resolution 95 (I) which contributed to the legal legacy. It consolidated legal output and increased its acceptance.

Legacy developed into a full-fledged institutional concept in the context of peacebuilding. It was shaped by experiences of the 1990s. The 2004 report of the UN Secretary-General on the Rule of Law and Transitional Justice in Conflict and Post-Conflict Societies highlighted the importance of legacy strategies in institutional planning. It noted that it is 'essential that, from the moment any future international or hybrid tribunal is established, consideration be given, as a priority, to the ultimate exit strategy and intended legacy in the country concerned'.[488]

The *ad hoc* (ICTY, ICTR) and others tribunals (SCSL, STL) have gradually included legacy programmes in their completion strategies in order to consolidate their record and mitigate their transitional nature.[489] The ICTY has defined legacy as 'that which the Tribunal will hand down to successors and others'.[490] It associated legacy with factors, such as the facts established by the tribunal, its archives, the contribution to the 'rule of law in the region', or jurisprudential legacy.[491] It recognized that its 'core work, i.e., the investigations, trials and the judgements' and 'long-term access to the Tribunal's records' are 'the fundamental basis of the Tribunal's legacy'.[492] The SCSL placed considerable emphasis on outreach, the impact of the Charles Taylor trial, and lessons learned.[493] The STL has defined legacy as the broader 'impact on a domestic or international level that an international or

[487] See Kevin Heller, 'Completion' in Reydams, Wouters, and Ryngaert (eds), *International Prosecutors* 886–925, 925.

[488] Report of Secretary General, The rule of law and transitional justice in conflict and post-conflict societies, para. 46.

[489] See generally OHCHR, *Rule of the Law Tools for Post-Conflict States* 4–6. On the legacies of the ICTY, see Carsten Stahn, Carmel Agius, Serge Brammertz, and Collen Rohan (eds), *Legacies of the International Criminal Tribunal for the Former Yugoslavia: A Multidisciplinary Approach* (Oxford: Oxford University Press, 2020).

[490] ICTY, 'Assessing the Legacy of the ICTY—Background Paper' (2010), at http://www.icty.org/en/features/legacy-conferences/international-conference-2010/background-paper.

[491] See ICTY, *Legacy of the ICTY in the Former Yugoslavia: Conference Proceedings, Sarajevo 6 November 2012* (The Hague: ICTY Outreach Programme, 2013).

[492] ICTY, Report of the President on the Conference: Assessing the Legacy of the ICTY, 27 April 2010, para. 11, http://www.icty.org/x/file/Press/Events/100427_legacyconference_pdt_report.pdf.

[493] See No Peace Without Justice, *Making Justice Count: Assessing the Impact and Legacy of the Special Court for Sierra Leone in Sierra Leone and Liberia* (Freetown: Special Court for Sierra Leone and No Peace Without Justice, 2012), 36.

hybrid tribunal leaves behind after its work is complete'.[494] The ICC has engaged with legacy as part of disengagement from situations under consideration. It has related the idea of legacy to the sustainability of justice intervention. It relied on the definition provided by the OHCHR which defines legacy as the 'lasting impact on bolstering the rule of law in a particular society, by conducting effective trials to contribute to ending impunity, while also strengthening domestic judicial capacity'.[495]

The implementation of legacy programmes cuts across judicial organs. Some aspects form part of judicial activity (e.g. transfer of cases) or prosecutorial strategy (e.g. sharing of evidence). Other parts fall with the responsibility of the Registry (e.g. outreach), or are outsourced to civil society organizations.

3.2.2.7.2 Approaches

In institutional discourse, legacy is approached from a functionalist perspective, as an object that exists and that can be transferred from institutions to recipients. This conception conveys a certain sense of ownership. For instance, the OHCHR compared legacy to 'software'. It mentions 'policies and processes that help to ensure the domestic justice system operates more effectively and efficiently, consistent with its international human rights obligations'.[496] They include 'substantive legal framework reform, professional development (e.g., cross-fertilization of expertise), and raising awareness of the role of courts as independent and well-functioning rule-of-law institutions, operating within a human rights framework and scrutinized by a strong civil society'.[497]

Current approaches are strongly focused on specific results or outcomes (i.e. specific uses of facts, laws, or record). But as rightly pointed out in scholarship,[498] legacy is a process of social construction. It differs from outreach. It does not arise simply from 'the policies and actions of the tribunals themselves'.[499] As Viviane Dittrich has stated, it is not only a bipolar relation between sender and recipient but relies on a more complex cycle of action[500] and reaction among different agents: the 'legacy object', the 'legacy creator', 'legacy preservers', and 'legacy addressees'.[501]

494 STL, *Glossary of Legal Terms* (Leidschendam: Outreach and Legacy Section, 2012), 234.

495 Report of the Court on complementarity: Completion of ICC activities in a situation country, ICC-ASP/12/32, 15 October 2013, para. 27.

496 Ibid.

497 Ibid.

498 See, for example, Viviane Dittrich 'The legacy of the ECCC' in Simon Meisenberg and Ignaz Stegmiller (eds), *The Extraordinary Chambers in the Courts of Cambodia: Assessing Their Contribution to International Criminal Law* (The Hague: TMC Asser Press, 2016) 123–58, 138.

499 Caitlin Reiger, 'Where to From Here for International Tribunals? Considering Legacy and Residual Issue', ICTJ Briefing, September 2009, 4, at https://www.ictj.org/sites/default/files/ICTJ-Global-Legacy-Tribunal-2009-English.pdf.

500 Dittrich identifies a cycle of legacies with three phases: creation, consolidation, and contestation. Dittrich, *Present at the Completion: Creating Legacies at the International Criminal Tribunals* 107.

501 Dittrich, 'Legacies in the making' 670.

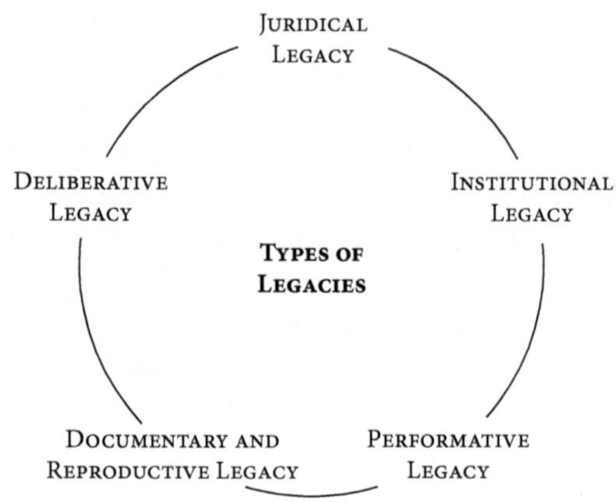

Figure 10 Types of legacies

It is shaped by practices of representation, production, reception, and contestation. It is grounded in social interaction and subjectivity, a relationship towards the past and the imagination of the recipient.[502] Legacy can be 'positive' or 'negative'. It evolves with and through perception and construction over time by different actors. It is thus more proper to speak of 'legacies'.[503]

3.2.2.7.3 Types of legacies

Legacy creation occurs in multiple forms. Certain practices are uncontested. For instance, archiving, case reporting or codification have a long tradition in international and domestic justice. Managerial contributions to legacy formation, such as influence over opinion, perpetuation and internalization of accountability strategies or law reform, are more questionable. It is helpful to distinguish at least, five different categories of legacy: (i) juridical legacy, (ii) institutional legacy, (iii) performative legacy, (iv) documentary and reproductive legacy, and (v) deliberative legacy (Figure 10).

Juridical legacy (e.g. judicial or legal output) is one of the most common forms of legacy in legal discourse. Institutions tend to claim that investigations and prosecutions and judicial work count among their most visible legacies. It is a powerful and comfortable means of self-justification since it defies purely quantitative assessments. It includes not only decisions and blackletter law (case law, judgments), but the broader performance and rendition of justice, the interpretive narratives created, and symbolic expression, such as award of collective reparation. Juridical legacy is not only directed towards offenders and victims but also towards a broader

[502] See Mégret, 'The Legacy of the ICTY as Seen through Some of its Actors and Observers' 1014 ('an evolving intellectual relationship that we construct with an object receding in the past').

[503] See Dittrich, 'Legacies in the making' 668.

global community. Interpersonal dimensions, such as the creation of professional communities, are an important part of this type of legacy. As anthropologist Nigel Eltringham has noted, it is not only reflected in texts, but 'carried by those who have worked at the Tribunal' (e.g. researchers, interpreters, and advocates).[504]

Institutional legacy is a second type of legacy. It relates to institutional roles and role models, including lessons learned. Experimentation with legal forms and shapes is part of this heritage. It includes not only physical features, images, or tangible institutional outputs, but also meanings created in the eyes of public imagination. For example, one aspect of the institutional legacy of the ICTY and the ICTR is that they illustrated a specific 'type of ad hoc, time-bound international criminal court' and the need for residual follow-up mechanisms 'to manage the rights, obligations, and essential functions' in the afterlife of a tribunal.[505] The daily work of judicial entities tends to create institutional insularity. Institutional legacies include didactic practices, such as demonstration effects or transfer of institutional 'lessons learned' or 'good practices'. The very concept of transmitting 'lessons' has a transformative function since it turns negative experiences into positives. It presents shortcomings as learning incentives for the future.

Performative legacy is a third type of legacy. It builds on the role of actors (e.g. Judges, parties, and participants) in proceedings and the narratives and counter-narratives produced through agency, including historical accounts.[506] Performative legacy does not build a definitive record of events per se but rather a 'historical record awaiting analysis'. As Martha Minow, has argued, such performances are partly a means 'to help the society—and the watching world—not merely recall but also re-member, that is, to reconstitute a community of humanity against which there can be crimes and within which victims and survivors can be reclaimed as worthy members'.[507]

Documentary and reproductive legacy relates to processes of reproducing knowledge, such as memorialization, archiving, outreach or transmission of proceedings (e.g. video-streaming of trials). It builds a bridge between legacy creator, legacy preservers, and legacy addressees. These techniques have been refined through new technologies and investments into memory-building. For instance, the legacy of Nuremberg was largely built without physical sites of remembrance, such as a peace museum or widely accessible archives. In Japan, sentiments about the Tokyo trial were most vividly reflected in a monument honoring Pal's

[504] Nigel Eltringham, 'A War Crimes Community: The Legacy of the International Criminal Tribunal for Rwanda' (2008) 14 *New England Journal of International & Comparative Law* 309–18, 311. See also Christensen, 'From symbolic surge to closing courts' 609.

[505] See Lu, 'Curtain call at Closing' 864, referring to the 'structural' legacy of the ICTR.

[506] Due to their adversarial nature, trials are an imperfect means for producing historical accounts. They are typically a forum in which opposing parties engage each other's narratives pursuant to 'disciplining civility rules'. See **section 5.1**.

[507] Martha Minow, 'The Work of Re-Membering: After Genocide and Mass Atrocity' (1999) 23 *Fordham International Law Journal* 429–39, 430.

dissenting opinion.[508] In modern contexts, such as Cambodia, Sierra Leone, or the former Yugoslavia,[509] memorialization has become a core feature of legacy strategies. The work of tribunals was complemented by sites of legal memory, such as targeted museums. These sites preserve evidence, demonstrate to the world what happened, and seek to promote learning about the past. They bear features of spectacle[510] or even become tourist attractions.

Archival work and access to archives are an integral part of legacy creation. Archives respond to a collective right to know. They are a 'treasure-trove of information about war crimes themselves, the perceptions and experiences of harm, the fluidity and lived realities of identity, violence and the relationship between them'.[511] They are increasingly treated as 'living instruments'.[512] They 'are never closed and never complete'. Rather 'every individual and every generation are allowed their own interpretation of the archive, to reinvent and reconstruct its view on and narrative of the past'.[513]

Legal archives do not create collective memory as such. Instead, they 'open a new transitional space in which it becomes possible to articulate new claims to justice'.[514] In some instances (e.g. the former Yugoslavia), they have served to establish a 'counter-discourse to public opinion "that commemorates conflictual communal memory"'.[515]

One of the risks of documentary and reproductive legacy is that it traces events and historical patterns through judicial record and story of the institution, rather than broader inquiries. As evidenced in Cambodia, constructed memorialization can turn into a form of governance.[516] It presents particular 'lenses for knowing' a particular period while implying that international criminal justice serves 'as a response to it'.[517] It requires 'translation into the heterogeneous legal cultures, institutions, and languages' of domestic societies.[518] The translation of experiences into

[508] See Mark Drumbl, 'Judge Pal with Jefferson Davis in Tokyo', Opinio Juris, 23 March 2019, at http://opiniojuris.org/2019/03/23/judge-pal-with-jefferson-davis-in-tokyo/.

[509] Giovanna M. Frisso, 'Winding Down the ICTY: The Impact of the Completion Strategy and the Residual Mechanism on Victims' (2011) 3 *Göttingen Journal of International Law* 1093–121.

[510] Nigel Eltringham, 'Spectators to the Spectacle of Law: The Formation of a "Validating Public" at the International Criminal Tribunal for Rwanda' (2012) 77 *Ethnos: Journal of Anthropology* 425–45.

[511] Doris Buss, 'Performing Legal Order: Some Feminist Thoughts on International Criminal Law' (2011) 11 *International Criminal Law Review* 409–23, 414.

[512] Eric Ketelaar, 'Archives as Spaces of Memory' (2008) 29 *Journal of the Society of Archivists* 9–27, 12.

[513] Eric Ketelaar, 'Truths, memories and histories in the archives of the International Criminal Tribunal for the Former Yugoslavia' in Harmen van der Wilt, Jeroen Vervliet, Göran Sluiter, and Johannes Houwink ten Cate (eds), *The Genocide Convention: The Legacy of 60 Years* (Leiden: Brill, 2012), 201–21, 210

[514] See Kirsten Campbell, 'The Laws of Memory: The ICTY, the Archive, and Transitional Justice' (2012) 22 *Social & Legal Studies* 247–69, 261.

[515] Ibid. 258.

[516] Manning, 'Governing Memory' 165.

[517] Ibid., 179.

[518] Campbell, 'The Laws of Memory' 257.

global memory may cause estrangement among local victims or survivors. For instance, early calls by the ECCC that 'Ordinary Khmer Rouge have nothing to fear' and their portrayal as victims of the regime contributed to critiques of selective memorialization.[519]

Legal institutions are in the broadest sense sites of social interaction which provide a public space for social reassociation.[520] Legacy is deliberative. It is created through discourse and reception. It is grounded in storytelling and social interaction with institutions as legacy objects. It is framed through competing narratives. It enables others to read and make their own decisions. It evolves over time and creates new frames of reference. The meaning is ultimately created in the eye of the spectator.

3.2.2.7.4 Institutional practices

In legal practice, there was a strong trend towards the professionalization of legacy work. The ICTY had a pioneering role in this effort.[521] It created targeted institutional posts (e.g. a 'Legacy Officer'). Didactic objectives were mixed with goals of sociopolitical transformation, for example, capacity-building and knowledge transfer.[522] The SCSL commissioned a study to survey its own performance and perception. Unsurprisingly, the report concluded with a rather flattering appraisal of the perception of the SCSL. It found that a 'large majority' (overall 83.92 per cent) of respondents believed 'that the SCSL has done a good job in bringing those responsible for the atrocities to justice'.[523] It defined a 'thick' version of legacy. Legacy was grounded in a perception survey. It found *inter alia* that

> [t]he majority (82.09%) of respondents overall believes that the SCSL has contributed to greater respect for human rights and rule of law...
>
> [a]n overall 66.89% of respondents believes that the work of the SCSL has had an impact on the work of national rule of law actors such as the police, the army, prison officials and the national judiciary...
>
> [a] sizeable majority (overall 70.01%) also believes that the SCSL has had an impact on the development of other peace-building mechanisms in their country.[524]

519 Manning, 'Governing Memory' 166.

520 Campbell, 'The Laws of Memory' 263.

521 See Fausto Pocar, 'Completion or Continuation Strategy?: Appraising Problems and Possible Developments in Building the Legacy of the ICTY' (2008) 6 *JICJ* 655–65, 661–3.

522 Official legacy elements included: (i) 'Strengthening of the National Jurisdictions and Accessibility of the Records'; (ii) 'Structural and Legal Reforms in the Region'; (iii) 'Referral of Cases and Transfer of Investigative Material'; and (iv) 'Engaging with Civil Society through the Tribunal's Outreach Programme'. See ICTY, 'Assessing the Legacy of the ICTY—Background Paper'.

523 No Peace Without Justice, *Making Justice Count* 29.

524 Ibid., 30.

Courts, like the SCSL, ECCC, or the ICC have rather uncritically relied on the rule-of-law-oriented legacy definition of the OHCHR, without questioning its underlying premise. This approach is marked by an inherent contradiction.

Many courts formally subscribe to the view that '[l]egacy must be domestically owned and driven'.[525] However, court-mandated efforts to bolster 'the rule of law' often leave little space for such ownership. They may involve 'reverse legacy', that is, 'capacity drain' from domestic systems.[526] International approaches are often more concerned with institutional or systemic legacy than processes of country-specific internalization. Legacy work is directed at reproduction and replication. It imagines a natural continuum between demonstration at the international level and domestic action. National authorities are deemed to be ready to 'pick up and effectively continue work' when international criminal institutions are 'exiting a given country'. However, this is not always the case. For example, Sarah Kendall and Sarah Nouwen have found that the ICTR had a more limited impact on the Rwandan domestic system than assumed in legacy discourse. They have argued that there was limited evidence of 'norm infiltration' in the classical sense, that is, 'a modeling of norms and practices in the Rwandan justice system on those of the ICTR':[527]

> Rather, having adopted an absolute anti-impunity policy for those who committed genocide against the Tutsi, the RPF government has sought to receive cases that might otherwise go unprosecuted by the ICTR or extraditing states, and it was the conditionality attached to the transfer of such cases that incentivized Rwanda to adopt these changes.[528]

Although formally addressed to local constituencies, legacy policies are typically oriented towards the implementation of global standards and internationally set practices.[529] Domestic action is funded, incentivized, or endorsed if it implements international practices and lessons learned on the international level.

Self-centred approaches towards legacy are in need of refinement. Achievements are all often encoded and performed in generic language (e.g. justice for victims). This sets in place a vicious circle: 'Once formulaic language is established . . ., deviations from this language damage the integrity of the court and erode its legacy.'[530]

525 OHCHR, *Rule of the Law Tools for Post-Conflict States* 41.
526 Ibid., 15.
527 Kendall and Nouwen, 'Speaking of Legacy' 226
528 Ibid., 226.
529 On dilemmas of global justice, see Sarah M.H. Nouwen and Wouter G. Werner, 'Monopolizing Global Justice: International Criminal Law as Challenge to Human Diversity' (2015) 13 *JICJ* 157–76157.
530 Amanda Potts and Anne Lise Kjær, 'Constructing Achievement in the International Criminal Tribunal for the Former Yugoslavia (ICTY): A Corpus-Based Critical Discourse Analysis' (2016) 29 *International Journal for the Semiotics of Law* 525–55, 552.

Attempts to frame legacy as technical assistance or outreach simplify the complexity of legacy processes. Legacies begin after an event. They cannot and should not be regulated by courts. The relationship between centre and periphery needs to be turned around. The work of international criminal courts should be considered as an object of legacy debates, rather than an element foreclosing debate. Legacy work should enable 'debates over memory, and potentially conflicting and multiple meanings and perspectives on the underlying events'.[531] It should leave space for individuals to frame a new story and transform experiences of trauma into hope.

Legacy work should be approached with modesty. It relies on a lot of speculation that is not necessarily backed by empirical verification. It involves 'hypotheses, setting forth how the Tribunal could have an impact, or assertions of hopes or normative opinions as to what its impact should be'.[532] As Nigel Eltringham has noted in relation to Rwanda, 'the legacy of which we can be more certain is also more modest: the jurisprudence celebrated by legal scholars, a historical record awaiting analysis, and a cadre of legal practitioners equipped for the future of international criminal justice'.[533]

Based on this logic, courts engaged in legacy building should pay more attention to the creation of a space for public debate and receptiveness rather than legacy production and replication. Legacy building requires more critical engagement with the processes through which perceptions and collective memory are formed, and the conditions under which they can provide a rupture with the past. Courts should not try become what Gary Alan Fine has called 'reputational entrepreneurs', actors 'who attempt to control the memory' of individuals.[534] Some of the strength of the legal process lies in its immediacy, human elements, and authenticity, and information. Filtering out transformative moments in trials, or key pieces of evidence, may speak more directly to prospective constituencies than technical legacy programmes. Many aspects of legacy are translated through individual narratives.[535]

[531] Martha Minow, *Between Vengeance and Forgiveness: Facing History After Genocide and. Mass Violence* (Boston, MA: Beacon Press, 1998), 139.

[532] Kendall and Nouwen, 'Speaking of Legacy' 217.

[533] Nigel Eltringham, 'A Legacy Deferred?: The International Criminal Tribunal for Rwanda at 20 years', E-International Relations, 29 April 2014, at https://www.e-ir.info/2014/04/29/a-legacy-deferred-the-international-criminal-tribunal-for-rwanda-at-20-years/.

[534] Gary Alan Fine, 'Reputational Entrepreneurs and the Memory of Incompetence: Melting Supporters, Partisan Warriors, and Images of President Harding' (1996) 101 *American Journal of Sociology* 1159–93.

[535] On a narrative account, based on experiences, see Mégret, 'The Legacy of the ICTY as Seen Through Some of its Actors and Observers' 1013; Nigel Eltringham, 'When We Walk Out, What Was It All About?': Views on New Beginnings from within the International Criminal Tribunal for Rwanda' (2014) 45 *Development and Change* 543–64.

3.3 Conclusions

Expressivism is part of the motivation behind the turn to international criminal institutions and an integral part of their actions. As Kerstin Bree Carlson has argued in her work on modelling justice, 'without a discursive connection between an institution, the peoples subject to its mandate, and the sovereigns that it serves, an institution is structurally imbalanced'.[536]

This relationship manifests itself at all stages of the lifecycle of institutions. The establishment of an institution is often highly symbolic in itself. It marks an event. It carries multiple meaning to different audiences. The history of international criminal justice illustrates that these meanings have differed considerably, ranging from calls for memory and remembrance of expressions of shame and apology, to acts of recreating community relations, manifestations of hope and belief, and articulations of protest. The very presence of institutions itself creates constituencies. They often carry on discourse even after formal closure.

Institutional action has ritualistic features. During their lifespan, international criminal institutions 'project an image of themselves as well as their creators'.[537] They do not only reflect the idea of a common conscience but help to shape it. They seek to 'entrench certain practices and modes of thought, naturalizing and making them seem self-evident through each repeated performance'.[538]

Their action communicates messages about types of criminality and victimization, crimes and their meanings, context, and lines of responsibility. The need for expression arises not only from the publicity of criminal proceedings. It is shaped by certain behavioural patterns identified in organizational theory (e.g. survival instinct, mimetic factors), the search for recognition and justification by stakeholders and professional communities, and processes of communication.[539]

International criminal institutions rely on communicative action in their work in order to reach their audiences and demonstrate their outcomes ('justice is seen to be done'). The essence of activities goes beyond overt judicial action. Traditional forms of judicial action are complemented by the formulation of prosecutorial strategies, the establishment of outreach practices, legacy programmes, or reparative practices.

Many legal actions, such as preliminary examinations, investigations, jurisdiction, and admissibility decisions or acts of cooperation, contain speech acts. They can produce new narrative subjects, entail commands or incentives for action,

[536] Kerstin Bree Carlson, *Model(ing) Justice: Perfecting the Promise of International Criminal Law*, 183.

[537] Dittrich, *Present at the Completion: Creating Legacies at the International Criminal Tribunals* 56.

[538] Benjamin Authers, Hilary Charlesworth, Marie-Bénédicte Dembour, and Emma Larking, 'Introduction to Humanity Rituals Special Issue' (2018) 9 *Humanity: An International Journal of Human Rights, Humanitarianism, and Development* 63–74, 67.

[539] See with respect to legacy, Dittrich, *Present at the Completion: Creating Legacies at the International Criminal Tribunals* 309.

or convey attitudes or emotions. Certain speech acts rely on prospective consequences or 'if' scenarios in order to reduce the gap between norms and implementation. For instance, preliminary examinations and complementarity function are based on hypothetical consequences of ICC action. Complementarity and cooperation encourage states to act 'as if' they take their commitments to international criminal justice seriously.

The expressive power of international criminal justice is particularly high since it operates in atrocity contexts. Institutional speech acts attract large public attention but any meaning or application of the law is likely to remain subject to dispute. This has repercussions for didactic ambitions. Domestic justifications of expressivism, such as the ideal fostering of constructive public dialogue in a liberal society,[540] cannot be taken for granted. The assertion of authority, legal reasoning, and information sharing are often insufficient to produce the intended effects. Moralizing discourse, high-flying references to universal legal norms or standards, or their suggested incorporation to domestic systems may face political, cultural, or psychological resistance. Micro-processes involving communicative relationships with different types of actors and engagement with experiences may offer better chances of success than grand educational theories.

Outreach and legacy practices have shown that expressivism may remain elitist or focus on 'the international' as the site of engagement and interconnection. Expressivism requires more nuanced discursive techniques, which rely on modesty, persuasion, and fostering engagement.[541] For instance, institutions should more openly engage with their own limitations (e.g. budget constraints, obstructions, external influences) in order to retain trust, and distinguish between outputs that they can deliver and broader values that they promote, such as 'truth, justice, accountability' or solidarity.[542] Soft powers, affective dimensions of justice, and perceptions of sincerity play an important role.

In most cases, institutions have resisted against completion or closure strategies.[543] They have looked partly at each other's works and failures, in order to learn from each other. When completion or disengagement became unavoidable, they developed strategies to outlive their institutional death. These strategies include compilations of jurisprudence, archival work, case or norm transfer, education of domestic actors, or sharing of practices. These experiences ensure the survival of the institutions as a social construct.

540 Sekhon, 'Pedagogical Prosecutor' 32.

541 See also Kotecha, 'The Art of Rhetoric' 962.

542 See also Institute for Integrated Transitions, 'Changing the Narrative The Role of Communications in Transitional Justice', Policy Brief (2019), 11, at https://www.ifit-transitions.org/resources/publications/major-publications-briefings/changing-the-narrative-the-role-of-communications-in-transitional-justice/changing-the-narrative-en.pdf/view.

543 For instance, the *ad hoc* tribunals and other courts (SCSL, ECCC, STL) have all adapted their mandate or developed new strategies to counter closure.

4

Procedural Expression

Judicial Theatre, Legal Performance, Discursive Justice

Criminal procedures and trials have traditionally been a focal point of expressivist theory. Human rights discourse views international criminal justice as instrument in the 'fight against impunity'. However, the role of proceedings is often less 'strictly repressive' than 'signifying or symbolic'.[1] An essential element of their value lies in their communicative functions.

Procedures shape the social process through which meaning is created.[2] They have a strong demonstrative function. They demonstrate that law is not simply 'in the books'. They create new social relations. For instance, they define relationships between agents in proceedings (e.g. victims and perpetrators), domestic and international spheres of responsibility, or constitute 'communities of suffering and fate'.[3] Participation of agents in proceedings and communicative processes related thereto are an inherent part of access to justice, answerability of crimes before the law,[4] and the legitimation of procedures.[5] Some voices claim that they serve not only to demonstrate fairness but to illustrate the virtues of 'deliberative democracy'.[6]

As Niklas Luhman has argued in his work on legitimation through procedure, legal procedures typically differ from rituals by their open outcome. Uncertainty is to some extent the 'driving force' of proceedings.[7] The legal process enjoys legitimacy as a process between agents because it may lead to spectrum of possible events.[8] It carries the promise of a decision and may gradually reduce uncertainty.

[1] See Diane Bernard, 'Faut-il croire en le droit (international pénal)? Religion et symbolique dans le projet de justice internationale pénale' (2016) 13 *Penal Field* 1–39, 1.

[2] See generally Jan M Broekman and Larry Catà Backer, *Lawyers Making Meaning: The Semiotics of Law in Legal Education II* (New York, NY: Springer, 2013).

[3] Frédéric Mégret, 'In Defense of Hybridity: Towards a Representational Theory of International Criminal Justice' (2005) 38 *Cornell International Law Journal* 725–51, 472.

[4] See Pablo De Greiff, 'Deliberative Democracy and Punishment' (2002) 5 *Buffalo Criminal Law Review* 373–403, 392 ('According to expressionism, what makes a trial, specifically, distinct from other judicial or psychiatric inquires, is "that the defendant should participate in his trial: he is called to answer the charges laid against him"').

[5] Niklas Luhmann, *Legitimation durch Verfahren* (Frankfurt: Suhrkamp, 1983) 55–135.

[6] See Marlies Glasius, 'Do International Criminal Courts Require Democratic Legitimacy?' (2012) 23 *EJIL Democratic Legitimacy* 43–66, 61 ('they can be seen as an expression of deliberative reason-giving, that could in principle persuade victims, the public, and even the offender of the version of affairs proposed by the judges, and, if applicable, the justness of the punishment in light of the offence').

[7] Luhmann, *Legitimation durch Verfahren* 116.

[8] Ibid., 45.

Justice as Message. Carsten Stahn, Oxford University Press (2020). © Carsten Stahn.
DOI: 10.1093/oso/9780198864189.001.0001

The force of the legal process as instrument of communication derives partly from its symbolic and interactive form. Agents in proceedings are connected through social contacts and role-taking. They do not encounter each other as private individuals, but in specific roles. Luhmann has called this the 'crater' of procedure ('*Trichter des Verfahrens*').[9] If parties engage in proceedings and assume the ascribed or expected roles, they cannot but accept the outcome.

The communicative relations go far beyond the mere relationship between judge, offender and victim.[10] They may be understood as an attempt to frame a collective conscience.[11] The value of proceedings lies not only in their ability to produce certain legal outcomes, such as acquittal and conviction punishment, but also in their contribution to the creation of social 'bonds' and relationships that may foster the goals of international criminal justice.[12]

Performance and communication play a key role in the legal process.[13] International criminal proceedings bear close synergies to 'morality plays'.[14] These performative dimensions are often misunderstood. Some scholars see the value of international criminal proceedings in their 'normative performance, including their role as transformative rituals.[15] For instance, David Luban has defended the 'dramatic force' and didactic features of trials.[16] Milner S. Ball has characterized the justice process as a particular type of 'theatre' which gives 'place to an expression of humanity'.[17] It is a medium through which the legal system stages itself. It presents 'an image of the manner in which citizens are to have parts of importance and dignity, to be taken seriously and with ceremonious, protective deference, and to have their rights and duties fairly recognized'.[18] Others are more sceptical towards

[9] Ibid., 115.

[10] They involve many of types of discursive relationships: communicative processes between norm producers, norm appliers, and norm addresses; communications between litigants in proceedings; or communications between judicial entitities and other legal actors, citizens, or professional communities.

[11] Salif Nimage, , 'An International Conscience Collective? A Durkheimian Analysis of International Criminal Law' (2007) 7 *International Criminal Law Review* 561–619, 610.

[12] Ibid., 610.

[13] There is a rich literature on trials and theatre and performance, see Yasco Horsman, *Theaters of Justice: Judging, Staging, and Working Through in Arendt, Brecht and Delbo* (Stanford, CA: Stanford University Press, 2011); Henning Grunwald, *Courtroom to Revolutionary Stage: Performance and Ideology in Weimar Political Trials* (Oxford: Oxford University Press, 2012); Martha Merill Umphrey, 'Law in Drag: Trials and Legal Performativity' (2011) 21 *Columbia Journal of Gender and Law* 114–29; Awol Allo, 'The 'Show' in the "Show Trial": Contextualizing the Politicization of the Courtroom (2010) 15 *Barry Law Review*, 41–72.

[14] Thurman Arnold, 'The criminal trial as a symbol of public morality', in Yale Kamisar, Fred E. Inbau, and Thurman Arnold (eds), *Criminal Justice in Our Time* (Charlottesville, VA: University Press of Virginia, 1965), 137–61, 143–4.

[15] Kate Leader, 'The Trial's the Thing: Performance and Legitimacy in International Criminal Trials' (2018) *Theoretical Criminology* 1–17, 12–13.

[16] David Luban, 'Fairness to rightness: Jurisdiction, legality, and the legitimacy of international criminal law' in Samantha Besson and John Tasioulas (eds), *The Philosophy of International Law* (Cambridge: Cambridge University Press, 2010), 569–88, 587.

[17] Milner S. Ball, 'The Play's the Thing: An Unscientific Reflection on Courts under the Rubric of Theater (1975) 28 *Stanford Law Review* 81–115, 115.

[18] Ibid., 113.

performative understandings, and in particular the analogy to 'theatre'. For instance, Hannah Arendt has cautioned that trials lose their virtue as performances of justice if they turn into mere 'show' or 'theatre'.[19]

In the legal literature, analogies to performance carry certain pejorative connotations. The idea that justice is 'theatre'[20] stands in contradiction to some of the basic premises of international criminal justice, namely its ambition to be real (rather than illusory), objective (rather than inter-subjective), impartial[21] (rather than guided by specific motives), and determined by a search for truth (rather than scripted).[22] The notion of 'show trials' raises concerns in relation to the fairness and dignity of defendants because of its classical association with staged 'political' trials.[23]

However, performances are not always 'harmful to the pursuit of justice'.[24] All trials are 'show trials' in the sense that they seek to demonstrate something. The real question is thus not whether trials should have performative features, but rather what type of performance they entail.[25] They may be 'shows in a positive sense'.[26] As Jessie Allen provocatively put it: 'International courts of human rights do not substitute spectacle for enforcement. Their success as law courts is dependent on that spectacle. The theater ... is what makes them real courts of law.'[27]

4.1 International Criminal Proceedings as Performative and Semiotic Processes

Legal proceedings share many features of classical dramas. They involve a space, an audience, and a plot, which is written through the interaction of participants.[28] The action takes place in a certain unity of time and place.[29] The

[19] Hannah Arendt, *Eichmann in Jerusalem: A Report on the Banality of Evil* (New York, NY: Penguin, 1977), 8.

[20] Jeremy Bentham criticized English common law courts for 'theatre of justice'. This image suggested that courts are illusory or insincere. See Jeremy Bentham, Rationale of Judicial Evidence, Book III, Chapter V, in William Tait Bowring (ed.), *The Works of Jeremy Bentham*, Vol. VI, 286 (Edinburgh: William Tait), 1838–43.

[21] This image is often represented by the blindfolded *Justitia*.

[22] See Erwin Griswold, 'The Standards of the Legal Profession: Canon 35 Should not Be Surrendered' (1962) 48 *American Bar Association Journal* 615–18, 616.

[23] Allo, 'The "Show" in the Show Trials' 66.

[24] Jessie Allen, 'Performing Justice' (2018) 2 *Emotions: History, Culture, Society* 52–70, 54.

[25] The spectrum ranges from predominantly legal justice (justice theatre) to 'show trials' in the negative sense. See Nils Christie, 'Crime Control as Drama' (1986) 13 *Journal of Law and Society* 1–8, 3 ('play is a good one, as long as it concentrates on the question of guilt').

[26] Allo, 'The "Show" in the Show Trials' 62.

[27] Jessie Allen, 'Theater of International Justice' (2012) 3 *Creighton International & Comparative Law Journal* 121–47, 131.

[28] Denis J. Brion, 'The criminal trial as theatre: The semiotic power of the image' in Anne Wagner and Richard K Sherwin (eds), *Law, Culture and Visual Studies* (New York, NY: Springer 2014), 329–59; Milner S. Ball, 'All the Law's a Stage' (1999) 11 *Cardozo Studies in Law and Literature* 215–21.

[29] Richard Harbinger, 'Trial by Drama' (1971) 55 *Judicature* 122–8.

courtroom audience shares the same physical space as judicial agents. There is some degree of separation between the individuals who are speaking and acting and their words and actions. Actions carry performative features because the 'acts, speech, and gestures do not originate entirely with individuals who do and say these things'.[30] Legal actions are shaped by legal rules, rituals, or expected forms of behaviour. They rely on previous cases, Courtroom performances, legal scripts, or existing policies (e.g. prosecutorial policies). They are not only part of the 'here and now', but in secret or imaginative dialogue with the past. They are part of a 'performance of tradition' that views the trial itself in 'as a bulwark of justice and authority'.[31]

4.1.1 Performative foundations

Criminal procedures gain their meaning not only through a projection of formal legal rules and juridical principles but through their relational dimensions. Performative theories are helpful to understand the expressive dimensions of legal procedures, including their visual, symbolic, and transformative features.[32] Guidance may be derived from the concepts of *mimesis*, *poiesis*, and *kinesis*, that is, 'imitation', 'construction', and 'dynamics',[33] which go back to Aristotle's concepts of narration.

Aristotle claimed in *Poetics* that classical drama is deemed to imitate actions of life (*mimesis*).[34] Criminal proceedings involve such imitation. They seek to reflect real-life events and reproduce the crime in proceedings, in order to reveal what actually happened. They involve a dual act: a reinstitution of the law, and a re-enactment of the crime, as it is understood in the form of the law. This process of representation is mediated through actors in the justice process, such as judges, prosecutors, defence lawyers, and victims. It refers back to previous ways of 'doing, acting, seeing and believing'.[35]

[30] Allen, 'Theater of International Justice' 139.

[31] Kate Leader, 'Bound and Gagged: The Performance of Tradition in the Adversarial Criminal Jury Trial' (2007) 11 *Philament* 1, and 13 (the 'performance of tradition is, therefore, far from "mere" theatrics; rather, it is a process that, through its exploitation of live performance, functions to sustain the mythology of a (fair) trial . . . This emphasis on repeated enaction manufactures, almost as a by-product, the power of the law.') at http://www.philamentjournal.com/wp-content/uploads/2016/05/LEADER_BoundGagged.pdf.

[32] See Julie Stone Peters, 'Law as performance: Historical interpretation, objects, lexicons, and other methodological problems' in Elizabeth S. Anker and Bernadette Meyler, *New Directions in Law and Literature* (New York, NY: Oxford University Press, 2017), 193–209, .

[33] See Dwight Conquergood 'Beyond the text: Towards a performative cultural politics' in Sheron J. Dailey (ed.), *The Future of Performance Studies: Visions and Revisions* (Annandale, VA: National Communication Association, 1998), 15–36, 31.

[34] See Elizabeth Bell, *Theories of Performance* (Thousand Oaks, CA: Sage, 2008), 12.

[35] Ibid., 17.

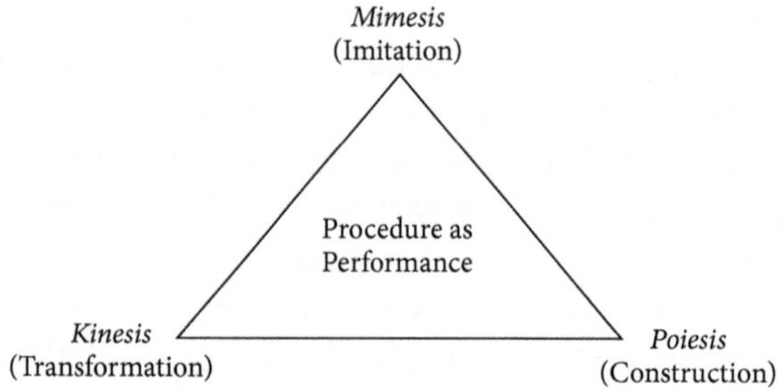

Figure 11 Procedure as performance

The reproduction of the crime involves an active process of construction (*poiesis*), that is, 'making' sense of events ('making not faking').[36] As Martha Merill Umphrey has observed, trials 'not only enact law, both theatrically and linguistically, in their very doing, but also performatively constitute the law they enact'.[37]

Proceedings seek to place the past into a common frame, but they also construct reality. Legal actions, such as the framing of cases and presentation of evidence, entail 'breaking and remaking'. Parties and proceedings rely on strategies to persuade audiences inside or outside the courtroom of their narratives. For instance, in the *Milošević* case, the Office of the Prosecutor (OTP) showed the Scorpions video not only for evidentiary purposes but rather to show the public what had happened.[38] Performative theorists make the point that criminal proceedings 'represent and replay social conflict and violence, turning history into dramatic narrative, fictionalizing social trauma, transforming it into the system of social representations, exchanges, surrogacies that make up the law'.[39] They institute new social relations, create identities, or produce new legal meanings.

This process, and performative exchange in proceedings, leads to a certain transformation; that is, movement, motion, fluidity (*kinesis*).[40] It alters society to a certain extent. For instance, certain narratives are confirmed while others are rejected. New information may emerge through party submissions, legal exchanges, disclosure, testimony, or examination of evidence. Decisions give effect to arguments, affirm authenticity, or create legal authority. Agents who interpret legal norms may attach new meanings to them. Ultimately, the trial as a whole may remake social or

[36] Victor Turner, *From Ritual to Theatre* (New York, NY: Performing Arts Journal Publications, 1982), 93.

[37] Umphrey, 'Law in Drag' 120.

[38] On the video, see Iva Vukušić, 'Nineteen Minutes of Horror: Insights from the Scorpions Execution Video' (2018) 12 *Genocide Studies and Prevention* 35–53.

[39] Julie Stone Peters, 'Legal Performance Good and Bad Law' (2008) 4 *Culture and the Humanities* 179–200, 185.

[40] Beatrice De Graaf, 'Terrorists on Trial: A Performative Perspective', Expert Paper, 30 March 2011, 7.

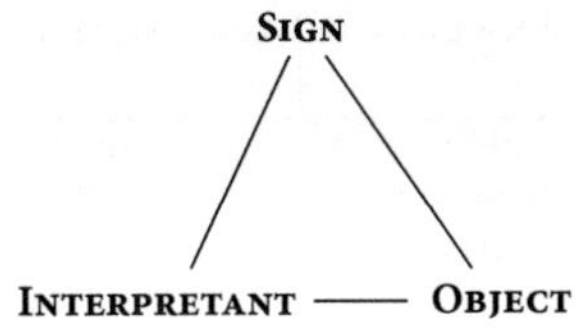

Figure 12 Sign theory, Peirce

legal rules. For example, the judgment, punishment, or sentencing relate not only to the defendant but also to imagined future offenders.

4.1.2 Procedures and sign theory

Criminal proceedings are semiotic processes[41] which involve signs and 'significations', practices which give meaning.[42] They are driven by the dynamics of interaction between agents. This interaction involves the production and communication of meaning. As Susan Tiefenbrun has argued:

> The words with which we give testimony … and interpret legal texts are mere signs—only indirect expressions of a reality at least one step removed from the thing itself. Therefore, speakers and listeners in a legal context are constantly engaged in a kind of informal interpretation process that can be described as semiotic analysis. Interpretation enables the parties to decode the messages and understand the explicit or implicit signs embedded in the legal discourse that confronts them and produces confusion.[43]

Signs are not only conveyed through use of language,[44] what actors say and perform, but also through non-verbal communication.

Some insights on the role of signs in legal processes may be derived from semiotics. A sign is something that stands for something. American philosopher and logician Charles Sanders Peirce, one of the leading semiotic theorists, has developed a triadic theory of signs.[45] He has argued that signs consist of three signifying elements: a sign, an object, and an interpretant.

[41] The notion derives from the Greek word semion (sign). See Susan Tiefenbrun, *Decoding International Law: Semiotics and the Humanities* (New York, NY: Oxford University Press, 2010).

[42] On 'signification' in cultural studies, see Stuart Hall, 'Encoding, Decoding' in Simon During (ed.), *The Cultural Studies Reader*, 2nd. edn (New York, NY: Routledge, 1993), 507–17.

[43] Susan W. Tiefenbrun, 'Legal Semiotics' (1986) 5 *Cardozo Arts & Entertainment Law Journal* 89–156, 98–9.

[44] Brenda Danet, 'Language in the Legal Process' (1980) 14 *Law & Society Review* 445–564.

[45] Charles Sanders Peirce, 'Logic as semiotic: The theory of signs' in Justis Buchler (ed.), *Philosophical Writings of Peirce* (New York, NY: Dover, 1955) 98–119.

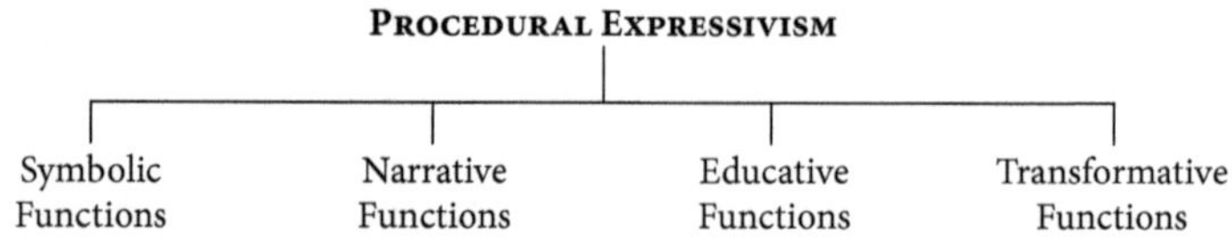

Figure 13 Procedural expressivism

The first one is the sign itself, that is, the sign vehicle or signifier. It can be a word or an utterance. The second one is the object that the sign refers to, the 'signified'. It encompasses the object related to the word or utterance. The interpretant is the most distinctive element of Peirce's theory. It relates to the understanding of the relation between sign and object. A sign can carry different meanings. The interpretant conveys the meaning which is signified by the sign. It is shaped by the interpreter's own conception of reality and events. The process of creating meaning is thus dynamic.[46]

Peirce's triadic structure of signs has continuing relevance for the understanding of international law as an evolving 'structure of meaning and knowledge':

> [O]bjects are known through signs, which, in their turn can only be understood in terms of yet other signs ... [S]ince an object is only known through mediation of a sign, which calls for further interpretation in terms of other signs, there can be no absolute beginning or definitive end of knowledge.[47]

This understanding helps to conceptualize the relational aspects of proceedings. It makes sense of the mediated nature of law, including the impediments that may arise in communication.[48]

Trials live through signals between parties and participants. They form a semiotic system of narration. For instance, an argument presented by legal parties constitutes a 'sign'. It becomes a sign of law through the interpretant, that is, its understanding as part of a system or structure of signs.[49] The interpretant is shaped by the institutional structure through which law is 'produced' and the procedural context in which law is 'embodied'.[50] It is formed by the meaning attached to certain signs by legal codes and supported by hypotheses of agents about such conventions, and the consequences attached to them.

[46] See also Vincent Colapietro, 'Peircean Semeiotic and Legal Practices: Rudimentary and "Rhetorical" Considerations' (2008) 21 *International Journal for the Semiotics of Law* 223–46, 240.

[47] Wouter G. Werner, 'Securitization and Judicial Review: A Semiotic Perspective on the Relation Between the Security Council and International Judicial Bodies' (2001) 14 *International Journal for the Semiotics of Law* 345–66, 365.

[48] Thomas Mathiesen, *Prison on Trial* (Winchester: Waterside Press, 2006) 65–8.

[49] Ibid., 66.

[50] Roger Cotterrell, 'The Sociological Concept of Law' (1983) 10 *Journal of Law and Society* 241–55.

During proceedings, these signs are meant to influence the position of other participants to proceedings, to persuade the judge, or to appeal to a broader public. Lawyers 'make meaning and attempt to manage it on behalf of their clients' or constituencies.[51] They use their legal skills to transform raw material into lines of argumentation that are accepted in legal discourse. These plots frame a history of their own, what Luhmann called a 'history of adjudication' (*Verfahrensgeschic hte*).[52] Every statement or argument made by lawyers determines the options for the other party.

Criminal procedures introduce a common ground between the social world and human subjects. The purpose of the trial to test *inter alia* whether the 'signs' communicated in speech (e.g. charges) are sufficiently related to objects in the real-life world (evidence). As the International Criminal Tribunal for the former Yugoslavia (ICTY) noted: 'Every criminal trial involves two issues: first, that the crimes charged have been committed and, second, that an accused is responsible for those crimes. The object of evidence is to ascertain the truth of the facts with respect to these two issues.'[53]
The criminal process as a whole is not 'just a system which prosecutes and punishes offenders against a law' but an 'institution' which produces certain 'designations of reality'.[54] It involves signs by institutions which communicate certain meanings, such as fair and equal treatment of offenders, as well as 'politics of signification'.[55]

Problems emerge when the 'signifier' and the 'signified object' lack a common interpretant. This has been of the striking problems in relation to testimony. International criminal procedure has suffered from testimonial deficiencies and evidentiary uncertainties. There are not only language barriers[56] but differences in the correlation between signs and objects. This makes it necessary to be sensitive to the emotive function of words.[57] Signs may be misinterpreted,[58] since different

[51] See Francis J. Mootz, 'Vico and Imagination: An Ingenious Approach to Educating Lawyers with Semiotic Sensibility' (2009) 22 *International Journal for the Semiotics of Law* 11–22, 21.

[52] Niklas Luhmann, Legitimation durch Verfahren (Frankfurt: Suhrkamp, 1983), 44–5.

[53] Prosecutor v. Brđanin, IT-99-36-T, 1 September 2004, para. 21.

[54] Mathiesen, *Prison on Trial* 67–8.

[55] Ibid., 67–8.

[56] See Leigh Swigart, 'Unseen and unsung: Language services at the International Criminal Court and their impact on institutional legitimacy' in Freya Baetens (ed.), *Legitimacy of Unseen Actors in International Adjudication* (Cambridge: Cambridge University Press, 2019), 272–96.

[57] In the *Akayesu* case, an expert witness testified that 'is a particular feature of the Rwandan culture that people are not always direct in answering questions, especially if the question is delicate. In such cases, the answers given will very often have to be "decoded" in order to be understood correctly. This interpretation will rely on the context, the particular speech community, the identity of and the relation between the orator and the listener, and the subject matter of the question.' See *Akayesu* Trial Judgment, para. 156.

[58] As Nancy Combs has noted, 'sometimes questions go unanswered' because 'witnesses do not understand the questions they are asked or the Western court personnel do not understand the answers that they receive'. Nancy Amoury Combs, 'Testimonial Deficiencies and Evidentiary Uncertainties in International Criminal Trials' (2009) 14 *UCLA Journal of International Law & Foreign Affairs* 235–73, 245.

cultures ascribe different meanings to the relation between sign and object.[59] In such cases, judges assume the role of an interpretant.

Judgments themselves may be viewed as signs. They have a mediating function. They are like 'mirrors', which invite others to look 'through the looking-glass'.[60] They point to future decisions. They provide incentives to other courts to apply these findings in related cases.[61]

4.2 Forms and Functions of Procedural Expressivism

Procedural expression involves different forms and functions.

4.2.1 Typology of functions

Procedural expressivism may be theorized through the lens of at least four broader functions: symbolic functions, narrative functions, educational functions, and transformative functions.

4.2.1.1 Symbolic functions

International criminal procedures are representational practices which allow individuals and institutions to engage with each other through the medium of law. As Shoshana Felman has argued, in international criminal justice, the function of a court 'is in its very *moral essence*, a *dramatic* function: not only that of "doing justice," but that of "*making justice seen*" in a larger moral and historically unique sense'.[62]

[59] Such problems emerged *inter alia* at the International Criminal Tribunal for Rwanda (ICTR) and the Special Court for Sierra Leone (SCSL). At the ICTR, interpreters struggled with the meaning of 'dates, times, distances and locations' given to events by witnesses and the use of the word *Inyenzi* (cockroach) which had relevance for genocidal intent, or cultural taboos associated with the concept of rape. See *Akayesu* Trial Judgment, paras 152–156. In Sierra Leone, cross-cultural discrepancies emerged *inter alia* in relation to the meaning of childhood. Defendants challenged the meaning of charges for child recruitment before the SCSL, based on cultural differences as to when a human being should be treated as a child and bears responsibility. Critics have noted that 'by prosecuting individuals for this crime, the Special Court arguably held those concerned to an alien standard of justice of which they knew nothing, imposing international norms and law on people, raised in a different culture, with contrasting moral ideas'. See Tim Kelsall, 'International Criminal Justice and Non-Western Cultures', Oxford Transitional Justice Research Working Paper Series, 12 April 2010, 2–3.

[60] See Ferry De Jong, 'The End of Doctrine? On the Symbolic Function of Doctrine in Substantive Criminal Law' (2011) 7 *Utrecht Law Review* 8–45, 38.

[61] See Marjolein Cupido, 'The Casuistry of International Criminal Law: Exploring A New Field of Research' (2015) 44 *Netherlands Journal of Legal Philosophy* 116–32, 126.

[62] Shoshana Felman, 'A Ghost in the House of Justice: Death and the Language of the Law' (2001) 13 *Yale Journal of Law & the Humanities* 241–82, 277–8; Shoshana Felman, *The Juridical Unconscious: Trials and Traumas in the Twentieth Century* (Cambridge: Harvard University Press, 2002), 162.

The principle of 'open justice' is key for the symbolic function. Public accessibility, visibility, and an audience reflect a will to see justice being done.[63]

Criminal procedures carry multiple symbolic meanings. They visualize or demonstrate atrocities. They show that criminal conduct is open to adjudication, condemnation, or reparation.[64] They imply certain messages about the form and types of justice that are required to address alleged violations. For instance, the fact that wrongdoing is treated in a formal criminal justice procedure, rather than a civil, military, or disciplinary procedure or a more flexible transitional justice mechanisms (e.g. truth and reconciliation commissions),[65] says something about the nature and gravity of the alleged conduct.[66]

In a more general sense, the application of criminal procedure may be seen as an expression of fairness[67] and procedural justice[68] in an attempt to convince others to respect law, even in the absence of formal enforcement procedures.[69] In this sense, criminal trials can 'be seen as normative demonstrations of the rule of law'.[70] The types of procedures applied, and the treatment of defendants, prosecutors, witnesses, and victims convey signals in relation to fairness standards.[71] They seek to counter the perception that the defendant is subject to a symbolic sacrifice.[72]

[63] See Denise Meyerson, 'Why Should Justice Be Seen to Be Done?' (2015) 34 *Criminal Justice Ethics* 64–86; Linda Mulcahy, *Legal Architecture: Justice, Due Process and the Place of Law* (Abingdon: GlassHouse, 2011); Jason Bosland and Jonathan Gill, 'The Principle of Open Justice and the Judicial Duty to Give Public Reasons' (2014) 38 *Melbourne University Law Review* 482–524.

[64] For instance, the Eichmann trial was not only a means to prove 'unimaginable facts', but, above all, as a medium to communicate 'thought-defying facts' to national and international audiences. The vivid testimony brought out by witnesses stood in stark to the bureaucratic rationalizations invoked by the defendant. See Felman, 'A Ghost in the House of Justice' 243.

[65] On criminal law institutions as response to 'cultures of impunity', see Payam Akhavan, 'Beyond Impunity: Can International Criminal Justice Prevent Future Atrocities?' (2001) 95 *AJIL* 7–31, 7.

[66] The symbolic dimensions of criminal proceedings go beyond artistic performances (i.e. theatre). They involve not only the power to re-enact events, but may inflict legal obligations or sanctions with real-life consequences. See Felman, 'A Ghost in the House of Justice' 264 ('A work of art cannot sentence to death.').

[67] Fairness needs to be assessed in a contextual way. It requires a balancing of interests, such as rights of victims and rights of accused, fairness and expeditiousness of proceedings, or crime control and due process more generally. See Mirjan Damaška, 'The Competing Visions of Fairness: The Basic Choice for International Criminal Tribunals' (2010) 36 *North Carolina Journal of International Law and Commercial Regulation*, 365–88, 380.

[68] There is an inherent connection between fairness and procedural justice. See Tom R. Tyler, 'Procedural Justice, Legitimacy, and the Effective Rule of Law' (2003) 30 *Crime and Justice* 283–357, 292–3; Fréderic Mégret, 'Beyond "Fairness": Understanding the Determinants of International Criminal Procedure' (2009) 14 *UCLA Journal of International Law and Foreign Affairs* 37–76.

[69] In practice, there is a tendency to assume that international procedures should symbolize the hightest standards or reflect 'ideal' human rights protections. However, as Mirjan Damaška has argued, this aspiration must be reconciled with the realities of atrocity crime contexts. See Damaška, 'Reflections on Fairness in International Criminal Justice' 611.

[70] See Lawrence Douglas, 'The Didactic Trial: Filtering History and Memory into the Courtroom' (2006) 14 *European Review* 513–22, 514.

[71] This is reflected in the famous image of the 'poisoned chalice'used at Nuremberg: 'To pass these defendants a poisoned chalice is to put it to our own lips.' On Jackson's influence, see Henry T. King Jr, 'Robert H. Jackson and the Triumph of Justice at Nuremberg' (2003) 35 *Case Western Reserve Journal of International Law* 263–72.

[72] John Borneman, *Settling Accounts: Violence, Justice, and Accountability in Postsocialist Europe* (Princeton, NJ: Princeton University Press, 1997).

The cases that are selected and pursued are often symbolic. They seek to strengthen the idea of accountability before the law. They stand for whole patterns of other cases that ought to be adjudicated but are left untreated by international criminal institutions or domestic courts.[73]

Proceedings entail messages about access to justice. They signal who is being affected by crime and who should be given a voice in the criminal process. An important element is the expression of repudiation, an action that rejects 'the permissibility of the treatment the victim experienced'.[74] It involves two elements: acknowledgment that 'wrongdoing occurred' and an acknowledgment that it requires condemnation.

4.2.1.2 Narrative functions

Throughout the legal process, international criminal proceedings rely on narrative form and diverse ways of narration.[75] They are a means to turn 'chaos' into order and provide a comprehensible story of events.[76] Courtroom interactions may be regarded as a set of stories which make up the story of the trial. They involve a high degree of procedural storytelling. Facts are rarely 'given', but rather created in the process of adjudication,[77] Proceedings require narration and evaluation, in order to connect social facts to legal concepts.[78]

International criminal justice has a strongly narrative culture. It relies in general on the principle of orality at trial. The testimony of each witness presents a story in itself, which is performed through the statement and aimed at persuading others.

The construction of facts is shaped by courtroom interaction. Prosecutors and defendants are 'required to construct their stories around the rules of evidence'.[79] Each party creates a narrative based on its own perception of the story, subject to the constraints of criminal procedure.[80] For instance, the charges presented by the

[73] Landsman attributes such an effect to the *Demjanjuk* case, arguing that US decisions in the case 'went beyond the guilt or innocence of a particular defendant, each one helped to complete the historical record on what America had done ... in response to the Holocaust'. Stephan Landsman, *Crimes of the Holocaust: The Law Confronts Hard Cases* (Philadelphia, PA University of Pennsylvania Press, 2005), 123.

[74] Colleen Murphy, *Conceptual Foundations of Transitional Justice* (Cambridge: Cambridge University Press, 2017), 181.

[75] On narratives, see Barrie Sander, 'History on Trial: Historical Narrative Pluralism Within and Beyond International Criminal Courts', (2018) 67 *ICLQ* 547–76.

[76] See Anette Bringedal Houge, 'Narrative Expressivism: A Criminological Approach to the Expressive Function of International Criminal Justice' (2019) 19 *Criminology & Criminal Justice* 277–93.

[77] On narrative fact-construction, see Bernard S. Jackson, 'Law, Fact and Narrative Coherence (Bernard S. Jackson, Law, Fact and Narrative Coherence (Merseyside: Deborah Charles Publications, 1988).

[78] See Peter Brooks and Paul Gerwitz, *Law's Stories: Narrative and Rhetoric in the Law* (New Haven, CT: Yale University Press, 1996).

[79] John D. Jackson, 'Law, Fact and Narrative Coherence: A Deep Look at Court Adjudication' (1990) 7 *International Journal for the Semiotics of Law* 81–95, 93.

[80] Osiel argues that defence counsel tell the story as a tragedy and prosecutors as a morality play. See Mark Osiel, *Mass Atrocity, Collective Memory, and Law* (New Brunswick, CT: Transaction Publishers, 1997), 3.

Prosecution entail narratives. They do not only relate facts to law but demonstrate 'the existence of specific relations between different facts and construct a particular narrative on the basis of which, if true, would cover all the legal elements of the charges with which it corresponds'.[81]

The Prosecutor must not only present a persuasive story but convince the judges that there is no other plausible reading of the evidence. The Defence may present counter-narratives.[82] Narratives are reinforced through the use of metaphors and images.[83] Together, these multiple stories form a broader story of the trial as a whole: 'Witnesses, lawyers, judges and historians seek to persuade by making truth-claims and these are assessed not merely by reference to the plausibility of the claims but by reference to the sincerity and integrity of the claimant.'[84]

The decisions which result from this process bear their own traces of storytelling.[85] They are not simply derived from an application of rule to the facts but are guided by the ambition to trace context and persuade others.[86] As Barrie Sander has argued, they may be addressed to multiple audiences,[87] including other courts and tribunals ('inter-court' narration'),[88] legal representatives of the parties, the defendant or victims ('intra-court' narration'),[89] or non-judicial entities ('narration 'beyond the courtroom').[90] For instance, Prosecutors or judges often seek to contribute to a 'norm nurturing process'[91] or the establishment of a broader pool of jurisprudence that sets footprints or path dependencies for other cases.[92]

[81] *Prosecutor v. Germain Katanga*, Judgment Pursuant to Article 74 of the Statute, ICC-01/04-01/07-3436-AnxI, Minority Opinion of Judge Christine Van den Wyngaert, 7 March 2014, para. 32.

[82] On the Karadžić trial, see Tim Meijers and Marlies Glasius, , 'Expression of Justice or Political Trial? Discursive Battles in the Karadžić Case (2013) 35 Human Rights *Quarterly* 720–52, 746 ('Karadžić is telling a story of himself as the defender of the Serbs as a historical victim, whereas the prosecution tells a story about how Karadžić bears the primary responsibility for the ethnic crimes in Bosnia.').

[83] For instance, metaphors, such as the image of the global child soldier or the ideal of universal culture heritage, are used in order to render violations capable of narration, spread information, and seek emulation.

[84] Jackson, 'Law, Fact and Narrative Coherence: A Deep Look at Court Adjudication' 87.

[85] Meijers and Glasius, 'Expression of Justice or Political Trial?' 746 ('At the end of the trial, judges will come with the version of the story they consider true beyond reasonable doubt.').

[86] Judge Elihu Lauterpacht made express reference to this narrative function in his separate opinion in the *Genocide* case. He noted: 'What will those in later years who are not well instructed in our contemporary history understand of the real thrust and significance of the Court's order if they cannot read therein some narrative of the circumstances which have led to it?' See ICJ, Application of the Convention on the Prevention and Punishment of the Crime of Genocide (*Bosnia and Herzegovina v. Serbia and Montenegro*), Order of 13 September 1993, Separate Opinion of Judge Lauterpacht, ICJ Reports 1993, 407, 425, para. 48.

[87] As has been rightly noted: '[e]ach of these audiences constitutes a particular semiotic group with its own narrativised conventions'. See Jackson, 'Law, Fact and Narrative Coherence: A Deep Look at Court Adjudication' 90.

[88] Sander, 'History on Trial' 550.

[89] See also Felman, *The Juridical Unconscious* 61.

[90] Sander, 'History on Trial' 568.

[91] Paul H. Robinson and John M. Darley, 'The Utility of Desert' (1997) 91 *Northwestern University Law Review* 453–99, 473, 477.

[92] Generally, legal decisions and judgments do not suffice to create new norms under international law. But judicial storytelling and narratives reflected in the reasoning contribute to norm nuturing or

Conceived in this narrative way, the criminal process gains a different perspective. It becomes

> eligible for the same kinds of questions that we put to fictional stories, such as questions about how the reader is positioned in relation to the characters, which characters are allowed to interact with each other, what kind of information is rendered inaccessible, and why some details are presented directly and others at second-hand.[93]

4.2.1.3 Educative functions

The educative function of international criminal procedures is one of the most debated elements of procedural expression. Such didactic rationales are mostly associated with truth-telling and historical clarification.

As Richard Wilson has shown, international criminal justice is marked by a paradox.[94] International criminal procedures are ill-equipped to provide comprehensive historical judgement, due to their inherent limitations. The very idea of individualizing responsibility sits uneasily with the purpose of establishing a historical record.[95] However, courts can hardly avoid creating a historical record.[96] They inevitably frame historical discourse and are thus formative of history itself.[97]

In general, there are three different positions on the interplay between history and the didactic rationales of trials.[98] Some scholars argue that history-telling is a legitimate goal of proceedings, namely part of their 'didactic legality'. They claim that historical clarification is necessary in order to understand the general context of atrocity, establish the contextual elements of crimes, and contribute to the

development of the law. On judicial development of the law, see ane Darcy, *Judges, Law and War: The Judicial Development of International Humanitarian Law* (Cambridge: Cambridge University Press, 2014), 21–81.

[93] Simon Stern, 'Narrative in the legal text: Judicial opinions and their narratives' in Michael Hanne and Robert Weisberg (eds), *Narrative and Metaphor in the Law* (Cambridge: Cambridge University Press, 2018), 121–39, 135.

[94] Richard Wilson, *Writing History in International Criminal Trials* (Cambridge: Cambridge University Press, 2011) 18.

[95] On the incompatibility theory', see ibid., 6–8.

[96] Barrie Sander, 'Unveiling the Historical Function of International Criminal Courts: Between Adjudicative and Sociopolitical Justice'(2018) 12 *International Journal of Transitional Justice* 334–55, 355. See also Leora Bilsky, 'The Judge and the Historian: Transnational Holocaust Litigation as a New Model' (2012) 24 *History and Memory* 117–56.

[97] See Douglas, 'The Didactic Trial' 514 ('The question is not whether the trial can serve the interests of history and memory, but how it can do so responsibly.'). See also Patricia M. Wald, 'Foreword: War Tales and War Trials' (2008) 106 *Michigan Law Review* 901–22, 911.

[98] See also Elinor Fry, 'The nature of international crimes and evidentiary challenges: Preserving quality while managing quantity' in Elies van Sliedregt and Sergey Vasiliev (eds), *Pluralism in International Criminal Law* (Oxford: Oxford University Press, 2014) 251–99, 253–65.

formation of collective memory,[99] keep 'the world's collective memory' of events alive.[100]

Other authorities questions whether procedures should be treated as a means to teach 'history lessons'. Hannah Arendt expressed this view most forcefully in her observations on the Eichmann trial when noting that the 'purpose of a trial is to render justice and nothing else'.[101] This position is grounded in a defence of the liberal foundations of trials ('liberal legalism'),[102] namely the idea that trials should focus on determinations on crimes and responsibility. Recognizing history-telling as didactic rationale would conflict with the rights of defendants, or extend the inherent the limits of criminal proceedings[103] which differ from historical methods.[104]

A third, intermediate position views historical clarification as useful didactic by-product of proceedings. This view recognizes that trials rely on historical and political analysis and engage in readings or interpretations of history.[105] The District Court of Jerusalem defended this approach in *Eichmann*.[106]

The close nexus between historical context and trials is not only reflected in judgments and legal decisions but also in speeches, opening statements, outreach practices, or witness statements. The particular value of the legal process lies in the fact that it ensures a certain degree of authenticity through testing of facts and evidence in the courtroom.[107]

[99] Douglas, *The Memory of Judgment: Making Law and History in the Trials of the Holocaust* (New Haven, CT: Yale University Press, 2001), 2; Osiel, *Mass Atrocity, Collective Memory and the Law* 2.

[100] Doris Buss, 'Expert witnesses and international war crimes trials: Making sense of large-scale violence in Rwanda' in Dubravaka Zarkov and Marlies Glasius (eds), *Narratives of Justice in and out of the Courtroom: Former Yugoslavia and Beyond* (The Hague: Springer, 2014), 23–44, 35.

[101] Hannah Arendt, *Eichmann in Jerusalem* 243.

[102] See Gary Bass, *Stay the Hand of Vengeance: The Politics of War Crimes Trials* (Princeton, NJ: Princeton University Press, 2000), 7–8.

[103] *Prosecutor v. Stanisić and Simatović*, Decision Pursuant to Rule 73 bis(D), IT-03-69-PT, 4 February 2008, para. 21 ('[T]he Tribunal was established to administer justice, and not to create a historical record'); *Prosecutor v. Karadžić*, Decision on the Accused's Holbrooke Agreement Motion, IT-95-5/18-T, 8 July 2009, para 46 ('The Chamber's purpose is not to serve the academic study of history.').

[104] For instance, context is selectively treated. Legal proceedings are governed by evidentiary regimes that are geared towards exclusion, rather than inclusion. The trial seeks to simplify social relations, and fit them into the rubrics of legal concepts (hierarchy, responsibility, causation). See Joachim S. Savelsberg and Ryan D. King, 'Law and Collective Memory' (2007) 3 *Annual Review Law Social Science* 189–211, 194 ('following the binary logic of criminal law, the defendant is guilty or not guilty, a gross simplification compared with social scientific standards').

[105] See also Richard Wilson, 'Humanity's Histories: Evaluating the Historical Accounts of International Tribunals and Truth Commissions' (2007) 80 *Politix* 31–58.

[106] See District Court of Jerusalem, *Israel v. Adolf Eichmann*, Criminal Case 40/61, Judgment, 11 December 1961, para. 2 ('Without a doubt the testimony given at this trial by survivors of the Holocaust, who pouted out their hearts as they stood in the witness box, will provide valuable material for research workers and historians, but as far as this Court is concerned, they are to be regarded as by products of the trial.').

[107] For instance, witnesses may be asked to give testimony under oath, documents are verified, and all evidence is assessed by judges.

It is more difficult to establish whether and how trials produce pedagogic effects through procedural expression.[108] Whether such effects occur depends on 'how the legal process imparts skills in judgment, adjudication, or investigation that empower people to apply lessons learned from one context to another and to critically evaluate conclusions drawn by various authorities'.[109]

There is a wide spectrum of opinion as to how international criminal procedures influence opinion. Some scholars argue that procedures contribute to historical clarification and may mitigate competing factual or legal claims as 'bookkeepers of history'.[110] For example, Court-established evidence, including forensic evidence, may be reflected in historical documentation and reduce divergence of opinion.[111] Others point to affective and cognitive features of criminal proceedings. For instance, Lawrence Douglas has insisted that trials 'actively re-impos[e] norms into spaces in which rule-based legality has been either radically evacuated or perverted'.[112] Milner Ball has argued that trials may have an educative effect, when 'they treat the parties as individuals', 'instead of deliberately undertaking to teach'. [113]

Other authorities stress the didactic effects that criminal proceedings produce through the public performance or drama that they produce. For example, Mark Osiel and Pablo de Greiff have defended the view that trials are communicative spaces which produce 'discursive solidarity'.[114] They build this argument on the premise that 'democracy begins in conversation'.[115] In their view, trials are lessons in deliberative democracy which teach engagement with counter-argument. They can foster 'micromobilization', 'interactions among actors in which meanings of past events and identities are formed'.[116] They emphasize that accountability is 'not just as a matter of conventional moral imperative, but also as a means for the community to reflect on its shared and reflexive experiences'.[117]

Criminal proceedings have thus undoubtedly didactic features. However, legal pedagogy is a process which evolves over time and goes far beyond the role of judicial entities.[118] As Bronwyn Leebaw has noted:

[108] See Bronwyn Leebaw, 'Justice and the Faithless: The Demand for Disobedience in International Criminal Law' (2018) 24 *European Journal of International Relations* 344–66, 356.

[109] Ibid., 356.

[110] See Savelsberg and King, 'Law and Collective Memory' 193 ('In addition to law's facilitation of such emotionally colored reinterpretations of history and its actors, legal trials also serve as bookkeepers of history.'). They argue that 'Franklin Roosevelt's eventual support for the Nuremberg Tribunal was clearly motivated by this understanding'. Ibid.

[111] Bass, *Stay the Hand of Vengeance* 302.

[112] Douglas, 'The Didactic Trial' 514.

[113] Milner S. Ball, *The Promise of American Law* (Athens, GA: University of Georgia Press, 1981) 56.

[114] Osiel, *Mass Atrocity, Collective Memory and the Law* 51.

[115] Ibid., 45.

[116] Savelsberg and King, 'Law and Collective Memory' 205.

[117] See Allo, 'The "Show" in the Show Trials' 60.

[118] Douglas, 'The Didactic Trial' 520.

> The pedagogical potential of international criminal justice is informed by the decisions of court officials, yet also shaped by the work of scholars, policymakers, and activists that draw attention to the limitations of war crimes investigations, push officials to expand them in new directions, or pursue new policies and protests in response to legal judgments.[119]

For example, legal decisions and judgments may inform future interpretations and meanings, provide guidance to other courts or train 'those participating in a legal order' to 'read the different signs that together make up 'the law'.[120] However, collective memory often takes a life of its own after the end of the legal process. Journalism, art, and media are often the 'first draft of history'.[121] They translate the complex performative functions of trials into publicly digestible messages. Trials come to be seen through other prisms. For example, the Nuremberg trial 'remains remembered in American popular imagination through the vehicle of the famous Hollywood movie, Judgment at Nuremberg, which, in fact, had nothing to do with the trial before the International Military Tribunal'.[122] Similarly, the Eichmann trial came to be understood and read largely through the medium Hannah Arendt's analysis as an observer.[123]

4.2.1.4 Transformative functions

International criminal proceedings have multiple transformative functions. They do not only clarify law or legal principles but translate social facts into the form and language of the law. The application of international criminal law 'transforms the lingually constituted public space' into 'a symbolically dimensioned legal space' that is governed by international legal rules.[124] This process enables legal agents to determine whether a certain social fact is 'in line' or in contravention with legal norms. It creates new categories through which we see the world. Proceedings produce knowledge by 'hearing, translating, weighing, and applying evidence to legal questions'.[125] They introduce classifications regarding the nature of crimes, the conduct of individuals, or their nexus to crimes. This process of knowledge

119 Leebaw, 'Justice and the faithless' 356.
120 De Jong, 'The end of Doctrine' 17.
121 See Thijs Bouwknegt, 'The international criminal trial record as historical source' in Nanci Adler (ed.), *Understanding the Age of Transitional Justice: Crimes, Courts, Commissions, and Chronicling* (New Brunswick, NJ: Rutgers University Press, 2018), 118–48.
122 Douglas, 'The Didactic Trial' 520.
123 Ibid., 521.
124 See De Jong, 'The End of Doctrine' 16.
125 See Doris Buss, 'Knowing Women: Translating Patriarchy in International Criminal Law' (2014) 23 *Social & Legal Studies* 73–92, 75 ('These practices take place not just at the moment of judgment but in the trial process itself (and earlier), as rules of evidence, investigative processes, court procedure, judicial customs, and individual actors structure how the accounts of what happened unfold and are given meaning.').

production[126] serves to tell a legally comprehensible story of 'the crime'[127] and to attach juridical effects to social facts.[128]

Legal truth-finding is a transformative process. International criminal proceedings do not necessarily 'reflect' truth but produce it.[129] Truth-finding involves social production. Trials deal not only with the 'empirical question whether something happened, but also with the reasons-seeking question of why something happened'.[130] Many facts are 'social facts'.[131] Parties to proceedings have different approaches to facts and events. Proceedings are marked by 'narrative pluralism'.[132] Witnesses often reframe their understandings in the context of proceedings. Truth is thus not only a matter of right and wrong or correspondence to reality[133] but a question of plausibility and coherence[134] and verification.[135] It emerges through communication, validation, and judgment.

[126] Ibid., 76 ('Knowledge is not simply encountered in international criminal law; it is also produced.').

[127] Robert Jackson framed it adequately when noting that the purpose of international criminal trials is to 'establish incredible events by credible evidence'. See also Patricia Wald, 'To "Establish Incredible Events by Credible Evidence": The Use of Affidavit Testimony in Yugoslavia War Crimes Tribunal Proceedings' (2001) 42 *Harvard Journal of International Law* 535–53.

[128] The translation of facts into narratives involves transformation, such as 'the suppression or subordination of certain of them and the highlighting of others, by characterization, motific repetition, variation of tone and point of view, alternative descriptive strategies, and the like'. Hayden White, 'The historical text as literary artifact' in Hayden White (ed.), *Tropics of Discourse: Essays in Cultural Criticism* (Baltimore, MD: Johns Hopkins University Press 1978) 81–100, 84.

[129] See Sander, 'History on Trial' 573.

[130] Ibid., 300.

[131] See Mirjan Damaška, 'Truth in Adjudication' (1998) 49 *Hastings Law Journal* 289–308, 291 ('most facts we seek to establish in adjudication are "social" facts rather than phenomena intrinsic to nature').

[132] Sander, 'History on Trial' 549.

[133] Realist schools ground truth in facts about the world and correspondances between propositions and reality (correspondence theories). They 'locate truth in the world', rather than beliefs of individuals. For the realist, 'truth is objective, and it does not rely on what anyone believes'. See Shannon Fyfe, 'Truth, testimony and epistemic injustice in international criminal law' in Morten Bergsmo and Emiliano J. Buis (eds), *Philosophical Foundations of International Criminal Law: Foundational Concepts* (Brussels: Torkel Opsahl Academic EPublisher, 2019) 269–308, 276. This approach is useful to understand fact-finding practices. For instance, the establishment of facts and circumstances in trials should be grounded in evidence that corresponds to reality.

[134] Coherence theories relate 'truth' to communicative processes and societal knowledge and belief, rather than correspondence to facts. See John D. Jackson, 'Theories of Truth Finding in Criminal Procedure: An Evolutionary Approach' (1988) 10 *Cardozo Law Review* 475–528, 514–20. They take into account that trials cannot be deemed to 'provide an exact reproduction of what is alleged to have occurred'. See Desmond S. Geer, 'Anything But the Truth? The Reliability of Testimony in Criminal Trials' (1971) 11 *British Journal of Criminology* 131–54, 140. They link truth to ways in which things are 'done in the world'. Propositions are deemed to be true if they cohere 'with the most comprehensive system of beliefs whose members imply each other'. See Richard L. Kirkham, *Theories of Truth: A Critical Introduction* (Cambridge, MA: MIT Press, 2001), 114. Truth becomes thus a question of plausibility, rather than a matter of being right or wrong. This approach helps to explain how truth about events may emerge through coherent narratives or stories. Truth emerges when statements are coherent enough to lead others to believe that they are true.

[135] Pragmatic theories argue that the truth is linked to ideas that humans can 'assimilate, validate, corroborate and verify'. See James William, 'Pragmatism's conception of truth' in Michael Lynch (ed.), *The Nature of Truth: Classic and Contemporary Perspectives* (Cambridge, MA: MIT Press, 2001), 211–28, 212–13. Truth-finding occurs through scientific inquiry, namely processes of investigation and verification, which frame beliefs. See Susan Haack, 'The Pragmatist Theory of Truth' (1976) 27 *British Journal for the Philosophy of Science* 231–49, 232. These theories help to understand the link between truth, testimony, and evidence. They suggest that fact-finding requires corroboration in order lead to 'a

Procedural 'truth' is an approximation.[136] There is typically not 'one version' of facts, or one layer of 'truth' that can be uncovered.[137] Rather, there are multiple truths. For instance, 'historical truth' and 'legal truth' do not always coincide. The strength of the criminal process lies in the fact that it offers a forum where contradictions and contestations may legitimately coexist. International criminal proceedings do not necessarily provide closure but 'should be viewed in more modest terms as a discursive beginning for the examination of particular episodes of mass violence'.[138]

International criminal proceedings are transformative in a relational sense: they alter relations between agents in proceedings. For instance, many international crimes are linked to political violence. They may marginalize victims because of their status, identity, or affiliation with certain groups. Proceedings may convey 'a moral message connected with validating' autonomy and dignity of victims'.[139] They recognize not only the harm inflicted[140] but also the status of victims as holders of rights or political subjects.[141] They may entail 'a demonstration of public commitment to the victim's dignity as an equal member in human community'.[142]

4.2.2 Modus operandi

International criminal procedures rely on different techniques in order to create expressivist effects. They include shaming and stigmatization, role play and performance, and the individualization of responsibility.

4.2.2.1 Shaming and stigmatization

A first key element is the power of shaming and stigmatization.[143] Shaming typically seeks to create moral consciousness, through the creation of in-groups and out-groups. Stigma involves social exclusion or discrimination. It is commonly

truthful verdict' or a 'truthful narrative for the historical record'. Fyfe, 'Truth, testimony and epistemic injustice in international criminal law' 299.

[136] It is a matter of 'probability', rather than 'absolute certainty'. See Allo, 'The "Show" in the Show Trials' 49.

[137] See also Frank Haldemann, 'Another King of Justice: Transitional Justice as Recognition' (2008) 41 *Cornell International Law Journal* 675–737, 726.

[138] Sander, 'History on Trial' 575.

[139] See Haldemann, 'Another King of Justice' 704.

[140] Silence may be perceived as a secondary violation, that is, as a sign of condonement or indifference. See Trudy Govier, 'What is acknowledgment and why is it important?' in Carol A.L. Prager and Trudy Govier (eds), *Dilemmas of Reconciliation: Cases and Concepts* (Waterloo: Wilfrid Laurier University Press, 2003), 65–89, 85.

[141] See also Murphy, *Conceptual Foundations of Transitional Justice*, 176 ('political wrongs are public acts communicating to victims that their views will not be heard and that they are not full members of a community').

[142] Haldemann, 'Another King of Justice' 704.

[143] Meijers and Glasius, 'Expression of Justice or Political Trial?' 749.

understood as 'severe social disapproval due to believed or actual individual characteristics, beliefs or behaviours that are against norms'.[144]

The justifications for such practices differ. Consequentialists defend practices of shaming and stigmatization by rational cost-benefit rationales. They argue that the physical or reputational risks associated with proceedings may deter perpetrators or prevent future crimes (e.g. special prevention, general prevention)[145] because they increase the potential costs of crimes and the probability of sanction.[146] Other theorists rely on psychology and persuasion. They argue that shame and stigma may curtail crime by convincing perpetrators that their 'behaviour is inconsistent with an identity to which they aspire'.[147] Both theories depend on intermediate factors. They rely on cognitive dispositions, such as the willingness of recipients to undertake rational analysis or openness to be persuaded.[148]

Acceptance is related to the political circumstances surrounding proceedings and varies considerably.[149] For example, in the context of the ICTY, which is generally considered as one of the more successful experiments in international criminal justice, 'participants felt free to disregard any aspect of the judicial "record" that did not conform to their perspective on the "truth" that happened during the war'.[150]

4.2.2.2 Performance

Performance is the second element of procedural expressivism.[151] It essential in order to enact justice (i.e. to make it seen) and may be conducive to persuasion or enforcement. International criminal proceedings rely on key elements of performance, 'actors, stages, scripts and audiences'.[152] They are necessary to exercise justice and 'make it seen to be done'.

The legal process relies on 'role play'. A trial would not be recognized as trial without a cast of agents which display 'various contradictory attitudes about crime and criminals'.[153] For instance, prosecutors, judges, or Defence counsel do not act

[144] See Christoph Lauber, 'Stigma and Discrimination against People with Mental Illness: A Critical Appraisal', (2008) 17 *Epidemiology and Psychiatric Sciences* 10–13.

[145] For a survey of German doctrine, see Markus Dubber and Tatjana Hörnle, *Criminal Law: A Comparative Approach* (Oxford: Oxford University Press, 2014), 18. See also **section 5.1.2.2.**

[146] Kathryn Sikkink, *The Justice Cascade: How Human Rights Prosecutions are Changing World Politics* (New York, NY: W.W. Norton & Co, 2011) 236.

[147] Thomas Risse and Kathryn Sikkink, 'The socialization of international human rights norms into domestic practices: introduction' in Thomas Risse, Steve Ropp, and Kathryn Sikkink (eds), *The Persistent Power of Human Rights: From Commitment to Compliance* (Cambridge: Cambridge University Press, 1999), 1–38, 11, 15.

[148] Murphy, *Conceptual Foundations of Transitional Justice* 184.

[149] See also Lynch, *Performances of Justice* 62.

[150] Laurel Fletcher and Harvey Weinstein, 'Violence and Social Repair: Rethinking the Contribution of Justice to Reconciliation' (2002) 24 *Human Rights Quarterly* 573–639, 600.

[151] See Gabrielle Lynch, *Performances of Justice: The Politics of Truth, Justice and Reconciliation* (Cambridge: Cambridge University Press, 2018), 60.

[152] Lynch, *Performances of Justice* 20.

[153] Thurman W. Arnold, *The Symbols of Government* ((New Haven, CT: Yale University Press, 1935) 147.

as individuals but instead in certain institutional roles, for example as public officials, officers of the Court, or representatives of the interests of clients, etc. These roles are necessary in order to understand their authority, speech acts, and actions in the courtroom. They give meaning to their action and the role of the trial as a whole. Trust in these roles may convince others to accept decisions with which they disagree.

Criminal proceedings have a 'stage'. They are performed in a particular space, namely the legal sphere and in particular courtroom environments. This space gives proceedings visibility and a particular identity. It is necessary for messages to be heard. These images may shape the perception of individuals.

Legal actions are 'scripted'. They are governed by formal legal sources and procedural rules. For instance, witness statements are re-enactments of events that have to follow procedural rules. Processes of legal interpretation are not entirely in the discretion of judicial agents but constrained by legal sources.[154] This form gives procedures specific authority and objectivity that is necessary to persuade others to comply.

International criminal proceedings are generally held in public. Publicity is both an institutional guarantee, designed to open criminal proceedings to public scrutiny, and part of the fair trial rights of defendants (right to a public hearing).[155] Key moments, such as trials or the delivery of judgments, are performed to audiences and/or broadcasted to the public sphere.[156] Audiences see what happens. Criminal proceedings create a plot in the eye of spectators that has a beginning, middle, and end. For instance, the trial 'has a protagonist, an antagonist, a proscenium and an audience, a "story to be told and a problem to be resolved", all "usually in three acts: plaintiff's case, defendant's case, and the third act, consisting of the summations, charge and the rendering of the verdict"'.[157]

This type of action, that is, public performance through legal procedures, may influence the perception of messages. Psychological studies, such as the Milgram or Zimbardo experiments have shown that individual attitudes may be shaped by institutional roles. The act of performing justice before a broad public may increase norm obedience[158] or institute a certain 'agentic' relationships between judicial

[154] See, for example, ICC Statute, Art. 21.

[155] See *inter alia* Art. 10 of the Universal Declaration of Human Rights, Art. 6 (1) of the European Convention on Human Rights and Art. 14 ICCPR.

[156] Judith Resnik, 'Bring Back Bentham: "Open Courts," "Terror Trials," and Public Sphere(s)' (2011) 5 *Law & Ethics of Human Rights* 4–69.

[157] See John E. Simonett, 'The Trial as One of the Performing Arts' (1966) 52 *American Bar Association Journal* 1145–7.

[158] Robert Cover has argued that judicial action may trigger norm obedience by virtue of performance. See Robert Cover, 'Violence and the Word' (1986) 95 *Yale Law Journal* 1601–29, 1615. However, compliance based on obedience to institutional authority has 'dark sides'. A good example is Socrates' legitimate challenge to authoritative moral norms or codes, based on moral consciousness. See Hannah Arendt, 'Thinking and Moral Considerations' (1971) 38 *Social Research* 417–46, 434.

actors and audiences (e.g. between tribunals and national judicial agents) that may be conducive to compliance.[159]

Finally, procedural expressivism relies on repetition. Performances derive their meaning from 'reiterative' practices, from 'repetition of the same'.[160] International criminal justice is enacted through the multiplication of 'courtroom performances' in other courts or through new media.[161]

4.2.2.3 Individualization of responsibility

Individualization of responsibility is a third key element of procedural expression in international criminal justice. It has become a mantra of international criminal proceedings. International criminal law focuses on individuals as responsible actors since states cannot be 'punished' in the traditional sense.[162] International criminal proceedings signal 'that atrocious or 'evil' acts in international relations are the direct responsibility of specific persons rather than states.[163] They are based on the idea that 'perpetrators assume responsibility for the wrong they committed'.[164] The core premise is that a 'crime is the act of a voluntary and responsible agent who chooses between the lawful and the unlawful'.[165]

The focus on individuals is convenient from a narrative perspective. It gives a human face to atrocities. The trial tells the story of the crime through the lens of many individualized stories of perpetrators and victims. They are woven into a meta-narrative.

Individualization expresses a particular type of responsibility before the law, namely the responsibility of the individual, as opposed to the responsibility of the state. International criminal justice tries to make up for the lack of state responsibility by promoting leadership responsibility, the responsibility of political or military leaders of states, armed groups, or organizations. The stigma associated with the responsibility of leaders casts an indirect shadow of blame on these entities as such.[166]

159 For an argument in relation to compliance by the Inter-American Court of Human Rights, see Allen, 'Theater of International Justice' 150.

160 Stone Peters, 'Legal Performance Good and Bad' 184.

161 Allen, 'Theater of International Justice' 151.

162 See Larry May and Shannon Fyfe, *International Criminal Tribunals: A Normative Defense* (Cambridge: Cambridge University Press, 2017), 78. For a discussion as to how states may be held accountable, see Anthony Lang, 'Crime and Punishment: Holding States Accountable' (2007) 21 *Ethics & International Affairs* 239–57.

163 See Kirsten Ainley, 'Individual agency and responsibility for Atrocity' in Renee Jeffery (ed.), *Confronting Evil in International Relations: Ethical Responses to Problems of Moral Agency* (Palgrave Macmillan: Basingstoke, 2008) 37–60, 46.

164 Murphy, *Conceptual Foundations of Transitional Justice* 181.

165 Craig Haney, 'Criminal Justice and the Nineteenth Century Paradigm: The Triumph of Psychological Individualism in the "Formative Era"' (1982) 6 *Law and Human Behaviour* 191–234, 194, 209.

166 May and Fyfe, *International Criminal Tribunals: A Normative Defense* 80.

This lens is an attractive option to counter sentiments of collective guilt.[167] The attribution of individual criminal responsibility to specific individuals has a certain exculpatory effect. The broader collectivity becomes a third party. However, it also has ambivalent effects.[168] Individual narratives may detract from the collective and group-based dimensions of atrocity crime. Defendants may come to be seen individuals accused of crimes and as representatives of collective evil, warranting condemnation.[169]

4.3 Performative Role of Agents

Criminal proceedings are shaped by the role of different agents. The starting point is the crime of the defendant and its context, which is described in the charges.[170] However, the spectrum of relations is much wider. International criminal justice involves a whole range of actors, including the Prosecution, the Defence, judges, different types of witnesses, as well as victims, and communication to a broader public.

4.3.1 Procedural context

The design of procedures and discursive structures influence the way in which actors and participants experience and evaluate proceedings.[171] For instance, perceptions of fairness of proceedings or the willingness to engage with messages sent through trials depend not only on 'winning or losing' one's case, but on communicative factors, such as the ability 'to tell one's story', 'being listened to', and 'being treated with respect in the process'.[172] The way in which actors in proceedings experience legal procedures depends on procedural traditions or cultures.

In inquisitorial systems, the legal process is generally organized as an impartial public inquiry rather than as a contest between opposing parties. This leaves less space for the Prosecution and the Defence to shape their cases and control

[167] See Christian Tomuschat, 'The Legacy of Nuremberg' (2006) *JICJ* 830–44, 841 ('By definition, a trial against a state would be based on the assumption of collective criminal guilt.').

[168] Osiel, *Making Sense of Mass Atrocities* 3.

[169] Expressivist practices should therefore 'be sensitive to whether a perpetrator was acting individually or as part of a group, and whether the harm stemming from wrongdoing was limited to individuals or was experienced by groups of which the individual is a part'. See Murphy, *Foundations of Transitional Justice* 167.

[170] Criminal proceedings frame cases and test allegations, based on the applicable procedural rules.

[171] Emilio Christodoulidis., 'The objection that cannot be heard: Communications and legitimacy in the courtroom' in Antony Duff, Lindsay Farmer, Sandra Marshall, and Victor Tadros (eds), *The Trial on Trial 1* (Oxford: Hart, 2004), 179–202, 181.

[172] Janet Ainsworth, 'Legal Discourse and Legal Narratives' (2015) 2 *Language and Law* 1–11, 7.

narratives at trial. Judges have a managerial role during proceedings, or may even be involved in case preparation (investigative judge). Proceedings are organized around a dossier which contains procedural activity and evidence. Written witness statements may be allowed as alternatives to oral testimony at trial. The process is inspired by the ideal to reveal an objective truth through inquiry. It relies on faith in the integrity of the investigation and public inquiry and the ability to pursue 'truth unprompted by partisan pressures'.[173]

In adversarial systems, the process is guided by the idea that the 'truth' emerges through contradictorial features, including submissions and evidence presented by the parties to a neutral adjudicator, and processes of contestation or contradiction at trial. The parties are the driving force of proceedings. Prosecution and Defence have the ability to conduct their own investigation. They rely on processes of disclosure to share their material and evidence. Witnesses are more frequently attached to the parties and their respective cases, rather than serving as witnesses of the court. There is a strong focus on orality at trial which is protected through constraints on admissibility of evidence and hearsay.

Orality may have certain benefits from an experiential perspective. It may *inter alia* 'promote positive perceptions in the public of the procedural fairness of the justice system by giving litigants and witnesses a more direct experience of being able to shape their own legal narratives and of having an opportunity to have their stories heard and respected in court'.[174] However, such benefits are undermined if proceedings turn into an adversarial battle, governed by confrontation, rather than mutual engagement. Adversariality increase risks of dramatization and spectacle, since proceedings may be 'driven by strategic considerations rather than communicative rationality'.[175]

International criminal proceedings are in many ways hybrid or *sui generis*. They do not follow one 'pure' ideal type, but borrow elements from different systems, in order to accommodate the international nature of crimes. In some cases, they define new rules or practices that are not found in any domestic system.

Pure adversarial structures are ill-suited to serve the communicative purposes of international criminal proceedings. As Awol K. Allol has observed:

> The 'either–or' binary communication at trial structurally removes the many possible explanations of a historical or political event. In an 'either-or' communicative space that is always prone to a fallacy of false dichotomy, which version of the

[173] Chrisje Brants, Stewart Field, and Nico Jörg, 'Are inquisitorial and adversarial systems converging?' in Christopher Harding, Philip Fennell, Hugh William, Nico Jörg, and Bert Swart (eds), *Criminal Justice in Europe: A Comparative Study* (Oxford: Clarendon Press, 1995), 41–56, 46.

[174] Ainsworth, 'Legal Discourse and Legal Narratives' 9.

[175] Allo, 'The "Show" in the Show Trial' 48.

pedagogy should be validated as the true version—the Court's, the Defendant's, or the Prosecution's?[176]

International criminal justice has sought to counter some of the aggressive features of the adversarial culture through managerial powers of judges, including control over the parties or the presentation of evidence, constraints on prosecutorial discretion, or use of expert witnesses. This approach is sometimes described as a system of 'tempered adversariality. It allows 'two passionately committed parties to adduce all relevant facts before a neutral adjudicator while allowing the adjudicator to play a secondary, but active, role in bringing out the evidence'.[177]

The common feature is that storytelling and performance of roles assigned by law is not an end in itself, but a means to an end. As Simon Stern has noted, a 'case is always a case of something', the 'legal ends, rather than specific details account for the case's significance from the judge's point of view'.[178]

Facts and events are traced in order to show something.[179] The narrative plot turns a chain of events into a causal sequence. It may contain counterfactuals or what linguists have called 'disnarration', active silencing of events or alternative stories.[180]

Ultimately, the legal process has a demonstrative function which 'bridges the story of the parties and the story of the law'.[181] It points to something beyond the status quo. This demonstration is grounded in '[law]s ability to abstract events from particular contexts and discover relationships that hold among all instances ... irrespective of the spatial and temporal context'.[182]

It conveys information or knowledge about morality, law, and justice to spectators.[183] It contains statements about the different narrators and narratives. In some cases, trials are attacks on the 'political projects' of defendants.[184]

176 Allo, 'The "Show" in the Show Trial' 67.

177 See Peter Carmichael Keen, 'Tempered Adversariality: The Judicial Role and Trial Theory in the International Criminal Tribunals' (2004) 17 *LJIL* 767–814, 811.

178 See Stern, 'Narrative in the Legal Text' 131.

179 Maksymilian Del Mar, 'Exemplarity and Narrativity in the Common Law Tradition' (2013) 25 *Law & Literature* 390–407.

180 See Gerald Prince, 'The Disnarrated' (1988) 22 *Style* 1–8, 1 ('The disnarrated consists of those passages in a narrative that consider what did not or does not take place.').

181 Stern, 'Narrative in the Legal Text' 131.

182 David Polkinghorne, *Narrative Knowing and the Human Sciences* (Albany, NY: SUNY Press, 1988), 21.

183 See De Graaf, 'Terrorists on Trial' 9, arguing that trials may entail a 'performance of justice', that is 'a show where the trial reveals injustice, where the verdict educates the public about the importance of the rule of law in a democratic society, creates a collective memory and sets standards for future conduct of states and people'.

184 See Gerry Simpson, 'Politics, sovereignty, remembrance' in Dominic McGoldrick, Peter Rowe, and Eric Donnelly (eds), *The Permanent International Criminal Court: Legal and Policy Issues* (Oxford: Hart, 2004), 47–63, 49.

4.3.2 The Prosecution: Moralizer, educator, and architect of blame

The role of the Prosecution bears performative features. Prosecutors are not only parties to proceedings but representatives of the public interest. Symbolic, narrative, and educational aspirations are part of their identity. The Prosecution represents multiple interests: community interests in the pursuit of criminal justice, interests of persons affected by international crimes, and in some cases also the interests of the Defence (e.g. investigation of exculpatory evidence). It speaks to different audiences: the judge, victims, the Defence, and the broader public.

4.3.2.1 Public function

In the international arena, prosecutors have an important symbolic function. As Frédéric Mégret has observed: 'The international criminal prosecutor is also a notable public and media figure, much more so than would typically be the case domestically, whose practices of confiding and granting interviews and issuing declarations considerably help him in channeling stigma strategically.'[185]

Their relative independence from national systems or states gives international prosecutors a broader platform and audience. The role of the International Criminal Court (ICC) Prosecutor is among the closest incarnations of the representation of imagined community interests and the role of civil society in international law.[186] Symbolically, the office represents a sort of 'global conscience' that can act independently of the will of states. It may be understood as a symbol that inspires belief in the idea of a legitimate international community.[187]

This role comes with conflicting expectations.[188] The Prosecution is often 'the organ of a tribunal that is most responsible—and perceived as most responsible—for realizing the tribunal's goals.'[189] Its mandate represents the '*raison d'être* of the tribunal.'[190] However, the prosecutorial function is also the 'most political' in

[185] Frédéric Mégret, 'Practices of Stigmatization' (2013) 76 *Law and Contemporary Problems* 287–318, 296.

[186] Edwin Bikundo has compared the ICC Prosecutor to an icon. See Edwin Bikundo, 'Humanity's exemplary justice: From *hostis* to *hostia humani generis*' in Britta van Beers, Luigi Corrias, and Wouter Werner (eds), *Humanity across International Law and Biolaw* (Cambridge: Cambridge University Press, 2014) 42–66, 48 ('All that is in order to visualize the invisible, and hear the inaudible international community through its icons as embodied representations of something that has its own existence, yet which is only visible and audible through those icons.').

[187] Tallgren, 'The Sensibility and Sense of International Criminal Law' (2002) 13 *EJIL* 561–95, 594–5.

[188] Kate Cronin-Furman, 'Managing Expectations: International Criminal Trials and the Prospects for Deterrence of Mass Atrocity' (2013) 7 *International Journal of Transitional Justice* 434–54.

[189] See Kevin Heller, 'Completion' in Reydams, Wouters, and Ryngaert (eds), *International Prosecutors*, 886–925, 909–10.

[190] Marieke Wierda and Anthony Triolo, 'Resources' in Reydams, Wouters, and Ryngaert (eds), *International Prosecutors*, 113–70, 114.

international criminal justice.[191] Whatever a Prosecutor does, he or she will be criticized from one side or the other. The accountability that prosecutors express is by its nature exemplary.[192] It serves as an illustration of broader patterns of criminality, including those which are not investigated or prosecuted.

International prosecutors are not merely executive or quasi-judicial actors that seek to apply and enforce the law. They are entitled to select situations and cases and enjoy a margin discretion in their choices. This discretion gives them political leverage and enables them to act as communicative agencies.[193] It opens space for dialogue with states, affected communities, and victims.[194] This communicative space goes beyond suspects, witnesses, and evidence relevant to the Prosecution's case. It is reflected in practices of cooperation, timing of justice intervention, accountability strategies (e.g. freezing of assets, complementary transitional justice approaches), or enforcement.

Many communications portray an image of the Prosecution itself or ideas about how it wants to be perceived. For instance, David Crane presented himself as servant of the 'people of Sierra Leone' which he considered as his 'clients'.[195] The ICC has actively used press releases and statements to display certain ideal images of its own role.[196] It has emphasized its alleged detachment from politics, its impartiality and transparency, its role as a universal court, and its care for victims.[197] As Jillian Dobson and Sofia Stolk have argued, such practices are not only a means to bolster moral authority but also techniques to externalize blame. They are 'tools to educate but also to repair mistakes', or rather 'to defer blame', and 'serve as a means to express ideas of and commitments to justice before or even in the entire absence of a trial'.[198]

Throughout pre-trial and trial proceedings, the Prosecution typically bears the burden of proof. This onus is a counterpart to the stigmatizing and coercive powers of prosecutors. It expresses the value placed on liberties of citizens and the presumption of innocence.

[191] See Luc Côté, 'Independence and Impartiality', in Luc Reydams, Jan Wouters, and Cedric Ryngaert (eds), *International Prosecutors* (Oxford: Oxford University Press, 2012) 319–415, , 321.

[192] Bikundo, 'Humanity's exemplary justice' 48–51.

[193] See **section 3.2.2**.

[194] See Jillian Dobson and Sofia Stolk, 'The Prosecutor's Important Announcements: The Communication of Moral Authority at the International Criminal Court' (2016) *Law, Culture and the Humanities* 1–20, 5–6 ('This narrative power is exercised, in part, through the communications of the OTP, in the format of its press releases, its statements to the United Nations and Assembly of States Parties and by granting interviews to various international media.').

[195] David M. Crane, 'The Special Court for Sierra Leone' in David Crane, Leila Sadat, and Michael Scharf (eds), *The Founders: Four Pioneering Individuals Who Launched the First Modern-Era International Criminal Tribunals* (Cambridge University Press, 2018), 74–93, 75 ('Yet my heart was with my client . . . the people of Sierra Leone').

[196] For a critique, see Dobson and Stolk, 'The Prosecutor's Important Announcements' 20.

[197] Ibid., 19.

[198] Ibid., 7.

4.3.2.2 Narrative functions

Prosecution discourse is characterized by certain macro-narratives that present a particular view of defendants and global events. As Tim Kelsall has argued, the Prosecution carves out 'a set of criminal acts from the continuous flow of political events'.[199] These narratives divide the world into a space of politics and a space of law.[200] They serve to stress the importance of proceedings and to legitimize the role of the Prosecution. They are a 'counter-performance' to the crime. They send a message that the trial can serve to overcome chaos. But they also produce questionable binaries.[201]

4.3.2.2.1 Perpetrator-related discourses

The defendant plays a central role in Prosecution narratives.[202] In practice, arguments about perpetrators are often connected to discourses about humanity. They serve as one of the main narrative functions of the criminal trial, namely to rehumanize behaviour.[203]

The representations of defendants in Prosecution narratives are often not descriptive but performative. They produce certain images that are deemed to reinforce the didactic functions of trials. The image of the 'ideal' perpetrator is marked by contradiction. As Sofia Stolk has noted, the 'stereotypical defendant is not only a monster but also a man. Human and inhuman at the same time'.[204]

This duality is reflected in Hannah Arendt's famous saying that Eichmann was 'the most abnormal monster the world had ever seen'.[205] It illustrates the dichotomies between humanity and inhumanity in discourse about perpetrators.

Narratives shift over time and follow a logic of inclusion and exclusion. When context and crimes are presented, the role of perpetrators is often demonized.

[199] Tim Kelsall, 'Politics, Anti-Politics, International Justice: Language and Power in the Special Court for Sierra Leone' (2006) 32 *Review of International Studies* 587–602, 593.

[200] Ibid., 593, pointing to David Crane's Opening remarks in the *Norman et al.* case as example ('The issues before you are not—cannot be political. We have not charged political crimes. The court of law—this Chamber must focus on the alleged acts of these jointly charged indictees; politics must remain barred from these proceedings.'). See ibid., 594, with reference to *Sesay et al.* ('We are not going to question whatever initial politics surrounded the RUF. We are going to show, however, that this abuse of a political process and the discontent of the citizens of Sierra Leone was a mask for these actors' own criminal purposes. This trial is not, cannot be, about this subterfuge of frustrated political aspirations, but about war crimes.').

[201] Kamari M. Clarke, 'Refiguring the Perpetrator: Culpability, History and International Criminal Law's Impunity Gap' 19 *International Journal of Human Rights* (2015) 592–614.

[202] See Damien Rogers, 'Prosecutors' opening statements: The rhetoric of law, politics, and silent war' in Nobuo Hayashi and Cecilia Bailliet (eds), *The Legitimacy of International Criminal Tribunals* (Cambridge: Cambridge University Press, 2017), 325–50.

[203] See Sofia Stolk, 'A Sophisticated Beast? On the Construction of an "Ideal" Perpetrator in the Opening Statements of International Criminal Trials' (2018) *EJIL* 677–701, 695 ('being labelled "a man"—a human being who is part of humanity—is one of the trial's highest stakes').

[204] Stolk, 'A Sophisticated Beast?' 696.

[205] Arendt, *Eichmann in Jerusalem* 276.

They are branded as outlaws ('enemies of humankind', 'evil', or 'monsters'),[206] or as extraordinary perpetrators who deviate from ordinary standards of behaviour.[207] A striking example is Jackson's depiction of Nazi defendants as 'living symbols of racial hatreds, of terrorism and violence, and of the arrogance and cruelty of power'. He qualified them as 'symbols of fierce nationalisms and of militarism, of intrigue and war-making which have embroiled Europeans generation after generation, crushing its manhood, destroying its homes, and impoverishing its life'.[208] Such metaphors have recurred in other contexts. For instance, in *Nuon Chea et al.*, the three defendants were described as 'malignant forces'.[209] SCSL Prosecutor David Crane branded Sierra Leonean Revolutionary United Front (RUF) perpetrators as 'dogs of war' and 'hounds from hell'. He also referred to 'beasts of impunity'[210]—a metaphor openly challenged by the Defence.[211] He noted: 'crimes in our joint indictment against Sesay, Kallon, and Gbao certainly defy any logic, any reason; the pure evil of these deeds of destruction are so horrific, terrible, and devastating in their scope, words in any language do not describe the offences committed by these indictees'.[212] Serge Brammertz qualified *Karadžić's* conviction to life imprisonment as 'an important message that justice can prevail over evil'.[213]

Such dehumanizing discourse pursues several demonstrative rationales. It is meant to convey stigma and 'othering'. It is deemed to break 'the cycles of collective blame that fuel group conflicts'.[214] It creates distances between perpetrators and

[206] Saira Mohamed, 'Of Monsters and Men: Perpetrator Trauma and Mass Atrocity' (2015)_115 *Columbia Law Review* 1157–216; Alexander Hinton, *Man or Monster? The Trial of a Khmer Rouge Torturer* (Durham, NC: Duke University Press, 2017).

[207] See Anette Bringedal Houge, 'Re-presentations of Defendant Perpetrators in Sexual War Violence Cases Before International and Military Criminal Courts' (2016) 56 *British Journal of Criminology* 419–37, 425.

[208] Robert Jackson, Nuremberg Trials, Opening Address for the United States, Nazi Conspiracy & Aggression, Volume I (Washington, DC: United States Government Printing Office, 1946), 115.

[209] *Prosecutor v. Chea, Sary and Samphan*, Trial Transcript, 002/19-09-2007-ECCC/TC, 21 November 2011, Opening statement of the Prosecution 'Let us never for one moment forget in this trial that these are the malignant forces and this is the tragic legacy that these three elderly people represent', 110–11.

[210] SCSL, RUF Trial, Opening statement of the Prosecution, SCSL—2004-15-PT, 5 July 2004, 4–5 at http://www.rscsl.org/Documents/Press/OTP/prosecutor-openingstatement070504a.pdf. ('Their alleged crimes against humanity cannot justly or practically be ignored, as they were the handmaidens to the beast—the beast of impunity that walked this burnt and pillaged land.').

[211] The Defence argued: '[T]here is something troubling about talking about impunity by itself because it invites us to say, "Well there clearly were," and this Court has judicially noticed "wide-scale humanitarian violations in Sierra Leone during the period of this conflict and someone must pay," and the phrase "beast of impunity" invites us to say, "Well we must find someone who canpay from among these Accused," ... when in fact the nature of impunity does not revolve [sic] such sacrifices, but rather a continued adherence to the rule of law and the burden of this Prosecution ... to prove a case against Morris Kallon.... The evidence about Morris Kallon will not demonstrate or even come close to suggesting that he is a hand-maiden of evil as has been suggested in this hall.' See Wanda M. Akin, 'Nuremberg, justice and the beast of impunity' in Herbert R. Reginbogin and Christoph Safferling (eds), *The Nuremberg Trials: International Criminal Law Since 1945* (München: KG Saur, 2006) 257–65, 258.

[212] RUF Trial, 'Opening statement of the Prosecution' 14.

[213] See Statement by the Prosecutor on the occasion of Karadžić Appeals Judgement, The Hague, 20 March 2019, at http://www.irmct.org/en/news/statement-prosecutor-occasion-karad%C5%BEi%C4%87-appeals-judgement.

[214] Mohamed, 'Of Monsters and Men' 1214.

human values. This distance is supposed to produce a didactic effect on society. It is a means to enable society to affirm its communal values to itself.[215] This message is meant to provide some comfort, namely to 'convince us all that we are different from them, that we share a common sense of decency and humanity, and that none of us could ever slide into that same darkness'.[216]

In sexual violence cases, prosecutors highlighted the particular gravity of crimes of defendants in comparison to others. As Anette Houge has pointed out, they used various types of stigmatization. The Prosecution argued that defendants '"relished" (*Radić*) in "heinous crimes" (*Zelenović*), which were seen as entertainment (*Radić, Graner*)'.[217] Crimes were qualified as 'shameless' (*Muhimana*), 'cruel' (*Kovač, Radić*), 'perverse' (*Radić*), 'sadistic' (*Landžo, Bralo, Kovač*), 'premeditated' (*Kovač, Kunarac*), 'horrible odysseys' (*Zelenović*).[218] *Delić* was described as a 'sadistic individual who, at times, displayed a total disregard for the sanctity of human life and dignity'.[219]

The branding of a crime as attack against humanity is meant to provide legitimation for prosecution. It demonstrates the importance of the trial, the moral underpinning of the prosecution case, or the legitimacy of an international forum or the use of universal jurisdiction.

However, reliance on 'us versus them' divides has also downsides. Stereotypical depictions of defendants can conflict with fundamental assumptions and rationales of criminal proceedings. For example, it is difficult to argue that a trial may educate a perpetrator or influence future behaviour if that same person is deemed to lack sufficient human capacity or rationality.[220] Treating perpetrators as 'monsters' complicates the claim that trials contribute to problem-solving.

The imagery of the 'ideal' perpetrator as evil is thus often connected to a prospect of 're-gaining humanity'.[221] This dual narrative presents certain advantages: to 'admit that perpetrators are not monsters' may 'encourage deeper examination of their choices and motivations, which can lead to more productive investigations of how to secure compliance with laws and resistance to campaigns of destruction'.[222]

It allows the Prosecution to argue that defendants enjoy the necessary cognitive skills and degree of rational choice to satisfy the conditions of individual criminal responsibility. It also facilitates motivations of sentencing. Sentencing signals that the perpetrator is 'nothing more than a mere mortal'.[223]

[215] Emile Durkheim, *The Division of Labour in Society* (George Simpson trans., New York, NY: The Free Press, 1947), 63.
[216] Mohamed, 'Of Monsters and Men' 1211.
[217] Houge, 'Re-presentations of Defendant Perpetrators in Sexual War Violence Cases' 426.
[218] Ibid., 426.
[219] *Delalić et al.* Trial Judgment, para. 1268.
[220] Stolk, 'A Sophisticated Beast?' 697.
[221] Ibid., 697.
[222] Mohamed, 'Of Monsters and Men' 1211.
[223] Mohamed, 'Of Monsters and Men' 1215.

4.3.2.2.2 Meta-narratives

Prosecution discourses relate the roles of defendants to a broader plot about atrocity situations. Such meta-narratives are necessary to build a theory of the individual case.[224] They complement the narrative function of charges.[225] They present the defendant as part of a broader whole. They portray crimes as ideological or political projects rather than just 'byproducts of war'.[226] In this context, law becomes intertwined with readings of history. As Richard Wilson has shown, practices navigate between 'monumental histories' and 'microscopic histories'.[227]

The attempt to frame entire conflicts in charges against individuals poses severe methodological problems. Prosecutors face a difficult choice as to how far they should engage with context in their case strategy. They may either limit 'their inquiries into the larger context to the very minimum required' or pursue 'a broader exposition of the larger picture', which creates 'a heightened risk of historical contextualization dwarfing the subject of individual culpability'.[228]

Narratives may become more informed by case strategy rather than historical accuracy. Meta-narratives are frequently told through the framework of modes of liability or mental elements of crimes, such as a common plan or policy or a shared purpose. In particular, the joint criminal enterprise (JCE) doctrine has provided a window of opportunity for the OTP to construct broad meta-narratives about the roles of perpetrators that later proved to be difficult to establish.

The ICTR presented a specific historical reading of the Rwandan genocide in *Akayesu*. It devoted thirty-three paragraphs to the 'historical context of the events in Rwanda in 1994'. OTP narratives of the conflict and the story told in the judgment relied heavily on the testimony of historian Alison Des Forges,[229] who served as background witness and became famous for her book, *Leave None to Tell the Story: Genocide in Rwanda*.[230] The judgment marked an attempt of ICTR

224 Wilson, 'Humanity's Histories' 43 ('Few prosecutors in international criminal justice arrive in the courtroom without a "theory of the case"—that is, explanation of why the crimes occurred in the first instance, and this theory is often based upon circumstantial and historical factors.').

225 See Predrag Dojcinović, 'The shifting status of grand narratives in war crimes trials and international law: History and politics in the courtroom' in Zarkov and Glasius (eds), *Narratives of Justice In and Out of the Courtroom*, 63–88.

226 See Marlies Glasius, 'Terror, terrorizing, terrorism: instilling fear as a crime in the cases of Radovan Karadzic and Charles Taylor' in Dubravaka Zarkov and Marlies Glasius (eds), *Narratives of Justice In and Out of the Courtroom: Former Yugoslavia and beyond* (The Hague: Springer, 2014) 45–61, 59.

227 Wilson, *Writing History in International Criminal Trials* 98–121.

228 Sander, 'Unveiling the Historical Function of International Criminal Courts' 348.

229 *Akayesu* Trial Judgment, paras 78–11. See also Doris Buss, 'Expert witnesses and international war crimes trials: Making sense of large-scale violence in Rwanda' in Dubravaka Zarkov and Marlies Glasius (eds), *Narratives of Justice in and out of the Courtroom: Former Yugoslavia and Beyond* (The Hague: Springer, 2014) 23–44, 42 ('This account of what happened in Rwanda in the 1990s, and the understanding of large-scale violence that it confirms, was substantially based at the outset on the research of several experts on Rwanda, including Alison Des Forges. Her testimony provided the basis on which the trial chamber was able to, first, depict the violence as inter-ethnic and constituting the international crime of genocide and second that the genocide was planned and then executed by a select group of elites.').

230 Alison Des Forges, *Leave None to Tell the Story: Genocide in Rwanda* (New York, NY: Human Rights Watch/Fédération Internationale des Ligues des Droits De l'Homme, 1999).

prosecutors and judges to 'make sense' of history. It presented the conflict essentially as an ethnic conflict between Hutu and Tutsi, which was fuelled by distinctions introduced under Belgian colonial rule and marked by deliberate action that incited ordinary Hutus to kill Tutsi.[231] The judgment stressed that 'although the genocide against the Tutsi occurred concomitantly' with the conflict between the Rwandan Armed Forces (RAF) and the Rwandan Patriotic Front (RPF), 'it was fundamentally different from the conflict'.[232] It noted that the genocide 'was organized and planned not only by the members of the RAF, but also by the political forces who were behind the "Hutu" power, that it was executed essentially by civilians including the armed militia and even ordinary citizens'. [233]

This narrative fits into the framing of genocide as an intent crime. However, some aspects of meta-narrative and, in particular, the question to what extent the genocide was planned prior to 1994 became more fluid over time.

In *Bagasora*, the Trial Chamber adopted a more cautious reading. It reflected the 'the more uneven, changing and arguably less intentional aspects of the genocide' which fit less clearly into legal boxes.[234] It stated that 'the process of a criminal trial cannot depict the entire picture of what happened in Rwanda, even in a case of this magnitude'.[235] It found that that there was not sufficient evidence to establish that there was a conspiracy among the defendants prior to 6 April 1994 to commit genocide.[236]

It stated that:

> When viewed against the backdrop of the targeted killings and massive slaughter perpetrated by civilian and military assailants between April and July 1994 as well as earlier cycles of violence, it is understandable why for many this evidence takes on new meaning and shows a prior conspiracy to commit genocide. Indeed, these preparations are completely consistent with a plan to commit genocide. However, they are also consistent with preparations for a political or military power struggle ... It cannot be excluded that the extended campaign of violence directed against Tutsis, as such, became an added or an altered component of these preparations.[237]

The ICTR struggled with the anthropological underpinnings of the genocide. Narratives about the ethnic foundations of the conflict shifted. *Akayesu* presented the conflict between Hutu and Tutsi as a rivalry between 'stable and permanent

[231] *Akayesu* Trial Judgment, para. 83.
[232] Ibid., para. 128.
[233] Ibid., para. 128.
[234] Buss, 'Expert Witnesses and International War Crimes Trials' 42.
[235] *Prosecutor v. Bagosora et al.*, Judgement & Sentence, ICTR-98-41-T, 18 December 2008, para. 5.
[236] Ibid., para. 2112.
[237] Ibid., para. 2110.

groups'. Later cases acknowledged that ethnicity is partially a social construct. They defended objective and subjective conceptions of ethnicity, grounded in perceptions.

The ICTY frequently embedded broader historical analysis in its framing of cases.[238] For instance, *Tadić*, the first case, started with an extensive study (sixty-nine pages) of the history of the Balkans conflict and the role of Bosnia in order to analyse to how *Tadić* fits into a broader JCE relating to the persecution of non-Serb civilians. *Krstić* told a micro-history of events in Srebrenica, in order to assess genocidal charges. This narrative informed later judgments.

In the *Milošević* case, the ICTY Prosecution used broad historical narratives about the creation of a 'greater Serbia' in order to establish responsibility for genocide. This meta-narrative was used to present the Serbian political and military leadership as members of an overarching joint criminal enterprise, with a common plan to create a 'centralized Serbian State encompassing the Serb populated areas of Croatia, and Bosnia and Herzegovina, and all of Kosovo'.[239]

Carla Del Ponte joined the indictments in relation to Kosovo, Croatia, and Bosnia and Herzegovina in order to present a comprehensive narrative of the Yugoslav conflict. She approached the trial with a means to write history. She noted:

> I recognise that this trial will make history, and we would do well to approach our task in the light of history. The history of the disintegration of the former Yugoslavia and the fratricidal conflicts of another age which brought it about is a complex process which must be written by many people.

The narrative of 'a Greater Serbia' was supported by an expert witness, historian Audrey Helfant Budding. A split Trial Chamber found evidence for the 'accused's advocacy of and support for the concept of a Greater Serbia',[240] in response to a Motion for Judgement of Acquittal. However, ultimately, this reading of history failed to establish sufficient ground for a JCE. Judges acknowledged that broad historical notions related to Serb nationalism are insufficient to prove genocidal intent. The Trial Chamber made this point clear in *Brđanin*. It noted that 'the Strategic Plan was to link Serb-populated areas in BiH together, to gain control over these areas and to create a separate Bosnian Serb state, from which most non-Serbs would be permanently removed, and that force and fear were used to implement it'.[241] It found that this did not suffice to establish

[238] See Robert Donia, 'Encountering the Past: History at the Yugoslav War Crimes Tribunal' (2004) *Journal of the International Institute* 1–7, 2–3.

[239] *Prosecutor v. Milošević*, Prosecution's Motion for Joinder, IT-99-37-PT, IT-01-50-PT, IT-01-51-PT, 27 November 2001, para. 113.

[240] *Prosecutor v. Milošević*, Decision on Motion for Judgement of Acquittal, IT-02-54-T, 16 June 2004, para. 288 (Judge Kwon dissenting).

[241] *Prosecutor v. Brđanin*, Judgment, IT-99-36-T, 1 September 2004, para. 981.

'an intention to do so by destroying the Bosnian Muslim and Bosnian Croat groups'.[242]

In *Šešelj*, the majority of the Trial Chamber openly questioned the criminal nature of the meta-narrative. It argued that the objective of the creation of Greater Serbia was more of a political venture than a criminal project. It criticized the Prosecution for 'a very fragmented reading of the events' relating to allegations regarding 'a criminal plan for a Greater Serbia, or an-entity-known by some such name'.[243] It concluded that the plan for a 'Greater Serbia' supported by Seselj constituted 'a priori a political and not a criminal goal'.[244] The Appeals Chamber corrected this reasoning in an *obiter dictum*,[245] but ultimately dismissed 'the Prosecution's arguments related to Seselj's acquittal for the commission of crimes through participation in a joint criminal enterprise'.[246]

The *Taylor* case before the SCSL showed a similar disconnect between historical meta-narrative and outcome. The Prosecution presented Charles Taylor as an overarching figure who formed a conspiracy with the RUF in Liberia in order to control West Africa, terrorize civilians and pillage diamonds.

In her closing brief at trial, Prosecutor Brenda Hollis presented the following meta-narrative:

> Charles Taylor, this intelligent, charismatic manipulator had his proxy forces and members of his Liberian forces carry out these crimes against helpless victims in Sierra Leone to achieve the objectives he shared with other members of the joint criminal enterprise in which he participated, to forcibly control the people and territory of Sierra Leone and to pillage its resources, in particular its diamonds. And they would do this through their agreed criminal means, the campaign of terror he waged on the innocent people of Sierra Leone with all its attendant crimes.[247]

Taylor was thus portrayed as a unifying figure who controlled the RUF rebels. His crimes were branded as acts of terror and exploitation. However, the story that emerged from trials shows a different historical reading.

The RUF trial challenged the reading of Taylor as a mastermind. It presented RUF leaders as main responsible and only awarded minor attention to Taylor's role.[248] In the *Taylor* trial, the notion and framing of the JCE remained blurry. It was unclear

[242] Ibid., para. 981.

[243] *Prosecutor v. Šešelj*, Judgment, IT-03-67-T, 31 March 2016, para. 229 (*Šešelj* Trial Judgment).

[244] *Šešelj* Trial Judgment, para. 230, paras 238 and 245.

[245] *Prosecutor v. Šešelj*, Judgment, MICT—16-99-A, 11 April 2018, para. 114.

[246] Ibid., para. 119.

[247] See Marlies Glasius and Tim Meijers, 'Constructions of Legitimacy: The Charles Taylor Trial' 239–40.

[248] Ibid., 251 ('In the Taylor case, the RUF rebels were largely portrayed as mindless killing machines who voluntary laid all their diamonds at Taylor's feet. During the RUF leaders' trials, meanwhile, full responsibility was placed with the RUF leadership and Taylor was a marginal figure.').

'whether fuelling the conflict was an intermediate aim, with the ultimate aim being self-enrichment, or whether the extraction and sale of diamonds was an intermediate aim, with the ultimate aim being control over Sierra Leone as well as Liberia'.[249]

The trial judgment rejected an important part of the Prosecution narrative. It denied that Taylor and RUF leader Foday Sankoh formed a joint criminal enterprise to commit crimes against the Sierra Leone population.[250] It convicted Taylor as an accessory for providing practical assistance, encouragement or moral support to the RUF in the commission of crimes. It specified that there was not sufficient evidence to show that 'the invasion of Sierra Leone was undertaken pursuant to a common purpose to terrorize the civilian population'.[251] The story that emerged from trial thus differed considerably from the grand narratives framed through the JCE claim.

The ICC Prosecution encountered methodological challenges in relation to its meta-narratives in the *Gbagbo* case. The main didactic rationale of the case was to show the impermissibility of post-electoral violence. The OTP wanted to 'send a strong signal to those who intend to, or attempt to accede to power, or to maintain themselves in power through violence and brutality'.[252]

The case strategy relied on a simplified history of the conflict in Côte d'Ivoire.[253] The main claim was that Laurent Gbagbo, his wife (Simone Gbagbo), and his former youth minister (Blé Goudé) had formed a common plan in October 2000 to 'keep him in power by all means', 'knowing that a freely-contested presidential election was inevitable'.[254] The OTP alleged that electoral violence carried out against pro-Ouattara supporters a decade later, namely in four events between December 2010 and April 2011, was a consequence of this plan; a means to allow Gbagbo to remain in power through criminal means. It sought to prove its case about the repression of political opposition through speeches and patterns of denial of crimes by his 'inner circle' that foreshadowed events in 2010. This argument contrasted with the narrative of Gbagbo, who presented himself as supporter of multi-party democracy in the country, and the voices of his supporters who claimed that his main goal was to protect democracy against armed rebel forces.

The plausibility of the OTP narrative was first contested at pre-trial. Judge Van den Wyngaert issued a dissent against the confirmation of charges. She noted

> There is no convincing evidence, in my view to show that Laurent Gbagbo at any point agreed with his alleged 'inner circle' to commit crimes against

249 Ibid., 249.

250 *Taylor* Trial Judgment, paras 2229, 2260.

251 Ibid., para. 2388.

252 See *Prosecutor v. Blé Goudé*, Confirmation of Charges Hearing, ICC-02/11-02/11-T-5-Red-ENG, 29 September 2014, 7–8.

253 See Thijs Bouwknegt, 'Gbabgo—An Acquittal Foretold', 31 January 2019, at https://www.justiceinfo.net/en/tribunals/icc/40156-gbagbo-an-acquittal-foretold.html.

254 *Prosecutor v. Gbabgo*, Corrected Version of Prosecutions's Pre-Trial Brief, 28 July 2015, para. 6. See also para. 5 ('objective of retaining power by, inter alia, repressing or violently attacking those who challenged his authority').

> innocent civilians . . . I also do not believe that it was foreseeable that the killing and raping of civilians would occur in the ordinary course of events . . . I am not persuaded . . . that there were substantial grounds to believe that Laurent Gbagbo, either alone or in concert with one or more members of the alleged 'inner circle' used the forces at his disposal to intentionally commit crimes against civilians . . . Although it might be argued that by sending military units into a densely populated civilian area, Laurent Gbagbo created and accepted a risk that innocent civilians might be harmed (i.e. dolus eventualis), this falls short in my view of actively instructing/instigating those troops to deliberately target civilians.[255]

At trial, the OTP struggled to support its historical narrative. The trial became partly about history.[256] The Defence argued that the OTP version of facts presented a one-sided history of events in Côte d'Ivoire. It developed its own counter-history and challenged the nexus of Gbagbo to the crimes committed in the four instances.

The fragile underpinning of the Prosecution's case narrative, lack of evidence, and turnaround of insider witnesses led to a collapse of the prosecution case in the midst of the trial. The OTP presented 2679 documents, including documentation relating to the 'inner circle' based on the presidential palace logbooks and Simone Gbagbo's diary, but it failed to establish a sufficient link between Gbagbo and the crimes. The majority concluded that there was no case to answer since the prosecution narrative was too detached from the charges.[257]

As critics have noted, the *Gbagbo* trial stands as an example of the instrumentalization of political history through law.[258] It showed how 'history is used in case theories and abused as rhetorical window-dressing for both legal and

[255] *Prosecutor v. Gbabgo and Blé Goudé*, Dissenting Opinion of Judge Christine Van den Wyngaert, ICC-02/11-01/11-656-Anx, 13 June 2014, paras 5–6.

[256] The Defence noted: 'In international proceedings, it is also history with a capital "H" that is being written. In fact, the situations in which the Court must intervene require it to take on board historical, sociological and political context without which the case cannot be fully understood. It is also a history of a country, a region and a people and its sufferings that is being written.' *Prosecutor v. Laurent Gbagbo*, Confirmation of Charges Hearing Transcript, ICC-02/11-01/11, 19 February 2013, 7.

[257] See *Prosecutor v. Gbagbo and Blé Goudé*, Reasons for oral decision of 15 January 2019 on the Requête de la Défense de Laurent Gbagbo afin qu'un jugement d'acquittement portant sur toutes les charges soit prononcé en faveur de Laurent Gbagbo et que sa mise en liberté immédiate soit ordonnée, and on the Blé Goudé Defence no case to answer motion, ICC-02/11-01/15-1263, 16 July 2019, Reasons of Judge Geoffrey Henderson, ICC-02/11-01/15-1263-AnxB-Red, para. 79 ('In this case, the Prosecutor seems to have started from the premise that her case theory is correct and that this theory provides the necessary coherence to link the disparate evidentiary elements she relies upon. However, this is putting the cart in front of the horse. In order to prove her case, the Prosecutor must first demonstrate the aforesaid connections and coherence. This has not been done.').

[258] Ibid., para. 5 ('The Prosecutor, in a Herculean effort, has attempted to bring within the scope of this single litigation several years of Ivorian history. This has proved to be overly ambitious.'); para. 77 ('the fundamental flaw of the Prosecutor's narrative is that she depicted the post-electoral crisis as a straightforward story about a leader who could not accept that he had come to the end of the line and was unwilling to hand over power to his natural successor').

extra-legal purposes'.[259] Judge Cuno Tarfusser confirmed this in vivid terms in his opinion:

> Day after day, document by document, witness after witness, the 'Prosecutor's case' has been revealed and exposed as a fragile, implausible theorem relying on shaky and doubtful bases, inspired by a Manichean and simplistic narrative of an Ivory Coast depicted as a 'polarised' society where one could draw a clear-cut line between the 'pro-Gbagbo', on the one hand, and the 'pro- Ouattara', on the other hand, the former from the South and of Christian faith, the latter from the North and of Muslim faith; a caricatured, 'one-sided' narrative, 'built around a unidimensional conception of the role of nationality, ethnicity, and religion (in the broadest sense) in Côte d'Ivoire in general and during the post-electoral crisis in particular', progressively destroyed by the innumerable elements to the contrary emerging from the testimonies.[260]

All of these experiences suggest that it is risky to base case theories on grand historical narratives. Legal concepts, like JCE, leave space or even send flawed incentives to build lofty constructions about criminal responsibility based on broadly conceived plans or policies. However, at trial, many of these meta-narratives failed or needed to be adjusted over time. It is thus misguided to present the establishment and articulation of historical narratives as foundations of trials. The evidence and structure of criminal proceedings are more conducive to the production of 'microscopic' histories.[261]

4.3.2.2.3 Commodification of suffering

Images of the perpetrator and meta-narratives are often reinforced by stories about the suffering of victims. Victims are collectivized or presented in abstract terms. This description provokes empathy through vulnerability, weakness, or dependence.[262] Norwegian criminologist Nils Christie has developed the concept of the 'ideal' victim to illustrate this imagery. The victim has a public status in society like a 'hero' or a 'traitor'.[263] According to Christie, the 'ideal' victim in domestic settings is a 'little old lady' who is weak, respectable, and cannot to be blamed for the harm

[259] Bouwknegt, 'The international criminal trial record as historical source' 147.

[260] *Prosecutor v. Gbagbo and Blé Goudé*, Reasons for oral decision of 15 January 2019 on the Requête de la Défense de Laurent Gbagbo afin qu'un jugement d'acquittement portant sur toutes les charges soit prononcé en faveur de Laurent Gbagbo et que sa mise en liberté immédiate soit ordonnée, and on the Blé Goudé Defence no case to answer motion, ICC-02/11-01/15-1263, 16 July 2019, Opinion of Judge Cuno Tarfusser, ICC-02/11-01/15-1263-AnxA, para. 12.

[261] Wilson, *Writing History in International Criminal Trials* 134, 219.

[262] Joris van Wijk, 'Who Is the "Little Old Lady" of International Crimes? Nils Christie's Concept of the Ideal Victim Reinterpreted' (2013) 19 *International Review of Victimology* 159–79; Christine Schwöbel-Patel, 'The "Ideal" Victim of International Criminal Law' (2018) 29 *EJIL* 703–24.

[263] Nils Christie, 'The ideal victim' in Ezzat A. Fattah (ed.) *From Crime Policy to Victim Policy* (London: Tavistock, 1986), 17–30.

inflicted on her. This image cannot be simply transposed to international criminal justice.[264] However, it opens important discussions about roles and labels associated with victimhood. Certain attributes can be found in prosecutorial narratives.

Prosecutors invoke victims in a generalized and decontextualized way in discourse in order to reinforce or justify the case for investigation or prosecution of international crimes. The 'ideal' victim is to extent a counterpart to the 'ideal' perpetrator. It reduces the complexity of the phenomenon in order to 'make it easier for the eye'.[265] This type of victim is typically vulnerable, innocent, and in need of care, that is, 'weak enough not to become a threat to other important interests'.[266] 'Ideal' victims are apolitical, silent (i.e. they do not protest), easy to blend into collective schemes, or spectacular.

Such features are recurring in prosecutorial narratives. Charging strategy or prosecutorial discourse focus on spectacular events and certain specific categories of victims (e.g. child soldiers, victims of sexual violence). For instance, in *Lubanga*, the OTP used 'the global child' as an archetype. It defended the relatively low sentence of fourteen years as 'a symbol of hope' and 'an important step towards bringing an end to the suffering of tens of thousands of children still forced to fight, to kill and to die in conflicts around the world'.[267] The individual victim became to some extent a 'universalised victim', emblematic of the harm and suffering caused to the international community as a whole.

In the *Katanga* case, the OTP used the interests of victims as a pattern of justification for the opening and closing of the case. It noted in its opening statement that 'this is a great moment, a great moment of hope for the victims who, for more than six years, have been waiting, waiting for justice to be served'.[268]

After the conviction, it agreed with the Defence on the withdrawal of the appeal against the judgment. It justified this move on the ground that 'Germain Katanga has ... played a part in addressing the need for accountability and justice as expressed by the victims', by 'acknowledging his participation in these crimes and in expressing his regret'.[269]

Such generalizations are tempting from a rhetorical point of view. They enable the Prosecution to justify its case as a humanitarian act and a means of catharsis. The fact that a victim is presented as suffering creates a moral justification for

264 Christie's idealized image has been been criticized from an empirical point of view. See James Dignan, 'Victims, victimization and victimology' in James Dignan (ed.), *Understanding Victims and Restorative Justice* (Maidenhead: Open University Press, 2005) 13–40, 18–20.

265 Tallgren, 'The Sensibility and Sense of International Criminal Law' 594.

266 Christie, 'The ideal victim' 21.

267 Statement of the Prosecutor of the International Criminal Court, Fatou Bensouda, following the Appeals Chamber decision on the verdict and sentence in the Lubanga case: Protecting children means preserving the future, 2 December 2014.

268 *Prosecutor v. Katanga and Ngudjolo Chui*. Opening Remarks, ICC-01/04-01/07, 24 November 2009, 39.

269 Statement of the Prosecutor of the International Criminal Court, Fatou Bensouda, on Germain Katanga's Notice of Discontinuance of his Appeal against his Judgment of Conviction, 25 June 2014.

action, that is, prosecution. It suggests that something ought to be done to remedy suffering. The cause of victims gives meaning to proceedings. It strengthens truth-finding and provides a restorative justification, that is, 'justice for victims'. Ultimately, the trial itself may be presented as a means to restore a sense of dignity.

However, this 'commodification of suffering' also has dark sides. The Prosecution takes ownership over the stories of victims. It treats them as objects rather than subjects. Such 'narrative ownership' may cause secondary types of victimization.[270] Prosecutorial ideal types neglect the complexities of victimhood. They are difficult to reconcile with nuanced victim-perpetrator identities, the idea that victims may be harmed and victimizers at the same time.[271] They blend out the fact that victimhood is culturally embedded. This may fuel a 'feminized, infantilized and racialized' conception of victimhood.[272]

4.3.2.3 Didactic functions

Didactic functions enable the Prosecution to present itself as a moral agent that promotes a broader public good. They are invoked in intra-Court and extra-Court relations.

During proceedings, prosecutors seek to elucidate facts and persuade judges and other parties and participants of their position. The presentation of evidence and the contradictorial engagement with the Defence is not only a technical exercise in law enforcement or a means to win a case but guided by motives of moral instruction. Cases are brought in order to teach certain lessons. The appeal to punishment is at least partly inspired by the hope to encourage critical cognitive reflection by defendants.

Many of these didactic rationales extend beyond the agents involved in proceedings. They seek to promote public engagement or drive normative change. These dimensions are often overinflated or morally ambiguous.

Prosecutors have asserted that their investigations or prosecutions are means to educate entire domestic societies about wrongdoing. For instance, in *Taylor*, the Prosecution defended its case as an exercise of democratic agency, aimed at countering arbitrary rule and promoting domestic capacity. The Prosecution claimed to be speaking for the 'people of Sierra Leone'. It claimed that the trial was 'above all else' about 'seeking justice for the people of Sierra Leone' and meant to demonstrate to the people that 'there are those in this world who are ready to uphold the law'.[273] This rhetoric implied that the OTP is empowered to speak on behalf of Sierra Leone society and legitimized to counter inequalities in the world.

270 Antony Pemberton, Pauline G.M. Aarten, and Eva Mulder, 'Stories as Property: Narrative Ownership as a Key Concept in Victims' Experiences with Criminal Justice' (2018) *Criminology & Criminal Justice* 1–17.

271 Mark Drumbl, 'Victims Who Victimize' (2016) 4 *London Review of International Law* 217–46, 218.

272 Schwöbel-Patel, 'The "Ideal" Victim of International Criminal Law' 724.

273 See Glasius and Meijers, 'Constructions of Legitimacy' 240.

The ICC has used similar messianic messages to promote its didactic qualities. For example, in the *Al Mahdi* case, the OTP stressed that cultural destruction is about more than 'walls and stones'[274] in order to promote greater international engagement in other conflicts, such as Syria. An ambiguous example of expressivist rhetoric is the engagement with electoral violence in Kenya. The OTP branded its own role as an educational means to manage post-election violence. In a press statement entitled 'Kenya can be an Example to the World', it noted that 'Kenya will show how to manage past violence and how to create a peaceful process for the upcoming elections in 2012. Kenya will be an example to the world.'[275] The statement implied that the ICC would teach a moral history lesson for other nations through the example of Kenya. Seven years later, the OTP had to concede that this promise was highly ambitious. It noted that the cause for justice in Kenya was 'eroded by a 'perfect storm' of witness interference and intense politicization of the Court legal mandate and work.'[276]

Proponents of moral education theories claim that even failed cases may teach important didactic lessons. However, such didactic rhetoric is deeply problematic since it creates the impression that cases and trials are designed to produce specific outcomes and that the OTP has the political power and moral authority to educate entire societies. Failures to achieve the objectives promised may have negative expressivist effects in relation to belief in deterrence or demonstration of justice. It is thus contested to what extent prosecutors should use proceedings and cases as a means to shape security politics or 'educate' the masses. Such an approach seeks to create empathy for the goals of the Prosecution but instrumentalizes the interests of those who are at the receiving end of prosecutorial strategies.[277]

Procedurally, didactic rationales are most visibly reflected in charging discretion and, in particular, in the defence of thematic charges. The idea of focusing charges on certain themes in order to draw attention to specific forms of atrocity has some merits. Selection is inherent in the prosecutorial function. International prosecutors need to prioritize certain crimes and patterns of victimization in atrocity contexts. This is reflected in the ICC prosecutorial strategy. It may be legitimate to emphasize certain categories of crimes for broader didactic purposes, that is, to show that they 'they are not considered serious domestically and their victims are not heard, and therefore their voices have been silenced'.[278]

[274] See **section 3.1.1.3**.

[275] ICC Press Release, 'ICC Prosecutor: Kenya Can be an Example to the World', 18 September 2009, at https://www.icc-cpi.int/Pages/item.aspx?name=pr452.

[276] Statement of the Prosecutor of the International Criminal Court, Fatou Bensiuda, regarding Trial Chamber's decision to vacate charges against William Samoei Ruto and Joshua Arap Sang without prejudice to their prosecution in the future, 6 April 2016.

[277] Bikundo, 'Humanity's exemplary justice' 62.

[278] Mohammad Hadi Zakerhossein, 'The al-Mahdi case and thematic prosecution, 7 September 2016, at https://justicehub.org/article/the-al-mahdi-case-and-thematic-prosecution/..

However, thematic charging also has trade-offs. Its educative rationale is primarily oriented towards global audiences. Using trials to promote certain under-prosecuted types of criminality speaks predominantly to other international or domestic jurisdictions, global organizations, or non-governmental organizations (NGOs). These prioritizations drawn may limit the expressivist effects of cases vis-a-vis the immediate victims of crime whose interests are not reflected. They might also be at odds with domestic cultural preferences.[279] For instance, a strong focus on sexual and gender-based violence emphasizes values such as individual autonomy, self-determination, and sexual freedom. This emphasis may stand in competition with local prioritizations (e.g. protection of life, security, access to food or services), or more community-oriented conceptions of conflict-related harm. It is thus partially a choice about audiences. Thematic charging may also undermine other expressivist effects. It may reduce expression of retribution or belief in deterrence and convey images of partial justice.[280]

4.3.3 Witnesses: Narrating facts and evidence

Witnesses are key to the success of international criminal proceedings. International criminal justice relies heavily on witness testimony to prove a crime base, context, or the link of defendants to crimes. The criminal process involves different types of witnesses such as victim witnesses, eyewitnesses, or insider witnesses, who may have experienced events, and other witnesses who provide general background, context, or scientific evidence (e.g. expert witnesses).

The role of witnesses is crucial for the evidence and fact-finding process. Their testimony and stories 'influence not just how facts are perceived but what facts are'.[281] Storytelling influences not only courtroom advocacy but also methods of proof. The assessment of the evidence in international criminal trials is heavily based on inferences. Narratives have an important role in this. They complement probability assessments.[282] The construction of a story is an important cognitive tool to assess the evidence.[283] This approach (narrative evidence theory)

[279] Tim Kelsall, *Culture under Cross-Examination: International Justice and the Special Court for Sierra Leone* (Cambridge: Cambridge University Press, 2009), 243–55.

[280] See Christopher Mahony, 'Prioritising International Sex Crimes before the Special Court for Sierra Leone: One more instrument of political manipulation?' in Morten Bergsmo (ed.), *Thematic Prosecution of International Sex Crimes* (Brussels: Torkel Opsahl Academic EPublisher, 2018) 61–85, 84.

[281] Lisa Kern Griffin, 'Narrative, Truth, and Trial' (2013) 101 *Georgetown Law Journal* 281–335, 287.

[282] On the Bayesian model, see Stephen E. Feinberg and Mark J. Schervish, 'The Relevance of Bayesian Inference for the Presentation of Statistical Evidence and for Legal Decisionmaking' (1986) 66 *Boston Uiniversity Law Review* 771–98.

[283] On the role of narratives in jury assessment, see Nancy Pennington and Reid Hastie, 'A Cognitive Theory of Juror Decision Making: The Story Model' (1991) 13 *Cardozo Law Review* 519–57, 542.

helps to provide explanations for evidence and to make sense of conflicting testimony.[284]

The narratives provided by witnesses organize the experiences and events at trial.[285] They bear performative features (i.e. *mimesis* and *poiesis*). [286] As anthropologist Michael Jackson has argued, storytelling is 'never simply giving voice to what is on one's mind or in one own's interests; one is realizing, or objectifying one own's experience in ways that others can relate to through experiences of their own'.[287]

Providing testimony reconstitutes events in a story. A useful comparison may be drawn to Walter Benjamin's distinction between lived experience (*Erlebnis*) and reflected experience (*Erfahrung*)[288] which has been digested in order to share it with others and make it comprehensible. In-court testimony does not relive events but reworks them in conjunction with others, and based on the speakers' imagination. Testimony is based on evolving memory. It may be transformed by discussions with others that reshape memories and narratives. It is 'an incremental process of redescription telling the same story each time with additional detail'.[289] It is thus important to understand not only what witnesses experienced but also what led them to see events in this way.[290]

The dynamic dimensions of witness stories and the development of memory may contrast with the intended role of testimony in the narratives of parties (e.g. Prosecution and Defence) or the broader plot of the trial. One of the dangers of international criminal proceedings is the discrepancy between testimony in court and previous witness statements. Often years pass between an original witness interview and the actual trial. For prosecutors, witnesses may be 'living time bombs'. Statements are thus carefully selected and prepared.

[284] Michael S. Pardo and Ronald J. Allen, 'Juridical Proof and the Best Explanation' (2008) 27 *Law & Philosophy* 223–68, 225. See also Mark Klamberg, *Evidence in International Criminal Trials* (Leiden: Brill/Nijhoff, 2013) 166–7.

[285] Robert P. Burns, *A Theory of the Trial* (Princeton, NJ: Princeton University Press, 1999), 222 ('narrative forms the deep structure of human action').

[286] Lieketso Mohoto, 'Theatrical Strategies of Storytelling, Bearing Witness and Testimony for Another: An Examination of Two South African Plays' (2015) 28 *South African Theatre Journal* 78–87.

[287] Michael Jackson, *The Politics of Storytelling: Violence, Transgression, and Intersubjectivity* (Copenhagen: Museum Tusculanum Press, 2015), 15.

[288] See Walter Benjamin, 'Erfahrung' in Rolf Tiedemann and Hermann Schweppenhäuser (eds), *Gesammelte Schriften*, Vol. ii.1, (Frankfurt am Main: Suhrkamp, 1991), 54–5. See also Ben Highmore, *Everyday Life and Cultural Theory: An Introduction* (London: Routledge, 2002) 66–7.

[289] See Nigel Eltringham, '"We are not a Truth Commission": Fragmented Narratives and the Historical Record at the International Criminal Tribunal for Rwanda' (2009) 11 *Journal of Genocide Research* 55–79, 61.

[290] International criminal courts and tribunals have relied on a number of indicators to assess the veracity of the testimony. They include: knowledge of the facts, time span between the event and testimony, internal consistency of the testimony, its coherence with other evidence, personal interests affecting the motivation to tell the truth, as well as demeanour, conduct, and character. See Kelsall, *Culture under Cross-Examination* 183.

The methodologies of storytelling differ from truth and reconciliation commissions.[291] For instance, in South Africa, the Truth and Reconciliation Commission heard oral testimonies without an overarching narrative or a decisive organizing principle.[292] It sought to reflect 'widest possible record of people's perceptions, stories, myths and experience'.[293] The process was perceived as 'quasi-theatrical event'.[294] It provided witnesses with the ability to present their own narrative: 'victims and perpetrators gave their testimony like actors delivering a private monologue [much like the client on a counsellor's couch]; [and] the public watched like an audience, waiting to hear how the devastatingly bleak narratives would resolve themselves'.[295]

International criminal proceedings involve more constructed and strategic uses of narratives. They apply a more legalistic style of storytelling in which the witness 'story' is polished. The Prosecution essentially wants the witness to retell the story framed in the charges. The statement is thus prepared and re-enacted. The legal process is more coercive. It 'does not permit witnesses to tell their own coherent narrative; it chops their stories into digestible parts, selects a handful of parts, and sorts and refines them to create a new narrative—the legal narrative'.[296]

The *ad hoc* tribunals have allowed substantive preparation of witnesses for trial, that is, conversations between the Prosecution or the Defence and a witness prior to testimony, comparison of projected testimony with earlier statements, or clarification of deficiencies or differences in recollection. Witness preparation was justified by pragmatic concerns, such as the weaknesses of human memory, the long periods of time between original statement and testimony, and objective of facilitating 'accurate, complete, orderly and efficient presentation of the evidence in the trial'.[297]

The ICC has criticized 'witness proofing', based on fears that pre-testimonial contacts with witnesses might compromise the integrity of evidence. In the *Lubanga* case, the Trial Chamber, presided by British Judge Fulford, decided that it is permitted to refresh memory, but prohibited to discuss the content of the witness statement in Court or any exhibits, since this could lead to a distortion of the truth

[291] As the ICTR put it: 'We are running a trial . . . We are not a truth commission', see Eltringham, 'We are not a Truth Commission' 55.

[292] On historical functions of truth commissions, see Charles S. Maier, 'Doing history, doing justice: The narrative of the historian and the truth commission' in Robert Rotberg and Dennis Thompson (eds), *Truth v. Justice: The Morality of Truth Commission* (Princeton, NJ: Princeton University Press, 2000), 261–78.

[293] On personal and narrative truth, see Truth and Reconciliation Commission of South Africa Report, Vol. 1 (Cape Town: Juta, 1998) 112.

[294] Mohoto, 'Theatrical Strategies of Storytelling' 81.

[295] Greg Homann, 'Preamble' in Greg Homann (ed.), *At this Stage: Plays from Post Apartheid South Africa* (Johannesburg: Wits University Press, 2009), 1, 11.

[296] Julie Mertus, 'The politics of memory and international trials for wartime rape' in Paul Gready (ed.), *Political Transition: Politics and Cultures* (London: Pluto Press, 2003), 227–65, 230.

[297] *Prosecutor v. Limaj and others*, Decision on Defence Motion on Prosecution Practice of 'Proofing' Witnesses, IT-03-66-T, 10 December 2004, para. 2.

('rehearsal of in-court testimony') and diminish the spontaneous nature of testimony.[298] This line of reasoning was questioned by Trial V in the Kenya cases.[299] It claimed that spontaneity of testimony is often a fiction when victims come to trial. It argued that risks of undue witness coaching might be mitigated by 'transparency', that is, a witness preparation protocol regulating duty of disclosure and video-recording, and effective 'use of cross-examination'.

The tendency to curtail the freedom and immediacy of witness testimony is driven by the adversarial nature of trials. It creates mixed experiences for witnesses.[300] As Kai Ambos has argued:

> the more informal and conversational witness interrogation by a judge, as practiced in modern civil law systems, may be more appropriate since it will put the witness at ease and thus create an atmosphere where she can tell her story, which in turn is more conducive to fact—and truth-finding.[301]

4.3.4 The Defence: Counter-performances and courtroom drama

The Defence is the procedural counterpart of the Prosecution. It needs to counter charges that are loaded with high moral stigma, including attacks on community values, human rights protections, and rights of victims. Traditionally, criminal trials have focused on the defendant as the centre of the trial. However, with the rise of restorative justice and victim-centric approaches, this role has changed. The defendant is one among several protagonists and may face arguments by the Prosecution and victims. This affects the 'disparity between the circumstances of the accusers and of the accused'.[302]

Mounting a Defence strategy is a heavy burden which requires different types of performance. The defendant is not only an object but a subject in proceedings, who may actively participate in the trial or choose to stay silent throughout

[298] *Prosecutor v. Lubanga*, Decision Regarding the Practices Used to Prepare and Familiarise Witnesses for Giving Testimony at Trial, ICC-01/04-01/06, 30 November 2007, paras 51–52.

[299] *Prosecutor v. Muthaura and Kenyatta*, Decision on Witness Preparation, ICC-01/09-02/11, 2 January 2013, para. 47 ('Chamber considers that the risk can be adequately addressed by appropriate safeguards'); *Prosecutor v. Ruto and Sang*, Decision on witness preparation, ICC-01/09-01/11, 2 January 2013, para. 43.

[300] Rebecca Horn, Simon Charters, and Saleem Vahidy, 'Testifying in an International War Crimes Tribunal: The Experience of Witnesses in the Special Court for Sierra Leone' (2009) 3 *International Journal of Transitional Justice* 135–49.

[301] Kai Ambos, Treatise on International Criminal Law: Vol. III: International Criminal Procedure (Oxford: Oxford University Press, 2016), 467.

[302] Robert H. Jackson, Opening Statement for the United States of America, On the Subject of International Military Tribunal No. I (21 November 1945), in Trial of the Major War Criminals before the International Military Tribunal, Nuremberg 14 November 1945—1 October 1946, Vol. 2 (1947), 101.

proceedings. The Defence as an institution is an agent of justice. It needs to respond to the charges. It may speak to different audiences than the Prosecution, including constituencies outside the courtroom, in order to contest the legitimacy of the trial itself.

4.3.4.1 Institutional function

In international criminal proceedings, the defendant has often a particular status. Many defendants are tried because of their special role as military, political, or institutional leader of state structures or organizations in international crimes. They are thus to some extent public symbols of past atrocities in the court of public opinion. The crimes that they represent may not only be related to their own wrongdoing but also symbolize the wrongs of others.

There is a risk that the ritual of the trial is perceived as a form of public 'sacrifice'[303] of the defendant. A sacrifice typically requires an object, an entity who performs the sacrifice (sacrifice), and an audience to whom it is directed (sacrifier).[304] Drawing on René Girard's theory on scapegoating,[305] some scholars have compared international criminal trials to performances in which the defendant is offered as a sacrifice to provide social catharsis, 'social bonding and the binding of violence'.[306]

This structural condition may affect the presumption of innocence or create an inherent confirmation bias. This explains why the Defence plays a crucial role from a justice perspective. A fair and effective Defence is not only necessary to protect the rights of defendant[307] but also serves to safeguard the interests of the criminal justice system as a whole. It protects the equality of arms between the Prosecution and the Defence and the rights of a defendant to a fair trial.

Each story has several sides. The Defence is essential for the integrity of proceedings and the process of truth-finding.[308] Its presence ensures that 'justice is done, and seen to be done'. It sends a message about the fair treatment of the defendant and future offenders.

The defendant is not only an object but a subject on proceedings.[309] The lack of engagement by the Defence may have negative effects from a performative point of view. For instance, if a defendant 'refuses to defend himself', it will be a 'lose–lose' situation for all. Refusing to defend is in itself 'politically performative'.[310] It

303 Henri Hubert and Marcel Mauss, *Sacrifice: Its Nature and Function*, trans. W.D. Halls (Chicago, IL: University of Chicago Press, 1964).

304 Ibid., 10–12.

305 René Girard, *The Scapegoat* (Baltimore, MD: Johns Hopkins University Press, 1986).

306 Bikundo, 'Humanity's exemplary justice' 62.

307 Björn Elberling, *The Defendant in International Criminal Proceedings: Between Law and Historiography* (Portland, OR: Hart Publishing, 2012).

308 See generally Colleen Rohan and Gentian Zyberi (eds), *Defense Perspectives on International Criminal Justice* (Cambridge: Cambridge University Press, 2017); Mayeul Hiéramente and Patricia Schneider (eds), *The Defence in International Criminal Trials* (Baden-Baden: Nomos, 2016).

309 See Ambos, *Treatise on International Criminal Law: Vol. III* 166.

310 Allo, 'The "Show" in the Show Trials' 66.

complicates the goal to see the trial as a means of communication with the defendant, or as an instrument to reintegrate offenders.

4.3.4.2 Defence narratives

Defence narratives are crucial to the success of trials. As Alexandra Natapoff has argued, 'it is through speech that defendants engage with the law, understand it and express anger, remorse, and their acceptance or rejection of the criminal justice process'.[311]

The Defence may win a case by contesting evidence and raising doubt. But it is often necessary to develop its own counter-narratives to events or to challenge the role or nexus of the defendant to crimes in order to confront the public stigma associated with charges. The success of a Defence strategy may require alternative narratives to the Prosecution and independent Defence investigations.[312]

Defence narratives contribute as much to the construction of the image of the perpetrator as Prosecution narratives.[313] The Defence often seeks to establish that the defendant is not an inhumane perpetrator but rather a victim of coercive circumstances, or an individual caring about humanity.[314] Defence narratives may suggest that the defendant could not have been expected to act differently, and that others placed in the same position might have acted in the same way. They reframe actions in order to distance themselves from the crimes,[315] diminish blameworthiness of actions, shift responsibility, or imply that, under the wrong conditions, anybody can turn into a perpetrator of international crimes.[316]

Methodologically, the discourse of the Defence is partially intended to challenge the idea of deviance. It seeks to fit the defendant into 'a morally defensible lens' by justifying action or stressing conformity to group dynamics in extraordinary circumstances.[317] Defendants may struggle with the paradox of an inverted world view. Actions that were deemed to be legitimate at their time and in their local contexts are now branded as instances of criminality.[318] Discursive reconstructions are meant to demonstrate an alternative vision of social reality and a different image

[311] Alexandra Natapoff, 'Speechless: The Silencing of Criminal Defendants' (2005) 80 *New York University Law Review* 1449–504, 1449.

[312] See generally Jenia Iontcheva Turner, 'Defense Perspectives on Law and Politics in International Criminal Trials' (2008) 48 *Virginia Journal of International Law'* 529–94.

[313] Mina Rauschenbach, Christian Staerkle, and Damien Scalia, 'Accused for Involvement in Collective Violence: The Discursive Reconstruction of Agency and Identity by Perpetrators of International Crimes' (2015) 37 *Political Psychology* 219–35.

[314] See Stolk, 'A Sophisticated Beast?' 692.

[315] On distancing, see Johanna Peetz, Gregory Gunn, and Anne Wilson, 'Crimes of the Past: Defensive Temporal Distancing in the Face of Past In-Group Wrongdoing' (2010) 36 *Personality and Social Psychology Bulletin* 598–611.

[316] For a survey, see Kristen Perrin, *Transcripts from the International Criminal Tribunal for the Former Yugoslavia: A Linguistic Interpretation of Sociological Patterns found in Court Data*, PhD Thesis (London: UCL, 2016) 176–263.

[317] Rauschenbach, Staerkle, and Scalia, 'Accused for Involvement in Collective Violence' 232.

[318] Akhavan, 'Beyond impunity' 7.

of the perpetrator. For instance, in *Lubanga*, the Defence actively supported the narrative of the Ituri conflict as ethnic, rather than economically driven conflict, in order to 'mount a necessity defence that mitigates the gravity of the crime'.[319]

Empirical studies of perpetrator discourse suggest that courtroom strategy is partly a means to assert control. It is used by individual accused to regain narrative ownership that has been framed by Prosecution stories and institutional narratives: 'Through their active positioning within various identity and power relations, [defendants] expect to regain part of the control they have lost through their experience of the international criminal justice system and subsequent detention.'[320]

In practice, defendants have adopted different strategies to counter Prosecution narratives. They include techniques to delegitimize institutions (e.g. through invocation of bias, hegemony, or flawed representation of the past), challenges to idealized Prosecution narratives, discursive reconstructions (e.g. images of victimhood, martyrdom), or attempts to bring a 'personal truth to the fore'.[321]

At the SCSL, defendants like Hinga Norm and Augustine Gbao took issue with 'attempt to depoliticise their actions', tried 'to reinsert questions of political context into the courtroom' and played 'to the public gallery'.[322]

At the ICTY, some Defence counsel have invoked 'chaos' or 'arguments to deny or mitigate blame.[323] For instance, in *Delić*, the Defence argued that 'truth is the first casualty in a war'.[324] Other Defence briefs referred to 'war chaos', 'orders', and 'war psychosis'.[325] These arguments suggest that defendants were 'out of control' or simple 'cogs' in a machine.

Other Defence teams have invoked political critiques and framed them as legal arguments. Some defendants have openly alleged that they were used as scapegoats. Others have argued that they are the subject of selective prosecution or contested the legality of the tribunal. Most of the objections were unsuccessful. Judges have been reluctant to rule that their own court or tribunal was unlawfully established. The threshold for selective prosecution is high. It requires a demonstration of discriminatory intent by the Prosecution,[326] which is hard to establish in light of prosecutorial discretion. More effective Defence techniques are challenges to the

[319] See Richard A. Wilson, 'Through the Lens of International Criminal Law: Comprehending the African Context of Crimes at the International Criminal Court' (2011) 11 *Studies in Ethnicity and Nationalism* 106–15, 107.

[320] Rauschenbach, Staerkle, and Scalia, 'Accused for Involvement in Collective Violence' 231.

[321] See Mina Rauschenbach, 'Individuals Accused of International Crimes as Delegitimized Agents of Truth' (2018) 28 *International Criminal Justice Review* 291–316, 308.

[322] See Kelsall, 'Politics, Anti-Politics, International Justice' 602, 596–601.

[323] Wilson, *Writing History in International Criminal Trials* 148–69.

[324] Houge, 'Re-presentations of Defendant Perpetrators in Sexual War Violence Cases' 428.

[325] Ibid., 433.

[326] The ICTY held that the defendant needs to 'demonstrate that the decision to prosecute him or to continue his prosecution was based on impermissible motives, such as race or religion, and that the Prosecution failed to prosecute similarly situated defendants'. See *Prosecutor v. Delalić et al.*, Judgment, IT-96-21-A, 20 February 2001, para. 607 (*Delalić* Appeal Judgment).

reliability of evidence, the credibility of witness testimony, including linkage evidence, or strategies to deny a sufficient nexus to crimes based on the role of others in the planning or commissions of crimes.

Self-representation is a popular strategy in international trials to challenge court authority, increase an adversarial culture, or express defiance. In several cases, defendants have decided to represent themselves in proceedings and used the trial as a stage to produce counter-histories. For instance, Milošević has presented an alternative account of the fall of Yugoslavia and implicated the West in crimes ('*tu quoque*'). He extended the audience beyond the courtroom and added new political frames to discourse. He quoted extensively from external sources (e.g. Wesley Clark) in order to distance himself from events and let others speak for him. He refused to recognize the authority of the ICTY as legitimate and 'real' court, referring to it as the 'so-called Tribunal'.[327] Ultimately, his speech sought to reassign blame and victimhood and redefine who deserves punishment. Karadžić played to Serbian audiences by presenting himself as a 'servant' of his people and challenging his involvement in relation to Srebrenica.[328] Both defendants benefited from media attention and the existence of a receptive audience for their discourses. They used speech as a means to maintain a leadership role and power over narratives. They portrayed 'the West' as the 'guilty party', drew attention to Serbian victimhood, and presented themselves as martyrs for the collective cause of the nation.[329] Other ICTY accused, like Vojislav Šešelj or Slobodan Praljak, used not only media channels to reinforce their case but published their own counter-histories, in order to mobilize domestic audiences.[330]

Several defendants have used the trial as a platform to express protest or obstruct proceedings.[331] There is a whole range of practices which may cause rupture and confrontation:

> [A] disruptive and discourteous attitude towards officers of the court; contempt for and aggressiveness towards witnesses and victims; a refusal to use legal language or otherwise adopt an 'internal' perspective on the law; constant 'politicization' of the trial and portrayal of the law 'externally' as a mere instrument of power politics; a refusal to discuss issues of fact and law regarding one's alleged criminal acts; refusal to discuss one's individual case as opposed to broader political and historical events.[332]

[327] Perrin, *Transcripts from the International Criminal Tribunal for the Former Yugoslavia* 202.

[328] See Meijers and Glasius, 'Expression of Justice or Political Trial?' 750.

[329] For an excellent survey, Izabela Steflja, 'The Production of the War Criminal Cult: Radovan Karadžić and Vojislav Šešelj at The Hague' (2018) 46 *Nationalities Papers* 52–68.

[330] Vladimir Petrović, 'The ICTY Library: War Criminals as Authors, Their Works as Sources' (2018) 28 *International Criminal Justice Review* 333–48. Praljak produced 18 works, *Šešelj* 63 volumes.

[331] Mégret, 'Practices of Stigmatization' 314.

[332] See Frédéric Mégret and Marika Giles Samson, 'Defiance, Defence, Repentance and What Lies Between' (2019) 17 *JICJ* 151–77, 155.

In Cambodia, Defence counsel Jacques Verges was accused by a member of the public of 'performing a circus, or a play in a theater'.[333] At the ICTY, Mladić interrupted proceedings through political speeches and was cut off by judges. Nuon Chea and Hissène Habré refused to appear at trial. Šešelj used courtroom drama and notions of conspiracy and self-sacrifice to attack the trial as forum of justice. He refused to attend court and went on hunger strike. Such techniques are grounded in a 'political', rather than a legal rationality.[334] They are used by defendants to portray themselves as martyrs or victims, to delay proceedings, or seek 'political vindication'.[335]

The ultimate performance of protest was Praljak's public suicide in the courtroom after the verdict which imitated Socrates' death. It was an act of resentment which challenged ICTY narratives regarding the Croatian war in Bosnia and the use of the trial as showcase to demonstrate that 'it is the world community that decides about the fate of war criminals'.[336]

Such practices run counter to the perception of the trial as a performance of justice.[337] As scholars have noted: 'If the defendant succeeds in delegitimizing the court in the eyes of (some of) the audiences, the entire expressivist potential towards those audiences will be undermined. If the court is not taken seriously, truth-telling and stigmatization of particular behaviours cannot succeed.'[338]

Judges have imposed limits on the modalities of self-representation in the courtroom in order to prevent the obstruction and delay of proceedings by defendants.

4.3.5 Judges: Fact-finders, meaning messengers, and directors of performance

Judges have an active role in the performance of justice. They typically exercise several functions simultaneously: They are fact-finders, interpreters, and managers. Their performative authority is related to their independence and impartiality, and their resistance to partisan approaches.

4.3.5.1 Fact-finding

Accurate fact-finding is a cornerstone of the criminal process. Judges act as the ultimate adjudicators of fact. They have to listen to all narratives and make sense

333 Rachel Hughes, 'Ordinary Theatre and Extraordinary Law at the Khmer Rouge Tribunal' (2015) 33 *Environment and Planning D: Society and Space* 714–31, 726.

334 Mégret and Samson, 'Defiance, Defence, Repentance and What Lies Between' 167.

335 Ibid. 156.

336 See Alexander Heinze, 'Slobodan Praljak's Suicide and International Criminal Justice' E-International Relations, 9 January 2018, at https://www.e-ir.info/2018/01/09/slobodan-praljaks-suicide-and-international-criminal-justice/.

337 Damaška, 'Reflections on Fairness in International Criminal Justice' 617.

338 Glasius and Meijers, 'Constructions of Legitimacy' 252.

of competing meanings. Their duty is to establish an accurate account of the facts. Judges need to test competing narratives and evaluate witness testimony.[339] They also have to analyse the motives of parties and participants and connect to the broader context. This requires an active role.

Judges are not supposed to fill shortcomings or failures in the Prosecution case to the detriment of the defendant. But they have independent powers of assessment. They have asserted these powers to question witnesses independently of the parties, to hear directly from victims as participants, or to call witnesses they consider relevant, in order to determine the truth.[340] This may give witnesses and victims a sense of value, dignity, or agency. Ultimately, the presumed rationality and impartiality of judicial fact-finding may send a counter-message to the emotional nature of testimony and identify meta-narratives that deviate from those presented by the parties.[341]

In the exercise of their powers, judges are more constrained than historians. Their findings are thus often mere starting points for future historical inquiry. They rely on the expertise of expert witnesses, who speak to context and history.

4.3.5.2 Judges as interpretant

The duty to apply and interpret the law is the most classical role of judges. Judges have the authority to determine the meaning of legal provisions and their application in individual cases. Their task bears resemblance with the role of the interpretant in Peirce's sign theory.[342] The judge gives meaning to the many signs and messages expressed by parties and participants in the application and interpretation of the law. As semiotic theorists have argued, interpretation is partly an act of decoding.[343] Representations by parties and participants are mediated through words, codes and sometimes ambiguous legal language. The judges 'unlock' the meanings. They do not only infer such meanings from established traditions but play an active role in defining the very conventions and rules that help to decipher the signals conveyed in the legal process. Ultimately the judges have to make a decision on the legal relevance of narratives.

339 See Wilson, *Humanity's Histories* 43.

340 See Guido Acquaviva, Nancy Combs, Mikaela Heikkilä, Suzannah Linton, Yvonne McDermott, and Sergey Vasiliev, 'Trial process' in Göran Sluiter, Håkan Friman, Suzannah Linton, Sergey Vasiliev, and Salvatore Zappalà (eds) *International Criminal Procedure* (Oxford: Oxford University Press, 2013), 489–938, 578.

341 On shifting attitudes of defendants, based on Court interactions, see Mégret and Samson, 'Defiance, Defence, Repentance and What Lies Between' 176.

342 See Tiefenbrun, *Decoding International Law* 39.

343 Ibid., 24 ('Interpretation (known in semiotic terms as decoding) is the systematic process of finding keys to hidden codes that unlock the doors to meaning. Interpretation is a major part of the legal process because of the volume and complexity of its codes and because of the indirect nature of legal language that, like ordinary language, merely represents reality through the mediation of words.').

In the exercise of their functions, judges have not confined themselves to a mere application of predetermined rules or traditions. They have acted as pioneers, engineers, and 'meaning managers'[344] due to the imperfections of the international legal framework, their expert authority, peer pressure, and influences by NGOs and justice constituencies, and strong moral incentives to create accountability systems for atrocity crime.[345]

Judges have been reluctant to accept the idea of a *non-liquet*, that is, the absence or insufficiency of law on a question at hand.[346] They have been eager to solve problems, give precision to norms, or if necessary extend the realm of law.

Due to the incomplete nature of rules of procedure and evidence, judges have almost inevitably been engaged in procedural law-making.[347] For instance, the *ad hoc* tribunals,[348] the SCSL, and the Kosovo Specialist Chambers were mandated to adopt their own rules of procedure. They have adopted 'recommendations'[349] and guidelines to reflect best practices and guide other tribunals. This practice is guided by the intent to develop a framework that provides the best 'epistemic fit' to international crimes.[350]

The judgment marks an attempt to produce a legally authoritative reading of words, signs, and signals expressed in the procedures. It translates the different narratives of the trial into one authoritative account. It is meant to provide a final narrative or sense of closure that extends beyond the individual submissions of parties[351] and responds to all participants in the case.

Separate and dissenting opinions play an important in the exercise of the judicial function. They serve to accommodate conflicting narratives and interpretations. They are an expression of the conscience and independence of judges, and a means to counter conviction bias and make the majority answerable for their claims.[352]

[344] See **section 3.2**.

[345] Beth van Schaack, 'Nullum Crimen Sine Lege: Judicial Lawmaking at the Intersection of Law and Morals' (2008) 97 *Georgetown Law Journal* 121–92.

[346] Julius Stone, 'Non Liquet and the Function of Law in the International Community' (1959) 35 *British Yearbook of International Law* 124–61.

[347] See Göran Sluiter, 'Procedural lawmaking at the international criminal tribunals' in Shane Darcy and Joseph Powderly (eds), *Judicial Creativity at the International Criminal Tribunals* (Oxford: Oxford University Press, 2010) 315–31.

[348] In *Tadić*, the ICTY stated that the Security Council surely expected that '[the Statute] would be supplemented, where advisable, by the rules which the Judges were mandated to adopt, especially for Trials and Appeals'. See *Tadić* Interlocutory Appeal 1995, para. 4.

[349] See *Prosecutor v. Gbagbo and Blé Goudé*, Judgment on the appeal of Mr Laurent Gbagbo against the decision of Trial Chamber I entitled 'Decision giving notice pursuant to Regulation 55(2) of the Regulations of the Court', ICC—02/11-01/15-369, 18 December 2015, para. 54.

[350] John Jackson, 'Finding the Best Epistemic Fit for International Criminal Tribunals' (2009) 7 *JICJ* 17–39.

[351] Robert Cryer, Hakan Friman, Darryl Robinson, and Elizabeth Wilmshurst, *An Introduction to International Criminal Law and Procedure* (3rd edn, Cambridge University Press, 2014), 38–40.

[352] See Hemi Mistry, 'The Paradox of Dissent: Judicial Dissent and the Projects of International Criminal Justice' (2015) 13 *JICJ* 449–74.

Separate opinions are a means to deviate from the strict frame of majority reasoning. They enable judges to expand on *obiter dicta* or to send messages 'to the community of international lawyers' or other addresses,[353] and to the other organs of the UN'. They may address points silenced in the reasoning of the judgment or engage judges and professional communities in a broader 'conversation' about alternative hypotheses or consequences of rulings.

Dissenting opinions are a means to voice dissent or engage with the limits of the law.[354] Some dissents have challenged evidentiary readings, criticized the argument of the majority, or contributed to the development of the law. Other, more fundamental dissents, like Pal's at Tokyo, have addressed broader problems that have not been discussed in the majority judgment or have provided fundamentally different accounts of the historical and political context of trials.[355] They may serve as counter-performances to traditional readings.

4.3.5.3 Managerial powers

Managerial powers of judges are essential to protect the integrity of proceedings and their role as legal performances of justice rather than drama. They enable procedural expressivism and impose constraints at the same time.

Judges have to secure fairness towards parties and participants and the fairness of the trial as a whole. Ultimately, they are bound to ensure 'that individuals are not convicted of offenses that do not adequately represent their level of responsibility'.[356]

Judges also have a role in controlling the use of resources. They watch over the expeditiousness of proceedings and may intervene to ensure that only sufficiently grave cases are investigated and or prosecuted internationally. This turns them into 'guardians of the relative exceptionality of stigma'.[357]

The procedure as a whole remains often dominated by the idea of competition between the case of the Prosecution and the case of the Defence. However, judges may take on a more active role in setting time limits, facilitating agreement, streamlining charges, limiting the number of witnesses heard, or controlling and expediting cases. They have used these powers to control testimony and reduce witness lists, limit the very possibility of witness participation, or silence defendants who sought to turn the trial into a 'solo show'.

353 Werner, 'Securitization and Judicial Review' 364.

354 In international criminal justice, typically the voice of a majority (e.g. two judges) is sufficient to enter a conviction, even if a minority (e.g. one judge) finds that the charges have not been proved beyond reasonable doubt.

355 See Neha Jain, 'Radical Dissents in International Criminal Trials' (2017) 28 *EJIL* 1163–8.

356 Mégret, 'Practices of Stigmatization' 296.

357 Ibid., 296.

4.3.6 Victims: Agents and objects between trauma and catharsis

International criminal justice has a conflicting relationship with the role of victims in proceedings.[358] Victims are important for the symbolism of trials. Traditionally, crimes have been conceived as crimes 'against order in society', but not as crimes 'against victims per se'.[359] The role of victims in proceedings is key for expressivist purposes. Victims are both a crucial audience and a constituency of trials. They are a means to create societal attachment. They have increasingly been recognized as active agents in proceedings. Their voices and experiences are heard in court. This move from 'passive object' to agency sends a message that the crime causes harm to concrete persons and communities.[360]

At the same time, the role of victims in truth-finding and their procedural rights are limited. The speech and narrative function of victims is highly mediated. Direct involvement of victim-survivors in the trial may be harmful since it carries a risk of re-traumatization. Victims may be presented through one-sided lenses, namely as objects of harm.[361] Courts face a constant dilemma: they struggle to accommodate the complexity of victims and victimization but they also cannot live without them.

4.3.6.1 Between symbolism and performance

The role of victims has undergone a conceptual revolution.[362] It navigates between symbolism and agency.[363] It is marked by a tension between the status as object and subject of proceedings.[364]

In a criminal trial, the story of victimization is traditionally told through the story of perpetrators and witnesses. The trial focuses on the facts of the crime and the responsibility of the defendant. The trend to make trials more victim-centred and is relatively novel at the international level. Victims have both a symbolic and a performative role.

As Maria Elander has shown, their role has been 'reconfigured' over time.[365] The recognition of a more performative role is a story in four acts (the 'abstract victim',

[358] Mahdev Mohan, 'The Paradox of Victim-Centrism: Victim Participation at the Khmer Rouge Tribunal,' (2009) 5 *International Criminal Law Review* 733–75.

[359] Benjamin Schiff, *Building the International Criminal Court* (Cambridge: Cambridge University Press, 2008), 32.

[360] Claire Garbett, 'From Passive Objects to Active Agents: Changing Conceptions of Victim Identities at the ICTY and ICC' (2016) 15 *Journal of Human Rights* 40–59.

[361] See Maria Elander, 'The Victim's Address: Expressivism and the Victim at the Extraordinary Chambers in the Courts of Cambodia' (2013) 7 *International Journal of Transitional Justice* 95–115, 101.

[362] Shoshana Felman, 'Theaters of Justice: Arendt in Jerusalem, the Eichmann Trial, and the Redefinition of Legal Meaning in the Wake of the Holocaust' (2000) 1 *Theoretical Inquiries in Law* 201–38.

[363] On agency, see Scott Kenney, 'Human Agency Revisited: The Paradoxical Experiences of Victims of Crime' (2004) 11 *International Review of Victimology* 225–57.

[364] Susanne Karstedt, 'From Absence to Presence, from Silence to Voice: Victims in International and Transitional Justice Since the Nuremberg Trials (2010) 17 *International Review of Victimology* 9–30.

[365] Maria Elander, *Figuring Victims in International Criminal Justice: The Case of the Khmer Rouge Tribunal in Figuring Victims in International Criminal Justice* (New York, NY: Routledge, 2018).

the victim as 'survivor testifier', the victim as witness,[366] and the victim as agent). In the early phase of international criminal justice, the victim was mainly 'absent' in proceedings. In Nuremberg in Tokyo, victims did not have an independent voice as speakers. Victims were simply objects or audiences.[367] The main idea was that the trial would reveal a truth to victims. Victims remained 'abstract' entities.[368]

In the *Eichmann* trial, prosecutors rediscovered the value the testimony by survivors. Victims were not simply deemed to be passive observers but were given a more active role as 'survivor testifier'. The prosecution invited more than 100 survivors to testify. They represented the facts.[369] They spoke in proceedings in different ways 'through the testimonies, through the speech of the Attorney General Hausner, and through a presence as audience at trial'.[370]

The involvement of survivors was a deliberate strategy. It was meant to provide a 'living record' and to convey narratives of heroism in order to constitute a social bond and reinforce the legitimacy of the birth of Israel as a nation. Lawrence Douglas saw it as an instrument to provide not only 'formal' but also narrative justice.[371] He qualified the trial as an attempt to provide 'representational justice to the Holocaust' through survivor testimony.[372]

At the *ad hoc* tribunals, victims were more broadly treated as witnesses. Victims selected by the parties, thereby contributed to the truth-finding process of the trial through their testimony. However, their contribution was constrained by the adversarial features of trials. Victims did not necessarily have an opportunity to relate their story and experiences. The testimony was heavily pre-scripted through the contours the case of the parties. It had thus a strategic rather than a 'representational' function. The strict rules of examination imposed constraints on the liberty of victims to deviate from the script of the trial and created risks of 'secondary victimization'.[373] Some observers claim that victims were indirectly silenced.[374]

Some of these limitations were addressed through the broader recognition of the autonomous role of victims in modern procedural instruments. At the ICC and the STL, victims were recognized as independent agents ('participants') in criminal proceedings whose voice is not tied to that of the parties. They are entitled to

[366] See generally Natalie von Wistinghausen, 'Victims as witnesses: Views from the defence' in Thorsten Bonacker and Christoph Safferling (eds), *Victims of International Crimes: An Interdisciplinary Discourse* (The Hague: Springer, 2013), 165–73.

[367] For an account, see Yael Danieli, 'Reappraising the Nuremberg Trials and Their Legacy: The Role of Victims in International Law (2006) 27 *Cardozo Law Review* 1633–49.

[368] Elander, *Figuring Victims in International Criminal Justice* 19.

[369] Haim Gouri, *Facing the Glass Booth: The Jerusalem Trial of Adolf Eichmann*, trans. Michael Swirsky (Detroit, MI: Wayne State University Press, 2004), 269.

[370] Ibid., 20.

[371] Douglas, *Memory of Judgment* 126.

[372] Douglas, *Memory of Judgment* 113.

[373] Marie-Bénédicte Dembour and Emily Haslam, 'Silencing Witnesses? Victim Witnesses at War Crimes Trials' (2014) 15 *EJIL* 151–77, 168.

[374] Ibid., 153.

present their own 'views and concerns' to the judges, independently of the story of the Prosecution or the Defence. In the *Bemba* trial, victims were allowed to 'participate at hearings and status conferences, to make opening and closing statements, to file written submissions, to introduce evidence, to question witnesses subject to a discrete written application decided upon in advance by the Chamber, and to have access to confidential documents in the record'.[375] This move illustrates that victims' stories are crucial to the truth-finding process. It entails a promise that the voice of victims may extend beyond witness testimony.

The procedural status as participants has important ramifications. It provides greater visibility to victims. It entails a certain formal recognition of the status as victim. It also has a denunciatory effect. It signals that the wrong done by the perpetrator caused concrete forms of harm to 'real' rather than 'abstract' victims.

Victim participation is based on the assumption that victim stories and perspectives can make criminal proceedings more meaningful. At the ICC, victims were even allowed to present their own evidence, based on the truth-finding powers of judges.[376]

From an expressivist perspective, victim participation pursues at least two important macro goals. Allowing victims to tell their story is a means to regain agency.[377] Theoretically, it may enable victims to gain self-respect, status, and recognition, and to present themselves as 'survivors', rather than vulnerable or passive victims.[378] Participation is also a means to strengthen community attachment (communion).[379] Participation in the trial as ritual may carry important symbolic meaning, irrespective of the punishment of the perpetrator. Victim statements may reconnect victims to their social communities or foster new bonds of attachment.

However, in practice, these objectives face significant challenges.[380] Victim participation continues to be characterized by a high degree of instrumentalization in the format of the criminal trial. The very idea of the victim as 'active agent' may not correspond to societal realities after conflict. The individualized and autonomous

375 *Prosecutor v. Bemba*, Judgment pursuant to Article 74 of the Statute, ICC-01/05-01/08, 21 March 2016, para. 24.

376 See *Prosecutor v. Lubanga*, Judgment on the appeals of The Prosecutor and The Defence against Trial Chamber I's Decision on Victims' Participation of 18 January 2008, ICC-01/04-01/06-1432, 11 July 2008, paras 3 and 4.

377 See generally Eva Mulder, Antony Pemberton, and Pauline G.M. Aarten, 'Beyond Retribution, Value Restoration and Procedural Justice: The Big Two of Agency and Communion in Victims Perspective on Justice' (2017) *Psychology, Crime and Law* 682–98.

378 Johanna Ray Vollhardt and Michal Bilewicz, 'After the Genocide: Psychological Perspectives on Victim, Bystander, and Perpetrator Groups' (2013) 69 *Journal of Social Issues* 1–15.

379 Mulder, Pemberton, and Aarten, 'Beyond Retribution, Value Restoration and Procedural Justice' 682–98.

380 On experiences, see Luke Moffett, 'Meaningful and Effective? Considering Victims' Interests Trough Participation at the International Criminal Court' (2015) 26 *Criminal Law Forum* 255–89; Eric Stover, Mychelle Balthazard, and Alexa Koenig, 'Confronting Duch: Civil Party Participation in Case 001 at the Extraordinary Chambers in the Courts of Cambodia' (2011) 93 *International Review of the Red Cross* 503–46.

notion of victimhood underlying claims of participation may contrast with competing local practices.[381]

The interests of victims do not necessarily coincide with the objectives of the trial. Their personal interests may detract from the narrow focus of the trial. Their story is appropriated by others in the course of proceedings.[382] Victimhood is trimmed to fit within the legal boundaries of the trial[383] and typically constrained by the scope of charges brought by the Prosecution. Victims are approached through the lens of 'harm and suffering'. There is a risk that courts take narrative ownership.[384] Ultimately, victims are thus both agents and objects. The criminal trial does not only offer prospects of agency but appropriates 'victim's grief, makes it its own and reenacts the grief over and over again through its focus on suffering and harm'.[385]

4.3.6.2 Narrative functions

In victimology,[386] it has become common to study victims and patterns of victimization through narratives.[387] Storytelling by victims in justice processes is sometimes regarded as a form of therapeutic expression ('testimony as catharsis').[388] Studies in social psychology suggest that victims and survivors need to tell their story in order to move on with their lives.[389] Silence about events or 'not telling' the story would perpetuate wrong inflicted through the crime and the injustice experienced. Therapeutic justifications of victim participation have increased in

[381] Garbett, 'From Passive Objects to Active Agents' 54 ('For example, local cultural practices may not enable particular groups of persons (women, for example) to hold a position as an automous subject.').

[382] See Pemberton, Aarten, and Mulder, 'Stories as Property' 1–17.

[383] For a critique, see Jan van Dijk, 'Free the Victim: A Critique of the Western Conception of Victimhood' (2009) 16 *International Journal of Victimology* 1–33.

[384] On the risks of 'stealing', see Nils Christie, 'Conflicts as Property (1977) 17 *The British Journal of Criminology* 1–15.

[385] Elander, 'The Victim's Address' 107. On the role of media, see Birgitta Höijer, 'The Discourse of Global Compassion: The Audience and Media Reporting of Human Suffering' (2004) 26 *Media, Culture and Society* 513–31

[386] Narrative victimology studies the 'interaction of the victim's story with the multitude of other stories that—particularly in and around justice processes—also concern the event that forms the nucleus of the story of victimization'. See Antony Pemberton, Eva Mulder, and Pauline G.M. Aarten, 'Stories of Injustice: Towards a Narrative Victimology' (2019) 16 *European Journal of Criminology* 391–412.

[387] Sveinung Sandberg and Thomas Ugelvik, 'The Past, Present, and Future of Narrative Criminology: A Review and an Invitation' (2016) 12 *Crime, Media, Culture: An International Journal* 129–36.

[388] See generally Jonathan Doak, 'The Therapeutic Dimension of Transitional Justice: Emotional Repair and Victim Satisfaction in International Trials and Truth Commissions' (2011) 11 *International Criminal Law Review* 263–98; Bruce J. Winick, 'Therapeutic Jurisprudence Perspectives on Dealing with Victims of Crime' (2009) 33 *Nova Law Review* 535–44; Carolyn C. Hartley, 'A Therapeutic Jurisprudence Approach to the Trial Process in Domestic Violence Felony Trials' (2003) 9 *Violence against Women* 410–37. See also South African Truth and Reconciliation Commission, Final Report, vol. 5 (1998), 351 ('healing potential of storytelling, of revealing the truth before a respectful audience and to an official body').

[389] Ervin Staub, 'Genocide and Mass Killing: Orgins, Prevention, Healing and Reconciliation', (2002) 21 *Political Psychology* 367–82, 376.

international criminal law discourse as of the 1990s.[390] However, it is often too easily assumed that international criminal proceedings constitute a suitable platform for victims to recount their stories or overcome trauma.[391]

The criminal justice process does not only offer discursive spaces, but also creates hierarchies among victims and types of victimization, silences alternative accounts, or poses risks of re-traumatization. Criminal trials are not per se restorative mechanisms.[392] Demonstration of harm and suffering is not a primary goal of the legal process in itself. Criminal proceedings differ from truth and reconciliation processes which award greater space to storytelling and personal experiences. The criminal process may cause stress for victims. Cross-examination or confrontations with the accused may cause particular fear and risks. For example, in the *Duch* trial, the defendant directly challenged the account of survivors.[393] In the *Lubanga* trial, former child soldier witness recanted their testimony in light of the trial experience. Victims may thus become victims of their narrative experiences.[394]

The retributive orientation of trials places limits on the forms of participation and narration. The possibility for victims to present their own story is limited.[395] The narratives of survivors of trauma may not fit within the logic of the law. Often, the language used by victims does not fully correlate with the requirements of the legal process.[396] Stories of victims do not matter as such, but only through their evidentiary value. Actual telling of experiences is rare. Arguments by victims who are allowed to participate in proceedings are used to support context, illustrate details of cases, demonstrate harm, or frame alternative legal arguments. Victim stories speak to the gravity of offences or the type of criminality committed. Individual

[390] For a survey, see John D. Ciorciari and Anne Heindel, 'Victim Testimony in International and Hybrid Criminal Courts: Narrative Opportunities, Challenges, and Fair Trial Demands, (2016) 56 *Virginia Journal of International Law* 266–338, 270–2.

[391] See Pemberton, Aarten, and Mulder, 'Stories as Property' 10, arguing that such an account misrepresents 'the role and impact of venting in therapy itself'. Critically, also Harvey Weinstein, 'The Myth of Closure, The Illusion of Reconciliation: Final Thoughts on Five Years as Co-Editor-In-Chief' (2011) 5 *International Journal of Transitional Justice* 1–10; David Mendeloff, 'Trauma and Vengeance: Assessing the Psychological and Emotional Effects of Post-Conflict Justice' (2009) 31 *Human Rights Quarterly* 592–623; Karen Brounéus, 'The Trauma of Truth Telling: Effects of Witnessing in the Rwandan Gacaca Courts on Psychological Health' (2010) 54 *Journal of Conflict Resolution* 408–37; Shanee G. Stepakoff, G. Shawn Reynolds, Simon Charters, and Nicola Henry, 'Self-reported Psychosocial Consequences of Testifying in a War Crimes Tribunal in Sierra Leone' (2015) 4 *International Perspectives in Psychology: Research, Practice, and Consultation* 161–81.

[392] Claire Garbett, 'The International Criminal Court and Restorative Justice: Victims, Participation and the Processes of Justice' (2017) 5 *Restorative Justice* 198–220, 215 ('victim participation is limited to ensure the retributive structure of the ICC's proceedings').

[393] Ciorciari and Heindel, 'Victim Testimony in International and Hybrid Criminal Courts' 296–7.

[394] Charles Trumbull IV, 'The Victims of Victim Participation in International Proceedings', 29 *Michigan Journal of International Law* 777–826, 810.

[395] Garbett, 'The International Criminal Court and Restorative Justice' 216 ('Victims rarely appear in person in the courtroom, and given the vast number of victims assigned to legal representatives, may not have their individual views and concerns expressed to the Chambers.').

[396] Ibid., 214–15.

statements, such as victim impact statements in domestic cases,[397] are more limited due to the high quantity of victims in international criminal cases. At the SCSL and the Extraordinary Chambers in the Courts of Camboidia (ECCC), victims of sexual violence felt that they were effectively silenced by proceedings.[398]

Victim statements are frequently grouped with other victim statements. The story of the individual is thus presented through a collective frame. It may easily become a group story, rather than an individual story.[399] This process entails disnarration of individual harm and suffering.[400]

Speech acts of victims are highly mediated. Victims have limited opportunity to address the offender directly.[401] In the *Bemba* trial, the ICC allowed three victims to convey their views and concerns via live video-link since their experiences were found to be representative of a broader pattern of harm.[402] However, collective representation is the norm.[403] This differentiates the ICC regime from restorative justice frameworks since victims 'do not participate in an 'encounter' with the accused: The ICC 'does not allow for an inclusive "problem-solving" approach to the resolution of crime'.[404]

There are fears that the 'personal appearance of a large number of victims' may 'affect the expeditiousness and fairness of the proceedings'.[405] Arguments of victims are typically presented through a legal representative. Meaningful contributions require direct and regular channels of interaction between victims and their legal representatives. The mediation of the communicative process takes away some of the authenticity. Legal representatives filter original speech, focus on legally relevant aspects, and may speak in a different language, adjusted to the legal framework of the trial. Victim discourse is contextualized, linked to legal plot.

397 Julian V. Roberts and Edna Erez, 'Communication in sentencing: Exploring the Expressive Function of Victim Impact Statements' (2004) 10 *International Review of Victimology* 223–44; Susan A. Bandes, 'Empathy, Narrative, and Victim Impact Statements' (1996) 63 *University of Chicago Law Review* 361–412.

398 Michelle Staggs Kelsall and Shanee Stepakoff, '"When We Wanted to Talk about Rape": Silencing Sexual Violence at the Social Court for Sierra Leone, (2007) *International Journal of Transitional Justice* 355–74. See also Nicola Henry, 'Witness to Rape: The Limits and Potential of International War Crimes Trials for Victims of Wartime Sexual Violence' (2009) 3 *International Journal of Transitional Justice* 114–34.

399 On community narratives, see Julian Rappaport, 'Community Narratives: Tales of Terror and Joy' (2000) 28 *American Journal of Community Psychology* 1–24.

400 Shonna Trinch, 'Disappearing Discourse: Performative Texts and Identity in Legal Contexts' (2010) 7 *Critical Inquiry in Language Studies* 207–29.

401 Garbett, 'The International Criminal Court and Restorative Justice' 209. ('Given the lack of direct participation by victims, there is no space for dialogue with the offender.').

402 *Prosecutor v. Bemba*, Decision on the supplemented applications by the legal representatives of victims to present evidence and the views and concerns of victims, ICC-01/05-01/08-2138, 22 February 2012, paras 39–51.

403 See Luke Moffett, Cheryl Lawther, Kieran McEvoy, Clara Sandoval, and Peter Dixon, 'Alternative Sanctions before the Special Jurisdiction for Peace: Reflections on International Law and Transitional Justice', 31 March 2019, pp. 36–9, at https://reparations.qub.ac.uk/assets/uploads/JEP-Report-Eng.pdf.

404 Garbett, 'The International Criminal Court and Restorative Justice' 213.

405 *Prosecutor v. Lubanga*, Decision on Victims' Participation, ICC-01/04-01/06-1119, 21 January 2008, para. 116.

This involves a process of translation which 'transforms the truths of the victims into a juridified truth'.[406]

The narrative function of victims is marked by a tension between active contribution to truth-telling and passive reception.[407] The form of the trial and its procedures limit the type of truth that is revealed. Shame and fear often cause discomfort or pose obstacles to the process of truth-finding. Certain types of victimization may be difficult to articulate in terms of speech. Judges have a catalytic function in stimulating and controlling victim statements. They may have the final say as narrators through engagement with victim narratives in the judgment.

In the context of the controversial decision not to authorize an investigation in relation to Afghanistan, victim representatives openly challenged the instrumentalization of the interests of victims by judges. The Pre-Trial Chamber stated that opening an investigation with limited prospects of success would not be in the interests of victims since it would 'result in creating frustration and possibly hostility vis-a-vis the Court'.[408] Victim representatives noted that it is disingenuous to speak of a 'victim-centred court' and express concern for victims in order to justify the arguably 'worst' decision a Chamber 'can take with regard to victims'.[409] Claiming that such a decision is in the interests of victims 'is profoundly misguided, if not disrespectful and patronizing'.[410] It illustrates that 'the Chamber has wholly ignored or disregarded the representations made by the victims'.[411]

The sentence is deemed to put an end to a particular vision of crime and victimization. However, due to the constraints of the trial, some sense of closure 'following a sentence is considerably more likely to be experienced by third-party observers than by victims themselves'.[412] In particular, victims who testified may easily be disappointed. As Refik Hodzić notes, based on experiences in Bosnia and Herzegovina:

> The act of testifying is a difficult experience for victims, though it might have a short-term 'therapeutic effect of some sort. Shortly after their testimony, many victims have experienced a sense of euphoria and a sense that justice may be provided through the judicial process in which they have participated. Subsequently, once the euphoria dissipates, victims tend to develop a strong sense of importance

[406] Sofia Stolk, 'The Victim, the International Criminal Court and the Search for Truth' (2015) 13 *JICJ* 973–94, 988.

[407] Ibid., 973–94.

[408] PTC II, Decision Pursuant to Article 15 of the Rome Statute on the Authorisation of an Investigation into the Situation in the Islamic Republic of Afghanistan, ICC-02/17-33, 12 April 2019, para. 96.

[409] Legal Representatives of Victims, Victims' Notice of Appeal of the 'Decision Pursuant to Article 15 of the Rome Statute on the Authorisation of an Investigation into the Situation in the Islamic Republic of Aghanistan', ICC-02/17-38, 10 June 2019, para. 23.

[410] Ibid., para. 25.

[411] Ibid., para. 25.

[412] Pemberton, Aarten, and Mulder, 'Stories as Property', 13.

> in the community and are often quite keen to discuss their testimony with neighbours and those they trust. However, these benefits might all diminish and give rise to embittered disappointment when the verdict is rendered and where sentences are perceived as inadequate, or where their testimony has not been fully accepted by the court. The majority of witnesses see these events as a sort of personal betrayal which might re-exacerbate their sense of vulnerability and helplessness.[413]

The actual contribution of victim narratives to the content of the criminal process is often limited. In many cases, victim statements add or support the Prosecution case. The added value lies in their ability to fill certain gaps in relation to the facts, framing or historical, and the cultural context of cases. As the International Federation for Human Rights has noted, this may be done in several ways:

> Legal representatives may identify and highlight gaps in the way the evidence is presented or in the factual or legal interpretation. Another way of filling in gaps is to present a different perspective (the victims') or communicating concerns that victims may have in respect to issues being decided upon by the Court.[414]

At the ICC, victim statements served *inter alia* to draw attention to local languages or to understand local habits. Victims also sought to broaden the evidentiary base of trials. For instance, in the *Katanga* case, victims introduced five pieces of evidence and called two witnesses.[415] In *Bemba*, victim representatives criticized the decision of the Prosecution not to pursue certain charges.[416]

4.3.7 Spectators: Constituencies, observers, and re-narrators

The dynamic of performances in the courtroom is shaped by the actual or presence of spectators.[417] This role is typically underestimated. The focus is placed on 'active, speaking participants' in proceedings, rather than 'spectators'.[418] Proceedings

[413] See Refik Hodzić, 'Living the Legacy of Mass Atrocities: Victims' Perspectives on War Crimes Trials', (2010) 8 *JICJ* 113–36, 125.

[414] FIDH, 'Five myths about victim Participation in ICC proceedings', December 2014, 9, at https://www.fidh.org/IMG/pdf/cpi649a.pdf.

[415] *Prosecutor v. Katanga*, Judgment pursuant to article 74 of the Statute, ICC-01/04-01/07-3436-tENG, 7 March 2014, paras 21–22.

[416] *Prosecutor v. Bemba*, Decision on the request of the legal representative of victims VPRS 3 and VPRS 6 to review an alleged decision of the Prosecutor not to proceed, ICC-01/04-582, 25 October 2010.

[417] On spectacle and trials in Argentina, see Diane Taylor, *Disappearing Acts: Spectacles of Gender and Nationalism in Argentina's 'Dirty War'* (Durham, NC: Duke University Press, 1997).

[418] Nigel Eltringham, 'Spectators to the Spectacle of Law: The Formation of a "Validating Public" at the International Criminal Tribunal for Rwanda' (2012) 77 *Ethnos: Journal of Anthropology* 425–45, 433.

implicate others. External spectators and the public are vital elements of international criminal proceedings. They provide a forum for speech.

The audience witnesses the narratives, drama, and gestures and gives recognition and validity to the proceedings. It provides them the character of rituals.[419] Agents in proceedings serve as ritual producers, whilst others serve as ritual constituencies.

As Antonio Cassese said, international criminal court and tribunals rely 'on the widespread publication of judicial acts and commentaries' for the fulfilment of their mandate: 'it is not enough for the International Tribunal simply to administer international criminal justice impartially and with due regard for the rights of the accused. It must also carry out this activity under the scrutiny of the international community.'[420]

International criminal proceedings address audiences beyond the physicality of the courtroom because they cover 'monumental events' of domestic and international relevance.[421] Publicity of proceedings is important from a performative perspective because it influences the way how are stories told, how they are perceived, and how they are replicated. Agents in proceedings are aware that they are also addressing a 'remote audience' who is 'watching the relay, reading the transcripts, or the journalistic digests of these events.'[422]

Publicity gives veracity to the evidence presented and the witnesses heard. It provides a role for the 'present audience' and 'the individual spectator' in the 'staging and shaping' of narratives through courtroom participants.[423] It serves democratic purposes.[424] The existence of a public audience provides important checks and balances against abuses or instrumentalization of proceedings. It becomes a witness to the fairness of proceedings and narratives of fact, truth, and responsibility.

The relationship with audiences has undergone transformation. The courtroom audience is the most immediate audience. It is generally rather small. It encompasses local or international visitors, NGOs, journalists, court monitors, persons with particular interests in proceedings, or curious spectators who watch proceedings from the public gallery. It is complemented by much larger remote

[419] See Gerd Baumann, 'Ritual Implicates "Others": Rereading Durkheim in a Plural Society' in Daniel de Coppet (ed.), *Understanding Rituals* (London: Routledge, 1992), 97–116, 111 ('Legal rituals ... depend on the outside witness to confer on them not only recognition but validity.'); Mark Cammack, 'Evidence Rules and the Ritual Functions of Trials: Saying Something of Something' (1992) 25 *Loyola Los Angeles Law Review* 783–96.

[420] Antonio Cassese, 'Foreword by the former President of the International Criminal Tribunal for the former Yugoslavia' (1997) 321 *International Review of the Red Cross* 602.

[421] Graham White, 'Witnessing Proceedings: The Hague War Crimes Tribunal, Narrative Indeterminacy, and the Public Audience' (2008) 52 *The Drama Review* 75–87. See also Mark Osiel, 'Public memories, publicly' in Carla Hesse and Robert Post (eds), *Human Rights in Transitions: Gettysburg to Bosnia* (New York, NY: Zone Books, 1999), 217–61, 219 ('monumental didactics').

[422] White, 'Witnessing Proceedings' 79.

[423] Ibid., 75.

[424] Cornelia Vismann, *Medien der Rechtsprechung* (Frankfurt am Main: Fischer, 2011).

audiences[425] who are not visible to courtroom participants and who follow proceedings through public media, such as radio or television. Such channels have become important tools to disseminate information or send messages. They multiply the number of spectators and help to preserve the trial record as a historical source.

Historically, this trend started in the 1960s. The *Eichmann* trial was the first televised international criminal trial. It was aired from Jerusalem in order to allow the world to watch and listen. The *ad hoc* tribunals and hybrid courts have integrated radio and TV media into their outreach strategy. For instance, the ICTY started to broadcast trial of Slobodan Milošević in 2003 in order to reach local audiences in Bosnia and Herzegovina and Republika Srpska. Today, most proceedings can be followed live through online streaming or edited video clips on social media. There is a strategy to make them known globally. The turn to new technologies has changed the role of legal performance: 'We live in a world in which law is constantly on view in our living rooms, acted and re-enacted, multiplied and refracted through its fictional and real instantiations.'[426]

This has modified the role of audiences. Immediate courtroom audiences are easy to control. They are subject to the disciplinary power of courts. As Nigel Eltringham has argued, the 'ideal' spectator is a 'silent' spectator' ('uniform, docile and quiescent') whose 'observing presence' has a 'validating' function that does not require 'reflective investment in courtroom activity'.[427] He or she is deemed to serve as 'key component in the building of the narratives of justice', namely as 'witness' of due process, and as 'student of didactics'.[428]

The multiplication of remote audiences has extended the reach of speech relations significantly beyond the 'courtroom', but also led to a partial loss of influence. For instance, the broadcasting of the *Milošević* trial confirmed reservations or biases against the tribunal by those in Serbia who perceived the trial as a performance of injustice.[429] It increased sympathy for Milošević in public perceptions and fostered nationalism. [430] Later, Šešelj claimed that his trial should be broadcast on national television in order to rally support for his case.

The increased use of new technologies as a space of conveying messages or staging trials as global events entails a broadening of speech relations. Spectators are not necessarily 'passive' or 'silent' observers but communicative agents of their own. Through social media, they become 'storytellers' in their own right.

425 White, 'Witnessing Proceedings' 78.
426 Stone Peters, 'Legal Performance Good and Bad' 200.
427 Eltringham, 'Spectators to the Spectacle of Law' 442, 439.
428 White, 'Witnessing Proceedings' 77–8.
429 On the perceptions of the ICC engagement in Kenya as 'performance of injustice', see Lynch, *Performances of Injustice* 57–90.
430 Joseph Lelyveld, 'The Defendant: Slobodan Milošević's Trail, and the Debate Surrounding International Courts', *The New Yorker*, 27 May 2002.

4.4 Performative versus Discursive Justice

One of the purposes of proceedings is to produce some form of justice.[431] In popular discourse, proceedings are often assessed by their outcomes, that is by conviction or acquittal, years of sentencing, etc. However, the virtue of international criminal proceedings lies partly in their ability to provide procedural justice.

4.4.1 Procedural and relational justice theories

Procedural justice looks beyond the application of law to the facts or the final outcome of proceedings. It is concerned with the criminal process as such. It takes into account that agents affected by criminal proceedings may respect outcomes and consider them as just, even if they disagree with them in the individual case, due to 'trust' in the value of proceedings.[432]

Many of the sociological foundations were explained by Luhmann. He argued that judicial systems legitimize themselves in society through the performance of court proceedings, even in relation to persons who do not follow proceedings.[433] He claimed that acceptance of procedural outcomes (e.g. decisions) depends not only on the quality of reasoning but on procedural role-taking, the contribution of actors to the legal process, their mutual engagement ('ceremonial integration'), and the performance of the legal process as a whole.[434]

In legal discourse, theories of procedural justice have become popular in domestic contexts in the mid-1970s.[435] They rely on the premise that psychological factors influence acceptance or compliance with procedures. Studies in domestic legal systems have shown that the way how actors are treated in the process is a key factor in the assessment as to whether justice was done in their eyes.[436] Perceptions of the fairness of proceedings as such may be more important for acceptance than the outcome of an individual case.[437]

Procedural justice is traditionally connected to two major elements: the decision-making process and the treatment of agents in proceedings. Trust in the

431 Simonett, 'The Trial as One of the Performing Arts' 1146 ('A trial if it is to be a good performance, must find truth, must give to each party what is his due, justice.').

432 Tom R. Tyler and Yuen J. Huo, *Trust in the Law: Encouraging Public Cooperation with the Police and Courts* (New York, NY: Russell Sage Foundation, 2002).

433 Luhmann, *Legitimation durch Verfahren* 121–8.

434 Ibid., 55–136.

435 John W. Thibaut and Laurens Walker, *Procedural Justice: A Psychological Analysis* (Hillsdale, NJ: Lawrence Erlbaum, 1975).

436 E. Allan Lind, Ruth Kanfer, and P. Christopher Early, 'Voice, Control, and Procedural Justice: Instrumental and Non-instrumental Concerns in Fairness Judgments' (1990) 59 *Journal of Personality and Social Psychology* 952–9.

437 Rebecca Hollander-Blumo and Tom R. Tyler, 'Procedural Justice in Negotiation: Procedural Fairness, Outcome Acceptance, and Integrative Potential' (2008) 33 *Law & Social Inquiry* 473–500.

decision-making process is influenced by several factors, including the understanding of the applicable norms and rules, the professional and unbiased nature of the legal process, and the voice of agents, their opportunity to be heard and tell their side of the story. For instance, empirical studies have shown that persons who take part in the criminal process, or are affected by it, 'want to feel that they have made a difference in it'.[438] The second element relates to the treatment of participants in the process. Participants wish to be treated with dignity and respect. Both elements need to be satisfied. Procedural justice relies therefore on four cardinal notions: 'voice, trustworthy motives, dignity and respect'.[439] The ICC reflected this understanding in its own justification of victim participation. It noted that 'by providing victims with an opportunity' to be 'part of the justice process' and 'by ensuring that consideration is given to their suffering', it is hoped 'that they will have confidence in the justice process and view it as relevant to their day to day existence rather than as remote, technical, and irrelevant'.[440]

Procedural justice is not only instrumental but 'relational',[441] driven by human dynamics and interpersonal and group relationships.[442] This relational dimension 'gives to justice a sense of purpose and vision for the values and behaviours which should characterize a just society'.[443] International criminal justice is not like a blindfolded *Justicia* who watches over fair trial and punishment through the scales of justice as an impartial and distant observer. Rather, it is an affective form of justice which emerges through active speech and relations and 'finds its expression in just behaviour'.[444] It connects experiences of individuals affected by crimes with actors and institutions that represent the shared norms damaged by the experience of victimization'[445] The relationship goes beyond that between offender and justice institution. The aspiration is 'not merely to punish, but to try to restore where possible relationships damaged by crime'.[446]

[438] Kimi Lynn King and James David Meernik, *The Witness Experience: Testimony at the ICTY and Its Impact* (Cambridge: Cambridge University Press, 2017) 35.

[439] See Sarah Bennett, Lorelei Hine, and Lorraine Mazerolle, 'Procedural Justice' Oxford Bibliographies, 26 April 2018, DOI: 10.1093/obo/9780195396607-0241; Steven L. Blader and Tom R. Tyler, 'A Four Component Model of Procedural Justice: Defining the Meaning of a "Fair" Process' (2003) 29 *Personality and Social Psychology Bulletin* 747–58.

[440] ICC Assembly of States Parties, Report of the Court on the Strategy in Relation to Victims, ICC-ASP/8/45, 10 November 2009, para. 46.

[441] See Samuel H. Pillsbury, *Imagining a Greater Justice: Criminal Violence, Punishment and Relational Justice* (New York, NY: Routledge, 2019).

[442] Relationalists claim that justice is grounded in certain social, political, or institutional relationships between persons. On relational and non-relational approaches to justice in political theory, see Megan Kime, *Theories of Global Justice: Relational and Non-Relational Approaches*, PhD Thesis (Sheffield: Sheffield University, 2009) 33–59, at http://etheses.whiterose.ac.uk/14531/1/521864.pdf.

[443] See Jubilee Policy Group, *Relational Justice: A Reform Dynamic for Criminal Justice* (Cambridge: Elitian Ltd, 1994) 11. See also Steven L. Blader and Tom R. Tyler, 'Relational models of procedural justice' in Russell S. Cropanzano and Maureen L. Ambrose (eds), *The Oxford Handbook of Justice in the Workplace* (Oxford: Oxford University Press, 2015) 351–67, 352.

[444] Jubilee Policy Group, *Relational Justice* 11.

[445] Ibid., 11.

[446] Ibid., 12. See also Samuel Pillsbury, 'What Is Relational Justice?', Loyola Law School, Los Angeles Legal Studies Research Paper No. 2019-09, 20 February 2019, 17.

Insights from social psychology suggest that experiences of procedural justice shape views on compliance and enforcement.[447] For example, Tom Tyler has traced the connection between procedural justice and compliance in *Why People Obey the Law*.[448] He has argued that criminal procedures send important symbolic signals as to how individuals are treated and valued in society. These signals provide incentives to respect the law because they create legitimate authority. Individuals respect such authority because they wish to be treated in the same way: Procedural justice 'conveys a positive message to justice recipients about their relationship with the entity enacting justice', while 'procedural injustice conveys a negative message about that relationship'.[449]

4.4.2 Imperfect discursive justice

Repair of relationships goes beyond the immediate judicial function of the criminal process. It may emerge through some of the communicative processes generated by proceedings. Criminologist Barbara Hudson has developed a theory of discursive justice in her book, *Justice in the Risk Society*. Drawing on Habermas, she has argued that justice must be

1. *relational*—'take account of relationships between individuals, groups and communities';
2. *discursive*—allowing 'claims and counter-claims, critiques and defences of existing values to be weighed against each other in undominated discourse',
3. *plurivocal*—mindful of 'the different voices of the plurality of identities and social groups' in pluralist contemporary societies;
4. *rights-regarding*—defensive of 'the rights of individuals and of communities'; and
5. *reflective*—based on 'the particulars of the individual case'. [450]

International criminal justice is often more performative than discursive. It is neither a mere gateway to punishment and sanction, nor a medium for dialogue, discursiveness, and persuasion, as suggested by restorative justice theories. It is an 'in-between'.

International criminal procedure contains many symbolic-expressive elements which seek to enhance compliance through relational messages in the sense of

[447] Tom R. Tyler and Jonathan Jackson, 'Popular Legitimacy and the Exercise of Legal Authority: Motivating Compliance, Cooperation, and Engagement' (2014) 20 *Psychology, Public Policy, and Law* 78–95.
[448] Tom R. Tyler, *Why People Obey the Law* (Princeton, NJ: Princeton University Press, 2006).
[449] Blader and Tyler, 'Relational models of procedural justice' 351.
[450] Barbara Hudson, *Justice in the Risk Society* (London: Sage Publications, 2003) 206.

Tyler. Procedures are performative, 'exemplary', and partly directed towards outside audiences. Procedural fairness and trial management by judges are meant to prevent that proceedings become a theatre of opinion or an instrumentalist 'show trial' in which 'the defendant has no chance of avoiding conviction and where the trial is managed entirely for an outside audience'.[451] However, the discursive structures are less open to dialogue than restorative justice models. Communications between parties and participants are controlled. Interaction is structured through 'discursive contestation'.

4.4.2.1 More symbolic than real

Many of the communicative elements are related to symbolic expression. International criminal proceedings are, at least symbolically, an attempt to fix 'broken relationships' or create new relational spaces.[452] As French philosopher Jean-Francois Lyotard has argued, the 'perfect crime' may not necessarily 'consist in killing the victim or the witnesses ... but rather in obtaining the silence of the witnesses, the deafness of the judges, and the inconsistency (insanity) of the testimony'.[453]

International criminal proceedings are deemed to counter this erasure in two ways: through the creation of relational spaces, in which agents interact, and symbolic recalibration of power structures (e.g. empowerment of victims).

4.4.2.1.1 Constitution of communicative spaces

The most immediate impact of international criminal proceedings is the creation of a communicative space. It is composed of very different speech communities.

International criminal proceedings create an internal 'speech community'.[454] It encompasses parties and participants in proceedings. This internal community emerges through performative action and collective speech acts. As Kristen Perrin has noted, 'although there is the feeling that individuals on the stand are giving an unbroken account of events', such events 'are in fact created not only by the witness or accused, but through the interjections of the judges and lawyers as well, however routine these interjections may seem'.[455]

This internal speech community is limited in scope and governed by the formal rules of the legal process. However, the symbolic-expressive relevance of international criminal procedure goes beyond this relational community. One of the main didactic ambitions is to pass messages to non-courtroom participants in

[451] Jeremy Peterson, 'Unpacking Show Trials: The Saddam Hussein Trial' (2007) 48 *Harvard International Law Journal* 257–92, 289.

[452] Theoretically, an international crime constitutes a breach of relations in international society. See **section 1.3**.

[453] Jean-Francois Lyotard, *The Differend: Phrases in Dispute*, transl. by Georges Van Den Abbeele (Minneapolis, MN: University of Minnesota Press, 1988), 8.

[454] Perrin, *Transcripts from the International Criminal Tribunal for the Former Yugoslavia* 46.

[455] Ibid., 46–7.

order to provide moral compass and to give sense to actions. The publicity of proceedings is a means to create a broader relational space that extends beyond legal interactions. It constitutes a public that is not only a spectator or passive listener of courtroom interactions but part of the plot.

Communication with external audiences is impeded by the plurality of voices. Proceedings convey parallel or even conflicting discourses. Prosecutors actively use storytelling, 'we' discourses and terms such as 'humanity', in order to draw audiences in, encourage them to take sides, or continue to write the stories of trials beyond the limited content of courtroom discourse. Their speech acts go beyond the individual case and are oriented towards global audiences. They seek to capture public imagination and to inspire a broader sense of communion in the abstract sense.

Defence discourses speak to other audiences. They put the emphasis on the individual case. They often seek to shift the lens from the individual to collective structures in order to create an alternative community of blame.[456] They present themselves as symbols of harm and stigma inflicted on specific communities or national identities. Through this collectivization, they reach out to their home constituencies or broader media. This discourse creates may create new distinction between 'in-groups' and 'out-groups' and form a parallel plot in public imagination.[457]

Victim discourse relates to yet another type of audience. It is deemed to ' "right" previously harmful relationships' and to contribute to providing 'repair' that cannot be achieved without 'those most affected by the crime'.[458] It is meant to connect global discourse to tangible local communities and to serve a means to rebuild communion. But this space is confined to victims who are 'able and willing' to make a contribution to discourse. Victims are predominantly viewed as 'persons who have suffered'.[459] Their speech acts are directed towards international audiences, or defendants, rather than their peers. In some contexts, the symbolic recognition of voice may have counterproductive effects in the societies affected by crime. It may entail perceptions of victimizations by others, challenge 'social practices of kinship and community', or 'antagonize familial or community relations'.[460]

International criminal proceedings create, therefore, a plurality of discursive relationships. They provide a communicative space for specific micro-communities. The idea of 'reforming attachments' in order to build 'a new community' is more fictional.

[456] Johanna Mannergren Selimovic, 'Challenges of Post-Conflict Coexistence: Narrating Truth and Justice in a Bosnian town' (2015) 36 *Political Psychology* 231–42.

[457] Rauschenbach, Staerklé, and Scalia, 'Accused for Involvement in Collective Violence' 210–21.

[458] Garbett, 'From Passive Objects to Active Agents' 44.

[459] Liesbeth Zegveld, 'Victims as a Third Party: Empowerment of Victims?'(2019) 19 *International Criminal Law Review* 321–45, 344.

[460] Garbett, 'From Passive Objects to Active Agents' 54.

4.4.2.1.2 Rehumanization and empowerment

A second promise of procedural justice is the readjustment of power relations. The treatment of offenders and the recognition of the voice of victims is meant to have a double transformative effect. Proceedings are deemed to rehumanize defendants and have an empowering effect on participants in proceedings.[461] In practice, both claims are often more symbolic than real.

Modern criminal proceedings treat the defendant as a subject, who must an opportunity to respond to allegations. The application of fairness and due process guarantees recognizes the offender as an equal member of international society rather than social outlaw. Liability theories operate on the assumption that defendants are rational beings who are capable of making moral decisions, that is, distinguishing rights and wrongs. Judgment and sentence are partially meant to deconstruct justifications of criminal behaviour, remove threats, and foster resocialization. However, such promises often contrast with continuing stigma or bias.

Upon conviction, international criminal courts and tribunals struggle to find states who would agree to carry out sentences. Even an acquittal is often only a 'pyrrhic victory.[462] As stated by Barbora Hola and Joris van Wijk, defendants continue to be 'international pariahs'.[463] At the ICTR and the ICC, some defendants were obliged to remain in detention after acquittal, since they were not able to return home in safety.

Participation in proceedings can be a means to equalize power relations and counter implicit social hierarchies created through crime. It requires respect of a plurality of speaking and listening positions. Empirical studies suggest that participation in proceedings may entail positive experiences.[464] Victims and witnesses who contribute to proceedings feel important. Participation may have important symbolic effects for victims, even if it is relatively passive: '[Victims] see the offender is 'smaller' than expected, or less scary. Having the perpetrator hear about the harm that was suffered by the victim may provide more satisfaction than solely telling the Court.'[465]

[461] For instance, the ICC booklet on victims states that victim participation 'can be an empowering experience for victims who would otherwise be left aside in the proceedings as passive observers'. See ICC, Victim's Booklet, 'Victims before the International Criminal Court: A guide for the participation of victims in the proceedings of the ICC', 21, at https://www.icc-cpi.int/about/victims/Documents/VPRS_Victim-s_booklet.pdf.

[462] On acquittals, see Marie-Sophie Devresse and Damien Scalia, 'An Outsider's View from Inside: The Experience of Acquittals before International Criminal Tribunals' (2019) 17 *JICJ* 179–98.

[463] Barbora Holà and Joris van Wijk, 'Acquittals in International Criminal Justice: Pyrrhic Victories?' (2017) 30 *LJIL* 241–61, 251.

[464] Kimi King and James Meernik, 'The Burden of Bearing Witness: The Impact of Testifying at War Crimes Tribunals' (2019) 63 *Journal of Conflict Resolution* 348–72, 362.

[465] Malini Laxminarayan, 'The International Criminal Court and Victim Well-being: A Restorative Approach?', 17 March 2015, at http://www.thehagueinstituteforglobaljustice.org/latest-insights/latest-insights/commentary/the-international-criminal-court-and-victim-well-being-a-restorative-approach/.

However, such experiences are related to a variety of factors, including expectations and post-testimony treatment. For instance, studies of ICTY witnesses suggests that the experience of witnesses differ according to many factors, such as motivation, fair treatment, external professional support, and the current situation. For example, Kimi King and James Meernik have concluded in their empirical study of witness attitudes that those witnesses 'who were highly motivated to testify and those who testified multiple times' had altogether less positive experiences.[466] At the ICTR, offenders received better medical treatment than witnesses or victims affected by crime. This has disempowering effects.

Experiences of victims differ from context to context. Studies of the *Duch* trial at the ECCC suggest that act of providing testimony as victim-witness or civil party is a 'multifaceted experience, fraught with unexpected challenges and emotional swings, rather than one that is wholly cathartic'.[467] It can be a positive experience, 'if the process is largely perceived as safe, respectful, and dignified'.[468] However, civil parties may 'lose faith' in a court 'if they believe that a sentence is too lenient or if they feel that a court has failed to provide reparations commensurate with the gravity of the crimes'.[469] Rachel Killean has found that procedural factors, such as ongoing information of victims, 'respect, expediency, and representation' have influenced experiences and attitudes of civil parties before the ECCC, but did not fully overcome grievances caused by 'unwelcome outcomes' of cases. [470]

Studies of experiential dimensions of victim participation in ICC proceedings show similar results. For example, a Berkeley-led study of 622 victim participants in the situations in Uganda, Democratic Republic of the Congo (DRC), Kenya, and Côte d'Ívoire has found that victims may find value in victim participation, even if they do not 'participate in person in trials'.[471] It concluded that satisfaction depends on a number of factors, such as the ability of proceedings to provide conviction and reparation, their length and 'personal interactions with ICC staff and their legal representatives'.[472] These findings suggest that the argument of empowerment may be true in a symbolic or legal sense but it faces many constraints from a broader experiential perspective.

[466] King and Meernik, 'The Burden of Bearing Witness' 366.
[467] Stover, Balthazard, and Koenig, 'Confronting Duch' 530.
[468] Ibid., 541.
[469] Ibid., 541.
[470] Rachel Killean, Procedural Justice in International Criminal Courts: Assessing Civil Parties' Perceptions of Justice at the Extraordinary Chambers in the Courts of Cambodia, (2016) 16 *International Criminal Law Review* 1–38, 32.
[471] Berkeley Human Rights Center, 'A Victim's Court?: A Study of 622 Victim Participants at the International Criminal Court' (Berkeley, CA: Human Rights Center, 2015), 3.
[472] Ibid., 3–4.

4.4.2.2 More expressive than dialogue-based

The structure of international criminal proceedings offers more space for discursive contestation, rather than mutual dialogue. In an ideal setting, discursive justice should allow an 'undominated discourse' of 'claims and counter-claims'.[473] But criminal procedures are 'bounded spaces' in which discourses conditions are constrained.[474] The legal process uses ordered forms of communication, in which stories and experiences are framed in 'rule-bound exchanges of rational arguments'.[475] The language is rationalized and coded. This limits the ability of actors to express their experiences in their own words.

International criminal proceedings provide a platform for expression but are not necessarily aimed at fostering mutual understanding or 'encounter' between offender and victims.[476] Parties and participants often talk at each other or to the judiciary and their audiences rather than with each other. The accused has a right to remain silent and does not have to engage with the allegations. In some instances, proceedings or trials can be held *in absentia*. For instance, charges may be confirmed in the absence of defendants. A partial absence in proceedings may be justified on grounds, such as disruptive behaviour in court or voluntary absence.[477]

The adversarial structure of procedures promotes confrontation of conflicting point of views, rather than 'collaborative-problem-solving'.[478] Judges may seek to encourage a common understanding of parties on certain elements of facts,[479] but each act in the courtroom pursues a distinct strategic rationale. It is guided by institutional roles, that is, certain positions that parties and participants are expected to defend due to their assigned function, that is, as prosecutor, Defence counsel, or victim representative. For instance, crimes and harm are presented through objective factual accounts rather than subjective narratives. Individual narratives are complemented by institutional narratives, 'central meaning-making practices' that seek to bring 'moral coherence' to social disorder and transform

473 Hudson, *Justice in the Risk Society* 206.

474 Pierre Bourdieu, 'The Force of Law: Toward a Sociology of the Juridical Field' (transl. by R. Terdiman) (1987) 38 *Hastings Law Journal* 805–53, 830.

475 Ibid., 830.

476 On 'encounter' and restorative justice, see Daniel van Ness and Karen Heetderks Strong, *Restoring Justice* (Concinatti: Anderson Publishing 1997), 67.

477 See Mohammad Hadi Zakerhossein and Anne-Marie De Brouwer, 'Diverse Approaches to Total and Partial In Absentia Trials by International Criminal Tribunals' (2015) 26 *Criminal Law Forum* 181–224, 220–13. The Appeals Chamber of the STL held that in exceptional circumstances, a trial may be held in absentia, namely 'where i) reasonable efforts have been taken to notify the accused personally; ii) the evidence as to notification satisfies the Trial Chamber that the accused actually knew of the proceedings against them; and that iii) it does so with such degree of specificity that the accused's absence means they must have elected not to attend the hearing and therefore have waived their right to be present'. See *Prosecutor v. Ayyash et al.*, Decision on Defence Appeals against Trial Chamber's Decision on Reconsideration of the Trial In Absentia Decision, STL-11-01/PT/AC/AR126.1, 1 November 2012, para. 31 (Trial in Absentia Decision).

478 Garbett, 'The International Criminal Court and Restorative Justice' 204.

479 See, for example, Adrian Fulford, 'Reflections of a Trial Judge' (2011) 22 *Criminal Law Forum* 215–23, 220.

'social relationships between people' through 'individual justice, truth-seeking, and acknowledgment'.[480]

International criminal trials are spaces where multiple views are heard and where multiple truths can coexist. Proceedings are not expected to produce a common agreement on outcomes. Offenders may enter an admission of guilt or show remorse, in order to diminish punishment. But they cannot be forced to apologize, show repentance, or 'make amends' for the crimes, in dialogue with victims.[481] Similarly, victims cannot be forced to forgive the offender. Trials are predicated on acceptance of differences, rather than agreement.[482] Any judgment is likely to be perceived as unjust to a certain degree by one of the participants in the process or audiences outside the courtroom. The trial is thus like a ritual, which enables insiders and outsiders to witness justice performance and make sense of contradictions. It creates new relational spaces for engagement with accountability, and at times a 'community of difference'.

4.4.2.3 More prospective than immediate

The type of justice that is produced is not final, but liminal. It is, as Jacques Derrida stated, based on a constant 'refounding' of law as horizon of expectation' and on many occasions a 'justice to-come'.[483]

In court testimony and the delivery of the judgment does not necessarily bring closure for witnesses, victims, or the accused. Parties and participants seek to have their version of the 'truth' confirmed. The strict form of the legal process impedes fully discursive justice. It limits opportunities of agents to share personal experiences or their side of the story.[484] This leaves a sense of incompletion or dissatisfaction.

Mina Rauschenbach has traced a certain 'mental journey' in the attitudes of defendants at the ICTY which navigates between expectation and disappointment. According to her findings, defendants have experienced the legal process as a trajectory which goes through several stages. It 'conveys initially high expectations, followed by the feelings of disillusion as well as perceptions of illegitimacy and unjust treatment'.[485] It often 'ends with descriptions of the strategies expressed' to 'disseminate their personal truth and to counter the judicial truths they consider to be imposed on them'.[486]

[480] Selimovic, 'Challenges of Post-Conflict Coexistence' 231–42.

[481] Garbett, 'The International Criminal Court and Restorative Justice' 205.

[482] Meijers and Glasius, 'Expression of Justice or Political Trial?' 749.

[483] Jacques Derrida, 'Force of Law: The Mystical Foundation of Authority' in Jacques Derrida, *Acts of Religion* (ed., Gil Anidjar) (New York, NY: Routledge, 2002), 230–98, 256–7 ('Justice remains to come ... it deploys the very dimension of events irreducibly to come ... Perhaps this is why justice, insofar as it is not only a juridical or political concept, opens up to the avenir the transformation, the recasting or refounding [la fondation] of law and politics.').

[484] Rauschenbach, 'Individuals Accused of International Crimes as Delegitimized Agents of Truth' 308.

[485] Ibid., 307.

[486] Ibid.

A very similar trend is visible in relation to experiences of victims. The application process triggers high expectations at the outset. For instance, the Berkeley study on victim perceptions found that the completion of an ICC application gave victims 'confidence that their experiences would be known at the court and aid in building a case against the accused'.[487] These expectations had to be gradually re-adjusted or declined throughout procedures. The study noted 'that most victims' joined ICC cases 'because they believe[d] that prosecutions will result in convictions and individual reparations'.[488] This led to 'unrealistic hopes for what the court can provide'.[489] Procedures gradually narrow the number of persons who may be admitted to participate in proceedings.[490] The sheer length of the judicial process creates frustrations.[491] The outcome of proceedings, that is, conviction and reparations, is determinative for perceptions. Acquittals, lack of reparation, or even symbolic reparation may cause disappointment.

These experiences emphasize the importance of communication and reason-giving throughout the legal process. It is important to update witnesses and victims on important developments in the trials in which they participate. Courts need to provide explanations for their actions, including decisions which limit participatory rights or decisions not to act.

Judgments themselves have an important social and civic role and a symbolic function. They provide legitimacy to the relevant institution and the preceding legal process. But they are imperfect as an instrument of rights vindication. Judgments reduce the contents of trials. The official record omits all 'gestures, hesitations, clothing, tone of voice, laughter, irony'.[492] It is virtually impossible to develop a narrative that is commonly shared by defendants, victims, and bystanders. Judgments struggle to remedy the harm that has been inflicted on the individual situations, or to restore all rights that have been violated. Judges have to take sides in the evaluation of facts and evidence. Their findings remain vulnerable to critique by parties and participants who have the impression that their narratives were not listened to, or whose claims were are fully addressed.

The effects of judgments often reach beyond the immediate case.[493] Judgments create novel relational spaces. They do not only contain findings on the guilt or innocence of the defendant but set 'aspirational standards for a broader set of the

487 Berkeley Human Rights Center, 'A Victim's Court?' 3.

488 Ibid., 5.

489 Ibid., 5.

490 See Garbett, 'The International Criminal Court and Restorative Justice' 208.

491 Berkeley Human Rights Center, 'A Victim's Court?' 4 ('Victim participants, like other observers of the ICC, complained about the inordinate length of the ICC judicial process. Many victim participants were concerned that they would die before verdicts or reparations decisions, and some worried that delays in proceedings could compromise their personal information and cause them security problems.').

492 James Clifford, *The Predicament of Culture: Twentieth Century Ethnography, Literature and Art* (Cambridge, MA: Harvard University Press, 1988), 290.

493 Saira Mohamed, 'Deviance, Aspiration, and the Stories We Tell: Reconciling Mass Atrocity and the Criminal Law' (2015) 124 *Yale Law Journal* 1628–89, 1676.

community'. They situate the case in a line of previous cases and encourage reflexivity. Judges send messages about rules should be applied in the future. As Rosa Aloisi and James Meernik have shown, some 'speak to other, would-be war criminals around the world'.[494] Others 'seize opportunities to move beyond the formal requirements of their opinions to adjudicate legal matters and speak to history'.[495] The effects are often felt only decades later.

4.5 Conclusions

The value of international criminal justice goes beyond punishment and sentencing. Procedural dimensions are of key importance. The justice that procedures produce does not solely derive from the fair and expeditious application of legal rules to social conduct but also from the performative enactments and experiences of participants in the process. It emerges through practices and public action which gives effect to competing rights or narratives.[496]

Performative elements play an important role in this process. The legal process navigates between performance and counter-performance, 'theatricality and antitheatricality'.[497] As Julie Stone Peters has argued, both elements are present: 'Theatricality is essential to the production of law. At the same time, theatricality in law often bears its historically negative charge: law is about accessing truth; theatre is about presenting lies.'[498]

In international criminal proceedings, actors behave in specific ways because of the roles that the law assigns to them. Each role serves different functions. The Prosecution case is to some extent a counter-performance to the crime. The Defence challenges or deconstructs Prosecution narratives. Witnesses or victims seek to gain some recognition of their experiences or reach some form of catharsis. Judges serve as listeners, interpretant, and guardians of the law.

Trials have important systemic meaning. They bear synergies to rituals and processes of 'redemptive sacrifice', which seek to renew community relations.[499] They do not only seek to condemn misconduct but are a means to offer redress, restoration, or reconciliation, or allow society to move on.[500] They are purificatory in the sense that they connect past and present, attribute blame, convey reprobation,

[494] Rosa Aloisi and James Meernik, *Judgment Day* (Cambridge: Cambridge University Press, 2017) 148.

[495] Ibid., 148–9.

[496] On performative justice, see Allen, 'Performing Justice' 52–70; Kersty Hobson, 'Enacting Environmental Justice in Singapore: Performing Justice and the Green Volunteer Network' (2006) 37 *Geoforum* 671–81, 673–4; Tazim Jamal and Rob Hales, 'Performative Justice: New Directions in Environmental and Social Justice' (2016) 76 *Geoforum* 176–80.

[497] Stone Peters, 'Legal Performance Good and Bad' 198.

[498] Ibid., 198.

[499] A sacrifice is a symbolic act of communication.

[500] See Bikundo, 'The International Criminal Court and Africa: Exemplary Justice' 37.

express harm and empathy, and promote connectivity. The communal sacrifice is not so much the 'offering' of the defendant as subject of proceedings but rather the burden of establishing fair and effective procedures and institutions to adjudicate this type of criminality, and the commitments, political costs, or compromises that are necessary to make such trials happen and endure.

Proceedings are partly an attempt to reveal truth or create communal meaning. These macro-goals must be approached with modesty, in light of international criminal law's narrow focus on individual responsibility for the criminal acts.[501] Such effects are often more distant than immediate. They depend on many intermediate factors and social processes. The social ties and dynamics that are created through the legal process are as important as its outcomes or substantive findings. As in the context of other performances, it is more realistic to view trials as a forum to open possibilities, rather than as a forum to provide closure. Trials are not 'master frames'. They create possibilities for future dialogue. They provide a new way to think about crimes and victimhood, may create 'a sense of responsibility' that can provoke action and reaction, or stimulate processes of memorialization.[502]

[501] For a critique of a sacralization of individual criminal responsibility, see Rauschenbach, Staerklé, and Scalia, 'Accused for Involvement in Collective Violence' 232–3.

[502] See Tine Destrooper, 'Performative Justice? The Role of Theatre and Performance in Facilitating Transitional Justice' (2018) *South African Theatre Journal*, 1–16, 9–11. See also William J. Booth, 'The Unforgotten: Memories of Justice' (2001) 95 *American Political Science Review* 777–91, 779 ('a venue for seeking the victory of the memory of justice over the will to forget').

5

Remedial Expression

Expressive Punishment and Repair of Harm

The justification of punishment is one of the biggest challenges of international criminal justice.[1] Paradoxically, the punishment of offenders is international crimes is often 'harder to justify' in terms of prevention or condemnation than 'the punishment of ordinary criminal offenders'.[2] Punishment is applied more selectively at the international level. Penal institutions are often detached from the social context where crime occurs. This distance may affect their authority in the eyes of affected states, victims, and offenders. Punishing bodies are not ingrained in the social fabric of domestic societies. Perpetrators may be less inclined to accept messages of condemnation.[3] In situations of political transition from conflict, penal frameworks and choices are negotiated or under construction in domestic societies.[4] Punishment is only one among many competing objectives.

The diverse goals of international criminal justice pull it in different directions. The justification of punishment depends partly on the conception of crimes. For instance, if a crime is predominantly viewed as 'a crime against order in society'[5] or as a violation of the international legal order, the expressive value of punishment lies in the affirmation of that society and the protection of legal norms. If the crime is viewed as a breach of a social contract between individuals or as an attack on individuals (as suggested by human rights law), the relational dimensions of punishment, including communication with victims, require further attention.

Existing theories of punishment are imperfect. They face difficulty to capture some of the structural features of macro or system criminality.[6] Offender-oriented approaches, which place the emphasis on punishment that reflects the culpability of the defendant and the gravity of crimes, reach their limits in relation to atrocity

[1] See Róisín Mulgrew, *Towards the Development of the International Penal System* (Cambridge: Cambridge University Press, 2013).

[2] Deirdre Golash, 'The justification of punishment in the international context' in Larry May and Zachary Hoskins (eds), *International Criminal Law and Philosophy* (Cambridge: Cambridge University Press, 2010) 201–23, 223.

[3] Ibid., 202.

[4] See Lily Rueda Guzman and Barbora Holá, , 'Punishment in Negotiated Transitions: The Case of the Colombian Peace Agreement with the FARC-EP' (2019) 19 *International Criminal Law Review* 127–59, 131.

[5] Benjamin Schiff, *Building the International Criminal Court* (Cambridge: Cambridge University Press, 2008), 32.

[6] Colleen Murphy, *Conceptual Foundations of Transitional Justice* (Cambridge: Cambridge University Press, 2017), 60.

Justice as Message. Carsten Stahn, Oxford University Press (2020). © Carsten Stahn.
DOI: 10.1093/oso/9780198864189.001.0001

crime. As the Supreme Court of Israel put in *Eichmann*, 'even as there is no word in human speech to describe deeds such as the deeds of the appellant, so there is no punishment under human law sufficiently grave to match the appellant's guilt'.[7] Victim-oriented approaches struggle with the problem of restoring 'what has been smashed'.[8]

Expressivism is a way to grapple with limits of punishment and repair to make these limits more digestible. It recognizes that punishment of perpetrators is not an end in itself.[9] As demonstrated earlier,[10] expressivist theories view punishment as a communicative gesture that is meant to affirm legal and societal norms and to convey messages of punishment to offenders and victims. This approach alters visions towards punishment. It renders punishment less perpetrator-centric. It provides space for a more holistic view of punishment, which includes expression of wrongdoing, process-related elements, and repair of harm as part of accountability measures. It accommodates alternatives to imprisonment and reparative practices, which encompass corrective and transformative elements.

5.1 Expressive Punishment

Trials and punishment are typically focused on the perpetrator. Expressive punishment involves a broader spectrum of considerations. It includes (i) expression of criminal wrongdoing; (ii) determination of culpability; (iii) the infliction of sanction (*poena*); (iv) communication of punishment; (v) and potential remedial measures (Figure 14).

5.1.1 Foundations

Expressivist theories emphasize that punishment carries symbolic relevance. It is not only a means to inflict suffering on the offender or an instrument 'for rationally controlling deviating conduct'[11] but a 'social convention' that expresses moral condemnation. International crimes may be deemed to hurt collective feelings or cause moral outrage. According to this logic, punishment has not only a denunciatory

[7] Supreme Court of Israel, *Attorney-General of the Government of Israel v. Adolf Eichmann*, Judgment, 29 May 1962 (1968) 36 *International Law Reports* 257, 341.

[8] See generally John C. Torpey, *Making Whole What Has Been Smashed: On Reparations Politics* (Cambridge, MA: Harvard University Press, 2006).

[9] On an expressive theory of punishment, see Bill Wringe, *An Expressive Theory of Punishment* (London: Palgrave Macmillian, 2016).

[10] See **section 2.1**.

[11] Immi Tallgren, 'The Durkheimian Spell of International Criminal Law?' (2013) *71 Revue interdisciplinaire d'études juridiques* 137–69, 156..

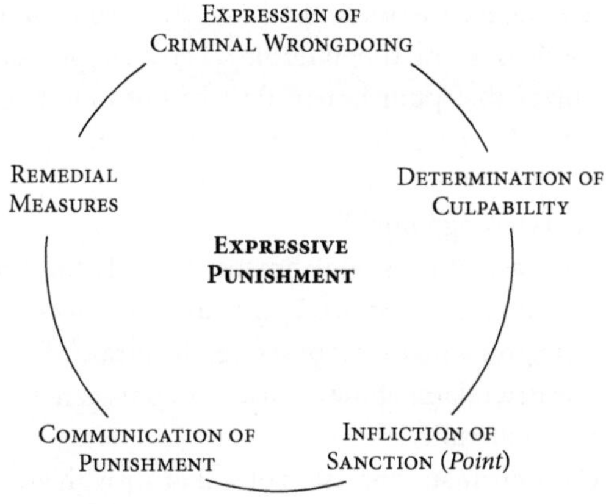

Figure 14 Expressive punishment

function[12] but a therapeutic effect for the 'international community'.[13] It affirms existing community sentiments or creates new values.[14] Ultimately, it is deemed to reinforce solidarity, make community members feel good, and contribute to prevention.[15] It is thus not necessarily the severity of punishment, but its broader expressive effects that make punishment special. The focus is partly on the communication, that is, the message that offenders are subject to accountability. For instance, sentencing practices can be qualified as attempts to express 'some kind of international moral consensus regarding the appropriate aims and penalties for international crimes'.[16]

Expressivist theories defend a communicative based understanding of punishment in relation to the offender. It includes communication of criminal wrongdoing and the message that the offender is subject to norms as other citizens.[17]

[12] On denunciation as form of expressive punishment, see Bill Wringe, 'Collective Agents and Communicative Theories of Punishment' (2012) 43 *Journal of Social Philosophy* 436–56, 443–4.

[13] Emile Durkheim, 'The rules of sociological method' in Steven Lukes (ed.), *The Rules of Sociological Method and Selected Texts on Sociology and its Method* (New York, NY: The Free Press, 1982), 31–163, 124 ('Thus, the essential function of punishment is not to make the guilty expiate his crime through suffering or to intimidate possible imitators through threats, but to buttress those consciences which violations of a rule can and must necessarily disturb in their faith-even though they themselves aren't aware of it; to show them that this faith continues to be justified.').

[14] Miriam J. Aukerman, 'Extraordinary Evil, Ordinary Crime: A Framework for Understanding Transitional Justice' (2002) 15 *Harvard Human Rights Journal* 39–97, 85.

[15] Ibid., 158 ('The expression of values is ideally believed to initiate or contribute to feelings of community, humanity, closure, or other collective therapeutic and structuring effects of criminal justice.').

[16] See Ralph Henham, 'Theorizing the Penality of Sentencing in International Criminal Trials' (2004) 8 *Theoretical Criminology* 429–463, 38.

[17] Klaus Günther, 'Criminal Law, Crime and Punishment as Communication', Normative Orders Working Paper 02/2014, 3–4, also published in Andrew. P. Simester, Antje du Bois Pedain, and Ulfrid Neumann (eds), *Liberal Criminal Theory. Essays for Andreas von Hirsch* (Oxford: Hart Publishing, 2014), 123–40, 22.

Unlike the trial, the sentence carries limited cognitive value in itself.[18] The communicative effect derives from the interplay between process and sentence. Expressivism recognizes that punishment derives not only from the gravity of sanction but partly from the process,[19] that is, a process that 'must be burdensome for the offender, not just for its own sake, but as a way of giving forceful expression to the recognition of his wrongdoing'.[20]

This communicative account of punishment supports the application of discretion in judicial sentencing decisions. It encourages processes of reintegrative shaming,[21] including expressions of remorse or guilty pleas.[22] For instance, expressions of repentance by defendants show a sense of moral agency. They may be read as signals of a 'return to humanity'.[23]

Punishment can be seen as an expression of solidarity with victims[24] or as an attempt to restore equality or dignity. The infliction of punishment entails an 'official recognition' that individuals have been 'wronged'.[25] Some experiments in domestic practice suggest that punishment may increase the social standing of victims, while its absence can have diminishing effect.[26]

It is questionable whether victims can be deemed to have a 'right to punishment'.[27] Their punitive claims are typically mediated through public authorities who serve as trustees of the interests of victims, and accommodated by a broader right of access to justice. However, victims may share their voice in relation to punishment. This is reflected in consideration of victim impact statements at trial. They open an 'avenue of communication' between 'the victim and the offender'.[28]

[18] Golash, 'The justification of punishment in the international context' 220 ('If offenders understand why they are being punished, it is only because of separate messages (such as conviction) verbally delivered.').

[19] For instance, Durkheim recognized that harsh or draconian penalties may stand in contradiction to the moral foundations of punishment. He rejected capital punishment because it sends a message of power and superiority to the defendant, rather than reinforcing engagement with the crime.

[20] Frank Haldemann, 'Another King of Justice: Transitional Justice as Recognition' (2008) 41 *Cornell International Law Journal* 675–737, 704.

[21] Such types of shaming stand in contrast to stigmatization. They do not simply brand the defendant as a 'bad person', but suggest that the perpetrator may be a 'good person' who 'did a bad thing'. See Toni Makkai and John Braithwaite, 'Reintegrative Shaming and Compliance with Regulatory Standards' (1994) 32 *Criminology* 361–85, 361.

[22] As the late Judge Cassese noted in *Erdemović*: 'by pleading guilty, the accused undoubtedly contributes to public advantage'. *Prosecutor v. Erdemović*, Separate and Dissenting Opinion of Judge Cassese, para. 8.

[23] Frédéric Mégret, 'The Repentant Defendant and the Potential of International Criminal Justice' (2018) 21 *Contemporary Justice Review* 432–54, 440.

[24] See also George P. Fletcher, 'The Place of Victims in the Theory of Retribution' (1999–2000) 3 *Buffalo Criminal Law Review* 51–64.

[25] Julian V. Roberts and Edna Erez, 'Communication in Sentencing: Exploring the Expressive function of Victim Impact Statements' (2004) 10 *International Review of Victimology* 223–44, 230.

[26] Kenworthey Bilz, 'Testing the Expressive Theory of Punishment' (2016) 13 *Journal of Empirical Legal Studies* 358–92.

[27] See Thomas Weigend, 'Die Strafe für das Opfer?—Zur Renaissance des Genugtuungsgedankens im Straf—und Strafverfahrensrecht' (2010) 1 *Rechtswissenschaft* 39–57.

[28] Roberts and Erez, 'Communication in Sentencing' 230.

Defenders of restorative justice argue that punitive measures should seek not only to right wrongs but to correct harms. For instance, Jean Hampton has claimed punishment should be viewed as a means to 're-establish the acknowledgment of the victim's worth damaged by the wrongdoing, and ... to repair the damage done to the victim's ability to realize her value'.[29] This rationale is most visibly reflected in reparation practices which complement sentences in specific contexts (e.g. International Criminal Court (ICC), Extraordinary Chambers in the Courts of Cambodia (ECCC), Extraordinary African Chambers).[30]

Expressivist theory provides some flexibility in relation to the modalities of penalty. It is a means to rethink the 'banality of punishment'.[31] Imprisonment is a 'conventional symbol' of disapproval.[32] In the context of system criminality and international crimes, social conventions are less firmly established.[33] Examples, such as South Africa or the Rwandan genocide, show that it is impossible to sanction all crimes through formal imprisonment. Imprisonment may be limited to particular offences or categories of offenders. Condemnation may be expressed in other forms.

As Barrie Sander has argued:

> A criminal justice process that includes a platform for the voices of victims to be heard and a judgment for the history of the events under examination to be narrated and the wrongful acts of individuals to be condemned can also show sincerity, particularly if complemented by other justice mechanisms such as preventative intervention, assistance to victims, and orders to make compensation.[34]

Some voices have suggested that punishment lies predominantly in condemnation rather than sanction. For example, William Schabas has noted that

[29] Jean Hampton, 'Correcting Harms versus Righting Wrongs: The Goal of Retribution' (1992) 39 *UCLA Law Review* 1659–702, 1684–85, 1686.

[30] It is disputed whether punishment itself restores equality between the victim and the offender. See Deidre Golash, *The Case Against Punishment: Retribution, Crime Prevention, and the Law* (New York, NY: New York University Press, 2005), 53 ('punishment represents a competitive victory over the offender').

[31] Gavin Dingwall and Tim Hillier, 'The Banality of Punishment: Context Specificity and Justifying Punishment of Extraordinary Crimes' (2010) 6 *International Journal of Punishment and Sentencing* 6–18.

[32] Golash, 'The justification of punishment in the international context' 219 ('Where punishment is the conventional vehicle for conveying deep social condemnation, not to punish can be taken as condonation of wrongful behavior.').

[33] Ibid., 219 ('the convention of punishing international crimes is not yet so deeply ingrained as to imply condonation by its absence. The international community has both used other kinds of formal condemnation and ignored a great deal of seriously wrongful behavior.').

[34] Barrie Sander, 'Justifying international criminal punishment: A critical perspective' in Morten Bergsmo and Emiliano J. Buis (eds), *Philosophical Foundations of International Criminal Law: Foundational Concepts* (Brussels: Torkel Opsahl Academic EPublisher, 2019, 167–240, 236.

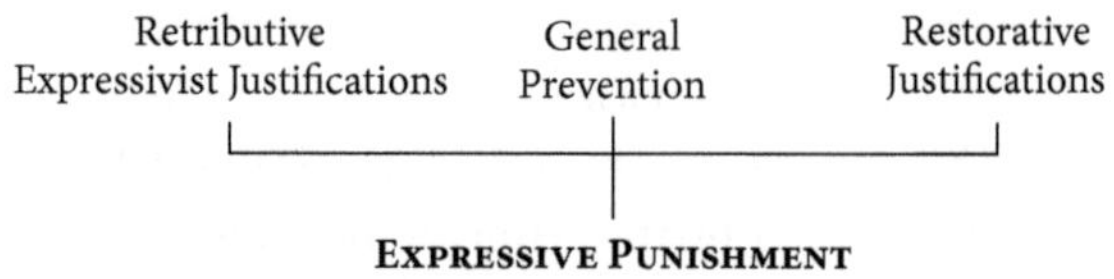

Figure 15 Justifications of expressive punishment

> [f]or the victims, and for the public in general, the thirst for justice may be better satisfied by society's condemnation of anti-social behaviour than by the actual punishment of the offenders. What is desired is a judgment, a declaration by society, and the identification and stigmatization of the perpetrator. This alone is often sufficient redress. What is actually done to the offender as a result of conviction may be far less important.[35]

The adequate modality of punishment may thus depend on what is socially understood to express condemnation.

5.1.2 Justifications of expressive punishment

Expressivist punishment is not grounded in one, but rather in a number of justifications of punishment: retributive-expressive justifications, prevention, and restorative rationales.[36]

5.1.2.1 Expressivism and retribution

Expressivism is most frequently invoked in conjunction with retributive arguments. Retribution is typically perpetrator-centred (Figure 15).[37] It starts from the premise that crimes inflict culpability on individuals which is remedied through the suffering of punishment. Punishment is justified 'in return' for crimes committed.[38] Philosophers, such as Kant or Hegel have suggested that punishment must reflect the harm that the criminal action inflicted on society, in order to provide justice and restore the legal order. Retributive concepts, such as guilt and desert, have been used to justify coercive authority by states.Kant has insisted that

[35] William Schabas, 'Sentencing by International Tribunals: A Human Rights Approach' (1996-97) 7 *Duke Journal of Comparative and International Law* 461–517, 502.

[36] It was never meant to provide a justification for punishment alone. See Dan M. Kahan, 'What Do Alternative Sanctions Mean?' (1996) 63 *University of Chicago Law Review* 591–653, 601; Robert D. Sloane, 'The Expressive Capacity of International Punishment: The Limits of the National Law Analogy and the Potential of International Criminal Law' (2007) 43 *Stanford Journal of International Law* 39–94, 601.

[37] Tobias R. Andrissek, *Vergeltung als Strafzweck* (Tübingen: Mohr Siebeck, 2017).

[38] Silvia D'Ascoli, *Sentencing in International Criminal Law* (Oxford: Hart, 2011) 64.

punishment should never be inflicted solely as a means to an end but is intrinsically related to guilt. He argued that a perpetrator must be punished because he or she violated a legal norm.[39]

In contemporary discourse, retribution has seen a revival, both at the international[40] and the domestic level.[41] Modern retributive approaches relate the justification of punishment more to the wrongdoing of the offender. Anglo-American approaches towards typically stress proportionality between punishment and the gravity of the offence. Romano-Germanic systems rely on the relationship between culpability and punishment (*Schuldprinzip*).[42] This reasoning is essential to justify an equivalence of personal culpability and punishment.[43] It serves as a limitation to the infliction of 'exemplary justice', that is, the use of offenders as prototypes.

Novel approaches base retribution on rationales other than than guilt or desert. For instance, Adil Haque has argued that retributive justifications of punishment should not only rely on the guilt of the offender, but also on the harm caused to victims and obligations owed to them.[44] Michael Pawlik has grounded retribution in the duties of offenders as citizens which go beyond inter-personal relations to victims.[45] He has claimed that individuals have a duty to contribute to common civil rights community in liberal societies. Punishment is justified to sanction disloyalty to such obligations. Other approaches view retribution as a means to an end. For example, Tonio Walter has argued that retribution is a legitimate aim of punishment since it institutionalizes retributive needs and contributes to societal peace.[46] Tobias Andrissek has expressly connected retributive theory to prevention: Retribution is necessary to secure cooperation of citizens and secure the legitimacy and foundation of state authority.[47] Some of

[39] Immanuel Kant, *The Metaphysics of Morals* (Mary Gregor ed. and trans., 1991) (1797), § 49 ('weil er verbrochen hat'). See Georg Mohr, 'Nur weil er verbrochen hat: Menschenwürde und Vergeltung in Kant's Strafrechtsphilosophie' in Heiner F. Klemme (ed.), *Kant und die Zukunft der europäischen Aufklärung* (Berlin: De Gruyter, 2009) 469–99.

[40] See e.g., Alexander Greenawalt, 'International Criminal Law for Retributivists' (2014) 35 *University of Pennsylvania Journal of International Law* 969–1044; Adil Ahmad Haque, 'Group Violence and Group Vengeance: Toward a Retributivist Theory of International Criminal Law' (2005) 9 *Buffalo Criminal Law Review* 273–328; Mordechai Kremnitzer, 'An Argument for Retributivism in International Criminal Law' in Floran Jessberger and Julia Geneuss (eds), *Why Punish Perpetrators of Mass Atrocities?* (New York: Cambridge University Press, 2020), 161–75.

[41] For a survey, see Roxin and Greco, *Strafrecht Band I: Allgemeiner Teil* 16–21.

[42] See Azuz Epik, *Strafzumessung bei Taten nach dem Völkerstrafgesetzbuch* (Tübingen: Mohr Siebeck, 2017) 82.

[43] The focus on culpability is necessary in order to avoid an extension of punishment based on preventive rationales. Allison Marston Danner, 'Constructing a Hierarchy of Crimes in International Criminal Law Sentencing' (2001) 87 *Virginia Law Review* 415–501, 453 ('retribution offers the Tribunals a sentencing method they can employ on a case-by-case basis without recourse to the complex calculations of costs and benefits endemic to the deterrent mode').

[44] See Haque, 'Group Violence and Group Vengeance', 278.

[45] See Michael Pawlik, *Person, Subjekt, Bürger* (Berlin: Duncker & Humblot, 2004), 90.

[46] Tonio Walter, 'Vergeltung als Strafzweck: Prävention und Resozialisierung als Pflichten der Kriminalpolitik' (2011) 7 *Zeitschrift für Internationale Strafrechtsdogmatik* 636–47, 646.

[47] Tobias Andrissek, Vergeltung als Strafzweck (Tübingen: Mohr Siebeck, 2017), 61–148.

these approaches come very close to theories of general prevention,[48] or are even branded as variations of the latter. [49]

5.1.2.1.1 Limits of retributive justifications of punishment

In international criminal justice, retribution is one of the 'main purposes of sentencing'[50] but it has many limitations.[51] They relate to the role of 'desert', selectivity of punishment and proportionality dilemmas.

A first problem is the narrow approach to punishment. Retribution is centred on punishment of the offender and conventional means of punishment. The 'just desert' argument is based on the assumption that penal sanction is mandatory in all circumstances. These parameters do not apply in an absolute sense to international criminal justice. Atrocity crimes require fuller range responses that go beyond perpetrators. The duty to prosecute core crimes needs to be balanced against other considerations, such as the mass nature of crimes, the availability of forums for trials, other competing objectives in situations of transition from conflict to peace (e.g. security, demobilization), and space for alternative mechanisms of justice.

A second concern relates to the principle of equality. Retribution that relies on the premise that justice is something objective that should be inflicted on all perpetrators. Its legitimacy rests on the principle of equal treatment of offenders. As critics note, retribution implies that perpetrators should be prosecuted out of debt owed to society even on a desert island that 'that decides to dissolve itself'.[52] This prerequisite is not fully convincing in international criminal justice, which is typically highly selective in nature and focused on punishment of the most serious crimes.[53]

A third difficulty concerns the determination of proportionate punishment. The *jus talionis* principle (i.e. a tit-for-tat) is ill-equipped to deal with the complexity of international crime. The idea that punishment can provide 'just deserts', that is, inflict what is due, is partly illusory in relation to crimes that transcend individuals, affect a global constituency and often cause irreparable harm. No punishment can adequately correct the wrong inherent in international crimes. The close interrelation between individual and collective responsibility makes it difficult to determine proportionate punishment. Relating retribution to the proportionality

[48] Roxin and Greco, *Strafrecht Band I: Allgemeiner Teil* 20.

[49] Angela Kalous, *Positive Generalprävention durch Vergeltung* (Regensburg: Roderer, 2000); Bernhard Haffke, *Tiefenpsychologie und Generalprävention – Eine strafrechtstheoretische Untersuchung* (Frankfurt: Sauerländer, 1976).

[50] *Delalić* Appeal Judgment, para. 799 et seq.

[51] See Sloane, 'The Expressive Capacity of International Punishment' 77 et seq.

[52] Kai Ambos, 'Prosecution of Former Nazi Camp Guards: About Restoring Society's Trust in Law and Participation in a Criminal Enterprise' *EJIL Talk*, 20 May 2013, at https://www.ejiltalk.org/prosecution-of-former-nazi-camp-guards-about-restoring-societys-trust-in-law-and-participation-in-a-criminal-enterprise/.

[53] See Drumbl, 'Collective Violence and Individual Punishment: The Criminality of Mass Atrocity' (2005) 99 *Northwestern University Law Review* 539–610, 539.

of punishment in relation to individual culpability, rather than the gravity of the crime as such, may mitigate discrepancies. As Robert Sloane has argued, 'collective features of ICL crimes arguably diminish culpability insofar as they diffuse moral responsibility and counsel distributing "guilt among the parties to a criminal transaction," mitigating each perpetrator's guilt in some proportion to that of the collective'.[54] But the application of the principle of proportionality entails serious risks, such as 'over-punishing small fish' and under-punishing the most responsible.[55]

International criminal justice is often marked by a discrepancy between the magnitude of crimes and expectations in relation to penalties.[56] Sentences are easily perceived as being too lenient. Penalties for international crimes are often equal or even lower than penalties for ordinary crimes (e.g. murder).[57] For instance, penalties inflicted by international criminal courts and tribunals may be lower than corresponding domestic penalties. As Jens David Ohlin has shown, one of the problems of a fully retributive approach is that it may be used to promote sentences that violate human rights, such as greater use of the death penalty in international criminal law.[58] This proposition has little attraction.[59] Punishment can serve as an approximation, but it is hardly ever equipped to match the harm caused by wrongdoing. As modern retributivists (e.g. Andrew von Hirsch) have emphasized, punishment is more an act of censure ('*Tadel*')[60] rather than retribution. Logically, even a comparatively low sentence may be retributive if it reflects recognition of responsibility for wrongdoing and inflicts suffering.

5.1.2.1.2 Retributive-expressive justifications

It is widely acknowledged that retribution alone does not suffice to justify punishment. As Kai Ambos has observed:

> [C]riminal law does not exist for its own sake but to avoid and solve interpersonal conflicts and, perhaps, even establish social peace ... A criminal sanction, useless for the society, cannot be justified and much less in a postmodern society, where criminal law is only one instrument among others to solve interpersonal conflicts.[61]

[54] Sloane, 'The Expressive Capacity of International Punishment' 59.

[55] Kremnitzer, 'An Argument for Retributivism in International Criminal Law' 172–74.

[56] See Mark A. Drumbl, *Atrocity, Punishment and International Law* (Cambridge: Cambridge University Press, 2007), 155 et seq.

[57] Ibid., 157 et seq.

[58] See Jens David Ohlin, 'Applying the Death Penalty to Crimes of Genocide' (2005) 99 *AJIL* 747–77.

[59] Margaret M. DeGuzman, 'Proportionate sentencing at the ICC' in Carsten Stahn (ed.), *The Law and Practice of the International Criminal Court* (Oxford: Oxford University Press, 2015), 932–62, 949.

[60] Andrew von Hirsch, *Censure and Sanctions* (Oxford: Oxford University Press, 1993); Jean-Claude Wolf and Ignace Haaz, 'Strafe als Tadel? Argumente pro und kontra', in Andreas von Hirsch, Ulfrid Neumann, and Kurt Seelmann (eds), *Strafe—Warum?* (Baden-Baden: Nomos, 2011), 69–78.

[61] Ambos, 'Prosecution of Former Nazi Camp Guards'.

Punishment is often justified by retributive-expressive justifications. Expressivist theory provides a slightly different justification for the infliction of punishment. It views punishment not necessarily as a 'just desert' but rather as a necessary societal reaction to crime that involves expression of reprobation. As highlighted earlier,[62] according to expressivist theory, certain crimes may be viewed as performative acts[63] that imply a message that cannot be ignored by society: 'Just as punishment addresses the offender and sends a message to her, to the community, and to the victim, the crime sends a message to the victim and to society too.'[64]

Retributive expressive accounts break the strict divide between deontological and consequentialist justifications of punishment.[65] They integrate retributive elements in the communicative justification of punishment. They stress that punishment involves not only norm affirmation, establishment of trust in society or community creation, but also messages in relation to individual wrongdoing and allocation of responsibility.[66] They rely on the idea of an adequate reaction to crime.[67] The crime determines both, the necessity of societal reaction, and the scope of punishment.

The criminal process and punishment provide a reaction to such acts, an objection to that message, in order to prevent the erosion of norms. Such an explanation may help to understand the nature of international criminal trials which are highly selective in nature. They often serve more to express legal condemnation in response to crimes, rather than to inflict 'just desert' on individual defendants for the magnitude of harm caused. Identification of culpability and allocation of responsibility are part of the communicative function of trials.[68] The nature of the crime and individual responsibility impose constraints for the allocation of responsibility and the communication of adequate punishment to offender and victims. As Feinberg has noted, expressivist justice requires that the 'condemnatory aspect of the punishment [must] suit the crime'.[69] Punishment affirms equality before the law. But its infliction is at the same limited by the principle of equality.

5.1.2.1.2.1 Punishment as repentance Some theorists ground the justification of punishment in communication with the defendant, including expression of repentance ('*Sühne*').[70] Antony Duff has developed a retributive account of

[62] See **section 2.1.**

[63] Ingeborg Puppe, 'Strafrecht als Kommunikation—Leistungen und Gefahren eines neuen Paradigmas in der Strafrechtsdogmatik' in Erich Samson, Friedrich Dencker, Peter Frisch, Helmut Frister, and Wolfram Reiß (eds), *Festschrift für Gerald Grünwald zum siebzigsten Geburtstag* (Baden-Baden: Nomos, 1999), 469–94, 473 et seq.

[64] Günther, 'Criminal Law, Crime and Punishment as Communication' 6–7.

[65] Daniela Demko, 'An expressive theory of international punishment for international crimes' in Florian Jessberger and Julia Geneuss (eds), *Why Punish Perpetrators of Mass Atrocities?* (New York: Cambridge University Press, 2020) 176–96, 192.

[66] Id., 190–1.

[67] See Georg Freund and Frauke Rostalski, *Strafrecht Allgemeiner Teil: Personale Straftatlehre*, 3rd edn (Berlin: Springer, 2019), 14--5; Frauke Rostalski, *Der Tatbegriff im Strafrecht* (Tübingen: Mohr Siebeck, 2019), 17–19; Tony Rostalki, *Alternativ legitimierte Verhaltensnormen* (Tübingen: Mohr Siebeck, 2019), 26–37.

[68] Demko, 'An Expressive Theory of International Punishment' 184.

[69] Joel Feinberg, 'The expressive function of punishment' in Joel Feinberg (ed.), *Doing and Deserving* (Princeton, NJ: Princeton University Press, 1970), 95–118, 118.

[70] See Hannah Maslen (ed.), *Remorse, Penal Theory and Sentencing* (Oxford: Hart, 2015).

punishment which relies on the concept of 'secular penance'.[71] His argument of 'penance' is grounded in the communicative nature of punishment, namely the purpose to influence the perpetrator through the act of punishment. It relies on the premise that the perpetrator can experience the norm violation only through an act of communication. Punishment is thus a means to foster understanding about the violations and to encourage the perpetrator to take responsibility for the actions.[72]

This justification combines retributive and expressivist arguments. However, it is more difficult to maintain in international criminal justice than in domestic contexts. The ability to convey such messages depends on whether or not the offender regards the penal institution as 'both legitimate and morally authoritative'.[73] Many high-level perpetrators have failed to recognize this authority or even built their own defence on challenging this legitimacy.[74] Low or mid-level perpetrators may not necessarily require acts of repentance, which reconnect them to communities since may have acted based on conformity pressures or lack the 'moral defects' that these theories presume.[75]

5.1.2.1.2.2 Retributive norm expression Other approaches relate punishment to the gravity of the offence and the culpability of the perpetrator, expression of disapproval, and condemnation to the offender,[76] and encouragement of states to assume their responsibility to protect human rights.[77] For example, Silvia D'Ascoli has argued that a 'retributive approach is justified' in international criminal justice because it 'conveys the message that there can be no justification and no tolerance for grave violations of human rights'.[78]

This reasoning is reflected in sentencing judgments.[79] In *Alexovski*, the International Criminal Tribunal for the former Yugoslavia (ICTY) Appeals Chamber noted that retribution 'is not to be understood as fulfilling a desire for revenge but as duly expressing the outrage of the international community at these crimes'.[80]

[71] See Antony Duff, *Punishment, Communication, and Community* (Oxford: Oxford University Press, 2001), 106.

[72] See Antony Duff, 'Penance, Punishment and the Limits of Community' (2003) 5 *Punishment & Society* 295–312, 301–2.

[73] Golash, 'The justification of punishment in the international context' 221.

[74] See **section 5.3**.

[75] Golash, 'The justification of punishment in the international context' 220–1.

[76] The ICTY stressed the importance of public denunciation of crimes the *Erdemović* case. It held that 'public reprobation and stigmatisation by the international community, which would thereby express its indignation over heinous crimes and denounce the perpetrators, [are] ... one of the essential functions of a prison sentence for a crime against humanity'. *Prosecutor v. Erdemović*, Sentencing Judgment, IT-96-22-T, 20 November 1996, para. 65.

[77] Kirsten J. Fisher, *Moral Accountability and International Criminal Law, Holding Agents of Atrocity Accountable to the World* (London: Routledge, 2011), 53 et seq.

[78] D'Ascoli, *Sentencing in International Criminal Law* 298.

[79] The ICC adopted a combined retributive–expressive approach in *Al Mahdi*. It justified punishment as 'an expression of the international community's condemnation of the crimes ... by way of imposition of a proportionate sentence [which] also acknowledges the harm to the victims and promotes the restoration of peace and reconciliation'. See *Prosecutor v. Al Mahdi*, Judgment and Sentence, ICC-01/12-01/15-171, 27 September 2016, para. 67.

[80] *Prosecutor v. Alexovski*, Judgment, IT-95-14/1-A, 24 March 2000, para. 185.

In the *Mrda* Sentencing judgment, the ICTY grounded retribution expressly in the need to temper feelings of hatred or desires of revenge by victims (victim hatred theory).[81] It noted:

> As a form of retribution, punishment expresses the society's condemnation of the criminal act and of the person who committed it and should be proportional to the seriousness of the crimes. The Tribunal's punishment thus conveys the indignation of humanity for the serious violations of international humanitarian law for which an accused was found guilty. In its retributive aspect, punishment may reduce the anger and sense of injustice caused by the commission of the crimes among victims and in their wider community.[82]

Punishment is thus not only meant to address the defendant, but to 'speak to the world at large' and victims.[83] However, such rationales (e.g. victim gratification)_ do not justify punishment as such. Measures, such as deprivation of freedom, require a justification that goes beyond norm expression or 'the communicative process itself'.[84] As Andreas Werkmeister has noted, the victim-related justifications are 'partly dependent on prevention':

> victims only have a reason to believe the message of punishment if they can assume that the penalty is capable of reaffirming and stabilising the infringed norm and thereby capable of preventing the offender or other potential offenders from future violations.[85]

5.1.2.2 Expressivism and prevention

Expressivism has strong synergies with prevention[86] which seeks to reinforce crime control.[87] It is sometimes expressly qualified as 'positive prevention'.[88]

[81] See Sander, 'Justifying international criminal punishment' 225.
[82] *Prosecutor v. Mrda*, Sentencing Judgment, IT-02-59-S, 31 March 2004, para. 14.
[83] Aloisi and Meernik, *Judgment Day* 167, 187.
[84] Andreas Werkmeister, 'The individual and the international community: an outline for a combined meso preventive theory of international punishment', in Florian Jessberger and Julia Geneuss (eds), *Why Punish Perpetrators of Mass Atrocities?* (New York: Cambridge University Press, 2020) 228–57, 243–4.
[85] Id., 244.
[86] Kai Ambos, *Treatise on International Criminal Law: Vol. I: Foundations and General Part* (Oxford: Oxford University Press, 2013) 71.
[87] See generally David Garland, *The Culture of Control: Crime and Social Order in Contemporary Society* (Chicago, IL: The University of Chicago Press, 2001).
[88] Kremnitzer, 'An Argument for Retributivism in International Criminal Law' 162.

The role of prevention in justifying punishment[89] may be traced back to the writings of Cesare Beccaria and Paul Johann Anselm von Feuerbach. Feuerbach argued that punishment is meant to induce 'psychological coercion' in society ('threat-based general prevention').[90] Modern approaches rely on a differentiated psychological model, which takes into account a variety of factors, such as risk calculation, moral influence, aspirations, and emotions.[91] Prevention is inherently tied to societal expectations about behaviour. It differs from specific deterrence. It is generally 'more concerned with the psychology of those obedient to the law than with the psychology of criminals'.[92]

General prevention builds on the didactic function of punishment.[93] It suggests that punishment is not only meant to encourage norm-abiding behavior through its dissuasive effect on offenders, but also a means to strengthen norm internalization, norm acceptance social commitment to norms.[94] It accepts that crime may be reduced through disapprobation rather than through mere threat of punishment. It relies on communication of messages, including messages 'about what would be risked by disobedience', and 'proclamations specifying that it is wrong to disobey'.[95] As Thomas Mathiesen has argued, punishment may be viewed as a threefold message:

> First, ... a message which intends to say that crime does not pay (deterrence). Secondly, ... a message which intends to say that you should avoid certain acts because they are morally improper or incorrect (moral education). Thirdly, ... a message which intends to say that you should get into the habit of avoiding certain acts (habit formation).[96]

[89] Rationales of general prevention have been used in legislative policy and sentencing practices. See generally Wilfried Bottke, *Assoziationsprävention: zur heutigen Diskussion der Strafzwecke* (Berlin: Duncker & Humblot, 1995). In domestic contexts, general prevention is sometimes criticized as punishment rationale since it is difficult to establish empirically. On empirical grounding in domestic law, see Michael Baurmann, 'Vorüberlegungen zu einer empirischen Theorie der positiven Generalprävention' (1994) 141 *Goltdammer's Archiv für Strafrecht* 368–84.

[90] On Feuerbach and psychological compulsion as motivation of punishment, see Luís Greco, *Lebendiges und Totes in Feuerbachs Straftheorie* (Berlin: Duncker & Humblot, 2009).

[91] Johannes Andenaes, 'General Preventive Effects of Punishment' (1966) 114 *University of Pennsylvania Law Review* 949–83, 955; David L. Bosco, 'The International Criminal Court and Crime Prevention: Byproduct or Conscious' (2011) 19 *Michigan State Journal of International Law* 163–200, 172.

[92] Andenaes, 'General Preventive Effects of Punishment' 955.

[93] Thomas Mathiesen, 'General prevention as communication' in Antony Duff and David Garland (eds), *A Reader on Punishment* (Oxford: Oxford University Press, 1994) 221–37.

[94] Michael Baurmann, 'Vorüberlegungen zu einer empirischen Theorie der positiven Generalprävention' (1994) 141 *Goltdammer's Archiv für Strafrecht* 368–84.

[95] Andenaes, 'General Preventive Effects of Punishment' 950.

[96] Thomas Mathiesen, *Prison on Trial* (Winchester: Waterside Press, 2006), 65.

Prevention plays a cardinal role in international criminal justice, which deals with macro criminality and violations that are deemed to affect peace and security.[97] For instance, the ICC Statute makes reference to it in the preamble and warrants of arrest.[98] It encompasses different dimensions: prevention aimed at deterring other potential offenders from committing crimes ('negative general prevention'), and prevention geared at reaffirming the validity common norms and encouraging law-abiding persons to comply with them ('positive general prevention').[99]

5.1.2.2.1 Negative general prevention

The first concept, 'negative general prevention', poses significant challenges in international criminal law. Such arguments are part of the rhetoric of international criminal justice. Some voices argue that 'elements of individual and general deterrence' form part of the communicative content of international punishment.[100] However, it is questionable whether they provide a basis for an expressive justification of punishment.[101] Theories of negative general prevention view criminal actions predominantly through a rational choice model.[102] Some judgments have expressly relied on such a logic. For instance, the International Criminal Tribunal for Rwanda (ICTR) noted that '[w]ith the sentence, an attempt is made to deter, that is, to discourage people from committing similar crimes. The main result sought is to discourage people from committing a second offence since the penalty should also result in discouraging other people from carrying out their criminal plan.'[103] Others judgments have interpreted punishment as a message of intolerance towards future violations.[104] For example, the Trial Chamber in *Kayishema and Ruzindana* used expressivist justifications of punishment to motivate sentencing. It noted that the judgment 'seeks to dissuade for good those who will be tempted in the future to perpetrate such atrocities by showing them that the international community is no longer willing to tolerate serious violations of international humanitarian law and human rights.'[105]

[97] On sentencing and prevention, see Christopher Slobogin, 'Prevention as the Primary Goal of Sentencing: The Modern Case for Indeterminate Dispositions in Criminal Cases' (2011) 48 *San Diego Law Review* 1127–72.

[98] See preamble, 'determined to put an end to impunity for the perpetrators of these crimes and thus to contribute to the prevention of such crimes'. See also ICC Statute, Article 58(c)(3).

[99] Tatjana Hörnle and Andreas von Hirsch, 'Positive Generalprävention und Tadel' (1995) 142 *Goltdammer's Archiv für Strafecht* 261–82.

[100] For such an approach, see Demko, 'An Expressive Theory of International Punishment' 186.

[101] For a critique, see Werkmeister, 'The Individual and the International Community' 248 ('Many international crimes continue to go unpunished after the establishment of the ICC, even if they become known').

[102] See Petra Wittig, *Der rationale Verbrecher: Der ökonomische Ansatz zur Erklärung kriminellen Verhaltens* (Berlin: Duncker & Humblot, 1993).

[103] *Prosecutor v. Rutaganira,* Judgment and Sentence, ICTR 95-1C-T, 14 March 2005, para. 110.

[104] See Aloisi and Meernik, *Judgment Day* 165.

[105] *Prosecutor v. Kayishema and Ruzindana,* ICTR-95-1-T, 21 May 1999, Judgment para. 2. See also *Prosecutor v. Kambanda,* Judgment and Sentence, ICTR 97-23-S, 4 September 1998, para. 28 ('dissuading for good those who will attempt in future to perpetrate such atrocities by showing them

Such arguments rely on a simplified vision of perpetrators. They are built on the assumption that potential perpetrators are rational agents that act according to cost/benefit analysis. This premise is questionable.[106]

International criminal justice faces a 'non-deterrability challenge'.[107] Many international crimes are not rational but driven by emotions that are difficult to understand by bystanders. Decisions are often founded in ideologies, passions, or belief that transcend rational calculus or ignore the threat punishment. Negative general prevention is difficult to prove. There is an epistemic dilemma: '[o]ne cannot ever know who actually is deterred by the existence of international criminal justice . . .; we can only know who was not'.[108]

In many cases, it is questionable whether perpetrators are actually influenced by the threat of punishment, the application of criminal procedures, or the infliction of punishment. In some instances, punishment at the international level may be a lesser evil or even be perceived as a reward.

Additional complications arise from the nature of macro-criminality. Leaders or mid-level perpetrators may be influenced by threats of punishment. Lower-level perpetrators are more likely to be influenced by their peers. Prevention may need to be directed at particular types of collectivities that pose special risks (e.g. leadership structures, criminal organizations) rather than isolated individuals, in order to produce effects.[109] Andreas Werkmeister has developed the concept of 'meso-prevention' (*Mesoprävention*) in order to distinguish between different addresses, i e. leaders who frame wrong norm of behaviour and followers who fail to show disobedience. He has argued that punishment is a form of communicative compensation ('intellectual crime damage')[110] that concerns those 'who are "indirectly" affected by a core'.[111] Preventive effects are influenced by a wide range of intermediate factors other than punishment that determine behaviour, including social context. They are even more difficult to verify than in domestic contexts.

Expressivist theory provides an alternative explanation to justify 'negative general prevention'. It justifies the idea of 'negative general prevention' by the ability to influence future-oriented attitudes through engagement with past behaviour. As Dan Kahan has argued, 'the law can discourage criminality not just by "raising the

that the international community was not ready to tolerate the serious violations of international humanitarian law and human right').

[106] See Mathiesen, *Prison on Trial* 74–5 ('general prevention functions in relation to those who do not "need" it. In relation to those who "need" it, it does not function.').

[107] Sander, 'Justifying international criminal punishment' 189.

[108] Dawn Rothe and Victoria Collins, 'The International Criminal Court: A pipe dream to end impunity?' in Dawn L. Rothe, James D. Meernik, and Thordis Ingadóttir (eds), *The Realities of International Criminal Justice* (Leiden: Brill, 2013), 191–209, 209.

[109] See Werkmeister, 'The Individual and the International Community' 249-256; id., *Straftheorien im Völkerstrafrecht* 365.

[110] Werkmeister, 'The Individual and the International Community' 245, 256.

[111] Id. 255.

cost" of such behavior through punishments, but also through instilling aversions to the kinds of behavior that the law prohibits'.[112]

This reasoning does not rely, to the same extent, on consequentialist reasoning, that is, cause and effect relations and balances of probability in relation to future behaviour. It implies that negative prevention is a possible consequence rather than a direct aim of international criminal justice. This assumption is more modest. It accepts that the expression of punishment may facilitate norm-abiding behaviour, but it does not argue that punishment as such is justified, because it reduces the frequency of crime. It avoids, therefore, some of the pitfalls of consequentialism.

5.1.2.2.2 Positive general prevention

Expressivism is very closely related to 'positive general prevention', which seeks to encourage norm promotion and moral education.[113] Norm expression is grounded in the idea that objection to criminal behaviour is necessary in order to maintain a peaceful society.[114] The authority to punish is related to prevention, namely the right and obligation to prevent future harm to others. One of the main strengths of international criminal justice is that it conveys a message that 'similar atrocities are wrong'.[115]

5.1.2.2.2.1 Links to expressivism 'Positive general prevention' has considerable significance in international criminal justice. International criminal justice loses its legitimacy without trust in its norms and institutions. A frequent objection to 'positive general prevention' is that its effects have not been empirically proven. However, it serves as motivating factor for behaviour and as an important justification for punishment.

International criminal justice is often exercised long after crimes have been committed, sometimes decades after atrocities (e.g. the Holocaust, Latin American dictatorships, Cambodia). In many cases, it can only be justified as an undertaking with a strongly preventive orientation. For instance, the punishment of elderly offenders decades after the facts, such as in Germany or Cambodia, cannot be justified by ideas of deterrence or resocialization of individuals. Positive general prevention takes these particularities into account. The value of expressivism lies in the fact that it helps to explain how 'positive general prevention' works.

[112] Dan M. Kahan, 'What Do Alternative Sanctions Mean?' (1996) 63 *University of Chicago Law Review* 591–653, 603.

[113] Ambos, *Treatise on International Criminal Law* 47–8; Demko, 'An Expressive Theory of International Punishment' 192, 184-185 ('International punishment expresses with great symbolism and emphasis, and with the communicative inclusion of the elements of positive affirmative general prevention, that no human being is above the law and that no one can hide behind collective, systemic and macro-criminal structures'). See also **section 1.1.4.**

[114] It relies on the premise that criminal procedures and punishment are necessary to reaffirm to society that norms violated through crimes are still valid.

[115] D'Ascoli, *Sentencing in International Criminal Law* 300.

'Positive general prevention' relies on the assumption that lack of punishment would not only 'shock' the moral conscience of law-abiding citizens but create inequality among offenders.[116] The ICTY expressly invoked 'affirmative prevention' in *Kupreškić et al.* The Trial Chamber held that a relevant sentencing purpose 'is to show the people of not only the former Yugoslavia but of the world in general, that there is no impunity for these types of crimes'.[117] This 'should be done in order to strengthen the resolve of all involved not to allow crimes against international humanitarian law to be committed as well as to create trust in and respect for the developing system of international justice'.[118]

Claus Roxin has argued that the theory of positive general prevention can be defended on the basis of three different rationales: its didactic effects ('*Lerneffekt*'), its contribution to re-establishment of trust ('*Vertrauenseffekt*'), and its pacificatory effect ('*Befriedungseffekt*').[119] These rationales are highly dependent on a communicative function of justice and require a long-term assessment.

Expressivism adds a missing link to the theory of positive general prevention. It recognizes that justice is partly a 'ritual' that needs to accommodate expectations of a wide range of stakeholders. It provides a framework to understand the modalities of positive general prevention.

5.1.2.2.2.2 Didactic justifications of general prevention International criminal justice does not only express moral outrage about the need to react to violations but also contains appeals to societal attitudes and values. The didactic functions of general prevention may be explained in at least three different ways: faith-building, norm communication, and encouragement of disobedience and civil courage (Figure 16).

In its most general version, international criminal justice may be understood as an attempt to contribute to the creation of a common global identity relating to the ban and prevention of international crimes. For example, David Koller has claimed that international criminal justice has an identity-creating or

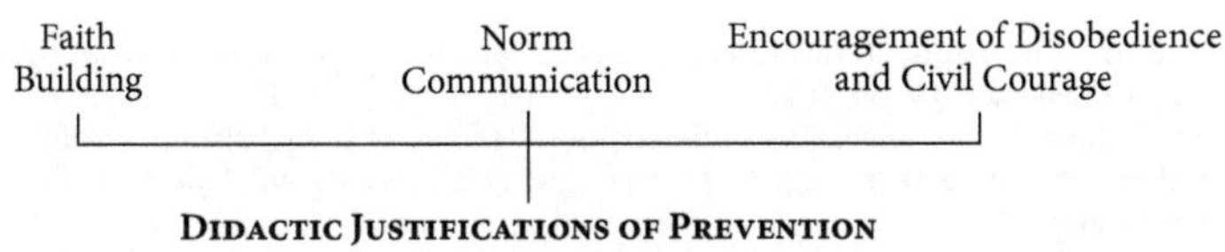

Figure 16 Didactic justifications of general prevention

[116] Ambos, *Treatise on International Criminal Law* 72.

[117] *Prosecutor v. Kupreškić et al.*, Judgment, IT-95-16-T, 14 January 2000, para. 848.

[118] Ibid.

[119] Roxin, 'Prevention, Censure and Responsibility' 23–42; Roxin and Greco, *Strafrecht Band I: Allgemeiner Teil* (2020), 31.

'faith-building' function.[120] According to this view, the virtue of punishment is related to the creation of a global moral ethics and its integrating function in relation to global society.[121] The didactic function lies in the formation of a system of prevention.[122]

A second school of thought relates didactic justifications of prevention to processes of norm communication, including 'legal and normative internalization of international human rights and humanitarian law'.[123] For example, Harmen Van der Wilt has argued that the main value of expressive theory is to communicate core values and ensure faith in the rule of law.[124] Sloane has made the argument that international criminal tribunals 'will deter most effectively', if they 'encourage the growth of national institutions, laws, and ethical norms that can be applied with greater regularity and frequency'.[125]

Other authorities go further and claim that the main didactic rationale of international criminal justice lies in its ability to create concrete expectations in relation to norm-abiding behaviour by individuals, namely to incentive individuals to demonstrate disobedience or resistance to international crimes.[126] They claim that the didactic function has a preventive effect only if it produces concrete consequences. For instance, Vasco Reuss has argued that encouragement of civil courage should be recognized as rationale of punishment. Reuss has stressed that global consciousness alone does not help to prevent crimes or save lives.[127] Actors need to subordinate their actions to moral imperatives and defend them in critical contexts.

This ambition has been voiced in the connection of post-Second World War trials. For instance, Fritz Bauer, one of the main driving forces behind the Frankfurt Auschwitz trials in Germany the 1960s,[128] has argued that these proceedings were meant to teach citizens to demonstrate resistance against state crime. He viewed these trials first and foremost as a message to members of German society, namely as a reminder that they should have behaved differently and objected to Nazi

[120] David Koller, 'The Faith of the International Criminal Lawyer' (2007) 40 *NYU Journal of International Law & Policy* 1019–69, 1057.

[121] On the term in German scholarship, see Jens Christian Müller-Tuckfeld, *Integrationsprävention: Studien zu einer Theorie der gesellschaftlichen Funktion des Strafrechts* (Frankfurt: Peter Lang, 1998).

[122] Christina Möller, *Völkerstrafrecht und Internationaler Strafgerichtshof. Kriminologische, straftheoretische und rechtspolitische Aspekte* (Münster: LIT Verlag, 2003) 526.

[123] Sloane, 'The Expressive Capacity of International Punishment' 44.

[124] See Van der Wilt, 'Why International Criminal Lawyers Should Read Mirjan Damaška' 99.

[125] Sloane, 'The Expressive Capacity of International Punishment' 75.

[126] See Bronwyn Leebaw, 'Justice and the Faithless: The Demand for Disobedience in International Criminal Law' (2018) 24 *European Journal of International Relations* 344–66.

[127] Vasco Reuss, 'Zivilcourage als Strafzweck des Völkerstrafrechts? Betroffenenbelange aus teleologischer Perspektive (2012) 45 *Kritische Justiz* 241–60, 245.

[128] See Fritz Bauer Institut and Katharina Rauschenberger (eds), *Rückkehr in Feindesland? Fritz Bauer in der deutschjüdischen Nachkriegsgeschichte* (Frankfurt: Campus Verlag, 2013).

rule,[129] even at the price of individual sacrifice.[130] In his view, the proceedings were ultimately designed to motivate civil courage.

In recent decades, the idea to promote disobedience as part of prevention has gained greater recognition. International criminal justice stigmatizes certain forms of obedience. Core provisions of international criminal law, such as the irrelevance of official capacity or restriction duress and superior order contain incentives to individuals to set aside self-interest and manifest disobedience in relation to unlawful conduct. Courts often use examples of disobedient behaviour (exemplary disobedience) to show that perpetrators had a moral choice and could have behaved differently.[131] Duties of disobedience apply, in particular, to persons holding positions of authority. Disobedience and resistance play a central role in international relations. As Bronwyn Leebaw has noted:

> [S]oldiers and civilian authorities are now required [under international criminal law] to refuse compliance with domestic laws and commands that might implicate them in crimes against humanity and to risk their own lives in order to prevent mass killings. International criminal law also demands disobedience from those who are likely to find this demand most challenging—soldiers with training aimed at producing habitual obedience, conformity, and desensitization to the shock of violence.[132]

Klaus Günther has argued that international criminal law 'demands and expects' citizens to display a critical attitude towards human rights violations, by virtue of their dual status as citizens of the domestic and the international legal order.[133] He claims that civic courage is a 'central part of the justification of international criminal law':

> Citizens have to examine their domestic law critically from the point of view of human rights, and they have to protest and resist against any transformation of their domestic law and its practice into a system of massive human rights violations.[134]

[129] Fritz Bauer, Manfred Jenke, and Walter Menningen, 'Zu den Naziverbrecher-Prozessen: "Globke ist im Ruhezustand"' (1963) 57 *Neue Wege: Beiträge zu Religion und Sozialismus* 281–91, 288 ('Deswegen ist es das A und O dieser Prozesse zu sagen: Ihr hättet Nein sagen müssen.').

[130] Ibid., 290 ('Recht verlangt von uns enen Kampf und ein gewisses Opfer. Ich sage, das ist der Inhalt dieser Prozesse—so schwer es ist und so schwer es eigentlich als bittere Medizin dem deutschen Volk hinuntergeht: Darum geht es—um die Zivilcourage im eigenen Volk, um den eigenen Kampf für das Recht mit eigenen persönlichen Opfern.').

[131] Leebaw, 'Justice and the faithless' 357.

[132] Ibid., 363.

[133] Klaus Günther, 'Positive general prevention and the idea of civic courage in international criminal law' in Florian Jessberger and Julia Geneuss (eds), *Why Punish Perpetrators of Mass Atrocities?* (New York: Cambridge University Press, 2020), 213–28, 222.

[134] Ibid., 222.

Reuss has expressly linked this argument to prevention. He has argued that resistance against abusive state power and creation of civil courage in global civil society form part of the preventive rationales of international criminal justice.[135] His argument is grounded in the claim that individuals are central in the prevention of crimes since states alone cannot be entrusted with the enforcement of international criminal norms.[136] He derived duties of civil courage from the horizontal application of human rights and the need to protect the dignity of victims of international crimes.[137]

Other voices are more sceptical.[138] The notion of civil courage is vague. There are many grey zones in relation to the scope of duties of disobedience. The spheres of responsibility are often blurred. It is unclear how far individual duties can be stretched, and to what extent civil courage must be guided by a subjective conviction that the action is justified.

Some of these problems became evident in the famous *Erdomović* case before the ICTY, which dealt with the controversial question of whether duress can be a defence to the killing of civilians. The case displayed divergent attitudes as to what can be expected from individuals in a situation of conflict.

The majority, Judges MacDonald and Vohrah, advocated a strict behavioural standard. They argued that Erdomović should have resisted the order to kill, even at the expense of his own fate, since law 'expects' a certain degree of 'heroism from its subjects'.[139] They claimed that 'soldiers or combatants are expected to exercise fortitude and a greater degree of resistance to a threat than civilians, at least when it is their own lives which are being threatened'.[140] Soldiers, 'by the very nature of their occupation, must have envisaged the possibility of violent death in pursuance of the cause for which they fight'.[141]

Judges Cassese filed a dissenting opinion. He adopted a more lenient standard in his. He argued international criminal justice does not require individuals to set 'a heroic example for mankind'.[142] He claimed that duties of disobedience are not absolute 'in situations where sacrifice of his own life would be to no avail', namely where 'the civilians, prisoners of war, etc., would be shot anyway'[143] since 'law is based on what society can reasonably expect of its members. It should not set

[135] Reuss, 'Zivilcourage als Strafzweck des Völkerstrafrechts? Betroffenenbelange aus teleologischer Perspektive' 257–9; Günther and Reuss, 'Legitimation des Völkerstrafrechts in Deutschland—Völkerstrafrecht als Bürgerstrafrecht' 127–63.

[136] Reuss, 'Zivilcourage als Strafzweck des Völkerstrafrechts?' 18–19.

[137] Ibid., 256.

[138] Möller, *Völkerstrafrecht und Internationaler Strafgerichtshof* 528 (arguing that the recognition of civil courage as preventive rationale is desirable, yet still unrealistic).

[139] *Prosecutor v. Erdemović*, Joint Separate Opionion of Judge MacDonald and Judge Vohrah, 7 October 1997, para. 85.

[140] Ibid., para. 84

[141] Ibid., para. 84.

[142] *Prosecutor v. Erdemović*, Separate and Dissenting Opinion of Judge Cassese, para. 44.

[143] Ibid., para. 44.

intractable standards of behaviour which require mankind to perform acts of martyrdom, and brand as criminal any behaviour falling below those standards.'[144]

The assumption that the didactic function of international criminal justice promotes civil courage remains highly aspirational.[145] International criminal justice contributes to 'a belief in individual responsibility' that 'may influence the decision-making of individuals' over time.[146]

5.1.2.2.2.3 Confidence-building and pacificatory effects The confidence-building and pacificatory effects associated with positive general prevention must be approached with modesty. In many cases, norm expression or infliction of punishment does not in itself create confidence. International criminal justice does not enjoy the same degree of democratic legitimacy as domestic justice institutions. It is often distant from the crimes. This limits its ability to create confidence through judicial action.[147] The practice of the ICTY is a pertinent example. It leaves significant doubts about whether international criminal justice can contribute to a 'rehabilitation' of communities. As Diane Orentlicher has argued, based on twenty-five years of experience, it has been very hard to establish that international criminal courts have a transformative impact on social beliefs:

> Psychological dynamics that operate in the most prosaic spheres of human endeavor—in particular, a human propensity to discredit information that challenges our collective self-esteem, our habitual reliance on trusted sources to interpret reality, and our resistance to information at odds with established beliefs—were at play in post-Milošević Serbia and postwar Bosnia. Similar dynamics are likely to operate in many countries, where basic norms of human decency have been so thoroughly debased as to give rise to war crimes prosecutions.[148]

Confidence-building occurs more indirectly and discretely. The acknowledgment and record of crimes do not automatically alter social belief. It expresses solidarity with victims of crimes. This expression may strengthen bonds between those who have not offended the norm.[149] It may have a certain de-escalating potential. It may

[144] Ibid., para. 47.

[145] See Ambos, *Treatise on International Criminal Law: Vol. I* 72.

[146] Koller, 'Faith of the International Criminal Lawyer' 1059.

[147] See Jan Holling, *Internationaler Strafgerichtshof und Verbrechensprävention* (Berlin: LIT, 2016) 138.

[148] See Diane Orentlicher, '25 Years of Contemporary War Crimes Tribunals', OUP Blog, 25 May 2018, at https://blog.oup.com/2018/05/25-years-contemporary-war-crimes-tribunals/; Diane Orentlicher, *Some Kind of Justice: The ICTY's Impact in Bosnia and Serbia* (Oxford: Oxford University Press, 2018).

[149] For instance, the individualization of responsibility is not only guided by retributive rationales, such as ensuring proportionate punishment, but 'intimately connected to wider communitarian concerns'. See Henham, 'Theorizing the Penality of Sentencing in International Criminal Trials' 444.

serve as a constraint on vengeance by its potential decollectivization of guilt and prevent a secondary victimization of victims.[150]

5.1.2.3 Expressivism and restorative justice

The justification of expressive punishment is further related to restorative rationales. Providing justice for victims is one of the key goals of international criminal justice.[151] As Salvatore Zappalà has observed, 'international criminal trials are not merely about punishing a few individuals. Rather, the purpose of international criminal justice is broader, comprising victim rehabilitation through participation and assuming a pedagogical dimension involving the affected communities'.[152]

Modern theories recognize that victims have a legitimate interest in punishment that needs to be taken into account in penal theories.[153] It is linked to rights, such as the right to truth, access to justice, and reparation.[154] Crimes entail messages that individuals, groups, and communities may be harmed.[155] Criminal trials constitute 'a sort of substitute for the desire of victims to punish the offender by themselves'.[156] Restorative justice relies on the premise that a criminal process should not only guarantee fair and effective justice towards the defendant but involve engagement with victims and others, in order to be meaningful.

The criminal process involves either symbolic recognition or direct engagement with victims as subjects.[157] Punishment has a more limited communicative effect. It does not undo the crime, but it has a corrective effect in relation to victims. It increases the probability that the perpetrator realizes the norm violation and compels the offender to 'experience' the harm inflicted on victims. It also implies a message about equality. It signals that offender and victims are equal citizens. As Jean Hampton has noted: 'by creating an event that counters the symbolic message sent by the crime, we symbolize the correct moral relationships among human beings, and thereby create the moral reality in which we believe'.[158]

150 Holling, *Internationaler Strafgerichtshof und Verbrechensprävention* 139.

151 See Ambos, *Treatise on International Criminal Law* 51–2.

152 Salvatore Zappalà, 'The Rights of Victims v. the Rights of the Accused' (2010) 8 *JICJ* 137–64, 162–3.

153 See Jan Philipp Reemtsma, *Das Recht des Opfers auf die Bestrafung des Täters—als Problem* (München: C.H. Beck, 1999).

154 These rights have their origin in human rights law, which typically governs relations between victim and states. They cannot be blindly transposed to international criminal proceedings. For instance, the UN Basic Principles and Guidelines on the Right to a Remedy and Reparation for Victims of Gross Violations, which provide a victim-oriented perspective on atrocity crime, were originally meant to provide guidance to states, rather than to establish firm entitlements in international criminal procedures.

155 Luke Moffett, Cheryl Lawther, Kieran McEvoy, Clara Sandoval, and Peter Dixon, 'Alternative Sanctions before the Special Jurisdiction for Peace: Reflections on International Law and Transitional Justice', 31 March 2019, 6.

156 Zappalà, 'The Rights of Victims v. the Rights of the Accused' 158.

157 See **section 5.3.5**.

158 Jean Hampton, 'An expressive theory of retribution' in Wesley Cragg (ed.), *Retributivism and Its Critics* (Stuttgart: F. Steiner Verlag, 1992), 1–25, 1, 19.

5.1.3 Expressivism and sentencing

In practice, expressivism is most frequently addressed as a concept in sentencing considerations. Sentencing has important symbolic meaning.[159] It is generally determined by a wide degree of judicial discretion. Expressivism plays *inter alia* a role in sentencing methodology and guilty pleas.

5.1.3.1 Sentencing methodology

International criminal justice lacks a catalogue of minimum or maximum sentences for crimes. The way how expressivism should influence sentencing methodology is disputed.[160]

Several scholars have argued that judges should pay more attention to the 'communicative aspects of the sentences they impose'.[161] For instance, Robert Sloane has made the argument that the 'absolute severity' of the sentence in quantitative terms may be less relevant than its 'relative severity as an expression of the condemnation'.[162] He argued that dissemination of the sentence 'to the broadest possible audience' in a persuasive form carries particular weight because it 'may contribute to the long-term project of preventing ICL crimes through mediums other than direct communication of a threat to potential criminals—for example, by its influence on national jurisprudence, rules of conduct integrated into military manuals distributed to soldiers, the media'.[163]

Sloane has postulated a defendant-relative reading of proportionality. He has argued that punishments should 'convey the right degree of international condemnation relative to other defendants' and crimes.[164]

Margaret deGuzman has gone a step further. She has proposed determining proportionality not only by retributive factors but also in light of preventive rationales. She has argued that the sentence should reflect the 'punishment necessary to express the international community's condemnation of crimes'[165] (preventive international proportionality). According to her, a prevention-oriented approach does necessarily require harsher punishment but rather better reasoning and explanation expressing condemnation.[166] She has suggested that 'judges should have

[159] Some have argued that it may mean 'more to victims, the accused and the public at large' than any other moments at trial'. See Mark B. Harmon and Fergal Gaynor, 'Ordinary Sentences for Extraordinary Crimes' (2007) 5 *JICJ* 683–721, 707.

[160] Expressivism provides *inter alia* an incentive to go beyond retributive rationales and to take into account the importance of norm dissemination or sensitivity to the messages sent through sentencing.

[161] DeGuzman, 'Proportionate Sentencing at the ICC' 957.

[162] Sloane, 'The Expressive Capacity of International Punishment' 77, 75 ('expressive value of ICL sentences—the extent to which they convey, reinforce, and encourage the growth of national legal and moral norms that conform to ICL—matters more than the relative severity of the punishment in any individual case').

[163] Ibid., 77.

[164] Ibid., 83.

[165] DeGuzman, 'Proportionate Sentencing at the ICC' 958.

[166] Ibid., 961.

discretion to impose harsher punishment whenever they believe the need for condemnation is particularly strong [which] may the case, for example, with respect to crimes involving sexual or gender violence [b]ecause such crimes are underpunished in many parts of the world'.[167]

This proposal is more critical from a due process perspective since it relates punishment to extrinsic social ends (i.e. the global need for greater punishment and the general harm caused through the crime rather than the culpability of the perpetrator.

Sentencing should not be oriented solely towards the global community (i.e. expression of global norms) but rather take into account the context of communities most affected by crime. These audiences are typically the first ones to criticize sentencing. Their norms and preferences are not determinative but may provide guidance in relation to expectations. For instance, the ICC Statute allows the Court to 'take into account national laws of States that would normally exercise jurisdiction over the crime' as part of its applicable law.[168]

International law provides limited criteria on the severity of sentences required for international crimes. It is controversial to what extent expressivism would require a minimum sentence. For instance, Colombia has relied on mitigated sentences as part of its approach towards peace and justice. FARC argued that it committed crimes a part of the resistance against the political order in Colombia. In peace settlements and efforts to end armed conflict, punishment competes with other rationales. It implicates not only the offender and the crime but society as a whole. Punishment becomes a means to subject actors once again to a peacetime legal order. This provides space for a more elastic vision of punishment. Some 'element of compromise' may be necessary in order to meet 'the competing objectives of effectively communicating condemnation and securing peace'. Often the 'best that can be hoped for' is an 'approximation whereby a significant degree of condemnation and social persuasion for reform is achieved'.[169]

Condemnation can be expressed through other means than strictly retributive proportionality (e.g. ban from political office, a criminal process, recognition of wrongdoing, reparation).[170] A finding of guilt may have strong expressive quality per se.[171] Lesser sentences may be acceptable if it is set out what ought to be achieved through punishment. What counts is the message of condemnation

[167] Ibid., 961.

[168] ICC Statute, Art. 21 (1) (c).

[169] See Paul Seils, 'Squaring Colombia's Circle: The Objectives of Punishment and the Pursuit of Peace', ICTJ Briefing, June 2015, 13.

[170] See James Stewart, 'The Role of the ICC in the Transitional Justice Process in Colombia', 30–31 May 2018, para. 143, at https://www.icc-cpi.int/iccdocs/otp/201805SpeechDP.pdf ('Sentences may achieve these goals in different ways, provided they reflect public condemnation of the criminal conduct and recognition of the suffering of victims, and contribute to deterrence.').

[171] Schabas, 'Sentencing by International Tribunals' 516.

sent through a combination of measures: criminal process, sanction, and repair of harm.[172]

The ICC Office of the Prosecutor (OTP) has encouraged a case-by-case assessment of reduced custodial sentences. ICC Deputy Prosecutor James Stewart has identified a number of factors might be used to guide this assessment. These include 'acknowledgement of criminal responsibility, demobilization and disarmament, guarantees of non-repetition, full participation in the process of establishing the truth about serious crimes, a possible temporary ban from taking part in public affairs, among other measures'.[173]

5.1.3.2 Sentencing narratives

Sentencing narratives are important as an instrument of communication since they try to analyse the circumstances and individual factors shaping the crime. Narrative analyses of sentencing stress that the process of sentencing 'does more than simply punish perpetrators', since it 'involves an assessment of the individuals concerned—or, narratives of the individuals concerned—in relation to the law'.[174]

As the ICTY noted in *Tadić*, according to the 'modern philosophy of penology', punishment 'should fit the offender and not merely the crime'.[175] Sentencing assessments need to assess appropriate punishment in relation to both the crime and the offender. They examine *inter alia* the 'gravity of the offence' the 'individual circumstances of the convicted person', as well as mitigating and aggravating factors.[176] This includes an assessment of the 'relative significance of the role of the [defendant] in the broader context of the conflict'.[177]

The actions of perpetrators are motivated by complex motivations, including professional socialization and group identification. Alette Smeulers has identified at least nine different archetypes of offenders. They include criminal masterminds, careerists, profiteers, fanatics, devoted warriors, professionals, sadists, followers, and compromised perpetrators.[178]

Sentencing marks an attempt to decontextualize, explain, and rationalize criminal behaviour. Sentences weave narrative plots together. They are 'an expression of the legal, political and moral values not just of the tribunals, but of

[172] Ibid., 514.

[173] See Stewart, 'The Role of the ICC in the Transitional Justice Process in Colombia', para. 147.

[174] Inger Skjelsbæk, 'The Military Perpetrator: A Narrative Analysis of Sentencing Judgments on Sexual Violence Offenders at the International Criminal Tribunal for the Former Yugoslavia' (2015) 3 *Journal of Social and Political Psychology*, 46–70, 51.

[175] *Prosecutor v. Tadić*, Sentencing Judgment, IT-94-1-T, 14 July 1997, para. 61.

[176] ICTY Statute, Art. 24.

[177] *Prosecutor v. Rukundo*, Judgment, ICTR-2001-70, 27 February 2009, para. 605.

[178] Alette Smeulers, 'Perpetrators of international crimes: Towards a typology' in Alette Smeulers and Roelof Haveman (eds), *Supranational Criminology: Towards a Criminology of International Crimes* (Antwerp: Intersentia, 2008), 233–63.

the international community, and as such, are intended to speak to the victims, the villains and the world'.[179]

Perpetrator discourse often seeks to justify behaviour by coercion or as a means to pursue a higher purpose. Actions are presented or perceived as necessary or even heroic behaviour. In light of this cognitive dissonance, perpetrators are under the impression that they are' doing the right thing'.[180] For example, Rudolf Höss, the first camp commander at Auschwitz, noted: '[w]hether the reason behind the extermination of the Jews was necessary or not was not something on which I could allow myself to form an opinion'.[181] Such discourse 'reverses the logic of reasoning applied by international criminal justice and humanitarian norms and reinterprets the situation to fit a morally defensible lens'.[182]

Sentencing narratives deconstruct such narratives. They mark an attempt to present 'evil not as the work of "lunatics"' but 'as actions with a clear and justified purpose—so defined by a context of cruelty'.[183] They are a means to treat defendants as rational subjects rather than objects of litigation and 'juridical' actors.[184]

They emphasize agency, choice, and action. They typically discard arguments which seek to justify or excuse behaviour by reference to coercive group dynamics or the necessity to obey orders. They tend to 'narrate' blameworthiness through the 'gravity' of the crime.[185]

For instance, sentencing motivations have discarded justifications of sexual and gender-based violence. Defendants have sought to present sexual violence as part of normal male behaviour in situations of social distress. Judges have rejected such chivalrous narratives. They have condemned falsely understood masculinities (e.g. 'boys will be boys' narratives).[186] They have also failed to recognize sexual crimes as mere 'opportunistic crimes', by contrasting behaviour of offenders to others. Some defendants were blamed for treating 'abuses as entertainment'[187] or carrying out sexual violence based on 'feelings of revenge'.[188]

[179] Aloisi and Meernik, *Judgment Day* 187.

[180] See Alette Smeulers, 'Why Serious International Crimes Might Not Seem "Manifestly Unlawful" to Low-level Perpetrators' (2019) 17 *JICJ* 105–23, 122.

[181] Rudolf Höss, *Commandant of Auschwitz: The Autobiography of Rudolph Hoess* (transl. Constantine Fitzgibbon) (London: Weidenfeld and Nicolson, 1959) 165.

[182] Mina Rauschenberg, Christian Staerklé, and Damien Scalia, 'Accused for Involvement in Collective Violence: The Discursive Reconstruction of Agency and Identity by Perpetrators of International Crimes' (2015) 37 *Political Psychology* 219–35, 232.

[183] James E. Waller, *Becoming Evil: How Ordinary People Commit Genocide and Mass Killing* (Oxford: Oxford University Press, 2007), 271.

[184] Alexandra Natapoff, 'Speechless: The Silencing of Criminal Defendants' (2005) 80 *New York University Law Review* 1449–504.

[185] See Shahram Dana, 'The Sentencing Legacy of the Special Court for Sierra Leone' (2014) 42 *Georgia Journal of International and Comparative Law* 617–86, 683–4 ('Just punishment and fair sentencing is no longer a disciplined legal exercie of judgment, but a gut check emotion.').

[186] Skjelsbæk, 'The Military Perpetrator' 55–8.

[187] On Mlado Radić, see *Prosecutor v. Kvočka et al.*, Judgment, IT-98-30/1-, 2 November 2001, para. 741.

[188] On Hazim Delić, see *Delalić et al.* Trial Judgment, para. 1269.

Sentencing decisions often portray crimes as part of a story of abuse of position, authority, and power.[189] Factors such as abuse of power, betrayal of trust, exploitation of resources for personal gain, or excessive brutality may qualify as aggravating factors. The argument that crimes are committed for a good or legitimate cause (e.g. a just war) has been rejected.

The most notorious example is the treatment of the Civil Defence Forces (CDF) defendants (e.g. Samuel Hinga Norman, Moinina Fofana, and Allieu Kondewa) by the Special Court for Sierra Leone (SCSL). CDF forces were perceived as 'national heroes' in Sierra Leone since they contributed to the ending of 'rebellion' and helped restore constitutional government after the civil war. The Trial Chamber considered that their 'legitimate cause' in fighting constituted a mitigating factor for purposes of sentencing. It stated that the CDF defendants acted with a 'sense of civic duty' and issued reduced sentences.[190] The Appeals Chamber overturned this reasoning, which reflected popular narratives. It rejected 'just cause' as a mitigating factor. It held that '[i]nternational humanitarian law specifically removes a part's political motive and the 'justness of a party's cause from consideration ... The political motivations of a combatant do not alter the demands on that combatant to ensure that their conduct complies with the law.'[191] It thereby challenged the narrative that consideration of the 'justness or propriety' of cause would send a proper message.[192]

5.1.3.3 Guilty pleas

Expressivist rationales play an important role in consideration of guilty pleas. Guilty pleas may provide a 'discount' in sentencing, based on the admission of responsibility by the defendant in relation to some or all of the charges.[193] They are important from an expressivist perspective because they contribute to norm affirmation and involve speech acts towards victims. By assuming responsibility, the defendant negates 'the negation of the norm' or makes amends towards victims. This creates a lesser need for the communication of punishment through the penalty. Rehabilitation becomes less acute in case of a guilty plea since the defendant shows signs of reform or starts to 'reconcile' himself/herself with those harmed by the crime.[194]

In domestic cases, guilty pleas often lead to reduced sentences because of efficiency considerations. They facilitate investigative work and cooperation with the

[189] Taylor Sentencing Judgment, para. 97 (referring to abuse of 'state machinery and public resources').

[190] *Prosecutor v. Fofana and Kondewa*, Judgment on the Sentencing of Moinina Fofana and Allieu Kondewa, SCSL-04-14-T, 9 October 2007, para. 94 (*Fofana and Kondewa* Sentencing Judgment).

[191] *Prosecutor v. Fofana and Kondewa*, Judgment, SCSL-04-14-A, 28 May 2008, para. 530.

[192] For the contrary view, see *Fofana and Kondewa* Sentencing Judgment, para. 96.

[193] See generally Nancy Amoury Combs, *Guilty Pleas in International Criminal Law: Constructing a Restorative Justice Approach* (Stanford, CA: Stanford University Press, 2007).

[194] Duff, *Punishment, Commmunication and Community* 106–12.

Prosecution and save judicial efforts in the establishment of punishment. In international criminal justice, they are connected to a broader range of rationales.

At the *ad hoc* tribunals, guilty pleas have initially been viewed with scepticism. They are difficult to reconcile with retributivism since they conflict with the idea of 'deserved punishment'. They were largely introduced on pragmatic grounds, namely to save time and costs, and reduce the length of proceedings.[195] But they have been gradually been defended on other grounds, including efficiency, expressivist functions, and peace-related grounds (e.g. reconciliation).[196] An apology may 'symbolically and publicly affirm victims' harm and acknowledge the criminal nature of the acts perpetrated against them'.[197] Expression of remorse and acknowledgment of responsibility qualify as mitigating factors for punishment. As the ICTR has noted:

> [A] guilty plea may have mitigating effects because it shows remorse and repentance and contributes to reconciliation, the establishment of the truth, the encouragement of other perpetrators to do so, the sparing of a lengthy investigation and trial and thus resources and time, and relieves witnesses from giving evidence in court.[198]

In theory, guilty pleas may support truth-telling and the didactic functions of proceedings. The acknowledgment of facts and responsibility by the defendant has a particular signalling towards domestic audiences, including those who are sceptical towards international criminal justice. For instance, in the *Plavšić* case, the ICTY interpreted the guilty as a sign of recognition of the legitimacy of the tribunal by the defendant.[199]

The attestation of the veracity of charges by the defendant carries a unique authenticity and may contribute to alternate perceptions of narratives and events.[200] Expressions of remorse may involve showing of repentance and ground judicial

[195] See Carla del Ponte, 'Investigation and Prosecution of Large-scale Crimes at the International Level: The Experience of the ICTY' (2006) 4 *JICJ* 539–58, 545–6. See also *Prosecutor v. Sikirica*, Sentencing Judgment, IT-95-8-S, 13 November 2001, para. 149.

[196] *Prosecutor v. Nikolić*, Sentencing Judgment, IT-02-60/1-S, 2 December 2003, para. 145. In the *Plavšić* sentencing judgment, the judges stated: '[A]cknowledgement and full disclosure of serious crimes are very important when establishing the truth in relation to such crimes. This, together with acceptance of responsibility for the committed wrongs, will promote reconciliation.' See *Prosecutor v. Plavšić*, Sentencing Judgment, IT-00-39&40/1-S, February 27, 2003, para. 80 (*Plavšić* Sentencing Judgment).

[197] Queen's University Belfast Human Rights Centre and the Redress Trust observations pursuant to Article 75(3) of the Statute and Rule 103 of the Rules, ICC-01/12-01/15, 2 December 2016, para. 81.

[198] *Prosecutor v. Bagaragaza*, Sentencing Judgment, ICTR-05-86-S, 17 November 2009, para. 38.

[199] *Plavšić*, Sentencing Judgment, para. 76.

[200] See Aloisi and Meernik, *Judgment Day* 175 ('guilty plea is thought to provide some measure of closure to the victims as well as advance a powerful counter-narrative to those who espouse ethnic hatred or revisionist histories that downplay the extent of and responsibility for the crimes committed in the Balkans, Rwanda and Sierra Leone').

proceedings more deeply in the 'authenticity of sentiments'.[201] Ultimately, this may 'protect victims from having to relive their experiences and re-open old wounds',[202] or even constitute a 'new norm' between victim and offender.

However, experiences with guilty pleas are mixed. At the ICTR, many defendants were reluctant to engage in guilty pleas because they shared concerns about the genocide narrative. As Nancy Comb has noted: 'High-level ICTR defendants, for instance, are so convinced of their innocence, so ideologically committed to their characterization of the Rwandan conflict, and so concerned about their place in the history books that virtually no sentence inducement will persuade them to plead guilty to genocide.'[203] Jean-Paul Kambanda, the former Prime Minister, pleaded guilty to charges, including genocide, but still received a sentence of life imprisonment. This created a 'legacy of distrust' among defendants.[204]

In Cambodia, Nuon Chea issued a half-hearted apology in Case 002/01. He noted in his final statement:

> Although the tragedy in the DK period was the result of the acts committed by those traitors in the name of Deputy Secretary of the Party that had the responsibility to disseminate and propagandize education about the CPK policy, I would like to sincerely apologize to the public, to the victims, their families, and all Cambodian people.[205]

The Chamber found that 'his failure to accept responsibility for his own wrongdoing' undermined the mitigating impact of the statement.[206]

At the ICTY, some guilty pleas lacked genuineness. For instance, Biljana Plavšić, the former President of the Republika Srpska, retracted her confession after benefiting from plea bargaining.[207] At trial, experts testified that her plea may have no less than four key benefits from an expressivist perspective:

> [F]irstly, as the plea of guilty was offered by a Serb nationalist and former political leader, Mrs. Plavšić's confession sends out a crucial message about the true criminal nature of the enterprise in which she was involved; secondly, by surrendering and pleading guilty, Mrs. Plavšić is also sending a powerful message about the legitimacy of the International Tribunal and its functions; thirdly, Mrs. Plavšić's

[201] See Mégret, 'The Repentant Defendant and the Potential of International Criminal Justice' 441.
[202] *Prosecutor v. Deronjić*, Sentencing Judgment, IT-02-61-S, 30 March 2004, para. 134.
[203] Nancy Combs, 'Procuring Guilty Pleas for International Crimes: The Limited Influence of Sentence Discounts' (2006) 59 *Vanderbilt Law Review* 69–151, 148.
[204] Ibid., 122.
[205] *Prosecutor v. Nuon Chea and Khieu Samphan*, Case 002/01 Judgement, 7 August 2014, para. 1092 (Case 002/01 Judgment).
[206] Ibid., para. 1093.
[207] Jelena Subotić, 'The Cruelty of False Remorse: Biljana Plavšić at The Hague' (2012) 36 *Southeastern Europe* 39–59.

> apology for her actions and her call on other leaders to examine their own conduct is of particular importance; and fourthly, the confession of guilt and acceptance of responsibility by Mrs. Plavšić may demonstrate to the victims of the persecutory campaign that someone has acknowledged their personal suffering.[208]

Plavšić started to reverse her alleged repentance when writing her memoirs in prison. After her release, she admitted that the plea was merely a strategic tool to achieve a mitigation of punishment. She noted: 'I sacrificed myself. I have done nothing wrong. I pleaded guilty to crimes against humanity so I could bargain for the other charges. If I hadn't, the trial would have lasted three, three-and-a-half years. Considering my age that wasn't an option.'[209] The guilty plea was thus a staged performance. It provided a lesson that it is not the bargaining process but rather the sincerity of expression that contributes to truth-telling functions of the trial.

Critics contend that guilty pleas may limit fact-finding and narrow or distort the historical record of proceedings. For instance, plea bargaining may limit consideration of charges of sexual or gender-based violence. Experiences suggest that 'many defendants refuse to admit sexual offences even where they are willing to admit other acts of violence'. As a consequence, 'many deals are made which result in withdrawing charges of sexual violence' and 'a huge number of sexual offences are not made part of the historical record established by the courts'.[210] The ICC Statute seeks to mitigate such risks, by allowing a 'more complete presentation of the facts of the case' at trial, despite an admission of guilt.[211]

The positive impact of an admission of responsibility depends on a number of factors,[212] including their timing, 'explicit statements of apology and regret' admitting personal responsibility, sincerity, 'willingness to make amends and promises to avoid future transgressions', as well as cultural factors.[213] The reception of guilty pleas is shaped by cultural practices. For instance, in East Timor, acknowledgment was motivated more by community and identity-related factors than sentencing discounts, since communities placed significant weight on confession and reconciliation in their approach towards justice.[214]

208 *Plavšić* Sentencing Judgment, para. 76.

209 Daniel Uggelberg Goldberg, 'Plavšić retracts war-crimes confession', Bosnian Institute, News & Analysis, 4 February 2009, at http://www.bosnia.org.uk/news/news_body.cfm?newsid=2544\.

210 See Regina Rauxloh, 'Negotiated History: The Historical Record in International Criminal Law and Plea Bargaining' (2010) 10 *International Criminal Law Review* 739–70, 754.

211 See ICC Statute, Art. 65 (4).

212 See generally Michael Cunningham, 'Saying Sorry: The Politics of Apology' (1999) 70 *The Political Quarterly* 285–93; Nicholas Tavuchis, *Mea Culpa: A Sociology of Apology and Reconciliation* (Stanford, CA: Stanford University Press, 1991).

213 Queen's University Belfast Human Rights Centre and the Redress Trust observations pursuant to Article 75(3) of the Statute and Rule 103 of the Rules, para. 80.

214 See Combs, 'Procuring Guilty Pleas for International Crimes' 136.

5.1.4 Alternatives to imprisonment

One of the strengths of expressivism is that allows for a more creative perspective on punishment. Imprisonment is the main type of penalty imposed in international criminal justice. For instance, in the *Celebici* case, the ICTY noted: 'Although long prison sentences are not the ideal, there may be situations which will necessitate sentencing an accused to long terms of imprisonment to ensure continued stability in the area.'[215] Imprisonment is a conventional, but rather a rudimentary form of punishment. The role of the prison as a social institution has come under critique. For instance, sociologist Thomas Mathiesen has argued that imprisonment cannot be reliably justified by classical rationales, such as rehabilitation, prevention, incapacitation or grounds of desert.[216] Duff has justified incarceration based on a communicative vision of punishment. He has claimed that imprisonment delivers a moral message of wrongdoing.[217] It signals a message about social exclusion. However, these classical rationales may not be fit for all types of perpetrators of international crimes and face limits in mass atrocity contexts.

Imprisonment is highly symbolic and conveys a strong message to the international community. But it may have negative effects. The experience of punishment may have counter-productive criminogenic effects. Imprisonment is 'disintegrative' and may increase 'deviant' identity or facilitate the creation of new criminal networks. The perception of punishment differs across audiences. For instance, for victims, incarceration in a Western prison, with access to healthcare and modern facilities, may not constitute a severe form of punishment. Imprisonment may impede restorative approaches towards punishment. For example, secluding perpetrators may render 'impossible any meaningful engagement between perpetrators and survivors' in local communities in post-conflict settings.[218] Communicative purposes of punishment, such as conveying moral wrongdoing or inflicting pain, can be expressed in other forms. Not all elements of the process or the sanction have to be punitive, in order to have expressive effect.

The situational context provides space for differentiated approaches. As Deirdre Golash has argued, the very 'convention of punishing international crimes' is 'not yet so deeply ingrained' as to require a formal criminal process and imprisonment for all perpetrators and categories of international crimes at all times.[219] Rather, the forum and scope of trials are calibrated in each context and adjusted to the

[215] *Delalić et al.* Trial Judgment, para. 1234.

[216] Mathiesen, *Prison on Trial* 9–26.

[217] Duff, *Trials and Punishment* 283 ('And even a short prison term, if administered and received in the right spirit, can provide a stimulus to and expression for a criminal's repentant understanding: the "short sharp shock" of a brief imprisonment, or even the "clang of the prison gate" itself, could ideally serve, not as a prudential deterrent, but as an adequately communicative and penitential punishment.').

[218] Phil Clark, *The Gacaca Courts, Post-Genocide Justice and Reconciliation in Rwanda* (Cambridge: Cambridge University Press, 2010) 346.

[219] Golash, 'The Justification of Punishment in the International Context' 219.

respective social context. The very concept of punishment may be regarded in a different light, depending on cultural practices.

The Latin word *poena* carries different meanings: 'pain, punishment, penalty'. Mark Drumbl has suggested that punishment can be understood in a more 'elastic' sense, namely as 'recrimination, shame, consequence, and sanction'.[220] Impunity would then be the absence of 'harmful consequences, recrimination, reparations, shame, or pain'.[221] In practice, at least three different alternatives to imprisonment have been tested: alternative sentences, trials without punishment, and punishments without trial.

5.1.4.1 Alternative sentences

In certain contexts, non-custodial sentences may be viable alternatives to custody. Alternative sentences 'sit somewhere between punishment and amnesty, in that they ensure that individuals are held responsible for their wrongful actions under international human rights and international criminal law, but their punishment is attenuated by the broad political goal of reconciliation'.[222]

They may constitute a complement to classic imprisonment in cases in which they pursue a legitimate public interest, involve investigation of crimes and determinations of responsibility.[223]

For instance, Colombia contemplated restrictions of freedoms and rights, rather than ordinary prison sentences as part of the Comprehensive System for Truth, Justice, Reparations and Non-Recurrence, negotiated with the FARC. Such alternatives sentences may be awarded if offender acknowledges full truth and responsibility in the early stages of the criminal proceedings. Such sanctions have a more restorative and reintegrating orientation.

The logic is based on a complex combination of rewards and threats that are deemed to persuade perpetrators to come forward, confess, and renounce the crime. It places the emphasis on punishment as didactic exercise and rational message, rather than infliction of suffering. As Lily Rueda Guzman and Barbora Holá have noted:

> The basic scheme is a combination of pull and push factors, aimed to compel perpetrators to behave in a certain way while at the same time to serve as a deterrent mechanism: If you do x (cease violence and disclose and recognise truth), then the State will offer y (restorative sanctions, amnesties and pardons) unless you do

[220] Mark Drumbl, 'Impunities' Washington and Lee Public Legal Studies Research Paper No. 2017-17, 3 November 2017, 1, 27.

[221] Ibid., 27.

[222] See Moffett, Lawther, McEvoy, Sandoval, and Dixon, 'Alternative Sanctions Before the Special Jurisdiction for Peace' 70.

[223] Ibid., 53.

z (not telling the truth and not contributing to reparation), in which case the State will take away y and will apply w (imprisonment) instead.[224]

The ICC OTP has not excluded the idea that such sanctions may be consistent 'with a genuine intent to bring the convicted persons to justice'.[225] It has suggested applying a case-by-case approach, It includes factors such as 'the usual national practice in sentencing for Rome Statute crimes, the proportionality of the sentence in relation to the gravity of the crime and the degree of responsibility of the offender, the type and degree of restrictions on liberty, any mitigating circumstances, the reasons the sentencing judge gave for passing the particular sentence'.[226]

5.1.4.2 Trials without punishment

A second way to express condemnation in the absence of incarceration is the use of trials for expressive, rather than immediately punitive purposes. Argentina tested this approach in order to address legal problems caused by amnesties laws. It used 'trials for truths' (*Juicios por la Verdad*) as a way to reconcile the conflict between amnesty and the right of access to justice. These trials are unique, non-punitive mechanisms of accountability. They were deemed to clarify the fate of disappeared persons and obtain a judicially verified narrative of facts. The judgments framed events in legal terms, recognized victims, and made information available for communication and education.

This approach marks a unique addition to classical punitive trials. It served as a counter-strategy to institutional forgetting. It differs from truth and reconciliation commissions through its judicial nature. As Sévane Garibian has argued, it offers 'a privileged place to the victims of such crimes; it allows them to take back a leading role in the proceedings, and to question the roles of the judge and the state, along with, more globally, that of retributive criminal justice'.[227]

5.1.4.3 Punishment without trial

A third approach is to express responsibility for wrongdoing, shame, and sanction through punishment without trial. For instance, testimony and appearance in truth commissions or local accountability mechanisms may constitute a form of punishment in the broader sense,[228] which complements classical punishment. Such alternative justice mechanisms are able to 'reach more than the select few, but

[224] Guzman and Barbora Holá, 'Punishment in Negotiated Transitions' 147–8.
[225] Stewart, 'The Role of the ICC in the Transitional Justice Process in Colombia', para. 149.
[226] Ibid., para. 150.
[227] Sévane Garibian, 'Ghosts Also Die: Resisting Disappearance through the "Right to the Truth" and the Juicios por la Verdad in Argentina' (2014) 12 *JICJ* 515–38, 536.
[228] Drumbl, 'Impunities' 22.

preserve the stigma of punishment by incorporating local beliefs and customs as accountability measures for a larger number of offenders'.[229]

Rwanda relied on special dispute resolution mechanisms, the *gacaca* courts,[230] in order to deal with the mass of genocide cases, provide truth-telling, and to restore social harmony in divided communities. Classical retributive justice, namely the 'continued imprisonment of 125,000 genocide suspects', was considered to be 'both untenable and undesirable'.[231] *Gacaca* courts complemented the ICTR and domestic criminal courts. Such proceedings were conducted 'not for the alleged perpetrator but for the victims, their families, and the community'.[232] They combined 'legal and non-legal objectives and methods'.[233] They were created 'not only with the aim of providing punishment' but to a reconstitute 'the Rwandan Society that had been destroyed by bad leaders'.[234] The proceedings marked a mid-way between retributive and restorative justice. They took place in various venues, including 'classrooms, conference rooms, or outdoors'.

The *gacaca* courts completed 1,958,634 cases, two-thirds of which related to property offences.[235] Punishment was deemed to promote engagement between offenders and survivors. The range of sanctions differed according to categories of crime and admission of guilt. The proceedings were deemed to encourage 'reintegrative shaming', through confession, apology, and forgiveness.[236] Sanctions for person-related crimes included imprisonment, as well as community service.[237] Half of the classical prison terms could be served through community service, that is, 'works of public interest', in case of confession of crimes. This included 'building (or rebuilding) homes for survivors, repairing roads and bridges, planting fauna, or creating terraces'.[238] Property-related offences were sanctioned by fines to be paid to victims, repayment of stolen goods, or community work.[239]

Broader conceptions of punishment might also be used in order to denounce or condemn the contributions of collective entities or legal persons (including corporate actors) to the commission of international crimes. This lens is sidelined in

[229] Linda M. Keller, 'Achieving Peace with Justice: The International Criminal Court and Ugandan Alternative Justice Mechanisms' (2007) 23 *Connecticut Journal of International Law* 209–79, 271.

[230] *Gacaca* means 'justice on the grass'.

[231] Max Rettig, 'Gacaca: Truth, Justice, and Reconciliation in Postconflict Rwanda?' (2008) 51 *African Studies Review* 25–50, 45.

[232] Hollie Nyseth Brehm, Christopher Uggen, and Jean-Damascène Gasanabo, 'Genocide, Justice, and Rwanda's Gacaca Courts' (2014) 30 *Journal of Contemporary Criminal Justice* 333–52, 339.

[233] Clark, *The Gacaca Courts, Post-Genocide Justice and Reconciliation in Rwanda* 27.

[234] See the Preamble of Organic Law No. 16/2004 of 19 June 2004 which established the organization, competence, and functioning of *gacaca* courts.

[235] Brehm, Uggen, and Gasanabo, 'Genocide, Justice, and Rwanda's Gacaca Courts' 339–340.

[236] Mark A. Drumbl, 'Punishment Postgenocide: From Guilt to Shame to "Civis" in Rwanda' (2000) 75 *New York University Law Review* 1221–326, 1263.

[237] See Brehm, Uggen, and Gasanabo, 'Genocide, Justice, and Rwanda's Gacaca Courts' 337.

[238] Ibid., 343.

[239] Ibid., 341–2.

criminal trials which focus heavily on the guilt of individuals. Kirsten Ainley has suggested applying additional accountability mechanisms in order to capture the criminality of collective entities and group structures. She has suggested relying on 'responsibility and truth commissions' to hold accountable collective drivers of conflict, such as 'political, military, media, and private sector actors, international organizations, and any others who could be said to bear some significant responsibility for the enabling conditions of atrocity'.[240] Accountability could be achieved through non-punitive measures, such as 'the naming of offenders (under carefully defined conditions) to generate condemnation of their acts, and such measures (recommended by the commission for implementation by political bodies) as the removal of certain persons from office, the restructuring or destruction of public or private institutions that facilitated atrocity, sanctions, reparations programs, and acts of atonement'.[241]

5.2 Repairing Harm

Reparative practices are increasingly recognized as an important addition to punishment, or an element of the international penal system in the broader sense.[242] As the ICC Appeals Chamber recognized, reparations reflect 'a need to go beyond the notion of punitive justice'.[243] They are arguably 'the most victim-centered' response to international crimes.[244]

In international law, duties to provide reparation to victims of violations have traditionally been framed as state obligations.[245] They have been centred on the state as duty-bearer, rather than state agents or individuals.[246] However, several

[240] Kirsten Ainley, 'Excesses of Responsibility: The Limits of Law and the Possibilities of Politics' (2011) 25 *Ethics and International Affairs* 407–31, 425.

[241] Ibid., 426.

[242] Mulgrew, *Towards the Development of the International Penal System* 260.

[243] *Prosecutor v. Lubanga*, Order for Reparations,, ICC-01/04-01/06-3129-AnxA, 3 March 2015, para. 1.

[244] Ruben Carranza, 'The Right to Reparations in Situations of Poverty,' International Center for Transitional Justice Briefing (September 2009), 4. See also Peter Dixon, 'The Role of Reparations in the Transition from Violence to Peace', *Oxford Research Encyclopedia of Politics* (2017), doi: 10.1093/acrefore/9780190228637.013.541, 2 ('Reparations are among the most tangible, victim-centric, and personal of processes in the transition from violence to peace, symbolizing the recognition that an individual has been harmed and has rights in the eyes of the state or international community.').

[245] See Christian Tomuschat, 'State responsibility and the individual right to compensation before national courts' in Andrew Clapham and Paola Gaeta (eds), *Oxford Handbook of International Law in Armed Conflict* (Oxford: Oxford University Press, 2014), 811–39, 821–8.

[246] Christian Tomuschat, 'Reparation for Victims of Grave Human Rights Violations' (2002) 10 *Tulane Journal of International and Comparative Law* 157–84; Christian Tomuschat, 'Individual reparation claims in instances of grave human rights violations: The position under general international law' in Albrecht Randelzhofer and C. Tomuschat (eds), *State Reponsibility and the Individual* (The Hague: Martinus Nijhoff, 1999) 1–25.

contemporary documents recognize that individuals may owe duties of reparation to victims of international crimes. For instance, the UN Basic Principles and Guidelines on the Right to a Remedy and Reparation for Victims state that natural or legal persons are liable to provide reparation for harm caused to victims of 'gross violations' of international human rights law and 'serious violations' of international humanitarian law.[247] In some courts, victims may seek reparation directly through a criminal process. For instance, victims were allowed to act as civil parties in the criminal process before the ECCC[248] and in *Habré*,[249] in order to seek not only punishment but also reparation. At the ICC, reparation is an integral part of criminal proceedings.

This reparative approach broadens the perspective on crime and wrongdoing beyond punishment. It shifts the focus from the agency of the offender and the violation of public norms (i.e. the 'faceless state') to the harm of victims and their needs. Providing reparations in criminal proceedings signals that crimes affect not only state-owned interests. It acknowledges the experience of suffering and harm and may express recognition, relief, and support of victims or victimized communities.[250] This affirmation may carry important psychological benefits for victims in addition to punishment. It recognizes that the crimes have been committed against them.[251] It also sends messages as to who deserves public redress for violations.[252] Reparation may be better equipped than punishment to confront wrongdoing to victims and to repair some of the harm caused to them as individuals. It may encompass measures to prevent a recurrence of violations, including commitments of offenders not to commit similar wrongs.[253]

Reparative practices aspire to the ideal of providing 'full and effective reparation'. The UN Basic principles promote 'adequate, effective and prompt reparation'.[254] Full and effective reparation should be provided 'as appropriate and proportional

[247] Basic Principles and Guidelines on the Right to a Remedy and Reparation for Victims of Gross Violations of International Human Rights Law and Serious Violations of International Humanitarian Law, UN Doc. A/RES/60/147, adopted and proclaimed by General Assembly resolution 60/147 of 16 December 2005, Principle 15.

[248] For an account, see Johanna Herman, 'Realities of Victim Participation: The Civil Party System in Practice at the Extraordinary Chambers in the Courts of Cambodia, (2013) 16 *Contemporary Justice Review* 461–81.

[249] Nader Diab, 'Challenges in the Implementation of the Reparation Award against Hissein Habré: Can the Spell of Unenforceable Awards across the Globe be Broken?' (2018) 16 *JICJ* 141–63.

[250] Haldemann, 'Another King of Justice' 705.

[251] Brandon Hamber, 'Narrowing the micro and macro: A psychological perspective on reparations in societies in transition' in Pablo de Greiff (ed.), *The Handbook of Reparations* (Oxford: Oxford University Press 2006) 560–89, 566.

[252] Peter J. Dixon, 'Reparations and the politics of recognition' in Christian De Vos, Sara Kendall, and Carsten Stahn (eds), *Contested Justice* (Cambridge: Cambridge University Press, 2015) 302–26, 326–51.

[253] Murphy, *Conceptual Foundations of Transitional Justice* 186.

[254] Basic Principles and Guidelines on the Right to a Remedy and Reparation for Victims of Gross Violations of International Human Rights Law and Serious Violations of International Humanitarian Law, Principle I (2)(c).

to the gravity of the violation and the circumstances of each case'.[255] However, 'reparation and, in particular, compensation must always be synchronized with the societal context'.[256] Like retributive punishment, reparative justice faces serious limitations in relation to international crimes. Individuals are unable to pay the 'debt' owed to victims. The ability of perpetrators to do harm exceeds the ability to repair. A criminal court can never fully satisfy victims' right to reparation. The harms inflicted 'explode the limits of the law'.[257] Resources to award material compensation are often limited. As Pablo De Greiff has argued, reparations must be approached with a sense of realism:

> [R]eparations programs, not least because of the financial difficulties that arise in cases with massive numbers of claimants, should not even attempt, and should always avoid using the vocabulary of, proportional compensation. There should not be anything in a reparations program that invites either their designers or their beneficiaries to interpret them as an effort to put a price on the life of victims or on the experiences of horror. Rather, they should be interpreted as making a contribution to the quality of life of survivors.[258]

Reparations should thus not only be approached in mere juridical terms but require a broader assessment. Many of their benefits and effects are expressive in nature. Reparations may deliver a counter-message to the violence of crimes. They are important because they 'say' something about how society cares for victims and what is owed to them. They involve statements about 'dignity and membership'.[259] As Margaret Urban Walker has clarified, the justification of reparations relies heavily on expressivist arguments:

> [P]art of what makes reparations effective is what reparations demonstrate and communicate to victims and to their societies about the recognition of wrong, responsibility, the standing of victims as rights-bearing citizens and in many cases about group membership and the standing of groups.[260]

[255] Ibid., Principle 18.

[256] See Christian Tomuschat, 'Darfur—Compensation for the Victims' (2005) 3 *JICJ* 579–89, 584.

[257] Lotte Kohler and Hans Saner (eds), *Hannah Arendt and Karl Jaspers: Correspondence: 1926–1969* (New York: Harcourt Brace International, 1992), 54.

[258] Pablo De Greiff, 'Justice and reparations' in Pablo De Greiff (ed.), *The Handbook of Reparations* (Oxford: Oxford University Press, 2006), 451–77, 466.

[259] See Cristian Corea, 'Integrating Development and Reparations for Victims of Massive Crimes', Center for Civil & Human Rights, University of Notre Dame, July 2014, 12–13, at https://klau.nd.edu/assets/136618/correareparations2.pdf.

[260] Margaret Urban Walker, 'Transformative Reparations? A Critical Look at a Current Trend in Thinking about Gender-Just Reparations' (2016) 10 *International Journal of Transitional Justice* 108–25, 119. See also Matiangai V.S. Sirleaf, 'Beyond Truth and Punishment in Transitional Justice' (2014) 54 *Virginia Journal of International Law* 223–96, 234.

Walker has distinguished two expressive functions that are inherent in 'all types of reparations'.[261] The first one, the 'vindicatory function' is retrospective. It relates to the communicative function of reparations, namely their ability to deliver a message to victims and offender, which recognizes wrongfulness of events and accountability of the perpetrator to victims.[262] The second ('exemplifying function') is more prospective; it is aimed at preventing violations. It is a message about standing and recognition of victim as such. It concerns the role of reparations to signal a 'kind of relationship between victim and responsible parties' that was 'rejected or lacking in the circumstances in which the wrong was done'.[263] It involves an attitude to take responsibility in other or future interactions.[264] Viewing reparation as a message, rather than a one-off act, underlines the need for continuity, namely its character as ongoing process.[265]

Symbolic and material elements are interrelated in reparation practices. Expressivism is useful to understand some of the constraints and weaknesses of reparative practices. It 'explains why material measures alone are usually insufficient and require a certain framing to be acceptable, and why perceived failures of inclusion, acknowledgment, attention and responsiveness in a reparations process in themselves can provoke outrage and leave bitterness and suspicion'.[266]

This theorization is also able to provide a realistic foundation for the application of reparation obligations to non-state actors. For instance, non-state armed groups may not be expected to repair harm in the same way as states since they lack institutional means and capacity to provide long-term reparation. However, reparations can take different forms. They can be understood as 'a form of responsibility whereby ownership of past actions is taken, harm is acknowledged, and a commitment to non-repetition is made'.[267] This may involve truth-telling, apologies, and commitments to non-violence.

5.2.1 Expressivist functions of reparations

Reparations play an important supplementary role in addition to punishment. Their goal is not necessarily to restore 'the status quo ante' but to affirm 'a new

[261] Margaret Urban Walker, 'The expressive burden of reparations: Putting meaning into money, words, and things' in Alice Maclachlan and Allen Speight (eds), *Justice, Responsibility and Reconciliation in the Wake of Conflict* (Dordrecht: Springer, 2013), 205–25, 211.

[262] Ibid., 208, 212.

[263] Ibid., 208.

[264] Ibid., 217.

[265] Corea, 'Integrating Development and Reparations for Victims of Massive Crimes' 17.

[266] Walker, 'Transformative Reparations?' 119.

[267] See Luke Moffett, Cheryl Lawther, Sunneva Gilmore, and Ebba Lekvall, 'The Limits of the Law: Putting Reparations into Practice' *EJIL Talk*, 2 July 2019, at https://www.ejiltalk.org/the-limits-of-the-law-putting-reparations-into-practice/.

baseline for moral and political engagement going forward'.[268] The harm inflicted on victims through crimes is not only physical but psychological and emotional as well. Reparations reflect in the broadest sense a 'recognition owed to fellow citizens whose fundamental rights have been violated'.[269] They involve forms of 'social recognition', such as recognition of responsibility and recognition of harm.[270] For instance, De Greiff has suggested that reparations recognize victims as holders of rights, and are deemed to inspire civic trust and solidarity.[271] Walker has argued that reparations are about reconstructing relationships. She has insisted that 'all measures of reparation' should be 'consistent with a message that recognizes, respects and vindicates victims as subjects of justice in their own right'.[272]

Reparations can be grounded in many of the justifications 'traditionally offered in favor of punishment'.[273] They send messages about accountability relationships, types of victimization and harm, and forms of repair. The different forms of recognition inherent in the award of reparations may potentially be 'far more valuable than the particular good or service actually being distributed'.[274] As the Truth and Reconciliation in Sierra Leone noted: 'while tangible reparations may alleviate some quotidian struggles of an individual, the trauma of an extended and especially violent war cannot automatically be removed through financial support'.[275]

Due to its detachment from local contexts, the lack of power to compel states to award reparation, and the focus on the responsibility of individual offenders, international criminal justice relies even to a greater extent than domestic reparation programmes on symbolism and effective communication strategies to convey the intended meanings.[276] Many aspects of the classical law on state duties in relation to reparation cannot be directly transposed to reparations between individual offenders and victims (Figure 17).

5.2.1.1 Messages about responsibility

Reparations differ from punishment. They are less distinctly criminal and bear more synergies with torts. They may reinforce a sense of condemnation of wrong.

[268] Margaret Urban Walker, 'Making reparations possible: Theorizing reparative justice' in Claudio Corradetti, Nir Eisikovits, and Jack Volpe Rotondi (eds), *Theorizing Transitional Justice* (London: Ashgate, 2015) 211–22, 217.

[269] De Greiff, 'Justice and reparations' 461.

[270] Hamber, 'Narrowing the micro and macro' 560–89.

[271] De Greiff, 'Justice and reparations' 460–4.

[272] Walker, 'Transformative Reparations?' 119.

[273] Geoffrey Sayre-McCord, 'Criminal Justice and Legal Reparations as an Alternative to Punishment' (2001) 11 *Philosophical Issues* 502–29, 503.

[274] See Dixon, 'Reparations and the politics of recognition' 326, 332.

[275] See Frédéric Mégret, 'The International Criminal Court Statute and the Failure to Mention Symbolic Reparation' (2009) 16 *International Review of Victimology* 127–47, 141.

[276] Ibid., 333. See also Urban Walker, 'Making Reparations Possible' 216.

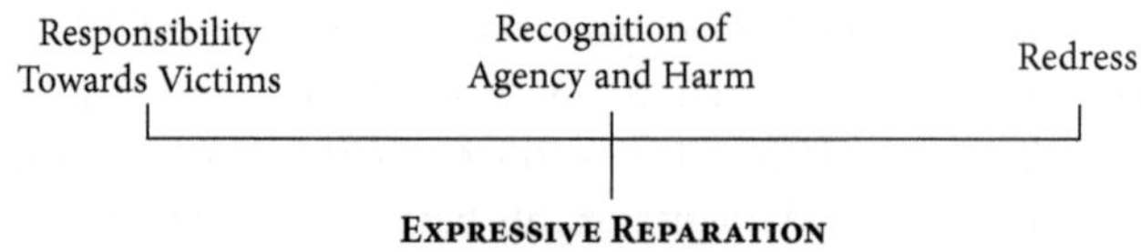

Figure 17 Expressivist functions of reparations

However, they are generally not meant to inflict 'pain (or harm)' on the offender. They are deemed to encourage perpetrators to make 'amends for the offence' or facilitate repair.[277] The award of reparation is partly a means to reinstate the standing of the offender as a member of society.[278] It might speak more directly to victims than punishment. Punishment is typically justified by general interests of society. Reparations are more directly aimed at righting wrongs and reaffirming victim's rights.[279]

In international criminal justice, the award of reparation is closely linked to the criminal process. This implies that reparations are framed through individual criminal responsibility. They are either awarded in proceedings following sentencing or as an annex to criminal proceedings.

The inclusion of reparations in criminal processes thickens the expression of accountability.[280] Reparations are partly about 'demonstrating (rather than establishing) relations of accountability'.[281] They signal that the offender is not only accountable for the crimes towards the public through a transparent procedure but subject to direct responsibility towards victims (principle of responsibility). The close nexus to responsibility distinguishes reparative measures from charity or assistance measures, which may be awarded based on need.[282] Legally, victims are entitled to reparations because they have been 'wronged', rather than because of their needs or vulnerability.[283]

> Strictly speaking, a development program is not a program of reparations. In fact, development programs have a very low reparative capacity, for they do not target

[277] Sayre-McCord, 'Criminal Justice and Legal Reparations as an Alternative to Punishment' 504 ('In committing a crime where there is a victim, the criminal has not only imposed a cost on the victim, he has also acted offensively in a way that calls for making amends and not merely for repayment.').

[278] Ibid., 505.

[279] Ibid., 514.

[280] Peter Dixon, 'Reparations, Assistance and the Experience of Justice: Lessons from Colombia and the Democratic Republic of the Congo', (2016) 10 *International Journal of Transitional Justice* 88–107, 95.

[281] See Walker, 'Making Reparations Possible' 217. Reparations express 'that something is owed to those against whom an offense has been committed'. See Sayre-McCord, 'Criminal Justice and Legal Reparations as an Alternative to Punishment' 519.

[282] See Frédéric Mégret, 'Justifying Compensation by the International Criminal Court's Victims Trust Fund: Lessons from Domestic Compensation Schemes' (2010) 36 *Brooklyn Journal of International Law* 124–204, 136.

[283] Naomi Roht-Arriaza and Kate Orlovsky, 'A complementary relationship: Reparations and development', in Pablo de Greiff and Roger Duthie (eds), *Transitional Justice and Development: Making Connections* (New York, NY: Social Science Research Council, 2009), 170–213, 172, 179.

victims specifically, and what they normally try to achieve is to satisfy basic and urgent needs, which makes their beneficiaries perceive such programs, correctly, as ones that distribute goods to which they have rights as citizens, and not necessarily as victims.[284]

The ICC specified the principle of accountability of the offender towards victims in its *Lubanga* Appeals Decision, which set out principles and procedures of reparation. The Chamber clarified that reparations are deemed to ensure that 'offenders account for their acts'.[285] It noted that 'the obligation to repair harm arises from the individual criminal responsibility for the crimes which caused the harm'.[286]

This individualized frame strengthens the expressivist dimensions of ICC reparation[287] but it also sets constraints. It establishes a 'perpetrator-centred' model which ties the scope of reparations to the content of the criminal trial. The scope of reparation is limited by the scope of conviction[288] and the principle of proportionality: 'A convicted person's liability for reparations must be proportionate to the harm caused and, inter alia, his or her participation in the commission of the crimes for which he or she was found guilty, in the specific circumstances of the case.'[289]

Victims are unable to seek remedies for harms that are not the result of the crimes that formed the subject of the conviction. This approach requires more detailed legal analysis and judicialization than more victim-oriented mass claim proceedings.

5.2.1.2 Recognition of agency and harm

A second important expressivist function of reparation is their recognition of ham.[290] International crimes impede agency and social interaction. The pain and suffering inflicted through crimes is often 'merely the beginning of sequelae that frequently include a deep sense of uncertainty and a debilitating and in some cases incapacitating sense of fear'.[291]

[284] De Greiff, 'Justice and reparations' 470.

[285] *Prosecutor v. Lubanga*, Judgment on the Appeals Against the 'Decision Establishing the Principles and Procedures to Be Applied to Reparations' of 7 August 2012, ICC-01/04-01/06-3129, 3 March 2015, para. 65 (*Lubanga* Judgment Principles Reparation).

[286] Ibid., para. 99.

[287] See Carsten Stahn, 'Reparative Justice after the Lubanga Appeal Judgment: New Prospects for Expressivism and Participatory Justice or "Juridified Victimhood" by Other Means?' (2015) 13 *JICJ* 801–13.

[288] The scope of liability for reparations shall 'not exceed the scope of the crimes' for which the offender found guilty. *Lubanga* Judgment Principles Reparation, para. 227.

[289] Ibid., para. 118.

[290] Dixon, 'Reparations, assistance and the experience of justice' 97.

[291] Pablo De Greiff, 'Articulating the Links between Transitional Justice and Development' Justice and Social Integration' in Pablo de Greiff and Roger Duthie (eds), *Transitional Justice and*

Reparations are a means to vindicate the 'moral status' of victims as human beings.[292] They recognize not only loss or damage suffered by victims but view crimes as attacks on victims' rights. As Peter Dixon has stressed, through reparations, 'categories of crime and victimisation in the courtroom become social categories of people on the ground. This is part of what makes them symbolically powerful'.[293]

The harm inflicted through crimes relates not only to direct victims but to broader constituencies. Reparations often 'symbolize' this harm more than accounting for it in quantitative terms.[294] For many survivors, their status of victimhood is related to social or economic marginalization. Reparations may be important to acknowledge harm, recognize agency and facilitate social integration. They illustrate that violations are taken seriously and represent victims 'not only as members of groups' but also 'as irreplaceable and unsubstitutable human beings'.[295] They may benefit society, by reaffirming the legal order and raising public consciousness about victimization, and convey messages of 'equality and respect' to victims, by protecting choices about forms of life.[296] For instance, an official public apology or the naming of victims in a judgment carries an important expressive meaning since it recognizes victims as subjects of justice in their own right. It also contributes to memorialization. The effects associated with recognition and expression of care[297] may be as important as material compensation, and express lasting acknowledgment.[298]

The award of reparations carries 'political' features since it engages with the standing and recognition of victims in society. Reparations need to accommodate complex victim identities. They shape historical narratives and involve decisions over distributive justice. They do not necessarily create trust, solidarity, or morally acceptable relations.[299] In some cases, they may represent a form of control over suffering or reproduce contested political narratives.[300] But they may trigger 'hope'. 'They establish the possibility of a respectful interaction in light of shared

Development: Making Connections (New York, NY: International Centre for Transitional Justice, 2009), 42.

[292] See Murphy, *Conceptual Foundations of Transitional Justice* 176 ('Reiterating the standing of victims as citizens of a political community and equal citizens—is critical to repudiate the wrongdoing that occurred and its impact.').

[293] Dixon, 'Reparations and the Politics of Recognition' 350.

[294] See Frédéric Mégret, 'Of Shrines, Memorials and Museums: Using the International Criminal Court's Victim Reparation and Assistance Regime to Promote Transitional Justice (2010)16 *Buffalo Human Rights Law Review* 1–56, 47.

[295] De Greiff, 'Justice and reparations' 460.

[296] Ibid., 463, and 460..

[297] Walker, 'Transformative Reparations?' 124.

[298] On missing persons, see Vasuki Nesiah, *The Missing: Action to Resolve the Problem of People Unaccounted for as a Result of Armed Conflict or Internal Violence and to Assist their Families* (Geneva: ICRC, 2002).

[299] Walker, 'Making Reparations Possible' 218.

[300] Claire Moon, '"Who'll Pay Reparations on My Soul?" Compensation, Social Control and Social Suffering,' (2012) 21 *Social and Legal Studies* 187–99.

standards, and they aim to motivate and energize thought, feeling, and action toward making that form of interaction reliable.'[301]

Reparation decisions are often unable to recognize the harm caused to victims or to provide 'corrective justice'.[302] However, they should be designed to 'recognize, relieve and support' victims.[303] As the ECCC has acknowledged, reparations have to be carefully crafted to ensure that they are 'aimed at conferring official recognition upon victims, and assisting to restore dignity and preserve the collective memory'.[304]

Efforts to provide reparation must be serious and sincere, acknowledge the experiences of victim, and be open to input by victims, in order to produce the desired social effects (e.g. inclusiveness, social solidarity).[305] The main test is whether they are able to affirm and demonstrate 'moral standing' through 'the effective delivery of concrete measures of repair that victims value'.[306]

5.2.1.3 Redress

A third expressive feature of reparations is their potential redistributive effect. Reparations differ from mere truth-telling practices or punishment of the offender by making decisions about redress and allocation of resources. They may directly change the situation of victims. This perspective is often lacking in the criminal process.

Reparations may provide not only symbolic but also certain material benefits to victims of crime. Experiences in the context of transitional justice suggest that '[t]ruth-telling in the absence of reparations can be seen by victims as an empty gesture, as cheap talk'.[307]

Material reparations include restitution, compensation,[308] and rehabilitation. They involve distributive choices in relation to individuals, groups, and communities. They designate who is seen to be deserving of reparation. The main dilemma in making these choices is selectivity.

Human rights law requires reparations to be awarded on a non-discriminatory basis. In classical human rights contexts, reparations are ordered against a state. In international criminal justice, reparations are ordered against individuals. This makes it difficult to award reparative measures which require structural state support or resources, including guarantees of non-repetition. The amount of reparations depends on the resources of convicted persons, assets seized, or voluntary

301 Margaret Urban Walker, 'Truth-Telling as Reparation' (2010) 41 *Metaphilosophy* 525-545, 532.

302 See generally Simon Robins, 'Failing Victims? The Limits of Transitional Justice in Addressing the Needs of Victims of Violations' (2017) 9 *Human Rights and International Legal Discourse* 41–58.

303 Walker, 'Transformative Reparations? 121.

304 *Prosecutor v. Kaing Guek Eav*, Judgment, 001/18-07-2007/ECCC/TC, 26 July 2010, para. 661, fn 1144 (*Duch* Trial Judgment).

305 Walker, 'Truth-Telling as Reparation' 533–4.

306 Walker, 'Transformative Reparations?' 125.

307 De Greiff, 'Justice and reparations' 461.

308 Frédéric Mégret, 'Justifying Compensation by the International Criminal Court's Victims Trust Fund' 123.

state contributions. This poses additional challenges from the perspective of distributive justice.

Reparation must be understood in a broader context. International crimes often harm individuals as part of a broader collective. Individual harms are inherently related to the harm caused to families or communities. This makes a compelling moral case for collective rather than individual forms of reparation, and a relational understanding of reparation, which focuses not only on specific individuals or groups but rather on the bonds between them and their broader role in society.[309]

In transitional justice contexts, states are often required to prioritize certain patterns of victimization in reparation programmes. They may focus on specific types of harms or specific offences, such as extrajudicial killings, enforced disappearances, torture, or sexual and gender-based violence, which pose continuing harm. In international criminal proceedings there are additional filters. Reparations are limited to those victims who made reparation claims in judicial proceedings. The scope of reparations is related to crimes and incidents which fall within the jurisdiction of courts and are reflected in the charges. These factors fragment the reparation process. Prosecutorial choices constrain reparation practices. Judicial filters may create different classes of victims eligible to receive reparation:

> '[S]uper victims' who, as a result of having suffered at the hands of someone convicted by the Court, benefit from a quite strong victim reparations regime; and 'ordinary victims' who, as a result of having suffered at the hands of someone not convicted (or not apprehended) by the Court will have to make do with whatever alternative system of reparation exists, if at all.[310]

The nature of crimes may make it necessary to divide reparation among specific groups of victims or affected communities, which may be more cost-effective than individual compensation. For instance, in Cambodia, nearly all Cambodians considered themselves victims of the Khmer Rouge regime.[311] The ECCC expressly limited reparations to collective and moral measures and excluded monetary compensation. The Trial Chamber explained this approach in the *Duch* case:

[309] Frédéric Mégret, 'The case for collective reparations before the ICC' in Jo-Anne M. Wemmers (ed.), *Reparations for Victims of Crimes against Humanity: The Healing Role of Reparation* (New York, NY: Routledge, 2014) 171–89.

[310] Frédéric Mégret, 'Reparations Before the ICC: The Need for Pragmatism and Creativity', ICC Forum 6 February 2012, at https://iccforum.com/reparations#Megret.

[311] Phuong Pham, Patrick Vinck, Mychelle Balthazard, Sokhom Hean, and Eric Stover, 'So We Will Never Forget: A Population-Based Survey of Attitudes about Social Reconstruction and the Extraordinary Chambers in the Courts of Cambodia' (Berkeley, CA: Human Rights Center, 2009), 2 ('Nearly all those who lived under the Khmer Rouge regime identified themselves as victims (93%), while half (51%) of those who did not live under the regime said they were victims.').

> Such departures from national law were considered necessary in view of the large number of Civil Parties expected before the ECCC and the inevitable difficulties of quantifying the full extent of losses suffered by an indeterminate class of victims. Reparations before the ECCC were therefore intended to be essentially symbolic ... rather than compensatory.[312]

Tensions may emerge if non-material reparation is combined with symbolic monetary compensation.[313] The expressive function of reparations creates a risk that 'individual victims may end up being more sensitive about how the reparations they receive stands in relation to reparation received by others, than about the amount in the absolute'.[314]

Distributive choices may conflict with the desire to strengthen agency and acknowledgment of victims. Differences between awards 'may send a message that the violation of the rights of some people is worse than the violation of the same rights of others, thereby undermining an important egalitarian concern and resulting in a hierarchy of victims'.[315]

The dependence on state actors and the strong focus on individual responsibility make it difficult to pursue more radical reparation projects that might be needed to address long-standing inequalities. For instance, issues such as land reform, property distribution, or targeting of societal stereotypes about gender roles can only be addressed in cooperation with states that are willing to engage with such reparative policies.

An additional impediment is the lack of reparation-specific infrastructure and know-how. Judicial entities lack the resources and knowledge to manage large-scale administrative reparation programmes for high quantities of victims. Ambitious reparations require coordination with domestic authorities, potential national reparation programmes, and non-governmental organizations (NGOs).

5.2.2 Expressive reparation practices

The strengths of awarding reparation through criminal processes lie in their communicative features and expressive forms.[316] Judicial procedures tend to speak in 'a universal voice of reason'.[317] The expressive possibilities of reparations go beyond

[312] Duch Trial Judgment, para. 661, fn 1144.

[313] In *Al Mahdi*, the ICC awarded symbolic reparation to Mali and UNESCO. See *Al Mahdi* Reparation Order, paras 53 and 106.

[314] Mégret, 'Reparations before the ICC: The Need for Pragmatism and Creativity'.

[315] De Greiff, 'Justice and reparations' 458.

[316] Maria Elander, 'The Victim's Address: Expressivism and the Victim at the Extraordinary Chambers in the Courts of Cambodia' (2013) 7 *International Journal of Transitional Justice* 95–115.

[317] Susan A. Bandes, 'Empathy, narrative, and Victim Impact Statements' (1996) 63 *The University of Chicago Law Review* 361–412, 385.

this narrow focus. Reparative measures contain a more direct focus on victims' needs, acknowledgment, and recognition.

One of the virtues of international criminal justice is its ability to provide symbolic expression.[318] Court-ordered reparations against perpetrators are unable to undo the harm or compensate for the suffering or damage inflicted.[319] Repairing harm requires a fuller scale of measures, including healthcare, education, administrative, economic, or political measures, provided through national programmes or aid and development measures. International criminal justice can give special meaning to material or immaterial forms of reparation. It is 'suited to offer compensation and reparation with a symbolic focus, adding additional gravitas to other modes of acknowledging the injustice experienced by victims of international crime'.[320]

The expressive potential of reparative measures goes beyond their concrete benefits or outcomes. They stand for a bigger idea or principle.[321] Some measures emphasize harm of victims, while others stress the value of individuals to society. The spectrum ranges from symbolic measures, such as public apologies, rites, and ceremonies or the establishment of memorials (e.g. naming of streets or monuments) to material measures. They may include individual and collective measures, such as compensation, rehabilitation, and community centres, creating burial sites for remains, access to healthcare or education. In all cases, the material and immaterial dimensions are closely interrelated. It is the public dimension which gives these measures meaning, by demonstrating 'what happened and who was victimized': 'Material measures must have some symbolic accompaniment to give them meaning. Nonetheless, reparations may comprise important symbolic gestures that do not have a significant material component.'[322] For example, compensation acquires meaning through the way in which it is awarded. As Yael Danieli put it: 'It's not the money but what the money signifies—vindication ... The money concretises for the victim the confirmation of responsibility, wrongfulness, he is not guilty, and somebody cares about it.'[323]

[318] Elisa Hoven and Saskia Scheibel, '"Justice for Victims" In Trials of Mass Crimes: Symbolism or Substance?' (2015) 21 *International Review of Victimology* 161–85, 162.

[319] Emily L. Camins, 'Needs or Rights? Exploring the Limitations of Individual Reparations for Violations of International Humanitarian Law' (2016) 10 *International Journal of Transitional Justice* 126–45.

[320] Antony Pemberton, Rianne M. Letschert, Anne-Marie de Brouwer, and Roloef H. Haveman, 'Coherence in International Criminal Justice: A Victimological Perspective' (2015) 15 *International Criminal Law Review* 339–68, 367.

[321] On symbolic aspects, see Roberts and Erez, 'Communication in sentencing: exploring the expressive function of Victim Impact Statements' 223–44; Tyler G. Okimoto and Michael Wenzel, 'The Symbolic Meaning of Transgressions: Towards a Unifying Framework of Justice Restoration' 25 *Advances in Group Processes* (2008) 291–326.

[322] Lisa Margarrell, *Reparations in Theory and Practice* (New York, NY: ICTJ, 2007), 5.

[323] Yael Danieli, 'Massive trauma and the healing role of reparative justice' in Carla Ferstman, Mariana Goetz, and Alan Stephens (eds), *Reparations for Victims of Genocide, War Crimes and Crimes against Humanity: Systems in Place and Systems in the Making* (Leiden: Brill, 2009), 59–60.

Reparations are sometimes associated with rationales of deterrence. For instance, the ICC noted in *Lubanga* that the 'wide publication of the decision may also serve to ... help deter crimes of this kind'.[324] However, viewing reparations as punitive measures with a deterrent ambition may be counterproductive. 'A cost–benefit analysis of reparations would shift the focus—instead, we would ask what level of punishment through reparations would be sufficient to deter future wrongdoers. This level may be completely unrelated to the victims' harm suffered.'[325]

The logic is reparations is rather related to forward-logic features of the expression of shame,[326] repair, and prevention. They are deemed to create empathy and bring people closer together. They open space for additional storytelling and social bonding. For instance, collective reparations may remedy harm to community structures. The establishment of victims' organizations and infrastructure and sites of memorialization may contribute to share experiences and build solidarity. The impact is thus closely related to preventive rationales, which are inherent in guarantees of non-repetition.

The forms of reparation can be more creative than punishment. They include socio-economic or cultural measures which may mitigate harm and 'give a more holistic meaning to the suffering of victims'.[327]

5.2.2.1 Participatory aspects

In reparation proceedings, victims are typically parties. This status has symbolic value for the institution awarding reparation: the court. It also serves to recognize victims as agents.[328] It sends messages to and about victims. Repair cannot be achieved without consultation and participation of victims in the reparations process.[329] Reparation proceedings carry an experiential dimension. This experience 'is as much about the way that they are treated, consulted and respected procedurally throughout the reparation process, as it is about the substantive remedy, material or otherwise, they may be granted as part of the end result'.[330]

324 *Lubanga* Judgment Principles Reparation, para. 238

325 Alina Balta and Nadia Banteka, 'The Al-Mahdi Reparations Order at the ICC: A Step towards Justice for Victims of Crimes against Cultural Heritage', Opinio Juris, 25 August 2017, at http://opiniojuris.org/2017/08/25/the-al-mahdi-reparations-order-at-the-icc-a-step-towards-justice-for-victims-of-crimes-against-cultural-heritage/.

326 John Braithwaite, *Crime, Shame and Reintegration* (Cambridge: Cambridge University Press, 1989).

327 Mégret, 'Of Shrines, Memorials and Museums' 53.

328 See Corea, 'Integrating development and reparations for victims of massive crimes', Center for Civil & Human Rights, University of Notre Dame, July 2014, 17.

329 See Walker, 'Transformative Reparations?' 124–5; Maria Suchkova, 'The Importance of a Participatory Reparations Process and its Relationship to the Principles of Reparation', University of Essex, Reparations Unit, Briefing Paper No. 5 (2011).

330 Dixon, 'Reparations, Assistance and the Experience of Justice' 99.

It is essential to seek input from victims in the award, and potentially in the implementation of reparations.[331] Such participation has symbolic value in itself[332] and conveys recognition of voice and agency.[333] It mitigates perceptions that courts are 'stealing' conflicts from victims, as cautioned by Nils Christie.[334] For example, studies on victim participation at the ECCC suggest that the recognition of a right to participate in reparation proceedings as a 'party' may increase a sense of empowerment or even mark a form of reparation.[335]

The ICC Statute provides expressly that '[b]efore making an [reparation] order under this article, the Court may invite and shall take account of representations from or on behalf of the convicted person, victims, other interested persons or interested States'.[336]

Consultations are necessary to gain a more holistic impression of the harm of victims. Actual reparation providers might have to go beyond grievances asserted in individual reparation claims. Domestic reparative practices suggest that consultations are necessary in order to assess needs and reparative possibilities in relation to individual and collective reparation.[337] Consultations are helpful to determine the scope of harms and potential needs and to test the feasibility of collective reparation measures. Collective reparations can be granted to victims, independently of individual requests for reparation. They may affect victims who did not participate in proceedings. The ICC Appeals Chamber specified that 'it is necessary to seek the victims' consent when a collective award is made, consistent with the principle, identified by the Trial Chamber, that '[r]eparations are entirely voluntary'.[338]

[331] See generally Jonathan Doak, 'The Therapeutic Dimension of Transitional Justice: Emotional Repair and Victim Satisfaction in International Trials and Truth Commissions' (2011) 11 *International Criminal Law Review* 263–98, 263–98.

[332] Luke Moffett, 'Elaborating Justice for Victims at the International Criminal Court: Beyond Rhetoric and the Hague' (2015) 13 *JICJ* 281–331. On a rights-based approach, see Liesbeth Zegveld, 'Victims as a Third Party: Empowerment of Victims?'(2019) *19 International Criminal Law Review* 321–45, 321–45. On 'healing', see Yael Danieli, 'Healing aspects of reparations and reparative justice for victims of crimes against humanity' in Jo-Anne Wemmers (ed.), *Reparation for Victims of Crimes Against Humanity: The Healing Role of Reparation* (London: Routledge), 7–21; Brandon Hamber, 'Does the truth heal? A psychological perspective on political strategies for dealing with the legacy of political violence' in Nigel Biggar (ed.), *Burying the Past: Making Peace and Doing Justice after Civil Conflict* (Washington, DC: Georgetown University Press, 2001), 131–48.

[333] See Brandon Hamber, 'The dilemmas of reparations: In search of a process-driven approach' in Stephan Parmentier, Koen De Feyter, Paul Lemmens, and Marc Bossuyt (eds), *Out of the Ashes: Reparation for Victims of Gross and Systematic Human Rights Violations* (Antwerp: Intersentia 2005), 135–49.

[334] Nils Christie, 'Conflicts as Property' (1977) 17 *The British Journal of Criminology* 1–15.

[335] Studies on civil party participation in Cambodia suggest that victims attached great importance to participation in court proceedings. See Elisa Hoven, Mareike Feiler, and Saskia Scheibel, 'Victims in Trials of Mass Crimes: A Multi-Perspective Study of Civil Party Participation at the Extraordinary Chambers in the Courts of Cambodia', Cologne Occasional Papers on International Peace and Security Law, 2013; Hoven and Scheibel, '"Justice for Victims" in Trials of Mass Crimes' 161, 181.

[336] ICC Statute, Article 75(3).

[337] Suchkova, 'The Importance of a Participatory Reparations Process and its Relationship to the Principles of Reparation' 12–13.

[338] *Lubanga* Judgment Principles Reparation, para. 160.

In light of the number of victims, it may be impossible to seek individual input from all victims.[339] Consultation is frequently carried through collective forums (e.g. community consultations, public consultations) or legal representatives.[340] Legal representatives exercise strong control over what narratives are presented.[341] Overall, the reparation process may thus be more an experience of being listened to rather than actively speaking.[342]

Access to reparations is related to effective outreach and communicative strategies. Legal decisions or project descriptions are often framed in a technical or foreign language. Victims may be ignorant about legal proceedings or reparative opportunities. Meaningful participation requires measures to enable victims to make informed decisions.[343]

5.2.2.2 Narrative features

The process of recognizing claims of victims and awarding reparation entails narrative features. It tells stories about victimhood when victims are identified, treated, and rewarded. Crimes mark a 'narrative rupture in the victim's life story'.[344] The reparation process affects how victims make sense of their experiences.

One of the difficulties is to recognize the complexity of victimhood through proceedings.[345] The ability of victims to convey their story directly is strongly mediated. Judicial proceedings can impose a particular narrative on victim experiences,[346] disnarrate harms, or create artificial labels of victimhood.[347]

The decision as to who is considered worthy of reparation does not only depend on characteristics of victimhood but contextual factors. For instance, in the *Lubanga* case, the number of victims entitled to receive reparation was limited,

339 In the *Lubanga* case, the Appeal Chamber held: 'When only collective reparations are awarded . . . a Trial Chamber is not required to rule on the merits of the individual requests for reparations.' Ibid., para. 152.

340 Dmytro Suprun, 'Legal Representation of Victims before the ICC: Developments, Challenges and Perspectives' (2016) 16 *International Criminal Law Review* 972–94.

341 Rachel Killean and Luke Moffett, 'Victim Legal Representation before the ICC and ECCC' (2017) 15 *JICJ* 713–40.

342 For a critique, see Zegveld, 'Victims as a Third Party: Empowerment of Victims?' 333.

343 See *Prosecutor v. Katanga*, Queen's University Belfast's Human Rights Centre and University of Ulster's Transitional Justice Institute Submissions on Reparation Issues pursuant to Article 75 of the Statute, para. 23.

344 Antony Pemberton, Pauline G.M. Aarten, and Eva Mulder, 'Stories as Property: Narrative Ownership as a Key Concept in Victims' Experiences with Criminal Justice' (2018) *Criminology & Criminal Justice* 1–17, 8.

345 See Luke Moffett, 'Reparations for 'Guilty Victims': Navigating Complex Identities of Victim–Perpetrators in Reparation Mechanisms' (2016) 10 *International Journal of Transitional Justice* 146–67.

346 Emily Haslam and Rod Edmunds, 'Victim Participation, Politics and the Construction of Victims at the International Criminal Court: Reflections on Proceedings in Banda and Jerbo' (2013) 14 *Melbourne Journal of International Law* 727–47.

347 See Tshepo Madlingozi, 'On Transitional Justice Entrepreneurs and the Production of Victims' (2010) 3 *Journal of Human Rights Practice* 208–28; Laurel Fletcher, 'Refracted justice: The imagined victim and the International Criminal Court' in De Vos, Kendall, and Stahn (eds), *Contested Justice*, 302–26.

in light of the narrow focus on charges relating to child recruitment. Reparations confirmed specific narratives over the ethnic foundations of the Ituri conflict and victim identities.[348] The case focused case predominantly perpetration and victimization within one group, the Hema population. Child soldiers were essentially portrayed as victims. Victims of sexual and gender-based violence were left aside. Leaders of the Lendu community expressed concerns about this narrative in a letter to the Prosecutor. They noted:

> [The focus] makes the Lendu community believe that there was no inter-ethnic war in Ituri between the Lendu and Hema peoples. This implies that that the children enlisted were Hema subjects, the victims would be the Hema relatives and brothers and the reparations in damages or interests whether individual or collective, would be done in the Hema community … What does this say about Lendu victims?[349]

Reparations were meant to reduce stigma.[350] The Trial Chamber wanted to order community-based reparations in order to extend the addressees of reparations. However, representatives of victims argued that community reparations would send a wrong message since the community accepted or collaborated in child recruitment.[351]

In Cambodia, reparative practices entrenched specific narratives about the past. For example, Vietnamese civil party applicants were initially excluded from the scope of reparations, because of the limited scope of charges.[352] The lack of focus at the ECCC on harm caused through sexual and gender violence (e.g. rape)[353] during the Khmer Rouge era rendered specific types of victimization 'invisible'.[354] The predominant narrative focused on state-arranged forced marriages[355] rather

348 Dixon, 'Reparations, 'Assistance and the Experience of Justice' 98.

349 See Olivia Bueno and Gilbert Angwandi, 'Steps towards Justice, Frustrated Hopes: Reflecting on the Impact of the ICC in Ituri', Discussion Paper International Refugee Rights Initiative and Association pour la promotion et la défense de la dignité des victims, 31 January 2012, 14, https://reliefweb.int/sites/reliefweb.int/files/resources/StepsTowardJusticeFinal.pdf, referring to 'Mot de la communauté Lendu à l'occasion de la visite du procureur de la cour penale internationale en Ituri du 08 au 11 juillet 2009'.

350 *Lubanga* Judgment Principles Reparation, paras 202–203.

351 *Prosecutor v. Lubanga*, Observations on the sentence and reparations by Victims a/0001/06, a/0003/06, a/0007/06, a/00049/06, a/0149/07, a/0155/07, a/0156/07, a/0162/07, a/0149/08, a/0404/08, a/0405/08, a/0406/08, a/0407/08, a/0409/08, a/0523/08, a/0610/08, a/0611/08, a/0053/09, a/0249/09, a/0292/09, a/0398/09 and a/1622/10', ICC-01/04-01/06-2864—tENG, 18 April 2012, para. 16.

352 Lyma Nguyen and Christoph Sperfeldt, 'Victim Participation and Minorities: Ethnic Vietnamese Civil Parties at the Extraordinary Chambers in the Courts of Cambodia' (2014) 14 *Macquarie Law Journal* 97–126, 110.

353 Emma Palmer and Sarah Williams, 'A "Shift in Attitude"? Institutional Change and Sexual and Gender-Based Crimes at the Extraordinary Chambers in the Courts of Cambodia' (2017) 19 *International Feminist Journal of Politics* 22–38.

354 Rachel Killean, 'Constructing Victimhood at the Khmer Rouge Tribunal: Visibility, Selectivity and Participation' (2018) 24 *International Review of Victimology* 273–96, 280.

355 Beini Ye, 'Forced Marriages as Mirrors of Cambodian Conflict Transformation' (2011) 23 *Peace Review: A Journal of Social Justice* 469–75.

than rape as a phenomenon under the Khmer Rouge regime.[356] Harms inflicted on the Khmer Krom minority remained peripheral.[357]

Victims are presented as helpless or vulnerable, in order to justify reparation.[358] There is a risk that their stories improperly transformed. Reparations convey the idea that crimes result merely from criminally minded individuals.[359] The story told through reparations is thus 'incomplete'. Trials may fail to reflect the extent to which ethnic differences and identities are instrumentalized by domestic actors for political or military purposes.[360]

Challenges to victims' narratives can be experienced as forms of secondary victimization or commodification of harm. At the African Extraordinary Chambers in Senegal, the government of Chad made a request to be accepted as civil party in the criminal case against Habré, its own former President. It argued that the 'state' had suffered harm from Habré's crimes and sought reparation.[361] This argument turned narratives of victimization around. The state presented itself as 'victim', rather than 'than taking responsibility ... for the crimes committed by a former regime'.[362] Ultimately, the request was rejected.

5.2.2.3 Symbolic compensation

Compensation is often a symbolic form of redress in international criminal justice. It is a substitute form of remedy. It responds to calls of victims for financial or economic repair. In many existing cases, defendants were found to be indigent or lacking the resources required to compensate harm. This makes it necessary to consider expressive measures.[363] International criminal justice is generally 'best suited to deliver compensation as a symbolic matter, while actual (monetary) compensation for those in urgent and dire need is more effectively and efficiently approached through other means'.[364]

Financial compensation 'speaks'. It is more like a fine, paid to individuals or harmed groups. It sanctions violations of civic trust, signals that perpetrators are

356 Rachel Killean, 'An Incomplete Narrative: Prosecuting Sexual Violence Crimes at the Extraordinary Chambers in the Courts of Cambodia' (2015) 13 JICJ 331–52, 341.

357 Mahdev Mohan, 'Reconstituting the 'Un-Person': The Khmer Krom and the Khmer Rouge Tribunal' (2008) 12 *Singapore Yearbook of International Law* 43–55.

358 Kieran McEvoy and Kirsten McConnachie, 'Victimology in Transitional Justice: Victimhood, Innocence and Hierarchy' (2012) 9 *European Journal of Criminology* 527–38.

359 For a critique, see Erin Baines, 'Spirits and Social Reconstruction after Mass Violence: Rethinking Transitional Justice' (2010) 109 *African Affairs* 409–30.

360 See Dixon, 'Reparations and the Politics of Recognition' 327, 342–4.

361 The government argued that *Habré* had stolen 10 million Euros.

362 Christoph Sperfeldt, 'The Trial against Hissène Habré: Networked Justice and Reparations at the Extraordinary African Chambers' (2017) 21 *International Journal of Human Rights* 1243–60, 1251.

363 For caution towards compensation, see Tomuschat, 'Dafur—Compensation for Victims' 587 ('Compensation payments do not contribute to a climate of internal understanding and conciliation if, at any moment, the threats of the past can materialize again.').

364 Pemberton, Letschert, De Brouwer, and Haveman, 'Coherence in International Criminal Justice' 364–5.

bound by law, expresses norm violations, and provides a tangible form of reparation, which may have personal value for victims.[365] It does not constitute a 'repayment' in the sense of tort litigation, but is rather an 'acknowledgment of the fact that this type of debt could never be repaid'.[366]

The ICC has in several cases expressly used symbolic compensation. In *Katanga,* judges awarded 297 victims with 'symbolic award of USD 250 compensation' in relation to harm occurred as part of the Bogoro attack.[367] The Legal Representative argued for a symbolic amount of one dollar. The Trial Chamber favoured 'a more substantial symbolic award' to make reparation 'meaningful to the victims, but not the source of tension within the community'.[368] It argued that 'the distribution of a symbolic amount by way of compensation gives acknowledgement, in a personal and symbolic sense, of the harm done and suffering occasioned'.[369]

In *Al Mahdi,* the Trial Chamber awarded individual compensation for victims with a close connection to the destroyed mausoleums, and symbolic compensation to third parties.[370] It found it appropriate 'to acknowledge the suffering endured by the Malian community and the international community as a whole as a result of the destruction of the Protected Buildings—all but one of which were UNESCO World Heritage Sites'.[371]

As a symbolic gesture, it ordered that one symbolic Euro should be paid to the Malian state and 'to the international community, which is best represented by UNESCO'.[372]

In other cases, the actual compensation ordered was more substantial, but 'symbolic', but it exceeded the capacity of the defendant to pay. It served thus more as an expression of redress, rather than actual recovery. It rests on the assumption that further resources may be identified or secured in the future. The ICC justified this approach by the distinction between personal liability and enforcement. It noted:

> A convicted person's financial circumstances may affect how a reparations award is enforced—such as by affording an option to make reasonable payments in installments—and the Chamber does not intend to impose hardships ... that

[365] See Ernesto Verdeya, 'A Normative Theory of Reparations in Transitional Democracies' (2006) 37 *Metaphilosophy* 449–68, 456, noting that compensation 'emphasizes the importance of remembering that victims are not merely a statistic but actual people'.

[366] Antony Pemberton, 'Occupy victimology: The relevance of David Graeber to the study of victims of crime' in Marc Groenhuijsen, Rianne Letschert, and Sylvia Hazenbroek (eds), *KLM Van Dijk: Liber Amoricum prof.dr.mr. J.J.M. van Dijk* (Nijmegen: Wolf Legal Publishers, 2012) 297–309, 305.

[367] *Prosecutor v. Katanga*, Order for Reparations pursuant to Article 75 of the Statute, ICC-01/04-01/07, 24 March 2017, para. 300 (*Katanga* Reparations Order).

[368] Ibid., para. 299.

[369] Ibid., para. 298.

[370] Francesca Capone, 'An Appraisal of the Al Mahdi Order on Reparations and Its Innovative Elements: Redress for Victims of Crimes against Cultural Heritage' (2018) 16 *JICJ* 645–61.

[371] *Prosecutor v. Al Mahdi*, Reparations Order, para. 53.

[372] Ibid., para. 106.

> make it impossible for [the defendant] to reintegrate into society upon his release. But the enforcement of reparations awards ... is beyond the ... question of setting ... personal liability.[373]

In the *Habré* case, the Court recognized that Habré's assets were insufficient to cover the amount of reparation stipulated. The Court recognized 7,396 victims as civil parties. The Court ordered Habré to pay compensation of 123 million euros to victims. It ordered compensation independently of the availability of funds in order to recognize harm and take into account any located or future assets.[374] It granted approximately 30,489 euros to victims of rape and sexual slavery, 22,867 euros to victims of torture and arbitrary detention and former prisoner of war, as well as 15,244 euros to family members of victims. It even acknowledged that victims who had not applied for reparation in proceedings might bring claims before the Trust Fund.

In *Lubanga*, the Chamber determined Lubanga's overall liability at 10 million USD.[375] The Chamber quantified the harm caused to 425 identified victims at 3.4 million USD, with an average harm of 8,000 USD per victim. It also awarded 6.6 million USD to estimated non-identified victims.[376]

5.2.2.4 Satisfaction

The ICC Statute contains no specific reference to satisfaction or symbolic reparation measures but they have played an important role in human rights reparations. The Inter-American Court of Human Rights (IACtHR) has developed a rich jurisprudence on satisfaction and collective reparation measures.[377] They are awarded in addition to other types of reparation or when restitution and compensation are insufficient.[378] For instance, apologies or commemorative practices have played an important role in transitional justice contexts to confront wrongdoing and improve community relations. 'They subtly deal with the selectivity problem since a transitional initiative of this kind, even though it may have been ordered

373 Ibid., para. 114.

374 Sperfeldt, 'The trial against Hissène Habré' 1253.

375 *Prosecutor v. Lubanga*, Corrected version of the 'Decision Setting the Size of the Reparations Award for which Thomas Lubanga Dyilo is Liable', ICC-01/04-01/06, 21 December 2017, para. 281.

376 Ibid., para. 304 ('[It] consists of his liability in respect of the 425 victims in the sample, amounting to USD 3,400,000, and his liability in respect of any other victims who may be identified, amounting to USD 6,600,000.'). The amount was later confirmed by the Appeals Chamber. See ICC, *Prosecutor v. Lubanga*, Judgment on the appeals against Trial Chamber II's 'Decision Setting the Size of the Reparations Award for which Thomas Lubanga Dyilo is Liable', ICC-01/04-01/06-3466-Red, 18 July 2019.

377 Diana Contreras-Garduño, 'Defining Beneficiaries of Collective Reparations: The Experience of the IACtHR' (2012) 4 *Amsterdam Law Forum* 40–57.

378 On collective reparation, see Nadia Tapia Navarro, 'Collective Reparations and the Limitations of International Criminal Justice to Respond to Mass Atrocity' (2018) 18 *International Criminal Law Review* 67–96, Christoph Sperfeldt, 'Collective Reparations at the Extraordinary Chambers in the Courts of Cambodia' (2012) 12 *International Criminal Law Review* 457–89.

for a specific sub-set of victims, could well end up being appropriated by many others.'[379]

The Basic Principles list different forms of satisfaction, including

> (d) An official declaration or a judicial decision restoring the dignity, the reputation and the rights of the victim and of persons closely connected with the victim; (e) Public apology, including acknowledgement of the facts and acceptance of responsibility; ... (g) Commemorations and tributes to the victims.[380]

Such measures have a representational function. Their value derives from the fact that they are 'carriers of meaning' and 'can help victims in particular and society in general make sense of the painful events of the past'.[381] As the Office of the UN Commissioner for Human Rights (OHCHR) has noted: 'Symbolic measures usually turn out to be so significant because, by making the memory of the victims a public matter, they disburden their families from their sense of obligation to keep the memory alive and allow them to move on.'[382]

In domestic contexts, public authorities have adopted a number of symbolic measures to express acknowledgment and recognition of victims in reparation programmes: individualized letters of apology, renaming of public spaces, or construction of museums or sites of memory.[383] For instance in Peru, the state issued apologies to registered victims, which affirmed their dignity and rights.[384]

5.2.2.4.1 Apologies and recognition of victims

The reparative options of international criminal courts and tribunals differ from national reparation programmes.[385] States or public authorities are typically not party to reparation proceedings against individuals. Judges do not make findings on state responsibility and cannot order states to issue an official apology,[386] even if

[379] See Frédéric Mégret, 'Reparations before the ICC' in Richard H. Steinberg (ed.), *Contemporary Issues Facing the International Criminal Court* (Leiden: Brill, 2016) 252–63, 259.

[380] Principle 22.

[381] Report by the Special Rapporteur on the promotion of truth, justice, reparation and guarantees of non-recurrence, Pablo de Greiff, A/69/518, 8 October 2014, para. 33.

[382] OHCHR, *Rule-of-Law Tools for Post-Conflict States: Reparations Programmes* (Geneva: United Nations, 2008), 23.

[383] Report by the Special Rapporteur on the promotion of truth, justice, reparation and guarantees of non-recurrence, Pablo de Greiff, A/69/518, 8 October 2014, 33.

[384] In *Gomes Lund et al. v. Brazil*, the IACtHR ordered Brazil to publish the official summary of the judgement issued by the Court in a newspaper with wide national circulation, and to publish the judgment in its entirety on an appropriate website of the state. See IACtHR, *Gomes Lund et al. v. Brazil*, Judgment, 24 November 2010, para. 273.

[385] For a critique of individual, as opposed to state-issued apologies, see Christian Tomuschat, 'The responsibility of other entities: Private individuals' in James Crawford, Alain Pellet, and Simon Olleson (eds), *The Law on International Responsibility* (Oxford: Oxford University Press, 2010), 317–30, 320.

[386] Michael R. Marrus, 'Official Apologies and the Quest for Historical Justice' (2007) 6 *Journal of Human Rights* 75–105.

crimes were committed as part of a state plan or policy. However, they have applied alternative techniques to provide satisfaction.[387]

In Cambodia, it was clear from the outset that that options for restitution and compensation were limited. The ECCC lacked jurisdiction to order an apology from the Royal Government of Cambodia,[388] but it applied symbolic reparations related to crimes committed by defendants. In Case 001, it included the name of all Civil Parties and their deceased relatives into the judgment. It also ordered making all statements of apology or acknowledgement of responsibility by the defendant public on the website.[389] These reparations fell short of expectations of victims,[390] since they were 'unlikely to yield significant tangible results for Civil Parties'.[391] Following the case, the ECCC Internal Rules were amended in order to allow a broader range of reparations. Internal Rules enabled the Victims Support Section (VSS) to carry out 'non-judicial measures in the form of projects to address the broader interests of victims'.[392] This regime allowed Civil Parties to seek additional moral and collective reparation measures in collaboration with the VSS, which are implemented with external funding. The Chamber clarified that such projects could start prior to the trial judgment. It recognized some of them as reparation upon conviction.[393]

In Case 002/02, the ECCC extended the narrative functions of reparations partly beyond the narrow confines of proceedings. It approved a reparation project which contained the stories of thirty civil parties who participated in the case but were not heard. It argued that a book compiling 'unheard stories' marked an important measure to recognize and acknowledge suffering.[394] It thereby engaged with the limits of trials through reparation.

At the ICC, apologies have played a significant role.[395] In the *Katanga* case, the defendant produced a public video in which he openly apologized to the victims of

[387] See generally Brent T. White, 'Say You're Sorry: Court-Ordered Apologies as a Civil Rights Remedy' (2006) 91 *Cornell Law Review* 1261–311. For a survey, see Diana Itza Odier-Contreras Garduño, *Collective Reparations Tensions and Dilemmas Between Collective Reparations and the Individual Right to Receive Reparations* (Antwerp: Intersentia, 2018), 195–208.

[388] *Duch* Trial Judgement, para. 663 ('The Chamber has no jurisdiction over Cambodian or other national authorities or international bodies. Nor can it properly impose obligations on or grant rights to persons or entities that were not parties to the proceedings before it. At most, the Chamber can merely encourage national authorities, the international community and other potential donors to show solidarity with the victims by providing financial and other forms of support that contributes to their rehabilitation, reintegration, and restoration of dignity.').

[389] Ibid., paras 682–683.

[390] Renée Jeffery, 'Beyond Repair?: Collective and Moral Reparations at the Khmer Rouge Tribunal' (2014) 13 *Journal of Human Rights* 103–19, 117.

[391] See Case 002/01 Judgement, para. 1112.

[392] Internal Rule 12*bis* (2).

[393] See Case 002/01 Judgement, para. 116.

[394] *Prosecutor v. Nuon Chea and Khieu Samphan*, Case 002/02 Judgment, 002/19-09-2007/ECCC/TC, 16 November 2018, para. 4426 (Case 002/02 Judgment).

[395] Apologies typically entail different dimensions: an acknowledgment of wrongdoing, expressions of remorse towards victims, a commitment to non-recurrence, and some form of repair.

the Bogoro attack. It received mixed reactions, since it was perceived as a trade-off for a mitigation of sentence.[396]

In *Al Mahdi*, the Trial Chamber recognized the defendant's apology as a form of satisfaction. It found his apology to be 'genuine, categorical and empathetic'.[397] It noted that the defendant had expressed remorse 'for the damage caused to his family, his community in Timbuktu, his country and the international community' and called upon others not to engage in destruction of cultural property.[398] The Chamber admitted that it is 'ultimately up to each individual victim to decide whether he or she considers Mr. Al Mahdi's apology to be sufficient'.[399] It ordered the Registry 'to produce an excerpt of the video of Mr. Al Mahdi's apology' and to post it on the ICC's website, together with the transcript, in order to enable victims to have access to it.[400]

Providing satisfaction through criminal processes is powerful because of its performative dimensions and its wide audience. The solemn nature of the courtroom and the global visibility of reparative measures attaches special meaning to acts of apology and recognition of victims. They may reach a broader public than domestic measures. However, the value of satisfaction depends on how it is conveyed and delivered. For instance, the value of apology decreases if it simply is seen as an attempt to gain a more lenient sentence. It is insufficient in the absence of other measures. As the legal representative of victims in *Al Mahdi* noted, 'apologies alone, as sincere as they may be, cannot make amends for the harm suffered and allow the victims to return to their previous lives and regain their dignity'.[401]

5.2.2.4.2 Memorialization

Memorialization is part of the 'symbolic-cultural landscape' of reparations.[402] It is closely linked to guarantees of non-recurrence.[403] Memory-related measures address a broader audience than the immediate victims of a case. They go 'to the core of the question of how a nation, or a people, choose to remember and to preserve their memory of events, which may shape their individual and/or national identity'.[404]

[396] The Legal Representative of victims stated: 'People should first sit down, make amends, and then apologise. If someone has been hurt, the wound must be treated and, once the person is cured, forgiveness can be sought.' See Legal Representative's observations on the reduction of sentence of Germain Katanga, ICC-01/04-01/07-3597-tENG, 18 September 2015, para. 54.

[397] *Al Mahdi*, Reparations Order, para. 70.

[398] *Al Mahdi*, Judgment and Sentence, para.103.

[399] *Al Mahdi*, Reparations Order, para. 69.

[400] Ibid., para. 71.

[401] *Prosecutor v. Al Mahdi*, Public redacted version of 'Submissions of the Legal Representative of Victims on the principles and forms of the right to reparation' dated 2 December 2016, ICC-01/12-01/15-190-Conf, 3 January 2017, para. 45.

[402] Report of the Special Rapporteur in the field of cultural rights, Farida Shaheed, 'Memorialization processes', A/HRC/25/49, 23 January 2014, para. 64.

[403] It relates discussions about the past to future non-recurrence.

[404] Queen's University Belfast Human Rights Centre and the Redress Trust observations pursuant to Article 75(3) of the Statute and Rule 103 of the Rules, ICC-01/12-01/15, 2 December 2016, para. 72.

Memorialization is an inherent part of transitional justice strategies. It is *inter alia* grounded in the right to truth (i.e. an 'interactive dialogical truth') and the civil, political, and cultural rights of victims.[405] It shares transformative features. It is a means to promote civic engagement, including reflection on historical narratives and resistance towards violence (e.g. resistance civil disobedience). Truth and reconciliation commissions have frequently recommended transforming former spaces of atrocity (e.g. detention centres) into places of memory. For instance, the Commission for Historical Clarification in Guatemala found that 'historical memory, both individual and collective, forms the basis of national identity'.[406] Remembrance of the victims 'is a fundamental aspect of this historical memory and permits the recovery of the values of, and the validity of the struggle for, human dignity'.[407]

It recommended *inter alia* the 'designation of a day of commemoration of the victims (National Day of Dignity for the Victims of the Violence)', the 'construction of monuments and public parks in memory of the victims', and 'the assigning of names of victims to educational centres, buildings and public highways'.[408] The IACtHR ordered the establishment of a monument to commemorate 'victims of gender-based murder' in Mexico, in order to preserve memory about the context of violence.[409] Other bodies have endorsed artistic activities, such as photographic and art exhibitions or performances as instruments of memorialization. For example, in Cambodia, reparative practice has relied on creative arts, because they can 'recreate and reimagine what was the past and ... also tell those stories, but in a way that ... is about creating dreams, creating a future, creating something that people can relate to'.[410]

In international criminal justice, memorialization is generally underdeveloped as a technique due to its cultural sensitivities and risks. The legal process seeks to produce objective interpretations, authoritative account of facts, or clear findings of harm and responsibility. Memorialization blurs the lines between objective facts and subjective interpretations and may construct new narratives. Memory is grounded in subjective processes and experiences. It is not a neutral space but

[405] See generally Arnaud Kurze and Christopher K. Lamont (eds), *New Critical Spaces in Transitional Justice: Gender, Art, and Memory* (Bloomington, IN: Indiana University Press, 2019).

[406] Report of the Commission for Historical Clarification, *Guatemala: Memory of Silence* (1999), 48, reprinted in (1999) 74 *Die Friedenswarte* 511–47. See generally Christian Tomuschat, 'Between national and international law: Guatemala's Historical Clarification Commission' in *Liber amicorum Günther Jaenicke* (Berlin: Springer, 1998), 991–1011; Christian Tomuschat, 'Fehlschlag oder Erfolg? Eine Bilanz der Arbeit der Wahrheitskommission in Guatemala' (1999) 74 *Die Friedenswarte* 433–55.

[407] Ibid.

[408] *Guatemala: Memory of Silence*, 49.

[409] IACtHR, *Gonzáles et al. ('Cotton Field') v. Mexico*, Judgment of 16 November 2009 (Preliminary Objection, Merits, Reparations, and Costs), paras 471–472.

[410] Rachel Hughes, 'Reparations of the Extraordinary Chambers in the Courts of Cambodia: A Brief Update', International Institute for Asian Studies, Newsletter, Vol. 80 (2018), at https://iias.asia/the-newsletter/article/reparations-extraordinary-chambers-courts-cambodia-brief-update.

is shaped by identity politics and conflicting narratives. It is a battlefield which involves struggles of ownership over meaning. One-sided narratives may erase memory, institutionalize forgetting, or produce 'mistruths'. Victims often disagree among themselves 'as to who and what to commemorate'.[411]

As Farida Shaheed, UN Special Rapporteur in the field of cultural rights, has noted, memorialization should be understood 'as processes that provide the necessary space for those affected to articulate their diverse narratives in culturally meaningful ways'.[412] It relies on the recognition of multiple truths and narratives, including complexities of victimhood and broader historical perspectives, in social dialogue.[413]

In the context of reparations, memorialization has been applied to physical objects[414] and cultural expressions. Monuments are sites of conscience which signal the 're-establishment of a sense of continuity for the survivors, and for the world'.[415] For instance, the preservation of former sites of atrocity and their transformation into memorial spaces may be an important measure to acknowledge harm, reflect a diversity of victim experiences, including local storytelling, maintain personal 'living' memory, provide survivors with an opportunity to reconnect to the past, and situate events in a broader historical context.[416] The ECCC has approved several projects of remembrance and memorialization. It has recognized them as reparation in cases in which they enjoyed sufficient consent and funding for implementation, including by external entities.

Judges have approved the request to recognize a national remembrance day as memory-related reparation. The request was first made in the *Duch* case, but rejected. In Case 002/01, the state consented to the idea. This allowed the Chamber to grant the request in the trial judgment. It recognized that 'provision of an official national holiday amounts to a nationwide and official acknowledgement of the harm suffered by the victims'.[417] It stated that '[p]ublic memorials may further assist to restore the dignity of victims, provide public acknowledgement of the crimes committed and harm suffered, and assist in healing the wounds of all

[411] Shaheed, 'Memorialization processes', para. 101.

[412] Ibid., para. 103.

[413] Impunity Watch has defended the 'principle of multiple narratives' based on two tenets: 'one is the fact of recognising that multiple narratives are constructive; the other is the importance of encouraging hidden narratives to be revealed. Impunity Watch, *Policy Brief: Guiding Principles of Memorialisation*, January 2013, 11.

[414] See Mégret, 'Of Shrines, Memorials and Museums' 35–50.

[415] Yael Danieli, 'Essential elements of healing after massive trauma: Complex needs voiced by victims/survivors' in Dennis Sullivan and Larry Tifft (eds), *Handbook of Restorative Justice* (New York, NY: Routledge, 2008), 343–54, 352.

[416] On Cambodia, see Cheryl Lawther, Rachel Killean, and Lauren Dempster, 'Whose Voices are Heard? Victimhood and Dark Tourism in Cambodia' April 2019, at https://pure.qub.ac.uk/portal/files/169818866/Whose_Voices_are_Heard_Report_FINAL.pdf.

[417] Case 002/01 Judgement, para. 1152.

victims by diffusing their effects far beyond the individuals who were admitted as Civil Parties'.[418]

It also approved the construction of a memorial in Phnom Penh to honor victims of forced evacuations. In Case 002/02, judges endorsed *inter alia* a popular multimedia project (the 'Courageous Turtle' project) as a form of judicial reparation. It relies on 'theatre performances, film screenings and photography exhibitions',[419] including a play which seeks to stimulate civil courage ('Stick out your head'). Memorial sites served not only as a means to let 'the world know' (e.g. 'dark tourism), but to preserve physical artifacts of the Khmer Rouge period, facilitate inquiry in relation to missing persons, and promote education.[420]

The ICC granted symbolic collective reparations in the *Lubanga* case. They included two forms of memory-related measures: the creation of commemoration centres in three communities and mobile memorialization projects relating to child soldiers.[421] They were meant to create awareness and acknowledgement of crimes and ongoing harms caused to victims and to reduce the stigma attached to former child soldiers within their (adopted) communities. They involved:

> community dialogue, artistic, cultural, and theatrical activities to promote awareness-raising about the convicted crimes and the harms suffered by child soldiers; children's rights and child protection; the negative consequences of enlisting, conscripting, and using children in hostilities; trans-generational and gender-related topics including as to the various forms in which former child soldiers and their families experience stigma, and to spread the message of reconciliation, non-repetition, and reintegration.[422]

In *Al Mahdi*, the Chamber admitted that 'most cultural property and cultural heritage are unique and of sentimental value' because of 'their purpose and symbolism'.[423] It prioritized individual awards, but it accepted that 'collective reparations can also include symbolic measures—such as a memorial, commemoration or forgiveness ceremony—to give public recognition of the moral harm suffered by the Timbuktu community and those within it'.[424] Such practices pose difficult

[418] Ibid.

[419] Case 002/02 Judgment, paras 4422 and 4456.

[420] Lawther, Killean, and Dempster, 'Whose Voices are Heard? Victimhood and Dark Tourism in Cambodia' 5–8.

[421] *Prosecutor v. Lubanga*, Order approving the proposed plan of the Trust Fund for Victims in relation to symbolic collective reparations, ICC-01/04-01/06-3251, 21 October 2016.

[422] *Prosecutor v. Lubanga*, Public Redacted version of Filing regarding symbolic collective reparations projects with confidential Annex: Draft Request for Proposals, ICC-01/04-01/06-3223-Conf, ICC-01/04-01/06-3223-Red, paras 29 and 41.

[423] *Al Mahdi*, Reparations Order, para. 22. The Chamber noted that the attack against the Protected Buildings destroyed and damaged not only physical structures, but 'rippled out into the community and diminished the link and identity the local community had with such valuable cultural heritage' (para. 19).

[424] Ibid., para. 90.

questions as to what notions of culture international criminal justice seeks to protect (e.g. 'international', 'domestic' or 'local' identity) and what happens if perceptions diverge.[425]

One of the inherent risks of memory-related measures is that they may cause resistance and contestations in domestic communities. These problems became apparent in *Katanga*. Victims' representatives were consulted about the feasibility of symbolic reparation. They rejected reparative practices, such as commemorative events or the erection of monuments, based on fears that they could 'cause fresh trauma or exacerbate social unrest'.[426]

5.2.2.4.3 Educative reparation measures

Educative measures are another form of expressive reparation.[427] They are often considered as priority by victims in reparative programmes.[428] They are not merely symbolic but material. They may enhance 'the capacity of citizens, especially—but not only adolescents and children, to think critically about the present and the past, ... and construct a better future'.[429] As Clara Ramírez-Barat and Roger Duthie have argued, they are an integral part of reparative practices because they may contribute to remembrance, transmit memory, mediate conflicting narratives about the past, 'nurture a culture of respect for human rights across generations',[430] promote the 'inclusion of victims as citizens',[431] or serve as a form of rehabilitation for victims (e.g. regain lost opportunities).[432] They have reintegrative value and express the 'educational impact of repressive policies and human rights violations on the lives of individuals and communities'.[433]

One of the strengths of educative measures is that they may transform the public space and address societal stereotypes (e.g. paternalistic attitudes, gender biases), promote a culture of tolerance and respect, and enable learning. Education adds to collective or symbolic reparation since it addresses some of the underlying factors conducive to crimes and material and may help repair social harm

[425] Mark A. Drumbl, 'From Timbuktu to The Hague and Beyond: The War Crime of Intentionally Attacking Cultural Property' (2017) 17 *JICJ* 77–99.

[426] *Katanga* Reparations Order, para. 301.

[427] See Clara Ramírez-Barat and Roger Duthie (eds), *Transitional Justice and Education: Learning Peace* (New York, NY: Social Science Research Council, November, 2016).

[428] Roger Duthie and Clara Ramírez-Barat, 'Education as Rehabilitation for Human Rights Violations' (2016) 5 *International Human Rights Law Review* 241–73, 246–7.

[429] Susana Frisancho and Félix Reátegui, 'Moral Education and Post-war Societies: The Peruvian Case' (2009) 38 *Journal of Moral Education* 421–43, 422.

[430] See Clara Ramírez-Barat and Roger Duthie, 'Education and Transitional Justice: Opportunities and Challenges for Peacebuilding' (New York, NY: ICTJ, 2015), 5, at https://www.ictj.org/sites/default/files/ICTJ-UNICEF-Report-EducationTJ-2015.pdf.

[431] Ibid., 12.

[432] See Duthie and Ramírez-Barat, 'Education as Rehabilitation for Human Rights Violations' 248–9.

[433] Ramírez-Barat and Duthie, 'Education and Transitional Justice: Opportunities and Challenges for Peacebuilding' 11.

done to communities.[434] For instance, in *Plan de Sanchez Massacre v. Guatemala*, the IACtHR established that reparation should include educational measures, in order to preserve cultural identity. It ordered the state to establish a programme relating to 'study and dissemination of the Maya-Achí culture in the affected communities through the Guatemalan Academy of Mayan Languages or a similar organization.'[435] In *Cantoral Benavides v. Peru*, it qualified education as a form of rehabilitation, which facilitates the reconstruction of life.[436]

In many contexts, education was part of domestic reparative programmes (e.g. Peru, Sierra Leone, East Timor, Colombia). General access to education does generally not amount to a reparative measure since it is a social service that states are deemed to provide.[437] Educative measures must rather address specific forms of harm, entail additional benefits, or imply acknowledgment of wrongdoing in order to qualify as reparation.[438] Reparations have included different types of educational measures: curriculum reforms, introduction of mandatory human rights education in state institutions, or education assistance for marginalized communities or youth and children who have suffered harm (e.g. children of children of 'disappeared' persons,[439] child soldiers)[440] or were excluded from educational benefits (e.g. apartheid).[441]

In international criminal justice, education has been mainly approached in the context of outreach and legacy strategies (e.g. ICTY, SCSL, Special Tribunal for Lebanon). However, it is increasingly recognized as a form of collective or individual reparation.

434 Alan Smith and Tony Vaux, *Education, Conflict and International Development* (London: Department for International Development, 2003).

435 IACtHR, *Plan de Sanchez Massacre v. Guatemala*, Judgment (Reparations), 19 November 2004, para. 110.

436 IACtHR, *Case of Cantoral-Benavides v. Peru*, Judgment (Reparations and Costs), 3 December 2001, paras 99(6) and 32. In the case *Ortega v. Mexico*, the Court noted that educational scholarships are reparations which recognize that 'harm continues and has resulted in significant alterations to their lives and also to their domestic relations and their relations with the community, which have affected their personal development.' See *Fernández Ortega et al. v. Mexico*, Judgment (Merits, Reparations, and Costs), 30 August 2010, para. 264.

437 Dyan Mazurana and Khristopher Carlson, 'Reparations as a means for recognizing and addressing crimes and grave rights violations against girls and boys during situations of armed conflict and under authoritarian and dictatorial regimes' in Ruth Rubio-Marin (ed.), *The Gender of Reparations: Unsettling Sexual Hierarchies While Redressing Human Rights Violations* (Cambridge: Cambridge University Press, 2009) 162–214, 196–97.

438 In Peru, educative measures were criticized for failing to communicate 'the rationale for these projects as an acknowledgment of harms suffered by the community as a result of the conflict.' See Duthie and Ramírez-Barat, 'Education as Rehabilitation for Human Rights Violations' 270.

439 The Commission on the Disappearance of Persons in Argentina mandated the state to pass laws 'to provide the children and/or relatives of the disappeared with economic assistance, study grants, social security, and employment.' See *Argentine National Commission on the Disappeared, Nunca Más: The Report of the Argentine National Commission on the Disappeared* (New York, NY: Farrar Straus Giroux, 1986), 446.

440 Mazurana and Carlson, 'Reparations as a means for recognizing and addressing crimes' 196.

441 Ramírez-Barat and Duthie, 'Education and Transitional Justice: Opportunities and Challenges for Peacebuilding' 9–20.

For example, the ECCC has recognized the close link between memorialization and education in its reparation practice. It stressed that '[p]ublic education regarding the suffering of victims and the nature of the Khmer Rouge regime is further likely to advance the goals of acknowledgment, remembrance, and awareness of the crimes committed and the suffering resulting therefrom and is therefore likely to benefit not only the Civil Parties, but also to generally contribute to national reconciliation'.[442]

It approved textbooks which rely on ECCC established evidence on the Khmer Rouge regime as reparative project, in order to provide 'the schools with an accurate basis for the discussion of events during the Democratic Kampuchea era'.[443] In Case 002/02, it endorsed projects on 'App-Learning on Khmer Rouge History' and 'Khmer Rouge History Education' in order to promote 'intergenerational dialogue', create 'appropriate spaces for interaction' (e.g. through digital media and artistic projects), and 'prevent the repetition of Civil Parties' and other DK survivors' experiences'.[444]

The ICC has made reference to educational measures in nearly all reparation orders. In *Lubanga*, the ICC recognized education as a form of rehabilitation for former child soldiers. It argued that access to education might mitigate feelings of shame and prevent further victimization in communities. It noted that '[r]ehabilitation of the victims of child recruitment should include measures that are directed at facilitating their reintegration into society, taking into account the differences in the impact of these crimes on girls and boys'.[445] These 'steps should include the provision of education and vocational training, along with sustainable work opportunities that promote a meaningful role in society'.[446]

In *Katanga*, the Court approved education assistance as a form of reparation. In *Al Mahdi*, the Chamber found that collective reparations may include 'community-based educational and awareness-raising programmes to promote Timbuktu's important and unique cultural heritage'.[447] In *Bemba*, it was suggested that the Trust Fund should 'implement a public campaign that raises awareness in specific communities in the [Central African Republic] about the discriminatory practices and negative stereotypes of women victims and their children'.[448]

The problem of educational measures is that they are highly dependent on context and may cause social tensions. Successful implementation often depends on some form of prior acknowledgment or sense of wrong in states or affected

[442] Judgment Case 002/01, para. 1156.
[443] Ibid., para. 1157
[444] Judgment Case 002/02, para. 4454
[445] *Prosecutor v. Lubanga*, Decision establishing the principles and procedures to be applied to reparations, ICC-01/04–01/06, 7 August 2012, para. 234.
[446] Ibid.
[447] *Al Mahdi*, Reparations Order, para. 83.
[448] *Prosecutor v. Bemba*, Submission by QUB Human Rights Centre on reparation issues pursuant to Article 75 of the Statute, ICC-01/05-01/08-3444, 17 October 2016, para. 89.

communities, where crimes have occurred and a willingness to engage and move on. It also requires adequate educational means and techniques which are able to accommodate disagreement and deliberation. Experiences suggest that oral history projects[449] or testimonies may be useful for educational purposes 'because they tell personal stories of how different people—potentially both victims and perpetrators of abuses—lived through and experienced a conflict period'.[450]

However, the scope of educative practices needs to go beyond the narrow histories or truth told through criminal proceedings. For instance, alternate accounts and 'stories of bystander behaviour, resistance against injustice, and solidarity with and support to victims' may have educative potential'.[451]

5.2.3 Dilemmas

Like punishment, reparative justice faces severe challenges. The judicial process is organized along binaries (e.g., perpetrator/victim, guilt/innocence). Reparative measures seek to break these divides. However, in reality, they are always likely to disappoint some.

Expressive reparative practices face some of the same dilemmas as other forms of expressivism. The underlying social aims (e.g. recognition of agency and dignity of victims, social transformation) exceed the reach of judicial bodies. Reparations are often highly complex projects that represent harm and victimization, shape identity politics, and frame memory. International criminal proceedings are less well-equipped than domestic reparation programmes to establish trust in states and public institutions. They lack procedures through which states can express public acknowledgment of responsibility or recognize harm.

Symbolic acts, such as apologies by the defendant or symbolic compensation awarded (with support of external actors), carry less weight than state apologies or reparation programmes. They only address 'some victims' and 'certain vulnerabilities'.[452] They struggle to address structural forms of violence, such as political inequality, poverty, or social injustice. They rely heavily on factors external to defendants, such as state consent, external funding, or links to assistance and development programmes. In case of the indigence of defendants and support through voluntary contributions, they are, to a large extent, expressions of care by international actors.

[449] See generally Alan McCully, 'History Teaching, Conflict and the Legacy of the Past' (2012) 7 *Education, Citizenship and Social Justice* 145–59, 156.

[450] Ramírez-Barat and Duthie, 'Education and Transitional Justice: Opportunities and Challenges for Peacebuilding' 20.

[451] Ibid., 17.

[452] Elander, 'The Victim's Address' 114.

Reparations proceedings provide limited means for victims to tell their individual stories, seek empowerment or catharsis.[453] Revealing does not necessarily produce healing. Defendants cannot be forced to make amends. The impact of apologies is related to performative elements.

Proceedings may become concerned more with the general image and message that courts send about themselves, rather than meaningful reparation to those affected. Critics note that they 'are instances of ritualized grief where a court picks up victims' grief, displays it and makes it its own while grieving the victims'.[454]

Reparations enable courts to justify their own existence and stress the 'importance of condemning the crimes in question'.[455] The underlying narratives are partly self-serving. They justify trials and empower agencies who are involved in the implementation of reparations.[456]

The social meaning associated with notions, such as 'reparation', may exceed their legal meaning. Expectations and needs of victims do neatly fit into the preconceived notions of restitution, compensation, satisfaction, rehabilitation, and guarantees of non-recurrence that are contemplated by the UN Basic Principles.[457] In practice, the trial process in itself may constitute a form of satisfaction. However, satisfaction is typically tied to a conviction. Acquittals have the opposite effect.

Reparations may inflict asymmetric proportion of blame on individual defendants. Courts try to apportion responsibility according to the individual contributions of defendants. However, they lack a clear methodology to do so. A limited number of defendants may come to carry the burden and social stigma of collective crimes as individuals, although criminality results from much broader group dynamics, state or organizational policies, or externally driven factors. A striking gap in existing reparation structures is the lack of responsibility of legal persons, including organizations and corporations that facilitated international crimes. The strong focus on individuals may blur the broader stories of conflict, or produce counterproductive exculpatory effects. It may sideline socio-economic causes or dimensions of conflict, such as foreign resource exploitation, corruption, or fight over land rights. Harm to the environment is blended out

[453] See Christine Van den Wyngaert, 'Victims Before International Criminal Courts: Some Views and Concerns of an ICC Trial judge' (2011) 44 *Case Western Reserve Journal of International Law* 475–96, 489 ('[A] criminal trial, unlike, for example, a truth and reconciliation commission, is not the appropriate forum for victims to express their feelings, as this would detract from the serenity of the trial and would not serve a useful purpose from the perspective of a criminal proceeding.').

[454] Elander, 'The Victim's Address' 115.

[455] John D. Ciorciari and Anne Heindel, 'Victim Testimony in International and Hybrid Criminal Courts: Narrative Opportunities, Challenges, and Fair Trial Demands' (2016) 56 *Virginia Journal of International Law* 266–338, 335.

[456] James Cockayne, 'Hybrids or Mongrels? Internationalized War Crimes Trials as Unsuccessful Degradation Ceremonies' (2005) 4 *Journal of Human Rights* 455–73.

[457] Phuong N. Pham and Patrick Vinck, 'Empirical Research and the Development and Assessment of Transitional Justice Mechanisms' (2007) 1 *International Journal of Transitional Justice* 231–48.

or marginalized due to the anthropocentric conception of victimhood in international criminal justice.[458]

The process of awarding reparation may entail identity conflicts and risk of misrepresentation. Some victims may be reluctant to identify themselves as victims. Others may challenge the way in which they are identified. The very notion of the victim may become 'a symbol around which contested notions of past violence and suffering are constructed and reproduced'.[459] Victims are grouped according to the narratives that are produced by the charges and the crimes selected for prosecution. They may contrast with subjective perceptions of identity and collectivity (e.g. indigenous or local communities), downplay the diversity of social attachments, or reduce the complexities of victimhood. For instance, in Cambodia, survivors recognized that 'many Khmer Rouge cadres were also victims of the Khmer Rouge'.[460]

In practice, there is a tendency to emphasize the needs of special categories of victims based on vulnerabilities (e.g. sexual violence, children). However, this very categorization may be problematic. For instance, proponents of gender justice prefer use the term 'survivor', rather than victim, in order to counter stereotypes about passivity and vulnerability.

The narratives that are told through reparations can cause secondary forms of victimization. As victimologists have pointed out, 'imposing a generic script on a victim's experience is at odds with the deeply personal process of coming to terms with the meaning of victimization in the context of an unfolding life story'.[461] For most victims, 'the strength of their own story is derived from its quality as a unique, authentic and special account of their own experience, not from its resemblance to a generic shorthand'.[462]

Administrative reparation programmes may be more effective in addressing harm and suffering than judicial reparations. The link between reparation and retribution is tied to a procedural rather than a distributive vision of justice. It relies on 'Western concepts of "justice for victims" that define justice mainly as an empowerment of victims through legal participation, risk neglecting the socio-economic realities of a post-conflict country'.[463] From a needs-based perspective, it might be more effective to assist victims of international crimes in the same way as victims of disaster, namely without establishment of criminal responsibility.

[458] See Matthew Gillett, 'Environmental damage and international criminal law' in Sébastien Jodoin and Marie-Claire Cordonier Segger (eds), *Sustainable Development, International Criminal Justice, and Treaty Implementation* (Cambridge: Cambridge University Press, 2013), 73–99; Frédéric Mégret, 'The Case for a General International Crime against the Environment' in ibid., 50–70.

[459] McEvoy and McConnachie, 'Victimology in Transitional Justice' 532.

[460] Lawther, Killean, and Dempster, 'Whose Voices are Heard? Victimhood and Dark Tourism in Cambodia' 8.

[461] Pemberton, Aarten, and Mulder, 'Stories as Property' 7.

[462] Ibid.

[463] Hoven and Scheibel, '"Justice for Victims" in Trials of Mass Crimes' 181.

5.3 Conclusions

Expressivism is a recurring concept in sentencing and reparation practice. It is rarely expressly invoked. It faces objections from several angles. Judges and courtroom lawyers are reluctant to admit the space for expressivist considerations in practice. They view themselves as judicial agents, rather than 'social and historical demigods promoting grand constitutive narratives'.[464] Defence counsel fear that expressivism may instrumentalize proceedings and treat defendants as objects rather than subjects of proceedings. Victims may remain opposed to the idea of symbolic reparation. Such reparations are easily perceived as less meaningful. In light of these factors, expressivism is typically not used as a justification of punishment in itself. It is a justice theory, rather than a punishment theory. It is invoked in combination with other punishment rationales or as a method to explain punishment. Its main utility lies in its ability to explain retribution or prevention in a way that avoids the pitfalls of consequentialism. It acknowledges that punishment relies on factors that cannot be quantified by outcomes (i.e. lower atrocity crime rates). Punishment is connected to the communication of the immorality of the atrocities and aspirational motives, such as the encouragement of moral courage or the expression of the social utility of punishment.

Punishment in itself has symbolic significance. It is not only a way to engage with the offender and the underlying crime but goes beyond the individual perpetrator. As sociologists have suggested, punishment is a social convention which bears ritualistic features. It symbolizes commitment to a system of norms and rights. The particular value of international criminal justice does not lie in the severity of punishment inflicted but rather in the publicity of the criminal process and the establishment of accountability towards a broader community. It is not solely concerned with retributive justice but also connected to restorative rationales. In some contexts, alternative sentences and broader forms of punishment may be more effective ways to convey expression of wrongdoing, re-establish social bonds, or secure prevention of crimes than lengthy terms of imprisonment. Harsh penalties, such as capital punishment, may be counterproductive from an expressivist perspective since they exclude the offender from humanity, conflict with human dignity, and sanction wrongdoing through novel or irreversible types of harm.

Judges have used expressivism as a method of reasoning and means of persuasion in relation to sentencing. They have been entrepreneurial in their approaches towards punishment and sentencing rationales. Punishment is partly a means to reconfirm authority. As Aloisi and Meernik have demonstrated in their empirical

[464] Mégret, 'Practices of Stigmatization' 294.

analysis of sentencing decisions, 'by referencing those elements of sentencing objectives and criteria that are most useful in ensuring judicial discretion, judges seek to strengthen the role of their institutions in advancing human rights and ensuring their judicial legacies'.[465] Sentencing serves at the same time as a means to release emotion. It portrays possibilities of alternative behaviour and seeks to make sense of the limits of the law.

The value of judgments as a means of communication with the offender is limited. Judgments often speak as much to the international community or expert audiences, as they do to the perpetrator. Their ability to communicate is constrained by the impersonal tone of judicial speech and technical language. Decisions engage only to a limited extent with broader historical narratives or the motivations of the defendant. Context is highly filtered and shaped through Prosecution narratives or witnesses. Judges have limited means to explore the criminological underpinnings of crime in sentencing. Punishment itself is often more a demonstration, an act expressing fair and proportionate punishment towards the defendant, rather than an educative measure itself.

Reparations are a way to strengthen communicative relations with victims beyond representation or participation in the courtroom. Studies on trauma in the aftermath of violence suggest that international crimes do not only shatter 'fundamental assumptions about the world and one's safety in it' but may also sever 'the sustaining connection between the self and the rest of humanity'.[466] Reparations are a means to establish such a sense of attachment. They are unable to restore the *status quo ante*, but they may create novel points of reference.

The way how reparations are awarded may be as important as their amount or scope. For instance, truth-telling or information on the whereabouts of missing persons provide an important form of satisfaction by virtue of the communication that they entail. Symbolism is an important aspect of reparations. Reparations gain meaning through the communicative and reparative gestures that they entail. Even modest forms of restitution, compensation, or repair of harm may gain value because of the messages that they send about acknowledgment of wrongdoing, the recognition of harm and responsibility, and the attempt to do justice. In cases where defendants are indigent, reparations may mark an expression of solidarity or care.

Reparations have additional value to punishment since they speak directly to victims individually or collectively. They may enable a more creative engagement with harm. For instance, education, memorialization, or performative arts may engage in a more holistic and accessible way with harm and address structural forms

[465] Aloisi and Meernik, *Judgment Day* 188.
[466] Susan J Brison, *Aftermath: Violence and the Remaking of the Self* (Princeton, NJ: Princeton University Press, 2002), 40.

of violence that are marginalized in criminal proceedings. They do not only contain expressions of wrongdoing and blame, based on binary structures, but are mediums to reflect on the complexities of crimes, agency, and victimhood. They may engage with victims in a fuller way (e.g. as political and human beings) than judicial proceedings.

6
International Criminal Law as Expressivist Justice
Meanings, Implications, and Critiques

Expressivist practices have a larger space in international criminal justice than traditionally assumed. Messages and messaging are inherent in law-making processes, institutional practices, adjudication, and reparation. The idea that expressivism is part and parcel of international criminal justice has initially met with scepticism because there is no coherent community to which laws and values can express.[1] However, this objection has lost part of its validity with the development of international criminal justice as a field.

For expressivists, international criminal justice is justified because it serves as 'an articulation of the appropriate reaction to criminal act on the part of a society'.[2] Domestic theories suggest that the value of criminal law derives partly from the relationships that it produces or reaffirms, that is, its ability to 'break down barriers of status and rank',[3] affirm the 'virtue of relationships in which people stand', or contribute to the formation of a political community.[4] This argument applies in different form also to the international context.[5] Accountability emerges in and through relations between different stakeholders (e.g. through listening, speaking, and engaging). These relations may create a transnational political community provide reassurance and reaffirmation of international criminal law's values (e.g. the need for prevention of crimes or response to moral wrongdoing), or 'help alter social morality.

Expressivism is part of the language, articulation, and representation through which legal agents and the field as a whole manifest themselves in relation to others. International criminal justice is constituting its own constituencies and audiences through practice. It involves not only communication and messaging

[1] See **section 1.1.3**.
[2] See Larry May and Shannon Fyfe, *International Criminal Tribunals: A Normative Defense* (Cambridge: Cambridge University Press, 2017), 51.
[3] Ibid.
[4] Antony Duff and Sandra Marshall, 'Public and private wrongs' in James Chalmers, Fiona Leverick, and Lindsay Farmer (eds), *Essays in Criminal Law in Honour of Sir Gerald Gordon* (Edinburgh: Edinburgh University Press, 2010), 70–85, 83–4.
[5] International criminal justice as a field is built on relations of 'injury, affect and responsibility'. See Nesam McMillan, 'Imagining the International: The Constitution of International as a Site of Crime, Justice and Community' (2016) 25 *Social & Legal Studies* 163–80, 170.

Justice as Message. Carsten Stahn, Oxford University Press (2020). © Carsten Stahn.
DOI: 10.1093/oso/9780198864189.001.0001

in the narrow sense but storytelling, performance, practices of representation, and theatric features. It offers a framework for the understanding of law as social practice (i.e. 'a way of being in the world')[6] and justice as a ritual and performative process.[7] It is a way of 'making meaning move across time'.[8]

6.1 Multidisciplinary Origins

Expressivist theories are relatively new in legal discourse. However, the concept has a long tradition in other disciplines. Its origins can be traced in multiple fields: classical rhetoric, sociology, speech act theory, performance, and semiotics.[9] These influences and interconnections have remained under-studied. Throughout much of the first half of the twentieth century, international law was more preoccupied with its own struggle for emancipation from politics rather than its connection to other disciplines. International criminal law gradually evolved from a project grounded in state interests and ethics into a broader field of law, with its own professional codes, semantics, procedures, and agents.

The recognition of expressivism as a theory underpinning international criminal justice was facilitated by the rise of the law and literature movement in the 1960s and communicative accounts of law, governance, and compliance. They have broadened the understanding of law in domestic discourse. Law was not only treated as a set of rules but also as a language, social practice, or culture which is formed by 'a community of speakers'.[10] This has opened the space for communicative understandings of punishment and criminal proceedings.

Expressivism has gained structural attention in domestic law and transitional justice discourse. Duff has stressed that expressivism is about process, rather than punishment. Continental criminal lawyers have linked it to ideas of norm affirmation (Günther Jakobs), retributive concepts (e.g., censure), and methods of positive general prevention (Claus Roxin, Klaus Günther). Transitional justice posed essential questions about the very meaning and societal impact of trials (e.g. why do we do what we do?). It explored to what extent trials can provide historical clarification, social bonding, deliberative democracy (e.g. Mark Osiel, Pablo De Greiff),

[6] Paul W. Kahn, *The Cultural Study of Law: Reconstructing Legal Scholarship* (Chicago, IL: University of Chicago Press, 1999), 36.

[7] Bernard J. Hibbitts, '"Coming to Our Senses": Communication and Legal Expression in Performance Cultures' (1992) 41 *Emory Law Journal* 873–960.

[8] Anne Orford, 'On International Legal Method' (2003) 1 *London Review of International Law* 166–97, 171–2.

[9] See **section 1.1**.

[10] James Boyd White, 'Law as Rhetoric, Rhetoric as Law: The Arts of Cultural and Communal Life' (1985) 52 *University of Chicago Law Review* 684–702, 691 ('The law is not merely a bureaucracy or a set of rules, but a community of speakers of a certain kind: a culture of argument, perpetually remade by its participants.').

reconciliation in post-conflict transitions (Colleen Murphy), and whether alternative accountability mechanisms promote truth-telling, local justice, and communal healing (e.g. Mark Drumbl).[11] This inquiry is multidisciplinary in nature. It connected the study of accountability and criminal law as a project of justice to narrative analysis, performative aspects of proceedings, and social and behavioural psychology.

International criminal justice has been marked by ad hocism, pragmatism, and faith in the validity of the project.[12] More critical attempts to make sense and meaning of international criminal law as justice started only later, namely with the emergence of the International Criminal Court (ICC), the completion of the work of *ad hoc* and hybrid tribunals, and inquiries about the effectiveness of courts and tribunals. Courts and tribunals have largely shied away from committing to a specific justice theory or identifying a grand justice narrative to justify their own existence. Fragments of justifications of punishment are reflected in sentencing decisions.[13] However, the virtue of the exercise of criminal jurisdiction has mainly been grounded in pragmatic considerations and theories of practice.

Institutions have approached justice 'not as something that simply is' but 'rather as something that is done'.[14] They have established outreach and legacy projects in order to communicate judicial narratives, publicize outcomes of proceedings, speak more directly to victims and local communities, and justify their own record. Victim participation has gained a more systemic space in proceedings, in order to bridge physical, geographic, and cultural distances and give victims a voice. Courts and prosecutors have pursued diplomatic channels of communication in order to mobilize political pressure for arrest and address non-cooperation by states. Images, press releases, broadcasting of proceedings, and social media are used to relate proceedings more closely to audiences and to present them in formats that are more accessible. They are multiplied through other channels (e.g. field offices, NGOs, other international organizations). These communicative and performative structures are strongly shaped by Court-centric needs,[15] one-sided messaging, and imperfect speech conditions in relation to defendants and victims. They are deemed to increase impact and memory and create shared experiences.

[11] See **section 1.1.4.**

[12] Barrie Sander, 'International Criminal Justice as Progress: From Faith to Critique' in Morten Bergsmo, Cheah Wui Ling, Song Tianying, and Yi Ping (eds), *Historical Origins of International Criminal Law: Vol. 4* (Brussels: Torkel Opsahl Academic EPublisher, 2015), 749–835.

[13] See **section 5.1.3.**

[14] Hibbitts, 'Coming to Our Senses' 959.

[15] Frédéric Mégret, 'The Anxieties of International Criminal Justice' (2016) 29 *LJIL* 197–221, 216 ('International criminal tribunals regularly showcase their achievements, notably on their websites and a whole line of institutional practices, such as the development of quantitative indicators, which can be seen as designed to reduce anxiety about what it is that the tribunals actually do in the world.').

6.2 Realist Motivations

The turn to expressivism is motivated by anxieties and fears[16] about international criminal justice as a project and an institutional urge for survival. Law is an instrument to 'counter fear, to reassure and appease constituencies'.[17] Expressivism is a method which contributes to this objective. It seeks to counter performative dimensions of crimes, provide societal reassurance, and produce positive meaning and experiences. It forms part of the ritualistic and purifying features of the field.

International criminal justice is directed towards the 'impossible'.[18] 'Impunity' is falsely portrayed as the *Grundnorm* of the field. Normative ambiguity or gaps in the law are perceived as a threat. International norms are expected to be able respond to novel types of criminality or new forms of crime. This creates an urge to engage in norm affirmation, gap filling, and narrative techniques to justify normative change.[19] The project is guided by moral ambition (e.g. 'Never again'). As Fréderic Mégret has observed, it 'cannot simply be',[20] but is action-oriented. It is meant to be seen to be acting and deemed to operate 'in ways that are reasonably meaningful, or succumb to crushing depression and melancholy'.[21] Expressivism is a strategy to show resistance to crimes, break 'silences', or mobilize empathy.

International criminal justice cannot automatically draw on the legitimacy of state authority in relation to punishment. Legal institutions are constantly required to justify themselves towards different audiences. They operate from the distance and may lack consent, authority, or the necessary social embedding in societies where crimes have been committed. They need to overcome more obstacles than domestic entities in order to trigger enforcement.[22] In practice, they are often only able to provide a 'signal', which requires further collective response.[23] They may need to earn acceptance on the international plane and domestically. They seek to gain legitimacy through practices of representation, namely by acting on behalf of certain constituencies, such as victims, states failing to exercise jurisdiction, or world society. The development of communicative structures and publicity is

[16] Andrea Bianchi, 'Fear's legal dimension: Counterterrorism and human rights' in Laurence Boisson de Chazournes and Marcel Kohen (eds), *International Law and the Quest for its Implementation—Le droit international et la quête de sa mise en oeuvre: Liber Amicorum Vera Gowlland-Debbas* (Leiden: Brill, 2010), 175–92.

[17] See Andrea Bianchi and Anne Saab, 'Fear and International Law-Making: An Exploratory Inquiry' (2019) 32 *LJIL* 351–65, 361.

[18] Mégret, 'Anxieties of International Criminal Justice' 199.

[19] Ibid., 205 ('More often than not, the "gap" is filled by an appeal to morality, natural law or its acceptable modern version, some broad historical telos or belief in, "world opinion".').

[20] Ibid., 200.

[21] Ibid., 200.

[22] See in relation to the IACtHR, Jessie Allen, 'Theater of International Justice' (2012) 3 *Creighton International & Comparative Law Journal* 121–47, 151.

[23] Frédéric Mégret, 'Practices of Stigmatization' (2013) 76 *Law and Contemporary Problems* 287–318, 311.

a means for institutions to 're-cast themselves as actors endowed with a certain democratic legitimacy'.[24] They are a way to persuade the diverse constituencies that the exercise of international criminal justice is in their interests.[25] However, their interests do not necessarily coincide. For instance, messages that appeal to 'international society' do not necessarily converge with those of 'domestic societies'.

Language barriers, legalistic discourse, or the adversarial nature of international criminal proceedings may impede communicative relationships with witnesses and victims or between victims and the offender. Judges and lawyers often seek to clarify their pronouncements and arguments by resorting to metaphors and stories.

6.3 Diverse Social Functions

Expressivism has at least two different broader social functions. The first one relates to community formation, social bonding, and formulation of societal aspirations. It builds on Durkheim's justification of criminal justice as instrument of building a collective conscience.[26] Expressivism serves as a means to continuingly reaffirm the purposes and ambitions of the field, and to encourage engagement and commitment to it. It is a means to transform the *status quo* and widen the spectrum of possibilities.

The second function is grounded in theories of practice[27] and the ambition to see 'law in action'. Expressivism makes the law real and tangible. International legal norms and instruments alone do not generate social practice. The different types of expression (normative, institutional, procedural, and remedial) give concrete shape and meanings to international criminal law. They authenticate or frame texts, attach social meaning to norms and legal concepts, and create audiences. Legal practices, such as interpretation, adjudication, or cooperation are performative acts that provide contours to roles assigned by law.[28] They create meaning, relate the law to audiences, and may encourage norm internalization or compliance.

[24] Mégret, 'Anxieties of International Criminal Justice' 207.

[25] Ibid., 209 ('international criminal tribunals engage in recurring patterns of proving that they speak for local societies, or at least for victims of international crimes. A whole range of institutional practices of communication and outreach are devoted to convincing those imagined as the ultimate constituents of international criminal justice that it is working with their interests genuinely at heart.').

[26] See **section 1.1.2**.

[27] For a practice approach in international relations scholarship, see, Emanuel Adler and Vincent Pouliot, *International Practices* (Cambridge: Cambridge University Press, 2011); Davide Nicolini, *Practice Theory, Work and Organization: An Introduction* (Oxford: Oxford University Press, 2013); Emanuel Adler and Vincent Pouliot, 'International Practices' (2011) 3 *International Theory* 1–36.

[28] Julie Stone Peters, 'Legal Performance: Good and Bad Law' (2008) 4 *Culture and the Humanities* 179–200.

6.3.1 Community formation, aspiration, and imagination

Like every field, international criminal justice is governed by the tension between reality and fiction. It deals with the past but produces forward-looking effects that may influence the decisions and actions of various actors. It creates intersubjective relationships and sends signals to future transgressors.

International criminal justice seeks to produce certain effects (e.g. deterrence, retribution, repair of harm). Expressivism does not postulate that such consequences occur or justify international criminal justice as a project but rather portrays them as aspirations. It embraces a different type of consequentialism than classical theories of justification. It views criminal justice as a means to prevent wrongdoing through the affirmation of punishment and didactic means which are meant to provide the broader public and offenders with grounds *not* to commit crimes. The justification is related to the ability to convey social meaning. The quantity of offenders or crimes prosecuted or the harshness of the penalty is less central than the affirmation of accountability and its process.

As Immi Tallgren has noted, 'clearly all law and legal systems, in general, are about symbolism and communication', but 'international criminal justice reaches the top of that pyramid'.[29] Expressivism takes some epistemic distance from facts and uses images, stories, language, and gestures to generate alternatives and possibilities. It uses moral postulates (e.g. 'should be') and fictions in order to enhance community formation and build a culture of accountability.[30] It takes into account that social transformation is not only driven by certainty, objective facts, and cognitive reason but tied to emotional connection and feelings of hope. Objectives, language, and community affiliations are not fixed and certain but fluid and constantly remade. For instance, legal proceedings create a community in space.

Expressivist practices are a necessary counterpart to technocratic and bureaucratic understandings of law, which seek to frame justice in terms of inputs, outputs, and measurable outcomes. Expressivism looks beyond reality. It plays with the power of imagination, which is an important element in legal work (e.g. interpretation, reading of facts, construction of arguments, engagement with other legal cultures).[31] It seeks to create excitement and remove barriers to social interaction. It may approach accountability from a fresh perspective, raise new questions, foster creative engagement with challenges, or create new audiences through the performance of law. It is not only a means to frame or affirm objectives of international criminal justice but a method to reaffirm the purpose of engaging with the field. For instance, court proceedings, testimony, and public hearings may produce a

[29] Immi Tallgren, 'Come and See? The Power of Images and International Criminal Justice' (2017) 17 *International Criminal Law Review* 259–80, 275.

[30] On law and persuasion, see Boyd White, 'Law as Rhetoric, Rhetoric as Law' 691.

[31] James White, *The Legal Imagination: Abridged Edition* (Chicago, IL: University of Chicago Press, [1973] 1985).

record which triggers community reactions or mobilizes social change. Metaphors are often more than rhetorical ornament. They are intended to provide intellectual stimulation, transform thought processes, or present a mirror to society.[32]

The very process of interaction, triggered through expressivist practice, is community-building. Communities are built on 'routines, words, tools, ways of doing things, stories, symbols, and discourse'.[33] They emerge not only through reason, persuasion, and empathy but also through time, communicative interactions, and repeated and cumulative practices.[34] Rituals and traces of periodicity are reflected in governance structures of international courts and tribunals (e.g. annual meetings, renewed vows of commitment through legal resolutions), review mechanisms, or the establishment of law enforcement networks.

Community formation occurs through discourse or conversation. As Monika Hakimi has argued, this process does not require consent but can encompass conflict. International law may construct a community 'not by consistently pressing for consensus or reconciliation but by at times doing almost the opposite: enabling the participants to disagree'.[35] Communities are 'constituted' through the participants' interactions.[36] In the most radical sense, the communication or conversation itself might be viewed as the community.[37]

6.3.2 Performing law

The second role of expressivism is its ability to perform law. It is a method to present law in a way that others (i.e. audiences) can understand (e.g. through words, messages, signs or images), and a process that allows them to participate and observe. It is grounded in the communicative relationship between law-making and regulation, adjudication and enforcement, and audiences who are deemed to show respect or allegiance to norms.

International criminal justice is not only a collection of rules and norms but a living project. It operates through processes of enactment and re-enactment. Norms are closely interrelated with processes of institutionalization. They aim to establish alternative worlds. There are to a certain degree 'afactual' and remain

[32] See Bernard Hibbitts, 'Making Sense of Metaphors: Visuality, Aurality and the Reconfiguration of American Legal Discourse' (1994) 16 *Cardozo Law Review* 229–356, 233–8.

[33] Emanuel Adler, *Communitarian International Relations: The Epistemic Foundations of International Relations* (New York, NY: Routledge, 2005) 15.

[34] See Allen, 'Theater of International Justice' 151 ('To understand how … officials might be affected, we have to think of their participation in, and observation of, multiple judicial hearing performances as part of a complex process that unfolds over a period of years.').

[35] Monica Hakimi, 'Constructing an International Community' (2017) 111 *AJIL* 317–56, 319–20.

[36] Ibid., 320.

[37] Ibid., 324–5 ('The community is constituted through their interactions about the joint project. These interactions have the potential to construct and fortify the group no matter whether they are harmonious or persistently conflictual.').

relevant even if they are not obeyed. Expressivism is a method to connect norms to reality, to affirm their existence, and to contribute to their realization.

Law does not only emerge from text but also from performance. Legal practice involves role play.[38] The performative dimensions of international criminal justice and its images are sometimes portrayed negatively as 'spectacles' of law. However, they also have something inherently positive. For instance, institutional histories suggest that international criminal institutions or trials are not ends in themselves but reactions to events, emotions, or neglects.[39] They often embody something bigger than their foundational instruments imply. They have performative force.

Expressivism serves at least four different functions from performative perspective. It 'embodies' the law by giving it concrete shape and form and relating to social reality and individual experiences. It 'locates' law by relating it to time and space. It contributes to memorialization by recalling and enacting law and embedding it in 'both individual and communal memory'.[40] It can also bring out the 'playful quality of law', reinforce allegiance, through 'physical participation, communal involvement' or the engagement of the senses by argument or ritual', or subvert the law (e.g. through misrepresentation).[41] This performative lens enables a fuller understanding of the functioning of international criminal justice as a field.

6.4 Strengths, Weaknesses, and Uncertainties

Expressivism is not a classical justification of justice or punishment on its own.[42] This justification depends on views on the value of criminal law as such, for example, whether it is seen as a punitive project (geared at providing justified punishment), an accountability project (aimed at promoting answerability and due process), or as an instrument of crime control and prevention. Expressivism is rather a means to explain how justice is produced and to ground diverse punishment rationales (e.g. retribution, deterrence, restorative justice).

One of the strengths of expressivism is that it is able to explain the strong turn towards norm expression in international criminal justice. Norm expression has enjoyed a prominent space in regulation and adjudication because it connects law to morals and ethics. It is not only reactive (i.e. a reactive attitude of society to the violation of norms or values) but transformational. It actively produces communities and constituencies through norm affirmation, norm projection, and norm

[38] See **section 4.3**.

[39] See **section 3.1**.

[40] See Bernard Hibbitts, 'De-scribing Law: Performance in the Constitution of Legality', Conference Paper, March 1996, at https://www.law.pitt.edu/archive/hibbitts/describ.htm.

[41] Ibid.

[42] See also James Edwards, 'Theories of Criminal Law', *The Stanford Encyclopedia of Philosophy* (Stanford: Stanford University, Fall 2018 Edition), sub. 3 (Justifications of Criminal Law).

internalization. Adjudication and regulatory processes involve narrative techniques and storytelling. They give meaning to the past, order facts and events in a sequence, identify historical marking points, arrange reasoning around sequences, and create plots.[43]

Expressivist theories shed a new light on the role and functioning of international criminal institutions. Institutions are not only functional entities with circumscribed mandates (e.g. investigation, adjudication, punishment, repair of harm), they are carriers of meaning. Sometimes the very establishment of the institution itself (i.e., the medium) is a message. Institutional practices involve performances and enactments. International criminal institutions use multiple types of speech acts to implement their objectives, demonstrate their effects, and justify their value and existence to constituencies and public audiences.[44] Enforcement may be 'induced by virtue of the performance of legal interpretation' rather than authority or binding legal force alone.[45]

Expressivism helps to understand the symbolic and performative dimensions of criminal procedures, including aesthetic and theatric features. International criminal proceedings rely on messaging and performance in order to reinforce certain virtues or ideas, such as the triumph of order over chaos, the solemn and binding nature of law, equality of individuals before the law, the necessity of impartiality and fairness in the delivery of justice, the need for agency and empowerment of victims, or the gradual rehumanization of perpetrators.[46] Legal actions, such as the interpretation, application, and enforcement of international criminal justice are shaped by roles that agents are expected to play by virtue of their mandates, affiliations, or professional responsibilities. This is not necessarily something bad. Proceedings themselves gain value through demonstration, performance, and repetition. Communication and persuasion are essential in this process. They may promote affective bonds and encourage compliance, even in cases of disagreement.

Dilemmas of punishment appear in a new light. Expressivism is a means to rethink the punitive dimensions of punishment. It is able to explain that punishment is often more a retributive gesture in international criminal justice, that is, a message with a signalling effect beyond the perpetrator, rather than a reflection of the evil of the crime. It accepts that accountability itself is a form of punishment. It is related to the publicity of condemnation, the impact of criminal proceedings on the civic status of offender, answerability towards victims, as well as prevention and encouragement of civil courage. This approach liberates international criminal

[43] See Hayden White, 'The Question of Narrative in Contemporary Historical Theory' (1984) 23 *History and Theory* 26–57.

[44] See **section 3.2**. The way in which crimes or modes of liability are articulated and performed through expressive processes may alter their originally intended meaning or produce new social meanings.

[45] Allen, 'Theater of International Justice' 149.

[46] See **section 4.2**.

justice from the dilemma of 'harsh punishment'. The public performance of trial and punishment is deemed to provide satisfaction to victims and the international community and to contribute to the prevention of future crimes.[47] Reparations send messages about agency, recognition, and repair. They involve education and memorialization. They are often 'mnemonic', aimed at preserving memory, and transformational.[48]

6.4.1 The macro idea: Justice as message

As a justice concept, expressivism has most synergies with procedural or discursive theories of justice[49] which suggest that justice may occur through communicative relationships, recognition of agency, participation in accountability processes, or social learning.

One of the novel contributions of expressivist theory is its emphasis on the value of justice as message. The idea of 'justice as message' suggests that there is merit in the establishment of a communicative relation between 'sender' and 'audience', the process of listening and answering, and the creation of a new deliberative space for engagement with criminality. Justice does not necessarily occur through legal decision-making or through some type closure found through proceedings at the end of trial but rather through the discursive structures created. It involves not only 'speaking rights to power'.[50] It can lie in the acknowledgment of formulation of specific narratives (e.g. through clarification of facts), the establishment of a common vocabulary for violations, the creation of accountability through speech relations (i.e. answerability to judges, victims), and the need to listen to the arguments of others, or the opening of a broader discursive space for continuing deliberation, engagement with violations, or the formulation of new behavioural norms or preventive strategies.

The idea of justice as message is able to acknowledge that justice is not absolute but intersubjective. It accommodates some of the paradoxes of international criminal justice. It recognizes that justice is an open-ended[51] and contested project since it involves different experiences. It implies that justice can emerge despite continuing contestation or societal disagreement. It removes international criminal justice from immediate enforcement pressures. It is able to ascribe meaning to justice procedures and rulings, even if they are not complied with domestically.

[47] See **section 5.1.2.**

[48] See **section 5.2.2.**

[49] See **section 4.4.**

[50] Alison Brysk, *Speaking Rights to Power—Constructing Political Will* (Oxford: Oxford University Press, 2013).

[51] Jacques Derrida, 'Force of Law: The Mystical Foundation of Authority' in Jacques Derrida, *Acts of Religion* (ed., Gil Anidjar) (New York, NY: Routledge, 2002), 230–98, 256–57.

It may mitigate problems of remoteness and selectivity by relying on the value of communication as a 'pathway' towards accountability'.[52] For instance, the fact of seeing justice performed internationally may serve as a form of satisfaction for victims, even if it is selective, since it sends a message to domestic constituencies. It may provide inspiration for domestic systems, strengthen accountability networks, promote civil courage, or affect a larger pool of cases beyond the limited number of proceedings before international courts.

The message bears synergies with Paul Celan's famous allegory of the poem as 'message in a bottle'. It is 'sent out in the—not always greatly hopeful—belief that somewhere and sometime it could wash up on land, on heartland'.[53] It becomes only fully known with time. It is addressed to recipients who may not be known by the sender. It requires deciphering, listening and reading and cannot be fully controlled by the speaker.

It contains certain recurring normative aspirations: (i) giving a voice to atrocity, rather than keeping silence; (ii) making violations speakable, rather than treating them as incomprehensible; (iii) reducing distance to crime, exposing experiential alterity, and promoting answerability of defendants; (iv) providing agency and redress to 'victims'; (v) fostering empathy, civic engagement, and moral imagination rather than disengagement; (vi) promoting remembrance, rather than forgetting; and (vii) and preventing repetition.[54]

6.4.2 The idea in practice

In practice, there are 'good' and 'bad' examples of messaging.[55] Generally, international criminal justice has been stronger as a project of normative expression and affirmation of beliefs in retributive justice than as a distributive or restorative project.

International criminal law has provided new ways to express crimes and criminality and make atrocities speakable. It has generated a whole list of new crime labels to stigmatize conduct and express harm, ranging from genocide or more distinct articulations of sexual and gender-based violence to the reconceptualization of typologies of conflict more generally. Normative expression has included different stages: norm enunciation, norm declaration, norm proscription, and norm

[52] Francesca Lessa, Tricia D. Olsen, Leigh A. Payne, Gabriel Pereira, and Andrew G. Reiter, 'Overcoming Impunity: Pathways to Accountability in Latin America' (2014) 8 *International Journal of Transitional Justice* 75–98.

[53] John Felstiner, *Paul Celan: Poet, Survivor, Jew* (New Haven, CT: Yale University Press, 1995), 115.

[54] Fuyuki Kurasawa, 'A Message in a Bottle: Bearing Witness as a Mode of Transnational Practice' (2009) 26 *Theory, Culture & Society* 92–111, 95.

[55] Some types of institutional, procedural, or remedial expressions may produce injustice. See generally Gabrielle Lynch, *Performances of Justice: The Politics of Truth, Justice and Reconciliation* (Cambridge: Cambridge University Press, 2018), 57–90.

enforcement. This normative expression creates novel conversations about the law in the public space and the import of a system that values international criminal justice. It gives practitioners a sense of purpose and comfort.

In some areas, expressivism has untapped potential. A prime example is environmental protection. International criminal justice treats environmental damage as a war crime, but sets a very highly threshold ('widespread, long term, and severe damage to the natural environment').[56] The International Law Commission (ILC) has recently suggested a Martens Clause in relation to the environment. It states: 'In cases not covered by international agreements, the environment remains under the protection and authority of the principles of international law derived from established custom, from the principles of humanity and from the dictates of public conscience.'[57] Such a clause could be an entry point for enhancing environmental protection during armed conflict in the future.

Global warming and climate change raise novel questions in relation to the notion of crime against humanity. The causes of climate change are often difficult to fit within the requirements of international criminal law.[58] However, certain types of displacement caused by climate might in the future be associated with the notion of crimes against humanity because of their consequences, such as mass displacement and food shortages.

The role of international criminal justice as a project of distributive justice is more limited. Many institutions have remained weak and dependent on state power. There are ongoing divides over the feasibility of international criminal justice in times of ongoing conflict, its elitist and self-referential nature (e.g. its detachment from local society, its closed professional culture), its production of normative and epistemic hierarchies, and its unequal effects. Key political actors remain reluctant to accept the authority of international justice institutions or continue to contest the idea of a *jus puniendi*. Others pay lip service to the rationales of international criminal justice while refusing to apply them if their own interests are at stake. The idea of expressing equality before the law through procedures is a powerful ambition. However, it is more symbolic than real due to the selectivity of international criminal justice which is distributive in the sense that it allocates blame to some individuals, while indirectly absolving others (e.g. collectivities). Selectivity may create unjust distributive effects. For instance, symbolic reparations may send ambiguous messages in relation to the recognition of victimhood.

[56] ICC Statute, Art. 8 (2) (b) (iv). The only recent environmental destruction which has been considered to meet this high threshold was burning of Kuwaiti oil fields by Iraqi forces during the 1991 Gulf War.

[57] See ILC, Protection of the environment in relation to armed conflicts, UN Doc. A/CN.4/L.937, 6 June 2019, Draft principle 12 (Martens Clause with respect to the protection of the environment in relation to armed conflict).

[58] See also Geoff Gilbert, 'International Criminal Law Is Not a Panacea—Why Proposed Climate Change Crimes Are Just Another Passenger on an Overcrowded Bandwagon' (2014) 14 *International Criminal Law Review* 551–87.

International criminal proceedings have gradually taken on more restorative elements with the rise of victim participation and reparation. However, international criminal justice has been more concerned with messaging to global constituencies, rather than communication with offenders or victims. Person-related forms of expressivism have remained at the periphery of the legal process (e.g. outreach, legacy, sentencing, reparation).[59] Two-way communications are the exception. Victims' rights are path-dependent on the scope of the Prosecution case. Victimhood itself is viewed through narrow accountability lenses or collective interests rather than individualized relationships. Reparations are powerful in their symbolic meaning, reparative gestures (e.g. satisfaction), or collective significance, but limited in their ability to remedy individual harm, provide restitution or compensation, or alter structural inequalities.[60]

The emphasis on symbolism and global expression limits societal relevance. For instance, institutions, such as the Nuremberg Military tribunal or the Special Tribunal for Lebanon (STL) left a more powerful legal rather than societal legacy. They are, to certain extent, echo chambers.

6.4.3 Limitations

There is still some degree of 'judicial romanticism' which imagines that 'major problems' can be solved 'by creating courts'.[61] Hardly any international criminal institutions have managed to realize proclaimed meta-objectives in the immediate or short term. Even relatively successful institutions, such as the International Criminal Tribunal for the former Yugoslavia (ICTY), have failed to mitigate divides in affected societies, during their time of existence, or in the immediate aftermath.

Many of the social-psychological assumptions that underlie expressivist thought require further investigation. It is not proven to what extent processes of stigmatization through international criminal justice enhance community formation or social solidarity. As noted in scholarship, 'the operation of stigma presupposes a somewhat unitary social sphere, one in which a particular "conscience collective" manifests itself to stigmatize certain crimes'.[62] Such conditions may exist in domestic societies, which share a common culture or tradition of shame and punishment, based on liberal conceptions of justice (e.g. individual guilt). However, the idea that Western liberal punishment reflects a collective conscience is more difficult to establish in relation to international society or cultures with broader conceptions of accountability.

[59] See **section 3.2.**

[60] See **section 5.2.3.**

[61] W. Michael Reisman, 'Institutions and Practices for Restoring and Maintaining Public Order' (1995) 6 *Duke Journal of Comparative and International Law*, 175–86, 175.

[62] Mégret, 'Practices of Stigmatization' 310–11.

Educational or didactic ambitions of trials face challenges, both empirically and as a matter of principle, and should not be overstated. Cognitive dissonance may impede openness to messages. There is a risk that expressivist practices reach and persuade only those audiences who already believe in the cause.[63] Scientists remain divided as to what extent international justice procedures have therapeutic effects on witnesses and victims. Existing studies seem to suggest that participation in proceedings may have positive effects.[64] However, they may also trigger retraumatization or disappointment or disillusion, such as in cases of acquittals or low sentences.

The focus on speech and action may have unintended negative effects. Expressivism can contribute to a certain hegemonization of international justice discourse through its speech acts and its silences. Crucial factors, such as the meaning and impact of silence, are not sufficiently studied or understood in institutional practices. Language philosophers have stressed that the active choice of words contains messages about words not spoken. For instance, Hans-Georg Gadamer has argued in *Truth and Method* that 'every word, as the event of a moment, carries with it the unsaid, to which it is related by responding and summoning'.[65] The 'unwritten' may speak as much as the written word.[66] Sociologist Boaventura de Sousa Santos has developed a 'sociology of absences'. He argued that social processes might actively create silences and render phenomena invisible.[67] This may also apply to international criminal practices. As Gerry Simpson has observed, international criminal trials can be conceived as 'law's official or semi-official monuments'.[68] Their absence can have negative signalling effects. The lack of prosecution may suggest that certain crimes may not be important enough to be stigmatized or remembered. However, even positive institutional action may create silences. For instance, the investigation and prosecution of specific forms of crimes or criminality may disnarrate other crimes. The focus on spectacular events or perpetrators may marginalize others, make them less visible, or render them 'non-existent'.[69]

63 See Stuart Ford, 'A Social Psychology Model of the Perceived Legitimacy of International Criminal Courts: Implications for the Success of Transitional Justice Mechanisms' (2012) 45 *Vanderbilt Journal of Transnational Law* 405–76, 409–11, 418–56; Dwight Conquergood, 'Performance theory, Hmong shamans, and cultural politics' in Janelleke G. Reinelt and Joseph R. Roach (eds) *Critical Theory and Performance* (Ann Arbor, MI: University of Michigan Press, 2007) 482–505.

64 See **section 4.3.5**.

65 Hans-Georg Gadamer, *Truth and Method* (London: Continuum, 2004) 454.

66 Christopher J. Knight, *Omissions are Not Accidents: Modern Apophaticism from Henry James to Jacques Derrida* (Toronto: University of Toronto Press, 2010), 5–6.

67 Boaventura de Sousa Santos, 'Nuestra America: Reinventing a Subaltern Paradigm of Recognition and Redistribution' (2001) 18 *Theory Culture Society* 185–217.

68 See Gerry Simpson, 'Unprecedents' in Immi Tallgren and Thomas Skouteris (eds), *New Histories of International Criminal Law: Retrials* (Oxford: Oxford University Press, 2019), 12–29, 24.

69 Ibid., 24 ('just as monuments un-remember acts of history, trials sometimes erase those "crimes" not juridified').

6.5 Contestations

The question to what extent justice processes should rely on messaging and performance to justify their *raison d'être*, induce normative change, or demonstrate certain effects remains contested.

Judicial entities send multiple messages, consciously or unconsciously. Their actions are part of a broad network of communicative relations, which include parties and participants to proceedings, judicial networks, as well as professional and epistemic communities. However, they prefer to be seen as juridical agents rather than as meaning messengers, or to be associated with very specific expressivist effects such as effectiveness or fairness. The idea that law is performed through judicial speech acts challenges traditional positivist understandings of law, the idea of courts as rational and apolitical actors, and assumptions about the objectivity and expertise of judges. Traditional judicial voices claim that courts should focus on the application of the law, rather than societal expectations, and stick to do what they are best at interpreting norms, balancing rights, adjudicating legal claims, and pronouncing judgments to parties and participants. The idea that judicial acts involve broader legal messaging or inherent political messages creates discomfort.[70]

Expressivist rationales are more accepted in relation to the role of Prosecution.[71] Prosecutors have judicial and non-judicial functions. They rely even more than judges on messaging in order to fulfil their diverse mandates.[72] The degree to which procedural expression is accepted differs according to legal traditions. Adversarial traditions view the Courtroom as arena for competing cases. They are more inclined to accept the use of messages and performative features by parties (e.g. Prosecution, Defence) as an integral part of proceedings, since parties are in control of the case. The Defence can mount counter-performances and rely on practices of self-representation. Inquisitorial systems place more emphasis on judge-led proceedings and the search for an objective truth guided by the judge and the role of parties as agents of justice. Courtroom performances may be seen as a distraction from the goals of the judicial process.

Prosecutors rely on messaging throughout the different stages of cases: analysis and atrocity alert, investigation, prosecution, and enforcement. They use expressivist practices in order to make most of the Prosecution's limited resources, maximize the impact of cases, gather empathy, mobilize cooperation, and shape future conduct. Fact-finding processes and investigations are not only internal working processes but meant to persuade other justice actors to take actions.[73] ICC

[70] See **section 1.2.4**.

[71] Nirej Sekhon, 'The Pedagogical Prosecutor' (2014) 44 *Seton Hall Law Review* 1–46, 33–4.

[72] See section 4.3.1.

[73] For instance, UN fact-finding commissions and investigative bodies, such as IIIM or Commission for International Justice and Accountability (CIJA) prepare materials, statements, or even case files, in order to mobilize national jurisdictions or other international entities to pursue accountability.

preliminary examinations have been expressly associated with complementarity rationales.[74] Charges are inherently expressivist in nature. They respond to the acts of defendants and messages of crimes, translate them into legal categories, establish narratives and portray the role of actors, and shape public consciousness and opinion.

The exercise of these functions involves diverse manifestations of power,[75] including the power to shape the ability of others to act and power over other actors.[76] Expressivist practice affects subjectivities and self-understandings. Representational and institutional practices map social phenomena as sites of atrocity, crime, or accountability. They give them a distinct 'international' identity and bring them within the realm of law. They are no longer 'ordinary' or 'local' matters but issues of international or global concern. They determine 'what harms are "appreciable" in the international sphere', and 'how people's suffering comes to matter'.[77] This mapping or demarcation of space involves productive power. It transforms meaning and creates struggles over exclusion and inclusion, the appropriate shape and the limits of law (e.g. legalism), or the instrumentalization of empathy.

Expressive language or affective imagery may produce false senses of universality, reduce complexities, marginalize alternative readings, or produce artificial binaries (e.g. victim/perpetrator divides, friends and enemies, winners and losers,), etc.[78] Expressivism is often more a one-sided process; a demonstration or performance 'to' others, rather than a discursive form of interaction 'with' others, based on dialogue and two-sided communication. This is reflected in norm projection,[79] institutional set-up,[80] procedural practices,[81] or repair of harm.[82]

It faces objections and contestations by those subjected to that power, including states, defendants or victims. The very idea of treating criminal trials as a means to form community relations contrasts with the idea of treating defendants are 'subjects' rather than 'objects' of justice. It makes proceedings similar to a public ritual (trial-as-sacrifice) in which a 'symbolically sacrificed outlaw' is investigated and prosecuted to build community relations.[83] Defendants have portrayed

[74] See **section 3.2**.

[75] Mégret, 'Practices of Stigmatization' 317–18 (International criminal justice 'has the power not only to convict a few distinct individuals but to stigmatize entire types of deviancy and, in the process, to help constitute a "normal" international society.')

[76] On this distinction, see Michael Barnett and Raymond Duvall, 'Power in International Politics' (2005) 59 *International Organization* 39–75, 43.,

[77] McMillan, 'Imagining the International' 175.

[78] See Sara Kendall, 'Critical orientations: A critique of international criminal court practice' in Christine Schwöbel-Patel (ed.), *Critical Approaches to International Criminal Law: An Introduction* (2014) 54–70, 56.

[79] See **section 2.2.3**.

[80] See **sections 3.1 and 3.2**.

[81] See **section 4.4**.

[82] See **section 5.2.2**.

[83] Alison Young, *Imagining Crime: Textual Outlaws and Criminal Conversations* (London: Sage Publications, 1996), 11.

themselves as scapegoats of the evil of entire populations. Objectives, such as 'reconciling effects, norm-dissemination and truth-telling cannot succeed', if the process is not perceived as legitimate.[84]

6.6 Implications

The fact that expressivism is subject to critique and contestation does not negate its virtue. Dispute and disagreement are inherent in international criminal justice as field. They are not necessarily deconstructive but can facilitate development over time or have a 'unifying' potential that builds a field.[85] However, there is need for critical self-inquiry.

International criminal institutions and non-governmental organizations (NGOs) have built an entire institutional machinery and vocabulary to stigmatize evil. It is important to reflect critically as to what messages international criminal justice is sending and what type of norm affirmation or justice is produced through communication. Much emphasis is placed on the forms or objects of international criminal justice. The context is often left aside. The receiving end of communications needs further attention. It should not be assumed that international criminal justice is built on shared assumptions (e.g. community notions, non-derogable norms, 'fight against impunity', liberal justice ideals). Such features emerge through processes of communication.[86] Some of the language or procedures evoke social or cultural biases that make international criminal justice suspect in the eyes of those that are subjected to it.

6.6.1 Embracing complexity

The conception of international criminal law as expressivist project entails a call to embrace complexity. Expressivism is able to recognize that justice is not built on a single truth but on several truths.[87] The idea of justice as message acknowledges that justice occurs in speech relations. It contains messaging and communication with the offender, victims, and other constituencies. The emphasis on intersubjective relations is able to take into account the complexity of justice procedures. It helps to explain the value of international criminal justice as a project, not through

[84] Tim Meijers and Marlies Glasius, 'Expression of Justice or Political Trial? Discursive Battles in the Karadžić Case (2013) 35 *Human Rights Quarterly* 720–52, 751.

[85] Monica Hakimi, 'Constructing an International Community' (2017) 111 *AJIL* 317–56, 319.

[86] Jared Wessel, 'International Law as Language—Towards a Neo New Haven School' (2010) 23 *International Journal of the Semiotics of Law* 123–44, 142–3.

[87] See **section 4.2.1.4.**

its assumed unity but through its plurality and differing voices. It can defend the project, even though it may be perceived differently by different agents.

6.6.2 Acknowledging imperfection

The idea of justice as message is able to acknowledge some of the weaknesses of international criminal justice. International criminal justice is a form of 'experimental justice'.[88] Existing justice theories are imperfect. Some voices doubt whether human structures are able to realize the idea of justice. Expressivism has a more modest point of departure. Viewing justice as message recognizes that international criminal justice is fundamentally about expressing justice. It is strongly mediated. It requires public articulation, persuasion, and performance in order to reach its objectives. For instance, a criminal trial does not necessarily provide retribution per se but expresses it. It does not realize fairness in an absolute sense. It rather demonstrates and expresses fairness towards different agents. It is not a distributive project per se. It communicates messages about choices and allocation of resources. It is not restorative as such but expresses messages about empowerment and agency. Trials do not per se help 'to avert future atrocities', but they may send signals that allow moving 'in this direction'.[89] The extent to which these speech acts, signals, or performances are seen or interpreted as justice depends on the context and the respective audience.

The process of creating justice extends far beyond the courtroom, both in space and time. As Gabrielle Lynch has noted, 'even a powerful performance [of justice] that engages a wide audience and which helps to reframe people's perceptions of institutions, processes and/or actors, will require ongoing evidence of transition and transformation through supportive performances and substantive change to sustain and build the semblance of legitimacy and credibility required'.[90]

6.6.3 Maintaining aspiration while resisting romanticization

The goals and ambitions of international criminal justice can and should be aspirational. Aspiration motivates normative, institutional, procedural, or remedial expression. It is necessary to promote social change.

[88] Jean-Marie Kamatali, 'The Challenge of Linking International Criminal Justice and National Reconciliation: The Case of the ICTR (2003) 16 *LJIL* 116–33.

[89] Saira Mohamed, 'Deviance, Aspiration, and the Stories We Tell: Reconciling Mass Atrocity and the Criminal Law' (2015) 124 *Yale Law Journal* 1628–89, 1680.

[90] Lynch, *Performances of Injustice* 21.

International criminal justice is more than a tool to condemn atrocities or to demonstrate deviance from legal norms and standards. It is 'an opportunity for understanding how individuals choose to perpetrate unspeakable crimes, articulating how we hope people will behave in the most demanding of circumstances, and shaping our beliefs about the way we ought to behave'.[91] It signals not only what individuals should not do but portrays how individuals should ideally behave. The success of international criminal justice cannot only be shown through action but through 'what does not happen'.[92]

International crimes are often justified by moral, utilitarian, or ideological justifications, such as the intent to protect certain communitarian or group interests or to maintain order and security. International criminal justice seeks to discard such justifications, by falsifying narratives, highlighting competing or superior interests, or projecting an alternative morality or way of behaviour.

Aspiration involves the need to pursue cases that are risky or may carry chances of failure. For instance, problems of enforcement do not detract from the duty to investigate or prosecute. There may be value in initiating investigations or proceedings against high-level officials, even in case of evidentiary limitations or limited chances of cooperation or compliance.

Aspiration in itself demonstrates virtue. It expresses institutional commitment to equality before the law or the attempt to promote conditions which facilitate the exercise of justice. This is part of the expressivist function. Prosecutors and courts and courts do not only need to decide where, when, and whom they investigate or prosecute, but also what message they send through such choices. Selection choices convey priorities. As Jonathan Hafetz has noted:

> [I]nternational criminal tribunals should seek to express the principle that no individual is above the law—both across and within situations—through their decisions to investigate and, where the evidence supports it, to prosecute. Even modest steps in this direction could contribute to an alternative narrative ... and help counter the perception that international criminal justice merely tracks the preferences of the strong and their supporters.[93]

However, it is necessary to strike a balance between practicality and aspiration. Aspirations should not be grounded in naive idealism.[94] International criminal

[91] Mohamed, 'Deviance, Aspiration, and the Stories We Tell' 1628.

[92] Payam Akhavan, 'The Rise, and Fall, and Rise, of International Criminal Justice, (2013) 11 *JICJ* 527–36, 531 ('The need for international tribunals is itself a failure ... Our ultimate aspiration should be a world in which the ICC remains idle for lack of cases.').

[93] Jonathan Hafetz, *Punishing Atrocities through a Fair Trial: International Criminal Law from Nuremberg to the Age of Global Terrorism* (Cambridge: Cambridge University Press, 2018), 156.

[94] Christian Tomuschat, *Human Rights: Between Idealism and Realism* (Oxford: Oxford University Press, 2014), 9–10.

justice has been complicit in framing wrong expectations about its own reach. High-flying discourses on ending impunity, outlawing evil, incapacitating political leaders, or providing catharsis for victims produce simplistic or false messages. They overinflate the power of justice. This is counterproductive since it creates inflated expectations and may undermine the expressivist potential of international criminal justice.

Legal concepts, such as crimes and modes of responsibility, which are used to express wrongdoing and punishment, need to be seen in context. As Payam Akhavan has noted, judicial romanticism about the ability of law to 'order' evil needs to reconciled with context-sensitive realism.[95]

Constructions of crimes and notions of responsibility must be framed in a realistic way which captures the reality of the context in which they apply. Structures enabling crimes, such as hierarchies, forms of organization and control, or group dynamics differ across entities. Many of the assumptions underpinning state-orchestrated crime or classical military structures, which shaped the emergence of international criminal law, cannot be automatically transposed to more decentralized or loosely organized armed groups or private actors. The legal framework concerning responsibility of non-state actors needs to be adjusted to distinct operating contexts. Perpetrators cannot be expected to be heroes. Models of liability should not overstretch the role of individuals in collective structures.

Negative or unintended side effects of stigmatization should be taken into account in institutional practices. Effects differ across audiences. For instance, the outlawing of perpetrators at the international level may strengthen their political weight domestically in the short-term. Trials may contribute to heroization of defendants. Timing is a key factor for the success of expressivist practices. Many long-term effects emerge through local processes and discourses rather than global norm production.

Procedural standards of proof must stay realistic. The search for perfection may be an enemy of the good. For instance, it cannot be expected that each incident or crime underpinning the contextual elements of international crimes should be proved individually. There is a need to see the forest for the trees. A narrative emerges through patterns and the interaction of different actions. A purely atomistic assessment of evidence, in which the value of each piece of evidence is assessed, is artificial. Evidence assessment requires a combination of individual and holistic assessments.[96]

95 Payam Akhavan, 'Are International Criminal Tribunals a Disincentive to Peace?: Reconciling Judicial Romanticism with Political Realism' (2009) 31 *Human Rights Quarterly* 624–54, 629 ('Just as the judicial romantics are not realistic about the limits of ritualistic ordering of overwhelming evil through criminal trials, the political realists often romanticize the profane rules of political conflict as inexorable outbursts of tribal hatred.').

96 See Yvonne McDermott, 'Strengthening the Evaluation of Evidence in International Criminal Trials' (2017) 17 *International Criminal Law Review* 682–702.

6.6.4 Do no harm: Minimizing cognitive bias, demonization, and orientalization

Many of the discourses and narratives of international criminal justice are guided by moral ambition, repetition, and replication, and the goal to leave a record that transcends the individual case. This type of agency creates certain motivational and behavioural biases.

Prosecutors and judges derive legitimacy from their autonomy and impartiality. However, the strong educational and punitive ambitions of the field, its heavy moral baggage and high societal expectations regarding moral agency, and the reproduction of images of violence and disorder make international criminal justice agents prone to numerous types of blind spots and biases that affect their speech acts and their preferences and beliefs.

Formally, international criminal justice is based on the presumption of innocence. However, in practice there is sometimes more a presumption of guilt,[97] or least a motivational bias to investigate and prosecute based on previous external information about the context or structure of crimes (e.g. reports by UN bodies, fact-finding missions, investigative commissions, or NGOs).

In the media, defendants are branded as 'war criminals' before conviction. The very establishment of an institution is taken as an affirmation of its own value. Creation and legal mandate are influenced by certain political macro goals, including extra-legal considerations. States and NGOs tend to view international criminal justice as an extension of the idea of creating peace and securing international human rights. No tribunal has questioned its own existence, even in the absence of real cases. Institutional practices or decisions are 'anchored' in the groundwork laid by other courts and tribunals.[98]

The principle of legality has been interpreted in a relaxed fashion.[99] The naissance of the field and the idea of taking the law out of the books have been driving factors in regulation and adjudication. States rarely reflect how changes in legal rules, attempts to expedite proceedings, or budget cuts impact the ability of the Defence. These conditions create risks of inattentional blindness or biases, such as the tendency to listen to or treat information in a way that supports existing preconceptions and to ignore readings that contradict them. This may affect assumptions about context, cause, and effect, evidentiary assessments, interpretation, or sentencing.

97 Moa Lidén, Minna Gräns, and Peter Juslin, 'The Presumption of Guilt in Suspect Interrogations: Apprehension as a Trigger of Confirmation Bias and Debiasing Techniques' (2018) 42 *Law and Human Behavior* 336–54.

98 On 'anchoring' in the domestic context, see Mark W. Bennett, 'Confronting Cognitive "Anchoring Effect" and "Blind Spot" Biases in Federal Sentencing: a Modest Solution for Reforming a Fundamental Flaw' (2014) 104 *Journal of Criminal Law & Criminology* 489–534.

99 See section 2.2.

Prosecutors are open to confirmation bias,[100] that is the 'seeking or interpreting of evidence in ways that are partial to existing beliefs, expectations, or a hypothesis in hand'.[101] External entities have their own vested interests in sharing information. For instance, state referrals in the ICC may be motivated by unstated intentions to get rid of prior military or political opponents. Public arrest and transfer of defendants, surrounded by broad media coverage, may influence the perception of crimes and suspects. It is essential to develop debiasing techniques which minimize the effect of potential confirmation bias on decision-making processes. This includes critical analysis of narratives, openness to diverse viewpoints, and perspective-taking, that is, the consciousness of the perspective of others. For instance, investigations must be crime-driven, rather than suspect-driven. Analysts and investigators need to 'remain aware of the interests and perspectives of the various agencies and to counter their influence by cultivating multiple information sources and always seek to corroborate all available information'.[102]

The investigation may primarily generate evidence that confirms guilt-confirming evidence if Prosecutors do not have a duty to look for exculpatory evidence. Evidence gathering must be subject to peer review and testing.

Judges have to counter unconscious conviction bias. As Justice Albie Sachs, former judge of the South African Constitutional Court, has observed, judging cannot 'properly be characterized as simply the application of pure reason to legal problems nor, at the other extreme, as the application of the personal will or passion of the judge'.[103] Rather, there is 'a complex interplay of forces—rational and emotional, conscious and unconscious—by which no judge [can] remain unaffected'.[104]

In international criminal justice, judges do not win a price for strict construction. There is the temptation to write history through judgments, or to portray the case in the line of a longer trajectory of criminality. Judgments have an 'anchoring' effect on subsequent decisions. Some doctrines, such as Joint Criminal Enterprise (JCE) III come close to 'guilt by association'.[105]

The publicity of pre-trial proceedings creates pressures to send a case to trial. Decisions on interim release pending trial have long been governed by a belief that detention is the rule, and liberty the exception.[106] Evidence assessment

[100] See Moa Lidén, Minna Gräns, and Peter Juslin, 'From Devil's Advocate to Crime Fighter: Confirmation Bias and Debiasing Techniques in Prosecutorial Decision-Making' (2019) 25 *Psychology, Crime & Law* 494–526.

[101] Raymond S. Nickerson, 'Confirmation Bias: A Ubiquitous Phenomenon in Many Guises' (1998) 2 *Review of General Psychology* 175–220.

[102] See Hiroto Fujiwara and Stephan Parmentier, 'Investigations' in Reydams, Wouters, and Ryngaert (eds), *International Prosecutors* 572–603, 582.

[103] Albie Sachs, *The Strange Alchemy of Life and Law* (New York, NY: Oxford University Press), 114.

[104] Ibid.

[105] Marston Danner and Jenny S. Martinez, 'Guilty Associations: Joint Criminal Enterprise, Command Responsibility, and the Development of International Criminal Law' (2005) 93 *California Law Review* 75–169.

[106] See Megan A. Fairlie, 'The Precedent of Pretrial Release at the ICTY: A Road Better Left Less Traveled' (2011) 33 *Fordham Journal of International Law* 1101–77.

is influenced by story construction, which weaves the evidence into a narrative. Sentencing motivations, which justify punishment, are partly by driven expressivist reasoning. Sentencing discretion is shaped by previous sentencing ranges. The risk of confirmation bias is often discarded by reference to the professional nature of judges. However, such biases are deeply ingrained in human behaviour and cognitive processes (e.g. memory). Minimizing them requires greater awareness and recognition that bias exists.

Stereotypes need to be unpacked. For instance, it is unhelpful to address atrocity crime through the denial of the humanity of the perpetrators or their demonization.[107] The defendant should not be a 'scapegoat' to showcase justice. Punishment should not be based on the 'typicality of the offender or the offense' but rather on the 'exercise of choice and judgment'.[108]

Storytelling practices must be aware of the risks of alienation. Situation and case narratives are presented as service to victims, formerly warring parties or the broader public. However, they have a darker side. They portray entire societies and countries as sites of conflict. The performative and aesthetic features of trial create a novel script which contrasts with lived experiences. Trials encourage witnesses and victims to frame their statements around a set of facts. As Alexander Hinton has cautioned, the ambition to deliver justice for the sake of order (e.g. good governance, rule of law) may not only create aspirations but a 'justice facade', which glosses over alternative histories, discards non-Western visions of justice, and diverts 'the attention from geopolitical interest, domestic manipulations, and structural violence'.[109] Greater attention needs to be paid to 'to what is masked' by the 'facade'.[110]

6.6.5 Revisiting language

The way in which language is used requires more attention. Legal discourse has struggled to engage with social concepts, such as gender, culture, ethnicity, or race, although they are part of the definition of crimes.

Notions such as race or destruction in the context of genocide have initially been understood in a biological/physical sense rather than as social constructs. Such readings pose difficulties. For instance, race is an outdated concept and scientifically disputed. It is contested whether race is a legitimate criterion of distinguishing

[107] Alexander Hinton, *Man or Monster? The Trial of a Khmer Rouge torturer* (Durham, NC: Duke University Press, 2017).
[108] Mohamed, 'Deviance, Aspiration, and the Stories We Tell' 1637.
[109] Alexander Hinton, *The Justice Facade: Trials of Transition in Cambodia* (Oxford: Oxford University Press, 2018) 7.
[110] Ibid., 23.

human species.[111] As the ICTY noted in *Krstić*, 'to attempt to differentiate each of the named groups on the basis of scientifically objective criteria' would be 'inconsistent with the object and purpose of the [Genocide] Convention'.[112]

The use of the concept of race has caused discomfort in modern practice.[113] Such notions require an evolutionary interpretation in order to avoid historical traps or biases. They have been given contemporary meaning by taking into account perceptions by perpetrators and victims, or reading them in the context of society.[114]

The 'gender' definition in the ICC Statute has been controversial since its adoption.[115] It is subject to critique since it relates gender to the 'two sexes, male and female'. This sex-based definition fails to capture gender-based identities that deviate from prescribed gender roles. It has been discussed in the context of the ILC Draft Articles on crimes against humanity. Governments and civil society criticized *inter alia* the binary vision of gender,[116] its 'opaque' and 'outdated' nature, and its deviation from 'more inclusive and more gender-sensitive definitions of 'gender'.[117] It was removed from the draft articles in 2019.[118]

Other terms should be dropped from the vocabulary or modified since they oversimplify or entrench stereotypes. For instance, the notion of 'managing expectations' is misguided. It portrays an overinflated sense of managerialism. It seems to imply that legal agents can control societal attitudes. Legal formalists question to what extent international criminal law should be driven by outside expectations. Where relevant, international criminal law should aspire to meet expectations rather than trying to manage them.

The concept of 'capacity-building' is taken from development discourse. It has a patronizing quality. It frames justice as an instrument of saviour and emancipation. It suggests that others lack agency and ability. Capacity is presented as something that can be passed on through education, cooperation, and social learning—like a good. The term hides the fact that capacity-building may have disempowering effects or create novel dependencies.

The use of the notion of 'victim' deserves caution. The term is often used in a generic way as if there was a unified or homogenous type of victimhood. If used in

[111] Sharona Hoffman, 'Is There a Place for Race as a Legal Concept?' (2004) 36 *Arizona State Law Journal* 1098–159.

[112] *Krstić* Trial Judgment, para. 556.

[113] See Randle de Falco and Frédéric Mégret, The Invisibility of Race at the ICC: Lessons from the US Criminal Justice System' (2019) 7 *London Review of International Law* 55–87.

[114] Carola Lingaas, 'Enhancing the effectiveness of the law of genocide' in Joanna Nicholson (ed.), *Strengthening the Validity of International Criminal Tribunals* (Leiden: Brill, 2018) 127–51

[115] For a survey, see Rosemary Grey, *Prosecuting Sexual and Gender-Based Crimes at the International Criminal Court* (Cambridge: Cambridge University Press, 2019) 95–122.

[116] UN General Assembly, International Law Commission, Seventy-First Session, UN. Doc. A/CN.4/726, 21 January 2019, 30.

[117] Ibid., at 31.

[118] See International Law Commission, Seventy-First Session, Crimes Against Humanity, UN Doc. A/CN.4/L.935, 15 May 2019.

the plural, it becomes a placeholder for an undefined, ideal, or imagined species of victim. Following Carl Schmitt's famous expression 'whoever invokes humanity wants to cheat'[119] one might say that whoever invokes 'victims' in the general sense might 'cheat' a little. It is important to specify which 'victims' are meant. Different types of victims have very different interests.

The turn to expressivism requires thus greater professional responsibility and sensitivity to the language used in messages and speech acts. Like other fields of international law, international criminal justice is in need of further 'decolonization'.

6.6.6 Rethinking law and learning

In the most general way, expressivism is an invitation to rethink the way in which we see law. International criminal justice as a field is constructed by discourses and stories. It does not require full coherence. It is shaped by contradictions and different discourses. It builds on dynamics of communication. As Martti Koskenniemi has noted, international law is 'a conversation about what to do, here and now'.[120] It permits multiple readings. This multiplicity is not a weakness of the law but a strength because it 'makes room for different voices, and gives a purchase by which culture may be modified in response to the demands of circumstance'.[121]

What constitutes international criminal law is not simply determined by states, treaty-making processes, or adjudication. It derives from a 'multiplicity of diverse communicative processes'.[122] The law we see is only the tip of the iceberg. The normative force of the field draws on moral philosophy and ethics, different types of politics, criminology, psychology, sociology, linguistics, and rhetoric techniques. The multidisciplinary foundations are hidden in the study of laws and institutions. They need to be brought out more clearly, in order to make sense of the prospects and limits of the field.

Lawyers need to engage with other ways of seeing the world. There is a trend to stay with what we know. Institutions need to develop structures for continuous learning and critical engagement with their own practices. Education and learning needs to be rethought. There is usefulness in seemingly 'useless knowledge'.

[119] Carl Schmitt, *The Concept of the Political: Expanded Edition* (Chicago: Chicago University Press, 2007), 54.

[120] Martti Koskenniemi, *From Apology to Utopia: The Structure of International Legal Argument* (Cambridge: Cambridge University Press, 2006), 544.

[121] James Boyd White, 'Law as Language: Reading Law and Reading Literature' (1981–82) 60 *Texas Law Review* 415–45, 444.

[122] See also Günther Teubner, 'The Two Faces of Janus: Rethinking Legal Pluralism' (1992)13 *Cardozo Law Review* 1443–62, 1450–1.

International criminal law cannot be understood solely by lawyers, nor should it be taught only by lawyers.[123] As Abraham Flexner has argued, institutions of learning 'should be devoted to the cultivation of curiosity'.[124] The 'less they are deflected by considerations of immediacy of application', the 'more likely they are to contribute to human welfare'.[125]

[123] Andrea Bianchi, 'The Unbearable Lightness of International Law' (2018) 6 *London Review of International Law* 335–59, 345.

[124] Abraham Flexner, 'The Usefulness of Useless Knowledge', Harper's Magazine, No 179 (June/November 1939) 544–52, 545.

[125] Ibid.

Index

Note: *For the benefit of digital users, indexed terms that span two pages (e.g., 52–53) may, on occasion, appear on only one of those pages.*
Figures are indicated by *f* following the page number